# FEUDS ABOUT FAMILIES

## Conservative, Centrist, Liberal, and Feminist Perspectives

### NIJOLE V. BENOKRAITIS, EDITOR
*University of Baltimore*

PRENTICE HALL, UPPER SADDLE RIVER, NEW JERSEY 07458

**Library of Congress Cataloging-in-Publication Data**

Feuds about families : conservative, centrist, liberal, and feminist perspectives / [selected by] Nijole V. Benokraitis.
    p.  cm.
    Includes bibliographical references.
    ISBN 0-13-912460-8
    1. Family—United States.  2. Marriage—United States.  3. Social values—United States.
4. Culture conflict—United States.  I. Benokraitis, Nijole V. (Nijole Vaicaitis)
HQ535.F48  2000
306.8'0973  21—dc21                                                                99-044976
                                                                                    CIP

*To all the college students,*
*across the ideological and political spectrum,*
*who read, think, and write critically:*
*Keep it up!*

© 2000 by Prentice-Hall, Inc.
Upper Saddle River, New Jersey 07458

Editorial Director: Charlyce Jones Owen
Editor in Chief: Nancy Roberts
Managing Editor: Sharon Chambliss
Marketing Manager: Christopher DeJohn
Project Manager: Serena Hoffman
Buyer: Mary Ann Gloriande
Cover Art Director: Jayne Conte
Cover Designer: Joe Sengotta
Cover art: Jane Sterrett/Stock Illustration Source

Printed in the United States of America

10  9  8  7  6  5  4  3  2  1

This book was set in 10/12 Palatino by DM Cradle Associates and was printed and bound by RR Donnelley & Sons. The cover was printed by Phoenix Color Corp.

ISBN 0-13-912460-8

Prentice-Hall International (UK) Limited, *London*
Prentice-Hall of Australia Pty. Limited, *Sydney*
Prentice-Hall Canada Inc., *Toronto*
Prentice-Hall Hispanoamericana, S.A., *Mexico*
Prentice-Hall of India Private Limited, *New Delhi*
Prentice-Hall of Japan, Inc., *Tokyo*
Pearson Education Asia Pte. Ltd., *Singapore*
Editora Prentice-Hall do Brasil, Ltda., *Rio de Janeiro*

# CONTENTS

# PREFACE

Over the years I've adopted a variety of "pro/con" readers to supplement whatever textbook I was using. The readers generated lively class discussions, but many of my students took an "it depends" position on most topics. As a result, I started considering how to incorporate more "it depends" material into my classes. This reader represents an effort to include a broader array of ideological and political perspectives on family issues.

The purpose of this reader is three-fold. First, *Feuds about Families: Conservative, Centrist, Liberal, and Feminist Perspectives* presents articles on 18 topics in a single, affordable source. There are a number of "opposing viewpoints" readers on the market; however excellent they might be, those books are done in debate format around a single issue. This reader, in contrast, presents three views on important and controversial marriage and family-related topics.

Second, this book encourages students to consider marriage and family issues through wider lenses. Marriage and family courses are often faulted for a lack of balance. One of the repeated complaints of conservative commentators, for example, is that college and university faculty bludgeon their hapless students with liberal dogma. Moderates often feel that their voices are altogether ignored in textbooks. And, while many of the "opposing viewpoints" readers use articles to illustrate a liberal perspective, "liberal" and "feminist" aren't synonymous. As a result, students are more likely to read liberal rather than feminist materials, especially in marriage and family courses. Many of our students who come from diverse backgrounds often feel that their views are ignored in textbooks and other course readings. I hope that students find "voices" in this reader that reflect their political and personal attitudes.

Finally, this anthology helps to develop critical thinking skills so that students can formulate more informed opinions. By offering articles from several political and ideological positions, it provides a forum for a broad range of discussions. Students and faculty can weigh the merits and flaws of each perspective and draw their own conclusions about marriage and family issues. One reviewer commented, for example, that "Our job as professors is to inform and teach, not proselytize. This is the reader's greatest strength to me."

## CRITERIA IN SELECTING READINGS

I used four criteria in selecting articles. The foremost and overriding criterion was readability, readability, readability. I've learned, during 30 years of teaching, that most students will simply not read material they don't understand.

Second, all the selections (with one exception) have been published during the 1990s. I gave the most recently published articles a higher priority although I don't equate "new" with "better." I have found, however, that subject matter that relies on 1980s information puts off many students. Many of the vital controversies (such as changing views about sex, men's roles, and stepfamilies) have shifted considerably during the last five years. I feel, therefore, that students' complaints about "dated information" are often justified.

Third, I did not want to rely on journalistic social science. Many of our students read such material on their own. College classes, it seems to me, should expose students to theoretical orientations that they don't encounter in the mainstream media. While journalists play a critical role in shaping public opinion, much of their writing is typically superficial (perhaps necessarily so because of overnight publishing deadlines). Often, moreover, the writing reflects opinions rather than conclusions based on research or a thoughtful analysis of empirical findings.

My fourth criterion changed as I delved deeper into the research. Initially, I assumed that sociological material would be plentiful and that there would be a mountain of subject matter published by academics. Wrong! After the first year's research, I had a stack of academic publications (though a number didn't meet my readability criterion) that reflected liberal and feminist perspectives on almost all of the chapters I wanted to cover but there were only a handful of academic articles for the centrist position and almost none for the conservative viewpoint.

For the conservative position (and to a lesser degree for the centrist perspective), there wasn't enough recent material on about half the topics that had been published by non-academic social scientists. Consequently, I decided to use some non-academic pieces that have been published by both social scientists and non-social scientists. I now had non-academic articles written by non-social scientists who represented either the Christian or secular Right. I decided to use pieces that were based on research rather than personal opinion. Using this criterion, practically all of the articles turned out to be those written by secular conservatives. And, when the research was negligible, I chose a few articles by writers (such as Laura Schlessinger and Carl Horowitz) who don't rely on empirical findings but who have influenced public opinion on family-related issues nationally.

I encountered similar but somewhat less daunting problems in selecting material for the centrist position. Because centrists seem more concerned about children in single-mother families than parenting regardless of family structure, I felt that the reading in Chapter 10 came as close to reflecting the centrist position as anything I found. To my knowledge, there are no published materials from the centrist position on four other topics ("Gay and Lesbian Families," "The Impact of Social Class," "Family Violence," and "Family Policies," especially in analyses of recent welfare reforms). For these chapters I decided to use "neutral" pieces by academic social scientists that provide some background for the conservative and liberal or feminist perspectives.

## The Organizing Framework

Like the selection criteria, the organizing framework changed and evolved as I worked on *Feuds about Families*. When reviewers evaluated the proposal for the reader, most raised two questions: (1) Should the continuum be broader? and (2) Who fits into each niche?

### Should the Continuum Be Broader?

Some of the reviewers suggested that I broaden the framework to present a much broader set of perspectives across the political and ideological continuum. Several reminded me, for example, that feminist perspectives include—among others—liberal feminism, radical feminism, cultural feminism, postmodern feminism, and multicultural feminism. Others noted that conservative conservatives and moderate conservatives might have different views on family issues. A few reviewers also observed that there are conservative moderates, moderate moderates, and liberal moderates. I agree that there is a much broader range of perspectives than the three presented in this reader, but I have to draw boundaries somewhere.

### Who Fits into Each Niche?

Some of the reviewers raised questions such as: "How does one decide that a specific article is validly placed in one slot rather than in another?" Except for the five articles noted earlier that appear to be scientific and "neutral," the authors of the centrist excerpts have identified themselves as communitarians, have been described as such by other centrists, or their selections come from centrist periodicals or books. I felt, moreover, that most of the centrists were "moderate" compared to conservative writers. Chapter 2 presents my typology and criteria for classifying readings as "conservative," "centrist," "liberal," or "feminist."

I realize that some readers may not agree with my classification system, with my selection criteria, or with all of my choices for the conservative, centrist, liberal/feminist selections. One reviewer mused, for example, that "It'd be interesting to get the reactions of the authors themselves in terms of their assigned niches."

## The Topics

This reader should be attractive to both undergraduate and graduate courses. Since the articles cover 18 important marriage and family topics, *Feuds about Families* can be adopted as a "stand alone" textbook. It can also be a useful anthology to accompany textbooks in such courses as Introductory Sociology, Marriage and the Family, Social Policy, Social Problems, Racial and Ethnic Relations, and Gender Roles because it encompasses most of the standard marriage/family topics that these courses cover. It can also be used in courses in social work, women's studies, public administration, political science, multicultural studies, government, and human resources because it addresses some of the most controversial family-related issues (such as family values, single-parent families, work, racial and ethnic diversity, family violence, and family policy).

## Pedagogical Features

This reader has three features that facilitate students' reading and reflection about the political and ideological controversies surrounding family issues. First, the introductions for Parts II to VI suggest some of the similarities, differences, and overlap (when it occurs) across the various perspectives. The Part introductions also include supplementary information that updates data cited in some of the articles, integrates recent empirical findings, and incorporates relevant or well-known studies that enhance students' understanding of the topics in each chapter.

Second, a brief introduction to each article highlights the key issues that students should keep in mind while reading a selection or a set of selections in a chapter. In many instances, these introductions "bridge" or contrast the three perspectives.

Third, three Critical Thinking Questions follow each article. I constructed at least two questions for each selection that encouraged critical thinking about the author's theoretical position, usage of data, or value assumptions. The questions at the end of the third article in each chapter often invite students to compare/contrast two or more of the perspectives.

## Acknowledgments

I am indebted to a number of people who have shaped *Feuds about Families*. At Prentice Hall, John Chillingworth, sociology editor, and Allison Westlake, John's administrative assistant, solicited reviewer comments and responded—always quickly and efficiently—to my questions and requests for information. After John left Prentice Hall, Nancy Roberts, editor-in-chief for social sciences, and Sharon Chambliss, managing editor for sociology, orchestrated the various tasks that were necessary to complete this project. Serena Hoffman, my production editor, provided meticulous attention to detail and kept me on schedule. Christopher DeJohn, marketing manager at Prentice Hall, and his staff have been responsive and energetic in launching this reader.

At the University of Baltimore, Brian Wyant, my graduate assistant, tracked down many of the articles and updated the information about the contributors. Linda Fair, our administrative wizard, facilitated my research and correspondence. The staff at Langsdale Library, as always, continues to be a most valuable (but undervalued) faculty resource. Our librarians resolved system-wide glitches, helped me access a veritable mountain of material, and provided generous support for my research and Internet-related questions.

I am grateful to Jennifer S. Barber (University of Michigan) and Shirley L. Zimmerman (University of Minnesota) for their insightful comments and suggestions on Chapter 2. Jennifer and Shirley posed challenging questions that helped me rethink some of my analysis.

A number of other faculty members reviewed the initial proposal and offered invaluable observations and much constructive criticism. These colleagues include Anita Glee Abscher (University of Central Oklahoma), Trudy B. Anderson (Texas A&M University at Kingsville), Mark A. Fine (University of Missouri), Richard L. Halpin (Jefferson Community College), Jane C. Hood (University of New Mexico), and Steven L. Nock (University of Virginia). I'm especially thankful to these reviewers for their quick responses when I badgered them with e-mail messages. Their availability and intellectual energy buoyed my sometimes sagging spirits when I encountered frustrating analytical dilemmas.

I thank David M. Klein (University of Notre Dame) for his suggestions and stimulating influence during several months of almost daily e-mail discussions. David took the time to argue with me, to think with me, and to push me to probe many of the gnarly and complex questions about political and ideological perspectives that I was tempted to ignore.

Norval D. Glenn (University of Texas) made substantive contributions throughout this book's labor pains and final birth. Norval was one of my highly respected instructors at the University of Texas during the early 1970s. We "reconnected" in 1996 when Norval was preparing his famous (some would say infamous) critiques of the major marriage/family textbooks, which were published in 1997. We considered working on this reader together because both of us felt that such an anthology would expand the "opposing viewpoints" standpoint. When Norval's schedule became overburdened, I carried on by myself. Throughout this endeavor, Norval has been generous with his time and his ideas. He sent me articles (especially for the conservative and centrist positions) that were not readily available and helped me grapple with a number of theoretical, ideological, and political conundrums. I am especially grateful, therefore, for his availability, input, and extensive e-mail dialogue throughout this reader's development.

Thank you, one and all. I look forward to, and will respond to, comments on this book. I can be contacted at:

University of Baltimore
1420 N. Charles Street
Baltimore, MD 21201
Voicemail: 410-837-5294
Fax: 410-837-5061
E-mail: nbenokraitis@ubmail.ubalt.edu

# CONTRIBUTORS

ENOLA AIRD is Acting Director of the Black Community Crusade for Children in Connecticut.

KATHERINE R. ALLEN is Professor of Family Studies in the Department of Human Development at Virginia Polytechnic Institute and State University.

ROSALIND C. BARNETT is Senior Scholar in Residence at the Murray Research Center at Radcliffe College.

JOHN BARTKOWSKI is Assistant Professor of Sociology at Mississippi State University in the Department of Sociology, Anthropology, and Social Work.

ROBERT BELLAH is Elliot Professor of Sociology Emeritus at the University of California at Berkeley.

NIJOLE V. BENOKRAITIS is Professor of Sociology at the University of Baltimore.

KAREN R. BLAISURE is Associate Professor of Family Studies in the Department of Family and Consumer Sciences at Western Michigan University.

DAVID BLANKENHORN is Founder and President of the Institute for American Values in New York City.

LAWRENCE F. BURTOFT is Senior Fellow, Family, Church and Society Public Policy Division, Focus on the Family, Colorado Springs, Colorado.

BETTY CARTER is Director of the Family Institute of Westchester in White Plains, New York, and Cofounder of the Women's Project in Family Therapy.

BRYCE J. CHRISTENSEN is the editor of *Family in America* newsletters at the Rockford Institute, Illinois.

STEPHANIE COONTZ, a historian, is a member of the faculty at the Evergreen State College in Olympia, Washington.

MARTIN DALY is Professor of Psychology at McMaster University in Hamilton, Ontario, Canada.

R. EMERSON DOBASH is Professor of Social Research, Department of Social Policy and Social Work, University of Manchester, Manchester, England.

RUSSELL P. DOBASH is Professor of Criminology and Social Policy, Department of Social Policy and Social Work, University of Manchester, Manchester, England.

WILLIAM J. DOHERTY is Professor of Family Social Science, College of Human Ecology, at the University of Minnesota at Twin Cities and is the director of the Marriage and Family Therapy program at the university.

KATHRYN EDIN is Assistant Professor of Sociology at the University of Pennsylvania.

CHRISTOPHER G. ELLISON is Associate Professor of Sociology at the University of Texas at Austin.

JEAN BETHKE ELSHTAIN is Professor of Social and Political Ethics, Divinity School, University of Chicago.

AMITAI ETZIONI is University Professor and Director of the George Washington Institute for Communitarian Policy Studies.

PATRICK F. FAGAN is William H. G. FitzGerald Senior Fellow in Family and Cultural Issues at the Heritage Foundation in Washington, D.C.

STEVEN FLANDERS is a court administrator and freelance writer in Pelham, New York.

MAGGIE GALLAGHER is a columnist, Universal Press Syndicate.

WILLIAM GALSTON is Professor of Public Affairs and Director of the Institute for Philosophy and Public Policy, University of Maryland at College Park.

RICHARD J. GELLES is Professor of Sociology and Psychology and Director of the Family Violence Research Program at the University of Rhode Island.

GEORGE GILDER writes for the *Wall Street Journal*, *National Review*, and *Forbes*.

MARY ANN GLENDON is Learned Hand Professor of Law, Harvard University Law School.

NORVAL D. GLENN is Ashbel Smith Professor of Sociology and Stiles Professor in American Studies at the University of Texas at Austin.

WILLIAM A. HETH is Associate Professor of New Testament and Greek at Taylor University, Upland, Indiana.

CARL F. HOROWITZ is a Washington correspondent for *Investor's Business Daily*.

LEON R. KASS is Addie Clark Harding Professor at the University of Chicago.

DEMIE KURZ is Assistant Professor of Sociology and Co-Director of the Women's Studies Program at the University of Pennsylvania.

LAURA LEIN is Senior Lecturer, Department of Anthropology, and Senior Lecturer and Research Scientist, the School of Social Work, the University of Texas at Austin.

DANA MACK is an affiliate scholar at the Institute for American Values, New York.

RICHARD MADSEN is Professor of Sociology, University of California at San Diego.

ANDREA MARTIN is a freelance writer.

SUSAN E. MAYER is Associate Professor in the Graduate School of Public Policy Studies at the University of Chicago.

MARTHA MINOW is law professor at Harvard University.

CHARLES MURRAY is Bradley Fellow at the American Enterprise Institute in Washington, D.C.

BARBARA F. OKUN is Professor in the Department of Counseling Psychology, Rehabilitation, and Special Education at Northeastern University, and Clinical Instructor of Psychology in the Department of Psychiatry at Harvard Medical School.

DENNIS K. ORTHNER is Professor of Sociology in the School of Social Work and Director of the Human Services Research Laboratory at the University of North Carolina at Chapel Hill.

PATRICIA PEARSON is a Canadian crime journalist.

JOAN K. PETERS is a journalist and novelist.

DAVID POPENOE is Professor of Sociology and Associate Dean for Social and Behavioral Sciences of the Faculty of Arts and Sciences at Rutgers University.

S. DuBOSE RAVENEL is a board-certified pediatrician in private practice in High Point, North Carolina.

CARYL RIVERS is Professor of Journalism at Boston University.

STACEY ROSENCRANTZ received her doctorate in Psychology at Stanford University.

ALICE ROSSI is Emeritus Faculty, Social and Demographic Research Institute, University of Massachusetts.

RUTH SIDEL is Professor of Sociology at Hunter College.

ARLENE SKOLNICK is Research Psychologist at the Institute of Human Development, University of California at Berkeley.

JUDITH STACEY is Professor of Sociology and Women's Studies at the University of California, Davis.

GLENN T. STANTON is Social Research Analyst in the Public Policy Division of Focus on the Family in Colorado Springs, Colorado.

THOMAS B. STODDARD (1949–1997) was Adjunct Professor of Law at New York University and Executive Director of the Lambda Legal Defense and Education Fund.

ROBERT P. STOKER is Associate Professor in the Department of Political Science, George Washington University.

MURRAY A. STRAUS is Founder and Codirector of the Family Research Laboratory at the University of New Hampshire.

WILLIAM SULLIVAN is Professor of Philosophy at La Salle College in Philadelphia.

ANN SWIDLER is Professor of Sociology, University of California at Berkeley.

CAROL TAVRIS is a psychologist with a private practice in Los Angeles.

ABIGAIL THERNSTROM is a Senior Fellow at the Manhattan Institute.

STEPHAN THERNSTROM is Professor of History at Harvard University.

STEVEN TIPTON is Professor of Sociology, Candler School of Theology, Emory University.

DEN A. TRUMBULL is a board-certified pediatrician in private practice in Montgomery, Alabama.

SARAH TURNER is a pseudonym. The author is Associate Professor of Education at a small liberal arts college in the East.

LYNET UTTAL is Assistant Professor in the Department of Child and Family Studies at the University of Wisconsin, Madison.

LINDA J. WAITE is Professor of Sociology and Director of the Center of Aging at the University of Chicago.

BARBARA DAFOE WHITEHEAD is a writer and a social analyst at the Institute for American Values in New York City.

JAMES Q. WILSON is Collins Professor of Management and Public Policy at the University of California at Los Angeles.

LAURA A. WILSON is Associate Professor in the School of Public Affairs, University of Baltimore.

MARTIN WILSON is Professor of Psychology at McMaster University in Hamilton, Ontario, Canada.

# I     INTRODUCTION

The first two chapters in Part I provide an analytical framework for understanding the recent debates about family issues. As Norval D. Glenn observes in Chapter 1, "No division into conservatives versus liberals or any similar dichotomous distinction fully captures the complexity of the factions and schools of thought." He begins by describing the two-category conservative-liberal classification that most people use to characterize the family. Glenn then includes a third ideological faction, communitarians (or centrists), who have played an increasingly prominent role in shaping public and political discussion on family issues. Using this three-category classification, Glenn illustrates how conservative, centrist, and liberal views differ on such topics as family relationships, divorce, abortion, gay rights, and family policy. He concludes the analysis with a discussion of the role of social science in framing the debates in the "family wars." Because feminists fit into several of the categories, Glenn subsumes them into the liberal category.

In Chapter 2, Nijole V. Benokraitis expands Norval Glenn's overview to include feminists. She describes some of the differences she sees between liberals and feminists, explains why her perception of centrists differs from Glenn's, and suggests how the four ideological factions influence family life. She concludes with examples of critical thinking questions about conservative, centrist, liberal, and feminist perspectives.

# 1 Who's Who in the Family Wars: A Characterization of the Major Ideological Factions

NORVAL D. GLENN

The battle lines in the heated debates about family issues in the United States defy simple description. No division into conservatives versus liberals or any similar dichotomous distinction fully captures the complexity of the factions and schools of thought. Beliefs, attitudes, and values about families fall into continua rather than into distinctly demarcated schools of thought, and there are several imperfectly correlated continua rather than just one.

Arguably the most basic and important of the continua are those that relate to attitudes toward family change. They deserve special attention because they are involved in almost every aspect of the debates; thus I turn to them first. Although the conservative-liberal distinction by itself is inadequate for mapping ideological variation, it is the best starting point for dealing with attitudes toward change.

## VARIATION IN ATTITUDES TOWARD CHANGE

The most widely used distinction between conservatives and liberals is based on how those two factions view change, and conservative and liberal participants in the "family wars" evince the usual differences in these attitudes. Conservatives want to "conserve" or preserve existing, or recently existing, social arrangements and behavior patterns, whereas liberals are more receptive to change. Conservatives

work to maintain the status quo, or to restore an earlier status quo, whereas liberals often actively promote change. The classic statement of the conservative view of the status quo comes from the eighteenth-century English poet Alexander Pope, who wrote:

> All nature is but art, unknown to thee
> All chance, direction, which thou canst not see;
> All discord, harmony not understood;
> All partial evil, universal good:
> And spite of pride, in erring reason's spite,
> One truth is clear, Whatever is, is right.[1]

A similar attitude is embodied in modern functionalist thought, at least some versions of which maintain that existing social institutions would not have come into being if they did not serve positive social functions. Liberals, by contrast, tend to believe that whatever change is occurring is for the better, and some give a functionalist-like explanation for change: If institutional change were not adaptive, and thus for the better, it would not occur.

These characterizations of conservatives and liberals are caricatures; few people believe that all aspects of all traditional social arrangements should be preserved, and few people regard all aspects of recent social change positively. However, a few prominent conservative and liberal participants in the current debates about family issues almost fit the caricatures.

A four-category rather than a two-category classification of attitudes toward change is sometimes used, in which case the categories of reactionary and radical are added to those of conservative and liberal. Rather than wanting to preserve the status quo, reactionaries want to re-create conditions that existed in the past. In practice, the distinction between conservatives and reactionaries is hard to apply, because most conservatives would like to roll back some recent changes and thus are reactionary to some extent. As the terms are usually used, the distinction between reactionary and conservative is one of degree rather than kind, reactionaries being the same as extreme conservatives. The distinction between liberals and radicals is less subtle, because radicals are more than just extreme liberals. Both radicals and extreme liberals want and work for substantial change, but they differ in how they pursue their goals. Liberals work within existing institutions, whereas radicals want to abolish present institutions and replace them with new ones. Whereas some radicals use violence to attain their goals, and use such tactics in academic debates as the fabrication of evidence, liberals reject such means.

Regardless of how many categories are used in classifying attitudes toward change, the most important distinction is between conservative and liberal. The difference between conservative and reactionary attitudes is not very clear, and only a very small percentage of Americans are radical. On college and university campuses, radical feminists are sometimes conspicuous participants in debates about gender and family issues, but radical perspectives are largely absent from public policy debates.

When the distinction between conservatives and liberals is made in terms of attitudes toward change, the other attitudinal and value differences between the two factions differ from time to time and from place to place. As long as institutional change continues in one direction, yesterday's liberals tend to become today's conservatives, as they defend their favored institutional arrangements from those who would replace them with still newer arrangements. A salient example is the case of the racial integrationists who were liberal activists during the civil rights movement of the 1960s. These people are now often called conservative when they express reservations about aspects of the multicultural movement and the trend toward what they consider to be racial and ethnic balkanization on college and university campuses. More closely related to family issues is the case of Betty Friedan, who more than any other person was responsible for initiating the modern feminist movement. Although her basic ideology has not changed, her expressed reservations about some recent developments in feminism have led some contemporary feminists to label her conservative.[2]

How the content of conservative and liberal thought can change in just two decades is illustrated by the data in Table 1, which are from American national surveys conducted in 1974 and 1994. In both surveys, the respondents were asked to rate themselves on a 7-point political ideology scale ranging from "extremely liberal" to "extremely conservative." I have combined those who said they were "extremely liberal" with those who said they were "liberal" (the combined category being labeled "liberal" in the table) and those who said they were "extremely conservative" with those who said they were "conservative" (labeled "conservative" in the table). On each of the three gender issues covered by the data, the responses of both liberals and conservatives changed considerably over the two decades in the direction of the attitudes more characteristic of liberals than of conservatives. On each issue, the 1994 responses of conservatives were, as a whole, very similar to the 1974 responses of liberals. In other words, in terms of a constant definition of liberal and conservative attitudes, on the three gender issues covered by the survey questions, conservatives were just as liberal in 1994 as liberals were in 1974.

**TABLE 1.** Responses (in Percent) of Liberals and Conservatives to Three Questions Concerning Gender Issues, 1974 and 1994, U.S. Adults

|  | Liberals | Conservatives |
|---|---|---|
|  | (n in parentheses) | |
| **Would vote for woman for president** | | |
| 1974 | 85.1 (221) | 72.1 (190) |
| 1994 | 96.3 (268) | 85.8 (379) |
| Change | +11.2 | +13.7 |
| **Agree that women should take care of running their homes and leave running the country to men** | | |
| 1974 | 23.3 (223) | 49.2 (195) |
| 1994 | 8.4 (273) | 19.8 (388) |
| Change | −14.9 | −29.4 |
| **Approve of a woman working outside the home when she has a husband who can support her** | | |
| 1974 | 75.8 (219) | 58.2 (189) |
| 1994 | 80.9 (272) | 76.9 (381) |
| Change | + 5.1 | +18.7 |

SOURCE: The 1974 and 1994 United States General Social Surveys conducted by the National Opinion Research Center at the University of Chicago.

## VARIATION IN ATTITUDES TOWARD FREEDOM VERSUS CONSTRAINT

Another very important dimension of disagreement in the "family wars" and in other current ideological debates concerns freedom versus constraint. To what extent should individuals be allowed to act as they please and to what extent should their actions be constrained for the benefit of others, for the community as a whole, and for the society as a whole? And to the extent that individual behavior is subject to constraint, or social control, what should be the locus of control? To what extent should control be exercised by governments—as opposed to such institutions as families and religious and economic institutions—and how should the governmental control be divided among federal, state, and local governments?

Ideological factions delineated on the basis of attitudes toward freedom versus constraint cannot be ranked on one continuum. Rather, some ideological factions, including both conservatives and liberals, favor high social control of some kinds of behavior and low control of other kinds. For instance, most conservatives advocate relatively little control over the behavior of persons engaged in "free enterprise" but relatively great control over sexual behavior and interpersonal relationships. In contrast, most liberals advocate considerable government regulation of business, and of persons engaged in business enterprise, but little control over personal behavior and relationships.

A rough and somewhat oversimplified depiction of the positions of five ideological factions concerning freedom versus constraint in regard to two spheres of human activity (economic and personal) is given in Figure 1. Authoritarians, who lack a major presence in contemporary American society, advocate high social control of both kinds of activity. At the other end of the continuum are libertarians, who advocate little control of both kinds of activities and who are a

**FIGURE 1.** Degree of Social Control of Two Kinds of Behavior Advocated by Five Ideological Factions

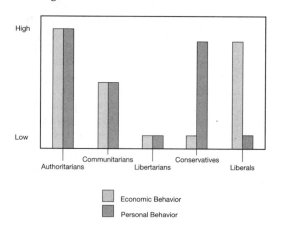

small but occasionally vocal faction in current ideological debates in the United States. In the middle of the continuum, advocating a moderate degree of control of both kinds of behavior, are communitarians, an increasingly important faction in elite and intellectual circles with whom a large percentage of the public agrees.[3] Taking inconsistent positions in regard to the two kinds of human activities are conservatives and liberals, both of whom are, of course, active and influential participants in all major ideological debates, including the family wars.

Liberals tend to favor a high degree of freedom for individuals to pursue self-interest as they relate to family members and friends, for instance, by taking the position that parents in unhappy marriages should not stay married for the sake of their children. On the other hand, liberals tend to criticize individualism and the pursuit of self-interest by entrepreneurs. Whereas liberals reject the idea, set forth by Adam Smith, that the "invisible hand" of the marketplace weaves together the self-interested striving of individuals in a way that furthers the common good, they believe in something akin to an invisible hand whereby self-interested individuals "looking out for number one" in their family and other interpersonal relationships contribute to the common good.

Conservatives are just as inconsistent as liberals, their views being a mirror image of those of liberals. For instance, conservatives favor free market economies, but they oppose a free mating market, by which adult men and women can freely compete for more desirable spouses and lovers as long as they live.

In pointing out that both liberals and conservatives fail to take consistent positions concerning the amount of freedom and constraint that should exist with respect to different spheres of human endeavor, I am not making a value judgment. Both factions have well-constructed rationales for the positions they take. One can argue that consistency in this respect is not a virtue, that freedom and constraint have differing effects on human well-being in the different spheres.

## COMPARISON OF THREE IDEOLOGICAL FACTIONS ON SELECTED FAMILY ISSUES

The most influential and conspicuous players in contemporary family debates in the United States are conservatives, liberals, and emerging centrist factions, such as communitarians and neoliberals.[4] Debates in Congress and in state legislatures usually pit conservatives against liberals, but centrists, some of whom call themselves moderate liberals or moderate conservatives, are increasingly prominent when family issues as well as other controversial topics are discussed. For instance, the Democratic Leadership Council, founded by President Clinton to represent the moderate wing of the Democratic party, advocates a "Third Way," which is distinctly different from either orthodox conservatism or orthodox liberalism.[5] On college and university campuses, and in the academic literature, conservative views are rare, and thus debates about family issues are largely between centrists and liberals.

In this section I first describe what I perceive to be the prevailing conservative position or positions on each issue discussed and then turn to the prevailing liberal views. Finally, I report positions taken by communitarians and neoliberals. Even though I deal to some extent with intrafaction diversity, I do not attempt to consider all views within each faction. Some readers who identify with each faction will find no discussion of their values and beliefs.

I have already given a general characterization of conservative and liberal views of change. Now I address how the major ideological factions view recent family change in the United States.

### Recent Family Change

The important recent family changes that are viewed differently by the major ideological factions include the steep increase in divorce that occurred in the 1960s and 1970s, the continuing increase in the percentage of babies that are born to unwed mothers, the increase in the percentage of persons who spend some of their preadult years in single-parent families and stepfamilies, and the increase in cohabitation of unmarried men and women.

Almost all conservatives view these changes negatively and emphasize evidence that the changes have had detrimental effects on the socialization and well-being of children and adolescents.[6] Most conservatives also argue that the changes have hurt present generations of adults and have had deleterious effects on society as a whole through contributing to crime and delinquency, violence, increased governmental costs, and reduced economic productivity.

Religious and secular conservatives arrive at similar conclusions concerning the undesirability of these and related family changes, but they do so for different reasons. To many religious conservatives, divorce, out-of-wedlock childbearing, and nonmarital sexual relations are undesirable because they are morally wrong—contrary to the will of God—regardless of their social and psychological consequences. In addition, religious conservatives tend to disapprove of abortion, homosexuality, and male-female equality in marriage, because they believe these activities and conditions are contrary to the will of God. In contrast, secular conservatives generally disapprove of these activities and conditions only to the extent that they perceive them to have undesirable social and psychological consequences—and many perceive no such consequences. The less extreme conservatives, who, although they may be religious, generally do not hold beliefs about family issues based in conservative religion, tend to approve of married mothers working outside the home, whereas the more extreme conservatives believe that married mothers should stay home, at least until their children are of school age.

Conservatives tend to attribute recent family change to different influences than do liberals, believing that it has resulted in large measure from changes in values and moral standards. Conservatives emphasize such cultural changes (which many persons in other ideological factions also believe have occurred) as a deemphasis of duty, obligation, and personal restraint and an increased emphasis on personal freedom and such goals as "self-actualization" and "personal growth."[7] Religious conservatives characterize these changes as aspects of the growth of "secular humanism," which, they believe, encourages devotion to self to the exclusion of devotion to God, country, and family. Both religious and secular conservatives tend also to attribute undesirable family change to the growth of the welfare state, which they believe has weakened families by taking over functions the families previously performed.[8]

Conservatives generally believe that recent changes in families can be, and should be, reversed. They believe that this reversal can be accomplished by a cultural movement to reestablish traditional family values and by dismantling, or partially dismantling, the welfare state. Some conservatives believe that such legislation as rescinding, or limiting access to, no-fault divorce can lead to a reinstitutionalization of marriage. Conservatives, with support from some moderates and liberals, recently led successful campaigns in Louisiana and Arizona to implement "covenant marriage," an optional form of marriage in which the spouses give up their right to no-fault divorce. Conservatives, in alliance with moderates and some liberals, are behind recent efforts to change public assistance programs to limit payments to unwed women who repeatedly give birth.

Most liberals, of course, take a much more sanguine view of recent family change, often denying, for instance, that such changes as the increase in the number of single-parent families have contributed substantially to delinquency, juvenile violence, poor achievement, and similar outcomes. When liberals do acknowledge possible undesirable consequences from family change, they often claim that the change is part and parcel of broader social changes, which include such trends as increased prosperity and a trend toward equality of men and women, that few persons would want to reverse.[9] In other words, the trends that concern conservatives are, according to this view, the costs of the transition into the postmodern world that must be accepted along with the benefits of the transition.

Furthermore, liberals tend to believe that recent family change, whether desirable or undesirable, has resulted from economic, technological, and demographic changes and thus that the family change cannot be reversed. The changes in family values, according to this view, are consequences rather than causes of structural family change.

Liberals generally strongly oppose efforts to dismantle, or partially dismantle, the welfare state. They, of course, favor welfare state policies and programs for other reasons, but they favor them especially as a means for ameliorating any undesirable consequences of family change.

Many liberals decry any attempts to reverse family change, not only because they think the attempts are futile but because they believe the attempts may have undesirable consequences. At least among academic liberals, there is much concern that discussion of problems in unconventional families will stigmatize persons in those families. A few liberals have accused persons concerned about recent family trends with having the hidden motive of wanting to reinstitute patriarchy.

Communitarians, neoliberals, and similar centrists agree with conservatives in believing that some recent family changes, including especially the growth of single-parent families, have had detrimental effects. At the same time, however, these centrists applaud the trend toward equalitarian marriages, and in contrast to many liberals, believe that equality in marriage and marital stability are not incompatible goals.[10] They generally do not disapprove of the employment of mothers outside the home or of the growing economic independence of women.

Most of these centrists agree with liberals that most recent family change can be attributed ultimately to economic, technological, and demographic change, but they also believe that values are not simply epiphenomenal. That is, they believe that values can have, and have had, effects on family structure. They reject economic and technological determinism and believe that there can be successful movements to change values and morals, and thus behavior. They point out that some of the reversal of family change that many liberals claim cannot occur is already occurring, examples being a recent decline in the birth rate among unmarried African American women and an increase in pro-marriage attitudes among high school seniors.[11]

Most of the dialogue on family issues in which communitarians and neoliberals have participated has been with liberals, some of whom view these centrists hardly more favorably than they view conservatives. Some liberals seem to perceive little difference between the centrists and conservatives. Others perceive considerable difference but focus their criticism on centrists, not because they dislike centrist ideas and values as much as they dislike conservative ones but because they perceive that centrist views are more influential in academia and in the mainstream media.[12] Regardless of how liberals view them, some of the differences between the new centrists and conservatives are arguably very important. For instance, hardly any communitarians or neoliberals favor male-headed families, whereas a substantial proportion of conservatives do. Furthermore, the new centrists generally do not favor a major dismantling of the welfare state, and their views are not based in conservative Christianity. Many of the prominent participants in the communitarian movement are Jewish or nonreligious, and most of the Christian partici-pants are affiliated with the liberal Protes-tant denominations or are moderate or liberal Catholics.

## Selected Specific Issues

*Obligations of family members to one another.* Conservatives emphasize duty, obligation, and personal responsibility in all social relationships but especially in family ones. According to the orthodox conservative view (with which not all con-servatives agree), family members owe one another unconditional love, children and adolescents owe their parents obedience and respect, and parents should put the needs of their offspring before their own needs. A corollary of this view is that when a family member is in need, financially or otherwise, family members should, if they can, meet that need. Government assistance should be a last resort.

Liberals are not opposed to duty, obliga-tion, and personal responsibility, but they place much less emphasis on these qualities than do conservatives. It is unlikely that a majority of liberals would say that parents should not place their preadult offspring's needs before their own, but many believe that parental self-sacrifice tends not to help the offspring. For instance, some argue that a parent who stays in a troubled marriage for the sake of the children is usually not able to be a good parent. A widespread liberal belief, promulgated especially by popular psychology and the self-help liter-ature, is that "looking out for number one" is requisite to looking out for anyone else, including one's children. According to the more extreme version of this view, self-sac-rifice for one's family that achieves its goal is impossible, or nearly so.

Communitarians and similar centrists are more similar to conservatives than to liberals on this issue. They believe that there has been an undesirable weakening of a sense of obligation and duty in American society, a decline in emphasis on what one should give to others and a corresponding but basically contradictory increase in a sense of what one is entitled to get from others. The main difference between com-munitarians and conservatives on this issue is that the former are more in favor of gov-ernment assistance to families and less inclined to blame family problems exclu-sively on a decline in feelings of obligation, duty, and responsibility.

*Divorce.* The orthodox conservative view on divorce is that it should be resorted to only if there is violence, gross misbe-havior by a spouse, or marital discord that does not yield to protracted and sincere efforts at resolution by both spouses. Many conservatives think that implementation of no-fault provisions for divorce was a mistake and that married couples with chil-dren should try to keep their marriages viable for the sake of the children. Many if not most conservatives believe that the recent increase in divorce and in the per-centage of adults who are unmarried has had serious negative social consequences.

Liberals, in contrast, are inclined to believe that divorce is justified if a spouse is dissatisfied with the marriage for any reason or perceives that divorcing will con-tribute to his or her personal growth or self-actualization. Some liberals (probably not a majority) believe that we should move closer to what Bernard Farber has called "permanent availability" on the marriage market.[13] Such a condition, toward which American society has moved substantially in recent decades, would exist if married persons felt free to leave their current mar-riage any time they perceived an opportu-nity to get a more desirable spouse. Liberals generally support no-fault divorce, do not believe that persons in troubled marriages should stay together for the sake of their children, and believe that the recent decrease in marital stability is adaptive and will not in the long run have negative con-sequences. They also tend to believe that any short-term negative consequences can and should be ameliorated by extension of the services of the welfare state.

Communitarians and neoliberals are somewhat more similar to conservatives than to liberals in their views of divorce. They agree with conservatives, for instance, in believing that the increase in divorce has had serious negative social consequences. They generally do not favor rescinding no-fault divorce provisions, but many do favor some form of "divorce law reform," such as extending the waiting period between the filing of a divorce petition and the granting of a divorce.

*Abortion.* The conservative position on abortion is that it is always wrong or is wrong except in the case of rape or incest or when the life of the mother is endangered. Religious conservatives are, as a whole, much more opposed to abortion than are secular conservatives, but both tend to view the widespread practice and acceptance of abortion as symptomatic of moral decline. Both tend to oppose the use of public funds to pay for abortions, and both tend to believe that parental consent should be required for abortions sought by adolescents.

The orthodox liberal position on abortion is that whether or not to terminate a pregnancy is a private matter to be decided by the woman and her physician. Liberals generally favor the use of public funds to pay for abortions desired by low-income women and oppose requiring parental consent for abortions sought by adolescents.

Communitarians and neoliberals are quite diverse in their views on abortion.[14] Many of them agree with conservatives that the widespread practice and acceptance of abortion is symptomatic of undesirable moral changes but oppose legal restrictions on abortion.

*Homosexuality and gay rights.* Religious and secular conservatives disagree at least as much in regard to issues relating to homosexuality as they do in regard to abortion. To religious conservatives, homosexual behavior is a sin, and homosexual orientation is based at least partially on choice. They believe that through religious faith and/or therapy, homosexuals can become straight. They, of course, oppose legislation prohibiting employment and other kinds of discrimination against homosexuals, and they strongly oppose allowing gays and lesbians to marry. Secular conservatives tend to join with religious ones in opposing legislation, and policies on the part of public employers, to extend the same benefits (such as participation in health insurance programs) to the "domestic partners" of homosexuals that are accorded the spouses of heterosexual employees.

The orthodox liberal position is that homosexual lifestyles are as acceptable as heterosexual ones, and that, in view of the history of discrimination against homosexuals, legislation to prevent such discrimination is needed. Many liberals, although not necessarily most, favor gay and lesbian marriage, and a larger proportion endorses extending benefits to the "domestic partners" of homosexual employees. Few liberals believe that sexual orientation is a matter of choice.

Communitarians and neoliberals are somewhat more similar to liberals than to conservatives on this issue. A fairly common position among these centrists is that although the term *marriage* should be reserved for heterosexual bonding, some kind of legal recognition of homosexual pairings is warranted. Communitarians often favor extending employee benefits to the "domestic partners" of homosexual persons but oppose such benefits for cohabiting heterosexual couples, who could marry if they wanted to.[15] Persons in these centrist factions rarely consider homosexuality to be a sin or believe that sexual orientation is a matter of choice.

*Family policy.* I have already discussed many of the stands that the three major ideological factions take in regard to policies regarding specific family issues. Here I need only give a broad characterization of the different policy positions.

According to conservatives, the number one rule to be followed by governments in dealing with family issues is to do no harm. They believe that many government policies and programs designed to help families hurt them instead. They also generally believe that most of the family-related public policies advocated by liberals only treat symptoms and do not deal with the basic causes of family problems. Most conservatives believe that government policies should promote and give preference to two-parent families; for instance, they believe that tax policy should encourage marriage. A common conservative view is that governments should not assume responsibility for the negative consequences of unwise family decisions of individuals. To do so, many conservatives argue, will encourage such decisions.

Liberals tend to agree that the family-related policies they advocate are ameliorative rather than aimed at reversing social changes that cause family problems. However, they claim that attempts to deal with "basic causes" tend to be both futile and oppressive and stigmatizing to people in unconventional families. They believe that societies should take collective responsibility for lessening the negative consequences of family decisions made by individuals, for two reasons: (1) The persons who make the decisions are only responding to structural conditions in the society and thus should not be held responsible for the decisions, and (2) the negative consequences are experienced by persons other than those who make the decisions, including especially children, such as those born out of wedlock.

Communitarians and neoliberals tend to agree with conservatives that it is a mistake to emphasize governmental policies designed to ameliorate the negative consequences of family change while doing nothing to reverse or retard the change, but they nevertheless generally favor the ameliorative policies. They agree with liberals that children should not be penalized for the actions or decisions of their parents.

However, they agree with conservatives in favoring "family-friendly" tax policies and in thinking that government policy should promote and give preference to two-parent families.

## SOCIAL SCIENCE AND THE FAMILY WARS

The recent heated debates in American society about family issues are, of course, of interest to social scientists as objects of study—especially to students of social conflict and social change. Moreover, family social scientists are frequently participants in the debates rather than detached observers of them, and all factions in the debates often look to the social scientific literature to find support for their positions. Implicit in much of the discussion of the issues is a belief that social science can provide resolution to at least some of the major disagreements. In order to assess the validity of that belief, it is necessary to examine the nature of ideology.

Ideology consists of both values and beliefs about the nature of reality. Values—notions about what is good and what is bad, what is desirable and what is undesirable—are of two basic kinds, ultimate and derivative. Ultimate values are those that do not depend on beliefs about empirical reality. If one is asked why one holds an ultimate value, the answer is not an empirical statement. Rather, the answer is something on the order of "It just is" or "It is the will of God." Examples of ultimate values are the beliefs that life is better than death and that happiness is better than unhappiness. Derivative values, in contrast, depend on an alleged consequence for one or more ultimate values. For instance, if someone says that divorce is undesirable because it increases the frequency of emotional problems among children and adolescents, that is a statement of a derivative value.

Science has nothing to say about the validity of ultimate values, but, of course, it can assess the alleged empirical relationships on which derivative values are based.

The descriptions of the ideologies of the opposing factions in the family wars given above include statements about both ultimate and derivative values, but a large proportion of the disagreements among the factions is amenable to empirical assessment. Much of the literature in the debates consists of statements of empirical fact, with or without supporting evidence from social scientific research.

One might think, therefore, that the major disagreements on family issues will soon be resolved by the accumulated evidence from social scientific research. That is not likely, a major reason being that evidence about cause and effect from social scientific research is almost never conclusive. The strongest evidence for causation comes from randomized experiments, in which the experimental stimulus (the effect of which is being assessed) is administered to an experimental group and is withheld from a control group, the two groups having been separated from one another randomly. Randomized experiments are rarely possible in social research. For instance, for ethical as well as other reasons, researchers cannot randomly divide children into two groups and subject one group to a parental separation and divorce while withholding that stimulus from the other group. Instead, they must let divorce occur where it may and then try statistically to equalize other influences on the children whose parents divorce and whose parents do not. Unfortunately, it is impossible to know whether or not all other major relevant influences have been equalized through statistical controls.

Given the impossibility of using ideal research designs to address the empirical issues debated in the family wars, much of the evidence from the research inevitably will be ambiguous and inconsistent. This situation allows considerable intrusion of ideological bias into interpretations of the evidence; it is easy for dogmatic adherents to particular ideological positions selectively to cite evidence that supports their positions. It is even possible for the same

purely descriptive findings that are consistent from study to study to be used to support contradictory ideological views, in the manner of saying that the glass is either half empty or half full. For instance, liberals may say, correctly, that a majority of young adults who experienced a preadult parental divorce are well adjusted. On the other hand, conservatives, citing the same body of evidence, may say, also correctly, that young adults who experienced a parental divorce are less likely to be well adjusted than those whose parents did not divorce.

The probabilistic nature of social scientific knowledge, and the inevitability of some ideological bias in the interpretation of social scientific evidence, may be discouraging, but they are not reasons for despair. Although the social scientific evidence for causal relationships is rarely conclusive, the preponderance of the evidence often strongly supports the existence of a particular causal relationship. Especially when research using different methods yields consistent results on an issue, one can often be confident, though not certain, about what affects what and to what extent.

If the necessity of basing policy on probabilistic knowledge makes one uncomfortable, it is useful to remember that every person in his or her personal life makes decisions on the basis of probabilistic knowledge every day. For instance, when we interact with other persons, we judge what reactions are likely to the things we say or do, but we never know for sure.

Another reason not to despair is that many social scientists are highly committed to objectivity, to letting the evidence lead where it may, regardless of what they wish it to show. There are numerous recent cases of social scientists changing their minds about controversial family issues on the basis of new research findings.[16]

Social science does not have to be "value-free" in order to be useful in resolving issues in the family wars. Strong adherence to ultimate values often provides the motivation to engage in social scientific study, and if there were not rather general public agreement on some ultimate values, there would be no support for social science. The values held by social scientists, and by those who interpret social scientific evidence, do not necessarily have pernicious effects unless there is dogmatic adherence to derivative values. Social scientists and policymakers who make use of social scientific findings should be unyielding in their commitment to ultimate values while keeping their commitment to derivative values tentative. Indeed, one cannot be true to one's ultimate values without being willing to change one's derivative values.

To the extent that the family wars entail conflicts of ultimate values, social science of course is unlikely to contribute to a resolution of the disagreements. However, given the degree to which the debates concern derivative values, social science is, and should be, very much involved.

## NOTES

1. *Essay on Man*, Epistle I. Although the "Whatever is, is right" line from Pope captures the essence of extreme conservatism, Pope is not known as a conservative political theorist.

2. Friedan's book, *The Feminine Mystique*, is widely regarded as a major stimulus for the rise of modern feminism, and when it was published in 1963, Friedan was unambiguously liberal. Her *The Second Stage*, published in 1981, led some feminists to reclassify her ideologically, although she did not retreat from any of the major stands she took in *The Feminine Mystique*. Recently, she has published articles in communitarian and other centrist journals. For instance, see Betty Friedan, "To Transcend Identity Politics: A New Paradigm," *The Responsive Community* 6 (Spring 1996): 4–8.

3. For a summary of communitarian views by a leading communitarian, see Amitai Etzioni, *The Spirit of Community: Rights, Responsibilities, and the Communitarian Agenda* (New York: Crown, 1993). For evidence that a majority of Americans agree with communitarian positions on several major social issues, see David Karp, "Americans as Communitarians: An Empirical Study," *The Responsive Community* 7 (Winter 1996/1997): 42–51. However, it is unlikely that a majority of Americans are familiar with the term *communitarian*.

4. I use the terms *communitarians* and *neoliberals* almost interchangeably, but the two groups differ in that communitarians have an organized movement and neoliberals do not. The term *neoliberal* is often applied to persons who do not identify with that term, and thus it is difficult to document the content of neoliberal thought.

A question frequently asked when I discuss ideological factions in my classes is where feminists fit in the scheme. The answer is that feminists do not fit into any scheme of mutually exclusive ideological categories, because there are feminists in more than one of the other categories. Most feminists are liberals, but some are centrists and others are radicals. Most liberals and centrists, and not a small proportion of conservatives, believe in such feminist goals as male-female equality of economic opportunity and male-female equality in marriage. However, the proportion who identify themselves as feminists is only about a third, even among liberals, according to the 1996 General Social Survey, and is only about 40 percent among liberal women.

5. The views of the Democratic Leadership Council are reported in a magazine, *The New Democrat*, and in a bulletin titled *The DLC Update*, which is distributed by fax at irregular intervals but sometimes as frequently as twice per week.

6. Arguably the most articulate expressions of conservative views on family issues are essays published in *The Family in America*, issued monthly for many years by the Rockford Institute Center on the Family in America and now published by the Howard Center for Family, Religion, and Society. An important recent book on family issues by a secular conservative is Richard Gill, *Posterity Lost: Progress, Ideology, and the Decline of the American Family* (New York: Rowman and Littlefield, 1997).

7. For a clear statement of a conservative view of these cultural changes, see Edward Hoffman, "Pop Psychology and the Rise of Anti-Child Ideology: 1966–1974," *The Family in America* 5 (August 1991): 1–10.

8. See David A. Hartman, "Uncle Sam: Seducer?" *The Family in America* 11 (July 1997): 1, 5–7.

9. See Arlene Skolnick, *Embattled Paradise: The American Family in an Age of Uncertainty* (New York: Basic Books, 1994); and Stephanie Coontz,

*The Way We Never Were* (New York: Basic Books, 1992).

10. For instance, see Norval Glenn, "Are Stable Marriages and Two-Parent Families Concordant with Male-Female Equality? An Affirmative Answer," featured presentation at the National Council on Family Relations Conference in Kansas City, November 7, 1996; and Pepper Schwartz, "Peer Marriage," *The Responsive Community* 8 (Summer 1998): 48–60.

11. U.S. Department of Commerce, Bureau of the Census, *Statistical Abstract of the United States: 1997* (Washington, DC: U.S. Government Printing Office, 1997), p. 79; and data from the Monitoring the Future Surveys conducted by the Survey Research Center at the University of Michigan.

12. For instance, see Judith Stacey, *In the Name of the Family: Rethinking Family Values in the Postmodern Age* (Boston: Beacon Press, 1996).

13. Bernard Farber, "The Future of the American Family: A Dialectical Account," *Journal of Family Issues* 8 (December 1987): 431–433.

14. Amitai Etzioni makes only an incidental reference to abortion in *The Spirit of Community* and takes no position in the debates about abortion.

15. Extension of benefits to "domestic partners" usually includes cohabiting heterosexual couples for a pragmatic reason—that is, including heterosexuals makes the policies less vulnerable to legal challenge.

16. Almost all of these changes have been away from orthodox liberal positions for a rather obvious reason. So few family social scientists have taken orthodox conservative positions that it is impossible for there to be much movement away from those positions.

# 2

# How Family Wars Affect Us: Four Models of Family Change and Their Consequences*

NIJOLE V. BENOKRAITIS

I recently presented a seminar on family values to about 100 faculty, staff, and students at the University of Baltimore. When I asked members of the audience about their political affiliations, approximately equal numbers identified themselves as conservative, moderate, or liberal. Only a few people indicated that they were "other." I then asked the attendees how many would describe themselves as feminists. About a third raised their hands, some more hesitatingly than others. After the presentation, some of the participants commented that they were probably more "other" than they had realized. One of the students sent me an e-mail message, for example, that "I said I was conservative, but I'm pretty liberal on some issues. I'm against abortion, but I think gay marriages should be legalized. I think all welfare benefits to unwed mothers should be cut off, but it's okay to have illegitimate children if you can support them yourself."

As this anecdote suggests, our personal views on family-related issues may reflect more than one ideological viewpoint. Overall, however, most people identify themselves with one of the major political perspectives. This chapter expands Norval Glenn's overview (see Chapter 1) of the major factions in the family wars in several ways. First, I propose that the family debates include four, not three, influential ideological perspectives that Glenn describes (even

though liberal and feminist views overlap). Second, I address what I call the "so what?" question that I often ask my students. That is, so what if there are two, three, four, or ten perspectives on family change? Who cares? Finally, I offer some general critical thinking questions about each perspective that you, the student, should keep in mind as you read this book. (Specific critical thinking questions will follow each article in Chapters 3 to 18).

## FOUR MODELS OF FAMILY CHANGE

As Glenn notes in Chapter 1, the same descriptive findings can be used to argue that the glass is half empty or half full.[1] An analysis of family change becomes even fuzzier, moreover, because the principal contestants in the family feuds "are not always explicit about their premises, and at times they advance rather inconsistent views."[2] I'll address inconsistent views later in this chapter. What, however, are the basic tenets of conservative, centrist, liberal, and feminist advocates in describing family change and proposing solutions? In my reading of the literature, and in doing the research for this reader, I saw four general perspectives on the changing family:

- *Conservatives* are alarmed that the family is declining and deteriorating morally because of the increased rates of divorce, out-of-wedlock births, and single-parent families.

* I am grateful to Jennifer S. Barber and Shirley L. Zimmerman for their comments on this chapter.

- *Centrists* feel that many of the family changes reflect decline and deterioration because "the massive erosion of fatherhood contributes mightily to many of the major problems of our time."[3]
- *Liberals* argue that the family is changing, not deteriorating, because family functions and gender roles have been adapting to economic transformations.
- *Feminists* assert that the family is stronger than ever because many women and men have more options than in the past.

You or your instructor may disagree with my typologies and conclusions. The classifications should be helpful, however, in providing a general framework for understanding the "family wars" debates.

## A Conservative Model: "The Family Is Declining and Deteriorating"

Conservatives see the family as falling apart because of a demise of family values, sexual promiscuity among teenagers as well as adults, and a general disintegration of the traditional family (see Table A). Conservative observers such as George Gilder, for example, blame much of the perceived family breakdown on women (see Chapter 5) because "the success or failure of civilized society depends on how well the women can transmit . . . values [such as the desire for male protection and support and a stable community life] to the men. . . . She is the vessel of the ultimate values of the nation."[4] Conservatives value traditional family gender roles (see Chapter 5) and feel that most Americans agree. They point to national polls, for example, which show that Americans overwhelmingly think it is better for children if the mother stays home.[5] Conservatives are reluctant to compensate mothers on welfare (see Chapter 18), however, and oppose federally funded childcare programs because they undermine the role of parents in the upbringing of their children.[6]

Conservatives applaud personal choice in economics but favor high social control of some kinds of behavior (see Chapter 1). Because conservatives, as a group, stress maintaining tradition and order, they want government to defend the community from perceived threats to its moral fiber.[7] Thus, most conservatives oppose government subsidies to unwed mothers and mother-headed families, as well as legislation (such as no-fault divorce and legalizing gay marriage) that threatens traditional definitions of the family and traditional "community standards."

Conservatives attribute many of our current societal ills to a decline in morality and, consequently, to the breakdown of the family. Most conservatives blame such problems as poverty, crime, drug use, societal violence, and high school dropouts to a demise of family values (see Table A). And, according to most conservatives, government interference dilutes parents' rights to

**TABLE A. Conservative Model: "The Family Is Declining/Deteriorating"**

| *Family changes are due to . . .* | *Consequences* | *Remedies* |
|---|---|---|
| • cultural and moral weakening<br>• demise of family values<br>• sexual promiscuity<br>• generous welfare benefits | • family breakdown (e.g., cohabitation, divorce, single mothers, out-of-wedlock births)<br>• school dropouts<br>• poverty<br>• crime<br>• drug use<br>• societal violence | • restore religious faith<br>• reinstitutionalize marriage<br>• cut welfare payments to unwed mothers and mother-headed families<br>• stigmatize divorce and out-of-wedlock birth<br>• return full-time mother to the home |

direct the upbringing and education of their children: Parents should have more control over sex education classes, curricula, and testing materials.

## A Centrist Model: "Many Aspects of the Family Are Declining or Deteriorating"

While conservatives focus on a return to traditional family structures and forms, centrists claim that some groups, especially families, should deemphasize the needs and rights of individuals and support "communal responsibility."[8] Centrists who feel that the family is in trouble cite such reasons as a lack of individual responsibility, a lack of parental commitment to the family, and just plain selfishness by adults who are more concerned about themselves than nurturing their children (see Table B and Chapter 4).

Many centrists argue that the family is deteriorating because most people place a higher priority on meeting their own individual needs rather than those of the family. Many adults, centrists maintain, arc unwilling to invest their psychological and financial resources when they do have children or give up on marriages too quickly when there are problems.[9] Centrists claim that a relentless pursuit of career goals and financial success lessens the attainment of marital and parental goals. That is, there has been a general increase of a sense of entitlement (what people believe they should receive from others) and a decline of a sense of duty (what people believe they should give to others). When married people focus almost exclusively on their personal gratification, such traditional institutional functions of marriage as the care and socialization of children become a lower priority.[10]

Communitarians, an influential group of centrists, see the family, not the individual, as the primary building block of a responsible society:

> The central thesis is that the common good of the community should take precedence over self-interested, autonomous individuals. For communitarians a sense of self (or social identity) is possible only within the context of some form of "communal life."[11]

As Glenn noted in Chapter 1, centrists (including communitarians) don't simply take positions midway between those of liberals and conservatives. Centrists agree with (secular) conservatives on some issues (such as eliminating no-fault divorce laws) and with liberals on other issues (such as providing paid leave for parents following a birth or an adoption). As I note in the Preface, centrists appear to be avoiding some of the most contentious debates, espe-

**TABLE B. Centrist Model: "Many Aspects of the Family Are Declining/Deteriorating"**

| Family changes are due to . . . | Consequences | Remedies |
| --- | --- | --- |
| • selfishness and "me-first" values<br>• rampant individualism<br>• parents' failure to nurture their children<br>• media and parental permissiveness | • children are not developing into responsible adults<br>• premature sexualization of children<br>• high divorce rates<br>• high out-of-wedlock birth rates<br>• father absence in the home | • promote self-help programs<br>• provide 6 months' paid leave for intact families following child's birth or adoption<br>• give two-parent households tax exemptions<br>• establish paternity at the time of birth and enforce child support payments<br>• prepare couples for marriage and discourage divorce<br>• campaign against teenage pregnancy |

cially on abortion, the legitimacy of gay families, and welfare reform.

I disagree with Glenn that centrists (and communitarians in particular) "believe that equality in marriage and marital stability are not incompatible goals" or that centrists "generally do not disapprove of the employment of mothers outside the home or of the growing economic independence of women." A number of centrists seem to blame many of the family's problems on mothers who work outside the home. If mothers stayed at home and took care of their children, many centrists maintain, we would have less delinquency, fewer high school dropouts, and more disciplined children (see the centrist positions in Chapters 9, 10, and 12).

Other "it's-the-employed-mother's-fault" centrist arguments are more subtle. Maggie Gallagher notes, for example, that "today the young woman who contemplates dropping out of the workforce to care for her own baby, even temporarily, must fight strong cultural forces that seek to keep her tied to the workplace." And, if women had good provider husbands, they could choose "to devote their talents and education and energy to the rearing of their chil-

dren, the nurturing of family relationships, and the building of community and neighborhood."[12] The implication is that the deteriorating family could be shored up if fathers were breadwinners and mothers were homemakers.

## The Liberal Model: "The Family Is Changing, not Deteriorating"

Conservatives seek a return to traditional family structures. Centrists emphasize the importance of group rather than individual rights that support two-parent families. Liberals, in contrast, endorse individual choice in personal matters. Most liberals accept a wide range of family forms (such as single-mother and gay/lesbian households) and maintain that the government should help the most disadvantaged groups, including unwed teenage mothers (see Table C).

Unlike conservatives and centrists, many liberals argue that the family has not deteriorated. Instead, liberals maintain, many of the changes we are experiencing are extensions of long-standing family patterns. Although more mothers have entered the labor force since 1970, the mother who

## TABLE C. Liberal Model: "The Family Is Changing, Not Deteriorating"

| Family changes are due to . . . | Consequences | Remedies |
|---|---|---|
| • economic structure<br>• changing demographic patterns<br>• changing family functions and gender roles<br>• greater acceptance of changing sexual mores | • current economy promotes material poverty among poor and "time poverty" among middle- and working-class families<br>• job insecurity and deteriorating employment opportunities in many sectors<br>• growth of two-earner families<br>• increase of employed mothers<br>• postponement of marriage | • facilitate women's employment through government-sponsored policies<br>• provide programs to help women and children become economically secure<br>• establish more training and job opportunities for low-income workers<br>• implement universal health insurance<br>• reform tax law to help dependents and unmarried couples<br>• intensify child support enforcement |

works outside the home is not a recent phenomenon. The number of married women in the labor force doubled between 1930 and 1980 but *quadrupled* between 1900 and 1904.[13] Some scholars contend that family problems such as desertion, illegitimacy, and child abuse have always existed. Family literature published during the 1930s, for example, included studies that document divorce, desertion, and family crises due to discord, delinquency, and depression.[14]

Similarly, liberals note that single-parent families have always existed. The percentage of single-parent households has doubled during the past three decades, but this number *tripled* between 1900 and 1950.[15] Divorce began to be more common during the eighteenth century, when parents could no longer control their adult married children, the importance of romantic love began to grow, and women began to have greater access to divorce.[16] Clearly, however, greater proportions of people divorce today than ever before and marriages are ending in divorce earlier. As a result, many singles are postponing marriage until they are older, more mature, and have stable careers.

Another major difference among conservatives, centrists, and liberals is that liberals tend to rely on government to solve numerous family-related dilemmas. Liberals argue that since government has created, or at least has done little to reduce, such problems as child poverty, homelessness, and working poor families (see Chapter 14), we need macro-level solutions for macro-level problems.

### The Feminist Model: "Many Families Are Stronger Than Ever" or "I'm Not Going Back to the Bad Old Days"

Although all feminists are probably liberals, all liberals are not feminists. Feminists challenge the notion (held by many liberals) that the traditional family where the father is the breadwinner and the mother is the full-time homemaker is either "natural" or desirable. Feminists point out that family life is diverse and that our notion of "the family" should be expanded to encompass families from many cultures and racial groups, including those with single heads of households, lesbian and gay families, stepfamilies, and grandparent-grandchild households (see Table D).

Like most liberals, feminists believe that many family-related problems are the consequence, not the cause, of societal changes. Instead of persisting in seeing the family as a source of social disarray, feminists maintain, conservatives and centrists should give "due weight to how social conditions affect the structure and viability of families."[17]

Feminists share some of the same concerns about families with the other political/ideological groups. Feminists agree with conservatives, for example, that the family is an important institution in U.S. society. They agree with centrists that children's well-being should be a high priority in our communities and in governmental programs. And they agree with liberals that many national policies have supported greedy corporations instead of providing institutional supports for low-income workers, children in single-parent households, and universal health insurance for all families.

Unlike the other political/ideological groups, however, feminists argue that women's and children's issues are often ignored despite all the rhetoric about family values. Many liberals, feminists argue, are still reluctant to implement workplace policies that encourage *both* men and women (married or divorced) to care for children and aging relatives, to lobby for legislation that eliminates gender gaps in salaries, and to provide quality day care for employed mothers (see Chapters 12, 13, and 14).

Some feminists are especially suspicious of the "new family values campaign" promoted by centrists. Judith

**TABLE D. Feminist Model: "The Family Is Stronger Than Ever" or "I'm Not Going Back to the Bad Old Days"**

| Family changes are due to . . . | Consequences* | Remedies |
|---|---|---|
| • women's drive for more equality in many institutions<br>• changing family definitions, forms, and gender roles<br>• women's challenging patriarchal systems<br>• lack of supportive kin, communities, and workplaces | • greater satisfaction in diverse family forms<br>• greater role flexibility across the life cycle<br>• divorce often leads to a "feminization of poverty"<br>• unfriendly work policies create domestic stress<br>• outdated family policies reinforce the division of labor in the home between the sexes as natural or inevitable | • develop more institutional supports for dual-earner and single-parent families<br>• legislate family-friendly workplace policies (such as flexible work time)<br>• enforce economic support from absent fathers<br>• provide quality child care for all families and decent housing in good neighborhoods for poor families<br>• raise women's wages and salaries to close the income gender gap<br>• implement universal health insurance for all families |

*Most feminists feel that the family is stronger than ever. They also argue that many policies are outdated and don't support changing family definitions, forms, and gender roles. Thus, this column reflects both positive and negative consequences of changing families.

Stacey believes, for example, that centrists perpetuate gender, race, and class inequalities: they are out of touch with working-class family life; their complaints about individualism reflect a criticism of women's growing independence; their concern about "fatherless families" is an attempt to decrease women's economic independence; and their promotion of marriage is an attack on black unwed mothers[18] (see Chapter 9).

### SO WHAT?

So far, I've summarized some of the most important characteristics of conservative, centrist, liberal, and feminist perspectives on family issues. The next question is "So what? Who cares if there *are* different views about the family?"

*You* should care because many family debates are often translated into laws and policies. I continuously remind my students, for example, that *ideas have conse-quences.* In 1980, for example, a hit-and-run driver killed a 13-year-old-girl in California. Although the driver had several drunk-driving crashes, the judge allowed the offender to serve time in a work camp and a halfway house instead of going to prison. A handful of California mothers, furious at the judge's ruling, organized Mothers Against Drunk Driving (MADD). Since 1980, MADD has been extremely influential in changing state laws to limit plea-bargaining and implement prison terms for drunk driving. Thus, ideas can have consequences.

Conservatives, centrists, liberals, and feminists who lobby for a variety of family-related "remedies" affect our family lives on a daily basis. In 1993, for example, President Clinton finally signed into law the Family and Medical Leave Act (FMLA) that was first introduced into Congress in 1985. Compared to similar laws in other countries, the FMLA was largely symbolic rather than actually helpful to working parents.[19] Since 1989, 17 industrialized countries have provided between 12 and 72 weeks of *paid* parental leave.[20] In Norway, Sweden, France, Japan, Belgium, Italy, Canada, Austria, Denmark, and other industrialized countries that are much less wealthy than the United States, the government and most companies offer subsidies to parents (divorced, single, or married), provide high-quality day care, and offer generous and paid childbirth benefits.[21]

Family-friendly policies don't "just happen," however, and especially not in the United States. Activists who endorse a particular view usually devote many years to lobbying and persuading others to support their position, to pressure legislators, and to vote for or against issues or congressional candidates who will shape family policy. That is, it may take years before an idea is translated into policy.

If you look at the "Remedies" column of Tables A to D, you'll see, again, that ideas have consequences. Political ideologies are often translated into family policies. Conservatives and centrists, for example, have played an influential role in changing the welfare system under the 1996 Personal Responsibility and Work Opportunity Reconciliation Act (see Chapter 18). Both groups have also been effective in encouraging some states to pass "covenant marriage" laws that discourage no-fault divorce and require couples to take counseling classes before getting married (see Chapter 8). Liberals pushed through the FMLA despite widespread resistance from conservatives. Feminists have promoted legislation against family violence, sexual harassment in the workplace, domestic partner benefits, and quality day-care programs.

Overall, when the full array of family issues is taken into account, there is much consistency between the explanations of family problems (first column) and the proposed remedies (third column) across the political and ideological spectra. Because they attribute family changes to the breakdown of traditional family structures and sexual promiscuity, conservatives propose such remedies as stigmatizing divorce and out-of-wedlock birth, cutting welfare support for unwed mothers and mother-headed families, and encouraging women to be full-time mothers.

Centrists, who are most concerned about the decline of two-parent families due to individual selfishness, endorse remedies that would provide tax exemptions for two-parent households, discourage divorce and father absence, and encourage current and prospective parents to be more responsible for their progeny.

Liberals attribute family changes and related problems to economic inequality and to changing family functions and gender roles rather than to individual frailty. Consequently, liberals offer such macro-level remedies as more training and job opportunities for low-income workers, tax credits to lift many unmarried couples and their children out of poverty, and increasing child support enforcement.

Feminists ascribe many changes in families to economic factors and a patriarchal system that devalues women's domestic caregiving and paid labor. Accordingly, feminists want reforms that encourage both women and men to engage in caregiving while being productive workers, to increase the wages of single mothers in low-paying jobs, to provide adequate child care, and to promote decent housing and hospitable neighborhoods for lower socioeconomic families.[22]

Note, however, that there may be inconsistencies *within* ideological and political perspectives. Consider, for example, the question of whether or not the government should intervene in family issues. Conservatives argue for government intervention in some family areas (such as abortion) but feel that government has no business intervening in family lives in other areas (such as welfare). Centrists maintain that children's well being is a primary concern, but support pro-family economic policies primarily for biological, "intact" families. Liberals and feminists argue that government has no right to interfere in childbearing decisions (such as abortion), but that government has a responsibility to support low-income families financially (through welfare, for example).

## SOME GENERAL CRITICAL THINKING QUESTIONS

Several of the faculty who reviewed the proposal for *Feuds About Families* urged me to identify my own political stance and ideological biases. Initially, I grumbled to myself that "I'm going to be objective. My personal views won't interfere." Such disclaimers are defensive and self-righteous, of course. No matter how objective your instructor, you, or I try to be, none of us (or the research that social scientists conduct) is really "value-neutral."

Generally, I consider myself somewhere between a liberal and a radical feminist[23] on many family-related issues. I agree with conservatives, however, that out-of-wedlock births, especially for teenagers, should be discouraged—not because illegitimate births are immoral, as many conservatives argue, but because teenagers (and even many young adults) are simply not prepared, emotionally and financially, to raise children. I also agree with centrists that the media foster sexual permissiveness (especially among teenagers) by its unrealistic portrayal of sex as safe and unencumbered by responsibility (see Chapter 10). I side with liberals who argue, for example, that economic inequality is at the root of many family-related problems (such as poverty and welfare). I identify most closely with feminists, however, because they emphasize family strength—in promoting human satisfaction and each family member's development—regardless of family form (married, divorced, cohabiting, or remarried). I also agree with feminists that our policies should help, not hurt, women and men who juggle work and family responsibilities.

After every selection in each chapter, I'll provide some critical thinking questions to spark class discussions and foster individual reflection. Overall, however, here are a few of the contradictions, inconsistencies, and general questions that I encountered as I prepared this reader:

### Conservatives

- Whose "family values" are important? Are the family values of two-parent households superior to those of divorced parents or never-married parents?
- Pro-life for whom? If conservatives insist on compulsory pregnancy, should they also be supporting welfare for poor families and mothers? And themselves adopting unwanted children who have not been aborted?
- If women are expected to be full-time mothers, how will young and uneducated men support their families on minimum-wage salaries?
- Does the state of children's physical and financial health depend, entirely, on a two-parent family? How do such non-family forces as the failings of our educational system as well as violent streets and neighborhoods affect children? And do two-parent homes guarantee that the parents won't be alcoholics, drug-users, or child abusers?

### Centrists

- Should community interests really override individual rights? Even if the relationship isn't violent, for example, should a spouse tolerate an alcoholic or otherwise "dysfunctional" partner who's participating only minimally in the child's upbringing?
- Are stepfamilies and gay/lesbian households really "deficient" compared to "intact" and traditional families?
- If two-parent families are critical, why haven't centrists advocated support for working-poor families who are living just above the poverty level?
- If divorce is so terrible, why are children of divorce in other countries (such as France and Sweden) doing well

financially, educationally, and emotionally?

## Liberals

- Because economic policies have disabled many families' functioning, why aren't liberals promoting family-friendly legislation that supports divorced parents and single mothers in the workplace?
- Are liberals depending too much on government to solve micro-level problems that may be due to parental irresponsibility across the income spectrum?
- Although there's a lot of rhetoric, what have liberals really done to improve the job opportunities and salary increases of low-income earners and working-poor families?
- Since they profess a commitment to raising healthy children, why do many liberal legislators fund pork-barrel projects in their own communities rather than passing legislation to build strong educational systems, to protect women and children from domestic violence, and to lift hardworking families out of poverty?

## Feminists

- Since most feminists say that they're interested in the intersections of race/ethnicity, class, sex, and sexual orientation, why is much of the research still about white, middle-class, and professional women?
- Although feminists have helped to implement domestic violence legislation, why do they often ignore family violence where mothers and wives are the offenders?
- How much effort have feminists devoted to the rights and concerns of traditional women, such as homemakers' social security benefits?
- Are feminists ignoring many family-related problems of men in lower socioeconomic classes because they focus, almost exclusively, on women's rather than peoples' rights?

In conclusion, you should be aware that all of the ideological groups (except feminists) are well funded in pursuing and implementing their political objectives. According to one researcher, there are at least 1,300 non-profit "think tanks" nationally. These think tanks perform five major roles: (1) they are a source of ideas for politicians; (2) they evaluate and publish books on policy proposals; (3) they evaluate government programs to determine if they are operating effectively and efficiently; (4) they serve as a source of personnel for incoming administrations; and (5) they often serve as "authoritative" sources of information for news organizations and educators.[24] The American Enterprise Institute and the Heritage Foundation, for example, fund conservative think tanks, the Institute for American Values funds centrists, and the Brookings Institution and the Urban Institute support liberals.

Many conservatives and centrists complain that academic institutions are too liberal. A recent report published by the National Committee for Responsive Philanthropy shows, however, that between 1992 and 1994, 12 conservative foundations funneled $210 million to a small group of privileged educational institutions. The contributions support specific curricular programs that promote conservative perspectives and finance students and faculty who espouse conservative views in their research and publications.[25] There are conservative, centrist, and liberal faculty in practically every higher education institution. Outside the classroom, similarly, we rarely read "neutral" material on family-related issues. I hope that the rest of this book enhances your awareness and understanding of the political controversies surrounding family issues. Consider the flaws and the strengths of the different positions as you read the articles in each chapter. Then, draw your own conclusions.

## NOTES

1. Based on my research for this reader, for example, I've noticed that conservatives, centrists, liberals, and feminists draw very different conclusions about the positive or negative effects of single-parent families and divorce from two publications: Sara McLanahan and Gary Sandefur, *Growing Up with a Single Parent: What Hurts and What Helps* (Cambridge, MA: Harvard University Press, 1994); and Paul R. Amato and Alan Booth, "Consequences of Parental Divorce and Marital Unhappiness for Adult Well-Being," *Social Forces* 69 (March 1991): 891–911.

2. Gideon Sjoberg, Norma Williams, Elizabeth Gill, and Kelly F. Himmel, "Family Life and Racial and Ethnic Diversity: An Assessment of Communitarianism, Liberalism, and Conservatism," *Journal of Family Issues* 16 (May 1995): 247.

3. David Popenoe, *Life Without Father: Compelling New Evidence That Fatherhood and Marriage Are Indispensable for the Good of Children and Society* (New York: Free Press, 1996), p. 1.

4. George Gilder, *Men and Marriage* (New York: Pelican Publishers, 1992), p. 8.

5. "Americans Believe Mom Is Best Child Care Provider," Family Research Council, *www.frc.org:80/infocus/if98b2cc.html* (accessed January 10, 1997).

6. " 'Family Time' Child Care Policy," Family Research Council, *www.frc.org/faq/faq5.html* (accessed January 22, 1999).

7. Marshall Fritz, *Beyond Left/Right* (Fresno, CA: Advocates for Self-Government, Inc: 1987).

8. Alan Wolfe, "Scholarship on Family Values: Weighing Competing Claims," *Chronicle of Higher Education*, January 23, 1998, p. B8.

9. See, for example, Steven Flanders, "The Benefits of Marriage," *The Public Interest* 124 (Summer 1996): 80–86; Maggie Gallagher, *The Abolition of Marriage: How We Destroy Lasting Love* (Washington, DC: Regnery, 1996); and David Blankenhorn, *Fatherless America: Confronting Our Most Urgent Social Problem* (New York: HarperCollins, 1995).

10. Norval D. Glenn, "Values, Attitudes, and the State of American Marriage," in *Promises to Keep: Decline and Renewal of Marriage in America*, ed. D. Popenoe, J. B. Elshtain, and D. Blankenhorn (Lanham, MD: Rowman & Littlefield, 1996), pp. 15–33.

11. Sjoberg et al., "Family Life and Racial and Ethnic Diversity," p. 248.

12. Gallagher, *The Abolition of Marriage*, pp. 183, 184.

13. David E. Stannard, "Changes in the American Family: Fiction and Reality," in *Changing Images of the Family*, ed. Virginia Tufte and Barbara Myerhoff (New Haven, CT: Yale University Press, 1979), pp. 83–98.

14. Carlfred B. Broderick, "To Arrive Where We Started: The Field of Family Studies in the 1930s," *Journal of Marriage and the Family* 50 (August 1988): 569–584.

15. Stannard, "Changes in the American Family," pp. 83–98.

16. Nancy F. Cott, "Eighteenth Century Family and Social Life Revealed in Massachusetts Divorce Records," *Journal of Social History* 10 (Fall 1976): 20–43.

17. Bonnie Thornton Dill, Maxine Baca Zinn, and Sandra Patton, "Feminism, Race, and the Politics of Family Values," *Report from the Institute for Philosophy & Public Policy* 13 (Summer 1993): 17.

18. Judith Stacey, *In the Name of the Family: Rethinking Family Values in the Postmodern Age* (Boston: Beacon Press, 1996).

19. For a critical evaluation of the FMLA that is still relevant today, see, for example, Melissa Kesler Gilbert and Nijole V. Benokraitis, "The Family and Medical Leave Act of 1988: One Step Forward and Two Steps Back?" *Family Perspective*, 8, no. 1 (1989): 57–73.

20. C. J. Ruhm and J. L. Teague, "Parental Leave Policies in Europe and North America," in *Gender and Family Issues in the Workplace*, ed. Francine D. Blau and Ronald G. Ehrenberg (New York: Russell Sage Foundation, 1997), pp. 133–156.

21. For a summary of family-friendly policies in these and other countries, see Nijole V. Benokraitis, *Marriages and Families: Changes, Choices, and Constraints*, 3rd ed. (Upper Saddle River, NJ: Prentice Hall, 1999), pp. 509–511.

22. Janet Z. Giele, "Decline of the Family: Conservative, Liberal, and Feminist Views," in *Promises to Keep: Decline and Renewal of Marriage in America*, ed. David Popenoe, Jean Bethke Elshtain, and David Blankenhorn (Lanham, MD: Rowman & Littlefield, 1996), pp. 89–115.

23. There are many feminisms. *Liberal feminism*, for example, emphasizes social and legal reform to create equal opportunities for women (and men) in the workplace, politics, and education. *Radical feminism* considers patriarchy to be the major cause of women's and children's low status and inequality. In a patriarchy, men generally hold the positions of power and authority—political, economic, legal, religious, educational, military, and domestic. Across all socioeconomic levels, males in patriarchal societies are considered heads of household and dominate the economic, social, and domestic spheres of family life.

24. Steven K. Wisensale, "The Family in the Think Tank," *Family Relations* 40 (April 1991): 199–207.

25. The academic institutions that have received the most generous grants from conservative think tanks during this period include the following: University of Chicago ($10.4 million), Harvard University ($9.7 million), George Mason University ($8.6 million), Yale University ($6 million), Claremont McKenna College ($3.1 million), Marquette University ($1.6 million), Boston University ($1.5 million), Cornell University ($1.4 million), Stanford University ($1.3 million), Georgetown University ($1.2 million), New York University ($1.1 million), University of California, Berkeley ($830,000), Columbia University ($852,725), Duquesne University ($484,000), and Hillsdale College ($451,000). Cited in Sally Covington, *Moving a Public Policy Agenda: The Strategic Philanthropy of Conservative Foundations* (Washington, DC: National Committee for Responsive Philanthropy, 1997), p. 8.

# II DEFINING MARRIAGE AND FAMILY ISSUES

About 25 years ago, a sociologist observed that family ties are likely to persist in our society because human beings need stability, continuity, and affection.[1] Most people, regardless of their political or ideological perspectives, would probably agree. As you saw in Chapter 2, conservatives, centrists, liberals, and feminists are all "pro-family." They all want family ties to be strong and feel that a family should provide stability and affection. The disagreement reflects how the various groups define "family ties" and "family." The three readings in this section illustrate some of the divergent views on what constitutes a family, what we mean by "family values," and which family gender roles are appropriate.

You'll notice that, across the three chapters, the "factions" make different assumptions about the family. Consequently, they draw different conclusions about "healthy" and "unhealthy" families. Conservatives, for example, equate the family with a traditional family form that includes the biological parents and their children. Traditional female and male roles are valued. Centrists emphasize the importance of the married couple and its children even if mothers and fathers don't play traditional roles. Compared to conservatives, for example, centrists are more accepting of employed mothers and on improving day-care accessibility. They feel, however, that the family would fare better if mothers placed a higher priority on raising their children. Liberals, in contrast, embrace a great variety of family structures:

> It is time to abandon once and for all the idol of "The Family" and to validate the great variety of families that people are actually living by. Mainstream culture . . . promotes a set of images of family and home that no longer bear much relation to either reality or the imaginings of a large part of the population. It is time to recognize the richness of our contemporary family cultures and to explore the possibilities that these open to all of us regardless of our class, race, or gender.[2]

Feminists, like liberals, approve of a variety of family forms. Feminists insist, moreover, that men should share in the housework and childrearing tasks.

## Chapter 3: Current Perspectives on the Family

In a recent article on the family, Frank Furstenberg, a prominent U.S. demographer and family sociologist, concluded that "the current situation falls somewhere between those who embrace the changes with complete sanguinity and an increasingly vocal group who see the meltdown of the so-called traditional family as an unmitigated disaster."[3] As Chapter 3 shows, however, the various political and ideological groups are much less middle-of-the-road in their views on the changing family.

In the first article, "The Breakdown of the Family," Patrick F. Fagan argues, as do many conservatives, that most of our societal problems, such as high crime rates, reflect a disintegration of the family. If, Fagan notes, we endorsed a traditional family structure where people marry before having children and women stayed at home to raise their children, we wouldn't experience a continuous rise of out-of-wedlock births, widespread premarital and nonmarital sex, and high divorce rates.

Centrists are as concerned about "family breakdown" as are conservatives. Both groups, moreover, feel that "intact" families provide a "moral cornerstone" in raising children. In contrast to conservatives, however, centrists believe that family disintegration reflects adults' placing a higher priority on their own individual needs rather than living up to family responsibilities.[4] Essentially, many centrists feel that "self-absorbed baby boomers" and a "me first" attitude have eroded family loyalty and altruism. Adults place more importance on pursuing their careers and professional interests than in raising their children.[5] As the article "A Communitarian Position on the Family" by Jean Elshtain and her colleagues shows, centrists feel that mothers and fathers should rededicate themselves to their children. Centrists believe, unlike most conservatives, that workplaces should provide greater flexibility for working parents. Centrists think, however, that the government should make it harder to get a divorce and should implement tax codes that support marriage.

Liberals and feminists agree with centrists that government policies should support families. They differ from both conservatives and centrists in three major ways, however. First, most liberals, especially feminists, define family more broadly: "If we define 'the family' as existing only during that short time of life spent as a married couple with children under eighteen, we are ignoring the lives of the vast majority of Americans."[6]

Second, liberals fault conservatives and centrists for lacking a historical context when they describe the family as being "in crisis."[7] Stephanie Coontz, in "Why We Miss the 1950s," maintains, for example, that the "traditional family" of the 1950s has been romanticized. She believes that blaming myriad social problems (such as poverty) on family forms deflects attention from defects in American society, especially its economy. If contemporary families enjoyed the same programs and family subsidies that the government provided to middle- and working-class families during the 1950s, she argues, most families would be financially secure and stable.

A third difference between liberals and centrists reflects government intervention. Centrists endorse government support (such as access to quality child care) for two-parent families. In contrast, feminists and most liberals believe that government should place a high priority on strengthening poor families—whether married, divorced, or headed by an unmarried mother.

## Chapter 4: Family Values

In May 1992, then-Vice President Dan Quayle delivered a speech in San Francisco on restoring basic values. He lambasted Murphy Brown, the central character in a popular television program, for having a baby outside of marriage:

> Ultimately . . . marriage is a moral issue that requires cultural consensus, and the use of social sanctions. Bearing babies irresponsibly is, simply, wrong. Failing to support children one has fathered is wrong. We must be unequivocal about this. . . . It doesn't help matters when prime time TV has Murphy Brown—a character who supposedly epitomizes today's intelligent, highly paid, professional woman—mocking the importance of fathers, by bearing a child alone, and calling it just another "lifestyle choice."[8]

About a year after the Quayle speech, Barbara Dafoe Whitehead, a widely read writer who identifies herself as a communitarian, published an article in *The Atlantic Monthly* entitled "Dan Quayle Was Right."[9] In the article, Whitehead claimed that, in contrast to "intact" and "stable" families, children of divorced, separated, or never-married parents are far more likely to live in poverty, drop out of school, become pregnant as teenagers, abuse drugs, and engage in such aggressive behavior as assaulting teachers and classmates.

The Whitehead article ignited a debate about family values that continues as we enter the next millennium. Like Whitehead, conservatives often blame a deterioration of family values on the rise in cohabitation, out-of-wedlock births, welfare, and divorce rates. As James Q. Wilson argues, in "The Family-Values Debate," for example, childrearing requires a commitment from both parents, and the commitment should be sealed through marital vows.

For the most part, centrists agree with conservatives that the growth of single-parent families has had a detrimental effect on families and has eroded traditional family values. According to Dennis K. Orthner, in "The Revolution in Family Norms," although cultural values have been changing slowly throughout the twentieth century, "We are now confronted by a veritable revolution in family norms." This revolution in family norms, Orthner believes, has created confusion in forming and maintaining adult relationships, especially in marriage. As a result, divorce is more acceptable. Stepfamily norms are vague, redivorce is common, and a search for individual happiness has replaced traditional family values.

Feminists and many liberals believe that the emphasis on "family values" reflects little more than a backlash—by both conservatives and centrists—in response to family changes. They feel that the push to "restore" the traditional nuclear family ostracizes many family forms, especially the children of unmarried mothers or divorced parents. Arlene Skolnick and Stacey Rosencrantz write in their article "The New Crusade for the Old Family" that "sooner or later, we are going to have to let go of the fantasy that we can restore the family of the 1950s."

Despite some of these heated debates on family values, most people feel that the family is a top priority. In a study of personal values in 35 countries, for example, Roper Starch Worldwide found that the respondents in 22 countries, including the United States, classified protecting the family as their top value. In the United States, the family was valued more than honesty, stable personal relationships, freedom, or friendship.[10]

## Chapter 5: Women's and Men's Family Roles

In June 1998, the Southern Baptist Convention adopted a resolution that delineated women's and men's family roles. A husband "has the God-given responsibility to provide for, to protect, and to lead his family." A wife is "to submit herself graciously to the servant leadership of her husband," to respect her husband, and "to serve as his helper in managing the household and nurturing the next generation."[11]

Most conservatives applaud such traditional family gender roles. The maternal role is paramount. A good mother should deny herself individual fulfillment to raise the children and perform domestic duties. Moreover, as George Gilder writes in "Women Should Domesticate Men for Marriage," because men are "innately" sexually promiscuous, women are responsible for maintaining the moral, aesthetic, religious, and nurturant values of the family and the community.

Centrists are somewhat more accepting of women's employment when it's absolutely necessary for the family's economic survival. They maintain, however, that families would be better off if mothers devoted more of their time to raising children. According to Maggie Gallagher, in "Gender Roles: A Taboo Subject," the "gender revolution" has promoted two-career couples and has eroded the happiness that traditional marital roles offer. As you'll see in later chapters, centrists express alarm over an increasingly "fatherless America"[12] where many men have abandoned their children, economically and emotionally. Centrists don't impugn divorced couples. For the most part, however, centrists favor a return to traditional gender roles with the father as the breadwinner and the mother as the full-time caregiver.

Liberals maintain that conservatives and centrists place too much emphasis on family structure and not enough on the emotional quality of the marital bond. In "Remaking Marriage and Family Roles," for example, Betty Carter and Joan Peters argue that the happiest couples are those where the relationships and power are egalitarian rather than traditional.

Some feminists allege, moreover, that the yearning for traditional gender roles "is nothing less than reestablishing control over women's lives." They believe that many male leaders "envision a day when households will once again be headed by men and women will fall into line, answering first to their husbands and then to God and country."[13] According to many feminists, the conservative and centrist emphasis on mom's staying home reflects a greater interest in dominating women's behavior than in improving children's well-being.

## NOTES

1. Mary Jo Bane, *Here to Stay: American Families in the Twentieth Century* (New York: Basic Books, 1976).

2. John R. Gillis, *A World of Their Own Making: Myth, Ritual, and the Quest for Family Values* (New York: Basic Books, 1996), p. 239.

3. Frank F. Furstenberg, Jr., "The Future of Marriage," *American Demographics* 18 (June 1996): 34.

4. For a discussion of the rights of individuals taking precedence over those of groups, including families, see Alan Wolfe, "Scholarship on Family Values: Weighing Competing Claims," *Chronicle of Higher Education*, January 23, 1998, pp. B7-B8.

5. Ibid.

6. Arlene Skolnick, *Embattled Paradise: The American Family in an Age of Uncertainty* (New York: Basic Books, 1991), p. 206.

7. See, for example, Chapters 1 and 2 in Edward L. Kain, *The Myth of Family Decline: Understanding Families in a World of Rapid Social Change* (Lexington, MA: Lexington Books, 1990).

8. Dan Quayle, "Restoring Basic Values: Strengthening the Family," *Vital Speeches of the Day*, 58 (June 1, 1992), p. 519.

9. Barbara Dafoe Whitehead, "Dan Quayle Was Right," *The Atlantic Monthly*, April 1993: pp. 47–84.

10. Roper Starch Worldwide, "Family Is Top Value for Most of World, Global Study Shows," *www.roper.com* (accessed October 18, 1998).

11. Time-Picayune Publishing Company, "Baptist Statement on Family," June 21, 1998, *http://web.lexis-nexis.com/univers* . . . (accessed June 23, 1998).

12. See, for example, David Blankenhorn, *Fatherless America: Confronting Our Most Urgent Social Problem* (New York: HarperPerennial, 1995); and David Popenoe, *Life Without Father* (New York: Free Press, 1996).

13. James Ridgeway, "Father Knows Best: Patriarchy Is Back, and Badder Than Ever," *Village Voice*, January 17, 1995, p. 15.

# 3 Current Perspectives on the Family

## Conservative: The Breakdown of the Family

PATRICK F. FAGAN, "The Breakdown of the Family," *http://www.heritage.org:80/ issues/chap6.pdf* (accessed January 10, 1999). Reproduced by permission of the Heritage Foundation and Patrick F. Fagan.

*According to Patrick Fagan and many other conservatives, most of our contemporary difficulties are due to the breakdown of the family. Fagan argues, for example, that we are experiencing a "societal erosion," reflected in high child abuse and crime rates. He attributes such problems to the rising out-of-wedlock births, early premarital sexual intercourse, high divorce rates, abortion, and employed mothers who don't spend enough time raising their children.*

### THE ISSUES

The family is the most fundamental of society's institutions, for it is within the family setting that character, morality, responsibility, ability, and wisdom are nurtured best in children. This is not news; yet, in America today, the family institution is being steadily dismantled, even held in disdain by many leaders in the political, academic, and media elite. And the insidious erosion has serious consequences:

- In 1950, for every 100 children born, 12 entered a broken family. Today, for every 100 children born, 60 will enter a broken family. Each year, about one million children experience the divorce of their parents, 1.25 million are born out of wedlock, and another 1.4 million are aborted. Child abuse is growing steadily, and child sexual abuse is growing fastest of all.

- In short, Americans are literally turning against their children. But adults suffer as well from the breakdown of the family institution. Studies clearly show that those who divorce suffer short life expectancies, poorer physical and psychological health, and lowered standards of living.[1]

The assault on the American family has not gone unnoticed. Conservative social scientists have begun to document the correlation between a family founded on a life-long marriage and low incidences of crime, addiction, abuse, illness, and underachievement. But increasingly, they encounter a problem in tracking such trends: Official government statistics on marriage, divorce, and correlates in child outcomes are being gathered and reported less frequently. In fact, statistics on marriage and divorce are no longer tracked in at least half of the states today.[2] This paucity of reliable information will make it more difficult to assess either the progress or the deterioration of the American family in the future. . . .

THE FACTS

### The Components of Family Breakdown

The American family has been weakened by two widespread patterns undermining marriage: giving birth to children out of wedlock and divorce. Both entail a rejection of marriage, though in different ways. Having children out of wedlock is a rejection of any initial commitment to a partner in marriage, and divorce is a rejection of marriage after that initial commitment has been made.

### Rising Rates of Out-of-Wedlock Birth

Among whites in 1995, 25.3 percent of births were out of wedlock, more than double the rate of 11 percent in 1980. Among blacks, 69.9 percent of births in 1995 were out of wedlock, up from 58 percent in 1980. In certain parts of the country, the rates of out-of-wedlock births for blacks are alarmingly high: 82.8 percent of births in Wisconsin in 1995 and almost 80 percent for blacks in most states surrounding the Great Lakes.[3]

For all demographic groups in all parts of the country, the trend in out-of-wedlock birth is the same: steadily upward. The changing demographics are propelled by changes in three factors:

1. A decline in the portion of women of childbearing age who are married;
2. An increase in the birth or fertility rate among non-married women; and
3. A decline in the birth or fertility rate among married women.

### Earlier Sexual Intercourse Outside of Marriage

As Chart 1 indicates, the increase in the birth rate among non-married women is propelled by the high levels of early sexual

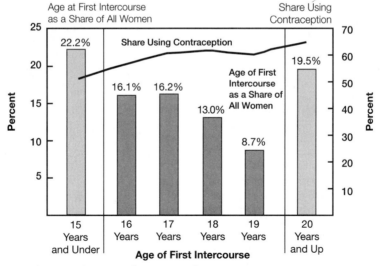

CHART 1. Age and Use of Contraception at First Intercourse for American Women

Note: The survey interviewed women aged 15–44.
Source: National Center for Health Statistics, *National Survey of Family Growth, 1995.*

intercourse and the use of contraception among teenagers—even very young teenagers—in America.

## Rising Rates of Divorce

Divorce is the second major cause of single-parent families, and Americans divorce at the highest rate among all nations of the world.[4] The number of children affected now seems to have leveled off at just over one million children per year. Though divorce reached its highest rate in 1978 and has dropped only slightly since then, the number of children living with single divorced parents continues to rise; in 1997, the number was 8.1 percent, up from 7.5 percent in 1993.[5]

## Abortions at Unacceptable Levels

Abortion is a sign of serious dysfunction in the sexual practices of the nation. So far, however, there has been only one large sample survey conducted to give a reliable snapshot of the rates of abortion within and outside of marriage. As reported in 1989 by the Alan Guttmacher Institute:[6]

- In 1988, women who were never married accounted for 63.3 percent of abortions; divorced women, 11.2 percent; women who were separated from their husbands, 6.4 percent; and married women whose husbands lived with them, 18.5 percent.

As the best approximation of abortion available from the research community, these same rates applied to the incidence of abortion since 1973 paint a grave picture of the number of surgical abortions of children:

- Of the 35.2 million surgical abortions of children performed since 1972, approximately 28.6 million (or 81 percent) occurred to women and teenagers who were committed neither to the child they had created nor to a spouse.

If policymakers and social activists seriously wish to bring about a reduction in the number of abortions today, they must focus on ways to reduce sexual intercourse outside of marriage. Efforts to provide contraceptives to children have not worked, as the National Campaign to Prevent Teen Pregnancy asserts.[7] To change the deplorable statistics cited above, the country must experience a cultural shift. Government agencies, policymakers, community leaders, teachers, religious leaders, actors, sports personalities, and parents will have to join their voices in support of sex after marriage. As effective teachers, the family, churches, and schools need to be encouraged to promote abstinence. Government action alone cannot deliver the cultural shift, though it certainly can help or hinder it. Of all the institutions that should lead in this effort, it is the churches and synagogues that must be up front, for that is their role.

## The Rising U.S. "Rejection Ratio"

Combining the demographic statistics for out-of-wedlock births, divorce, and early sexual intercourse provides a disturbing picture of the fractured American family (see Chart 2). The proportion of children who are being denied a nurturing and full family life by their parents is increasing. The ratio of children who suffer from such rejections has risen dramatically: from 12 out of every 100 children born in 1950 to over 58 for every 100 children born in 1992.

Sadly, it is possible to conclude that parents themselves have sharply diminished the strength of their families. In broken families, beneath the rejection of a child lies a fundamental rejection by the child's parents of each other. As a result, more and more Americans today are part of second, third, and even fourth generation broken families whose fathers and mothers, having rejected their commitment to each other, are now alienated from each other. This alienation weakens both their children's ability to value commitment to the family and (even more so) their ability to commit themselves to others. And when the rates of abortion—the ultimate rejection

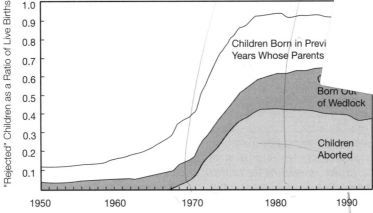

**CHART 2.** Annual Child Rejection Ratio: Children of Divorce, Ab[...]
and Out-of-Wedlock Births Compared with Live Births per Year

Note: A value of less than 1.0 indicates the number of rejected children is less than the number of children born. A value of 1.0 indicates both groups are of equal size.

Sources: National Center for Health Statistics data series, Alan Guttmacher Institute.

of a child—are added to this equation, the picture becomes even more stark.

## Family Time Famine

The amount of conversation and the level of interaction between parents and children has an enormous impact on a child's development. Even in intact families, however, children suffer from a lack of intimate time with their parents. One of the sad consequences of the breakdown of society today is that, to pay the bills or fulfill their higher expectations for material comforts, more mothers work outside the home. This fact, coupled with the numbers of single-parent families and the rising of divorce, means there has been a tragic reduction in "family time."

Adequate time with parents is critical for the development of every child, especially for self-esteem and confidence. The reduction of time between parents and children is cause for grave concern. It attenuates the most important relationship to a child and correspondingly deprives him of the strength he derives from his parents. As

Harvard University child psychiatrist Robert Coles puts it, "The frenzied need of children to have possessions isn't only a function of the ads they see on TV. It's a function of their hunger for what they aren't getting—their parents' time."[8]

- By 1990, parents were, on average, available 10 hours less per week to their children than they were in 1980 and 40 percent less than they were in 1965.[9]
- In a Massachusetts Mutual poll, 33 percent of parents said they did not spend enough time with their preschool children and 46 percent said they did not spend enough time with their teenagers.[10]
- A 1990 *Los Angeles Times* poll found that 57 percent of all fathers and 55 percent of all mothers felt guilty about spending too little time with their children. The poll also found that 73 percent of all married couples would have one parent stay home full-time with the children "if money were not an issue."[11]
- A 1990 Yankelovich poll found that 57 percent of mothers would give up work

ely if they no longer needed the
y.[12]

ecting the concern about mothers'
sence, a 1998 poll by Wirthlin Worldwide found that 86 percent of mothers
believe their children would do best if
they were cared for by their mothers
rather than by day care providers. Similarly an increasing number of parents
think too many children are being raised
in child care.[13]

There are many side effects. For instance,
one of the by-products of this situation of
attention to children is juvenile delinquency. Dr. James Allen Fox, Dean of the
College of Criminal Justice at Northeastern
University in Boston, stated at a 1995 congressional hearing on juvenile delinquency
that:

> I think it's a matter of supervision . . . one of
> the important elements that we are not talking
> about. . . . For example at this point 57% of
> the children in this country do not have full
> time parental supervision. . . . Almost 45% of
> the juvenile violent crimes occur between
> 3:00 in the afternoon and dinnertime. [They]
> are unsupervised in the neighborhood.[14]

One of the biggest factors driving the
dearth of family time is the growing
absence of mothers.

## Day Care Not the Answer

When mothers are away from their infant
children more than 20 hours each week, the
effect is an increase in the risk of attenua-
tion of early infant attachment, which in
turn further increases the risk that the child
will be unable to form close and satisfying
intimate relationships in the teen years and
adulthood.[15] Day care is no substitute for
time with mother.

Most Americans understand the importance a mother plays in a child's development. For example, polls commissioned by
the Family Research Council and conducted by Wirthlin Worldwide found that
Americans view care by a child's own
mother as the single most desirable form of
child care. Furthermore, they consider care

by a government-run day-care center as the
least desirable. According to these polls,
parents ranked the different options as
follows, from most desirable to least desirable:

1. Care by a child's own mother.
2. Care by the child's own grandmother or
   other family member.
3. Care by the child's own parents who
   work split shifts.
4. Care by a church-run center.
5. Care by a trusted neighbor or family
   friend.
6. Care by a day-care provider in the home.
7. Care by a nanny or *au pair*.
8. Care by a commercial day-care center.
9. Care by a government-run day-care
   center.[16] . . .

## THE EFFECTS OF SOCIAL CHANGE

### Effects of Marriage Breakdown on Child Development

Children pay a high price for their parents'
inability to commit to each other. Among
the principal effects are:[17]

- Lower newborn health and increased
  risk of early infant death;
- Retarded cognitive and verbal develop-
  ment;
- Lowered educational achievement;
- Lowered levels of job attainment;
- Increased ability to control impulses;
- Warped social development;
- Increased dependency on welfare;
- Increased exposure to crime; and
- Increased risk of being physically or sex-
  ually abused.[18]

### Effects of Marriage Breakdown on Adults

Adults also suffer from the breakup of their
marriages.[19] Some of the effects include:

- **Shorter life expectancies**. Married
  people have consistently lower death
  rates from disease, suicide, and accident
  mortality.[20] The death rate among non-
  smoking divorced men is almost the

same as it is for men who smoke at least two packs of cigarettes a day. Overall, the premature death rate is four times higher among divorced white men than among their married counterparts.[21]

- **Poorer physical health**. Divorced and separated people experience acute conditions such as infections and parasite diseases, respiratory illnesses, digestive disorders, and severe injuries significantly more frequently than other marital status groups.[22]

- **Poorer psychological health**. The divorced suffer from higher levels of stress and exhibit more psychiatric disorders like depression, which in turn have a profound impact on their physical well-being, including depressed immunological capacities.[23]

- **Lower economic well-being**. Only women who are very poor and go on Aid to Families with Dependent Children (AFDC), or who work longer hours after they are divorced than they did before they were divorced, experience an increase in income after divorce.[24] The poverty rate for black female-headed families is five times the rate for married black Americans, at 53.9 percent.[25] By contrast, married black Americans are steadily moving above the poverty level; the poverty rate among married blacks, in 1994 figures, is at 11.4 percent and is closing in on the 8.3 percent rate found among white married Americans.

## Broken Families and the Pathway to Crime

The breakdown of the family, added to the breakdown of the community, has a long-term effect on crime. The risk that a child will become a criminal increases as the child experiences the following:[26]

1. **In early childhood,** the child experiences parental neglect or abandonment in different combinations of fatherlessness, the absence of a mother's love, parental fighting and domestic violence, lack of parental supervision and discipline, out-right rejection, parental abuse and neglect, or parents who commit crimes.

2. **In the mid-childhood years,** the child is drawn to embryonic gangs of young aggressive children who are rejected by their peers and who seek out other alienated children; they fail in school, lose interest in education, and begin to run wild.

3. **In the early teenage years,** the embryonic gang of grade school changes into a gang of tough, exploitative teenagers who gradually become better at committing crimes.

4. **In the mid-teenage years,** violence emerges as a way of life within the gang as the teenagers become more expert and learn how to commit crimes without getting caught.

5. **In the late teenage years and early adulthood,** the former child—now a criminal—fathers his own child, stays with the mother for a while, but eventually abandons her and their child; the mother's background is similar to the young father's, and the child is raised not knowing any other existence.

The greater the number of single-parent families, the more likely it is that increasing numbers of children will experience this pathway to crime.

- Overall, a 10 percent increase in illegitimacy is associated with a 17 percent increase in violent teenage crime. With the continued rise in illegitimacy, more and more violent teenage criminals will be walking America's streets in the future. And with the appearance of these criminals, Americans will be forced to give up more and more of their everyday freedom as their level of fear rises. In addition, they will be forced to pay for the growing social and economic costs of this explosion in juvenile delinquency and crime.

## Broken Families and Child Abuse

Rising rates of serious child abuse follow the rising rates of marriage breakdown. Although national surveys on the relationship between marriage, cohabitation, and child abuse have not been conducted in the United States, serious studies in Britain indicate a startling relationship. Compared with children in traditional intact, married families, children are:[27]

- **Six times** more likely to be abused in blended (divorced and remarried) families;
- **Fourteen** times more likely to be abused in single mother/living alone families;
- **Twenty times** more likely to be abused in families where the natural parents cohabit; and
- **Thirty-three times** more likely to be abused when the mother cohabits with a boyfriend.

In the United States, the absence of marriage is most pronounced in the lower income groups. Among the poor, marriage is virtually disappearing. Of the 20 million children living with single parents, 12.6 million live in the poorest families. Sadly, the rates of abuse follow the absence of marriage. . . .

## Effects of Marriage Breakdown on the Community

When the number of single-parent families in a community reaches about 30 percent, the community begins to break down and the rate of crime begins to soar. The community changes from a supportive environment to one that jeopardizes the development of children.

The virtual extinction of two-parent families in poor inner-city neighborhoods has contributed greatly to the collapse of those neighborhoods. The absence of fathers means there is no adult male to give financial support, a guiding hand, or protection for children. The result is the prevalence of gangs of violent young men, young girls vulnerable to abuse, children having children, and mindless violent crime. A state-by-state analysis indicates that, in general, a 10 percent increase in the percentage of children living in single-parent homes (including divorces) is accompanied by a 17 percent increase in juvenile crime.[28]

Researchers have noted for some time that violent crime, among both teenagers and adults, is concentrated most heavily in urban neighborhoods that are characterized by a very high proportion of single-parent families.[29] Researchers today find that a neighborhood comprised primarily of single-parent families invariably is a chaotic and crime-ridden community[30] where gangs assume control.[31] Under such conditions, parental supervision of adolescent and pre-adolescent children is almost impossible.[32] Children raised in these neighborhoods are likely to learn, accept, and use physical violence to satisfy their wants and needs.[33]

In addition, institutions in poor neighborhoods that once provided help and guidance to those who may have lacked it at home have been crowded out by the burgeoning welfare state. Caring people in the community have been replaced by entitlement programs that emphasize rights and rules, not community and responsibility.

### NOTES

1. David B. Larson, James P. Swyers, and Susan S. Larson, "The Costly Consequences of Divorce: Assessing the Clinical, Economic and Public Health Impacts of Marital Disruption in the United States," National Institute for Healthcare Research, Rockville, Maryland, 1995, pp. 43–49.

2. According to officials at the National Center for Health Statistics, it is not possible to get accurate data on marriage and divorce statistics from 27 states.

3. National Center for Health Statistics, *Monthly Vital Statistics Report, Report of Final Natality Statistics*, 1995, Vol. 45, No. 11 (June 10, 1997), and earlier editions.

4. Bureau of the Census, U.S. Department of Commerce, *Children's Well Being: An International Comparison*, 1990, pp. 8, 9, 35.

5. Bureau of the Census, U.S. Department of Commerce, *Current Population Survey*, 1993, 1997.

6. Stanley K. Henshaw *et al.*,"Characteristics and Private Contraceptive Use of U.S. Abortion Patients," *Family Planning Perspectives*, Vol. 20, No. 4 (July/August 1989), p. 162.

7. Douglas Kirby, "No Easy Answer: Research Findings on Program to Reduce Teen Pregnancy," National Campaign to Prevent Teen Pregnancy, Washington, D.C., 1997.

8. Quoted by William R. Mattox, Jr., "The Parent Trap," *Policy Review*, No. 55 (Winter 1991), p. 10.

9. From research on personal time diaries by sociologist John Robinson of the University of Maryland. See Mattox, "The Parent Trap," pp. 6–13.

10. Family Research Council, "Family Time: What Americans Want," *In Focus*, December 1995.

11. *Ibid.*

12. *Ibid.*

13. Family Research Council, "Americans Believe Mom Is Best Child Care Provider," *In Focus*, No .1F98B2CC, 1998.

14. Dr. James Allen Fox, testimony at hearing on juvenile drug use, Committee on the Judiciary, U.S. Senate, December 20, 1995.

15. "Babies who start day care early in life and spend more than 20 hours per week in non-parental care develop avoidant attachments somewhat more often than other babies do." From Virginia Colin, *Infant Attachment: What We Know: A Literature Review*, Department of Health and Human Services, Washington, D.C., April 1991, p. 81.

16. Family Research Council, "Americans Believe Mom is Best."

17. Patrick F. Fagan, "Rising Illegitimacy: America's Social Catastrophe," Heritage Foundation *F.Y.I.* No. 19/94, June 29, 1994.

18. Patrick F. Fagan, "The Child Abuse Crisis: The Disintegration of Marriage, Family, and the American Community," Heritage Foundation *Backgrounder* No. 1115, June 3, 1997, pp. 9,10.

19. Summarized from an overview of the divorce literature in Larson *et al.*, "The Costly Consequences of Divorce."

20. *Ibid.*, pp. 43–49.

21. *Ibid.*, pp. 58–59.

22. *Ibid.*, pp. 58–61.

23. *Ibid.*, pp. 62–70.

24. *Ibid.*, pp. 72–75.

25. Bureau of the Census, U.S. Department of Commerce, "Income, Poverty, and Valuation of Noncash Benefits: 1994," No. P60189, Table B7.

26. Patrick F. Fagan, "The Real Root Causes of Violent Crime: The Breakdown of Marriage, Family and Community," Heritage Foundation *Backgrounder* No. 1026, March 17, 1995.

27. Robert Whelan, "Broken Homes and Battered Children: A Study of the Relationship Between Child Abuse and Family Type," Family Education Trust, Oxford, United Kingdom, 1994.

28. Fagan, "The Real Root Causes of Violent Crime," pp. 9–10.

29. Clifford Robert Shaw, *Juvenile Delinquency and Urban Areas* (Chicago: University of Chicago, 1942); cited in Jeffrey Fagan and Sandra Wexler, "Family Origins of Violent Delinquents," *Criminology*, Vol. 25, No. 3 (1987), pp. 643–669.

30. Douglas Smith and G. Roger Jarjoura, "Social Structure and Criminal Victimization," *Journal of Research in Crime and Delinquency*, Vol. 25 (February 1988), pp. 27–52; Anne Hill and June O'Neill, *Underclass Behavior in the United States: Measurement and Analysis of Determinants* (New York: City University of New York, Baruch College, March 1990).

31. Fagan and Wexler, "Family Origins of Violent Delinquents."

32. Albert J. Reis, Jr., "Why Are Communities Important in Understanding Crime?" in Albert J. Reis, Jr., and Michael Tonry, eds., *Communities and Crime* (Chicago: University of Chicago, 1986), p. 133.

33. Elton J. Jackson, Charles Tittle, and M. J. Burke, "Offense Specific Models of Differential Association," paper presented at annual meeting of the American Society of Criminology, 1984; cited in Fagan and Wexler, "Family Origins of Violent Delinquents." See also Rodney Stark, "Deviant Places: A Theory of the Ecology of Crime," *Criminology*, Vol. 25 (1987), pp. 893–909.

## CRITICAL THINKING QUESTIONS

1. According to Fagan, "the increase in the birth rate among non-married women is propelled by the high levels of early sexual intercourse and the use of contraception among teenagers." Contraception, however, typically decreases birth rates. Is this a contradiction? Or not?

2. In describing "fractured families," Fagan coins the phrase "rejection ratio." This ratio includes aborted embryos, children born out of wedlock, and children of divorced parents. Do you agree that decisions such as abortion, not marrying, and getting a divorce characterize a rejection of children? Explain why or why not.

3. Fagan believes that the most desirable form of childcare is by the child's mother. He also argues that the father's absence results, among other problems, in a child's criminal activities. Would he agree, then, that we should support stay-at-home mothers who are on welfare? That we should encourage all biological fathers to remain in the home?

# 3 Current Perspectives on the Family

## *Centrist:* A Communitarian Position on the Family

JEAN BETHKE ELSHTAIN, ENOLA AIRD, AMITAI ETZIONI, WILLIAM GALSTON, MARY ANN GLENDON, MARTHA MINOW, AND ALICE ROSSI, "A Communitarian Position Paper on the Family" (Washington, DC: The Communitarian Network, 1993). Reproduced with the permission of Jean Bethke Elshtain.

*Communitarians believe that responsible, intact families are the cornerstones of the "moral and social formation of children." Consequently, they propose providing quality parental care for children, implementing pro-family economic policies, enhancing marital stability, reinforcing parental responsibility, reining in children's premature sexualization, and curbing the excessive society-wide individualism that endangers many children's well-being.*

### PREAMBLE

The 1992 election has focused long overdue attention on the subject of families and family values. Yet there can be little doubt that the use of pro-family arguments as attack weapons by some has done a profound disservice to the cause of America's families.

We, the undersigned, are determined to do what we can to redirect the public dialogue along a more constructive course. Our purpose is to demean no one, but rather to promote the common good by supporting families in the vital work they do. Each of us championed the needs of families long before they came to be abused as political pawns. We rise to speak for the younger generation, for American families, and for the family that America might yet be.

We, the undersigned, believe:

- that *the well-being of our nation's children is a prime responsibility of parents;*
- that too many parents are failing to discharge this responsibility adequately;
- that society *is not fostering a family-friendly environment and has a responsibility to do so;* economic pressures on parents, especially mothers, are mounting and the popular culture is making the raising of children an ever more challenging task;
- that as a result of these societal and parental failures, too many of our children are being deprived of their opportunity to develop into responsible adults and contributing citizens;
- that this deprivation constitutes a profound threat to the health of our common life; and that therefore,

- we must act with urgent shared purpose to strengthen families in order to improve the prospects for our children and community.

While we do not agree with one another on every detail of each policy recommendation set forth below, *we stand united in our belief that our nation dares not further delay the implementation—through personal commitment, the voluntary institutions of civil society, and public action—of a coherent pro-family agenda.*

Government cannot intervene to promote child welfare while remaining neutral about the family. Recognizing the family as the cornerstone of the moral and social formation of children, we believe the following perspectives must inform specific measures to be taken:

- economic, welfare, and human service policies should help, not hinder parents in their child-rearing responsibilities;
- all programs should *encourage self-help* rather than promoting and deepening dependency;
- all sectors of our society—parents, government, business, educators, voluntary organizations, and health care providers—should be encouraged and offered incentives to work together to receive the ethic of personal and shared commitment to children and families; and,
- as *The Responsive Communitarian Platform* states, "the weights of the historical, sociological, and psychological evidence suggests that on average *two-parent families are better to discharge their child-raising duties* if only because there are more hands—and voices—available for the task."

### RECOMMENDATIONS

#### 1. Toward a Coherent Care Policy: Infants at Home; Focusing Public Support on Quality Care for Children

The new President should formulate a coherent family policy that will include two dovetailed main parts: bonding for infants

with their parents at home at least until age one and improved child care facilities for older children and for those infants whose parents face unusual circumstances. This policy would replace the current tendency to deal in isolation, as if unrelated, with policies concerning family leave and child care centers.

*1.1 The best place for infants is at home, where they can bond with their parents.* Most children who bonded with their parents in the first year of their lives are reported to be doing better by practically all social, intellectual, and other behavioral measurements than those who were largely brought up in the first year of their lives outside the home. Strong and growing evidence indicates that most infants (younger than age one) develop stronger attachments to their parents than to child care personnel. There may be a need for more study but we suggest that the accumulated evidence supports this conclusion.

It follows that several measures should be enacted that would move us as quickly as possible toward enabling parents to be with their infants during the critical first years of life.

**We need a family leave policy which allows parents to be parents—providing their children with a real "head start"—while avoiding regulations and requirements that could devastate small business.**

A ninety-day unpaid leave to allow parents to care for a new or sick child in businesses with fifty or more employees represents a good first step, but more should be done. Ninety days are far from enough. Many industrialized societies provide a full year of paid leave to a parent of a newborn child. Over time, as fiscal and economic circumstances permit, we strongly recommend a phase-in of at least six months of publicly provided paid leave for parents following child birth or adoption and an additional six months unpaid leave for those employed with more than fifty employees. Smaller businesses should be given tax incentives to encourage them to provide a similar leave program.

**We support policies that ease the tension between work place and parental responsibilities and relieve the time crunch now experienced by so many families.**

Forty hours remains the official work-week norm, but too many middle class families must put in many extra hours just to stay even, while wage earners in lower middle class and working poor families must frequently hold several jobs. The resulting time squeeze makes it difficult for parents to properly discharge their responsibilities. It also exerts pressure on organizations which depend heavily on volunteers—the network of informal associations that served families and communities in the past. Families flourish in a solid communitarian environment; when community deteriorates, families suffer.

Accordingly, we urge adoption of corporate policies that *encourage flex-time and home work* arrangements that permit parents to better mesh family and work responsibilities and spend more time with their children. We turn below to the economic pressures that parents experience and which push many parents to work long hours and hold multiple jobs. However, declining real wages are not the only problem.

*We also must call attention to cultural values which exaggerate the time crunch experienced by American families.* For too many parents, long work-hours are not simply a reflection of economic pressure but also of excessive careerism or acquisitiveness. What these parents, and the communities that they live and work within, need is a change of their "habits of the heart," a change which reaffirms the value of children. We call on parents to recommit themselves to their work as nurturers and stewards of the next generation and to put their children first. We call on their friends and neighbors to appreciate those who are dedicated to their—and our—children.

*1.2 Public resources committed to care centers for older children and special cases must focus on sharply reducing turnover and improving the quality of the personnel.* Far too much out-of-home child care is being provided by poorly qualified persons for whom it is just another minimum wage job. At the same time, excessive reliance on the state and on licensing systems that impeded small, informal neighborhood and community child-care arrangements would only exacerbate the problem. To enhance accountability and reduce costs, parents should be expected to contribute, where feasible, at least four hours a week to the child-care centers in which their children are placed.

## 2. Empowering Parents: Toward Pro-Family Economic Policies

When the economy is allowed to deteriorate, the loser includes not just our competitiveness and our general standard of living, but also our children and families. Economic downturns amplify family strains, increase abuse and divorce, force many families to seek two pay checks even if one or both parents wish to dedicate more time to their children, and plunge millions of families into poverty. Economic policies that return our country to a path of sustainable economic growth would count families among their leading beneficiaries, and in particular would help children both by lifting many out of poverty and by providing more of them with more stable homes. *For the sake of our families and children, therefore, the next administration must put in place a program of investment and growth to replace the frequent use of recessions to deal with inflation.*

Beyond general economic trends, there are specific developments that harm children and families which need to and can be corrected. Accordingly, we suggest the following measures:

*2.1 Child allowances are better than increased tax exemptions, but increased tax exemptions are better than inaction.* Economists have shown that families with

...are carrying an ever-...urden. In 1948, a family of ...ian income paid only 0.3% ...income taxes, while in 1989 ...y paid 9.1%. Increasing the ...or children by $500 has been ...by the Bush Administration to remedy, in part, this anti-children trend. *We rank this measure as second best; child allowance is better and more fair.*

It is true that parents would have extra cash in their pockets if the child exemption is increased. Such a tax cut, however, discriminates against families that dedicate more time to their children and hence have less taxable income. Parents whose income declined because they decided that one of them would stay at home while the children are young, parents who share one job, or work less overtime, or are less career-committed because they are especially dedicated to their children—are disadvantaged by such changes in tax laws. An increase in the exemption favors those families in which both parents work outside the household, thus dedicating less time to their children but gaining a higher joint income (which makes the tax exemption more valuable).

By contrast, a child allowance would aid all families by putting money directly into the pockets of parents. Such allowances, common in Europe, do not discriminate between those who work at home and those who work outside the home; they provide a fixed amount, say, $600 per child to all parents. (To reduce costs and enhance social justice, these monies are best treated as taxable income.)

What is at issue here is not the often-repeated debate over whether single parents can bring up a child properly, whether divorce hurts children more or less than "bad" marriages, and certainly not whether women have a right to work outside the household. At issue is whether the government should enact public policies that discriminate against those who wish to maintain child-oriented families and reward those that have decided to be two-paycheck families for economic, careerist, or other reasons—especially if both are gainfully employed full time. Parents should be able to choose between working at home and outside the home, but *government tax policies should not be used to favor families who earn more because both parents work outside the home* when there are young children in the family.

Finally, we must also *note that increased tax exemptions reward especially the rich, rain some favors on the middle classes, and do nothing for those with low incomes or no income, the real poor.* Child allowance treats all families as equals. For those who argue that child allowance is more expensive, we say that we favor a revenue-neutral switch whereby *the government would dedicate to child allowance the same revenues that would be lost if the tax exemption for children is increased* (about $24 billion over the next five years under the Republican plan.) In this way, child allowance would not cost a penny more than increased tax exemptions (of course, the cash grant would have to be lower than the amount of tax credit since it would also be directed toward low-income parents). Alternatively, a refundable earned federal tax credit could be used and phased out as income increases.

*2.2 The IRS should be used to ensure that deadbeat parents live up to their responsibilities, and all states should establish paternity at the time of birth.* Single-parent families often face financial hardship. This hardship is particularly burdensome when an absent parent does not contribute to his or her fair share of the parent rearing the children. In these cases, the task of parenting becomes all that much harder. Moreover, many of these families end up on welfare, posing an additional burden to the over-extended state and federal governments.

To remedy this problem and send a strong signal to absent parents that they bear important responsibilities toward their children, we support the following federal and state efforts. First, Congress should pass legislation pursuant to the Downey/Hyde Plan which would use the Internal Revenue Service to dock wages from parents (primarily fathers) who have crossed state lines to avoid paying child support. Second, all states should try to establish paternity at the time of birth and include both parents on a child's birth certificate to insure that fathers do not avoid their parental responsibilities.

### 3. Strengthening the Tie That Binds

We support measures and norms that recognize the psychological and economic needs of children and *enhance family stability*. We recognize the reasons that propel aggrieved individuals to seek divorce. But we also believe that our widespread "culture of divorce" does little to help sustain couples through inevitable periods of marital stress.

*3.1 We call attention to, and congratulate, religious organizations that provide systemic preparation before marriage takes place and counseling when divorce threatens.* Many churches will not marry couples who fail to attend preparatory discussions. Others provide venues in which couples can form mutually sustaining communities and renew their vows.

We *applaud and encourage expansion of the efforts to secular organizations such as family resource centers* and other community groups to offer courses and seminars on preparing for and strengthening marriages and meeting the challenges of parenting.

We *encourage schools* to offer family life courses by the late elementary years so that young people can focus early on the joys and responsibilities of family life and the challenge of parenting.

We *urge all government agencies issuing marriage licenses* to offer referrals to courses on marriage and parenting for prospective couples and community resources for families and parents.

*3.2 We call for a change in divorce laws to favor children and slow the rush to divorce.* Changes in family structure over the past generation are strongly correlated with rising rates of poverty among children. Divorce under current laws often spells economic hardship for custodial parents and above all for their minor children. Existing legal structures do not adequately recognize the difference between divorce involving only adults and those where children are affected.

*For divorces where children are involved we need a new set of rules based on the principle of "children first."* Issues of property division between the parents should not even be considered until adequate provision has been made for the needs of minor children. Second, as outlined above, child support awards must be systematically increased and effectively enforced, with increased federal participation if needed to bolster state-based efforts. A parent should be able to divorce a spouse if a marriage has irretrievably broken down, but *a parent should never be allowed to divorce a child*.

*3.3 We should also reexamine all other laws with an eye to their impact on the culture of divorce.* Current Social Security rules encourage divorce by substantially increasing (up to 200 percent) the total benefits a couple receives after divorce. This is undesirable because older people serve as role models for the young, because the elderly who have divorced are more prone to illness and accident and less satisfied with their lives, and because Social Security rules affect people of all ages through their impact on Supplemental Security Income (SSI). *This premium on divorce should be eliminated.*

### 4. Toward a New, Communitarian Family: Equal Rights and Responsibilities

*4.1 Nothing in this statement should be read as treating women (or mothers) as having lesser rights or more responsibilities than men (or fathers).* We do not seek a return to traditional families, to discriminate against women, or the notion that parenting is only a mother's job. We strongly support, and recognize as morally correct, *the fundamental equality of fathers and mothers: both command the same basic rights and responsibilities.*

If there is any systemic difference between fathers and mothers it is that many more fathers neglect their children than do mothers. For instance: very few fathers take family leave in those corporations where it is available. *Both fathers and mothers must rededicate themselves to their children,* for the sake of the children, the long-run satisfaction of the parents, and the quality of the community in which we all live.

*4.2 We must fundamentally reform our welfare system to reinforce rather than undermine family stability and personal responsibility.* While many factors are at work, there is little doubt that current welfare structures tend to exacerbate tendencies toward single-parent households with all their attendant problems. Credible studies show a strong correlation between marriage, completion of high school, and subsequent long-term employment. Unfortunately, the present system promotes forms of clientage that tend to erode family and community solidarity as well as individual responsibility.

Parenting under modern conditions is difficult enough for two dedicated people to handle. Facing that task alone—all too often in deteriorated housing, broken down neighborhoods, poverty, or drug dependency—is harder still. The results can be tragic: high infant mortality rates, substandard child health and educational attainment, and intergenerational cycles of poverty, in urban as well as rural areas.

While there is no single "silver bullet" solution to this problem, we support increased state, local, and community-based efforts to reform welfare. We believe that local welfare reform efforts should be guided by the following objectives. First, in trying to break the cycle of dependency which some single-families fall into, local efforts should emphasize incentives for parents who find jobs and leave welfare, and encourage their children to act responsibly. Second, while in principle we do not favor penalizing the poor or anybody else, if welfare parents consistently act irresponsibly, we see some justification in gradually reducing their benefits. Finally, local reform should receive significant federal encouragement and support. For example, the burdensome, complex waiver requirements limiting state-based innovation in welfare policy should be relaxed and simplified.

### 5. Restoring Childhood: Putting an End to Premature Sexualization

**We should initiate a comprehensive campaign—involving schools, community organizations, and families themselves—against teenage pregnancy and premature sexualization of the child.**

We are stunned at widespread reports of girls as young as seven starving themselves to meet culturally dictated images of female desirability. Studies indicate the preoccupation of the young with physical attractiveness and sexual appeal has grown during the past several decades. The ethos of self-indulgence and sexual objectification has become self-destructive.

All sexual education efforts must stress personal and social responsibility. The heart of our message must not be safe sex or mere technique, but rather responsible behavior as one feature of our mature identity.

This message should be reinforced—or at the very least not undermined—by media targeted to children and teenagers. Rather than accepting the cynical evasion of the 1990 National Children's Television Act that has characterized the response of all too many broadcasters, the next administration should fully enforce its letter and spirit.

### 6. A Culture of Familialism

**Finally, we must re-create a workable public philosophy, reflecting our deepest values, as the essential context within which families can be strengthened and celebrated.**

As Americans, we rightly cherish our individual freedom. But we cannot live without communitarian roots: families, communities, religious and secular associations, and various social movements. Children growing up outside a richly textured, interconnected network of human relations are deprived of a most precious gift, society itself.

America's families are being weakened at a time when faith in all our public institutions is faltering. The level of civic trust is on the wane. Young people lament the absence of heroes with whom to identify. Some think we have lost confidence in the promise of democracy itself. If we as a nation continue to fail the parents of our children, this loss of hope can only deepen.

We preach neither gloom nor nostalgia. We applaud the changes of the past generation that have loosened rigid assumptions about the role of men and women. We seek no return to a previous epoch. But we are disturbed that too many policy analysts, opinion makers, and elected officials continue to paint a rosy picture of change while refusing to confront the worsening condition of the American family.

That condition can be simply put: the well-being of America's children is declining. Were we engaged in a comprehensive discussion of policies and cultural norms that could promote child welfare right here, we would need to turn to a number of issues beyond the scope of this position paper. Our focus here is that we believe that stable intact families make vital contributions to the nurturing of future citizens. Our children are in peril in a large measure because they are less and less assured of the sustained care, support, and safety that comes only with order in their immediate family.

In short, children are bearing the brunt of a profound cultural shift toward excessive individualism, whose negative features we are now in a position to observe and whose continuing costs will last longer than our own lifetimes. As civic educators, citizens, and parents, we believe the time has come to look unflinchingly at the social costs of the fast-paced alterations of fan. life in recent decades and to commit our selves to taking the steps necessary to set things right with our children and families.

Although the family is the locus of private life, it is also critical to public identity. Here as elsewhere, the testimony of parents and scholars converges. Families teach us our first lessons in responsibility and reciprocity. In the primary setting of the family, we either learn or fail to learn what it means to give and take; to trust or to mistrust; to practice self-restraint or self-indulgence; to be unreliable or reliable. It is for that reason, if no other, that we must begin to make the vital connections between "public" policies and "private" families, and craft policies that support families.

The family of which we speak is not an isolated unit, but rather an institution nested in a wider social context that either sustains or weakens it. Without supportive society, families can best function with difficulty. But today, on balance, American society puts negative pressure—cultural as well as economic—on mothers and fathers.

When parents are asked to tell their stories, they lament that it is harder to do a decent job rearing children in a culture that they regard as unfriendly to families. The overwhelming majority of Americans believe that being a parent is much more difficult than it used to be. Pessimism about the decline of family values is increasing. While expert and official debate tends to focus on work-place and child-care issues, the grass-roots conversation revolves around cultural issues. Parents express a pervasive fear that they have less and less time to spend on the moral task of child-rearing and that, as a result, their children are succumbing to the values of an excessively individualistic, materialistic, and sex-obsessed culture.

## IN CONCLUSION

We do not argue that the government is the cause of children's problems, nor that gov-

action is the only problem ... . We do believe that greater ... such as prenatal care, women ... trition, and early childhood ... ucation would yield signifi-cant returns. We also believe that an effective pro-family agenda must be backed by resources. We believe that to reverse the tide, we must be willing to invest wisely in proven programs that can help children and strengthen families.

We want to set aside sterile debates between liberals and conservatives and get down to the business of strengthening families. The most important single indicator of childhood problems—from poor health to poverty to behavioral problems to school drop-out to criminality—is whether or not a child grows up in a stable, functioning family. With out-of-wedlock birth rates approaching 80 percent in some areas, we can anticipate a further rise in all these negative consequences unless something is done, soon.

Being a mother or father isn't just another "life-style choice," but rather an ethical vocation of the weightiest sort. A responsive community must act to smooth the path for parents so that the joys of family life might be more easily felt and its burdens more fairly borne. Social policies cannot turn the world upside down. Nonetheless, we must act together in ways that reflect our shared commitments to all those now engaged in the task of child-rearing and to the children whose well-being depends on that task being well done.

## CRITICAL THINKING QUESTIONS

1. Compare the conservative perspective on the family (see the article by Patrick F. Fagan) with the centrist position presented here. What are the similarities between the two views? What are the differences?

2. The authors of this article maintain that two-paycheck families, especially those with very young children, are less child-oriented, given time constraints, than parents who stay at home and "bond" with their infants at least until age 1. What else, besides acquisitiveness and "excessive individualism," might explain two-paycheck families? Does the document acknowledge these other factors?

3. What kinds of benefits do centrists attribute to marital stability? What kinds of problems do they ascribe to divorce and single-parent households? What kind of evidence do they use to support their conclusions?

# 3 Current Perspectives on the Family

## *Liberal/Feminist:* Why We Miss the 1950s

*Stephanie Coontz sympathizes with a recent national poll in which Americans chose the 1950s more than any other decade as the best time for raising children. Even when contemporary parents grew up in unhappy families, she notes, they associate the 1950s with fewer complicated choices for children and parents, clearer expectations about forming and maintaining families, and greater consensus about acceptable family norms. Coontz questions, however, whether such nostalgia is historically accurate. She also maintains that recent economic changes, not individual behavior, have transformed family life.*

### THE 1950S FAMILY EXPERIMENT

The key to understanding the successes, failures, and comparatively short life of 1950s family forms and values is to understand the period as one of *experimentation* with the possibilities of a new kind of family, not as the expression of some long-standing tradition. At the end of the 1940s, the divorce rate, which had been rising steadily since the 1890s, dropped sharply; the age of marriage fell to a 100-year low; and the birth rate soared. Women who had worked during the depression or World War II quit their jobs as soon as they became pregnant, which meant quite a few women were specializing in child raising; fewer women remained childless during the 1950s than in any decade since the late nineteenth century. The timing and spacing of childbearing became far more compressed, so that the young mothers were likely to have two or more children in diapers at once, with no older sibling to help in their care. At the same time, again for the first time in 100 years, the educational gap between young middle-class women and men increased, while job segregation for working men and women seems to have peaked. These demographic changes increased the dependence of women on marriage, in contrast to gradual trends in the opposite direction since the early twentieth century.[1]

The result was that family life and gender roles became much more predictable, orderly, and settled in the 1950s than they were either twenty years earlier or would be twenty years later. Only slightly more than one in four marriages ended in divorce during the 1950s. Very few young people spent any extended period of time in a nonfamily setting: They moved from their parents' family into their own family, after just a brief experience with independent living, and they started having children soon after marriage. Whereas two-thirds of women aged 20 to 24 were not yet married in 1990, only 28 percent of women this age were still single in 1960.[2]

Ninety percent of all the households in the country were families in the 1950s, in comparison with only 71 percent by 1990. Eighty-six percent of all children lived in two-parent homes in 1950, as opposed to just 72 percent in 1990. And the percentage living with both biological parents—rather than, say, a parent and stepparent—was dramatically higher than it had been at the turn of the century or is today: seventy percent in 1950, compared with only 50 percent in 1990. Nearly 60 percent of kids—an all-time high—were born into male breadwinner–female homemaker families; only a minority of the rest had mothers who worked in the paid labor force.[3]

If the organization and uniformity of family life in the 1950s were new, so were the values, especially the emphasis on putting all one's emotional and financial eggs in the small basket of the immediate nuclear family. Right up through the 1940s, ties of work, friendship, neighborhood, ethnicity, extended kin, and voluntary organizations were as important a source of identity for most Americans, and sometimes a *more* important source of obligation, than marriage and the nuclear family. All this changed in the postwar era. The spread of suburbs and automobiles, combined with the destruction of older ethnic neighborhoods in many cities, led to the decline of the neighborhood social club. Young couples moved away from parents and kin, cutting ties with traditional extrafamilial networks that might compete for their attention. A critical factor in this trend was the emergence of a group of family sociologists and marriage counselors who followed Talcott Parsons in claiming that the nuclear family, built on a sharp division of labor between husband and wife, was the cornerstone of modern society. . . .

The 1950s sitcoms were aimed at young couples who had married in haste, women who had tasted new freedoms during World War II and given up their jobs with regret, veterans whose children resented their attempts to reassert paternal authority, and individuals disturbed by the changing racial and ethnic mix of postwar America. The message was clear: Buy these ranch houses, Hotpoint appliances, and child-raising ideals; relate to your spouse like this; get a new car to wash with your kids on Sunday afternoons; organize your dinners like that—and you too can escape from the conflicts of race, class, and political witch hunts into harmonious families where father knows best, mothers are never bored or irritated, and teenagers rush to the dinner table each night, eager to get their latest dose of parental wisdom.

Many families found it possible to put together a good imitation of this way of living during the 1950s and 1960s. Couples were often able to construct marriages that were much more harmonious than those in which they had grown up, and to devote far more time to their children. Even when marriages were deeply unhappy, as many were, the new stability, economic security, and educational advantages parents were able to offer their kids counted for a lot in people's assessment of their life satisfaction. And in some matters, ignorance could be bliss: The lack of media coverage of problems such as abuse or incest was terribly hard on the casualties, but it protected more fortunate families from knowledge and fear of many social ills.[4]

There was tremendous hostility to people who could be defined as "others": Jews, African Americans, Puerto Ricans, the poor, gays or lesbians, and "the red menace." Yet on a day-to-day basis, the civility that prevailed in homogeneous neighborhoods allowed people to ignore larger patterns of racial and political repression. Racial clashes were ever-present in the 1950s, sometimes escalating into full-scale antiblack riots, but individual homicide rates fell to almost half the levels of the 1930s. As nuclear families moved into the suburbs, they retreated from social activism but entered voluntary relationships with people who had children the same age; they became involved in PTAs together, joined bridge clubs, went bowling. There does seem to have been a stronger sense of neighborly commonalities than many of us feel today. Even though this local community was often the product of exclusion or repression, it sometimes looks attractive to modern Americans whose commutes are getting longer and whose family or work patterns give them little in common with their neighbors.[5]

The optimism that allowed many families to rise above their internal difficulties and to put limits on their individualistic values during the 1950s came from the sense that America was on a dramatically different trajectory than it had been in the past, an upward and expansionary path that had already taken people to better places than they had ever seen before and would certainly take their children even further. This confidence that almost everyone could look forward to a better future stands in sharp contrast to how most contemporary Americans feel, and it explains why a period in which many people were much worse off than today sometimes still looks like a better period for families than our own.

Throughout the 1950s, poverty was higher than it is today, but it was less concentrated in pockets of blight existing side-by-side with extremes of wealth, and, unlike today, it was falling rather than rising. At the end of the 1930s, almost two-thirds of the population had incomes below the poverty standards of the day, while only one in eight had a middle-class income (defined as two to five times the poverty line). By 1960, a majority of the population had climbed into the middle-income range.[6]

Unmarried people were hardly sexually abstinent in the 1950s, but the age of first intercourse was somewhat higher than it is now, and despite a tripling of nonmarital birth rates between 1940 and 1958, more than 70 percent of nonmarital pregnancies led to weddings before the child was born.

Teenage birth rates were almost twice as high in 1957 as in the 1990s, but most teen births were to married couples, and the effect of teen pregnancy in reducing further schooling for young people did not hurt their life prospects the way it does today. High school graduation rates were lower in the 1950s than they are today and minority students had far worse test scores, but there were jobs for people who dropped out of high school or graduated without good reading skills—jobs that actually had a future. People entering the job market in the 1950s had no way of knowing that they would be the last generation to have a good shot at reaching middle-class status without the benefit of postsecondary schooling.

Millions of men from impoverished, rural, unemployed, or poorly educated family backgrounds found steady jobs in the steel, auto, appliance, construction, and shipping industries. Lower middle-class men went further on in college during the 1950s than they would have been able to expect in earlier decades, enabling them to make the transition to secure white-collar work. The experience of shared sacrifices in the depression and war, reinforced by a New Deal-inspired belief in the ability of government to make life better, gave people a sense of hope for the future. Confidence in government, business, education, and other institutions was on the rise. This general optimism affected people's experience and assessment of family life. It is no wonder modern Americans yearn for a similar sense of hope.

But before we sign on to any attempts to turn the family clock back to the 1950s we should note that the family successes and community solidarities of the 1950s rested on a totally different set of political and economic conditions than we have today. Contrary to widespread belief, the 1950s was not an age of laissez-faire government and free market competition. A major cause of the social mobility of young families in the 1950s was that federal assistance programs were much more generous and widespread than they are today.

In the most ambitious and successful affirmative action program ever adopted in America, 40 percent of young men were eligible for veterans' benefits, and these benefits were far more extensive than those available to Vietnam-era vets. Financed in part by a federal income tax on the rich that went up to 87 percent and a corporate tax rate of 52 percent, such benefits provided quite a jump start for a generation of young families. The GI bill paid most tuition costs for vets who attended college, doubling the percentage of college students from prewar levels. At the other end of our life span, Social Security began to build up a significant safety net for the elderly, formerly the poorest segment of the population. Starting in 1950, the federal government regularly mandated raises in the minimum wage to keep pace with inflation. The minimum wage may have been only $1.40 as late as 1968, but a person who worked for that amount full-time, year-round, earned 118 percent of the poverty figure for a family of three. By 1995, a full-time minimum-wage worker could earn only 72 percent of the poverty level.[7]

An important source of the economic expansion of the 1950s was that public works spending at all levels of government comprised nearly 20 percent of total expenditures in 1950, as compared to less than 7 percent in 1984. Between 1950 and 1960, nonmilitary, nonresidential public construction rose by 58 percent. Construction expenditures for new schools (in dollar amounts adjusted for inflation) rose by 72 percent; funding on sewers and waterworks rose by 46 percent. Government paid 90 percent of the costs of building the new Interstate Highway System. These programs opened up suburbia to growing numbers of middle-class Americans and created secure, well-paying jobs for blue-collar workers.[8]

Government also reorganized home financing, underwriting low down payments and long-term mortgages that had been rejected as bad business by private industry. To do this, government put public assets behind housing lending programs, created two new national financial institutions to facilitate home loans, allowed veterans to put down payments as low as a dollar on a house, and offered tax breaks to people who bought homes. The National Education Defense Act funded the socioeconomic mobility of thousands of young men who trained themselves for well-paying jobs in such fields as engineering.[9]

Unlike contemporary welfare programs, government investment in 1950s families was not just for immediate subsistence but encouraged long-term asset development, rewarding people for increasing their investment in homes and education. Thus it was far less likely that such families or individuals would ever fall back to where they started, even after a string of bad luck. Subsidies for higher education were greater the longer people stayed in school and the more expensive the school they selected. Mortgage deductions got bigger as people traded up to better houses.[10]

These social and political support systems magnified the impact of the postwar economic boom. "In the years between 1947 and 1973," reports economist Robert Kuttner, "the median paycheck more than doubled, and the bottom 20 percent enjoyed the greatest gains." High rates of unionization meant that blue-collar workers were making much more financial progress than most of their counterparts today. In 1952, when eager home buyers flocked to the opening of Levittown, Pennsylvania, the largest planned community yet constructed, "it took a factory worker one day to earn enough money to pay the closing costs on a new Levittown house, then selling for $10,000." By 1991, such a home was selling for $100,000 or more, and it took a factory worker *eighteen weeks* to earn enough money for just the closing costs.[11]

The legacy of the union struggle of the 1930s and 1940s, combined with government support for raising people's living standards, set limits on corporations that have disappeared in recent decades. Corporations paid 23 percent of federal income taxes in the 1950s, as compared to just 9.2 percent in 1991. Big companies earned higher profit margins than smaller firms, partly due to their dominance of the market, partly to America's postwar economic advantage. They chose (or were forced) to share these extra earnings, which economists call "rents," with employees. Economists at the Brookings Institution and Harvard University estimate that 70 percent of such corporate rents were passed on to workers at all levels of the firm, benefiting secretaries and janitors as well as CEOs. Corporations routinely retained workers even in slack periods, as a way of ensuring workplace stability. Although they often received more generous tax breaks from communities than they gave back in investment, at least they kept their plants and employment offices in the same place. AT&T, for example, received much of the technology it used to finance its postwar expansion from publicly funded communications research conducted as part of the war effort, and, as current AT&T Chairman Robert Allen puts it, there "used to be lifelong commitment on the employee's part and on our part." Today, however, he admits, "the contract doesn't exist anymore."[12]

Television trivia experts still argue over exactly what the fathers in many 1950s sitcoms did for a living. Whatever it was, though, they obviously didn't have to worry about downsizing. If most married people stayed in long-term relationships during the 1950s, so did most corporations, sticking with the communities they grew up in and the employees they originally hired. Corporations were not constantly relocating in search of cheap labor during the 1950s; unlike today, increases in worker productivity usually led to increases in wages. The number of workers covered by corporate pension plans and health benefits increased steadily. So did limits on the work week. There is good reason that people look back to the 1950s as a less hurried age: The average American was

working a shorter workday in the 1950s than his or her counterpart today, when a quarter of the workforce puts in 49 or more hours a week.[13]

So politicians are practicing quite a double standard when they tell us to return to the family forms of the 1950s while they do nothing to restore the job programs and family subsidies of that era, the limits on corporate relocation and financial wheeling-dealing, the much higher share of taxes paid by corporations then, the availability of union jobs for noncollege youth, and the subsidies for higher education such as the National Defense Education Act loans. Furthermore, they're not telling the whole story when they claim that the 1950s was the most prosperous time for families and the most secure decade for children. Instead, playing to our understandable nostalgia for a time when things seemed to be getting better, not worse, they engage in a tricky chronological shell game with their figures, diverting our attention from two important points. First, many individuals, families, and groups were excluded from the economic prosperity, family optimism, and social civility of the 1950s. Second, the all-time high point of child well-being and family economic security came not during the 1950s but *at the end of the 1960s*.

We now know that 1950s family culture was not only nontraditional; it was also not idyllic. In important ways, the stability of family and community life during the 1950s rested on pervasive discrimination against women, gays, political dissidents, non-Christians, and racial or ethnic minorities, as well as on a systematic cover-up of the underside of many families. Families that were harmonious and fair of their own free will may have been able to function more easily in the fifties, but few alternatives existed for members of discordant or oppressive families. Victims of child abuse, incest, alcoholism, spousal rape, and wife battering had no recourse, no place to go, until well into the 1960s.[14]

At the end of the 1950s, despite ten years of economic growth, 27.3 percent of the nation's children were poor, including those in white "underclass" communities such as Appalachia. Almost 50 percent of married-couple African-American families were impoverished—a figure far higher than today. It's no wonder African Americans are not likely to pick the 1950s as a golden age, even in comparison with the setbacks they experienced in the 1980s. When blacks moved north to find jobs in the postwar urban manufacturing boom they met vicious harassment and violence, first to prevent them from moving out of the central cities, then to exclude them from public space such as parks or beaches.

In Philadelphia, for example, the City of Brotherly Love, there were more than 200 racial incidents over housing in the first six months of 1955 alone. The Federal Housing Authority, such a boon to white working-class families, refused to insure homes in all-black or in racially mixed neighborhoods. Two-thirds of the city dwellers evicted by the urban renewal projects of the decade were African Americans and Latinos; government did almost nothing to help such displaced families find substitute housing.[15]

Women were unable to take out loans or even credit cards in their own names. They were excluded from juries in many states. A lack of options outside marriage led some women to remain in desperately unhappy unions that were often not in the best interests of their children or themselves. Even women in happy marriages often felt humiliated by the constant messages they received that their whole lives had to revolve around a man. "You are not ready when he calls—miss one turn," was a rule in the Barbie game marketed to 1950s girls; "he criticizes your hairdo—go to the beauty shop." Episodes of *Father Knows Best* advised young women: "The worst thing you can do is to try to beat a man at his own game. You just beat the women at theirs." One character on the show told women to always ask themselves, "Are you after a job or a man? You can't have both."[16]

## THE FIFTIES EXPERIMENT COMES TO AN END

The social stability of the 1950s, then, was a response to the stick of racism, sexism, and repression as well as the carrot of economic opportunity and government aid. Because social protest mounted in the 1960s and unsettling challenges were posed to the gender roles and sexual mores of the previous decade, many people forget that families continued to make gains throughout the 1960s and into the first few years of the 1970s. By 1969, child poverty was down to 14 percent, its lowest level ever; it hovered just above that marker until 1975, when it began its steady climb up to contemporary figures (22 percent in 1993; 21.2 percent in 1994). The high point of health and nutrition for poor children was reached in the early 1970s.[17]

So commentators are being misleading when they claim that the 1950s was the golden age of American families. They are disregarding the number of people who were excluded during that decade and ignoring the socioeconomic gains that continued to be made through the 1960s. But they are quite right to note that the improvements of the 1950s and 1960s came to an end at some point in the 1970s (though not for the elderly, who continued to make progress).

Ironically, it was the children of those stable, enduring, supposedly idyllic 1950s families, the recipients of so much maternal time and attention, that pioneered the sharp break with their parents' family forms and gender roles in the 1970s. This was not because they were led astray by some youthful Murphy Brown in her student rebel days or inadvertently spoiled by parents who read too many of Dr. Spock's child-raising manuals.

Partly, the departure from 1950s family arrangements was a logical extension of trends and beliefs pioneered in the 1950s, or of inherent contradictions in those patterns. For example, early and close-spaced child-bearing freed more wives up to join the labor force, and married women began to flock to work. By 1960, more than 40 percent of women over the age of 16 held a job, and working mothers were the fastest growing component of the labor force. The educational aspirations and opportunities that opened up for kids of the baby boom could not be confined to males, and many tight-knit, male-breadwinner, nuclear families in the 1950s instilled in their daughters the ambition to be something other than a homemaker.[18]

Another part of the transformation was a shift in values. Most people would probably agree that some changes in values were urgently needed: the extension of civil rights to racial minorities and to women; a rejection of property rights in children by parents and in women by husbands; a reaction against the political intolerance and the wasteful materialism of 1950s culture. Other changes in values remain more controversial: opposition to American intervention abroad; repudiation of the traditional sexual double standard; rebellion against what many young people saw as the hypocrisy of parents who preached sexual morality but ignored social immorality such as racism and militarism.

Still other developments, such as the growth of me-first individualism, are widely regarded as problematic by people on all points along the political spectrum. It's worth noting, though, that the origins of antisocial individualism and self-indulgent consumerism lay at least as much in the family values of the 1950s as in the youth rebellion of the 1960s. The marketing experts who never allowed the kids in *Ozzie and Harriet* sitcoms to be shown drinking milk, for fear of offending soft-drink companies that might sponsor the show in syndication, were ultimately the same people who slightly later invested billions of dollars to channel sexual rebelliousness and a depoliticized individualism into mainstream culture.

There were big cultural changes brewing by the beginning of the 1970s, and tremendous upheavals in social, sexual, and family values. And yes, there were sometimes reckless or simply laughable excesses in some of the early experiments with new gender roles, family forms, and personal expression. But the excesses of 1950s gender roles and family forms were every bit as repellent and stupid as the excesses of the sixties: Just watch a dating etiquette film of the time period, or recall that therapists of the day often told victims of incest that they were merely having unconscious oedipal fantasies.

Ultimately, though, changes in values were not what brought the 1950s family experiment to an end. The postwar family compacts between husbands and wives, parents and children, young and old, were based on the postwar social compact between government, corporations, and workers. While there was some discontent with those family bargains among women and youth, the old relations did not really start to unravel until people began to face the erosion of the corporate wage bargain and government broke its tacit societal bargain that it would continue to invest in jobs and education for the younger generation.

In the 1970s, new economic trends began to clash with all the social expectations that 1950s families had instilled in their children. That clash, not the willful abandonment of responsibility and commitment, has been the primary cause of both family rearrangements and the growing social problems that are usually attributed to such family changes, but in fact have *separate* origins.

The reversal of the wage and family bargain of the 1950s began in the late 1960s, with a gradual rise in inequality among young male workers. As inflation picked up toward the end of the Vietnam War, young male breadwinner families started losing ground in real wages. In the cities, the labor supply grew faster than the manufacturing jobs that African-Americans and Latinos had moved there to find. Then in the early 1970s, the biggest generation in history hit the housing market, setting off a bidding war for single-family homes. While overall price increases averaged 170 percent between 1972 and 1987, the average price of a new home rose by 294 percent. People who had bought homes before the rise saw their personal worth climb dramatically, especially since the cost of maintaining a home actually fell. But other people were saddled with crushing mortgages. Meanwhile, as Europe and Japan recovered from the devastation of World War II, America's competitive international position began to weaken. Sharp increases in oil prices in 1973 helped kick off a series of three recessions. Average weekly earnings of U.S. workers, on the rise since 1950, peaked in 1972 and 1973, then started a steady decline that has yet to be checked.[19]

How did families handle these pressures? As economists Gordon Berlin and Andrew Sum explain, most families "kept their standard of living up even while individual real wages were falling by doing the following four things: they postponed marriage, both spouses entered the labor market, they had fewer children, and they went into debt."[20]

Often, these behaviors led to changed family values, but they hardly represented a conscious rebellion against the past. Instead, American families were facing a *conflict* between two values they had dutifully absorbed in the 1950s. On the one hand, experts had told them that the best way to have a happy family was to have the husband work and the wife stay home. On the other hand, the media's descriptions of happiness had revolved around mother using the latest cooking and cleaning appliances, dad washing the car with the kids, and the kids hanging out in the comforts and spaciousness of an up-to-date home. By the mid-1970s, maintaining the prescribed family *lifestyle* meant for many couples giving up the prescribed family *form*. They married later, postponed children, and curbed their fertility; the wives went out to work. Such changes in family forms and values in the early 1970s were just as widespread among people who

*accepted* the 1950s family dream as among those who rebelled against it.

Because more people went to work in the 1970s, or worked longer hours, per capita income continued to increase even while real wages fell. But this created other problems. Disruptions of the old pathways from school to marriage to childbearing became more common. Marital conflict and breakup increased. For two-parent families, rising household income, soaring housing values, and growing payroll and excise taxes left them paying more in taxes without seeing any payoffs in government investments that increased their personal security, their leisure, or their access to social capital. Back in the 1940s, points out political analyst Kevin Phillips, the tax rate gap between a median-income family and a rich family "was enormous." By the 1970s, moderate- and middle-income taxpayers were paying almost as much as the rich. As rich families and corporations paid a smaller share of the tax burden, and middle-income families watched a larger portion of their stagnant incomes go to taxes, antigovernment and antispending sentiment grew. By 1974–1975, bankers and bondholders in New York City began demanding layoffs of city workers and cutbacks of social services as a condition for lending the money that had historically financed urban growth.[21] . . .

From 1965 to 1969, net investment in public works by federal, state, and local government averaged 2.3 percent of the gross national product. From 1975 to 1979 it averaged only 0.7 percent; between 1980 and 1984 it was 0.4 percent. Cutbacks in unemployment insurance programs caused the proportion of unemployed workers receiving unemployment compensation "to drop to record lows in seven of the ten years from 1980 to 1990." Welfare ceased to provide anything remotely resembling a viable fallback for families in economic distress. Cash benefits in the typical state lost more than half their purchasing power between 1970 and 1996. Meanwhile real wages continued to slide, resulting in a dramatic rollback of the gains made from 1947 to 1973. In each year from 1991 to 1994, average real wages were lower than they had been at any time between 1963 and 1990.[22]

Of course, there were other important factors working to change family life in the 1960s and 1970s, such as the civil rights movement, the sexual revolution, government military spending, the controversy over the war in Vietnam, the women's movement, and the acceleration of individualism. The impact of these is a subject of much controversy. But it is vital to remember the economic backdrop against which the reconfiguration of family life and gender roles proceeded in the 1970s and 1980s.

Under the pressures of these economic conditions, many good innovations in family life were distorted, while some already problematic changes were made worse. Liberating and positive changes in gender roles and family relations continued to occur, but people often had to pay a higher price for their gains than they might otherwise have expected. Behaviors that would have been purely emancipating options in the earlier economic climate sometimes became grinding necessities, as when women who had fought for the choice to work suddenly found that they couldn't choose not to. The resultant strains, turmoil, and confusion about the future drastically affected people's family options and attitudes. But these value changes cannot be understood apart from the economic pressures that families and individuals increasingly faced.

Initially, many economists thought that the economic reverses of the 1970s were an ironic but temporary consequence of 1950s family patterns. Richard Easterlin has argued that young men entering the job market in the 1950s were in an especially fortunate position because the low fertility of their parents' generation put them in a seller's market as the postwar economy expanded its demand for labor. Companies seeking to increase production were competing for workers and therefore had to raise wages.[23]

But the workers hired in the 1950s gave birth to the baby-boom generation. Between 1950 and 1970, the school-age population more than doubled. In the postwar economic and political climate, this population boom fueled prosperity, stimulating the construction of roads, schools, homes, sewer systems, and factories to churn out family consumer goods. Baby-boom children benefitted from this economic expansion, and in the process developed high expectations about their own standard of living. When these youngsters became the next generation of workers, however, they faced a very different situation than their parents. With many more young men in competition for good jobs and resources, says Esterlin, the job and housing markets were far less favorable to young men starting families than they had been in the 1950s and 1960s. In consequence, the real wages of baby-boom workers began to fall, and their chances of experiencing poverty began to rise.

## NOTES

1. Arlene Skolnick and Stacey Rosencrantz, "The New Crusade for the Old Family," *American Prospect*, Summer 1994, p. 65; Andrew Cherlin, "Changing Family and Household: Contemporary Lessons from Historical Research," *Annual Review of Sociology* 9 (1983), pp. 54–58; Sam Roberts, *Who We Are: A Portrait of America Based on the Latest Census* (New York: Times Books, 1995), p. 45; Donald Hernandez, *America's Children: Resources from Family, Government, and the Economy* (New York: Russell Sage, 1993), pp. 128, 132.

2. Arthur Norton and Louisa Miller, *Marriage, Divorce, and Remarriage in the 1990s*, Current Population Reports Series P23–180 (Washington, D.C.: Bureau of the Census, October 1992); Roberts, *Who We Are* (1995 ed.), pp. 50–53; Frank Levy, "Incomes and Income Inequality," in Reynolds Farley, ed., *State of the Union: America in the 1990s*, vol. 1 (New York: Russell Sage, 1995), p. 120.

3. Dennis Hogan and Daniel Lichter, "Children and Youth: Living Arrangements and Welfare," in Farley, ed., *State of the Union*, vol. 2, p. 99;

Richard Gelles, *Contemporary Families: A Sociological View* (Thousand Oaks, Calif.: Sage, 1995), p. 115; Hernandez, *America's Children*, p. 102. The fact that only a small percentage of children had mothers in the paid labor force, though a full 40 percent did not live in male breadwinner–female homemaker families, was because some children had mothers who worked, unpaid, in farms or family businesses, or fathers who were unemployed, or the children were not living with both parents.

4. For discussion of the discontents, and often searing misery, that were considered normal in a "good-enough" marriage in the 1950s and 1960s, see Lillian Rubin, *Worlds of Pain: Life in the Working-Class Family* (New York: Basic Books, 1976); Mirra Komarovsky, *Blue Collar Marriage* (New Haven, Conn.: Vintage, 1962); Elaine Tyler May, *Homeward Bound: American Families in the Cold War Era* (New York: Basic Books, 1988).

5. See Robert Putnam, "The Strange Disappearance of Civic America," *American Prospect*, Winter 1996. For a glowing if somewhat lopsided picture of 1950s community solidarities, see Alan Ehrenhalt, *The Lost City: Discovering the Forgotten Virtues of Community in the Chicago of the 1950s* (New York: Basic Books, 1995). For a chilling account of communities uniting against perceived outsiders, in the same city, see Arnold Hirsch, *Making the Second Ghetto: Race and Housing in Chicago, 1940–1960* (Cambridge, Mass.: Harvard University Press, 1983). On homicide rates, see "Study Finds United States No. 1 in Violence," *Olympian*, November 13, 1992; *New York Times*, November 13, 1992, p. A9; and Douglas Lee Eckberg, "Estimates of Early Twentieth-Century U.S. Homicide Rates: An Econometric Forecasting Approach," *Demography* 32 (1995), p. 14. On lengthening commutes, see "It's Taking Longer to Get to Work," *Olympian*, December 6, 1995.

6. The figures in this and the following paragraph come from Levy, "Incomes and Income Inequality," pp. 1–57; Richard May and Kathryn Porter, "Poverty and Income Trends, 1994," Washington, D.C.: Center on Budget and Policy Priorities, March 1996; Reynolds Farley, *The New American Reality: Who We Are, How We Got Here, Where We Are Going* (New York: Russell Sage, 1996), pp. 83–85; Gelles, *Contemporary Families*, p. 115; David Grissmer, Sheila Nataraj Kirby, Mark Bender, and Stephanie Williamson, *Student Achievement and*

*the Changing American Family*, Rand Institute on Education and Training (Santa Monica, Calif.: Rand, 1994), p. 106.

7. William Chafe, *The Unfinished Journey: America Since World War II* (New York: Oxford University Press, 1986), pp. 113, 143; Marc Linder, "Eisenhower-Era Marxist-Confiscatory Taxation: Requiem for the Rhetoric of Rate Reduction for the Rich," *Tulane Law Review 70* (1996), p. 917; Barry Bluestone and Teresa Ghilarducci, "Rewarding Work: Feasible Antipoverty Policy," *American Prospect* 28 (1996), p. 42; Theda Skocpol, "Delivering for Young Families," *American Prospect* 28 (1996), p. 67.

8. Joel Tarr, "The Evolution of the Urban Infrastructure in the Nineteenth and Twentieth Centuries," in Royce Hanson, ed., *Perspectives on Urban Infrastructure* (Washington, D.C.: National Academy Press, 1984); Mark Aldrich, *A History of Public Works Investment in the United States*, report prepared by the CPNSAD Research Corporation for the U.S. Department of Commerce, April 1980.

9. For more information on this government financing, see Kenneth Jackson, *Crabgrass Frontier: The Suburbanization of the United States* (New York: Oxford University Press, 1985); and Stephanie Coontz, *The Way We Never Were: American Families and the Nostalgia Trap* (New York: Basic Books, 1992), chapter 4.

10. John Cook and Laura Sherman, "Economic Security Among America's Poor: The Impact of State Welfare Waivers on Asset Accumulation," Center on Hunger, Poverty, and Nutrition Policy, Tufts University, May 1996.

11. Robert Kuttner, "The Incredible Shrinking American Paycheck," *Washington Post National Weekly Edition*, November 6–12, 1995, p. 23; Donald Bartlett and James Steele, *America: What Went Wrong?* (Kansas City: Andrews McMeel, 1992), p. 20.

12. Richard Barnet, "Lords of the Global Economy," *Nation*, December 19, 1994, p. 756; Clay Chandler, "U.S. Corporations: Good Citizens or Bad?" *Washington Post National Weekly Edition*, May 20–26, 1996, p. 16; Steven Pearlstein, "No More Mr. Nice Guy: Corporate America Has Done an About-Face in How It Pays and Treats Employees," *Washington Post National Weekly Edition*, December 18–24, 1995, p. 10; Robert Kuttner, "Ducking Class Warfare," *Washington Post National Weekly Edition*, March 11–17, 1996, p. 5; Henry Allen, "Ha! So Much for

Loyalty," *Washington Post National Weekly Edition*, March 4–10, 1996, p. 11.

13. Ehrenhalt, *The Lost City* , pp. 11–12; Jeremy Rifken, *The End of Work: The Decline of the Global Labor Force and the Dawn of the Post-Market Era* (New York: G.P. Putnam's Sons, 1995), pp. 169, 170, 231; Juliet Schorr, *The Overworked American: The Unexpected Decline of Leisure* (New York: Basic Books, 1991).

14. For documentation that these problems existed, see chapter 2 of *The Way We Never Were*.

15. The poverty figures come from census data collected in *The State of America's Children Yearbook, 1996* (Washington, D.C.: Children's Defense Fund, 1996), p. 77. See also Hirsch, *Making the Second Ghetto*; Raymond Mohl, "Making the Second Ghetto in Metropolitan Miami, 1940–1960," *Journal of Urban History* 25 (1995), p. 396; Micaela di Leonardo, "Boys on the Hood," *Nation*, August 17–24, 1992, p. 180; Jackson, *Crabgrass Frontier*, pp. 226–227.

16. Susan Douglas, *Where the Girls Are: Growing Up Female with the Mass Media* (New York: Times Books, 1994), pp. 25, 37.

17. *The State of America's Children Yearbook, 1966*, p. 77; May and Porter, "Poverty and Income Trends: 1994," p. 23; Sara McLanahan et al., *Losing Ground: A Critique*, University of Wisconsin Institute for Research on Poverty, Special Report No. 38, 1985.

18. For studies of how both middle-class and working-class women in the 1950s quickly departed from, or never quite accepted, the predominant image of women, see Joanne Meyerowitz, ed., *Not June Cleaver: Women and Gender in Postwar America, 1945–1960* (Philadelphia: Temple University Press, 1994).

19. Lynn Karoly, "The Trend in Inequality Among Families, Individuals, and Workers in the United States: A Twenty-Five Year Perspective," in Sheldon Danziger and Peter Gottschalk, eds., *Rising Inequality in America* (New York: Russel Sage, 1993), pp. 48, 77–78; Michael Bernstein and David Adler, eds., *Understanding American Economic Decline* (New York: Cambridge University Press, 1994); Geoffrey Holtz, *Welcome to the Jungle: The Why Behind "Generation X"* (New York: St. Martin's Press, 1995), p. 167; "Widening Wage Inequality," *Urban Institute Policy and Research Report*, Winter/Spring 1995, p. 4.

20. Gordon Berlin and Andrew Sum, *Toward a More Perfect Union: Basic Skills, Poor Families, and Our Economic Future* (New York: Ford Foundation, 1988), pp. 5–6.

21. Kevin Phillips, "Down and Out: Can The Middle Class Rise Again?" *New York Times Magazine*, January 10, 1993, p. 32.

22. Kevin Phillips, *Boiling Point: Republicans, Democrats, and the Decline of Middle-Class Prosperity* (New York: Random House, 1993); "Making America's Economy Competitive Again" (Washington, D.C.: Rebuild America Coalition, 1992), p.8; "Statement on Key Welfare Reform Issues: The Empirical Evidence," Tufts University Center on Hunger, Poverty, and Nutrition Policy, 1995, pp. 13–14; May and Porter, "Poverty and Income Trends: 1994," p. 87; Robert Pear, "Typical Relief Check Worth Half That of 1970," *New York Times*, November 27, 1996, p. A10.

23. Richard Easterlin, *Birth and Fortune: The Impact of Numbers on Personal Welfare* (Chicago: University of Chicago Press, 1987).

## CRITICAL THINKING QUESTIONS

1. Coontz argues that the 1950s family culture was neither idyllic nor as traditional as many people think. What evidence does she present to support this conclusion?

2. According to Coontz, some family forms (such as two-paycheck families) have changed in response to economic pressures. Does this mean, then, that two-earner families are inevitable? Or, as many conservatives and centrists argue, are parents sacrificing their children to maintain expensive lifestyles?

3. Should we resuscitate some aspects of the 1950s family as we enter the twenty-first century? Support your position using the conservative, centrist, and liberal/feminist selections in this chapter.

# 4  Family Values

## *Conservative:* The Family-Values Debate

JAMES Q. WILSON, "The Family-Values Debate," *Commentary*, April 1, 1993, pp. 24–31. Copyright James Q. Wilson. Reprinted by permission; all rights reserved.

*When you hear the term* family values, *what images come to mind? Do your family, friends, and classmates agree with your perceptions? Although many people use the term, few define it. In this article, James Q. Wilson explains what many conservatives mean by family values, why he and others feel that family values have deteriorated, and suggests how to restore the traditional family.*

There are two views about the contemporary American family, one held by the public and the other by policy elites. In his presidential campaign, Bill Clinton appeared to endorse the public's view. It remains to be seen which view President Clinton will support.

The public's view is this: the family is the place in which the most basic values are instilled in children. In recent years, however, these values have become less secure, in part because the family has become weaker and in part because rivals for its influence—notably television and movies—have gotten stronger. One way the family has become weaker is that more and more children are being raised in one-parent families, and often that one parent is a teenage girl. Another way is that parents, whether in one- or two-parent families, are spending less time with their children and are providing poorer discipline. Because family values are so important, political candidates should talk about them, though it is not clear that the government can do much about them. Overwhelmingly, Amer-icans think that it is better for children if one parent stays home and does not work, even if that means having less money.[1]

No such consensus is found among scholars or policy-makers. That in itself is revealing. Beliefs about families that most people regard as virtually self-evident are hotly disputed among people whose job it is to study or support families.

A good example of the elite argument began last fall on the front page of the *Washington Post*, where a reporter quoted certain social scientists as saying that the conventional two-parent family was not as important for the healthy development of children as was once supposed. This prompted David Popenoe, a professor at Rutgers who has written extensively on family issues, to publish in the *New York Times* an op-ed piece challenging the scholars cited in the *Post*. Popenoe asserted that "dozens'" of studies had come to the opposite conclusion, and that the weight of the evidence "decisively" supported the view that two-parent families are better than single-parent families.

Decisively to him, perhaps, but not to others. Judith Stacey, another professor of sociology, responded in a letter to the *Times* that the value of a two-parent family was merely a "widely shared prejudice" not confirmed by empirical studies; Popenoe, she said, was trying to convert "misguided nostalgia for 'Ozzie-and-Harriet'-land into social-scientific truth." Arlene and Jerome Skolnick, two more professors, acknowledged that although Popenoe might be correct, saying so publicly would "needlessly stigmatize children raised in families that don't meet the 'Ozzie-and-Harriet' model." After all, the Skolnicks observed, a man raised outside that model had just been elected President of the United States.

The views of Stacey and the Skolnicks are by no means unrepresentative of academic thinking on this subject. Barbara Dafoe Whitehead recently surveyed the most prominent textbooks on marriage and the family. Here is my paraphrase of her summary of what she found:

The life course is full of exciting options. These include living in a commune, having a group marriage, being a single parent, or living together. Marriage is one life-style choice, but before choosing it people weigh its costs and benefits against other options. Divorce is a part of the normal family cycle and is neither deviant nor tragic. Rather, it can serve as a foundation for individual renewal and new beginnings. Marriage itself should not be regarded as a special, privileged institution; on the contrary, it must catch up with the diverse, pluralistic society in which we live. For example, same-sex marriages often involve more sharing and equality than do heterosexual relationships. But even in the conventional family, the relationships between husband and wife need to be defined after carefully negotiating agreements that protect each person's separate interests and rights.[2]

Many politicians and reporters echo these sentiments and carry the argument one step further. Not only do poor Ozzie and Harriet (surely the most maligned figures in the history of television) stand for nostalgic prejudice and stigmatizing error,

they represent a kind of family that in fact scarcely exists. Congresswoman Pat Schroeder has been quoted as saying that only about 7 percent of all American families fit the Ozzie-and-Harriet model. Our daily newspapers frequently assert that most children will not grow up in a two-parent family. The message is clear: not only is the two-parent family not especially good for children, but fortunately it is also fast disappearing.

Yet whether or not the two-parent family is good for children, it is plainly false that this kind of family has become a historical relic. For while there has been a dramatic increase in the proportion of children, especially black children who will spend some or even most of their youth in single-parent families, the vast majority of children—nationally, about 73 percent—live in a home with married parents. Today, the mothers in those families are more likely to work than once was the case, though most do not work full time. (I am old enough to remember that even Harriet worked, at least in real life. She was a singer.)

The proponents of the relic theory fail to use statistics accurately. The way they arrive at the discovery that only 7 percent of all families fit the Ozzie-and-Harriet model is by calculating what proportion of all families consists *exactly* of a father, mother, and two (not three or four) children, and in which the mother never works, not even for two weeks during the year helping out with the Christmas rush at the post office.

The language in which the debate over two-parent families is carried on suggests that something more than scholarly uncertainty is at stake. If all we cared about were the effects of one- versus two-parent families on the lives of children, there would still be a debate, but it would not be conducted on op-ed pages in tones of barely controlled anger. Nor would it be couched in slogans about television characters or supported by misleading statistics.

What is at stake, of course, is the role of women. To defend the two-parent family is to defend, the critics worry, an institution in which the woman is subordinated to her husband, confined to domestic chores with no opportunity to pursue a career, and taught to indoctrinate her children with a belief in the rightness of this arrangement. To some critics, the woman here is not simply constrained, she is abused. The traditional family, in this view, is an arena in which men are free to hit, rape, and exploit women. To defend the traditional family is to defend sexism. And since single-parent families are disproportionately headed by black women, criticizing such families is not only sexist but racist. . . .

The main theme of much of the writing about marriage and families during the 1970s and 1980s was that of individual rights. Just as polities were only legitimate when they respected individual rights, so also marriages were worthy of respect only when they were based on a recognition of rights.

This view impressed itself on many who were not scholars, as is evident from an essay published in 1973 in the *Harvard Educational Review.* It urged that the "legal status of infancy . . . be abolished" so that a child would be endowed with all the rights of an adult. Even more, any law that classified people as children and treated them differently from adults "should be considered suspect." As a result, the state "would no longer be able to assume the rationality of regulations based on age." The author of this essay was Hillary Rodham.

A rights-based, individualistic view of marriage is questionable in its own terms, but these theoretical questions would become insuperable objections if it could be shown that children are harmed by growing up in mother-only, or communal, or swinging, or divorced households. The academic study of families during the 1970s, however, did not produce an unchallenged body of evidence demonstrating that this was the case. There were several studies that attempted to measure the impact of mother-only families on their children's school attainment, job success,

and personal conduct, but many discovered either no effects or ones that were ambiguous or equivocal. . . .

The evidence that single-parent families are bad for children has mounted. There will never be anything like conclusive proof of this proposition unless we randomly assign babies at birth to single- and two-parent families of various economic and ethnic circumstances and then watch them grow up. Happily the laws and customs of this country make such an experiment unlikely. Short of that, the best evidence comes from longitudinal studies that follow children as they grow up in whatever kind of family nature has provided.

One example: when the 5,000 children born in the United Kingdom during the first week of March 1946 were followed for three decades, those raised in families broken by divorce or desertion were more likely than those living in two-parent families to become delinquent.[3]

A second example: for many years, Sheppard Kellam and his colleagues at Johns Hopkins University followed several hundred poor, black, first-grade children in a depressed neighborhood in Chicago. Each child lived in one of several different family types, depending on how many and what kinds of adults were present. In about one-third of families the mother was the only adult present; in another third there was both a mother and a father. (Only a tiny fraction was headed by a father with no mother present.) The remainder was made up of various combinations of mothers, grandparents, uncles, aunts, adult brothers and sisters, and various unrelated adults. By the time the children entered the third grade, those who lived with their mothers alone were the worst off in terms of their socialization. After ten years, the boys who had grown up in mother-only families (which by then made up about half the total) reported more delinquencies, regardless of family income, than those who had grown up in families with multiple adults, especially a father.[4]

By 1986, when Rolf and Magda Loeber of the University of Pittsburgh reviewed 23 studies assessing the relationship of parental absence (usually, father absence) to juvenile delinquency, they found an effect, though smaller than the one caused by discord within a two-parent family.[5] One problem with their overall conclusion was that they lumped together families where the biological father had never been present with those in which he left, as a result of separation, divorce, or death, while the child was growing up. Inspecting their data suggests that if the latter cases are omitted, the connection between family status and criminality is strengthened a bit: fathers never present create greater hazards than fathers who depart (owing to death or divorce) later in the child's life. The greatest hazard of all is found in families where the parents have the greatest number of problems—they are absent, discordant, rejecting, incompetent, and criminal.

The most recent important study of family structure was done in 1988 by the Department of Health and Human Services. It surveyed the family arrangements of more than 60,000 children living in households all over the country. Interviews were conducted in order to identify any childhood problems in health, schoolwork, and personal conduct. These results were tabulated according to the age, sex, and ethnicity of the child, and the income and marital status of the parents.

The results were striking. At every income level save the very highest (over $50,000 per year), for both sexes and for whites, blacks, and Hispanics alike, children living with a never-married or a divorced mother were substantially worse off than those living in two-parent families. Compared to children living with both biological parents, children in single-parent families were twice as likely to have been expelled or suspended from school, to display emotional or behavioral problems, and to have problems with their peers; they were also much more likely to engage in antisocial behavior. These differences were about as wide in households earning over $35,000 a year as they were in those making less than $10,000.[6]

Charles Murray of the American Enterprise Institute has been looking at the people whose lives have been followed by the National Longitudinal Study of Youth (NLSY) since they were in high school (they are now in their late twenties or early thirties). The NLSY not only keeps careful records of the schooling, jobs, and income of these young adults, it also looks at the home environment in which they are raising any children they may have. These home observations rate emotional quality, parental involvement in child care, style of discipline, and the like. The homes, thus observed, can be ranked from best to worst.

Murray has compared the home environments with the economic status of the parents and the legal status of the child. The odds of the children living in the worst home environments were powerfully affected by two things: whether the parents were married when they had the baby and whether they were regular welfare recipients. The child of an unmarried woman who was a chronic welfare recipient had one chance in six of growing up in the worst—that is, emotionally the worst—environment. The child of a married woman who never went on welfare had only one chance in 42.[7]

Being poor hurts children. Living in a rotten neighborhood hurts them. Having cold or neglectful parents certainly hurts them. But so also does being illegitimate and living on welfare. This is generally true for whites as well as blacks.

And so also does being a teenage mother. For many years, Frank Furstenberg of the University of Pennsylvania and his colleagues have been following 300 teenage mothers living in Baltimore. What they have found supports the public's view. Teenage girls who have babies fare much worse than ones who postpone childbearing, and this is true even among girls of the same socioeconomic background and academic aptitude. They are more likely to go on welfare, and less likely to enter into a stable marriage. The children of teenage mothers, compared with those of older ones, tend to have more trouble in school, to be more aggressive, and to have less self-control. This is especially true of boys.[8]

We have always had teenage mothers, and in some less-developed societies that is the norm. What is new and troubling about the present situation is the vast increase in the number of teenage mothers and their concentration in the same neighborhoods. A girl with a baby presents one kind of problem when she is either a rarity or is embedded in an extended family that provides guidance and assistance from older women living with her. She presents a very different and much more serious problem when she is one of thousands of similarly situated youngsters living in the same neighborhood or public-housing project, trying to maintain an independent household on welfare.

A lot more light will be shed on these issues when Sara McLanahan at Princeton and Gary Sandefur at the University of Wisconsin publish their careful analysis of the best available longitudinal data bases.[9] There are at least four of these files—the already-mentioned National Longitudinal Study of Youth; the Panel Study of Income Dynamics; the High School and Beyond Study; and the National Survey of Families and Households. McLanahan and Sandefur are looking at the effect of family structure, after controlling for income, race, and education, on such things as a child's chances of graduating from high school, a girl's chances of becoming a teenage mother, and a boy's chances of being idle (that is, neither working nor in school). Their results so far suggest that children who grow up in single-parent families do less well than those who grow up in intact families, and that this is true whether they are white or black, rich or poor, boys or girls. These other factors make a difference—it is better to be white than black, rich than poor—but so does family status.

I think that the American people are right in their view of families. When they look at the dramatic increase in divorce, single-parent families, and illegitimate children that has taken place over the last 30 years, they see families in decline. They do not need studies to tell them that these outcomes are generally bad, because they have had these outcomes happen to them or to people they know. Divorce may sometimes be the right and necessary remedy for fundamentally flawed marriages and for the conditions created by an abusive or neglectful spouse, but in general divorce makes people worse off: the woman becomes poorer and the children more distressed. Properly raising a child is an enormous responsibility that often taxes the efforts and energies of two parents; one parent is likely to be overwhelmed. Children born out of wedlock are in the great majority of cases children born into poverty. Millions of people are living testimony to these bleak facts. If scholars say that the evidence is not conclusive, so much the worse for scholars. But now, I believe, scholars are starting to find hard facts to support popular impressions.

The debate over the effects of family structure continues, albeit with some prospect of a consensus emerging some time in the near future. But there is not even a glimmer of such an accord with respect to the other hot topic in family studies—day care. The dominant view among child psychologists is that day care is not harmful. For a long time Professor Jay Belsky of Pennsylvania State University shared that view. When he changed his mind, he was excoriated. He is now of the opinion that day care, especially in the first year of life, is harmful in some respects to some children.

In a widely-reported 1988 article, Belsky reviewed all the studies measuring the effect of nonmaternal care on attachment and social development and concluded that, subject to many caveats,

> entry into [day] care in the first year of life for twenty hours or more per week is a "risk factor" for the development of insecure attachment in infancy and heightened aggressiveness, noncompliance, and with-

drawal in the preschool and early school years.[10]

By "risk factor" Belsky meant that the child in day care was somewhat more likely to experience these adverse outcomes than would a similar child under parental care, especially if the day care was not of high quality.

Some critics argued with Belsky on scientific grounds, saying that the evidence was less clearcut than he suggested, that the measure of emotional well-being he used (observing how a child reacts after it is separated from its mother) was flawed, that children turn out well in cultures where nonparental care is commonplace, and that whatever ill effects exist (if any) do not last.

But many attacked him politically, and even the scholarly critiques had a sharp edge to them. As with family structure, what is at stake in this controversy are not just facts and interpretations but philosophy and policy: if day care has bad effects, then women ought to care for their children in their own homes. And that is a politically-incorrect conclusion. Many scholars feel, I believe, that to support the claim of family decline is to give aid and comfort to conservative politicians and religious leaders who bemoan that decline and call for the reassertion of "traditional values." In short, what is at stake is Murphy Brown.

## THE CHANGING CULTURE

Both teenage pregnancies and single-parent families have increased dramatically since the 1950s. Changes in the economy and in the provision of welfare benefits explain some of this growth but not all or even most of it. There are no doubt some features peculiar to American society that explain some of it, but since the decline of the family—that is, in lasting marriages and legitimate births—has happened in many nations, it cannot be entirely the result of American policies or peculiarities.

We are witnessing a profound, worldwide, long-term change in the family that is likely to continue for a long time. The causes of that change are not entirely understood, but probably involve two main forces: a shift in the family's economic function and a shift in the culture in which it is embedded. The family no longer is the unit that manages economic production, as it was when agriculture was the dominant form of production, nor is it any longer the principal provider of support for the elderly or education for the young.

At the same time, the family no longer exercises as much control over its members as it once did, and broader kinship groupings (clans, tribes, and extended families) no longer exercise as much control over nuclear families. . . . This emancipation has proceeded episodically and unevenly, but relentlessly. Liberal political theory has celebrated the individual and constrained the state, but it has been silent about the family. . . .

Family—and kinship generally—are the fundamental organizing facts of all human societies, primitive or advanced, and have been such for tens of thousands of years. The family is the product of evolutionary processes that have selected against people who are inclined to abandon their offspring and for people who are prepared to care for them, and to provide this caring within kinship systems defined primarily along genetic lines. If kinship were a cultural artifact, we could as easily define it on the basis of height, athletic skill, or political status, and children would be raised in all manner of collectives, ranging from state-run orphanages to market-supplied foster homes. Orphanages and foster homes do of course exist, but only as matters of last resort designed (with great public anxiety) to provide care when the biological family does not exist or cannot function.

If the family were merely a convenience and if it responded entirely to economic circumstances, the current debate over family policy would be far less rancorous than it is. Liberals would urge that we professionalize child-rearing through day care; conservatives would urge that we subsidize it through earned-income tax credits. Liberals would define the welfare problem as entirely a matter of poverty and recommend more generous benefits as the solution; conservatives would define it as entirely a matter of dependency and recommend slashing benefits as the solution. Liberals would assume that the problem is that families have too little money, conservatives that families get such money as they have from the state. There would still be a battle, but in the end it would come down to some negotiated compromise involving trade-offs among benefit levels, eligibility rules, and the public-private mix of child-care providers.

But once one conceives of the family problem as involving to a significant degree the conflict between a universal feature of human society and a profound cultural challenge to the power of that institution, the issue takes on a different character. To the extent that one believes in the cultural challenge—that is, in individual emancipation and individual choice—one tends to question the legitimacy and influence of the family. To the extent that one believes in the family, one is led to question some or all parts of the cultural challenge.

That is why the debate over "family values" has been so strident. On both sides people feel that it is the central battle in the culture war that now grips Americans (or at least American elites). They are absolutely right. To many liberals, family values means a reassertion of male authority, a reduction in the hard-earned rights of women, and a license for abusive or neglectful parents to mistreat their children free of prompt and decisive social intervention. For some liberals, family values means something even more troubling: that human nature is less malleable than is implied by the doctrine of environmental determinism and cultural relativism—that it is to some significant degree fixed, immutable. To many conservatives, family values is the main line of resistance against homosexual marriages, bureaucratized

child care, and compulsory sex education in the schools. For some conservatives, the family means a defense against the very idea of a planned society.

Now, reasonable people—say, the typical mother or father—will take a less stark view of the alternatives. They will agree with conservatives that the family is the central institution of society, incapable of being replaced or even much modified without disastrous consequences. They will be troubled by same-sex marriages, upset by teenage girls becoming mothers, angered by public subsidies for illegitimate births, and outraged by the distribution of condoms and explicit sex-education manuals to elementary-school children. But they will agree with many liberals that we ought not to confine women to domestic roles or make them subservient to male power, and that we ought to recognize and cope with the financial hardships that young couples have today when they try to live on one income in a big city.

On one issue most parents will squarely identify with the conservative side, and it is, in my view, the central issue. They will want our leaders, the media, television programs, and motion pictures to take their side in the war over what the family is. It is not one of several alternative lifestyles; it is not an arena in which rights are negotiated; it is not an old-fashioned and reactionary barrier to a promiscuous sex life; it is not a set of cost-benefit calculations. *It is a commitment.*

It is a commitment required for child-rearing and thus for any realistic prospect of human happiness. It is a commitment that may be entered into after romantic experimentation and with some misgivings about lost freedoms, but once entered into it is a commitment that persists for richer or for poorer, in sickness and in health, for better or for worse. It is a commitment for which there is no feasible substitute, and hence no child ought lightly to be brought into a world where that commitment—from both parents—is absent. It is a commitment that often is joyfully enlivened by mutual love and deepening friendship, but it is a commitment even when these things are absent.

There is no way to prepare for the commitment other than to make it. The idea that a man and a woman can live together without a commitment in order to see if they would like each other after they make the commitment is preposterous. Living together may inform you as to whether your partner snores or is an alcoholic or sleeps late; it may be fun and exciting; it may even be the best you can manage in an imperfect world. But it is not a way of finding out how married life will be, because married life is shaped by the fact that the couple has made a solemn vow before their family and friends that this is for keeps and that any children will be their joint and permanent responsibility. It changes everything.

Despite high divorce rates and a good deal of sleeping around, most people understand this. Certainly women understand it, since one of their most common complaints about the men they know is that they will not make a commitment. You bet they won't, not if they can get sex, cooking, and companionship on a trial basis, all the while keeping their eyes peeled for a better opportunity elsewhere. Marriage is in large measure a device for reining in the predatory sexuality of males. It works quite imperfectly, as is evident from the fact that men are more likely than women to have extramarital affairs and to abandon their spouses because a younger or more exciting possibility has presented herself. But it works better than anything else mankind has been able to invent. . . .

The legal system has also altered child-custody rules so that, instead of being automatically assigned to the father (as was the case in the 19th century, when the father was thought to "own" all the family's property including the child), the child is now assigned by the judge on the basis of its "best interests." In the vast majority of cases, that means with the mother. I sometimes wonder what would happen to

family stability if every father knew for certain that, should the marriage end, he would have to take custody of the children. My guess is: more committed fathers.

These cultural and legal changes, all aimed at individualizing and empowering family members, have had an effect. In 1951, 51 percent of all Americans agreed with the statement that "parents who don't get along should not stay together because there are children in the family." By 1985, 86 percent agreed.[11] Still, these changes have not devastated modern families. The shopping malls, baseball stadiums, and movie theaters are filled with them doing what families have always done. That fact is a measure of the innate power of the family bond.

Yet the capacity for resisting these changes is unequally distributed in society. Christopher Jencks of Northwestern University puts it this way:

> Now that the mass media, the schools, and even the churches have begun to treat single parenthood as a regrettable but inescapable part of modern life, we can hardly expect the respectable poor to carry on the struggle against illegitimacy and desertion with their old fervor. They still deplore such behavior, but they cannot make it morally taboo. Once the two-parent norm loses its moral sanctity, the selfish considerations that always pulled poor parents apart often become overwhelming.[12]

## NOTES

1. Evidence for these beliefs can be found in the poll data gathered in the *American Enterprise,* September/October 1992, pp. 85–86.

2. Paraphrased from Barbara Dafoe Whitehead, *The Expert's Story of Marriage,* Institute for American Values, Publication No. WP14 (August 1992), pp. 11–12. Whitehead supplies references to the texts she summarizes. She does not endorse—just the opposite!—the views she has compiled.

3. M. E. J. Wadsworth, *Roots of Delinquency,* Barnes & Noble (1979).

4. Sheppard Kellam *et al.,* "The Long-Term Evolution of the Family Structure of Teenage and

Older Mothers," *Journal of Marriage and the Family*, vol. 44 (1982), pp. 539–554; Kellam *et al.*, "Family Structure and the Mental Health of Children," *Archives of General Psychiatry*, vol. 34 (1977), pp. 1012–1022; Margaret Ensminger *et al.*, "School and Family Origins of Delinquency: Comparisons by Sex," in Katherine T. Van Dusen and Sarnoff A. Mednick, eds., *Prospective Studies of Crime and Delinquency*, Kluwer-Nijhoff (1983).

5. "Family Factors as Correlates and Predictors of Juvenile Conduct Problems and Delinquency," in Michael Tonry and Norval Morris, eds., *Crime and Justice: An Annual Review of Research*, University of Chicago Press (1986), pp. 29–149.

6. Deborah A. Dawson, "Family Structure and Children's Health: United States, 1988," *Vital and Health Statistics*, Series 10, No. 178 (June 1991).

7. "Reducing Poverty and Reducing the Underclass: Different Problems, Different Solutions," paper presented to the Conference on Reducing Poverty in America, January 15, 1993, at the Anderson Graduate School of Management, UCLA.

8. Frank F. Furstenberg, Jr., Jeanne Brooks-Gunn, and Lindsay Chase-Lansdale, "Teenage Pregnancy and Childbearing," *American Psychologist*, vol. 44 (1989), pp. 313–320.

9. *Uncertain Childhood, Uncertain Future* (Harvard University Press, forthcoming).

10. "The 'Effects' of Infant Day Care Reconsidered," *Early Childhood Research Quarterly*, vol. 3 (1988), pp 235–272. For a response, see Tiffany Field, *Infancy*, Harvard University Press (1990), pp. 90–93.

11. David Popenoe, "The Family Condition of America," paper prepared for a Brookings Institution seminar on values and public policy (March 1992), citing a study by Norval Glenn.

12. "Deadly Neighborhoods," *The New Republic*, June 13, 1988, pp. 23–32.

## CRITICAL THINKING QUESTIONS

1. Much of the debate over family values hinges on one's definition of the family. How does Wilson define family? What kinds of households (including yours, perhaps) does his definition exclude?

2. What, according to Wilson, are the major indicators that family values are declining? Is socioeconomic status important or inconsequential in many of the problems that Wilson attributes to deteriorating family values?

3. Wilson argues that no child ought to be brought into the world if the parents aren't married. Does this imply, then, that we should encourage unmarried women to have abortions? What about women who become pregnant as the couple begins divorce proceedings? Should we, also, require the states that recognize common-law marriages as legal to repeal such legislation?

# 4    Family Values

## Centrist: The Revolution in Family Norms

DENNIS K. ORTHNER, "The Family in Transition," in *Rebuilding the Nest: A New Commitment to the American Family*, ed. David Blankenhorn, Steven Bayme, and Jean Bethke Elshtain (Milwaukee, WI: Family Service America, 1990), pp. 94–105. Reproduced by permission of Manticore Publishers.

*Like James Q. Wilson (see his article "The Family-Values Debate"), many centrists believe that traditional family values are in decline. In this selection, however, Dennis K. Orthner proposes that family norms, not values, have changed most dramatically since the 1950s. Many contemporary family problems, he maintains, reflect confusion about adult relationships and responsibilities because we no longer have clear-cut expectations about dating, mate selection, marriage, and even divorce. As a result, the family is more vulnerable today than in the past.*

### CHANGING FAMILY VALUES AND BELIEFS

Cultural values have changed significantly over the past century. In his discourse on "New Rules," Daniel Yankelovich refers to the "giant plates of the culture" that have been shifting dramatically over this century.[1] Like the geological theory of plate tectonics, these cultural plates sometimes shift position, grind against each other, and promote instabilities in basic values and beliefs—creating, in short, the cultural equivalent of an earthquake. . . .

Many of the core values that have been changing are related to the family, including the high priority given to independence instead of marriage, to individual freedom over collective interests, to personal pleasure instead of nurturance, and to instrumental commitments instead of intrinsic commitments.

### The Value of Marriage vs. Independence

Those who speculate that the family system is declining claim that marriage as an ideal is less important today. They suggest that positive values associated with voluntary singleness have become more common, making marriage more of a choice than a necessity among those who traditionally have been in the marriage market. If this is true, marriage as a valued institution is indeed in trouble and other forms of non-marital living arrangements may replace marriage in the future. . . .

Although the percentage of adults who are single and cohabiting has increased, this appears to be the result of marriage delays and the increased use of cohabitation as a testing phase in courtship. The overall marriage rate may have declined from the 95% pinnacle of the 1970s to an 85% to 90% rate, but this percentage is still high by world standards. Somewhat more traditional societies than our own, such as Ireland and Australia, have considerably lower marriage rates,[2] but they are not usually considered in "decline." If anything, the value of marriage as a preferable living arrangement appears to be holding its own during this time of institutional transition.

## Individualism vs. Collectivism

A second concern is that individualism has become so strong in America that interest in the collectivities of family and community has declined. Robert Bellah and his colleagues note that "individualism lies at the very core of American culture. . . . We believe in the dignity, indeed the sacredness, of the individual. . . . Our highest and noblest aspirations, not only for ourselves, but for those we care about, for our society and for the world, are closely linked to our individualism."[3] David Popenoe worries, however, that "cultural trends associated with the growing importance placed on 'self-fulfillment' . . . could be regarded as another important contributor to the high family-dissolution rate."[4] . . .

If individualism has been such a dominant feature of American life, how has it manifested itself in the family? . . . Without a strong tradition of extended-family households in America, we created from the very beginning a pattern of relatively independent households with quite strong helping networks across kin and friend lines. If these helping networks have been eroding, then we can assume that individualism has indeed triumphed over collective interests, at least in the family arena.

Studies conducted during the 1950s found a strong sense of obligation among family members to help other family members.[5] This finding surprised some researchers, because they too had come to believe that familism had declined in favor of individualism. These researchers discovered frequent visitations between families, financial help being given to younger and older families, help with child care and other household tasks, and frequent exchanges of advice. . . .

The situation today is not that different. Visits among relatives, especially with parents, have not declined significantly since the 1950s. More than half (53%) of adults with living parents see them at least once a month, and a similar percentage (51%) agree that aging parents should live with their adult children.[6] . . .

This is not a gloomy picture of rampant individualism. Rather, it suggests that collective interests remain strong in American families, even within the context of a culture that promotes individual interests. There is little evidence that Americans are giving up on familism.

## Commitment vs. Autonomy

Autonomy is often prized because it reflects a level of competence typically associated with adulthood and maturity. Although commitments imply reciprocal obligations, autonomy promises the freedom to enter and leave obligations based solely on self-defined interests. . . .

One commonly used framework in family theory and family therapy is built on the assumption of balance between autonomy and commitments. In their "circumplex" model of family behavior, David H. Olson and his colleagues assume that extremes in either family-member autonomy (disengagement) or cohesion (enmeshment) have negative consequences.[7] Their research suggests that families whose members have balanced interests in separateness and togetherness are the most likely to report being satisfied and the most likely to stay married.

The inability of many couples to sustain lifelong commitments is often taken as evidence that family commitments are not as strong today as they once were. Furthermore, a large proportion of youth and adults worry that this trend will continue. . . . Nevertheless, it is difficult to sort out a general sense of pessimism from a personal sense of optimism about their own relationships. The vast majority of adults (71%)

believe that "marriage is a lifelong commitment that should not be ended except under extreme circumstances."[8] Even more Americans (85%) say they would remarry their spouses if they had to do it all over again.[9] Even the divorced and separated hold positive ambitions: most people who can do so will remarry and 81% still believe that marriage is a commitment for life.

These statistics do not indicate that Americans are running away from marriage and commitment. Instead, they indicate an underlying search for meaningful commitments and a healthy fear of the negative consequences if these do not last. Perhaps social scientists have been all too successful in pronouncing the decline in commitments: the fear of marital failure has continued to rise through the 1980s even though divorce rates have stabilized, even declined, in the past decade and a half. . . .

It is true that the balance between autonomy and commitment in American society continues to shift. But the shift is not away from commitments, as some have alleged, but rather toward different types of commitment—those that provide mutual and balanced gratifications for all family members.

### Nurturance vs. Narcissism

Have Americans lapsed into a narcissistic binge, retaining little concern for anyone other than themselves? . . . Have we lost any of our capacity to nurture other adults or children? Has the basic social value of supporting others been eroded? This question is crucial; indeed, if the modern family has shifted its primary functions away from meeting instrumental needs toward meeting expressive needs, then its ability to provide nurturance for its members has become the mainstay of its existence.

The evidence that modern men and women are no longer interested in nurturing others but only themselves is scanty. The data supporting this claim are largely impressionistic and qualitative. Expressed desires for intimate relationships have not decreased. Nor have persons who have left unsatisfactory relationships turned against the search for intimacy with others. Summarizing the results of their landmark study of divorced men and women, Mavis Hetherington, Martha Cox, and Roger Cox state:

> The divorced individuals wanted sustained, meaningful relationships and were not satisfied with a series of superficial encounters. The formation of lasting intimate relations, involving deep concern and a willingness to make sacrifices for the partner, as well as a strong attachment and desire to be near the person, was a strong factor in happiness, self-esteem, and feelings of competence in sexual relations for both divorced men and women.[10]

On balance, the lives and circumstances of children have not declined to the extent that the public perceives. But there is little question that most adults feel collectively guilty about their lack of attention to the nurturance needs of children. Yet, when parents were asked if they wished they could be free from the responsibilities of child rearing, only 8% agreed and 71% disagreed.[11] This is not the picture of parental and societal neglect that some would like to paint, but it does suggest that more attention must be focused on the needs of children.

Overall, the data suggest that needs for adult and child nurturance remain strong in our society. The issues being raised over the rearing and nurturance of children reflect an undercurrent of concern that is now being transformed into more support services for parents and their children. The increased emphasis on narcissism and selfishness that has been suggested by some does not appear to be a strong cultural value at this time, although it may reflect heightened opportunities for personal freedom during adolescence and young adulthood.

### CHANGING FAMILY NORMS

Although basic family values have not changed dramatically, the norms of family behavior have, in fact, undergone dramatic transformations. Family norms, as I define them here, refer to the behavioral expectations associated with the statuses and roles of family members. Whereas values are attached to beliefs, norms are attached to and directly guide behavior. (Also, behavioral changes can change norms.) Thus, norms guide our actions; they serve as cues to appropriate and inappropriate behavior.

Many contemporary family problems are not tied to value transitions at all. Instead, they represent norm transitions. To a large extent, family processes today are confused by conflicting, incongruent, and absent family norms. The rules of family behavior have changed so dramatically in some areas that many men, women, and children do not know how to respond to one another's expectations. With so many alternative cues to guide behavior, confusion is more the rule than the exception in intimate relationships.

This ambiguity in norms leads to confusion and stress in many families. Several studies have found that couples with congruent role expectations are much more likely to be satisfied and stable in their marriages than are couples with incongruent expectations.[12] Other studies show that congruency between norms and behaviors have important psychological consequences. For example, a study of depression in married women found that the least depressed women were those who were employed and preferred to be as well as those who were not employed and preferred not to be. The wives who were employed, but not by choice, were significantly more depressed; the most depressed were those who were not employed but who wanted to be.[13]

Another normative change is the shift away from ascribed family roles toward achieved family roles. Family roles— mother, father, son, daughter—are no longer defined by larger societal norms. Instead, each role is customized; it is defined within the context of the particular family system. My role as a father, for example, is defined more by the expecta-

tions my wife and children have of me than by society's notion of what a father should do for his family. Although this gives me more freedom to develop a father role that is rewarding and personally enjoyable, it also increases the level of anxiety associated with the role because my success as a father is contingent upon ongoing and ever-changing reinforcements.

**Relational Formation Norms**

The norms that guide dating, courtship, and mate selection have also changed dramatically and quickly. Major differences exist between children and their parents concerning the behaviors that are expected to dominate adolescence and young adulthood. Dating has been replaced by "going out" and by group events that do not follow the rules that were traditionally associated with dating in the 1950s and 1960s.

Sexual norms have also changed. Although the proportion of adolescents engaging in sexual intercourse has increased somewhat, the changes in the norms associated with this behavior are even more revolutionary. The proportion of adults who believed in total sexual abstinence before marriage dropped from 80% to only 30% between 1963 and 1975. Among adults who responded to the national General Social Surveys, in 1969, 68% believed that premarital sex was wrong, compared with only 39% in 1985.[14] . . .

Norms linking pregnancy and marriage have also changed. In the 1960s, youth who became pregnant were expected to get married prior to childbirth. More than one-half of them did. In contrast, by the 1980s more children were being conceived outside of marriage, but less than one-third of these conceptions resulted in the mother's being married by the time of the birth.[15]

Even marital norms have undergone significant transformations. Marriage has become less associated with the confirmation of commitment between partners, and nonmarital cohabitation has become so common that some observers now consider it a stage in the family life cycle—more a choice than a deviation from normal patterns. A 1989 survey found that 31% of American adults consider living together before marriage to be "O.K.," whereas 37% consider it "always wrong." However, age is a major factor in these attitudes. Among those younger than 30, 43% consider living together an acceptable arrangement; only 11% of those older than 60 agree with this position.[16]

These changes suggest a high level of confusion concerning courtship and sexual norms, leaving many avenues for interpretation open to those who are developing relationships or observing these relationships. Without adequate societal guidelines, deviations and confusion concerning what is considered to be acceptable behavior are likely to be considerable.

### Relational Maintenance Norms

The ambiguity of relational norms is also reflected in marriage and other adult relationships. These expectations are so confusing that most social scientists have given up on attempting to describe the traditional family life cycle. . . .

Today, only a minority of families follows what was once the traditional pattern of getting married, having children, mothers staying at home with the children, children leaving home, and the couple living to old age and death together. . . . Nowhere is the ambiguity in family norms more apparent than in the emerging roles of mothers and fathers. . . . Parenthood has not only become more voluntary, the role expectations of parents themselves are much less clear. Women, in particular, are less sure about how to incorporate parenting, marriage, and employment into their lives.

Data from recent surveys indicate considerable disagreement over emerging norms affecting the personal and family roles of American women. Only one out of four adults (23%) approves of mothers with preschool children working full time and nearly half (46%) believe that a preschool

child will suffer if the mother is employed. Furthermore, 70% of the women under age 30 say they want a family and a career, up from 52% who felt that way in 1964.[17]

Men too are experiencing pressure to change their roles and to accommodate new norms of work, fathering, and being a husband. Men are no longer encouraged to be absent from the home. However, norms for new fathering and homemaking roles are not yet well entrenched. On the one hand, more than one-half of American men (54%) say that the most satisfying accomplishment for a man today is being a father,[18] a situation that has resulted in a noticeable shift toward fathers participating more in children's activities. On the other hand, Frank Furstenburg[19] refers to the development of a "good-dad, bad-dad complex," in which fathers now feel more free to be involved with their children but they also feel more free to leave an unhappy home situation.

### Relational Dissolution Norms

As a result of the divorce rate rising for the past several decades and remaining stable at a comparatively high level since the mid-1970s, norms and expectations surrounding divorce also remain relatively unclear. Nearly all couples hope that they will stay married to the same partner. But the acceptance of divorce as an alternative to marital unhappiness has certainly increased. . . .

Frank Furstenberg and Graham Spanier contend that we are experiencing a paradigm shift in family norms in which "conjugal succession" is increasingly being accepted, although not preferred: "Divorce has become so commonplace that it represents, for much of the population, an optional stage in an increasingly variable conjugal career."[20] This paradigm shift is largely the result of changes in family status and the lack of clear-cut norms associated with family status. . . .

Because most divorced persons remarry, the ambiguity in family norms is carried into new relationships. Even though they are much more common, stepfamily patterns are not yet well defined. Cynthia Fuchs Epstein observes that "new stepfamily ties are not institutionalized and there are no established norms regarding 'proper' behavior in them."[21] Thus each new blended family has to make up its own rules, creating a situation in which all the parties must customize family norms based on uniquely derived rules, as opposed to adopting well-defined social rules. Given this situation, it is little wonder that stepfamily relationships are often strained and that second marriages experience even higher divorce rates than do first marriages.

## The Revolution in Family Norms

We are now confronted by a veritable revolution in family norms. While the dominant values undergirding the family have been slowly shifting, norms of family behavior have moved more quickly to take advantage of the freedoms permitted by greater independence and autonomy. The family system that had once been called "the haven" and "respite" from the changes occurring in other organizations, notably business and government, is now even more vulnerable to the status and role confusion in the larger society.

These normative issues have become the new battleground in public debate. What is considered "pro-family" can be interpreted as ultraliberal, ultraconservative, or somewhere in between. Though some family advocates argue about family "values," the real debate generally focuses on norms and expectations of family members, most often parents. Answers to James A. Levine's plaintive question *Who Will Raise the Children?*[22] are not framed in terms of whether children should be taken care of. We all agree that they should. What we disagree about is whether this responsibility, which fairly recently was solely the responsibility of mothers, should now be shared more by fathers and other caregivers. I do not believe that the value associated with children has been diminished that much. What has changed are the expectations regarding the responsibilities for their nurturance.

The norms guiding marriage are increasingly similar to the norms affecting other intimate relationships. John Scanzoni[23] refers to a new family paradigm emerging around norms that include what he calls "sexually bonded close relationships." Among couples without children, he finds the normative patterns of men and women to be very similar and the processes of relational development, maintenance, and disillusion increasingly indistinguishable. Robert Weiss observes that

> marriage is increasingly becoming like cohabitation. The woman may wear a wedding ring, but her name and, of course, her job will be unaffected. . . . For the woman who is a professional or executive, or on her way to becoming one of these, it is no longer possible to use the survey research rule that the social status of a married woman is that of her husband.[24]

As a society we are moving toward relational norms that do not prescribe clear-cut expectations, but in which more latitude for normative flexibility is permitted childless couples, whether married or not. When a third party enters the picture, namely children, some of this flexibility is lost. Many members of our society are still trying to determine how the major indicator of relational transformation, which used to take place with marriage, can now be parenthood. Perhaps the greater attention now being given to child-custody arrangements instead of divorce is evidence of growing societal control over some of the freedom men and women have acquired, especially in the area of parental norms and responsibilities.

## NOTES

1. Daniel Yankelovich, *New Rules: Searching for Self-Fulfillment in a World Turned Upside Down* (New York: Random House, 1981).

2. Peter McDonald, "Families in the Future: The Pursuit of Personal Autonomy," *Family Matters* 22 (1988), pp. 40–44.

3. Robert N. Bellah, Richard Madsen, William M. Sullivan, Ann Swidler, and Steven M. Tipton,

*Habits of the Heart* (New York: Harper and Row, 1985), p. 142.

4. David Popenoe, *Disturbing the Nest: Family Change and Decline in Modern Societies* (New York: Aldine de Gruyter, 1988), p. 289.

5. Marvin Sussman, "The Help Pattern in the Middle-Class Family," *American Sociological Review* 15 (1953), pp. 22–28. Eugene Litwak, "Geographic Mobility and Extended Family Cohesion," *American Sociological Review* 25 (1960), pp. 385–394

6. National Opinion Research Center, "General Social Survey" (Chapel Hill, NC: Institute for Research in the Social Sciences, 1988).

7. David H. Olson, Hamilton I. McCubbin, H. L. Barnes, A. S. Larsen, M. J. Muxen, and M. A. Wilson, *Families: What Makes Them Work* (Beverly Hills, CA: Sage Publications, 1983).

8. Larry Bumpass and James Sweet, *National Survey of Families and Households* (Madison, WI: University of Wisconsin, 1988).

9. Daniel Weiss, "100% American," *Good Housekeeping* (No. 207, 1988), p. 120.

10. Mavis Hetherington, Martha Cox, and Roger Cox, "Divorced Fathers," *Psychology Today* (April 1977), p. 42.

11. Bumpass and Sweet, op. cit.

12. Gary L. Bowen and Dennis K. Orthner, "Sex Role Congruency and Marital Quality," *Journal of Marriage and the Family* 45 (1983), pp. 223–230; G. Levinger, "Compatibility in Relationships," *Social Science* 71 (1986), pp. 173–177; Olson, et al., op. cit.

13. Catherine E. Ross, John Mirowsky, and Joan Huber, "Dividing Work, Sharing Work and In-between: Marriage Patterns and Depression," *American Sociological Review* 48 (1983), pp. 809–823.

14. National Opinion Research Center, "General Social Survey," op. cit.

15. Martin O'Connell and Carolyn C. Rogers, "Out-of-Wedlock Births, Premarital Pregnancies and Their Effect on Family Formation and Dissolution," *Family Planning Perspectives* 16 (1984), pp. 157–162.

16. CBS News/The New York Times Poll, *Attitudes toward Marriage*, February 13, 1989.

17. Lewis Harris, *Inside America* (New York: Vintage Books, 1987).

18. Weiss, op. cit.

19. Frank F. Furstenberg, Jr., and Gretchen A. Condran, "Family Change and Adolescent Well-being: A Reexamination of U.S. Trends," in Cherlin, op. cit., pp. 117–156.

20. Frank F. Furstenberg, Jr., and Graham G. Spanier, *Recycling the Family: Remarriage after Divorce* (Newbury Park, CA: Sage Publications, 1984), p. 47.

21. Cynthia Fuchs Epstein, "Toward a Family Policy: Changes in Mothers' Lives," in Cherlin, op. cit., p. 181.

22. James A. Levine, *Who Will Raise the Children?* (New York: Bantam, 1976).

23. John Scanzoni, "Families in the 1980s: Time to Refocus Our Thinking," *Journal of Family Issues* 8 (1987), pp. 394–421.

24. Ibid., p. 465.

## CRITICAL THINKING QUESTIONS

1. What is the difference, according to Orthner, between family values and family norms? Since values "chart the course for the behavior" of family members, can norms operate independently of values?

2. Orthner believes that the transition of family norms has created much "confusion and stress in many families." Is it possible, however, that changing norms can also strengthen marital relationships and parental commitments to their children?

3. How do Wilson's (see his article) and Orthner's perceptions of family values differ? How are they similar?

# 4   Family Values

## Liberal/Feminist: The New Crusade for the Old Family

ARLENE SKOLNICK AND STACEY ROSENCRANTZ, "The New Crusade for the Old Family." Reprinted with permission from *The American Prospect*, no. 18 (Summer 1994): 59–65. Copyright © 1994 The American Prospect, P.O. Box 383080, Cambridge, MA 02138. All rights reserved.

*As you saw in the articles by Wilson and Orthner, conservatives and centrists tend to equate traditional family values and norms with biological, two-parent families. Arlene Skolnick and Stacey Rosencrantz argue that restoring family values and the two-parent family won't solve America's social problems because "the research literature is far more complicated than the family restorationists have let on." Instead of applauding only nuclear families, Skolnick and Rosencrantz maintain, we should value families regardless of their structure and recognize the diversity of family life.*

What is the root cause in America of poverty, crime, drug abuse, gang warfare, urban decay, and failing schools? According to op-ed pundits, Sunday talking heads, radio call-in shows, and politicians in both parties, the answer is the growing number of children being raised by single parents, especially by mothers who never married in the first place. Restore family values and the two-parent family, and America's social problems will be substantially solved.

By the close of the 1992 presidential campaign, the war over family values seemed to fade. Dan Quayle's attack on Murphy Brown's single motherhood stirred more ridicule on late night talk shows than moral panic. The public clearly preferred Bill Clinton's focus on the economy and his more inclusive version of the family theme: "family values" means "valuing families," no matter what their form—traditional, extended, two-parent, one-parent.

Yet Clinton's victory was quickly followed by a new bipartisan crusade to restore the two-parent family by discouraging divorce as well as out-of-wedlock childbearing. The conservative right has for years equated family values with the traditional image of the nuclear family. The new crusade drew people from across the spectrum—Democrats as well as Republicans, conservatives, liberals, and communitarians. Eventually, even President Clinton joined in, remarking that he had reread Quayle's speech and "found a lot of good things in it."

While the new family restorationists do not agree on a program for reducing the number of single-parent families, they generally use a language of moral failure and cultural decline to account for family change. Many want to revive the stigma that used to surround divorce and single motherhood. To change the cultural climate, they call for government and media campaigns like those that have discouraged smoking and drinking. They propose to make divorce harder or slower or even, as the late Christopher Lasch proposed, to outlaw divorce by parents with minor children. And some have also advocated restricting welfare benefits for unmarried mothers or eliminating benefits entirely for mothers who have an additional out-of-wedlock child.

Focusing attention on the needs and problems of families raising children could be enormously positive. But the current crusade draws on the family values scripts of the 1980s, posing the issue in a divisive way (are you against the two-parent family?) and painting critics into an antifamily corner. Restricting legal channels for divorce, cutting off welfare to unmarried mothers, and restoring the old censorious attitudes toward single parenthood may harm many children and deepen the very social ills we are trying to remedy.

There's nothing new in blaming social problems on "the breakdown of the family" or in making the "fallen woman" and her bastard child into objects of scorn and pity. Throughout our history, public policies made divorce difficult to obtain and penalized unwed parents and often their children. In the 1960s and 1970s, however, public opinion turned more tolerant and legal systems throughout the West became unwilling to brand some children as "illegitimate" and deprive them of rights due others. Now we are being told that this new tolerance was a mistake.

Most Americans, even those most committed to greater equality between women and men, are deeply uneasy about recent family changes and worried about crime and violence. The new case for the old family owes much of its persuasive power to the authority of social science. "The evidence is in," declares Barbara Dafoe Whitehead, author of a much-discussed article, "Dan Quayle Was Right," which appeared in the April 1993 *Atlantic Monthly*. Divorce and single-parent families, Whitehead argues, are damaging both children and the social fabric. Another family restorationist, Karl Zinsmeister, a fellow at the American Enterprise Institute, refers to "a mountain of evidence" showing that children of divorce end up intellectually, physically, and emotionally scarred for life.

Despite these strong claims of scientific backing, the research literature is far more complicated than the family restorationists have let on. Whitehead says, "The debate about family structure is not simply about the social-scientific evidence. It is also a debate over deeply held and often conflicting values." Unfortunately, the family restorationists' values have colored their reading of the evidence.

Few would deny that the divorce of one's parents is a painful experience and that children blessed with two "good enough" parents generally have an easier time growing up than others. Raising a child from infancy to successful adulthood can be a daunting task even for two people. But to decide what policies would improve children's lives, we need to answer a number of prior questions:

- Are children who grow up in a one-parent home markedly worse off than those who live with both parents?
- If such children are so disadvantaged, is the source of their problems family structure or some other factor that may have existed earlier or be associated with it?
- How effectively can public policies promote a particular form of family and discourage others? Will policies intended to stigmatize and reduce or prevent divorce or single parenthood cause unintended harm to children's well-being? Would positive measures to help single-parent families or reduce the stress that accompanies marital disruption be of more benefit to children?

Finally, is there a direct link, as so many believe, between family structure and what a *Newsweek* writer calls a "nauseating buffet" of social pathologies, especially crime, violence, and drugs? In his Murphy

Brown speech, given in the wake of the Los Angeles riots, Quayle argued that it wasn't poverty but a "poverty of values" that had led to family breakdown, which in turn caused the violence. The one sentence about Murphy Brown in the speech—borrowed incidentally from an op-ed by Whitehead—overshadowed the rest of the message. Charles Murray was more successful at linking family values with fear of crime. In a *Wall Street Journal* article, he warned that because of rising white illegitimacy rates, a "coming white underclass" was going to engulf the rest of society in the kind of anarchy found in the inner cities. But what is the evidence for this incendiary claim? And why do countries with similar trends in family structure not suffer from the social deterioration that plagues us?

The family restorationists do not provide clear answers to these questions. And the answers found in the research literature do not support their extreme statements about the consequences of family structure or some of the drastic policies they propose to change it.

Of course, it's always possible to raise methodological questions about a line of research or to interpret findings in more ways than one. The perfect study, like the perfect crime, is an elusive goal. But some of the family restorationists seem to misunderstand the social science enterprise in ways that seriously undermine their conclusions. For example, they trumpet findings about correlations between family structure and poverty, or lower academic achievement, or behavior problems, as proof of their arguments. Doing so, however, ignores the principle taught in elementary statistics that correlation does not prove causation.

For example, suppose we find that increased ice cream consumption is correlated with increases in drownings. The cause, of course, has nothing to do with ice cream but everything to do with the weather: people swim more and eat more ice cream in the summer. Similarly, single parenthood may be correlated with many problems affecting children, but the causes may lie elsewhere—for example, in economic and emotional problems affecting parents that lead to difficulties raising children and greater chances of divorce. Making it hard for such parents to divorce may no more improve the children's lives than banning ice cream would reduce drowning. Also, causation can and often does go in two directions. Poor women are more likely to have out-of-wedlock babies—this is one of the oldest correlates of poverty—but raising the child may impede them from escaping poverty. In short, finding a correlation between two variables is only a starting point for further analysis.

The social science research itself is also plagued by methodological problems. Most available studies of divorce, for example, are based on well-educated white families; some are based on families who have sought clinical help or become embroiled in legal conflict. Such families may hardly be representative. Comparing one study with another is notoriously difficult because they use different measures to assess children of different ages after differing periods have elapsed since the divorce. Some studies, such as Judith Wallerstein's widely cited work on the harm of divorce reported in the 1989 book *Second Chances* by Wallerstein and Sandra Blakeslee, use no comparison groups at all. Others compare divorced families with intact families—both happy and unhappy—when a more appropriate comparison would be with couples that are unhappily married.

In addition, the family restorationists and some researchers lump together children of divorce and children whose parents never married. Yet never-married mothers are generally younger, poorer, and less educated than divorced mothers. And by some measures children living with never-married mothers are worse off than those living in divorced families.

The restorationists paint a far darker and more simplistic picture of the impact of divorce on children than does the research literature. Researchers agree that around the time their parents separate almost all children go through a period of distress. Within two or three years, most have recovered. The great majority of children of divorce do not appear to be impaired in their development. While some children do suffer lasting harm, the family restorationists exaggerate the extent and prevalence of long-term effects. For example, they may state that children of divorce face twice or three times the psychological risk of children in intact families. But the doubling of a risk may mean an increase from 2 to 4 percent, 10 to 20 percent, or from 30 to 60 percent. The effects of divorce tend to be in the smaller range.

In fact, a meta-analysis of divorce findings published in 1991 in the *Psychological Bulletin* reported very small differences between children from divorced and intact families in such measures of well-being as school achievement, psychological adjustment, self concept, and relations with parents and peers. (A "meta-analysis" combines data from separate studies into larger samples to make the findings more reliable.) Further, the more methodologically sophisticated studies—that is, those that controlled for other variables such as income and parental conflict—reported the smallest differences.

In general, researchers who interview or observe children of divorce report more findings of distress than those who use data from large sample surveys. Yet even in the clinical studies the majority of children develop normally. One point that researchers agree on is that children vary greatly in response to divorce, depending on their circumstances, age, and psychological traits and temperament.

Where differences between children of divorce and those in stable two-parent families show up, they may be due, not to the divorce itself, but to circumstances before, during, and after the legal undoing of the marital bond. Most researchers now view divorce not as a single event but as an unfolding process. The child will usually endure parental conflict, estrangement, and emotional upset, separation from one parent, and economic' deprivation. Often divorce means moving away from home, neighborhood, and school. Particular children may go through more or fewer such jolts than others.

Researchers have known for some time that children from intact homes with high conflict between the parents often have similar or even worse problems than children of divorced parents. Recent studies in this country as well as in Australia and Sweden confirm that marital discord between the parents is a major influence on children's well-being, whether or not a divorce occurs.

Some of the family restorationists recognize that children in high-conflict families might be better off if their parents divorced than if they stayed together. They want to discourage or limit divorce by parents who are simply bored or unfulfilled. But how should we draw the line between unfulfilling and conflict-ridden marriages? And who should do the drawing?

High-conflict marriages are not necessarily violent or even dramatically quarrelsome like the couple in Edward Albee's *Who's Afraid of Virginia Woolf?* One major recent study operationally defined a high-conflict family as one in which a spouse said the marriage was "not too happy" or the couple had arguments about five out of nine topics, including money, sex, chores, and in-laws. A number of recent studies do show that even moderate levels of marital dissatisfaction can have a detrimental effect on the quality of parenting.

The most critical factor in a child's well-being in any form of family is a close, nurturant relationship with at least one parent. For most children of divorce, this means the mother. Her ability to function as parent is in turn influenced by her physical and psychological well-being. Depression, anger, or stress can make a mother irritable, inconsistent, and in general less able to cope with her children and their problems, whether or not marital difficulties lead to divorce.

Until recently, the typical study of children of divorce began after the separation took place. However, two important studies—one directed by Jack Block and another by Andrew Cherlin—examined data on children long before their parents divorced. These studies found that child problems usually attributed to the divorce could be seen months and even years earlier. Usually, these results are assumed to reflect the impact of family conflict on children. But in a recent book analyzing divorce trends around the world, William J. Goode offers another possibility:

> . . . the research not only shows that many of the so-called effects of divorce were present before the marriage, but suggests an even more radical hypothesis: in at least a sizeable number of families the problems that children generate may create parental conflict and thereby increase the likelihood of divorce.

The problems of never-married single mothers and their children set off some of today's hottest buttons—sex, gender, race, and welfare. Dan Quayle's attack on Murphy Brown confused the issue. It is true that more single, educated, middle-class women are having children. The rate nearly tripled in the last decade among women in professional or managerial occupations. But despite this increase, only 8 percent of professional-status women are never-married, Murphy Brown mothers. Out-of-wedlock births continue to be far more prevalent among the less educated, the poor, and racial minorities.

Most people take the correlation between single parenthood and poverty as proof of a causal relation between the two. But the story is more complex. In his book *America's Children*, Donald Hernandez of the Census Bureau shows that if we take into account the income of fathers in divorced and unwed families, the increase in single mothers since 1959 probably accounts for only 2 to 4 percentage points of today's childhood poverty rates. As Kristen Luker has pointed out ("Dubious Conceptions: The Controversy over Teen Pregnancy," *The American Prospect*, No. 5, Spring 1991), the assumption that early childbearing causes poverty and school dropouts is backward; these conditions are as much cause as effect.

Elijah Anderson, Linda Burton, William Julius Wilson, and other urban sociologists have shown the causal connections linking economic conditions and racial stigma with out-of-wedlock births and the prevalence of single-mother families in the inner cities. Cut off from the rest of society, with little or no hope of stable, family-supporting jobs, young men prove their manhood through an "oppositional culture" based on machismo and sexual prowess. Young women, with little hope of either a husband or economic independence, drift into early sexual relationships, pregnancy, and childbirth.

Middle-class families have also been shaken by economic change. The family restorationists, however, have little to say about the impact of economic forces on families. In her *Atlantic* article, Whitehead mentions—almost as an afterthought—that the loss of good jobs has deprived high school graduates across the country as well as inner-city young people of the ability to support families. "Improving job opportunities for young men," she writes, "would enhance their ability and presumably their willingness to form lasting marriages." Yet these considerations do not affect the main thrust of her arguments supporting Quayle's contention that the poor suffer from a "poverty of values."

There is no shortage of evidence on the impact of economic hardship on families. The studies of ghetto problems have their counterparts in a spate of recent books about other groups.[1] Much quantitative research reinforces these analyses. As Glen Elder and others have found, using data from the Great Depression to the 1980s, economic conditions such as unemployment are linked to children's problems through their parent's emotional states. Economic stress often leads to depression and demoralization, which in turn lead to marital conflict and such problems in childraising as harsh discipline, angry outbursts, and rejection. Child abuse and neglect as well as alcoholism and drug use increase with economic stress.

New research has confirmed earlier findings that poverty and inadequate income are major threats to children's well-being and development. Poverty has a deep impact because it affects not only the parent's psychological functioning but is linked to poor health and nutrition in parents and children, impaired readiness for education, bad housing, the stress of dangerous neighborhoods, and poor schools as well as the stigma of being poor. One recent study comparing black and white children across income levels found that family income and poverty were powerful determinants of children's cognitive development and behavior, controlling for other differences such as family structure and maternal schooling.

Child poverty in the United States, as the family restorationists point out, is higher than it was two decades ago among whites as well as blacks. It is also much higher in the United States than in other Western countries. But it is not an unalterable fact of nature that children born to single mothers have to grow up in poverty. Whereas our policies express disapproval of the parents, the policies of other Western countries support the well-being of the children.

The family structure debate raises larger questions about the changes in family, gender, and sexuality in the past three decades—what to think about them, what language to use in talking about them. The language of moral decay will not suffice. Many of the nation's churches and synagogues are rethinking ancient habits and codes to accommodate new conceptions of women's equality and new versions of morality and responsibility in an age of sexual relationships outside of marriage and between partners of the same gender.

The nation as a whole is long overdue for a serious discussion of the upheaval in American family life since the 1960s and how to mitigate its social and personal costs, especially to children. The point of reference should not be the lost family of a mythical past conjured up by our nostalgic yearnings but the more realistic vision offered by the rich body of historical scholarship since the 1970s. From the beginning, American families have been diverse, on-the-go, buffeted by social and economic change. The gap between family values and actual behavior has always been wide.

Such a discussion should also reflect an awareness that the family trends we have experienced over the past three decades are not unique. Every other Western country has experienced similar changes in women's roles and family structure. The trends are rooted in the development of the advanced industrial societies. As Andrew Cherlin puts it, "We can no more keep wives at home or slash the divorce rate than we can shut down our cities and send everyone back to the farm."

However, our response to family change has been unique. No other country has experienced anything like the cultural warfare that has made the family one of the most explosive issues in American society. Most other countries, including our cultural sibling Canada, have adapted pragmatically to change and developed policies in support of working parents, single-parent families, and all families raising children. Teenagers in these countries have fewer abortions and out-of-wedlock births, not because they have less sex, but because sex education and contraceptives are widely available.

Sooner or later, we are going to have to let go of the fantasy that we can restore the family of the 1950s. Given the cultural shocks of the past three decades and the quiet depression we have endured since the mid-1970s, it's little wonder that we have been enveloped by a haze of nostalgia. Yet the family patterns of the 1950s Americans now take as the standard for judging family normality were actually a deviation from long-term trends. Since the nineteenth century, the age at marriage, divorce rate, and women's labor force participation had been rising. In the 1950s however, the age of marriage declined, the divorce rate leveled off, the proportion of the population married reached a new high, and the American birth rate approached that of India. After the 1950s, the long-term historical trends resumed.

Most of us would not want to reverse all the trends that have helped to transform family life—declining mortality rates, rising educational levels for both men and women, reliable contraception, and greater opportunities for women. Barring a major cataclysm, the changes in family life are now too deeply woven into American lives to be reversed by "just say no!" campaigns or even by the kinds of changes in divorce and welfare laws that the restorationists propose.

## NOTES

1. John E. Schwarz and Thomas J. Volgy's *The Forgotten Americans* portrays the fast growing population of working poor, people who "play by the rules" but remain below the poverty line. Lillian Rubin's *Families on the Fault Line* documents the impact on working-class families of the decline of well-paying manufacturing jobs. Katherine Newman's ethnographic studies, *Falling from Grace* and *Declining Fortunes*, document the effects of downward mobility in middle-class families.

## CRITICAL THINKING QUESTIONS

1. What are "family restorationists"? Why do Skolnick and Rosencrantz describe family restorationists as advocating "punitive and coercive prescriptions" for many contemporary families?

2. The authors don't deny that depression, anger, or stress can make a mother irritable, inconsistent, and less able to cope with her children. Does this support the conservative and centrist views (see Wilson's and Orthner's articles in this chapter) that single-mother households, especially, are "bad for children"?

3. Skolnick and Rosencrantz note that the family trends we have experienced over the past three decades—such as single-parent families and out-of-wedlock births among teenagers—are not unique. Thus, we shouldn't blame our social problems on nontraditional families. How would Wilson and Orthner respond to this argument?

# 5 Women's and Men's Family Roles

## *Conservative:* Women Should Domesticate Men for Marriage

GEORGE GILDER, *Men and Marriage* (Gretna, LA: Pelican, 1986), pp. 167–173. Reproduced with permission of Pelican Publishing Company.

*Most conservatives believe that traditional family gender roles—where the husband is the breadwinner and the wife is the full-time mother—promote family stability, order, and continuity. Not only is the woman's place in the home, George Gilder maintains, but women should tame men's "innate" and "rampant" sexual promiscuity and aggressiveness by enticing them to the domestic values of hearth and home.*

Women's activities are far richer in intellectual and social challenges than most academic writers comprehend. It is foolish to imagine that these complex roles and relationships can be abolished or assumed by outside agencies. The woman's role is nothing less than the hub of the human community. All the other work—the business and politics and entertainment and service performed in the society—finds its ultimate test in the quality of the home. The home is where we finally and privately live, where we express our individuality, where we display our aesthetic choices, where we make and enjoy love, and where we cultivate our children as individuals.

The central position of the woman in the home parallels her central position in all civilized society. Both derive from her necessary role in procreation and from the most primary and inviolable of human ties, the one between mother and child. In those extraordinary circumstances when this tie is broken—as with some disintegrating tribes—the group tends to sink to a totally bestial and amoral chaos.[1]

Most of the characteristics we define as humane and individual originate in the mother's love for her children. Men have no ties to the long-term human community so deep or tenacious as the mother's to her child. Originating in this love are the other civilizing concerns of maternity: the desire for male protection and support, the hope for a stable community life, and the aspiration toward a better long-term future. The success or failure of civilized society depends on how well the women can transmit these values to the men.

This essential female role has become much more sophisticated and refined in the modern world. But its essence is the same. The woman assumes charge of what may be described as the domestic values of the community—its moral, aesthetic, religious, nurturant, social, and sexual concerns. In these values consist the ultimate goals of human life—all those matters that we consider of such supreme importance that we do not ascribe a financial worth to them. Paramount is the worth of the human individual life, enshrined in the home, and in the connection between a woman and child. These values transcend the marketplace. In fact to enter them in commercial traffic is considered a major evil in civilized society. Whether proposing to sell a baby or a body or a religious blessing, one commits a major moral offense.

This woman's role is deeply individual. Only a specific woman can bear a specific child, and her tie to it is personal and unbreakable. When she raises the child she imparts in privacy her own individual values. She can create children who transcend consensus and prefigure the future: children of private singularity rather than "child-development policy." She is the vessel of the ultimate values of the nation. The community is largely what she is and what she demands in men. She does her work because it is of primary rather than instrumental value. The woman in the home with her child is the last bastion against the amorality of the technocratic marketplace when it strays from the moral foundations of capitalism.

In recent years, the existence of a distinctive feminine role in ethics has been discovered by feminists. Seeking to answer male psychologists who regard masculine defense of justice and equality as the highest level of moral development, female scholars have offered a contrary case for the moral perceptions of women. The leading work in this field is *In a Different Voice*, by Carol Gilligan of Harvard.[2] She postulates a uniquely feminine moral sense rooted in webs of relationship and responsibility, in intimacy and caring, rather than in rules and abstractions.

Gilligan's point is valuable and true and her book is full of interesting evidence for it. But contrary to her egalitarian vision, women's moral sense is not merely an equal counterpoint to masculine ideals.

Stemming from her umbilical link to new life itself and from a passionate sense of the value and potential of that life, the woman's morality is the ultimate basis of all morality. The man's recognition of the preciousness and equality of individuals is learned from women and originates with the feminine concern for relationships, beginning in the womb and at the breast. This concern contrasts sharply with his own experience of hierarchy and preference, aggression and lust, and the sense of sexual and personal dispensability he experiences as a single man. Just as outside male activity is regarded in all societies as most important in instrumental terms, women's concerns are morally paramount, by the very fact that they are female, part of the unimpeachable realm of life's creation and protection.

What is true for individual moral issues is also true for the practical needs of a nation: the maternal role remains paramount. There is no way to shunt off child care to the "society" or to substantially reduce its burdens. If children lack the close attention of mothers and the disciplines and guidance of fathers, they tend to become barbarians or wastrels who burden or threaten society rather than do its work. Raising children to be productive and responsible citizens takes persistent and unrelenting effort. The prisons, reformatories, foster homes, mental institutions, and welfare rolls of America already groan under the burden of children relinquished to "society" to raise and support. In the sense of becoming self-sufficient, all too many of these children never grow up at all. To reproduce the true means of production—men and women who can uphold civilization rather than subvert it—the diligent love of mothers is indispensable. In fact, the only remedy for the "overpopulation" in female-headed families is the creation of a larger population of children brought up by two active and attentive parents.

Crucial to the sexual liberals' dream of escape from family burdens is zero population growth. Because each individual no longer depends on his children to support him in old age, many observers seem to imagine that children are less important than they were in the past. But substantially fewer offspring are a possibility only for a while in modern welfare states. No less than in the past, the new generations will have to support the old. The only difference is that now the medium is coercive taxation and social security rather than filial duty.

With some 15 percent of couples infertile and others child-free by choice, in order to raise enough workers to support the social programs of retirees, each fertile woman must still bear more than two children. In order to prevent a substantial decline in the quality of children—their willingness to work hard and contribute to society in the face of high taxes and a generous dole—women must devote long hours to raising and disciplining the new generation. The decline in the quantity of children demands a rise in the quality of their contributions to society—a rise in their diligence and productivity.

This female responsibility, as Gilligan observes, entails difficult sacrifices of freedom and autonomy.[3] Other researchers, notably Jessie Bernard, have noted that these sacrifices produce a significantly elevated incidence of emotional stress and neurosis among full-time housewives, particularly when their children are young.[4] Some of this anxiety clearly reflects the sharp rise in expenses and tax burdens incurred by families raising children. Some of the problem is simply hard and grueling work. Part of the distress, though, may derive from the media's widespread disparagement of traditional women. Margaret Mead found that women are most contented not when they are granted "influence, power, and wealth," but when "the female role of wife and mother is exalted." A devaluing of "the sensuous creative significance" of woman's role, she wrote, makes women become unhappy in the home.[5] But regardless of the source of this stress, Gilligan's point is correct.

Women do make great sacrifices, and these sacrifices are essential to society.

Some theorists list sexual restraint high among these sacrifices. But women's sexual restraint is necessary for the fulfillment of their larger sexuality in families, which cannot normally survive the birth of children by men other than the family provider. In general, a man will not support a woman while she philanders.

Contrary to the assumption of most analysts, it is men who make the major sexual sacrifice. The man renounces his dream of short-term sexual freedom and self-fulfillment—his male sexuality and self-expression—in order to serve a woman and family for a lifetime. It is a traumatic act of giving up his most profound yearning, his bent for the hunt and the chase, the motorbike and the open road, the male group escape to a primal mode of predatory and immediate excitements. His most powerful impulse—the theme of every male song and story—this combination of lust and wanderlust is the very life force that drives him through his youth. He surrenders it only with pain. This male sacrifice, no less than the woman's work in the home, is essential to civilization.

Just as the female role cannot be shared or relinquished, the male role also remains vital to social survival. For centuries to come, men will have to make heroic efforts. On forty-hour weeks, most men cannot even support a family of four. They must train at night and on weekends; they must save as they can for future ventures of entrepreneurship; they must often perform more than one job. They must make time as best they can to see and guide their children. They must shun the consolations of alcohol and leisure, sexual indulgence and flight. They must live for the perennial demands of the provider role.

Unlike the woman's role, the man's tends to be relatively fungible and derivative. He does not give himself to a web of unique personal relationships so much as to a set of functions and technologies. Just as any particular hunter might kill an animal, so within obvious bounds any workman can be trained to do most jobs. The man makes himself replaceable. For most of his early years at the job site, individuality is an obstacle to earnings. He must sacrifice it to support his wife and children. He must eschew his desire to be an athlete or poet, a death-defying ranger or mountaineer, a cocksman and Casanova, and settle down to become a functionary defined by a single job, and a father whose children are earned by his work. Not his own moral vision but the marketplace defines the value of that work.

Extraordinary men transcend many of these constraints early in their careers and many men eventually rise to significant roles of leadership and self-expression. But even then jobs rarely afford room for the whole man. Even highly paid work often creates what Ortega y Gasset called "barbarians of specialization."[6] One may become a scientist, a doctor, an engineer, or a lawyer, for example, chiefly by narrowing the mind, by excluding personal idiosyncrasies and visions in order to master the disciplines and technicalities of the trade. In some cases, exceptionally successful specialization may bring some of the satisfactions won, for example, by the great athlete. Nevertheless, this process usually does not make a man interesting or whole. In fact, he is likely to succeed precisely to the extent that he is willing to subordinate himself to the narrow imperatives of his specialty, precisely to the extent that he forgoes the distractions and impulses of the full personality.

Among men, the term *dilettante* is a pejorative. Yet, because the range of human knowledge and experience is so broad, the best that most people can ever achieve, if they respond as whole persons to their lives, is the curiosity, openness, and eclectic knowledge of the dilettante. Most men have to deny themselves this form of individual fulfillment. They have to limit themselves, at great psychological cost, in order to fit the functions of the economic division of labor. Most of them

endure their submission to the marketplace chiefly in order to make enough money to sustain a home, to earn a place in the household, to be needed by women. This effort most of the time means a lifetime of hard labor.

As with the woman's role, what is true in most specific cases is still more true on the level of general rules and expectations across the entire society. On forty-hour weeks the world dissolves into chaos and decay, famine and war. All the major accomplishments of civilization spring from the obsessions of men whom the sociologists would now disdain as "workaholics." To overcome the Malthusian trap of rising populations, or to escape the closing circle of ecological decline, or to control the threat of nuclear holocaust, or to halt the plagues and famines that still afflict the globe, men must give their lives to unrelenting effort, day in and day out, focused on goals in the distant future. They must create new technologies faster than the world creates new challenges. They must struggle against scarcity, entropy, and natural disaster. They must overcome the sabotage of socialists who would steal and redistribute their product. They must resist disease and temptation. All too often they must die without achieving their ends. But their sacrifices bring others closer to the goal.

Nothing that has been written in the annals of feminism gives the slightest indication that this is a role that women want or are prepared to perform. The feminists demand liberation. The male role means bondage to the demands of the workplace and the needs of the family. Most of the research of sociologists complains that men's work is already too hard, too dangerous, too destructive of mental health and wholeness. It all too often leads to sickness and "worlds of pain," demoralization and relatively early death. The men's role that feminists seek is not the real role of men but the male role of the Marxist dream in which "society" does the work.

## NOTES

1. See the story of the Ik tribe in Colin Turnbull, *The Mountain People* (New York: Simon & Schuster, 1972), pp. 290–295 and passim.

2. Carol Gilligan, *In a Different Voice: Psychological Theory and Women's Development* (Cambridge, Mass.: Harvard University Press, 1982). In attacking the shallow notions of male maturation and male moral superiority offered by developmental psychologists, Gilligan performs an important service. But her alternative moral view comes perilously close to a slough of situational ethics. In her interesting comparison of George Eliot's *Mill on the Floss* (1860) with Margaret Drabble's retelling of the tale in *The Waterfall* (1969), Gilligan can even condone the stealing of another woman's husband. The most telling female offense against the sexual constitution, this violation is at the root of the princess's problem in chapter 5 of this book and a source of the breakdown of monogamy that causes so many problems for women in modern society.

3. Ibid., pp. 70–71 and passim.

4. Jessie Bernard, *The Future of Marriage* (New York: World, 1972), pp. 336, 338, 339.

5. Margaret Mead, *Male and Female: A Study of the Sexes in a Changing World* (New York: Morrow, 1949), quoted from the paperback (New York: Dell, 1968), p. 110.

6. Jose Ortega y Gasset, *The Revolt of the Masses* (New York: Norton, 1932), pp. 94–95.

## CRITICAL THINKING QUESTIONS

1. Gilder implies that wives are born but husbands must be made. If this depiction of men is true, don't women have better things to do with their lives than to socialize men who are sexually and emotionally immature? Also, is it stereotypical or valid to describe men as sexually and emotionally immature?

2. If it is men who make the major sexual sacrifice by marrying, does this mean that monogamy, especially marriage, is an unnatural state for men? If this is the case, should married women accept their husbands' infidelity?

3. If a woman is "the vessel of the ultimate values of the nation," shouldn't women, not men, be in the marketplace and in powerful positions to stop the ecological decline, to control the threat of nuclear holocaust, and to remedy some of the other problems that "still afflict the globe"?

# 5 Women's and Men's Family Roles

## *Centrist:* Gender Roles: A Taboo Subject

*A consistent theme among conservatives and many centrists is that the erosion of traditional gender roles has weakened the family. As a result, according to Maggie Gallagher, marriage as an institution holds fewer rewards for both women and men. Although Gallagher acknowledges that many mothers must be employed to ensure their family's economic survival, she believes that millions of middle-class married women with very young children "are turned out of home and thrust into the marketplace" because of feminist pressures to pursue careers. Gallagher maintains that these women should have more choices, especially the right to stay home.*

Our society recoils at the very idea of sex roles. Not just the sex role as it was defined in the fifties, which many women found too confining, but the idea of the sex role itself. We rebel against any explicit attempt to create for gender a story or purpose—a socially shared meaning. We view social roles as imposed by society on people. They restrict and confine us. Sex roles, in particular, perpetuate unfair and unequal distribution of power, money, and influence between men and women. We are reluctant to acknowledge or to describe our behavior in terms of sex roles, except in a pejorative sense, as a prelude to their final abolition.

But in reality, whether they know it or not, people like roles in life for the same reason they are drawn to them in movies, sitcoms, novels, plays, and even sporting events: Without roles, there can be no plot. Artists, intellectuals, journalists, academics, and sports heroes create character types and story lines that we enjoy vicariously and later use to flesh out our own life plots.

Drawing on resources and materials that culture provides, people are constantly creating, demolishing, modifying, and re-creating roles that define their lives, because roles in life—as on the stage—help transform random and chaotic experience into a story, a purpose. Without stories our lives make no sense, and thus we cannot define success, nor know how to act well or what it means to do right.

Many women who recoil at the mention of sex roles enjoy very much playing other roles: the avant-garde revolutionary, say, or the hard-driving corporate careerist, or the sexually wild woman. They may also enjoy playing more conventional roles: devoted mother, playful aunt, good neighbor, caring friend, citizen–activist.

The current intense distrust of sex roles grew out of the circumstances of a particular generation of American women, which saw both a tremendous surge in affluence and a huge increase in the number of women (and men) with college educations, at the very same time that sex roles began to take a particularly strong and, for some women, oppressive form: Just as many women acquired the money and skills to move beyond domestic pursuits, child experts began to insist that mothers be available to their children nearly constantly or risk psychological damage. Many elite women found the disparity between their desires and the range of roles offered to them too great. They rebelled, not just against the particular 1950s vision of sex roles, but against the idea of the sex role itself—which is to say against the idea that society and culture should attach any importance, or ascribe any set of meanings, to gender.

Each individual man or woman is now supposed to define for himself or herself what it means to be a man or a woman; he or she is to be the architect of his or her own sex.

When I was eighteen, such a breathtaking challenge seemed exhilarating. As I grew older, I began to suspect that we are never so deluded as when we imagine we are creating ourselves out of nothing. Such people, far from being authentic, self-made originals, are usually merely caught up in great waves of culture of which they remain studiously unaware—blinded by the sight of themselves posing as independent thinkers, while their ideas and ideals shift every five years, or ten, with every shifting current. They sail with the tide, and they never know they are at sea.

Now I wonder: Does it make any more sense to ask people to define their gender for themselves *ex nihilo* than it does to ask a man to figure out on his own—without education, apprenticeship, or direction— what it means to be a good carpenter? To be sure, such self-defined carpenters would have ample scope for personal innovation. But would their houses stand?

Social roles emerge because there are jobs that need to be done; the roles contain much of the information the individuals need to perform those jobs well. Sex roles per se came under attack when we lost the notion that sex had any important function. When sex was redefined as a recreational sideline—a hobby, like model trains or watching sports, which may have intense meaning for a private individual, but is without social significance—the notion of sex roles was redefined as an intolerably oppressive infringement of individual rights.

Sex roles are not fixed, in the sense of being unalterable. They do change in different cultures and in the same culture at different times in response to changing circumstances. Within certain limits (almost everywhere, men specialize in violence, and also in protection from violence, while women have the main responsibility for the care of babies), there is in sex a certain magnificent diversity.

But because sex is not merely a personal but a transcendent desire, because in sex the opportunities for drama are (to put it mildly) greatly magnified, because sexual culture plays such a large part in shaping the culture as a whole, because sex is *not* just a personal pastime but a social force, and above all because sex does produce babies on a regular basis, the sex role in some form regularly emerges in all cultures. Sex difference evolves but never dissolves.

Even today, at the heart of marriage is an unacknowledged exchange of sexual gifts: the promise by a man and a woman to care for each other and for any children that ensue from their union. Less so today, perhaps, than in the past, but still to an astonishing degree, in marriage men and women diversify: Women divert at least some of their energy to caring for children; men redouble their work efforts in order to permit women to do so.

Children, when they arrive in marriage, affect men's and women's work patterns differently. In general, men work more and make more after they become a father, while mothers, on average, work fewer paid hours and earn less.[1] Working fathers with children under six are more than four times as likely as working mothers to work at least fifty hours a week.[2]

Today's great sexual wage gap is not between men and women—single men and women make equivalent salaries—but between married men and singles of either sex.[3] Married men make 70 percent more than a single of either sex.[4]

What explains this huge gap? Is it merely, as some argue, that more successful men are more likely to marry? Or does marriage itself, by giving men's work a new meaning—in other words by giving men a sex role—make men more productive?[5] A recent study by economists Sanders D. Korenman and David Neumark sought to discover why "married men earn substantially more per hour worked than men who are not currently married." Married men, they found, experienced faster wage growth for the first ten to twenty years of marriage, and this growth could not be explained by location, union membership, changes in labor market experience, number of dependents, or occupation. Moreover, marriage increased "by almost 50 percent the probability of recent hires receiving one of the top two performance ratings," even after controlling for education, location, and prior experience. The researchers concluded that "marriage per se makes workers more productive" (or at least male workers).[6] Other studies have found a reverse effect for divorce: Women become more committed workers and men less committed workers in the aftermath of divorce.[7]

In recent decades, the greater amount of time women rather than men have devoted to child rearing has been construed mostly as an exercise in dependence. Marriage, according to the now-conventional wisdom, was structured to benefit men at the expense of women. Thus in 1971 Germaine Greer denounced marriage for creating "the prison of domesticity." Andrea Dworkin excoriated a system in which "every married man, no matter how poor, owned one slave—his wife." And Susan Brownmiller announced that marriage and rape were so entwined that it was "largely impossible to separate them out."[8] Jessie Bernard, a distinguished sociologist, argued with great success that there are two marriages—"his" and "hers"—and that of the two, his is much better.[9] And recently two influential experts maintained, in a typical sentiment, "With all its supposed attributes, the traditional family more often than not enslaved women. It reduced her to a breeder and caretaker of children, a servant to her spouse, a cleaning lady and, at times, a victim of the labor market."[10]

If this conventional wisdom were correct, American wives should be much happier than before. The old sex roles have been, if not abolished, at least diminished. Between 1982 and 1992 the proportion of families that met the strict test of "traditional"—married-couple families in which the husband works and the wife does not—plunged from 43 percent to 24 percent of all families.[11] In 1960 only 20 percent of all mothers with children under age six were in the labor force. Today 60 percent of mothers with young children work, at least part time.[12]

But this liberation of women from marital dependency has not increased the happiness of women, especially younger married women who are most likely to find themselves in such liberated circumstances. As noted in Chapter 8, "The Bad Marriage," the percentage of younger married women who describe themselves as "very happy" has dropped dramatically. Between the early seventies and the mid-eighties, the proportion of married women ages eighteen to thirty-one who said they were "very happy" unexpectedly plummeted from 44 percent to less than 35 percent. Meanwhile, the happiness rates of single men in this age group almost tripled, soaring from 11 percent to 31 percent in the same period.

Moreover, despite the erosion of the breadwinner role, the flood of women into the workforce, the decline in patriarchal authority, and the increased risk of divorce (much of it initiated by women), the proportion of married men who say they are "very happy" has not changed at all. As Norval Glenn notes, "It appears that recent changes . . . have led to a distinct decline in the happiness of women, but have had no net effect on the happiness of men as a whole."[13]

Not only are marriages not happier as a result of the divorce and the gender revolutions, they are, on average, distinctly less happy for one sex—and not the sex the experts would predict. According to the data on marital happiness, it seems that we are restructuring our social institution to benefit the least productive and most dangerous element of the population—single men—at the direct expense of younger married women.

This is less surprising when we note that the recent massive influx of women into the workforce for the most part did not stem from personal choice. For some women, of course, a career undoubtedly represents a devoutly sought-after choice. But for many other women, these same statistics of rising labor force participation by young mothers are not signs of freedom and progress, but indicators of constraint and decline. For the first time in our history, regardless of their wishes, millions of middle-class married women with very young children are being turned out of the home and thrust into the marketplace.

And these stressed and distressed mothers are not a small group of women. Only one in three mothers who work full time believes she can spend "the right amount of time" with her family.[14] A majority of working mothers say they would prefer to work part time or not at all.[15] When asked whether they personally would prefer to be part of a two-earner couple or a one-earner couple, Americans opt for the one-earner couple by a margin of almost two to one—54 percent to 31

percent.[16] As Stephanie Coontz, no cheerleader of the traditional family, notes, "The percentage of women who say they would prefer to stay home with their children if they could afford to do so rose from 33 percent in 1986 to 56 percent in 1990."[17] And that preference has proved surprisingly enduring. In the most recent prestigious Roper polls, 53 percent of women said they would prefer to be at home.[18]

Perhaps it is no accident that women's love affair with the workforce ended just as working mothers ceased to be unusual. When mothers first entered the labor force in large numbers, they were doing more than holding down a job—they were advancing a revolution. The career woman was interesting and different. Professional work was a distinguishing mark, a mark of unusual ambition. Women had an intriguing new role to try out.

Today's women cannot envision their work in this exciting way—they are not transforming the world, they are pulling down a desk. And it turns out that many jobs (from computer clerk to corporate lawyer) are a lot less interesting than advertised. Like their husbands, today's working mothers do it for the money.

The usual interpretation of the higher divorce rates among two full-time working spouses is that work enables women to escape unhappy marriages. This happy explanation of the relative fragility of two-career marriages is, I think, overly optimistic. For one thing, the rise of working women has not eliminated the fundamental economics of divorce. Working women who divorce still face a substantial drop in their standard of living. After all, if you needed two incomes to make ends meet, you are unlikely to feel very happy about your standard of living with only one income.

Part of the relative instability of two-career couples may be due to self-selection: Wives with less traditional attitudes may be more likely to both work full time and divorce. But there is another explanation that has been mostly ignored: Full-time working women, especially women who are working against their wishes, may be more prone to divorce because they *get less* from marriage.

A woman at home (part or full time) who chooses divorce must give up her entire way of life. By contrast, a wife who works full time and divorces can simply continue to do what she is doing anyway. Life may get a little harder—or even a lot harder—but for a wife with a full-time job, a change in her marital status does not seem to entail a radical transformation of her day-to-day lifestyle.

It may seem odd to think of full-time working wives as *getting less* from marriage than homemakers. But there is considerable evidence that many women see it just that way. Even for many mothers who choose to work, the choice is driven not by desire, but by fear.

Elaine Stassen, a young wife who, in her late twenties, left her job to care for her infant son, is typical. Though her marriage seemed sound, she was afraid of being abandoned and so returned to graduate school to prepare herself to earn a better salary. "I got my degree so I could feel that if anything happened I could survive and take care of Jamie."[19] Work was supposed to be a route to power, autonomy, and independence. Instead, for many women like Elaine, the decision to work is increasingly impelled by a pervasive anxiety. Whatever sense of control they might gain from work, they lose from living in a society that no longer upholds and sustains marriage, a society in which their most important relationship is no longer dependable or under their control.

Not infrequently the younger women with whom I spoke were practicing a kind of "defensive" careerism, working "not because they wanted to but because they were afraid not to," comments Catherine Johnson.[20] This is just one of many unhappy synergisms driving up the divorce rate: As the divorce rate rises, more and more women, out of anxiety for their own and their children's security, choose to work.

But the more women in the workplace, the more the divorce rate rises, creating a vicious cycle in which all women end up, not with more economic security, but with less and less.

Today the young woman who contemplates dropping out of the workforce to care for her own baby, even temporarily, must fight strong cultural forces that seek to keep her tied to the workplace. In the wake of our rebellion against sex roles, many husbands are no longer willing to make the sacrifices—financial or leisure time—that would allow their wives to stay at home. Sometimes the strongest objections come from the women's own mothers. "You are your only security," one mother (herself happily married for over thirty years) warned her daughter. Mothers who trusted their own husbands for many years have witnessed the changes and no longer trust their daughters' husbands to care for them.

Although the new stereotype paints housewives as bored or depressed, research literature tells a different, more complicated story. What matters most to the well-being of mothers and their children is neither working nor not working. What is important is real choice. The least depressed women are those who work because they prefer to and those who stay home because they prefer to. Conversely, the wives most likely to succumb to depression are those who are employed against their wishes or those who have no job, but want one.[21] Similarly, one of the most consistent findings of day-care research is that when women are happy to be working, kids tend to do fine; but when mothers are forced to work against their wishes, their children suffer.[22]

An inordinate fear of the 1950s' sex roles has blinded us to this simple equation: If work is to be a choice, women must have husbands willing to support them, financially or emotionally, in that choice. It is sex roles, albeit in a modified, flexible form, that set women free. When husbands are able and willing to be primary breadwinners, women have more options, not fewer. Unlike their husbands, women may choose to devote themselves to more interesting, rather than more lucrative, work. With good provider husbands, they can shape their work lives around the family if they wish, rather than being forced to make their families bow to the needs of the corporation. They can choose to devote their talents and education and energy to the rearing of their children, the nurturing of family relationships, and the building of community and neighborhood. They may even have the leisure (unknown to full-time working mothers) to cultivate artistic, cultural, and intellectual interests.

If all married mothers are all working because they want to, then there is nothing the government can or should do about it. But if middle-class, married mothers are now working because they must, new questions emerge: Why is our generation of women so much poorer than our mothers', with no choice but to work? And what, if anything, can be done about it?

## NOTES

1. Frank F. Furstenberg, Jr., "Good Dads—Bad Dads: Two Faces of Fatherhood," in *The Changing American Family and Public Policy,* ed. Andrew J. Cherlin (Washington, D.C.: The Urban Institute Press, 1988), 195.

2. Anna Quindlen, "Public and Private: Men at Work," *New York Times,* February 18, 1990, 19.

3. For the original and more definitive exploration of the relation between sex and work for men, see George Gilder's *Men and Marriage* (Gretna, LA: Pelican Publishing Company, 1986).

4. Ibid.

5. Ibid.

6. Sanders D. Korenman and David Newmark, *Does Marriage Really Make Men More Productive?* Finance and Economics Discussion Series, no. 29 (Washington, D.C.: Division of Research and Statistics, Federal Reserve Board, May 1988).

7. Terry Lunn, "The Impact of Divorce on Work," *Personnel Management* (February 1990): 28–31.

8. Bryce J. Christensen, "'Love in the Ruins?' The Future of Marriage in Modern America,"

*The Retreat of Marriage: Causes and Consequences* (Lanham, MD: University Press of America, 1990), 75–96.

9. Jessie Bernard, *The Future of Marriage* (New York: World Publishing, 1972), 51.

10. Sol Gordon and Craig W. Snyder, *A Guidebook to Better Sexual Health* (Boston: Allyn and Bacon, 1989), 358.

11. Bureau of the Census, "Fertility of American Women: June 1992," in *Star-Ledger,* July 14, 1993.

12. Ibid.

13. Ibid.

14. National Commission on Children, *Speaking of Kids: A National Survey of Children and Parents* (Washington, D.C.: National Commission on Children, 1991).

15. Ibid.

16. Family Research Council, "Earners Per-Family Appears to Be Bigger Concern Than Work-Hours Per-Family," *In Focus.*

17. Stephanie Coontz, *The Way We Never Were: American Families and the Nostalgia Trap* (New York: Basic Books, 1992).

18. Bernice Kanner, "Advertisers Take Aim at Women at Home," *New York Times,* January 2, 1995.

19. Catherine Johnson, *Lucky in Love: The Secrets of Happy Couples and How Their Marriages Thrive* (New York: Penguin Books, 1992), 201–202.

20. Ibid., 202.

21. Arlene Skolnik, *Embattled Paradise: The American Family in an Age of Uncertainty* (New York: Basic Books, 1991), 210.

22. Ibid.

## CRITICAL THINKING QUESTIONS

1. One of the problems today, according to Gallagher, is that each individual is now supposed to define for himself or herself what it means to be a man or a woman. She also writes that "a majority of working mothers say they would prefer to work part time or not at all." So, do most of us have more choices or more constraints now than in the past in terms of our family gender roles?

2. Gallagher attributes many women's marital unhappiness to "being turned out of the home and thrust into the market-

place." Are there other possible reasons for married women's unhappiness? (See, for example, the following article by Carter and Peters.)

3. If husbands worked harder as primary breadwinners, Gallagher argues, women would have more options—not to work, for example, but to raise their children and to build better neighborhoods. Shouldn't men have similar choices? Also, how might socioeconomic differences affect mothers' and fathers' gender-role options?

# 5 Women's and Men's Family Roles

## *Liberal/Feminist:* Remaking Marriage and Family Roles

BETTY CARTER AND JOAN K. PETERS, "Remaking Marriage and Family," as originally appeard in *Ms.* (November/December 1996): 56–65. Reprinted with permission of Pocket Books, a division of Simon & Schuster, Inc., from *Love, Honor and Negotiate* by Betty Carter and Joan Peters. Copyright © 1996 by Betty Carter and Joan Peters.

*Many couples are struggling to balance family and work responsibilities. One of the problems in juggling such roles, according to the authors, is that many people are caught between traditional gender roles and a changing world. Particularly after marital partners have children, societal expectations pressure many couples to "backslide" into traditional marriages that reduce the woman's power in a once equal marriage. Betty Carter and Joan K. Peters feel that the workplace should be more flexible and support men's greater participation in domestic life.*

When I started my work with couples in the seventies, I assumed that since women now worked and considered themselves the equals of men, we'd solved the gender problems I had struggled with in the early years of my own marriage. In therapy, I treated every marriage as if it were as unique as a snowflake. But as I began to notice the repetition of complaints, I couldn't help but realize that I was caught in a blizzard of sex-role issues that had not gone away.

The more I explored couples' "communication" problems, the more I found that one of the main things they can't communicate about is the power to make decisions. The more I questioned younger couples, the more I heard about their constant arguments. The more I questioned them about the content of their arguments, the more I heard about who spends what money, who does what housework and child care, and—if both partners work—whose work comes first. Or else I heard about the backlash from these conflicts in their sex lives—if they still had any. Older couples complained about the emptiness between them or argued bitterly about every detail of their lives. But the more I questioned them, the more I heard from the women about how much they resented their husbands' highhandedness or indifference to family life. The men, on the other hand, were defensively dismissive of these complaints.

Finally, I began to see the reason for this pattern—*most American couples backslide into traditional sex roles as soon as their children are born.* Women cut back at work, quit, or play superwoman because they are *automatically* the ones in charge of children. Meanwhile, men toil even more to "be good providers," ending up the bewildered breadwinner. Many are just furious because of what they see as their spouse's incessant complaints. And the divorce rates skyrocket.

I saw all this, but I was stymied. There was no way to use traditional family therapy theory to respond to the problems of gender. So, with a few like-minded colleagues— Marianne Walters, Peggy Papp, and Olga Silverstein—in 1977 I cofounded the Women's Project in Family Therapy, where we developed our own techniques. But it meant thinking in an entirely new way for a family systems therapist. To explain the new thinking, though, I should first describe what family systems therapy is.

Family systems therapy was developed in the fifties as an improvement on individual therapy. The classic Freudian approach treats the individual in a vacuum, as if a person has an emotional problem within himself or herself. Family systems theorists say that the individual doesn't exist alone emotionally but in dynamic relationship with other family members. This means that emotional problems exist not inside the person who happens to exhibit or experience the problem but among all the family members.

Except in rare circumstances, the family is the most powerful emotional system we ever belong to. It shapes and continues to determine the course and outcome of our lives. A three- or four-generation family operates as a finely tuned system with roles and rules for functioning as a unit. For example, if one member behaves "irresponsibly," an "overresponsible" member will step in and pick up the slack; if one person is silent and withdrawn, another is usually the one to talk and engage, and vice versa— the sequences are circular.

Everyone in the family maintains problem behavior, such as that of an alcoholic father or depressed mother or runaway son. They don't do this because they want or need to but because their "common sense" responses to the problem are also part of the problem. The wife who empties her husband's bottles of scotch, the husband who suggests his wife go on antidepressants, and the parents who send their runaway son to therapy to "get fixed" are all trying to be helpful. But they're only making the problem worse, partly because these "solutions" imply that the person's symptom is the problem. Instead of looking for the factors in the family system that are producing the person's anxiety or depression, they try to get rid of the symptoms.

Most people don't realize the extent to which the marriage and family we create is a product of the family we were raised in, whether we are trying to recreate that original family or do the opposite. Our family relationships—the gears that run the clock, so to speak—are highly patterned and reciprocal. Rules are spoken and unspoken. They are based on our family history, which produces themes, stories, taboos, myths, secrets, heroes, and rebels. This history is passed on, consciously and unconsciously, to the next generation and to all new marriages.

That's what we mean when we say that family relationships aren't optional. They're also not equal or fair. You might say that our original family is like a hand of cards dealt by fate. And that our life's task, emotionally, is dealing with this hand.

For all these reasons, the family therapist will help patients actively work out problems with their parents on the assumption that, as I always put it, if you can work them out with your parents, you can work them out with anyone. And you'd better, I tell them, because your parents will always play a significant, if silent, part in all your relationships, particularly in your marriage. The more unresolved the problems of the past, the more they influence the present.

Even when people flee their "families of origin," as we call them, the impact of the family doesn't end. In fact, it actually increases. Not speaking to family members who caused us difficulty may temporarily relieve the pain of trying to deal with them. But the poison of the cutoff spreads throughout the family as members expend enormous emotional energy taking sides, justifying some people's actions and vilifying others. Every subsequent family event takes place in the shadow of the cutoff, and when the conflict that supposedly caused it is almost forgotten, what remains are families whose members are disconnected from one another and who live with broken hearts or hearts covered with calluses. Worst of all, the legacy suggests to future generations that family members we disagree with should be discarded. This is not a healthy resolution of conflict.

The other side of the coin—what we call enmeshment or fusion—comes up when family members become overinvolved and entangled in their relationships, taking inappropriate responsibility for one another, wanting peace at any price, insisting on ignoring differences through denial and compromise. There is no "live and let live" in this smothering system.

Family therapists normally believe that for a person to have a mature relationship with family members, he or she must be authentically true to self—even in ways that may break the family rules—while still having a meaningful personal connection. Of course, as anyone who has ever tried to achieve this with parents, spouses, and siblings knows, it is very difficult to do. Most of us will spend a lifetime trying to do it. Family therapy just helps us move in that direction.

But the family context wasn't enough to explain the gender complaints I was constantly hearing. So I had to discover on my own that family systems therapy—like Freudian therapy—wasn't drawing a large enough picture. Marriages, I realized, were not only two people enmeshed in family structures, they were also families enmeshed in cultural structures—structures that often exert unbearable pressures on these families, making spouses blame each other for what are really social problems.

Each family tries to teach its members the "right way" to live in our time and the "right values" to have about things like money, marriage, work, parenting, and sex. A family does this without realizing the degree to which these "truths" are dictated by the family's place in our very stratified

culture—for example, their race, gender, ethnicity, social class, or sexual orientation—and how those values play out not only against the family, but also within it.

Without an understanding of the impact of family and cultural beliefs, couples are left with the crazy idea that they are inventing themselves and their lives, or that they could, if only their spouses would change. It is this false notion of independence that leads to marital power struggles and, often, divorce.

Improved communication is supposed to solve a couple's problems, but in the majority of cases, it cannot. For example, if a woman who works outside the home still does the lion's share of housework and child care, communication can only name the problem or identify the source of the wife's unhappiness. Unless the talk leads to a change in how the couple divide up housework and child care, it won't help at all. Too often, "communication" can become an argument without end and lead to mutual blame and psychological name-calling. With a cultural perspective on their problems, as well as a psychological one, couples can start to evaluate their problems in the context of their families and our culture.

American culture intrudes upon the inner sanctum of marriage. On one hand, it has given us new expectations of marriage; on the other, it has failed to allow the new marriage to fulfill these expectations. The American economy requires that most husbands and wives work outside the home but offers little workplace or social support for the two-earner family. And couples have changed—but not enough.

That's why I've come to believe in resolutions that combine the personal, social, and political. First, we have to give up the myths that women can't have it all except by doing it all and that men don't have to do it all but can have it all. We seriously have to question the idea that men's careers must never be disturbed and that mothering is different from—and more involving than—fathering.

The problem with contemporary marriage is that the lives of men and, especially, women have changed dramatically, radically, in this century, but the rules about marriage have not. Partly because of economics and partly because of the women's movement, women's behavior has changed drastically since the sixties. The vast majority of women are now in the workforce and half of them are providing as much—or more—of the family's income as their husbands. But men's behavior has changed far less. For personal, social, and economic reasons, they have not accommodated themselves to women's working by participating equally in the home. Although they now "accept" that a woman will work, they also "expect" her to be a homemaker. It is this lag in men's role change (combined with women's ambivalence about insisting on greater change) that results in contradictory wishes that weaken so many marriages.

In addition to blaming their husbands, women in this predicament often blame the women's movement for "taking away their 'right' to stay home." Instead of joining with other women to find support and solutions, they join the backlash that paints feminism as the enemy of men and family. Some may end up losing themselves in the excesses of the self-help movement, focusing on their "codependency" or their "inner child," as if these were the real problems in their marriages.

Men in these harried marriages also blame women. Instead of helping men to become more involved with the daily emotional and practical lives of their families, the men's movement blames contemporary women for "making them marginal." Spokesmen encourage men to take back their rightful place at the "head" of the family. As my colleague and friend Marianne Walters points out, the men's movement is about "male bonding" against women's "domination," not about developing men's capacities for emotional connection with wives and children and adjusting to equal partnership.

The changes women have made by coming into the world of work and politics have been a step up for them, a gain of power. For men, however, family involvement seems like a step down, a loss of power. This standstill reflects our continued valuing of power over connectedness and the continued association of power and money. Yet men have everything to gain by being more emotionally engaged in their lives.

While the traditional definition of masculinity is surely being challenged, it still holds sway in most men's lives. And the rules for "man the provider" are still very slippery. Is his wife fully committed to being a coprovider for life, or will she suddenly decide she has to stay home with the children? If his children are a priority for him, will he be penalized at work for taking paternity or family emergency leaves?

Men are also often afraid of the intimacy of family life. They are afraid that they don't know how to be intimate, and they're afraid of their own feelings, which they've been taught to suppress. Intimacy and connection have traditionally been the feminine sphere. Recognizing that "feminine" part of himself threatens a man's identity.

Unfortunately, avoiding intimacy also means that men cut themselves off from their deepest feelings, from their spouses, and from their children. Men who don't "feel" are as haunted and unhappy as women who aren't autonomous. They might grin and bear it, drink, gamble, have affairs, or become TV zombies, but escape is never satisfying. The demons are there when the high or the numbness wears off.

What does finally motivate men to change? Recognizing their own pain. Most men I work with begin to realize how much they suffered because their own fathers were distant and overworked. In their own longing and pain, they find the will to be a different kind of husband and father.

Men's reluctance to change has certainly been an obstacle to family life today. But to a large extent, society hasn't allowed them to change. It certainly hasn't helped them. If there is a villain in the contemporary marriage problem, it is our society. Women at work and men in the family are this century's revolution and problem. Society pays lip service to equality and to marriage, but there has been so little support of the two-paycheck marriage that I've come to think of the American workplace as the iron vise squeezing the life out of otherwise resilient, viable couples.

It's taken me a lifetime to realize that how we live and work as a nation is our own choice. And mostly I feel as if we don't even try to make our lives better, though it wouldn't be so very difficult to do so; we did it in the early part of the twentieth century by legislating an eight-hour workday and workplace safety standards. But now, women—who suffer most—don't dare challenge the status quo for fear we might sound "unrealistic"' or "unable to make the grade in a man's world."

The Family and Medical Leave Act of 1993 sounded good, but it didn't actually change our lives. In the first place, the legislation only applies to companies with more than 50 employees, while most Americans work for smaller ones. Second, employers can exempt "key employees," so women and men who want to take parental leave can kiss the best jobs good-bye. Third, the provision is for three months of unpaid leave with the birth of a child or a medical emergency. If parents need the income, they can't take off. But still, we don't join together to challenge the workplace rules that leave no time for family. And one thing we need, desperately, is more time with our families.

The real reason most parents don't take sufficient time off when a child is born or a family member is ill is because they are afraid of losing their jobs. Justifiably. As much talk as there has been in the business community about the "work-family" problem, there's been precious little action. Why?

- Because many companies believe that work-family programs are too costly,

even though it has been proven that companies don't actually lose money.
- Because most bosses are male, and they just don't see what the problem is. Or if there is some problem for working mothers, their bosses believe it's up to the mothers to solve it.
- Because women don't yet have enough power in the business community to change the work-family conflict.

Add to these problems several more: over half of all working women still earn less than $25,000 a year; child care is expensive and often of very poor quality; there are few after-school programs, no elder care for infirm parents, and no coverage on school holidays. And giving in to economic pressure, or careerism, or greed, parents work so much overtime that they often can't be home to put their children to sleep, let alone eat dinner with them.

In the past, the Puritan work ethic caused no conflict because the wife was the homemaker. Now that nearly everyone works, home life is often as hectic as work. Work has become the center of our universe, our raison d'etrê, even though most salaries today no longer buy either the free time or the upward mobility enjoyed by many of our parents. Today both partners usually have to work just to stay in place. But—and here's the shock—most don't really have to work as hard as they do.

And so here we are, striving so fiercely and working such long hours for security, only to find ourselves feeling lost in an obsessive concern with marketplace values and an out-of-control whirlwind of activity that we don't know how to stop long enough to take care of our relationships.

Whenever asked, people here in the United States say that family life and betterment of society are more important than having a nice home, car, and clothes. Clearly, our beat-the-clock lives are not in sync with our deep belief in family and community. The result is that not only do we suffer from overwork, but we also betray ourselves daily. Overworked Americans cannot raise their children well, cannot contribute to their communities, and cannot sustain the companionship they once found in their marriages. They also can't live according to their expressed values; they just don't have the time.

Society also drives us. We don't want to be workaholics, but we just can't stop. In a Los Angeles *Times* survey, nearly 40 percent of men say they would change jobs to have more family and personal time; and in another survey, cited by *Time* magazine, half of the men interviewed said they would refuse a promotion that involved sacrificing family time. The problem is they can't work fewer hours or refuse the promotion and hold on to their jobs. Even more women than men would give up money and status if they could have more family time. But they can't.

The lucky few can work shorter hours if they let themselves, but the average couple have to work outside the home at inflexible jobs, confronting a terrible choice between work and family. Clearly, sweeping changes are necessary.

What would improve the workplace for people who also want fulfilling personal and family lives? In the last several years, social critics and workers have come up with a list of suggestions. These are the most frequently cited:

- On-Site Day Care. Or: subsidies or discounts at child care centers near the workplace.
- Flextime. This allows employees to choose their hours and days. Compressed workweeks help, too, especially when there's a long commute.
- No Mandatory Overtime.
- Family Leave. What would a really supportive plan look like? Swedes are guaranteed 15 months of paid parental leave after the birth or adoption of a child, four months paid leave for sick children under 12, and the right to work part-time without losing their job or benefits until their children are 12.
- Telecommuting. Many companies are now experimenting with employees

working at home two or more days a week. Some companies go a step further to the "ultimate flexibility" of the virtual office. With laptops, e-mail, cellular phones, and beepers, people can work wherever they work best.

Given how much better family support programs could make the lives of today's men, women, and children, wouldn't it be wonderful if the men's movement turned its energies to advocating such programs? Men could bond by sharing fathering problems and the challenges of their new roles. Men's groups could explore the work-family problem to see how business today might support them as fathers and equal partners in their marriages. Finally, men could use the very real power they have to campaign for changes in the workplace.

As a culture, we have begun to understand the importance of connectedness and what we have lost by devaluing it. This is one of the reasons why the issue of "family values" strikes home for so many people. But family values need not be defined according to a notion of rigid family norms and traditional sex roles. Real family values are more appropriately defined as those created by parents who are as involved in their marriage and their children as they are in their own achievement. Real family values are reflected by a family's involvement in society and by a society that supports the needs of its families whatever those families might look like: two-paycheck marriages, single-parent households, remarried couples with their children, gay and lesbian couples with children, as well as traditional wage earner-homemaker partners.

The so-called family values debate now raging has become a code phrase to signify support for the traditional family structure of yesterday. But wage-earner father/stay-at-home mother is a family structure few of today's families want or can afford. Nor do women want the contemporary variation on that structure that "allows" wives to work if the family needs the income but preserves the traditional role of husband-money manager and wife-homemaker. We cannot turn the clock back to a marriage contract meant for a different social system. But we can certainly uphold family values. Who could possibly be against "family values" if it means what it always has: adults caring about each other and teaching their children to be loving, responsible, productive people? Bad values, an equal opportunity problem, can be learned from family or peers in the slums, in the heartland, in school, in the corporation, or the country club.

The traditional nuclear family structure led to an extremely high divorce rate, and certainly produced at least as much alcoholism, drug addiction, incest, and physical abuse as any other family structure. It could exist only through the sacrifice of women's autonomy. We need to strengthen the family values in the actual present-day structures of the American family. And this view was upheld recently by the men and women interviewed in a national survey. The vast majority of them did not define family values as having a traditional family. Nine out of ten of the women interviewed said, "Society should value all types of families." And the families that make up these new structures must in turn make their voices heard in their local communities and in the American polity.

## CRITICAL THINKING QUESTIONS

1. Why, according to the authors, do most American married couples backslide into traditional sex roles as soon as their children are born? How does this position differ from Gallagher's in the previous selection?

2. The authors believe that men are reluctant to participate in domestic tasks because they "don't have to do it all but can have it all." Would they agree with Gilder (see his article in this chapter) that it's up to women to "domesticate" men?

3. Carter and Peters advocate society-wide changes rather than counseling men to be more caring and collaborative. Does this suggest that marital therapy is ineffective in changing gender-role behavior and other family-related issues?

# III LOVE, SEX, AND MARRIAGE

Most conservatives believe that love, sex, and marriage go together. Religious conservatives emphasize the sanctity of marriage as a sacrament. Secular conservatives often point to the research studies that show higher divorce rates among cohabitants than among people who have not cohabited before marriage.[1] Centrists have little to say about love or sex. They emphasize, however, that marriage is crucial because it has positive effects on the partners' physical and mental health and children's well-being. While liberals and feminists support the institution of marriage, they think that people should be free to develop relationships that are most conducive to the growth and happiness of themselves and their partners.[2] Feminists particularly note that marriage is more beneficial for men than it is for women. Especially in abusive or controlling marriages, feminists argue, love often justifies keeping women and children trapped in unhealthy relationships.

## Chapter 6: Love and Courtship

A number of conservatives lament our society's focus on sex rather than love: "It may be a sign of our times that everyone seems to be talking openly about sex, but we seem to be embarrassed to talk about love . . . Sex is almost always available, but love is a lot harder to find."[3] Even when people are in love, love rarely leads to courtship and marriage. Instead, as Leon R. Kass observes in "The End of Courtship," "those who reach the altar seem to have stumbled upon it by accident." Some of the reasons for the demise of love, traditional courtship, and marriage, according to Kass, include feminism, the sexual revolution, and the growth of sexual technology during the 1960s; a greater acceptance of out-of-wedlock births, divorce, infidelity, and abortion; and cultural attitudes that celebrate youth and independence rather than responsible adulthood, especially a commitment to marriage and family life.

Centrists such as Robert N. Bellah and his colleagues ("Love and Individualism") attribute the decline of love—and, consequently, marriage—to a growth of utilitarian individualism. "Sharing is the essence of love," they write. Love requires people to lose a sense of their own identity because mutual sacrifices and responsibilities become a higher priority. While many people seek intimacy, according to these authors, they are unwilling to sacrifice the independence and freedom that "losing oneself" requires. Conservatives and centrists are similar; both groups contend that narcissism and self-realization have taken precedence over the commitment and obligation that characterize love.

Liberals and feminists are less enthusiastic about love's benefits in intimate relationships. In "Women as Love's Experts and Love's Victims," Carol Tavris points out, for example, that the "feminization of love" and the "masculinization of silence" discourage the expression of love between women and men. In effect, then, our cultural expectations and gender-role stereotypes (rather than narcissism or individualism) stifle love in many relationships. Many liberals and feminists also note that we often use love to justify, excuse, control, and manipulate:

> Parents who physically abuse their children say they love their children. Husbands who beat their wives claim they love them. In the name of love people sometimes commit violent acts of passion. In the name of love we sometimes overprotect and overindulge our children, preventing them from experiencing necessary developmental changes to the fullest degree. . . . In the name of love husbands neglect their wives and wives their husbands, failing to take the time and effort to show signs of daily caring and loving acceptance.[4]

Many conservatives and centrists believe that maintaining one's self-identity dampens love. In contrast, many liberals and feminists argue that love, especially when it's controlling and possessive, can wilt a person's development and self-identity.

## Chapter 7: Sex and Cohabitation

The numbers of cohabitants have climbed from 19 percent in 1970 to 30 percent in 1996. These numbers are expected to increase to 32 percent in 2005 due to a greater acceptance of living together and young adults' postponing marriage. There were almost 4.3 million unmarried-couple households in 1998.[5] An estimated 370,000 men and women over age 65 live together rather than marry because Social Security laws, pension benefits, homeownership capital gains taxes, and Medicaid eligibility rules can erode seniors' financial security.[6] Large numbers of people in the 45 to 64 age group also cohabit.[7]

While seniors and middle-aged people make up a large proportion of those "shacking up," conservatives and centrists denounce nonmarital sex and cohabitation only among younger couples. Both conservatives and centrists are mute about cohabitants ages 45 and over, I assume, because their unions are unlikely to result in childbirth. People over age 65 receive "legitimate" welfare benefits (such as Medicare). In contrast, younger women receive "illegitimate" welfare (see Chapter 18) because most of the biological fathers don't support the mothers or their out-of-wedlock children.[8] Most importantly, perhaps, conservatives and centrists oppose nonmarital sex and cohabitation for younger but not older populations because such unions may not result in marriage.[9]

Many conservatives are also concerned that "sexual indulgence without commitment" (reflected in cohabitation rather than marriage) results in abortion.[10] As a result, they endorse sexual abstinence until marriage and oppose sex education programs in schools, especially those that distribute information about contraception.[11] In contrast, many liberals argue that sex education and providing contraceptives in middle schools and high schools decrease the number of unwanted pregnancies and abortions.[12]

According to conservatives such as Laura Schlessinger ("Stupid Cohabitation: The Ultimate Female Self-Delusion"), many cohabiting women feel that live-in relationships will eventually lead to marriage. Thus, according to Schlessinger, they endure men who don't respect them and live with men who aren't very interested in maintaining the woman's or the couple's children either financially or emotionally.

Even worse, some conservatives point out, cohabitation is a major factor in child abuse. Because cohabitation implies a lack of commitment, the risk of child abuse is 20 times higher between a mother and her boyfriend in a common-law marriage than in traditional married families and 33 times higher if the single mother is cohabiting with a boyfriend.[13] Some conservatives note that "living together may not be such a good idea after all" because, as some studies show, cohabiting couples experience more conflict in their relationship. It is not clear, however, whether many conservatives are more concerned about the conflict and violence or the cohabitation. As one writer states, for example, "We should rethink the current view that living together is just one of several available lifestyle choices. . . . Cohabitation is risky—especially to young women and children. If a man isn't husband material or if he refuses to marry, it may not be a good idea to live with him either."[14] Although the writer feels that the offenders should be punished and the victims should be protected, the message seems to be one of "If you weren't cohabiting, you wouldn't be abused."

Conservatives (and many centrists) also note that cohabiting couples are less likely to have stable, satisfying marriages and a higher risk of divorce if they do marry. Conservatives often point to academic studies that show a higher divorce rate for cohabitants than for noncohabitants and conclude that "couples who engage in sex before marriage are more likely to break up than couples who save sex for marriage."[15]

Unlike conservatives, centrists don't seem to attribute a variety of outcomes (such as domestic violence and abortion) to sex and cohabitation. Like conservatives, however, centrists are opposed to cohabitation because only about half of such unions result in marriage. That is, the media endorses singlehood, casual sex, and cohabitation instead of promoting images of responsible adults who make a permanent commitment, marry, and raise children.[16]

In addition, centrists argue, many marital counselors undermine marriage—and, by implication, promote post-divorce cohabitation—by encouraging people to dissolve rather than repair their unions. In "How Therapists Threaten Marriages," for example, William J. Doherty maintains that many therapists view marriage simply as a "lifestyle choice" rather than a lifetime covenant. Because many marriage counselors embrace "the reigning ethic of individualism,"

Doherty posits, they promote the value of personal satisfaction and autonomy rather than foster collaboration and obligation within the marital relationship.

Because most liberals and feminists support a variety of family forms (see Chapters 2 and 4), they don't reject unmarried-couple households as "abnormal." While cohabitation has its drawbacks, it also provides many benefits. For example, cohabitants can dissolve the relationship without legal problems, can mature and prevent an unhappy marriage that ends in divorce, and can develop a meaningful relationship instead of playing superficial dating games.[17] Although marriage has its advantages, writes Andrea Martin in "Why Get Married?" cohabitation often reflects a "sound fiscal decision" because many of our tax laws and other governmental policies discourage marriage.

Many liberals point out that marriage and cohabitation vary greatly by socioeconomic level. People with stable employment, high earnings, and who have completed college are more likely to marry than to cohabit.[18] Among cohabitants, people who are employed full time or have completed high school are also among the most likely to marry.[19] Young women who plan to finish college and who believe that wives should be homemakers might also cohabit and postpone marriage.[20] In effect, then, decisions to cohabit or marry may reflect a combination of economic, educational, and attitudinal dimensions.

## Chapter 8: Marriage

Is marriage losing its appeal? According to a recent Census Bureau report, about 56 percent of all American adults were married and living with their partners in 1998, down from 68 percent in 1970, 62 percent in 1980, and 59 percent in 1990.[21] The number of married adults has gone down since the 1970s due to a rise in divorce, the number of people who have never been married, and many young adults' postponing marriage to pursue education and careers. The typical U.S. adult, however, is married and living with her or his spouse.

How observers interpret the declining marriage rates varies across ideological perspectives. Most conservatives see the declining marriage rates as "alarming." Steven Flanders maintains, for example, that marriage and the traditional family benefit the individual, the community, and the state for social, economic, and moral reasons ("The Benefits of Marriage"). As you saw in Chapters 3 and 4, most conservatives feel that marriage can deter many social problems. Marriage is important, they assert, because "broken and unformed families are the most important root cause of violence, crime, drug abuse, and academic failure."[22]

Centrists agree with conservatives. For example, Linda J. Waite argues in "Social Science Finds: 'Marriage Matters' " that marriage "typically provides important and substantial benefits, benefits not enjoyed by those who live alone or cohabit." Like conservatives, centrists emphasize that intact, two-parent families are especially beneficial for children because they decrease child poverty and increase children's access "to the time and attention of two adults in two-parent families."

In contrast to conservatives and centrists, many liberals are not surprised by the declining marriage rates. In 1850, John Humphrey Noyes wrote that marriage is similar to slavery because "it is an arbitrary institution, and contrary to natural liberty."[23] A few writers would like to abolish marriage altogether because marriage is "no longer relevant to our society":

> Most of us long for a fulfilling relationship, a union in which there is perfect love, perfect companionship and perfect compatibility. The exceptions who want to go through life alone prove the rule. But the institution of marriage does not insure against loneliness and isolation, nor does it guarantee love, happiness or sexual satisfaction. The only guarantee that marriage offers is that once the register is signed the parties are henceforth legally tied to each other, no longer free to act as single people, and the knot will be quite difficult to untie.[24]

Such a stance, albeit interesting, is not one that many liberals endorse. Some feminists object to calling marriage a contract. A contract represents an agreement between parties for equal responsibilities and privileges on both sides.[25] In contrast, most marriages reflect unequal power and decision-making between husbands and wives. In the case of employed mothers, for instance, marriage brings few benefits if the mother is still the one who performs almost all of the child-rearing and the household chores.[26]

Feminists, especially, are more concerned about the quality of the marital relationship than its presence or absence. They contend that egalitarian relationships produce happier wives and husbands. As Karen R. Blaisure and Katherine R. Allen show, however, marital equality can be elusive even in feminist marriages where both partners are consciously monitoring the relationship to achieve equality ("Feminism and Marital Equality"). As you saw in Chapters 3 to 5, many conservatives and centrists aren't very enthusiastic about women's economic independence because they are less likely to marry and more likely to divorce. Liberals, on the other hand, question the benefits of marriage if the woman helps support the family *and* does almost all of the housework *and* is responsible for raising the children *and* the marital bond is unsatisfying.

Some researchers predict that marriage will decline even further in the next century because many people simply can't afford to marry. Frank Furstenberg writes, for example, that we should back up our "sanctimonious calls for traditional . . . family values" with resources that support marriage:

> This includes moving toward a society that offers secure, remunerative jobs, as well as better child-care options and more flexible schedules so people can accept those jobs. Otherwise, the institution of marriage as we knew it in this century will in the twenty-first century become a practice of the privileged. Marriage could become a luxury item that most Americans cannot afford.[27]

## NOTES

1. For a good review of some of this literature, see, for example, Susan L. Brown and Alan Booth, "Cohabitation versus Marriage: A Comparison of Relationship Quality," *Journal of Marriage and the Family* 58 (August 1996): 668–679; and Steven L. Nock, "A Comparison of Marriages and Cohabiting Relationships," *Journal of Family Issues* 16 (January 1995): 53–76.

2. For one of the "classic" discussions of the destructiveness of marriage, see Lawrence Casler, *Is Marriage Necessary?* (New York: Human Sciences Press, 1974).

3. Thomas Sowell, "Love and Other Four-Letter Words," *Forbes*, January 1, 1996, p. 64.

4. John Fulling Crosby, *Illusion and Disillusion: The Self in Love and Marriage*, 4th ed. (Belmont, CA: Wadsworth, 1991), p. 106.

5. Terry A. Lugaila, "Marital Status and Living Arrangements: March 1998 (Update)," U.S. Department of Commerce, *http://www.census.gov* (accessed February 2, 1999).

6. See, for example, Elizabeth Fenner, "Why Seniors Don't Marry," *Money* (July 1995), p. 96, *http://boka.umd.edu800/WebZ* (accessed February 6, 1999).

7. See Rebecca Gronvold Hatch, *Aging and Cohabitation* (New York: Garland, 1995).

8. Randal D. Day and Wade C. Mackey, "The Mother-State-Child 'Family': Cul-de-sac or Path to the Future?" *The Family in America* 2 (March 1988): 1–8. See also David Popenoe, *Life Without Father* (New York: Free Press, 1996).

9. See, for example, Mitch Finley, "Cohabitation: A Perplexing Pastoral Problem," *America*, July 31, 1993, pp. 16–18; David Blankenhorn, *Fatherless America: Confronting Our Most Urgent Social Problem* (New York: HarperPerennial, 1995); and David Popenoe, *Life Without Father.*

10. See Stephen G. Post, "Abortion and the Triumph of Eros," *America*, April 28, 1990, pp. 427–428, 438.

11. Andrés Tapia, "Abstinence: The Radical Choice for Sex Ed," *Christianity Today*, February 8, 1993, pp. 24–26.

12. See Jane Mauldon and Kristen Luker, "Does Liberalism Cause Sex?" *The American Prospect*, no. 24 (Winter 1996): 80–85.

13. Patrick F. Fagan, "The Child Abuse Crisis: The Disintegration of Marriage, Family, and the American Community," The Heritage Foundation Roe Backgrounder No. 1115, May 15, 1997, *http://www.heritageorg:80//library/categories/family/bg1115.html* (accessed November 8, 1998).

14. Roger Sider, "Living Together Risky for Young Women and Children," *Grand Rapids Press*, January 25, 1999, *smartmarriages@his.com* (accessed January 28, 1999).

15. Family Research Council, "Saving Sex for Marriage Reduces the Risk of Divorce," *http://www.frc.org/infocus/if94i5ab.html* (accessed January 22, 1999).

16. For a conservative view on how popular culture dilutes parents' moral authority in the home, see Kenneth A. Myers, "Popular Culture and the Family: How Mass-Mediated Culture Weakens the Ties That Bind," Family Research Council, *http://www.frc.org:80/fampol/fp98hcu.html* (accessed January 10, 1999).

17. See Nijole V. Benokraitis, *Marriages and Families: Changes, Choices, and Constraints*, 3rd ed. (Upper Saddle River, NJ: Prentice Hall, 1999): 223–224.

18. Arland Thornton, William G. Axinn, and J. Teachman, "The Influence of School Enrollment and Accumulation on Cohabitation and Marriage in Early Adulthood," *American Sociological Review* 60 (October 1995): 762–774.

19. Wendy D. and Pamela J. Smock, "Why Marry? Race and the Transition to Marriage Among Cohabitors," *Demography* 32 (November 1995): 509–520.

20. See Jennifer S. Barber and William G. Axinn, "Gender Role Attitudes and Marriage Among Young Women," *Sociological Quarterly* 39 (Winter 1998): 11–32.

21. Terry A. Lugaila, "Marital Status and Living Arrangements: March 1998 (Update)," U.S. Department of Commerce, Current Population Reports, December 1998, *www.census.gov* (accessed February 6, 1999).

22. David W. Murray, "Talking Points on Social and Economic Benefits of Marriage," Linthicum, MD: Chesapeake Research Institute, mimeo., Spring 1994.

23. John Humphrey Noyes, *Slavery and Marriage: A Debate* (Oneida, NY, 1850).

24. Liz Hodkinson, *Unholy Matrimony: The Case for Abolishing Marriage* (London: Columbus Books, 1988), p. 10.

25. See, for example, pp. 154–188 in Carole Pateman, *The Sexual Contract* (Cambridge: Polity Press, 1988).

26. See, for example, David H. Demo and Alan C. Acock, "Family Diversity and the Division of Domestic Labor: How Much Have Things Really Changed?" *Family Relations* 42 (July 1993): 323–331; B. Manke, B. L. Seery, A. C. Crouter, and S. M. McHale, "The Three Corners of Domestic Labor: Mothers', Fathers', and Children's Weekday and Weekend Housework," *Journal of Marriage and the Family* 56 (August 1994): 657–668.

27. Frank F. Furstenberg, Jr., "The Future of Marriage," *American Demographics* 18 (June 1996): 40.

# 6   Love and Courtship

## Conservative: The End of Courtship

LEON R. KASS, "The End of Courtship," is excerpted with permission of the author from *The Public Interest*, no. 126 (Winter 1997): 39–63. © 1997 by National Affairs, Inc..

*Courtship is dead, claims Leon R. Kass. Some of the reasons for its demise include sexual technology, divorce, feminism, narcissism, adult immaturity, and men's innate promiscuity. The situation isn't hopeless, however, Kass concludes, and he offers suggestions for reviving courtship that leads to marriage.*

In the current wars over the state of American culture, few battlegrounds have seen more action than that of "family values"—sex, marriage, and child-rearing. Passions run high about sexual harassment, condom distribution in schools, pornography, abortion, gay marriage, and other efforts to alter the definition of "a family." Many people are distressed over the record-high rates of divorce, illegitimacy, teenage pregnancy, marital infidelity, and premarital promiscuity. On some issues, there is even an emerging consensus that something is drastically wrong: Though they may differ on what is to be done, people on both the left and the right have come to regard the break-up of marriage as a leading cause of the neglect, indeed, of the psychic and moral maiming, of America's children.

But while various people are talking about tracking down "dead-beat dads" or reestablishing orphanages or doing something to slow the rate of divorce—all remedies for marital failure—very little attention is being paid to what makes for marital success. Still less are we attending to the ways and mores of entering into marriage, that is, to wooing or courtship.

There is, of course, good reason for this neglect. The very terms—"wooing," "courting," "suitors"—are archaic; and if the words barely exist, it is because the phenomena have all but disappeared. Today, there are no socially prescribed forms of conduct that help guide young men and women in the direction of matrimony. This is true not just for the lower or under classes. Even—indeed especially—the elite, those who in previous generations would have defined the conventions in these matters, lack a cultural script whose denouement is marriage. To be sure, there are still exceptions to be found, say, in closed religious communities or among new immigrants from parts of the world that still practice arranged marriage. But for most of America's middle- and upper-class youth—the privileged, college-educated and graduated—there are no known explicit, or even tacit, social paths directed at marriage. People still get married—though later, less frequently, more hesitantly, and by and large, less successfully.

People still get married in churches and synagogues—though often with ceremonies of their own creation. But for the great majority, the way to the altar is uncharted territory: It's every couple on its own bottom, without a compass, often without a goal. Those who reach the altar seem to have stumbled upon it by accident.

## THEN AND NOW

Things were not always like this; in fact, one suspects things were *never* like this, not here, not anywhere. We live, in this respect as in so many others, in utterly novel and unprecedented times. Until what seems like only yesterday, young people were groomed for marriage, and the paths leading to it were culturally well set out, at least in rough outline. In polite society, at the beginning of this century, our grandfathers came a-calling and a-wooing at the homes of our grandmothers, under conditions set by the woman, operating from strength on her own turf. A generation later, courting couples began to go out on "dates," in public and increasingly on the man's terms, given that he had the income to pay for dinner and dancing. To be sure, some people "played the field," and in the prewar years, dating on college campuses became a matter more of proving popularity than of proving suitability for marriage. But, especially after the war, "going-steady" was a regular feature of high-school and college life; the age of marriage dropped considerably, and high-school or college sweethearts often married right after, or even before, graduation. Finding a mate, no less than getting an education that would enable him to support her, was at least a tacit goal of many a male undergraduate; many a young woman, so the joke had it, went to college mainly for her MRS. degree, a charge whose truth was proof against libel for legions of college coeds well into the 1960s.[1]

In other respects as well, the young remained culturally attached to the claims of "real life." Though times were good, fresh memory kept alive the poverty of the recent Great Depression and the deaths and dislocations of the war; necessity and the urgencies of life were not out of sight, even for fortunate youth. Opportunity was knocking, the world and adulthood were beckoning, and most of us stepped forward into married life readily, eagerly, and, truth to tell, without much pondering. We were simply doing—some sooner, some later—what our parents had done, indeed, what all our forebears had done.

Not so today. Now the vast majority go to college, but very few—women or men—go with the hope, or even the wish, of finding a marriage partner. Many do not expect to find there even a path to a career; they often require several years of postgraduate "time off" to figure out what they are going to do with themselves. Sexually active—in truth, hyperactive—they flop about from one relationship to another. To the bewildered eye of this admittedly much-too-old but still romantic observer, they manage to appear all at once casual and carefree and grim and humorless about getting along with the opposite sex. The young men, nervous predators, act as if any woman is equally good: They are given not to falling in love with one, but to scoring in bed with many. And in this sporting attitude, they are now matched by some female trophy hunters.

But most young women strike me as sad, lonely, and confused; hoping for something more, they are not enjoying their hard-won sexual liberation as much as liberation theory says they should.[2] Never mind wooing, today's collegians do not even make dates or other forward-looking commitments to see one another; in this, as in so many other ways, they reveal their blindness to the meaning of the passing of time. Those very few who couple off seriously and get married upon graduation as we, their parents, once did are looked upon as freaks.

After college, the scene is even more remarkable and bizarre: singles bars, personal "partner wanted" ads (almost never mentioning marriage as a goal), men practicing serial monogamy (or what someone has aptly renamed "rotating polygamy"), women chronically disappointed in the failure of men "to commit." For the first time in human history, mature women by the tens of thousands live the entire decade of their twenties—their most fertile years—neither in the homes of their fathers nor in the homes of their husbands; unprotected, lonely, and out of sync with their inborn nature. Some women positively welcome this state of affairs, but most do not; resenting the personal price they pay for their worldly independence, they nevertheless try to put a good face on things and take refuge in work or feminist ideology. As age 30 comes and goes, they begin to allow themselves to hear their biological clock ticking, and, if husbands continue to be lacking, single motherhood by the hand of science is now an option. Meanwhile, the bachelor herd continues its youthful prowl, with real life in suspended animation, living out what Kay Hymowitz, a contributing editor of *City Journal*, has called a "postmodern postadolescence."

Those women and men who get lucky enter into what the personal ads call LTRs—long-term relationships—sometimes cohabiting, sometimes not, usually to discover how short an LTR can be. When, after a series of such affairs, marriage happens to them, they enter upon it guardedly and suspiciously, with prenuptial agreements, no common surname, and separate bank accounts.

Courtship, anyone? Don't be ridiculous.

## RECENT OBSTACLES TO COURTSHIP

. . . . Here is a (partial) list of the recent changes that hamper courtship and marriage: the sexual revolution, made possible especially by effective female contraception; the ideology of feminism and the changing educational and occupational status of women; the destigmatization of bastardy, divorce, infidelity, and abortion; the general erosion of shame and awe regarding sexual matters, exemplified most vividly in the ubiquitous and voyeuristic presentation of sexual activity in movies and on television; widespread morally neutral sex education in schools; the explosive increase in the numbers of young people whose parents have been divorced (and in those born out of wedlock, who have never known their father); great increases in geographic mobility, with a resulting loosening of ties to place and extended family of origin; and, harder to describe precisely, a popular culture that celebrates youth and independence not as a transient stage en route to adulthood but as "the time of our lives," imitable at all ages, and an ethos that lacks transcendent aspirations and asks of us no devotion to family, God, or country, encouraging us simply to soak up the pleasures of the present.

The change most immediately devastating for wooing is probably the sexual revolution. For why would a man court a woman for marriage when she may be sexually enjoyed, and regularly, without it? Contrary to what the youth of the sixties believed, they were not the first to feel the power of sexual desire. Many, perhaps even most, men in earlier times avidly sought sexual pleasure prior to and outside of marriage. But they usually distinguished, as did the culture generally, between women one fooled around with and women one married, between a woman of easy virtue and a woman of virtue simply. Only respectable women were respected; one no more wanted a loose woman for one's partner than for one's mother.

The supreme virtue of the virtuous woman was modesty, a form of sexual self-control, manifested not only in chastity but in decorous dress and manner, speech and deed, and in reticence in the display of her well-banked affections. A virtue, as it were, made for courtship, it served simultaneously as a source of attraction and a spur to manly ardor, a guard against a woman's own desires, as well as a defense against unworthy suitors. A fine woman understood that giving her body (in earlier times, even her kiss) meant giving her heart, which was too precious to be bestowed on anyone who would not prove himself worthy, at the very least by pledging himself in marriage to be her defender and lover forever.

Once female modesty became a first casualty of the sexual revolution, even women eager for marriage lost their greatest power to hold and to discipline their prospective mates. For it is a woman's refusal of sexual importunings, coupled with hints or promises of later gratification, that is generally a necessary condition of transforming a man's lust into love. Women also lost the capacity to discover their own genuine longings and best interests. For only by holding herself in reserve does a woman gain the distance and self-command needed to discern what and whom she truly wants, and to insist that the ardent suitor measure up. While there has always been sex without love, easy and early sexual satisfaction makes love and real intimacy less, not more, likely—for both men and women. Everyone's prospects for marriage were—are—sacrificed on the altar of pleasure now.

## SEXUAL TECHNOLOGY AND TECHNIQUE

The sexual revolution that liberated (especially) female sexual desire from the confines of marriage, and even from love and intimacy, would almost certainly not have occurred had there not been available cheap and effective female birth control—the pill—which for the first time severed female sexual activity from its generative consequences. Thanks to technology, a woman could declare herself free from the teleological meaning of her sexuality—as free as a man appears to be from his. Her menstrual cycle, since puberty a regular reminder of her natural maternal destiny, is now anovulatory and directed instead by her will and her medications, serving goals only of pleasure and convenience, enjoyable without apparent risk to personal health and safety. Woman on the pill is thus not only freed from the practical risk of pregnancy; she has, wittingly or not, begun to redefine the meaning of her own womanliness. Her sexuality unlinked to procreation, its exercise no longer needs to be concerned with the character of her partner and whether he is suitable to be the father and co-rearer of her yet-to-be-born children. Female sexuality becomes, like male, unlinked to the future. The new woman's anthem: Girls just want to have fun. Ironically, but absolutely predictably, the chemicals devised to assist in family planning keep many a potential family from forming, at least with a proper matrimonial beginning.

Sex education in our elementary and secondary schools is an independent yet related obstacle to courtship and marriage. Taking for granted, and thereby ratifying, precocious sexual activity among teenagers (and even pre-teens), most programs of sex education in public schools have a twofold aim: the prevention of teenage pregnancy and the prevention of venereal disease, especially AIDS. While some programs also encourage abstinence or non-coital sex, most are concerned with teaching techniques for "safe sex"; offspring (and disease) are thus treated as (equally) avoidable side effects of sexuality, whose true purpose is only individual pleasure. (This I myself did not learn until our younger daughter so enlightened me, after she learned it from her seventh-grade biology teacher.) The entire approach of sex education is technocratic and, at best, morally neutral; in many cases, it explicitly opposes traditional morals while moralistically insisting on the equal acceptability of any and all forms of sexual expression, provided only that they are not coerced. No effort is made to teach the importance of marriage as the proper home for sexual intimacy.

But perhaps still worse than such amorality—and amorality on this subject is itself morally culpable—is the failure of sex education to attempt to inform and elevate the erotic imagination of the young. On the contrary, the very attention to physiology and technique is deadly to the imagination. True sex education is an education of the heart; it concerns itself with beautiful and worthy beloveds, with elevating transports of the soul. The energy of sexual desire, if properly sublimated, is transformable into genuine and lofty longings—not only for love and romance but for all the other higher human yearnings. The sonnets and plays of Shakespeare, the poetry of Keats and Shelley, and the novels of Jane Austen can incline a heart to woo, and even show one whom and how. What kind of wooers can one hope to cultivate from reading the sex manuals—or from watching the unsublimated and unsublime sexual athleticism of the popular culture?

Decent sex education at home is also compromised, given that most parents of today's adolescents were themselves happy sexual revolutionaries. Dad may now be terribly concerned that his daughter not become promiscuous in high school or college, but he probably remains glad for the sexual favors bestowed on him by numerous coeds when he was on campus. If he speaks at all, he will likely settle for admonitions to play it safe and lessons about condoms and the pill. And Mom, a feminist and career woman, is concerned only that her daughter have sex on her own terms, not her boyfriend's. If chastity begins at home, it has lost its teachers and exemplars.

## CRIPPLED BY DIVORCE

The ubiquitous experience of divorce is also deadly for courtship and marriage. Some people try to argue, wishfully against the empirical evidence, that children of divorce will marry better than their parents because they know how important it is to choose well. But the deck is stacked against them. Not only are many of them frightened of marriage, in whose likely permanence they simply do not believe, but they are often maimed for love and intimacy. They have had no successful models to imitate; worse, their capacity for trust and love has been severely crippled by the betrayal of the primal trust all children naturally repose in their parents, to provide that durable, reliable, and absolutely trustworthy haven of permanent and unconditional love in an otherwise often unloving and undependable world.

Countless students at the University of Chicago have told me and my wife that the divorce of their parents has been the most devastating and life-shaping event of their lives. They are conscious of the fact that they enter into relationships guardedly and tentatively; for good reason, they believe that they must always be looking out for number one. Accordingly, they feel little sense of devotion to another, and, their own needs unmet, they are not generally eager for or partial to children. They are not good bets for promise keeping, and they haven't enough margin for generous service. And many of the fatherless men are themselves unmanned for fatherhood, except in the purely biological sense. Even where they dream of meeting a true love, these children of divorce have a hard time finding, winning, and committing themselves to the right one.

It is surely the fear of making a mistake in marriage, and the desire to avoid a later divorce, that leads some people to undertake cohabitation, sometimes understood by the couple to be a "trial marriage"—although they are often one or both of them self-deceived (or other-deceiving). It is far easier, so the argument goes, to get to know one another by cohabiting than by the artificial systems of courting or dating of yesteryear. But such arrangements, even when they eventuate in matrimony, are, precisely because they are a trial, not a trial of *marriage*. Marriage is not something one tries on for size, and then decides whether to keep; it is rather something one decides with a promise, and then bends every effort to keep.

Lacking the formalized and public ritual, and especially the vows or promises of permanence (or "commitment") that subtly but surely shape all aspects of genuine marital life, cohabitation is an arrangement of convenience, with each partner taken on approval and returnable at will. Many are, in fact, just playing house—sex and meals shared with the rent. When long-cohabiting couples do later marry, whether to legitimate prospective offspring, satisfy parental wishes, or just because "it now seems right," post-marital life is generally regarded and experienced as a continuation of the same, not as a true change of estate. The formal rite of passage that is the wedding ceremony is, however welcome and joyous, also something of a mockery: Everyone, not only the youngest child present, wonders, if only in embarrassed silence, "Why is this night different from all other nights?" Given that they have more or less drifted into marriage, it should come as no great surprise that couples who have lived together before marriage have a higher, *not* lower, rate of divorce than those who have not. Too much familiarity? Disenchantment? Or is it rather the lack of wooing—that is, that marriage was not seen from the start as the sought-for relationship, as the goal that beckoned and guided the process of getting-to-know-you?

## FEMINISM AGAINST MARRIAGE

That the cause of courtship has been severely damaged by feminist ideology and attitudes goes almost without saying. Even leaving aside the radical attacks on traditional sex roles, on the worth of motherhood or the vanishing art of homemaking, and sometimes even on the whole male race, the reconception of all relations between the sexes as relations based on power is simply deadly for love. Anyone who has ever loved or been loved knows the difference between love and the will to power, no matter what the cynics say. But the cynical new theories, and the resulting push toward androgyny, surely inhibit the growth of love.

On the one side, there is a rise in female assertiveness and efforts at empowerment, with a consequent need to deny all womanly dependence and the kind of vulnerability that calls for the protection of strong and loving men, protection such men were once—and would still be—willing to provide. On the other side, we see the enfeeblement of men, who, contrary to the dominant ideology, are not likely to become better lovers, husbands, or fathers if they too become feminists or fellow-travelers. On the contrary, many men now cynically exploit women's demands for equal power by letting them look after themselves—pay their own way, hold their own doors, fight their own battles, travel after dark by themselves. These ever-so-sensitive males will defend not a woman's honor but her right to learn the manly art of self-defense. In the present climate, those increasingly rare men who are still inclined to be gentlemen must dissemble their generosity as submissiveness.

Even in the absence of the love-poisoning doctrines of radical feminism, the otherwise welcome changes in women's education and employment have also been problematic for courtship. True, better educated women can, other things being equal, be more interesting and engaging partners for better educated men; and the possibility of genuine friendship between husband and wife—one that could survive the end of the child-rearing years—is, at least in principle, much more likely now that women have equal access to higher education. But everything depends on the spirit and the purpose of such education, and whether it makes and keeps a high place for private life. . . .

The problem is not woman's desire for meaningful work. It is rather the ordering of one's loves. Many women have managed to combine work and family; the difficulty is finally not work but careers, or, rather, careerism. Careerism, now an equal-opportunity affliction, is surely no friend to love or marriage; and the careerist character of higher education is greater than ever. Women are under special pressures to prove they can be as dedicated to their work as men. Likewise, in the workplace, they must do man's work like a man, and for man's pay and perquisites. Consequently, they are compelled to regard private life—and especially marriage, homemaking, and family—as lesser goods, to be pursued only by those lesser women who can aspire no higher than "baking cookies." Besides, many women in such circumstances have nothing left to give, "no time to get involved." And marriage, should it come for careerist women, is often compromised from the start, what with the difficulty of finding two worthy jobs in the same city, or commuter marriage, or the need to negotiate or get hired help for every domestic and familial task.

Besides these greater conflicts of time and energy, the economic independence of women, however welcome on other grounds, is itself not an asset for marital stability, as both the woman and the man can more readily contemplate leaving a marriage. Indeed, a woman's earning power can become her own worst enemy when the children are born. Many professional women who would like to stay home with their new babies nonetheless work full-time. Tragically, some cling to their economic independence because they worry that their husbands will leave them for another woman before the children are grown. What are these women looking for in prospective husbands? Do their own career preoccupations obscure their own prospective maternal wishes and needs? Indeed, what understanding of marriage informed their decision to marry in the first place?

## NOT READY FOR ADULTHOOD

This question in fact represents a more subtle, but most profound, impediment to wooing and marriage: deep uncertainty about what marriage is and means, and what purpose it serves. In previous generations, people chose to marry, but they were not compelled also to choose what marriage meant. Is it a sacrament, a covenant, or a contract based on calculation of mutual advantage? Is it properly founded on *eros*, friendship, or economic advantage? Is marriage a vehicle for personal fulfillment and private happiness, a vocation of mutual service, or a task to love the one whom it has been given me to love? Are marital vows still to be regarded as binding promises that both are duty-bound to keep or, rather, as quaint expressions of current hopes and predictions that, should they be mistaken, can easily be nullified? Having in so many cases already given their bodies to one another—not to speak of the previous others—how does one understand the link between marriage and conjugal fidelity? And what, finally, of that first purpose of marriage, procreation, for whose sake societies everywhere have instituted and safeguarded this institution? For, truth to tell, were it not for the important obligations to care for and rear the next generation, no society would finally much care about who couples with whom, or for how long.

This brings me to what is probably the deepest and most intractable obstacle to courtship and marriage: a set of cultural attitudes and sensibilities that obscure and even deny the fundamental difference between youth and adulthood. Marriage, especially when seen as the institution designed to provide for the next generation, is most definitely the business of adults, by which I mean, people who are serious about life, people who aspire to go outward and forward to embrace and to assume responsibility for the future. To be sure, most college graduates do go out, find jobs, and become self-supporting (though, astonishingly, a great many do return to live at home). But, though out of the nest, they don't have a course to fly. They do not experience their lives as a trajectory, with an inner meaning partly given by the life cycle itself. The carefreeness and independence of youth they do not see as a stage on the way to maturity, in which they then take responsibility for the world and especially, as parents, for the new lives that will replace them. The necessities of aging and mortality are out of sight; few feel the call to serve a higher goal or some transcendent purpose.

The view of life as play has often characterized the young. But, remarkably, today this is not something regrettable, to be outgrown as soon as possible; for their narcissistic absorption in themselves and in immediate pleasures and present experiences, the young are not condemned but are even envied by many of their elders. Parents and children wear the same cool clothes, speak the same lingo, listen to the same music. Youth, not adulthood, is the cultural ideal, at least as celebrated in the popular culture. Yes, everyone feels themselves to be always growing, as a result of this failed relationship or that change of job. But very few aspire to be fully grown-up, and the culture does not demand it of them, not least because many prominent grown-ups would gladly change places with today's 20-somethings. Why should a young man be eager to take his father's place, if he sees his father running away from it with all deliberate speed? . . . .

## THE NATURAL OBSTACLE

Not all the obstacles to courtship and marriage are cultural. At bottom, there is also the deeply ingrained, natural waywardness and unruliness of the human male. Sociobiologists were not the first to discover that males have a penchant for promiscuity and polygyny—this was well known to biblical religion. Men are also naturally more restless and ambitious than women; lacking woman's powerful and immediate link to life's generative answer to mortality, men flee from the fear of death into heroic deed, great quests, or sheer distraction after distraction. One can make a good case that biblical religion is, not least, an attempt to domesticate male sexuality and male erotic longings, and to put them in the service of transmitting a righteous and holy way of life through countless generations.

For as long as American society kept strong its uneasy union between modern liberal political principles and Judeo-Christian moral and social beliefs, marriage and the family could be sustained and could even prosper. But the gender-neutral individualism of our political teaching has, it seems, at last won the day, and the result has been male "liberation"—from domestication, from civility, from responsible self-command. Contemporary liberals and conservatives alike are trying to figure out how to get men "to commit" to marriage, or to keep their marital vows, or to stay home with the children, but their own androgynous view of humankind prevents them from seeing how hard it has always been to make a monogamous husband and devoted father out of the human male.

Ogden Nash had it right: "Hogamus higamus, men are polygamous; higamus hogamus, women monogamous." To make naturally polygamous men accept the conventional institution of monogamous marriage has been the work of centuries of Western civilization, with social sanctions, backed by religious teachings and authority, as major instruments of the transformation, and with female modesty as the crucial civilizing device. As these mores and sanctions disappear, courtship gives way to seduction and possession, and men become again the sexually, familially, and civically irresponsible creatures they are naturally always in danger of being. At the top of the social ladder, executives walk out on their families and take up with trophy wives. At the bottom of the scale, low-status males, utterly uncivilized by marriage, return to the fighting gangs, taking young women as prizes for their prowess. Rebarbarization is just around the corner. Courtship, anyone?

## WHY IT MATTERS

Given the enormous new social impediments to courtship and marriage, and given also that they are firmly and deeply rooted in the cultural soil of modernity, not to say human nature itself, one might simply decide to declare the cause lost. In fact, many people would be only too glad to do so. For they condemn the old ways as repressive, inegalitarian, sexist, patriarchal, boring, artificial, and unnecessary. Some urge us to go with the flow; others hopefully believe that new modes and orders will emerge, well-suited to our new conditions of liberation and equality. Just as new cultural meanings are today being "constructed" for sexuality and gender, so too new cultural definitions can be invented for "marriage," "paternity and maternity," and "family." Nothing truly important, so the argument goes, will be lost.

New arrangements can perhaps be fashioned. But it is simply wrong that nothing important will be lost; indeed, many things of great importance have already been lost, and, as I have indicated, at tremendous cost in personal happiness, child welfare, and civic peace. This should come as no surprise. For the new arrangements that constitute the cultural void created by the demise of courtship and dating rest on serious and destructive errors regarding the human condition: errors about the meaning of human sexuality, errors about the nature of marriage, errors about what constitutes a fully human life.

Sexual desire, in human beings as in animals, points to an end that is partly hidden from, and finally at odds with, the self-serving individual. Sexuality as such means perishability and serves replacement. The salmon swimming upstream to spawn and die tell the universal story: Sex is bound up with death, to which it holds a partial answer in procreation. This truth the salmon and the other animals practice blindly; only the human being can understand what it means. According to the story of the Garden of Eden, our humanization is in fact coincident with the recognition of our sexual nakedness and all that it implies: shame at our needy incompleteness, unruly self-division, and finitude;

awe before the eternal; hope in the self-transcending possibilities of children and a relationship to the divine. For a human being to treat sex as a desire like hunger— not to mention as sport—is then to live a deception.

Thus how shallow an understanding of sexuality is embodied in our current clamoring for "safe sex." Sex is by its nature unsafe. All interpersonal relations are necessarily risky, and serious ones especially so. And to give oneself to another, body and soul, is hardly playing it safe. Sexuality is at its core profoundly "unsafe," and it is only thanks to contraception that we are encouraged to forget its inherent "dangers." These go beyond the hazards of venereal disease, which are always a reminder and a symbol of the high stakes involved, and beyond the risks of pregnancy and the pains and dangers of childbirth to the mother. To repeat, sexuality itself means mortality—equally for both man and woman. Whether we know it or not, when we are sexually active we are voting with our genitalia for our own demise. "Safe sex" is the self-delusion of shallow souls.

It is for this reason that procreation remains at the core of a proper understanding of marriage. Mutual pleasure and mutual service between husband and wife are, of course, part of the story. So too are mutual admiration and esteem, especially where the partners are deserving. A friendship of shared pursuits and pastimes enhances any marriage, all the more so when the joint activities exercise deeper human capacities. But it is precisely the common project of procreation that holds together what sexual differentiation sometimes threatens to drive apart. Through children, a good common to both husband and wife, male and female achieve some genuine unification (beyond the mere sexual "union" that fails to do so): The two become one through sharing generous (not needy) love for this third being as good. Flesh of their flesh, the child is the parents' own commingled being externalized and given a separate and persisting existence; unification is enhanced also by their commingled work of rearing. Providing an opening to the future beyond the grave, carrying not only our seed but also our names, our ways, and our hopes that they will surpass us in goodness and happiness, children are a testament to the possibility of transcendence. Gender duality and sexual desire, which first draws our love upward and outside of ourselves, finally provide for the partial overcoming of the confinement and limitation of perishable embodiment altogether. It is as the supreme institution devoted to this renewal of human possibility that marriage finds its deepest meaning and highest function.

There is no substitute for the contribution that the shared work of raising children makes to the singular friendship and love of husband and wife. Precisely because of its central procreative mission, and, even more, because children are yours for a lifetime, this is a friendship that cannot be had with any other person. Uniquely, it is a friendship that does not fly from, but rather embraces wholeheartedly, the finitude of its members, affirming without resentment the truth of our human condition. Not by mistake did God create a woman—rather than a dialectic partner—to cure Adam's aloneness; not by accident does the same biblical Hebrew verb mean both to know sexually and to know the truth—including the generative truth about the meaning of being man and woman.[3]

Marriage and procreation are, therefore, at the heart of a serious and flourishing human life, if not for everyone at least for the vast majority. Most of us know from our own experience that life becomes truly serious when we become responsible for the lives of others for whose being in the world we have said, "We do." It is fatherhood and motherhood that teach most of us what it took to bring us into our own adulthood. And it is the desire to give not only life but a good way of life to our children that opens us toward a serious concern for the true, the good, and even the holy. Parental love of children leads once wayward sheep back into the fold of church and synagogue. In the best case, it can even be the beginning of the sanctification of life—yes, even in modern times.

The earlier forms of courtship, leading men and women to the altar, understood these deeper truths about human sexuality, marriage, and the higher possibilities for human life. Courtship provided rituals of growing up, for making clear the meaning of one's own human sexual nature, and for entering into the ceremonial and customary world of ritual and sanctification. Courtship disciplined sexual desire and romantic attraction, provided opportunities for mutual learning about one another's character, fostered salutary illusions that inspired admiration and devotion, and, by locating wooer and wooed in their familial settings, taught the intergenerational meaning of erotic activity. It pointed the way to the answers to life's biggest questions: Where are you going? Who is going with you? How—in what manner—are you both going to go?

The practices of today's men and women do not accomplish these purposes, and they and their marriages, when they get around to them, are weaker as a result. There may be no going back to the earlier forms of courtship, but no one should be rejoicing over this fact. Anyone serious about "designing" new cultural forms to replace those now defunct must bear the burden of finding some alternative means of serving all these necessary goals.

## A REVOLUTION NEEDED?

. . . . Real reform in the direction of sanity would require a restoration of cultural gravity about sex, marriage, and the life cycle. The restigmatization of illegitimacy and promiscuity would help. A reversal of recent anti-natalist prejudices, implicit in the practice of abortion, and a correction of current anti-generative sex education, would also help, as would the revalorization of marriage as a personal, as well as a cultural, ideal. Parents of pubescent children could contribute to a truly humanizing sex education by elevating their erotic imagination through exposure to an older and more edifying literature. Parents of college-bound young people, especially those with strong religious and family values, could direct their children to religiously affiliated colleges that attract like-minded people.

Even in deracinated and cosmopolitan universities like my own, faculty could legitimate the importance of courtship and marriage by offering courses on the subject aimed at making the students more thoughtful about their own life-shaping choices. Even better, they could teach without ideological or methodological preoccupations the world's great literature, elevating the longings and refining the sensibilities of their students and furnishing their souls with numerous examples of lives seriously led and loves faithfully followed. Religious institutions could provide earlier and better instruction for adolescents on the meaning of sex and marriage, as well as suitable opportunities for co-religionists to mix and, God willing, match. Absent newly discovered congregational and communal support, individual parents will generally be helpless before the onslaught of the popular culture.

Under present democratic conditions, with families not what they used to be, anything that contributes to promoting a lasting friendship between husband and wife should be cultivated. A budding couple today needs even better skills at reading character and greater opportunities for showing it than were necessary in a world that had lots of family members looking on. Paradoxically, encouragement of earlier marriage, and earlier child-bearing, might in many cases be helpful—the young couple, as it were, growing up together before either partner could become jaded or distrustful from too much premarital expe-rience, not only of "relationships" but of life. Training for careers by women could be postponed until after the early motherhood years—perhaps even supported publicly by something like a GI Bill of Rights for mothers who had stayed home until their children reached school age.

But it would appear to require a revolution to restore the conditions most necessary for successful courtship: a desire in America's youth for mature adulthood (which means for marriage and parenthood), an appreciation of the unique character of the marital bond, understood as linked to generation, and a restoration of sexual self-restraint generally and of female modesty in particular.

Frankly, I do not see how this last, most crucial, prerequisite can be recovered, nor do I see how one can sensibly do without it. As Tocqueville rightly noted, it is women who are the teachers of mores; it is largely through the purity of her morals, self-regulated, that woman wields her influence, both before and after marriage. Men, as Rousseau put it, will always do what is pleasing to women, but only if women suitably control and channel their own considerable sexual power. Is there perhaps some nascent young feminist out there who would like to make her name great and who will seize the golden opportunity for advancing the truest interest of women (and men and children) by raising (again) the radical banner, "Not until you marry me"? And, while I'm dreaming, why not also, "Not without my parents' blessings"?

## NOTES

1. A fine history of these transformations has been written by Beth L. Bailey, *From Front Porch to Back Seat: Courtship in Twentieth Century America* (Baltimore: Johns Hopkins University Press, 1988).

2. Readers removed from the college scene should revisit Allan Bloom's profound analysis of relationships in his *The Closing of the Amer-*

*ican Mind* (New York: Simon & Schuster, 1987). Bloom was concerned with the effect of the new arrangements on the possibility for liberal education, not for marriage, my current concern.

3. I recognize that there are happily monogamous marriages that remain childless, some by choice, others by bad luck, and that some people will feel the pull of and yield to a higher calling, be it art, philosophy, or the celibate priesthood, seeking or serving some other transcendent voice. But the former often feel cheated by their childlessness, frequently going to extraordinary lengths to conceive or adopt a child. A childless and grandchildless old age is a sadness and a deprivation, even where it is a price willingly paid by couples who deliberately do not procreate. . . .

## CRITICAL THINKING QUESTIONS

1. Kass recognizes that many people see "courting" and "wooing" as archaic. What, however, were some of the benefits of traditional wooing practices in the past?

2. Kass suggests that women had (and could again have) greater power and control in relation to men when they practice sexual self-restraint and modesty. What does he mean? Do you agree with his position?

3. Kass offers a number of suggestions for restoring traditional courtship practices. Should the recommendations be implemented?

# 6    Love and Courtship

## *Centrist:* Love and Individualism

ROBERT N. BELLAH, RICHARD MADSEN, WILLIAM M. SULLIVAN, ANN SWIDLER, AND STEVEN M. TIPTON, *Habits of the Heart: Individualism and Commitment to American Life* (New York: Harper & Row, 1985), pp. 90–93, 107–110. © 1985, 1996 Regents of the University of California. Reproduced by permission.

*According to Robert N. Bellah and his associates, the "cancerous" growth of individualism in the United States threatens our commitment to each other and to our communities. Since love and marriage are seen primarily in terms of psychological gratification, for example, they result in unstable relationships that dislodge people from family and broader societal obligations.*

### LOVE AND THE SELF

Americans believe in love as the basis for enduring relationships. A 1970 survey found that 96 percent of all Americans held to the ideal of two people sharing a life and a home together. When the same question was asked in 1980, the same percentage agreed. Yet when a national sample was asked in 1978 whether "most couples getting married today expect to remain married for the rest of their lives," 60 percent said no.[1] Love and commitment, it appears, are desirable, but not easy. For, in addition to believing in love, we Americans believe in the self. Indeed, there are few criteria for action outside the self. The love

The authors' conclusions are based on interviews with over 200 people, 1979 to 1984, in San Jose, San Diego, and San Francisco, California; a major southern city; a Boston suburb; and two political organizations in Philadelphia and Santa Monica, California.

that must hold us together is rooted in the vicissitudes of our subjectivity. No wonder we don't believe marriage is easy today.

Yet when things go well, love seems so natural it hardly requires explanation. A love relationship is good because it works, because it "feels right," because it is where one feels most at home. Marge and Fred Rowan have been married for twelve years and have two children. They were high school sweethearts. When asked to say how they decided to marry, Fred says "there wasn't a lot of discussion." Marge was always "the kind of girl I wanted to marry" and "somewhere along the line" he just assumed "that's where our relationship was headed." There may be reasons, both practical and romantic, for marrying the person one does, but they are almost afterthoughts. What matters is the growing sense that the relationship is natural, right. One does not so much choose as simply accept what already is. Marge, Fred's wife, describes having the sense, before she married, that Fred was the "right person." "It was, like he said, very unspoken, but absolutely that's exactly how we felt. Fred was always 'my guy.' He was just 'mine.'" They were "right on ever since high school," and even when she tried to date someone else in college, "I felt stupid about it because I knew I was in love with Fred. I didn't want to be with anybody else."

Searching for a definition of "real love" becomes pointless if one "feels good" enough about one's relationship. After all, what one is looking for is the "right place" for oneself. As Fred says, "It just felt right, and it was like being caught in the flow. That's just the way it was. It wasn't a matter of deciding, so there could be no uncertainty." A relationship of the kind Fred and Marge describe seems so natural, so spontaneous that it carries a powerful sense of inevitability. For them, their relationship embodies a deep sense of their own identity, and thus a sense that the self has found its right place in the world. Love embodies one's real self in such a spontaneous, natural relationship, the self can be both grounded and free.

Not every couple finds the easy certainty of love that Fred and Marge convey. But most couples want a similar combination of spontaneity and solidity, freedom and intimacy. Many speak of sharing—thoughts, feelings, tasks, values, or life goals—as the greatest virtue in a relationship. Nan Pfautz, a divorced secretary in her mid-forties, describes how, after being alone for many years, she fell deeply in love. "I think it was the sharing, the real sharing of feelings. I don't think I've ever done that with another man." Nan knew that she loved Bill because "I let all my barriers down. I really was able to be myself with him—very, very comfortable. I could be as gross as I wanted or I could be as funny as I wanted, as silly as I wanted. I didn't worry about, or have to worry—or didn't anyway—about what his reaction was going to be. I was just me. I was free to be me." The natural sharing of one's real self is, then, the essence of love.

But the very sharing that promises to be the fulfillment of love can also threaten the self. The danger is that one will, in sharing too completely with another, "lose oneself." Nan struggled with this problem during her marriage, and afterward still found difficulty achieving the right balance between sharing and being separate. "Before my relationship with Bill, seven, eight years ago now, I seemed to want to hang on to people too much. It was almost as though I devoured them. I wanted them totally to be mine, and I wanted to be totally theirs, with no individuality. Melding . . . I lost all of myself that way and had nothing of *me* left."

How is it that one can "lose" oneself in love, and what are the consequences of that loss? Nan says she lost herself when she lost her "own goals." At first, her marriage was "very good. It was very give and take in those days. It really was. We went skiing the first time together, and I didn't like skiing. From then on, he went skiing on his own, and I did something I wanted to do." Thus not losing yourself has something to do with having a sense of your own interests. What can be lost are a set of independent preferences and the will to pursue them. With the birth of her son, Nan became absorbed in the mother role, and stopped asserting herself. She became "someone to walk on. Very dull and uninteresting, not enthused about anything. Oh, I was terrible. I wouldn't have wanted to be around me at all." The ironic consequence of passively adapting to others' needs is that one becomes less valuable, less interesting, less desirable. Nan's story is particularly interesting because her behavior conformed fairly well to the earlier ideology of "woman's sphere," where unselfish devotion was the ideal of wifely behavior. But giving up one's self, a subtle shift in emphasis from "unselfishness," may, in the contemporary middle class, as in Nan's case, lead to losing precisely the self that was loved—and perhaps losing one's husband.

A younger woman, Melinda Da Silva, married only a few years, has a similar way of describing her difficulties in the first years of her marriage. She acted out the role of the good wife, trying continually to please her husband. "The only way I knew to be was how my mother was a wife. You love your husband and this was the belief that I had, you do all these things for him. This is the way you show him that you love him—to be a good wife, and the fear that if you don't do all these things, you're not a good wife, and maybe you don't love your husband." Trying so hard to be a good wife, Melinda failed to put her *self* into the relationship. In trying so hard to "show Thomas that I loved him," she "was putting aside anything that I thought in trying to figure out what he thought. Everything was just all put aside." What Melinda had "put aside" was her willingness to express her own opinions and act on her own judgment, even about how best to please her husband.

Melinda sought help from a marriage counselor, and came to feel that the problem with her marriage was less her husband than the loss of her self. "That's all I thought about, was what he wanted, thinking that he would love me more if I did what he wanted. I began to realize when Thomas and I went in for counseling I wouldn't voice my opinion, and I was doing things just for him and ignoring things for myself. The very things I was doing to get his approval were causing him to view me less favorably." Thus losing a sense of who one is and what one wants can make one less attractive and less interesting. To be a person worth loving, one must assert one's individuality. Melinda could "give a lot to our marriage" only when she "felt better" about herself. Having an independent self is a necessary precondition to joining fully in a relationship.

Love, then, creates a dilemma for Americans. In some ways, love is the quintessential expression of individuality and freedom. At the same time, it offers intimacy, mutuality, and sharing. In the ideal love relationship, these two aspects of love are perfectly joined—love is both absolutely free and completely shared. Such moments of perfect harmony among free individuals are rare, however. The sharing and commitment in a love relationship can seem, for some, to swallow up the individual, making her (more often than him) lose sight of her own interests, opinions, and desires. Paradoxically, since love is supposed to be a spontaneous choice by free individuals, someone who has "lost" herself cannot really love, or cannot contribute to a real love relationship. Losing a sense of one's self may also lead to being exploited, or even abandoned, by the person one loves.

. . . For the classic utilitarian individualist, the only valid contract is one based on negotiation between individuals acting in their own self-interest. For the expressive individualist, a relationship is created by full sharing of authentic feelings. But both in hard bargaining over a contract and in the spontaneous sharing of therapeutically sophisticated lovers, the principle is in basic ways the same. No binding obligations and no wider social understanding justify a relationship. It exists only as the expression of the choices of the free selves who make it up. And should it no longer meet their needs, it must end.

### LOVE AND INDIVIDUALISM

How Americans think about love is central to the ways we define the meaning of our own lives in relation to the wider society. For most of us, the bond to spouse and children is our most fundamental social tie. The habits and modes of thought that govern intimate relationships are thus one of the central places where we may come to understand the cultural legacy with which we face the challenges of contemporary social life. Yet in spite of its great importance, love is also, increasingly, a source of insecurity, confusion, and uncertainty.[2] The problems we have in thinking about love are an embodiment of the difficulty we have thinking about social attachment in general.

A deeply ingrained individualism lies behind much contemporary understanding of love. The idea that people must take responsibility for deciding what they want and finding relationships that will meet their needs is widespread. In this sometimes somber utilitarianism, individuals may want lasting relationships, but such relationships are possible only so long as they meet the needs of the two people involved. All individuals can do is be clear about their own needs and avoid neurotic demands for such unrealizable goods as a lover who will give and ask nothing in return.

Such a utilitarian attitude seems plausible for those in the throes of divorce or for single people trying to negotiate a world of short-term relationships. It is one solution to the difficulties of self-preservation in a world where broader expectations may lead to disappointment or make one vulnerable to exploitation. Then love becomes no more than an exchange, with no binding rules except the obligation of full and open communication. A relationship should give each partner what he or she needs while it lasts, and if the relationship ends, at least both partners will have received a reasonable return on their investment.

While utilitarian individualism plays a part in the therapeutic attitude, the full significance of the therapeutic view of the world lies in its expressive individualism, an expanded view of the nature and possibilities of the self. Love then becomes the mutual exploration of infinitely rich, complex, and exciting selves. Many of our respondents stress that their own relationships are much better than their parents' marriages were. They insist on greater intimacy, sharing of feelings, and willingness to "work through" problems than their parents found possible.

It is true that the evangelical Christians we interviewed and others who maintain continuity with a religious tradition—liberal Protestant, Catholic, and Jewish traditions as well—find relationships deepened by being part of a wider set of purposes and meanings the partners share. [Some] say that their marriages are strong because they share commitment to the religious beliefs of their respective churches with their wives.

Accepting religious authority as a way of resolving the uncertainties and dilemmas of personal life was relatively unusual among those to whom we talked, as was the extreme version of the therapeutic attitude that puts self-realization ahead of attachment to others. But in the middle-class members of America's mainstream, we found therapeutic language very prevalent, even among those who also retain attachment to other modes of thinking about and experiencing the world. Therapeutic understandings fit many aspects of traditional American individualism, particularly the assumption that social bonds can be firm only if they rest on the free, self-interested choices of individuals. Thus even Americans who do not share the quest for self-actualization find the idea of loving in spite of, not because of, social constraints very appealing.

On the whole, even the most secure, happily married of our respondents had difficulty when they sought a language in which to articulate their reasons for commitments that went beyond the self. These confusions were particularly clear when they discussed problems of sacrifice and obligation. While they wanted to maintain enduring relationships, they resisted the notion that such relationships might involve obligations that went beyond the wishes of the partners. Instead, they insisted on the "obligation" to communicate one's wishes and feelings honestly and to attempt to deal with problems in the relationship. They had few ideas of the substantive obligations partners in a relationship might develop. Ted Oster began to hint at some of these when he discussed how having lived your life with someone, having a shared history, bound you to her in ways that went beyond the feelings of the moment. He seemed to reach for the idea that the interests, and indeed the selves of the partners, are no longer fully separable in a long-lasting relationship, but his utilitarian individualist language kept pulling him back. In the end, he oscillated between the idea that it might in some larger sense be wrong to leave his marriage and the simple idea that he and Debby would stay together because they were well suited to each other.

Similarly, while the evangelical Christians welcomed the idea of sacrifice as an expression of Christian love, many others were uncomfortable with the idea. It was not that they were unwilling to make compromises or sacrifices for their spouses, but they were troubled by the ideal of self-denial the term "sacrifice" implied. If you really wanted to do something for the person you loved, they said, it would not be a sacrifice. Since the only measure of the good is what is good for the self, something that is really a burden to the self cannot be part of love. Rather, if one is in touch with one's true feelings, one will do something for one's beloved only if one really wants to, and then, by definition, it cannot be a sacrifice. Without a wider set of cultural traditions, then, it was hard for people to find a way to say why genuine attachment to others might require the risk of hurt, loss, or sacrifice. They clung to an optimistic view in which love might require hard work, but could never create real costs to the self. They tended instead to believe that therapeutic work on the self could turn what some might regard as sacrifices into freely chosen benefits. What proved most elusive to our respondents, and what remains most poignantly difficult in the wider American culture, are ways of understanding the world that could overcome the sharp distinction between self and other.

## NOTES

1. Daniel Yankelovich, *New Rules: Searching for Self-Fulfillment in a World Turned Upside Down* (New York: Random House, 1981).
2. Ibid., pp. 103–105.

## CRITICAL THINKING QUESTIONS

1. What is the "dilemma" that love creates? Why, for example, do the authors see utilitarian individualism and expressive individualism as problematic for enduring relationships?

2. The authors claim that our emphasis on individuality and intimacy jeopardizes marital obligations and commitment. What other factors might explain our sometimes-fragile marital relationships?

3. Are all of us equally as selfish and self-centered as the authors claim? Is it possible, for example, that the small sample—based largely on middle-class Californians—is not representative of the larger population?

# 6 Love and Courtship

## *Liberal/Feminist:* Women as Love's Experts and Love's Victims

CAROL TAVRIS, *The Mismeasure of Woman* (New York: Simon & Schuster, 1992), pp. 246–254, 256–259. © 1992 by Carol Tavris. This usage granted by permission of Simon & Schuster and Lescher & Lescher, Ltd.

*There are no differences between women and men in the emotions they feel or in how intensely they feel them. The differences in expression emerge, however, because women are expected to reveal their emotions and men are expected to suppress theirs. According to Carol Tavris, this results in stereotypes about women as intimacy experts and stereotypes about men as aloof and unloving.*

A friend of mine, whom I will call Roberta, has been mildly unhappy for years about one flaw in her otherwise excellent husband, Henry. The flaw rises and falls in importance to her, depending on Roberta's state of mind and general stresses, but it has long been a chronic irritant. Henry's problem is that he doesn't like to "chitchat," as he puts it. This means, Roberta explains, that he doesn't like to gossip about friends and family, he doesn't like to analyze his marriage on a weekly or even yearly basis, he doesn't like to talk about his feelings, and the only time he ever said "I love you" was back in 1974, when he proposed marriage. Once, pressed to reveal his passions, Henry said, "I vote with my feet. If I didn't love you, I wouldn't be here. "

Instead of killing Henry at that moment, which was her inclination, Roberta did what she usually does: She called a woman friend, and they met for lunch to discuss Henry. Several hours later, Roberta emerged refreshed, invigorated, and prepared to cope with Henry for another few months.

• • •

When I was growing up, the stereotype was that men had all the great and true friendships: Damon and Pythias, Hamlet and Horatio, Butch Cassidy and the Sundance Kid. Male friendships were said to be based on male bonding, true and faithful camaraderie, and sturdy affection, whereas women's friendships were shallow, trivial, competitive, and vain. Anthropologist Lionel Tiger advanced his view, in *Men in Groups*, that "male bonding" originated in prehistoric male hunting groups and lingers today in their modern equivalents: sports, politics, business, and bars. Because females do not "bond" in the same way, their friendships are a shadow of the real (male) thing.

When I was growing up, the stereotype said that men were the great romantics, the great lovers. Devoted Rhett Butler was more admirable than the heartless Scarlett; adoring Cyrano de Bergerac was superior to the superficial Roxanne; self-sacrificing Sydney Carton did the far, far better thing than his Lucie would ever do. Women, being interested mainly in marrying a meal ticket, were said to be pragmatic and fickle. What did they know of true love?

When I was growing up, social scientists maintained that men were "instrumental" and "task-oriented," whereas women were "expressive" and "person-oriented." This was a fancier way of saying that men were best suited for work and women were best suited for motherhood. Experts explained that such a division of emotional and physical labor was an ideal arrangement for family life, although, overall and if the truth be told, being expressive and person-oriented was not as healthy or desirable as being instrumental and task-oriented.

With the rise of cultural feminism in the late 1970s and 1980s, many people began to argue that women's ways of expressing love and having friendships were better and healthier than men's. They no longer regarded women's ease with self-disclosure and talking about feelings as evidence of weakness but of strength. [Some researchers have] argued persuasively that women are better at love because of their skill at connection, whereas men have trouble with attachments because they are reared to overvalue independence and fear connection. Studies were finding that women's style of intimacy brought them moral support, protected their mental and physical health, and made them easier to talk to. Both men and women, it was found, feel better after talking things over with a woman.

As a result, it was not long before we saw the rise of the "deficit approach" to men's ability to love. A typical article of the 1970s lamented "The inexpressive male: A tragedy of American society," and new theories suggested that men have a "trained incapacity to share."[1] Research began emphasizing the competition, rivalry, emotional inhibition, and aggression that men

bring to their friendships and love affairs, in contrast to the emotional honesty and mutual support that women bring to theirs.

Today, it is female friendships that are celebrated as being deep, intimate, and true, based as they are on shared feelings and confidences and on women's allegedly greater capacity for connection with others. Today, male friendships are scorned for being superficial and trivial, based as they are on shared interest in, say, the Detroit Tigers, Michelle Pfeiffer, and classic E-type Jaguars. Today, love is the one domain in which women are thought to excel and to represent the healthy model of normalcy, while men are pathologized—the poor souls who can't love, don't express themselves, and won't allow themselves to become intimate. Roberta, with her emotional demands for "talk" and "love," used to be the problem. Now, for many women, she is the solution, and it is Henry who is the problem.

The new stereotype of Woman as Intimacy Expert is part of the women-are-better movement that has transformed activities formerly thought to illustrate female deficiency into female strength. On the surface, the stereotype praises women, and certainly it validates much that is true of women's experience. Yet both sexes sacrifice a great deal to maintain this stereotype, and the reasons that it has prevailed throughout our society have little to do with either gender's native abilities or deficits. To find the reasons, we need to stop asking "Which sex is better at love? Whose emotional style is better?" and ask instead: What are the consequences for women and men of the belief that women are the intimacy experts, the love experts? What are the consequences in a family when one partner demands and pursues intimacy, and the other retreats into silence? Why, if women's ways of loving are so normal and desirable, aren't men rushing out to buy books to fix themselves, books called *Men Who Love Too Little?*

It is not my intention to take away from women the one area in which they have approval to excel: the realm of nurturance, love, and caretaking. Although "women's ways of loving" have much to commend them, they must be put in perspective. The misunderstandings between women and men on matters of love and intimacy are often very funny, but they are no joke. They are part of a system that relegates the sexes to separate spheres of expertise: the intimate world of love for her, the public world of work for him. This schism is unfortunate for all concerned, because the two spheres, which represent equally valuable activities, are not equally valued in our society. Women's alleged superiority in love is a sop given to women in a system that regards love and care as fluffy topics to begin with, suitable for women's magazines, greeting cards, and sermons.

## THE FEMINIZING OF LOVE

Dear Abby: Another St. Valentine's Day has come and gone without flowers, candy or any kind of a valentine from my husband. I'm 25 and he is 26, and we've been married for three years. I'd have been thrilled if he had brought me a flower—or even handed me a valentine—but he ignored the day completely. . . . He's a super guy, hard-working and decent, so maybe I shouldn't complain. But it sure would have felt great to have been remembered on St. Valentine's Day. Any suggestions?[2]

—Nobody's Valentine

"Nobody's Valentine" is in good company, but I wonder whether she would be consoled to know that 85 percent of all valentine cards are purchased by women.[3] This is a fascinating statistic. Why aren't more men buying valentines? And why do so many women want them so much?

"Nobody's Valentine" is the target audience for countless books and articles that offer to help women learn to understand, manage, or change men and get them to be more "loving," at least as women define loving—by revealing their feelings. The cover line on an issue of *Self* magazine is typical: Right after "Breakthrough! The easiest diet!" and "6 Steps to a GREAT BODY!" is *Get him to talk—tonight.*"

Of course, for all the women who are asking, "Why won't he talk to me? Why won't he say he loves me?" there is a corresponding number of men who are complaining, "Why doesn't she shut up? Why does she keep needing reassurance that I love her?" Many women say that their greatest wish for their marriages is that their husbands be more intimate, better at communication. "If only my husband would tell me what he is thinking," they say, "everything would be perfect." For their part, men say, "If only she were happy, if only she would stop complaining, everything would be fine. She expects me to read her mind and know why she is unhappy; I'm truly baffled by what she says she wants."

Underlying these reciprocal complaints is the real problem: that men and women tend to define intimacy and express love differently. For many men, love is action: doing things for the other person. For many women, love is talking: acknowledging the immediate feeling of the other person's adorableness.

For example, psychotherapist Richard Driscoll, in *The Binds That Tie*, describes the following scene: A wife, Paula, asks her husband, Don, if he "really" loves her. Don tries to give her an honest answer: "'I know I want to be married to you. I am satisfied to go to work every morning, because I know that I am supporting you and that you are there for me. I would never want to leave you, and I would never want you to leave me. Is that what you mean by love?' This answer leaves her unsatisfied. " 'But why can't you say you *love* me?'" Yet, as Driscoll points out, Don did in fact say he loved her, but in his own words rather than in her words.

Paula did not see this, says Driscoll, because "she thinks of love as a feeling" and "he thinks of it as a commitment to being with a woman and working to provide for her."[4] This is one reason, he believes, that many men are reluctant to say "I love you," at least with the frequency women do. Repeating this phrase daily or on demand from a woman, says Driscoll, "sounds stupid to them. After it has been said once, these gents argue, there's no reason to repeat it over and over like a trained seal yapping on cue from a handler."[5]

Here is another husband, participating with his wife in a study of love. He says:

> What does she want? Proof? She's got it, hasn't she? Would I be knocking myself out to get things for her—like to keep up this house—if I didn't love her? Why does a man do things like that if not because he loves his wife and kids? I swear, I can't figure what she wants.

But his wife says:

> It is not enough that he supports us and takes care of us. I appreciate that, but I want him to share things with me. I need for him to tell me his feelings.[6]

What men *do*, every day of their lives, simply doesn't feel like love to this wife, to Driscoll's client Paula, and to Nobody's Valentine, who knows but discounts the fact that her husband is "hard-working and decent."

The resulting misunderstandings between couples occur daily in countless households. In one study, seven couples recorded their activities and marital satisfaction for several days.[7] Every day, they noted down how often the spouse did a helpful chore, like cooking a good meal or repairing a faucet; how often the spouse expressed affection; and how satisfied they were feeling with the marriage. The wives thought their marital relations were best on days when their husbands had verbally expressed affection to them, regardless of what the husbands *did*. But the husbands' degree of satisfaction depended on their wives' deeds, not on their affectionate words!

The researchers then directed the husbands to step up the frequency of expressions of love toward their wives, and asked the wives to keep track of any such demonstrations they noticed. After a while, they called up the husbands whose wives said there had been no change, and asked them why they had not complied with instructions. One husband replied huffily that he certainly had complied . . . by washing his wife's car. The husband thought that was a perfectly good way to express his love for her, but she, of course, hadn't a clue.

The doing-versus-talking distinction in the emotional styles of males and females begins in childhood, when boys tend to develop what psychologists call "side-by-side" relationships, in which intimacy means sharing the same activity—sports, games, watching a movie or sports event together, bantering and joking. Girls tend to prefer "face-to-face" relationships, in which intimacy means revealing ideas and emotions in a heart-to-heart exchange. As adults, women may have a tough time understanding that for many men a "shared intimate activity" can be something as banal as watching TV or being in the same room together doing different things. Words are irrelevant, even superfluous. As a woman I interviewed said:

> My husband and I have a custom of reading the papers and having coffee together every morning. He loves to listen to music in the background, so the radio is usually on. I don't like the music especially—I'd rather have quiet—but I know how much he does. One morning, though, the radio was annoying me, so I got up to read the paper in the other room. My husband protested immediately—"Where are you going?" I said I was leaving so he could enjoy his concert. "Never mind the music," he said, rather crossly, "come back here and I'll turn it off." His tone made me feel cranky, until I realized what he was really saying—he'd rather share the morning with me than with the radio.

This woman is fortunate that she got his message. Being together comfortably is the soul of intimacy to him.

For most women, in contrast, intimacy rests on talk—both "deep talk" about significant feelings and worries and "small talk" about daily events. Without it, many women feel like unwatered plants; they wither. So do their relationships. A common refrain in the explanations divorced women give for the failure of their marriages is "lack of communication." A bad marriage, they say, is by definition one in which there is "no talking."[8]

Moreover, women demand a particular kind of talk. When men talk to each other or to women, they tend to discuss relatively impersonal matters, such as cars, sports, work, and politics. When they reveal anything about themselves, it tends to be their strengths and achievements. Women like to talk about personal matters, such as their feelings and relationships; they are willing, often eager, to reveal weaknesses and fears. When a woman is worried, the first thing she does is call a friend to discuss it. When a man is worried, the first thing he does is distract himself by watching TV, playing racquetball, or drinking with his buddies.

In short, some of the basic functions of talk are different for men and women. For many men, the purpose of talking about feelings and problems is to solve them; for many women, the purpose of talking is to talk—simply to share the feeling. When women report the benefits of intimate conversation, they list relief from stress, feeling better, and self-improvement. The benefits that men report are more constructive, such as getting advice or help in solving problems. Thus, when a woman describes her worries, fears, or anger about a problem, she is often seeking confirmation of her *feeling*; the man interprets her talk as a request for *help*.[9]

In her book *You Just Don't Understand*, Deborah Tannen describes the story of a woman, Eve, who had had a lump removed from her breast. Eve tells her sister, a woman friend, and her husband, Mark, how upsetting it was to undergo the operation, and how unhappy she is with the stitches and the changed contour of her breast. The sister says, "I know. When I had my operation I felt the same way." The friend says, "I know. It's like your body has

been violated." But Mark says, "You can have plastic surgery to cover up the scar and restore the shape of your breast." Mark's comment makes Eve feel hurt and angry; she thinks it means he is disgusted with how she looks. But of course he thinks *she* is disgusted with the way she looks and he wants to be helpful. "Eve wanted the gift of understanding," Tannen observes, "but Mark gave her the gift of advice. He was taking the role of problem solver, whereas she simply wanted confirmation for her feelings."[10]

Men and women speak different languages of love, but in psychotherapy, research, and popular lore, the female language has become the dominant one. Women appear to be better than men at intimacy because intimacy is defined as what women do: talk, express feelings, and disclose personal concerns. Intimacy is rarely defined as sharing activities, being helpful, doing useful work, or enjoying companionable silence. Because of this bias, men rarely get credit for the kinds of loving actions that are more typical of them.

"Part of the reason that men seem so much less loving than women," argues Francesca Cancian, a sociologist and author of *Love in America*, "is that men's behavior is measured with a feminine ruler."[11] Many social scientists, she shows, use what she calls "a feminized definition of love" in their research: For instance, they label practical activities and helping the spouse as "instrumental behavior" and expressing feelings as "affectionate behavior." This distinction, she observes, thereby denies the affectionate aspect of practical help.

Yet most men are more likely than women to agree with statements like "When she needs help I help her" and "She would rather spend her time with me than with anyone else" as evidence of the love in their relationships. Many men define "commitment" not as constant reassurances of love, but as the daily work they do to support their families. "Many working-class women agree with men that a man's job is something he does out of love for his family," Cancian observes. "But middle-class women and social scientists rarely recognize men's practical help as a form of love."[12]

. . . When men do speak for themselves, their styles of intimacy are as effective as women's in producing feelings of emotional closeness and meaningful connection. Psychologist Scott Swain conducted a study in which he defined intimacy as any action in a friendship "that connotes a positive and mutual sense of meaning and importance to the participants." The participants, not the observers, got to define what intimacy meant to them, and "any action" would do. One young man said that his most intimate experiences with other men consisted of "a lot of outdoor-type things—fishing, hunting, Tom-Sawyer-type things."[13]

Swain's interviews reveal how different male intimacy is from the female standard. Men use the degree of comfort and relaxation they feel with other men as an index of closeness, says Swain. One interviewee explained that he was "more relaxed around guys. You don't have to watch what you say. . . . I wouldn't be careful I shouldn't say something like this, or I shouldn't do this. That's because with the guys, they're just like you."[14] When asked to recall a "meaningful" time with men friends, another young man said:

> The fun things come to mind. We rented a VCR and some movies and watched those, and just all the laughing together comes to mind as most memorable. As to the most meaningful, those also come pretty close to being the most meaningful, because there was just total relaxation there. That I felt no need to worry. There's no need to worry about anyone making conversation. The conversation will come. And we can laugh at each other, and you can laugh at yourself, which is handy.[15]

When they were asked to describe the "most meaningful occasion spent with a same-sex friend," the men mentioned twenty-six events, of which twenty were spent in "an activity other than talking"— fishing, playing guitars, diving, drinking, weightlifting, winning a court case, being with a close friend whose sister had died. "Can't think of just one thing that stood out in my mind," one man said. "It was more like a push-pull type thing. Like I'd pull him through things and he'd pull me through things."[16]

Several men said that intimacy with women friends is "just talking"; the talk that women like is, to them, "the lighter side of things." For many men, actions speak louder than words and carry greater value for the friendship, as they do in love relationships. They do not need to say to each other, "I like you"; being invited to a game or another activity *means* "I like you." (Many parents try to teach their daughters this fact about boys, explaining that if a boy puts a frog in a girl's lunchbox, it means he likes her. Girls find this hard to believe.) Men convey affection to one another, adds Swain, with "physical gestures, laughing at jokes, doing one another favors, keeping in touch, 'doing stuff,' teasing, and just being around friends."[17]

Of all these expressions of affection and closeness, perhaps the one that women tend to understand least is men's language of teasing and "joking around." Here, for example, is an exchange between a worried mother and Dr. Joyce Brothers:

> Dear Dr. Brothers: Our 14-year-old son loves to tease his young sister. While he has a lively sense of humor, she often doesn't appreciate it, and this becomes the cause of some really unpleasant quarrels. Is there anything we can do about this?

Joyce Brothers, being a woman and a psychologist, uses a female yardstick to measure this boy's behavior:

> Teasing often is not simple harmless fun. It can be a way of masking hostility, a kind of hit-and-run attack. . . . Ask your son how he'd like it if he were constantly the butt of jokes or if these same tricks were played on him. . . . Discourage the "teasing" and try to get your son to explore what's behind it.[18]

Notice that the direction of the intervention here is to change the boy's way into the girl's way. Joyce Brothers does not advise the parents, "Discourage your daughter's humorlessness and try to get her to explore the reasons she takes her brother's teasing so seriously." The son *does* know what it's like to be the butt of jokes, because that is how boys and men express many of their feelings to one another. Girls and women keep looking for the meaning "behind" the jokes, a doomed enterprise that makes women seem, to men, overly literal and humorless. To many women, like Joyce Brothers, it is obvious that the boy's teasing is hostile and demeaning. To many men, it is just as obvious that the boy's teasing is his way of being affectionate while also being appropriately masculine.

Men use jokes, teasing, and "horsing around" as ways of creating bonds of cama-raderie and in-group knowledge. Jokes communicate affection (and other feelings) indirectly, so no one can accuse the speaker of being wimpy or soft; they protect the speaker from the risk of rejection (or coun-terattack) that a straightforward remark might evoke. One of my husband's golfing friends, on hearing that my husband's son would be playing with them that day, said, "That's good; I hope he's a better player than you are." It's the kind of teasing remark that few women would say to a female friend—it would be regarded as a hurtful putdown—but my husband laughed and knew it to mean "I enjoy golfing with you and like you very much, even if you do beat me more often than I like."

Among men friends, Swain concludes, joking "camouflages the hidden agenda of closeness." Most men recognize the hidden agenda, but many women do not. In Swain's study, for example, one man had learned to waterski from his best friend. He had trouble getting the knack of it, but by joking the friend removed competitive pressure and worries about failure:

> We were just able to make jokes about it, and we laughed at each other all day. And it finally worked out. I mean it was great for me to be that frustrated and that up-tight about it

and know the only thing he was going to do was laugh at me.[19]

Of course, men also use jokes to create distance and to express anger or contempt; women who encroach on traditionally male territory do not mistake the hostility behind the sexist put-downs that they are expected to tolerate with "good humor." But the ambiguity in much of male teasing is the reason that jokes are such a good disguise for love and attachment: The speaker can always claim the listener didn't understand his intention. Most males become fluent in joke-speak and its many meanings by ado-lescence. They know that "What a jerk!," coming from a friend when they fall off a bicycle, conveys amused affection, but the same remark from a passing stranger is an act of hostility.

### NOTES

1. On the inexpressive male, see Jack O. Balswick and Charles W. Peek, "The Inexpres-sive Male: A Tragedy of American Society," in *The Forty-Nine Percent Majority: The Male Sex Role*, ed. D.S. David and R. Brannon (Reading, MA: Addison-Wesley, 1976); and Mirra Komarovsky wrote of men's "trained inca-pacity to share" in *Blue-Collar Marriage* (New York: Vintage, 1964).

2. "Dear Abby," *Los Angeles Times*, March 14, 1990, p. E3.

3. This statistic is from Harper's Index, *Harper's* magazine, February 1991, p. 19. The Index cited Hallmark Cards.

4. Richard Driscoll, *The Binds That Tie* (Lex-ington, MA: Lexington Books, 1991), p. 61.

5. Ibid., p. 62.

6. This couple is cited in Francesca M. Cancian, *Love in America: Gender and Self-Development* (Cam-bridge: Cambridge University Press, 1987), p. 76.

7. Thomas A. Wills, Robert L. Weiss, and Gerald R. Patterson, "A Behavioral Analysis of the Determinants of Marital Satisfaction," *Journal of Consulting and Clinical Psychology* 42 (1974): 802–811.

8. Catherine K. Riessman, "When Gender Is Not Enough: Women Interviewing Women," *Gender and Society* 1 (1987): 97.

9. On the different functions of talk, see Robin T. Lakoff, *Talking Power: The Politics of Language* (New York: Basic Books, 1990); Daniel N. Maltz and Ruth A. Borker, "A Cultural Approach to Male-Female Miscommunication," in *Language and Social Identity*, ed. J. J. Gumperz (Cambridge: Cambridge University Press, 1982); and Deborah Tannen, *You Just Don't Understand* (New York: William Morrow, 1990).

10. Tannen, *You Just Don't Understand*, pp. 49-50.

11. Cancian, *Love in America*, p. 74.

12. Ibid., p. 76.

13. Scott Swain, "Covert Intimacy: Closeness in Men's Friendships," in *Gender in Intimate Relationships*, ed. B. J. Risman and P. Schwartz (Belmont, CA: Wadsworth, 1989).

14. Ibid., p. 75.

15. Ibid.

16. Ibid., p. 77.

17. Ibid., p. 80.

18. *Los Angeles Times*, January 28, 1991, p. C3.

19. Swain, "Covert Intimacy," p. 72.

## CRITICAL THINKING QUESTIONS

1. Why is "woman as intimacy expert" a stereotype?

2. How does this stereotype reinforce gender-role behavior in private and public "spheres of expertise"?

3. Kass argued (in the earlier selection) that women have a "natural maternal destiny" and men are "naturally promiscuous." Bellah and his colleagues maintain that both women's and men's emphasis on individual intimacy discourages long-term commitments. How does Tavris's perspective challenge both of these conclusions?

# 7 Sex and Cohabitation

## *Conservative:* Stupid Cohabitation: The Ultimate Female Self-Delusion

LAURA SCHLESSINGER, *Ten Stupid Things Women Do to Mess Up Their Lives.* © 1994 by Laura C. Schlessinger. Reprinted by permission of Villard Books, a division of Random House, Inc.

*Religious conservatives object to "shacking up" because it is sinful and immoral and trivializes the sacrament of marriage. Secular conservatives oppose cohabitation because it often results in out-of-wedlock births and in breakups rather than marriage. In addition, Laura Schlessinger maintains, women who choose living together are acting like stupid, submissive victims.*

When I began working on radio some fifteen years ago, it was rare for a caller to admit she was shacking up with a guy. There seems to have been a relaxation of values and norms. Today, living-in no longer has a stigma attached to it.

The conventional wisdom in favor of living-in before marriage is that it allows the couple to get to know each other, make a better marital choice, and lay a more solid conjugal foundation than men and women who marry cold turkey.

Could this thinking be wrong?

### IS LIVING-IN THE KISS OF DEATH TO A RELATIONSHIP?

According to psychologist David G. Myers, Ph.D., author of *The Pursuit of Happiness,* seven recent studies concur that couples who cohabit with their spouses-to-be have a higher divorce rate than those who don't. Three national surveys illustrate this: A U.S. survey of 13,000 adults found that couples who lived together before marriage were one-third more likely to separate or divorce within a decade. A Canadian national survey of 5,300 women found that those who cohabited were 54 percent more likely to divorce within fifteen years. And a Swedish study of 4,300 women found cohabitation linked with an 80 percent greater risk of divorce.

### WHY PLAY RUSSIAN ROULETTE WITH YOUR LIFE?

Now, you and I both know how easy it is to discount all that data! You simply say, "But my situation is different."

Well, for some of you, that's true! There are those successful transitions. It happens. But it is not the rule. So why are you willing, even eager, to play Russian roulette with your life? Why? Desperation. Fear of not having somebody—of not having a life if a man doesn't want you.

In our dialogues you always come to admit it. How about saving yourself the stress of finding it out the hard way?

Perhaps waiting and growing in maturity, independence, and security-of-self are too tough to do—especially when you are young and needy and hoping to escape an unhappy past.

## I LOVE HIM, BUT I JUST DON'T TRUST HIM . . .

Jessica, a nineteen-year-old aspiring dancer, came from a troubled family in which her father had played around. Her upbringing had provided her with very little security and an exaggerated inability to trust. Despite that, she had been living with her boyfriend for four months and claimed she was in love with him, although she had trouble believing in his caring and fidelity. In her words, she was "hoping for something beautiful," i.e., marriage, as proof of his caring.

I pointed out to Jessica that she was very insecure and that part of what often makes very young women move in with a man early is their hope that by association (preferably marriage) with the fellow, they will feel better about themselves and about life. And you know something? It never, never works that way.

## LIVING-IN AS A RETARDANT TO MATURITY

Jessica's primary job is to build her self-esteem and competency, so that when she chooses somebody, it isn't out of a desperate need to heal the hurts of the past. It should be out of a desire to share herself, her life's experience. And that's why, in the long run, I don't think personal maturity is benefited by these living-in arrangements—especially at Jessica's age and with her history of loss and betrayal.

## WHEN HOPE CAN HURT YOU

There are exceptions to everything in life, infinite combinations and permutations to experience. For the most part, living-in is usually entered into, as Jessica did, with fantasy and hopefulness and an agenda that isn't even admitted to the self. Look at Jessica's "wanting something beautiful." There is almost inevitably the vain hope that being with a man will make something magical happen.

And Jessica's not alone in that. Everybody fantasizes at some time about bypassing the hard work of growing up and growing stronger.

But nobody can—not if they want to find some fulfillment in this life. When Jessica does the work and learns to take care of herself, she won't have to hope for something beautiful. She'll be creating it.

## ONLY YOU CAN MAKE YOU HAPPY

Listen, the phrase is "happily ever after." All of us girls grew up with that promise. So when you're an unhappy young girl, what better remedy than living-in with a man? The problem is that happiness just isn't won that easily—and it's not a matter of who *you* are with but who *he* is with (i.e., you!).

You and only you have the power, the sole power, to make you happy. When you blindly leap for a man, you generally end up repeating, reliving, the pain you've been trying to flee. That's why Jessica is agonizing over not being able to trust her man no matter what her instinct tells her.

## DENIAL AND LIVING-IN

Denial is a big factor in this living-in arrangement. And the styles of that denial—as you'll see in the course of this chapter—run the gamut from denial of one's own true needs and wants to denial of what he is about.

One quote from a caller named Jane highlights the latter: "I feel he does love me, but he holds back" is her explanation for the live-in boyfriend's desire to sex-swap with other couples. Sadly, she goes on to say, "I might do that for him if I knew how we stood . . ."

## IF HE REALLY LOVED ME, WOULDN'T HE MARRY ME?

Moving in with a man when you don't know how he feels is to try to make him feel something toward you. That's demeaning and stupid. It is about you auditioning.

Diana knew that. She and her boyfriend had been together for over a year and had been living together for five months. Although she claimed they constantly talked about marriage, a truer version would be that the "they" was really her. Her lover responded to her entreaties by saying he wanted to marry her but he didn't know when because he didn't "feel ready." . . .

## WHAT AM I STILL DOING HERE IF HE DOESN'T WANT ME?

Jean, thirty, a part-time student with an independent income, had been living rent-free with her boyfriend for a year and a half. Prior to that, she'd been separated from her now ex-husband and hadn't been meeting many men. When she connected with her present guy and they became close, she thought, Well, this seems to feel good. "So we became closer, and I moved in." At this point, I couldn't figure out why she'd called.

As she talked, the reality of her situation became increasingly upsetting. Although Jean had no children, the man's seventeen- and thirteen-year-olds were living with them, but the father was adamant—sometimes almost violent—about Jean keeping her distance from them.

"What does that mean?" I asked her. "You're not supposed to talk to them? Give them orders?"

"He doesn't want me to participate in their lives at all," she replied. "He always tells me, 'I just want you to take care of me. Don't worry about them.'"

I still wasn't absolutely certain why Jean had called—until she mentioned that her man "goes through spells" when he wants her to leave, then relents. When she added, "I try to convince him that we have so much going for each other," I told her, "You can't convince somebody of that. They are the measure of what they think and feel. Having that argument is a waste of time and demeaning to you." . . .

## LIVING-IN = GIVING IN

Women, remember, self-esteem is centered in the will to overcome circumstance, not to give in to being overcome. As in Jean's case, the giving in often takes the form of living-in. The results may be twofold: a roof over the head—and a sinkhole under the heart. Women have to know of their alternatives to selling themselves. And they have to be able to use their courage and creativity in ways that make them choosers, not beggars.

## DON'T EVER SETTLE FOR LESS

Women ask me quite often how to get a man to respect them, to treat them with respect. My answer is always the same: Never settle for or permit less. If he can't rise to that occasion, dump him. Conversions only come from within. But some women just don't seem to get that message. They just keep hopin' and tryin', like Yolanda.

## I THOUGHT I WAS IN A MONOGAMOUS RELATIONSHIP!

Yolanda, a thirty-eight-year-old social-services technician, called to discuss the fact that her live-in boyfriend of three years had admitted to spending the weekend with another woman. She was horrified that her fantasies of a monogamous relationship were dashed now that she knew he was fooling around.

I pointed out to Yolanda that when you move in with a man without a commitment, he already knows one crucial thing: He doesn't have to do much to get you. Then he fools around, and you stay, and he learns something more: He doesn't have to do much to keep you, either. And that has to be crushing to your self-respect.

Yolanda came across as a nice person, educated, a professional, who meant something in the world. I urged her to hold out for the right man, a man who would make a commitment to her, and added that she wasn't going to find one while she was frittering away her time—out of desperation—with a man who didn't seem to respect her or to be interested in pleasing her—only himself. She was clearly furious at him and disillusioned and had the financial means to move out. I only hope she had the emotional ones as well.

## MAKE NO MISTAKE, COMMITMENT *IS* A BIG DEAL

Now, you might well argue: "Big deal, a commitment. Commitments don't stop people from being abusive, unloving, unfaithful, or just plain annoying. Commitments don't even stop people from dumping each other. So—big deal."

Well, the statistics prove that commitment is a big deal; as I quoted earlier in this chapter, ". . . . compared to couples who don't cohabit with their spouses-to-be, those who do have higher divorce rates."

## A SOLID FOUNDATION REQUIRES TIME, EFFORT, AND SACRIFICE

The interesting question is Why? There are probably many forces at work here, worthy of a book to itself, but I feel strongly that the main contributors are maturity, patience, and the ability to postpone gratification.

When people aren't willing to put in the time and effort to build a foundation, to build something solid and meaningful, they are usually not the ones to persist with effort and sacrifice to develop it and keep it going.

Having sex-too-soon, moving in without commitments or life plans in concert, are the behaviors of basically immature, let-me-feel-good-right-now-because-I-want-it-therefore-it-is kind of people. The immaturity has to do also with not having developed an esteem and identity that permit you to be right out there with the truth of your needs and feelings.

You're scared, so you play it "safe." And then you find out that *safe* doesn't always have the big payoff! That's what my caller Sharon found out.

## WHEN YOU WANT A FAMILY AND HE DOESN'T

Sharon told me she had originally decided to move in with her boyfriend because she wanted "to get to know him better." And in fact, over the course of a couple of years, they had become close. In her words, "It's the ultimate, ideal relationship. He's wonderful to me and I believe I am to him. We are very supportive of each other, have a lot in common, and we enjoy each other's company." So why was she calling?

The problem was that Sharon had moved in without marriage in her mind (consciously, at least), and the subject hadn't been discussed. Now she found herself wanting marriage and a family, but her boyfriend didn't feel he was up to the enhanced responsibilities. And he was emphatic about it. In order not to rock the boat, Sharon seemed willing to put her own desires on the back burner, but I cautioned her that as time passed, she might get increasingly frustrated—and angry at him.

"And that isn't fair," I advised her, "because every step of the way, you made the choices. Like many women, you've been lying to yourself in the hope that the relationship will evolve. That's a calculated risk. If you're able to erase the notion of marriage and babies from your mind, that's one thing. But if you're kidding yourself in order not to lose him, that's a mistake!

## IMMEDIATE LOSSES/LONG-TERM GAINS

Imagine the choices Sharon is now facing— agonizing choices: to leave a satisfying relationship or not; to leave someone she loves and enjoys to seek another who will more match what she now dares to dream—marriage and family. The immediate losses are obvious. The long-term gain is unpredictable. Often, when a woman states her intent to jump ship, suddenly the man, not wanting to experience great loss either, decides to start paddling faster.

## GOOD DECISIONS
## REQUIRE OBJECTIVITY

Nonetheless, as we go through life, growing, changing, maturing, this type of crossroads experience is expected, typical, and human. No surprise. That's not the element that concerns me—that's just real life. My concern is that when relationships prematurely take on elements of sexuality and living-in, it makes it more difficult to have the objectivity required to make good decisions.

## YOU'RE TOO BUSY MAKING SURE
## HE WANTS YOU TO QUESTION
## WHETHER YOU WANT HIM

Women do not move in to check out the guy from closer range. Women move in to be protected, taken care of, to be wanted. And when you are in that mind-set, you can't for a moment wonder (especially not out loud) if you even want the guy—you're too busy making sure he wants you.

Controlling, petty, selfish, insecure, destructive, immature, and hurtful behaviors of the man in question become things to work around rather than qualities to examine to decide on his worthiness to you! It is harder to ask yourself the very important question "Is this how I want to live the rest of my life?" when you are already dug in!

## DATING AS A LEASE WITH
## AN OPTION TO BUY

Dating—not living-in—is supposed to be about learning and discerning. Dating is supposed to be a kind of lease with option—so don't get sexual and cohabit right away and change the meaning of dating to a "lease with premature obligations" situation!

## THE RETURN OF THE LIVING DREAD:
## "BUT I . . ."

Since our dating and love chapters we haven't invoked the old reliable "But he said," as motivation for our stupid choices. Let's do it now.

Dana, a thirty-three-year-old divorcée with two children, called to say she was considering leaving a five-year relationship. She and her kids were living with the boyfriend, who had a problem: He was not divorced. "He's been pretty much back and forth for several years," she told me, "because, I'd say, of guilt. He is very Catholic. I'm not. Maybe that's just an excuse I . . . anyway, I feel like I'm coaching him all the time, 'Did you talk to the attorney? Did you talk to the therapist?'"

To make matters worse, his wife wouldn't allow his kids to visit his new household, which meant that any time the fellow spent with them, such as holidays, were awful for Dana and her daughters. "And if he is with us, he might as well not be because he's so depressed," Dana told me. "And in this past year he has done nothing legally to change things."

When I asked her why she moved in to begin with, she responded, "Because he kept telling me everything was going to change. And I . . . I just believed him." To which I countered, "That's like jumping off the end of a swimming pool, saying, 'He told me there would be water in it by the time I hit bottom!'"

## YOU DON'T REALLY HAVE
## A MAN, ANYWAY

This is what I advised Dana: "I think that no matter what he does to straighten himself out, you and the children have got to get your own place and start leading your own lives. That would be a better climate for your kids—first of all, because I don't think the decisions you are making are good for them. I think it would be a step forward from where you are now. Especially in terms of maturity and how to handle grown-up situations of commitment and attachment.

"Dana, he is weak, and you've made it easy for him. You must know by now, it doesn't matter what he promises. Until he has fixed his life and shown some strength and integrity and maturity to handle that appropriately, you don't have much of a man anyway."

## I FEEL GREAT ABOUT MOVING
## IN—EXCEPT FOR THESE
## NAGGING DOUBTS . . .

Nicole knew I wasn't an advocate of living-in when she called, but she claimed, as many do, "We have a little bit more of a situation than that." Whatever that meant—because when I asked her directly, "Nicole, are you trying to convince yourself to move in?" she responded, "Well, I want to—but there is still a part of me that is hesitating."

DR. LAURA: Listen to that part of you. When you guys are both ready to make that commitment, make it! The indication is that living-in doesn't work if you think it's supposed to help you work on how to be together. And I've got to tell you I think it's a stupid idea. The only reason I would live with somebody is if I didn't want to get married.

NICOLE: Well, I do want to marry him. But he says it's a big step for him.

DR. LAURA: Then wait till he's ready to take that step. A commitment is a social statement and an inner promise—if he's not ready, pretending that he is by moving in won't make it so!

NICOLE: I'm trying to compromise.

DR. LAURA: I don't even believe I heard you say that! No compromise, honey. Don't you compromise yourself. If you want to get married and you feel this is the guy, date him, enjoy him, and see if in time you both feel the desire for that commitment. If he doesn't want to get married and you do and you move in to play marriage, you really have compromised—and gained nothing.

NICOLE: I think I knew all this!

DR. LAURA: Well, you certainly knew how I felt about this living-in issue before you called. So maybe you wanted some confirmation. Good for you! And don't back down when he flashes his baby browns at you. Okay?

NICOLE: Okay, thanks.

## HE'S THE ONE WHO SHOULD FEEL
## GUILTY, NOT YOU!

So he says it is a big step for him and she is supposed to feel guilty and greedy for wanting more. Women, don't let yourselves be beguiled and manipulated by that. And don't tolerate the injunction that you are being manipulative. Grown-ups should know that they don't get the goodies legitimately unless they have earned them. Look out for the word *compromise* if it ends up meaning you give up what is precious to you so that maybe you'll get what you want later.

You will live to regret it—Jackie did!

## LIVING TOGETHER AND MATURITY GO HAND IN HAND

To sum up: People have problems. There are no relationships without problems. The issue is whether people have the maturity and the commitment to hang in there with each other and work out the problems. Or do they have the inner strength and courage to admit to a mistake and let go. That's what makes the difference.

A living-in arrangement does not inherently have that kind of commitment; nor is it a further step in that direction. Living-in is more a convenience and a fantasy; typically the former for men, the latter for women. As you've surely guessed by now, I'm very agin' it. Let's get pragmatic: Statistics show that living-in doesn't ensure a quality, long-lasting marriage, probably because the attitude of one of the partners is more "Let's see if this feels good to me every day," and the attitude of the other is "I'll be careful, lest he not feel good about me today." The true tragedy is when the more-available sex brings forth a child into this situation. The child usually ends up the product of a never-was but still-broken home.

## LOVE IS ABOUT A LOT MORE THAN PASSION

So, couples have problems. But with maturity, caring, and commitment, they can get through them. Those are the relationships that last and grow into love. Because love isn't instant. It takes years and working through problems together and growth and nurturing each other's growth. That's what grows love, and it involves a lot more than passion. It takes commitment.

### CRITICAL THINKING QUESTIONS

1. Schlessinger maintains that women shack up not because they love the guy but because they're stupid. Why does she reach this conclusion? What evidence does she use to support her argument?

2. Are there other explanations for women's cohabitation besides those that Schlessinger posits?

3. Are there any *advantages* for women and *disadvantages* for men in living-in arrangements that Schlessinger doesn't address?

# 7    Sex and Cohabitation

## *Centrist:* How Therapists Threaten Marriages

WILLIAM J. DOHERTY, "How Therapists Threaten Marriages," *The Responsive Community* 7:3 (Summer 1997): 31–42.

*Should you or someone you know seek counseling if the marriage is in trouble? Probably not, according to William J. Doherty, because marital therapy can be hazardous to one's health. Doherty maintains that many therapists are morally neutral, have been trained to work primarily with individuals rather than couples, and are likely to give up prematurely on the marital therapy and the marriage itself.*

Soon after her wedding Marsha felt something was terribly wrong with her marriage. She and her husband Paul had moved across the country following a big church wedding in their home town. Marsha was obsessed with fears that she had made a big mistake in marrying Paul. She focused on Paul's ambivalence about the Christian faith, his avoidance of personal topics of communication, and his tendency to criticize her when she expressed her worries and fears. Marsha sought help at the university student counseling center where she and Paul were graduate students. The counselor worked with her alone for a few sessions and then invited Paul in for marital therapy. Paul, who was frustrated and angry about how distant and fretful Marsha had become, was a reluctant participant in the counseling.

In addition to the marital problems, Marsha was suffering from clinical depression: she could not sleep or concentrate, she felt sad all the time, and she felt like a failure. Medication began to relieve some of these symptoms, but she was still upset about the state of her marriage. After a highly charged session with this distressed wife and angry, reluctant husband, the counselor met with Marsha separately the next week. She told Marsha that she would not recover fully from her depression until she started to "trust her feelings" about the marriage. What follows is how Marsha later recounted the conversation with the counselor:

MARSHA: What do you mean, trust my feelings?

COUNSELOR: You know you are not happy in your marriage.

MARSHA: Yes, that's true.

COUNSELOR: Perhaps you need a separation in order to figure out whether you really want this marriage.

MARSHA: But I love Paul and I am committed to him.

COUNSELOR: The choice is yours, but I doubt that you will begin to feel better until you start to trust your feelings and pay attention to your unhappiness.

MARSHA: Are you saying I should get a divorce?

COUNSELOR: I'm just urging you to trust your feelings of unhappiness.

A stunned Marsha decided not to return to that counselor, a decision the counselor no doubt perceived as reflecting Marsha's unwillingness to take responsibility for her own happiness.

Two aspects of Marsha and Paul's case stand out. First, the couple saw a counselor who was not well trained in marital therapy. Any licensed mental health professional can dabble in marital therapy, but most therapists are far more comfortable working with individuals. When marriage problems are formidable or the course of treatment difficult, these therapists pull the plug on the conjoint sessions (involving both spouses) in favor of separate individual therapy sessions. Often they refer one of the spouses to a colleague for separate individual therapy, with this rationale: "You both have too many individual problems to be able to work on your relationship at this point." Of course, the couple is living together in this relationship seven days a week and has no choice but to "work on it" continually.

The unspoken reason for this shift in treatment modality, especially if it occurs early in the marital therapy, is generally that the therapist feels incompetent with the case, especially in dealing with a reluctant husband who is not therapy-savvy and says he is there only to salvage his marriage. This husband lacks a personal, psychological agenda. When he gets turfed off to another therapist to do his "individual" work, he balks, thereby confirming to his wife and her therapist that he is unwilling to work on his own "issues"' and thereby do his part to save the marriage. The marriage is often doomed at this point, an iatrogenic effect of poor marital therapy.

The second noteworthy feature of Marsha and Paul's case is the strong indi-

vidualistic and anti-commitment orientation of the therapist. Like most psychotherapists, she viewed only the individual as her client. She perceived no responsibilities beyond promoting this individual's immediate needs and agenda. The therapist not only ignored obligations to other stakeholders in the client's life, but also did not give proper weight to the role that sustained commitments play in making our lives satisfying over the long run. No doubt the therapist viewed herself as "neutral" on the issue of marital commitment. But, as I pointed out in *Soul Searching: Why Psychotherapy Must Promote Moral Responsibility*, claiming neutrality on commitment and other moral issues in American society means that the therapist likely embraces the reigning ethic of individualism. There is nothing neutral about asking a newly married, depressed woman, "Are you happy in your marriage?" and urging her to trust her frightened and confused feelings. No self-respecting therapist would urge a suicidal patient to "trust your feelings about how worthless your life is," but many well-regarded therapists play cheerleader for a divorce even when the couple has not yet made a serious effort to understand their problems and restore the health of their marriage. Therapist-assisted marital suicide has become part of the standard paradigm of contemporary psychotherapy.

A postscript to this case: Marsha talked to her priest during this crisis. The priest urged her to wait to see if her depression was causing the marital problem or if the marital problem was causing the depression—a prudent bit of advice. But a few minutes later, the priest brought up the possibility of an annulment if the marriage was causing the depression. Marsha was even more stunned than she had been by the therapist.

Some marriages, of course, are dead on arrival in the therapist's office, in which case the therapist's job is to help with the healthiest possible untangling for all involved parties, especially the children.

Some marriages are emotionally and physically abusive, with little chance for recovery. Some marriages appear salvageable, but one of the parties has already made up his or her mind to leave. I am not suggesting that the therapist harangue the reluctant spouse or urge an abused wife to keep her commitment in the face of debilitating abuse. Divorce is a necessary safety valve for terminally ill marriages, and in some cases, divorce is what morality demands. (I think of a woman who discovered her husband and co-parent was a pedophile, and he would not seek treatment.) My critique focuses on the practice of therapists, many of whom lack good skills in helping couples, and who philosophically view marriage as a venue for personal fulfillment stripped of ethical obligation, and similarly view divorce as a strictly private, self-interested choice with no important stakeholders other than the individual adult client.

### HOW DID WE GET HERE?

Marriage counseling (now termed "marital therapy" in the profession) was born in the 1930s and 1940s in an era of worry about the viability of modern "companionate" marriages. The early marriage counselors were mostly gynecologists, educators, and clergy. Of course psychiatrists treated many distressed married people, but did not see their primary responsibility as assisting the marriage. It was not until the 1950s that marriage counselors began to work with both spouses together in one session. Prior to then, it was considered inappropriate treatment, and even unethical, to have both partners in the sessions, because this would destroy the powerful one-to-one psychological transference dynamics deemed necessary for successful treatment of the individual problems that were feeding the marital problems.

During the 1950s and early 1960s, "conjoint" marriage counseling became more widespread as therapists began to appreciate the power of working on relationship patterns directly in the session. The American Association of Marriage Counselors grew in numbers as credentialed psychotherapists joined clergy who specialized in marriage counseling. Interestingly, marriage counseling as a professional activity developed independently of "family therapy," which grew out of psychiatry's experiments with family treatment for mental health disorders. (Only in the 1970s did the associations of marriage counselors and family therapists merge into the American Association for Marriage and Family Therapy.)

Prior to the U.S. cultural revolution of the late 1960s and 1970s, many marital therapists saw their task as saving marriages. Divorce was seen as an unequivocal treatment failure. There was little recognition of spouse abuse and the ways in which a stable but destructive marriage can undermine spouses' emotional health and create domestic hell for children. The individual tended to get lost in the marriage. Early feminist critics of marital therapy were quick to point out how this treatment approach could be dangerous to a woman's health. Women were often held responsible for the problems, since family relationships were supposed to be their forte, and women were implicitly encouraged to follow the then-popular cultural value that parents should stay together for the sake of the children. In addition, some clergy counselors added a religious rationale to the support of stable marriages, to the dismay of critics who saw this as making people feel guilty before God for salvaging their mental and physical health from a toxic marriage.

Research and professional literature on marital therapy burgeoned during the 1970s, during the era of skyrocketing divorce rates. Sobered by feminist critics and enamored with the 1970s cult of individual fulfillment, marital therapists largely rejected the "marriage saver" image. The 1980s brought a wealth of research studies on marital communication, marital distress, and effective treatment techniques. Marital therapists who were trained in these new techniques viewed themselves as performing a form of mental health treatment that not only helped marriages but also the individual well-being of the spouses. But on the value of preserving marital commitment if possible, the field was mostly "neutral"—which means embracing a contractual, individualist model of commitment. A decision about divorce became just like any other lifestyle decision such as changing jobs; the therapist's job entailed simply helping people sort out their needs and priorities.

As therapists during the 1970s and 1980s experienced their own divorces and those of colleagues, they increasingly saw divorce as a bona fide lifestyle option and a potential pathway to personal growth. The self-help books written by therapists reflected this positive orientation to divorce. In the term coined by Barbara Dafoe Whitehead in her book *The Divorce Culture*, therapists followed the popular culture in embracing the "expressive divorce" as an enlightened way to start a new life when the old marriage was in disrepair. Although they were concerned for a couple's children, most therapists believed that children would do fine if their parents did what was best for themselves. I term this "trickle down psychological economics," which works for the children just as well as the other trickle down model has worked for the poor in American society.

### WHERE WE ARE TODAY

The 1990s have witnessed marital therapy become mainstream as more professionals practice it, more couples seek it out, and some insurance companies pay for it. National political leaders make no apologies for having benefited from marriage (and family) therapy. The decade of the 1990s has also seen a movement back toward espousing the value of marital commitment and the therapist's role in pro-

moting it. This was first seen in Michele Weiner-Davis's early 1990s work on solution-oriented therapy for highly distressed couples. "Divorce Busting" is what she titled her training workshops, and later her popular book. She and others began to take a deliberately pro-marriage stance, much to the dismay of established leaders in the field. Having come to a "middle" point of encouraging neither divorce nor staying together, many leaders in marital therapy saw this new pro-marriage stance as a conservative backlash against feminism and emancipated individualism. If marriage and divorce are primarily lifestyle choices, and if a bad but stable marriage is destructive for all involved, why should therapists be in the business of saving marriages?

In the 1990s—a decade of backlashes and counter-backlashes—there has also been an assault on the use of the term "marriage" among scholars and practitioners. The critique is that "marriage" marginalizes cohabiting couples and especially gay and lesbian couples. Most marital therapists, when giving professional presentations, use the term "couples therapy" or "couples counseling." The list of presentations at national conferences of marriage and family therapists contains multiple references to "couples" and scant references to "marriage." I have no doubt that the profession of marriage and family therapy (now credentialed in 37 states as an independent mental health profession) would take a different name if it were being created in the late 1990s. "Family" is still okay, as long as a variety of family structures are included in the definition, but "marriage" is out because it is not inclusive.

This trend away from using the word "marriage" is unfortunate, because the term "couple" carries no connotations of moral commitment and lifetime covenant. My daughter and her boyfriend were a "couple" during their summer after high school, but the relationship did not survive their going to different colleges. Is this relationship morally equivalent to Marsha and Paul's, or to a long-married couple with children? Even if we use the term "committed couple" or "committed relationship," we beg the question of how deep and permanent the commitment. Rather than lower the bar for marital commitment by abandoning the term "marriage," why not expand the definition of marriage to include gay and lesbian couples who wish to make a permanent, moral commitment to each other? Why not make the marriage umbrella larger without sacrificing its essential values, instead of folding the umbrella and watering down the precious moral dimension of this unique, for-better-or-for-worse human relationship?

## GIVING COMMITMENT ITS DUE

My own work has offered a communitarian critique of the individualist ethic of psychotherapy in the United States. Although the focus of this article is on marital therapy as a treatment modality, I believe that all psychotherapy for individuals who are married is, in part, marital therapy, even if only one spouse participates. This is because issues of personal need versus marital bonds and obligations are inevitably present in individual therapy. Furthermore, I am convinced that there is widespread and invisible harm done to marriages by many individual-oriented psychotherapists. Consider the following example:

Monica was stunned when Rob, her husband of 18 years, announced that he was having an affair with her best friend and wanted an "open marriage." When Monica declined this invitation, Rob bolted from the house and was found the next day wandering around aimlessly in a nearby woods. He spent two weeks in a mental hospital for an acute, psychotic depression, and was released to outpatient treatment. Although he claimed during his hospitalization that he wanted a divorce, his therapist had the good sense to urge him to not make any major decisions until he was feeling better. Meanwhile, Monica was

beside herself with grief, fear, and anger. She had two young children at home, a demanding job, and was struggling with lupus, a chronic illness she had been diagnosed with 12 months earlier. Indeed, Rob had never been able to cope with her diagnosis, or with his own job loss six months afterward. (He was now working again.)

Clearly, this couple had been through huge stresses in the past year, including a relocation to a different city where they had no support systems in place. Rob was acting in a completely uncharacteristic way for a former straight-arrow man with strong religious and moral values. Monica was depressed, agitated, and confused. She sought out recommendations to find the best psychotherapist available in her city. He turned out to be a highly regarded clinical psychologist. Rob was continuing in individual outpatient psychotherapy, while living alone in an apartment. He still wanted a divorce.

As Monica later recounted the story, her therapist, after two sessions of assessment and crisis intervention, suggested that she pursue the divorce that Rob said he wanted. She resisted, pointing out that this was a long-term marriage with young children, and that she was hoping that the real Rob would reemerge from his midlife crisis. She suspected that the affair with her friend would be short-lived (which it was). She was angry and terribly hurt, she said, but determined to not give up on an 18-year marriage after only one month of hell. The therapist, according to Monica, interpreted her resistance to "moving on with her life" as stemming from her inability to "grieve" for the end of her marriage. He then connected this inability to grieve to the loss of her mother when Monica was a small child; Monica's difficulty in letting go of a failed marriage stemmed from unfinished mourning from the death of her mother.

Fortunately, Monica had the strength to fire the therapist. Not many clients would be able to do that, especially in the face of such expert pathologizing of their moral commitment. And equally fortunately, she and Rob found a good marital therapist who saw them through their crisis and onward to a recovered and ultimately healthier marriage.

This kind of appalling therapist behavior occurs every day in clinical practice. A depressed wife of a verbally abusive husband who was not dealing well with his Parkinson's Disease was told at the end of the first, and only, therapy session that her husband would never change and that she would either have to live with the abuse or get out. She was grievously offended that this young therapist was so cavalier about her commitment to a man she had loved for 40 years, and who was now infirm with Parkinson's Disease. She came to me to find a way to salvage a committed but nonabusive marriage. When I invited her husband to join us, he turned out to be more flexible than the other therapist had imagined. He too was committed to the marriage and needed his wife immensely.

These illustrations should not be dismissed as examples of random bad therapy or incompetent therapists. They stem from a pervasive bias among many individual-oriented therapists against sustaining marital commitment in the face of a now-toxic relationship. From this perspective, abandoning a bad marriage is akin to selling a mutual fund that, although once good for you, is now a money loser. The main techniques of this kind of therapy are twofold: (a) walk clients through a cost-benefit analysis with regards to staying married—what is in it for me to stay or leave? and (b) ask clients if they are happy and if not, then why are they staying married? If those questions yield what appears to be an irrational commitment in the face of marital pathology, as the therapist believed to be true for Monica, then the therapist falls back on pathologizing the reasons for this commitment. It takes extraordinary conviction to weather such "help" from a therapist.

These therapist questions and observations are value-laden wolves in neutral sheep's clothing. The cost-benefit questions in particular brook no consideration of the needs of anyone else in this decision. I was trained in the 1970s to dismiss clients' spontaneous moral language ("I don't know if a divorce would be fair to the children") by telling them that if parents take care of themselves, the children will do fine. And then I would move the conversation back to the safer ground of self-interest. That's how most of us learned to do therapy years ago, and it's still widespread practice.

## A COMMUNITARIAN APPROACH TO MARITAL THERAPY

The first plank in a communitarian platform for marital therapy would be for therapists, both those who work only with individuals and those who work with couples, to recognize and affirm the moral nature of marital commitment. This stance moves therapists beyond the guise of neutrality, which in fact covers an implicit contractual, self-interested approach to marital commitment. Divorce, from a communitarian perspective, is sometimes necessary when great harm would be caused by staying in the marriage. Particularly in the presence of minor children, the decision to divorce would be akin to amputating a limb; to be avoided if at all possible by sustained, alternative treatments, but pursued if necessary to save the person's life.

The second plank affirms that personal health and psychological well-being are indeed central dimensions of marriage and important goals of therapy. There is no inherent contradiction between emphasizing the moral nature of marital commitment and promoting the value of personal satisfaction and autonomy within the marital relationship. These moral and personal elements together define the unique power of marriage in contemporary life.

The third plank is that it is a fundamental moral obligation to seek marital therapy when marital distress is serious enough to threaten the marriage. We need a cultural ethic that would make it just as irresponsible to terminate a marriage without seeking professional help as it would be to let someone die without seeing a physician.

The fourth plank holds that promoting marital health should be seen as an important part of health care, because we now know the medical and psychological ravages of failed marriages for most adults and children. And the health care system should support this kind of treatment as an essential part of health care, instead of regarding marital therapy as an "uncovered benefit."

The fifth plank concerns the importance of education for marriage and early intervention to prevent serious marital problems. We need a public health campaign to monitor the health of the nation's marriages and to promote community efforts to help couples enhance the knowledge, attitudes, values, and skills needed to make caring, collaborative, and committed marriage possible. There are many well-tested courses and programs in marriage education across the country that can fill this need. Information about these courses and programs needs to be disseminated.

The sixth plank asserts that therapists should help spouses hold each other accountable for treating their spouse in a fair and caring way in the marriage. Although commitment is the linchpin of marriage, justice and caring are essential moral elements as well. A communitarian approach to marital therapy would incorporate feminist insights into gender-based inequality in contemporary marriages. It would be sensitive to how women are often expected to assume major responsibility for the marriage and the children, and then are criticized for being over-responsible. When a husband declines to do his fair share of family work on the grounds that "it's not my thing," the therapist should see this as a cop-out from his moral responsibilities, not just as a self-interested bargaining position with his

wife. Communitarians promote more than marital stability; they promote caring, collaborative, and equitable marital unions that are good for the well-being of the spouses as individuals.

The seventh plank is based on the prevalence of therapist-assisted marital suicide. We need a consumer awareness movement about the potential hazards of individual or marital therapy to the well-being of a marriage. Consumers should be given guidelines about how to interview a potential therapist on the phone, with questions such as "What are your values about the importance of keeping a marriage together when there are problems?" If the therapist responds only with the rhetoric of individual self-determination ("I try to help both parties decide what they need to do for themselves"), the consumer can ask if the therapist has any personal values about the importance of marital commitment. If the therapist hedges, then call another therapist. (Look elsewhere too if the therapist says that marriages should be held together no matter what the consequences.) Consumers should also be aware that many therapists who primarily work with individuals are not competent in marital therapy and thus are likely to give up prematurely on the marital therapy and the marriage itself. It is best to see a therapist who has had special training in working with couples.

Many therapists are now reconsidering their approach to marital commitment. They have been entranced by a cultural mirage about what constitutes the good life in the late 20th century, and they are beginning to rethink their ill-begotten moral neutrality in the face of disturbing levels of family and community breakdown. A communitarian critique and reformulation of marital therapy can point the way to a new kind of marriage covenant that views moral responsibility, sustained commitments, and personal fulfillment as a garment seamlessly sewn, not a piece of Velcro designed for ease of separation.

## CRITICAL THINKING QUESTIONS

1. What does Doherty mean when he says that many therapists are morally neutral on the issue of marital commitment? Why does he see such neutrality as a problem?

2. On the one hand, individualism is a highly prized characteristic ("Make up *your* own mind" or "Do what *you* think is right"). On the other hand, Doherty blames the "individualistic ethic of marital therapy in the United States" for ruining many salvageable marriages. Does Doherty's position suggest that marriage requires giving up one's individual rights?

3. Among his communitarian "planks," Doherty endorses marriage education programs across the country. Is it possible, however, that such programs might increase the likelihood of cohabitation and discourage getting married because marriage may seem too daunting?

# 7    Sex and Cohabitation

## *Liberal/Feminist:* Why Get Married?

ANDREA MARTIN, "Why Get Married?" *The Utne Reader* (January/February 1996): 17–18. Reprinted by permission from *Utne Reader* and the author.

*In the previous articles, Schlessinger accuses women of being "stupid" for cohabiting rather than marrying, and Doherty implies that incompetent marital therapists encourage divorce, and, consequently, cohabitation. In contrast, Andrea Martin contends that "living in sin" makes sense because U.S. economic policies reward cohabitation but penalize marriage and remarriage.*

About 3.5 million unmarried opposite-sex couples are living together in the United States today, up from 2 million a decade ago. If you think this is merely an explosion of passionate anti-authoritarianism, guess again: Many of the couples who are joining the boom may simply be making a sound fiscal decision.

Some observers link the widespread acceptance of cohabitation with recognition that the economics of marriage are often unfavorable. To begin with, there's a 50 percent chance that a marriage will fail, and divorce is expensive. Beyond that, tax laws and other government policies—in a country that says it wants strong families—may actually be discouraging marriage.

It's well known that the poor are often victims of tax and government-benefit marriage penalties. When marriage reduces welfare eligibility, many decide against it. In addition, as Joseph Spiers notes in *Fortune* (July 11, 1994), married low-wage workers may be at an income-tax disadvantage. For example, the standard deduction and Earned Income Credit are often lower for working couples than for two singles.

Spiers concludes that "the task of welfare reform might get easier if government first removes this disincentive to build stable families."

The problem persists higher up on the economic ladder, too. In *Forbes* (May 22, 1995), Janet Novack describes tax penalties that affect well-to-do couples, including income taxes higher than singles pay and business expense ceilings that don't double for marrieds. "[Had] Congress set about to create a tax code to encourage people to avoid marriage, it could scarcely have done a better job," says Novack. She concludes: "We hate to say it, but if you are a prosperous person contemplating marriage with a well-heeled partner, maybe you should forget the ceremony and just move in together."

Middle-aged couples of more modest means face another hurdle if either partner is divorced or widowed and has college-age children. Colleges routinely include stepparents' income in calculating whether a student will receive financial aid and, if so, how much. This forces potential stepparents to take on burdensome responsibilities for children who are not their own, and it may result in the denial of aid. Divorced parents have to decide between remarriage and their children's education.

In the American Association of Retired Persons magazine *Modern Maturity* (May/June 1995), Linda Stern describes the various marriage and remarriage penalties that threaten older people: Social Security earnings limits, capital gains exclusions on home sales, and Medicaid eligibility limits, for example. As a result, unmarried couples quietly move in together and enjoy companionship, while long-married couples sometimes divorce in order to avoid financial disaster.

Are these penalties causing cohabitation? It's impossible to say for sure, but the fact that older couples are an important part of the boom suggests a connection. "The Census Bureau estimates that the percentage of cohabiting unmarried couples has doubled since 1980, and older couples are keeping pace," writes Stern. "In 1993 some 416,000 couples reported that they were unmarried, living together, and over 45. That compares with 228,000 who fit the description in 1980." And in the *New York Times* (July 6, 1995), Jennifer Steinhauer reports on the research of Professor Larry Bumpass of the University of Wisconsin, who found that the biggest increase in couples choosing to live together was not among twenty-somethings, but among people over 35. Bumpass found that 49 percent of his subjects between 35 and 39 are living with someone, up from 34 percent in the late 1980s. Among people 50 to 54, the practice has doubled. Using data from his survey, Bumpass showed that only a small segment of people disapprove of

cohabitation and sex outside marriage. He concluded that "the trends we have been observing are very likely to continue, with a declining emphasis on marriage."

Of course, marriage still has its advantages, beyond obvious ones like greater emotional security and social and religious approval. It can be a social welfare system, providing health insurance and retirement security to a spouse who otherwise would have none. For couples in which one person earns most of the family income, tax laws are favorable to marriage.

But overall, official economic policy makes marriage a bad option for too many people. Those who determine our income taxes, government benefits, and institutional practices must remember that marriage is an economic as well as a social arrangement. In a society in which many marriages have failed, financial security is tenuous, and living together is acceptable, we can no longer assume that the institution of marriage will survive the burdens it has carried in the past. Moving toward marriage-neutral tax and benefit policies would, in the long run, lay a better foundation for true family values.

## CRITICAL THINKING QUESTIONS

1. How, according to Martin, do most U.S. tax laws discourage getting married?

2. If marriage triggers economic penalties, why do almost 90 percent of us marry at least once during our lifetimes?

3. Why do Schlessinger and Martin draw such different conclusions about the advantages and disadvantages of cohabitation?

# 8　Marriage

## *Conservative:* The Benefits of Marriage

STEVEN FLANDERS, "The Benefits of Marriage," *The Public Interest*, no. 124 (Summer 1996): 80–86. © 1996 by National Affairs, Inc. Reprinted by permission of the author.

*As you saw in Chapters 6 and 7, conservatives are alarmed that many people have separated sex and procreation from the institution of marriage. Steven Flanders expands this position by arguing that both the state and the general public benefit from traditional families. Thus, private institutions, legislatures, and other public bodies should reward traditional families, restrain divorce, and penalize nontraditional families.*

In a sane or sensible society, marriage is more an answer than a question. Of course, it is never the only answer: In any culture, a noticeable minority never marry, some because they resist for their own reasons what their culture and their families urge upon them and others for want of the right opportunity. But I venture to say that for most of humanity, past and present, the only real question here is when, or to whom. Whether to marry has been little more a question than whether to be born or whether to die.

The *New York Times* last spring printed a striking dispatch from a demographers' conference in San Francisco that carried to a new level of desperation the quest for an answer to a question that should not be asked. If the quoted researchers are to be taken seriously ("Studies Find Big Benefits in Marriage," April 10, 1995), we can all look forward to the gradual dissolution of the family and, perhaps, of civilization as well. These social scientists, it would seem, have abandoned the social or cultural claim

of marriage as the usual accompaniment of maturation, perhaps even the definition of the ascent out of adolescence. Instead, they try, through empirical efforts that (as reported) were both misguided and incompetent, to persuade us that marriage is good for us, like diet or exercise. They claim that marriage is in our individual interests simply on instrumental grounds.

Without a doubt, the marriage institution is in our collective interests. As a matter of individual choice, however, its practical claim upon our fellow citizens and ourselves becomes weaker each year. Sad to say, the quoted researchers faithfully reflect an atomized culture in which one's own interest is about all the basis available to justify any of life's choices, large or small. Among the other forces that have undermined marriage, I would emphasize the pervasive assault on sex roles in late twentieth-century America. If young women and men cannot see themselves naturally embracing the familiar roles of wife, mother, husband, father, then marriage becomes a kind of consumer choice, to be weighed against other claims upon one's money and time.

If that's what marriage is up against, we're all doomed. Or, more precisely, our heirs are, and theirs; for it will take a couple of generations before marriage's cultural props erode, at which time it will become clear that marriage is a loser—in purely instrumental terms. When this happens, we will have fulfilled the prediction made by the young Daniel Patrick Moynihan a generation ago, the prediction Charles Murray reminds us of today: A community that allows a large number of young men to grow up without fathers asks for and gets chaos. But Moynihan—then—was making a grim prediction that he hoped to forestall, of a minority of a minority community.

I would be the very last to dispute that marriage has its joys and its benefits. Unfortunately, they are mostly available outside marriage as well, at least in the short term and before the onset of old age. Marriage is disabling in lots of obvious ways: professional, sexual, economic. The married must consult, share, and be faithful, or at least offer some pretense of these. Yet, even the pretense must be a nuisance, and the reality is positively confining, in the sense that it restricts choices and opportunities.

If marriage is a misfortune in the realm of consumer choice, then children are a disaster. If we were to regard children as fabulously expensive pets, there would be no buyers. The price tag for each child might be placed at roughly one-quarter of a million dollars. A rule of thumb might be that middle-class families ultimately spend on each child about what they spend on their house.

Why do we marry? Why do we procreate? Out of self-interest? To make ourselves healthy? Hardly. We do these things out of love, and because they are our connection with future generations, with past generations, and perhaps with the infinite. But all of this is jeopardized as our culture of narcissism increasingly denies the validity of inherited marriage roles, deeming them coercive or, at least, confining. Living and making a life with the opposite sex has its charms of course, but, truth be told, easier, cheaper, less-demanding and less-confining alternative lifestyles abound.

Over the past 30 years, we have detached sex and procreation from the institution of marriage. Large numbers of American children are now born out of wedlock; in many communities, the number is more than half.

Well-meaning meddlers in legislatures and the courts may soon detach child rearing from marriage as well. The New York Court of Appeals last November issued a four-to-three decision that authorized in two cases adoption by a natural mother's unmarried partner. In one of the cases, it was a heterosexual partner who wished to adopt his partner's infant; in the other, a lesbian partner who wished to do the same. The majority, focusing on the statutory standard of "the best interests of the child," concluded: "The rule otherwise would mean that the thousands of New York children actually being raised in homes headed by two unmarried persons could have only one legal parent, not the two who want them." Hailing this "momentous" decision by Chief Judge Judith Kaye, the *New York Times* editorialized: "It will bolster the legal standing of the state's non-traditional families."

True enough. But, if child rearing works without marriage, why bother with the wedding ceremony at all? Indeed, those who might be inclined, even unconsciously, to duck the obligations of the marriage contract can now claim that cohabitation-plus-adoption is essentially the same as marriage. The equivocator's dream, this decision offers the wandering male a complete justification for his lifestyle choice. And, for the wandering female who finds pleasure and comfort in intimacy with other women, as well as with men, this decision may tip the scales for them too: Men and marriage are unnecessary.

Notably, neither side in this case articulated the important fact that "adoption" in these contexts is quite different from the traditional adoptions that legislatures presumably had in mind when fashioning the adoption statutes now in place in New York and other states. The majority sensibly relies on the fact that "the pattern of amendments since the end of World War II evidences a successive expansion of the categories of persons entitled to adopt regardless of their marital status or sexual orientation." This pattern presumably responds to an effort to maximize, or at least to increase, the number of eligible homes, so that infants who otherwise have inadequate or no care may be adopted. But adoption by the live-in partner of an unmarried mother has a different purpose altogether: to establish legal entitlements and obligations that mimic those of marriage. It is an effort that is profoundly subversive of the institution of marriage. A decision that doubtless improved the legal position, and perhaps the prospects, of the children directly before the court may contribute to an accelerating enfeeblement of marriage.

Also notable, the majority opinion commits a casual, yet significant, logical error that it shares with many who legislate on behalf of "non-traditional families." Judge Kaye seems to imagine that the cases before her are broadly representative of unmarried couples with children. But there is no evidence for this. It may be true, though certainly regrettable, that "at least 1.2 of the 3.5 million American households which consist of an unmarried adult couple have children under 15 years old, a more than six-fold increase since 1970." This hardly means that very many of those "headed by two unmarried persons" include "two who want (the children)." The vast majority of these households are arrangements of convenience, including, hopefully, one partner (nearly always the mother) who wants the children and another who is indifferent—on the good days.

If we must treat marriage within the calculus of interest, the best answer is that it is the State that benefits from marriage. This is a jarring notion. Our Anglo-American legal tradition and political culture generally do not treat the State—I capitalize this word to capture its German quality—as a distinguishable interest, conceptually distinct from the interests of the citizenry.

But it can hardly be doubted that the State has an interest in sustaining and encouraging a citizenry who are law-abiding and self-sufficient, who avoid self-destructive behavior, who vote intelligently and otherwise participate in communal governance. Citizens who break the law or evade it impose significant costs on the State that must catch, prosecute, and imprison the criminals. Those who receive welfare and other direct public-assistance benefits, inadequate though all of these may be, are also costly to the State. While no one would claim that the "benefits" to the State of a law-abiding citizenry follow directly from child rearing as practiced within all marriages, there is no shortage of evidence that a stable marriage, in general, is the best place to raise children.

I would only be persuaded otherwise if I were shown a citizenry roughly comparable to our own which had indeed abandoned the claims and obligations of marriage, and seemed to be nonetheless bumping along satisfactorily. Let us imagine that by the year 2050 the Swedes, say, had largely eliminated marriage. (They seem already to be well along in this.) Let us suppose further that they brought up nearly all of their children without spectacular ill effects in some combination of communal settings, casual couplings, and long-term homosexual and heterosexual pairings. Then perhaps someone could fairly propose that the interest I identify is illusory.

But nothing short of this would do, so I consider my hypothesis safe, at least for my own lifetime. The safe course is for the trustees of the interests of the State to resist efforts that would entitle "life partners" of the unmarried to the same benefits (health insurance and life insurance, in addition to more central rights like adoption) as the married. It long has been, and should still be, a major role of the State to support and preserve the family.

If it is easy to articulate a State interest in the institution of marriage, it is almost as easy to identify a similar interest of society. Indeed, not only do we all share an interest in the success of other people's marriages. Clearly, we share the State's interest in the law-abiding and self-sufficient qualities of our fellow citizens. For the most part, however, the benefits of marriages to society are less measurable than are those to the State.

A good place to begin is with public places. Most of us are acutely aware of a palpable decline in public civility, which keeps the young, the old, the defenseless, and many of the rest of us from enjoying our parks and other public spaces. This is a development that would have been unimaginable a generation ago. Not all of this can be traced to changes in family life or family organization. However, to demonstrate a shared stake of our fellow citizens in the integrity of the marriage bond, an assertion of universal or exclusive causality is not necessary. I need only claim what seems undeniable: a connection at least in part between antisocial behavior that destroys public spaces and facilities, making them forbidding and uninviting, and the less steady and effective child-rearing settings and practices that the progressive collapse of marriage has encouraged.

Some other costs to society are measurable enough. Expenditures for security gear, for moves to flee crime, for failed investments brought about by middle-class flight—these are the costs of social breakdown which might well have been averted had the marriage institution better survived.

Modern-day heirs of Tocqueville are concerned about the decline in those mediating civil institutions that seemed, to their mentor, to be the glory of our uniquely autonomous civic culture. They should be especially concerned about marriage, which may be the bedrock private civil institution.

It is not too difficult to imagine that without it, a century or so hence, "bowling alone" will be the least of our problems.

Let no one assume that the institution of marriage can take care of itself. Marriage seems to have lost entirely the cultural moorings that once brought young people together with a kind of inevitability. Why did they bother? They married not only for sex and for procreation but for more transcendent reasons. To avoid it or to miss it would be to step outside the familiar, the natural, the appropriate.

I have no solutions, only palliatives. I would begin with the old idea that marriage is a *moral* institution. Indeed, a long marriage, far from being something natural or inevitable or simply the spinning out of a series of actions in response to self-interest, is closer to the opposite: an unfolding of the life cycle that embodies not only joys and growth but especially obligations met, temptations resisted, and provocations accommodated or ignored. It may even embody a search for transcendence. Ordinary couples are entitled to approbation and perhaps more than that, not only on unique ceremonial occasions like fiftieth wedding anniversaries, but always. And no one should hesitate to express strong disapproval of the actions of those who abandon a marriage in a wanton fashion. We should also cherish what forms and ceremonies still remain. For nearly all ceremonies of any antiquity, and most without, serve as markers for the life cycle, generally in intimate relation to marriage and the married.

Marriage, recognized as fragile and endangered, should be an explicit frame of reference for the actions of legislatures and other public bodies. Because marriage benefits the State, as well as civil society, no legislator should hesitate to offer benefits in return. I will not try to define how far the State interest in marriage should be embodied in legislation. But I would discourage the State and private institutions from providing the unmarried with the same benefits as the married. And, of course,

I would resist efforts to sanctify in law either homosexual or other "non-traditional" marriages, or the novel forms of adoption discussed earlier. I would also support proposals to restrain divorce.

I predict that marriage, if it remains a consumer commodity, will fail. The great exception will be immigrants and their children, unless they too over time learn the American way of marriage. Thus, in a perverse extension of our national tradition of renewal and revitalization through immigration, the fate of marriage in America depends upon our newest citizens. The rest of us may find ourselves with a great deal to learn from them.

## CRITICAL THINKING QUESTIONS

1. How, according to Flanders, does the state and general public benefit from marriage? Are individuals' benefits less important than those of the state and the general public?

2. If marriage roles are *inherited*, why do people divorce? And if married couples have children to establish connections to past and future generations, are they guilty of treating their children like commodities?

3. Flanders blames the decline of public civility and the increase in crime on the collapse of the family. Are there other possible explanations?

# 8   Marriage

## *Centrist:* Social Science Finds: "Marriage Matters"

LINDA J. WAITE, "Social Science Finds: 'Marriage Matters.' " Originally appeared in *The Responsive Community* 6, no. 3 (Summer 1996). Reprinted with permission.

*Flanders' article focused on the benefits of marriage for the state and the general public. Here Linda J. Waite examines the benefits of marriage for individuals. She argues that marriage improves our health, wealth, and sex life and our children's well-being. She recommends that, as a society, we "pull some policy levers" to reinforce the institution of marriage.*

As we are all too aware, the last few decades have witnessed a decline in the popularity of marriage. This trend has not escaped the notice of politicians and pundits. But when critics point to the high social costs and taxpayer burden imposed by disintegrating "family values," they overlook the fact that individuals do not simply make the decisions that lead to unwed parenthood, marriage, or divorce on the basis of what is good for society. Individuals weight the costs and benefits of each of these choices to themselves—and sometimes their children. But how much is truly known about these costs and benefits, either by the individuals making the choices or demographers like myself who study them. Put differently, what are the implications, for individuals, of the current increases in nonmarriage? If we think of marriage as an insurance policy—which it is, in some respects—does it matter if more people are uninsured, or are insured with a term rather than a whole-life policy? I shall argue that it does matter, because marriage typically provides important and substan-

tial benefits, benefits not enjoyed by those who live alone or cohabit.

A quick look at marriage patterns today compared to, say, 1950 shows the extent of recent changes. Figures from the Census Bureau show that in 1950, at the height of the baby boom, about a third of white men and women were not married. Some were waiting to marry for the first time, some were divorced or widowed and not remarried. But virtually everyone married at least once at some point in their lives, generally in their early twenties.

In 1950 the proportion of black men and women not married was approximately equal to the proportion unmarried among whites, but since that time the marriage behavior of blacks and whites has diverged dramatically. By 1993, 61 percent of black women and 58 percent of black men were not married, compared to 38 percent of white men and 41 percent of white women. So, in contrast to 1950 when only a little over one black adult in three was not married, now a majority of black adults are unmarried. Insofar as marriage "matters," black men and women are much less likely than whites to share in the benefits, and much less likely today than they were a generation ago.

The decline in marriage is directly connected to the rise in cohabitation—living with someone in a sexual relationship without being married. Although Americans are less likely to be married today than they were several decades ago, if we count both marriage and cohabitation, they are about as likely to be "coupled." If cohabitation provides the same benefits to the individuals as marriage does, then we do not need to be concerned about this shift. But we may be replacing a valuable social institution with one that demands and offers less.

Perhaps the most disturbing change in marriage appears in its relationship to parenthood. Today a third of all births occur to women who are not married, with huge but shrinking differences between blacks and whites in this behavior. One in five births to white mothers and two-thirds of births to black mothers currently take place outside marriage. Although about a quarter of the white unmarried mothers are living with someone when they give birth, so that their children are born into two-parent—if unmarried—families, very few black children born to unmarried mothers live with fathers too.

I believe that these changes in marriage behavior are a cause for concern, because in a number of important ways married men and women do better than those who are unmarried. And I believe that the evidence suggests that they do better because they are married.

## MARRIAGE AND HEALTH

The case for marriage is quite strong. Consider the issues of longevity and health. With economist Lee Lillard, I used a large national survey to follow men and women over a 20-year period. We watched them get married, get divorced, and remarry. We observed the death of spouses and of the individuals themselves. And we compared deaths of married men and women to those who were not married. We found that once we took other factors into account, married men and women faced lower risks of dying at any point than those who have never married or whose previous marriage has ended. Widowed women were much better off than divorced women or those who had never married, although they were still disadvantaged when compared with married women. But all men who were not currently married faced significantly higher risks of dying than married men, regardless of marital history. Other scholars have found disadvantages in death rates for unmarried adults in a number of countries besides the United States.

How does marriage lengthen life? First, marriage appears to reduce risky and unhealthy behaviors. For example, according to University of Texas sociologist Debra Umberson, married men show much lower rates of problem drinking than unmarried men. Umberson also found that both married men and women are less likely to take risks that could lead to injury than are the unmarried. Second, as we will see below, marriage increases material well-being—income, assets, and wealth. These can be used to purchase better medical care, better diet, and safer surroundings, which lengthen life. This material improvement seems to be especially important for women.

Third, marriage provides individuals—especially men—with someone who monitors their health and health-related behaviors and who encourages them to drink and smoke less, to eat a healthier diet, to get enough sleep, and to generally take care of their health. In addition, husbands and wives offer each other moral support that helps in dealing with stressful situations. Married men especially seem to be motivated to avoid risky behaviors and to take care of their health by the sense of meaning that marriage gives to their lives and the sense of obligation to others that it brings.

## MORE WEALTH, BETTER WAGES—FOR MOST

Married individuals also seem to fare better when it comes to wealth. One comprehensive measure of financial well-being—household wealth—includes pension and Social Security wealth, real and financial assets, and the value of the primary residence. According to economist James Smith, in 1992 married men and women ages 51–60 had median wealth of about $66,000 per spouse, compared to $42,000 for the widowed, $35,000 for those who had never married, $34,000 among those who were divorced, and only $7,600 for those who were separated. Although married couples have higher incomes than others, this fact accounts for only about a quarter of their greater wealth.

How does marriage increase wealth? Married couples can share many household goods and services, such as a TV and heat, so the cost to each individual is lower than if each one purchased and used the same items individually. So the married spend less than the same individuals would for the same style of life if they lived separately. Second, married people produce more than the same individuals would if single. Each spouse can develop some skills and neglect others, because each can count on the other to take responsibility for some of the household work. The resulting specialization increases efficiency. We see below that this specialization leads to higher wages for men. Married couples also seem to save more at the same level of income than do single people.

The impact of marriage is again beneficial—although in this case not for all involved—when one looks at labor market outcomes. According to recent research by economist Kermit Daniel, both black and white men receive a wage premium if they are married: 4.5 percent for black men and 6.3 percent for white men. Black women receive a marriage premium of almost 3 percent. White women, however, pay a marriage *penalty*, in hourly wages, of over 4 percent. In addition, men appear to receive some of the benefit of marriage if they cohabit, but women do not.

Why should marriage increase men's wages? Some researchers think that marriage makes men more productive at work, leading to higher wages. Wives may assist husbands directly with their work, offer advice or support, or take over household tasks, freeing husbands' times and energy for work. Also, as I mentioned earlier, being married reduces drinking, substance abuse, and other unhealthy behaviors that may affect men's job performance. Finally, marriage increases men's incentives to perform well at work, in order to meet obligations to family members.

For women, Daniel finds that marriage and presence of children together seem to affect wages, and the effects depend on the woman's race. Childless black women earn substantially more money if they are married but the "marriage premium" drops with each child they have. Among white women only the childless receive a marriage premium. Once white women become mothers, marriage decreases their earnings compared to remaining single (with children), with very large negative effects of marriage on women's earnings for those with two children or more. White married women often choose to reduce hours of work when they have children. They also make less per hour than either unmarried mothers or childless wives.

Up to this point, all the consequences of marriage for the individuals involved have been unambiguously positive—better health, longer life, more wealth, and higher earnings. But the effects of marriage and children on white women's wages are mixed, at best. Marriage and cohabitation increase women's time spent on housework; married motherhood reduces their time in the labor force and lowers their wages. Although the family as a whole might be better off with this allocation of women's time, women generally share their husbands' market earnings only when they are married. Financial well-being declines dramatically for women and their children after divorce and widowhood; women whose marriages have ended are often quite disadvantaged financially by their investment in their husbands and children rather than in their own earning power. Recent changes in divorce law—the rise in no-fault divorce and the move away from alimony—seem to have exacerbated this situation, even while increases in women's education and work experience have moderated it.

## IMPROVED INTIMACY

Another benefit of married life is an improved sex life. Married men and women report very active sex lives—as do those who are cohabiting. But the married appear to be more satisfied with sex than others. More married men say that they find sex with their wives to be extremely physically pleasurable than do cohabiting men or single men say the same about sex with their partners. The high levels of married men's physical satisfaction with their sex lives contradicts the popular view that sexual novelty or variety improves sex for men. Physical satisfaction with sex is about the same for married women, cohabiting women, and single women with sex partners.

In addition to reporting more active and more physically fulfilling sex lives than the unmarried, married men and women say that they are more emotionally satisfied with their sex lives than do those who are single or cohabiting. Although cohabitants report levels of sexual activity as high as the married, both cohabiting men and women report lower levels of emotional satisfaction with their sex lives. And those who are sexually active but single report the lowest emotional satisfaction with it.

How does marriage improve one's sex life? Marriage and cohabitation provide individuals with a readily available sexual partner with whom they have an established, ongoing sexual relationship. This reduces the costs—in some sense—of any particular sexual contact, and leads to higher levels of sexual activity. Since married couples expect to carry on their sex lives for many years, and since the vast majority of married couples are monogamous, husbands and wives have strong incentives to learn what pleases their partner in bed and to become good at it. But I would argue that more than "skills" are at issue here. The long-term contract implicit in marriage—which is not implicit in cohabitation—facilitates emotional investment in the relationship, which should affect both frequency of and satisfaction with sex. So the wife or husband who knows what the spouse wants is also highly motivated to provide it, both because sexual satisfaction in one's partner brings similar rewards to oneself and because the emotional commitment to the partner makes satisfying him or her important in itself.

## THE IMPACT OF MARRIAGE ON CHILDREN

To this point we have focused on the consequences of marriage for adults—the men and women who choose to marry (and stay married) or not. But such choices have consequences for the children born to these adults. Sociologists Sara McLanahan and Gary Sandefur compare children raised in intact, two-parent families with those raised in one-parent families, which could result either from disruption of marriage or from unmarried childbearing. They find that approximately twice as many children raised in one-parent families than children from two-parent families drop out of high school without finishing. Children raised in one-parent families are also more likely to have a birth themselves while teenagers, and to be "idle"—both out of school and out of the labor force—as young adults.

Not surprisingly, children living outside an intact marriage are also more likely to be poor. McLanahan and Sandefur calculated poverty rates for children in two-parent families—including stepfamilies—and for single-parent families. They found very high rates of poverty for single-parent families, especially among blacks. Donald Hernandez, chief of marriage and family statistics at the Census Bureau, claims that the rise in mother-only families since 1959 is an important cause of increases in poverty among children.

Clearly poverty, in and of itself, is a bad outcome for children. In addition, however, McLanahan and Sandefur estimate that the lower incomes of single-parent families account for only half of the negative impact for children in these families. The other half comes from children's access—or lack of access—to the time and attention of two adults in two-parent families. Children in one-parent families spend less time with their fathers (this is not surprising given that they do not live with them), but they also spend less time with their mothers than children in two-parent families. Single-parent families and stepfamilies also move much more frequently than two-parent families, disrupting children's social and academic environments. Finally, children who spend part of their childhood in a single-parent family report substantially lower quality relationships with their parents as adults and have less frequent contact with them, according to demographer Diane Lye.

## CORRELATION VERSUS CAUSALITY

The obvious question, when one looks at all these "benefits" of marriage, is whether marriage is responsible for these differences. If all, or almost all, of the benefits of marriage arise because those who enjoy better health, live longer lives, or earn higher wages anyway are more likely to marry, then marriage is not "causing" any changes in these outcomes. In such a case, we as a society and we as individuals could remain neutral about each person's decision to marry or not, to divorce or remain

married. But scholars from many fields who have examined the issues have come to the opposite conclusion. Daniel found that only half of the higher wages that married men enjoy could be explained by selectivity; he thus concluded that the other half is causal. In the area of mental health, social psychologist Catherine Ross—summarizing her own research and that of other social scientists—wrote, "The positive effect of marriage on well-being is strong and consistent, and the selection of the psychologically healthy into marriage or the psychologically unhealthy out of marriage cannot explain the effect." Thus marriage itself can be assumed to have independent positive effects on its participants.

So, we must ask, what is it about marriage that causes these benefits? I think that four factors are key. First, the institution of marriage involves a long-term contract—" 'til death do us part." This contract allows the partners to make choices that carry immediate costs but eventually bring benefits. The time horizon implied by marriage makes it sensible—a rational choice is at work here—for individuals to develop some skills and to neglect others because they count on their spouse to fill in where they are weak. The institution of marriage helps individuals honor this long-term contract by providing social support for the couple as a couple and by imposing social and economic costs on those who dissolve their union.

Second, marriage assumes a sharing of economic and social resources and what we can think of as co-insurance. Spouses act as a sort of small insurance pool against life's uncertainties, reducing their need to protect themselves—by themselves—from unexpected events.

Third, married couples benefit—as do cohabiting couples—from economies of scale.

Fourth, marriage connects people to other individuals, to their social groups (such as in-laws), and to other social institutions (such as churches and synagogues) which are themselves a source of benefits.

These connections provide individuals with a sense of obligation to others, which gives life meaning beyond oneself.

Cohabitation has some but not all of the characteristics of marriage and so carries some but not all of the benefits. Cohabitation does not generally imply a lifetime commitment to stay together; a significant number of cohabiting couples disagree on the future of their relationship. Frances Goldscheider and Gail Kaufman believe that the shift to cohabitation from marriage signals "declining commitment within unions, of men and women to each other and to their relationship as an enduring unit, in exchange for more freedom, primarily for men." Perhaps as a result, many view cohabitation as an especially poor bargain for women.

The uncertainty that accompanies cohabitation makes both investment in the relationship and specialization with this partner much riskier than in marriage and so reduces them. Cohabitants are much less likely to assume that each partner is responsible for supporting himself or herself financially. And whereas marriage connects individuals to other important social institutions, cohabitation seems to distance them from these institutions.

Of course, all these observations concern only the average benefits of marriage. Clearly, some marriages produce substantially higher benefits for those involved. Some marriages produce no benefits and even cause harm to the men, women, and children involved. That fact needs to be recognized.

## REVERSING THE TREND

Having stated this qualification, we must still ask, if the average marriage produces all of these benefits for individuals, why has it declined? Although this issue remains a subject of much research and speculation, a number of factors have been mentioned as contributing. For one, because of increases in women's employment, there is less specialization by spouses now than in the past; this reduces the benefits of marriage.

Clearly, employed wives have less time and energy to focus on their husbands, and are less financially and emotionally dependent on marriage than wives who work only in the home. In addition, high divorce rates decrease people's certainty about the long-run stability of their marriage, and this may reduce their willingness to invest in it, which in turn increases the chance they divorce—a sort of self-fulfilling prophecy. Also, changes in divorce laws have shifted much of the financial burden for the breakup of the marriage to women, making investment within the marriage (such as supporting a husband in medical school) a riskier proposition for them.

Men, in turn, may find marriage and parenthood a less attractive option when they know that divorce is common, because they may face the loss of contact with their children if their marriage dissolves. Further, women's increased earnings and young men's declining financial well-being may have made women less dependent on men's financial support and made young men less able to provide it. Finally, public policies that support single mothers and changing attitudes toward sex outside the marriage, toward unmarried childbearing, and toward divorce have all been implicated in the decline in marriage. This brief list does not exhaust the possibilities, but merely mentions some of them.

So how can this trend be reversed? First, as evidence accumulates and is communicated to individuals, some people will change their behavior as a result. Some will do so simply because of their new understanding of the costs and benefits, to them, of the choices involved. In addition, we have seen that attitudes frequently change toward behaviors that have been shown to have negative consequences. The attitude change then raises the social cost of the newly stigmatized behavior.

In addition, though, we as a society can pull some policy levers to encourage or discourage behaviors. Public policies that include asset tests (Medicaid is a good example) act to exclude the married, as do

AFDC programs and most states. The "marriage penalty" in the tax code is another example. These and other policies reinforce or undermine the institution of marriage. If, as I have argued, marriage produces individuals who drink less, smoke less, abuse substances less, live longer, earn more, are wealthier, and have children who do better, we need to give more thought and effort to supporting this valuable social institution.

## CRITICAL THINKING QUESTIONS

1. How does Waite measure "health"? Are there other measures of health? Does Waite's evidence show that married partners enjoy *equal* health benefits?

2. Does Waite define "correlation" and "causality"? Can she really conclude that marriage *causes* better health and increased wealth?

3. Cohabitants are much more likely than married couples to be financially self-sufficient and many (white) women pay a "marriage penalty." Does this mean that marriage is an economic liability for most women? Also, if employed wives are less financially and emotionally dependent on marriage than housewives are, why do employed women marry?

# 8    Marriage

## *Liberal/Feminist:* Feminism and Marital Equality

KAREN R. BLAISURE AND KATHERINE R. ALLEN, "Feminists and the Ideology and Practice of Marital Equality," *Journal of Marriage and the Family* 57 (February 1995): 5–19. Copyrighted 1995 by The National Council on Family Relations, Minneapolis, MN 55421. Reprinted by permission.

*Many conservatives and some centrists blame feminists for undermining marriage and promoting "alternative lifestyles" (see Chapters 3, 4, and 5). Karen R. Blaisure and Katherine R. Allen show, in contrast, that feminist attitudes can improve the quality of the marital relationship for both partners. A feminist ideology, nonetheless, does not guarantee that wives and husbands will be egalitarian in all domestic spheres.*

In her 1972 book, *The Future of Marriage,* and again in the second edition (1982), Bernard concluded that the future viability of marriage will depend upon "upgrading" marriage for women. After reviewing the literature on marriage, she declared that two marriages exist, his and hers, and that marriage is more attractive and healthier for the former than for the latter. Bernard (1982) was optimistic that couples were struggling to improve marriage to make it beneficial for both spouses, although achieving an equal division of employment and family work was "still more talked about than practiced" (p. 300). According to more recent research, equality between marital partners continues to reflect incongruency between ideology and practice. Individual couples may experience more congruency between talk and action, but for the majority of married couples, the discrepancy remains. . . .

Hochschild (1989) noted the incongruency between ideology and practice in marriage when she considered "the second shift" (i.e., housework, parental responsibilities, and domestic management). While 18% of the men studied shared the work of the second shift equally with their wives, the majority did not. However, even though research such as Hochschild's reports a continued incongruency for the majority of couples, it also indicates that, for some couples, congruency between the ideology and the practice of marital equality is possible (Gilbert, 1993; Jump & Haas, 1987). Among the men who subscribed to an egalitarian ideology, 70% shared equally, while only 22% of the men subscribing to a traditional ideology and 3% of men subscribing to a transitional ideology shared equally. Certainly an ideology of marital equality increases the possibility of sharing family work, although it is not a guarantee.

## FEMINISM AND MARRIAGE

Feminism highlights first and foremost the oppressive character of structural inequality based on gender (Osmond & Thorne, 1993). . . . Gender becomes, along with race, sexual orientation, class, and age, an organizing category of peoples' lives.

Feminist analyses have provided an excellent critique of relationships as gendered constructions. Over the past two decades, feminists have demonstrated the problematic nature of marital and family life for women (Glenn, 1987). Women are the marital partners responsible for a family's emotional intimacy, for adapting their sexual desires to their husbands', for monitoring the relationship and resolving conflict from a subordinate position, and for being as independent as possible without threatening their husbands' status (Fishman, 1983; Thompson & Walker, 1989). Feminism has provided a critique of traditional gender-structured marriage, resulting in an awareness of its overwhelming cost to women in financial, emotional, and physical dimensions. The problematic nature of marriage for women has been linked to its centrality in patriarchy, the devaluation of women's work, and the hierarchy of gender (Ferree, 1990; Glenn, 1987).

Previously published research indicates a higher involvement of men in family life when married to women with equal or higher education, income, and status (Jump & Haas, 1987, Perry-Jenkins & Crouter, 1990). When the wife's career as well as the husband's organizes family life, the chances of marital equality are increased (Atkinson & Boles, 1984; Haas, 1980). . . .

Using the concept of distributive justice, Thompson (1991) sought to explain why women fail to consider the imbalanced division of family work as unfair. By examining "women's sense of fairness," the imbalance and its excuse become evident. Rather than counting time and tasks, Thompson argued that women want care from their husbands in the form of doing disliked tasks, covering for the women at home so they can have personal time, and responding to requests for help. In addition, by making within-gender comparisons, women consider themselves to be better off than other women with husbands who do less. Finally, justifications for unequal distribution of family work, such as attributing family work to women's personal needs, function to obscure women's entitlement to relational equality.

This present study asks what happens to the practice of marriage when wives and husbands agree on the goal of equality. Specifically, how do feminist women and men practice marriage? Is there a sharing of the second shift? Does a feminist ideology of marital equality result in a marital "upgrade" for women? For feminist couples, does the ideology of marital equality translate into the practice of marital equality? . . .

### Data Collection

Over the course of 8 months, intensive efforts were made to find couples in heterosexual marriages who were self-identified feminists prior to marriage and currently and who had been married for at least 5 years. Volunteers were recruited through advertisements and snowball sampling (Rubin, 1983; Taylor & Bogdan, 1984). Advertisements were placed in regional weekly and monthly newsletters of the National Organization for Women (NOW) and in local newspapers. Announcements were made monthly at a regional NOW meeting, and two professors at a local university announced the study to graduate classes during the fall semester of 1991.

Telephone or face-to-face pilot interviews were done with one or both partners of 23 couples who volunteered for the study. Volunteers were asked questions concerning feminism, length of marriage, and willingness to participate in joint and individual interviews. . . . Ten of the initial 23 couples met the requirements for participation and provided, on average, 6 hours of interview time per couple, or 4 hours of interview time per person. A joint interview was completed with each couple to obtain an initial description of their daily lives and a history of their marriage, as well as to provide an opportunity to observe the couple interacting. During subsequent individual interviews, participants were asked to clarify information presented in the joint interview, to talk more about the influence of their feminist beliefs on their marriage, and to note satisfactions and dissatisfactions with their marriage. Interviewing occurred in two sessions, one joint and one individual, for each participant, and took place in the participant's home or office. . . .

This research design allowed for joint and individual interviews, providing the opportunity for the interviewer to observe partners interacting as well as for the spouses to talk in confidence. Furthermore, joint interviews allowed couples to elaborate on and clarify relational events and thus offer a shared or disparate view of their experiences (Daly, 1992).

**Description of Participants**

The selection criteria, including the requirement of self-identification as a feminist and the means of recruitment via newspaper and NOW advertising, resulted in a homogeneous group. The 20 participants interviewed for this study were white and well educated. The median and mode age was 36. All but two women had degrees equivalent or higher than their husbands. Nine couples had children, and three couples had children from previous marriages. The median length of marriage was 10 years. Participants claimed the label of feminist currently, and both members of the couple considered themselves feminists before marriage. . . . The participants understood feminism to be the belief in equality, a promotion of women and their strengths, and a political movement dedicated to

changing society for the betterment of women and men.

ELIZABETH: Feminism is basically highly conscious of autonomy and a person's potential for self-development. Feminism remains at its heart seeing the wholeness and the value of the female and wanting women to have these political, social, economic, religious [rights].

**RESULTS**

This study confirms a distinction between ideology and practice of equality within heterosexual marriage and feminists. The practice of marital equality in terms of outcome—that is, sharing the second shift (Hochschild, 1989)—does not automatically flow from a stated feminist ideology of equality. However, couples in this study demonstrated some of the ways in which the gap between the ideology and practice of marital equality can be narrowed and possibly closed.

This analysis revealed that all couples participated in at least three processes of vigilance that reinforced the creation of their marriages as supportive locations for feminist thought and practice. However, couples differed in the extent to which they participated in two additional processes of vigilance that further promoted the practice of equality. These five processes are described below following a discussion on how feminist beliefs blend with marriage.

**Upgrading Marriage Through Vigilance**

Couples reported practicing vigilance, defined as an attending to and a monitoring of equality, within and outside of their relationship. This vigilance began prior to their marriage, and for some, prior to meeting their partner. Women reported feeling empowered to choose their spouse wisely. Feminism offered criteria for the women to use when determining the extent to which they felt comfortable in a relationship.

BARB: I don't want to get involved in a relationship if I have to worry about what I say or I have to go really gently to put feelers out to see how they feel about things.

ELIZABETH: Feminism gives me the strength to demand: Either I get the treatment I think is adequate partnering or I leave. Feminism is a very important part of my life.

Feminism provided women with a screening criterion to assess men as potential partners willing to attend to issues surrounding equality. Wives and husbands clearly stated the importance of having similar world views in choosing to marry one another. Miriam and Larry's discussion of their similarities was typical of all of the participants.

MIRIAM: Feminism is a view that we share. If we didn't share this view, we probably wouldn't have gotten married. So, it was important that we share it in order to be a happy couple. Feminism probably informs our decisions that we make and steers us as a couple in certain directions and away from other choices.

LARRY: In order to get married to someone I had to make sure that almost all our beliefs were completely congruent.

Ruth addressed the importance of entering marriage after acquiring an education, work experience, and self-knowledge, a process she termed "coming into my own."

RUTH: If you look at the traditional understanding of marriage where the man owns a woman, everything is in a man's name, the children take the father's name, that's oppressive. But if you can think of marriage as the commitment of two equals, you see what I am saying about waiting until I was 30 to get married, and how awful it would have been if I had gotten married in my twenties. I met Paul at a point when I had finally come into

my own, when I had found a career and a lifestyle that I felt comfortable with. I felt sufficient in and of myself. I decided that even though I wanted to one day get married and have children that I might not do that and that would be okay because I enjoyed what I did.

Foremost, due to their shared ideology, all participants considered themselves to be moving toward something better than what traditional marriage offered. Their dissatisfaction with traditional marriage resulted from observing marriages of friends and family, being aware of its costs to women, and experiencing such marriages with prior spouses. Feminism was identified by these women and men as a crucial component in making their relationship satisfying. They felt benefited by their marriages and believed them to be superior to traditional marriage. Women and men said that others had commented on how strong and supportive the couples' marriages appeared, although they questioned the couples' preferences for having different names, separate recreational interests, or friends of the other sex.

Moving toward something better translated into women being able to have their own identities while in marriage, and men being able to have connection with family members. Women talked about feminism helping them to have a sense of self in marriage.

JENNIFER: Being married is not oppressive to me. But part of that is, I'm not Mrs. E. I'm not his possession. And I see having his name as being his possession. He's not Mr. N. He's not my possession.

Men described feeling close to their children and to their partners. In explaining why he wanted to marry Jennifer and the benefits of blending marriage and feminism:

CALVIN: I feel a real emotional attachment and wanted to spend the rest of my life with her. . . . I don't see a contradiction in feminism and marriage. From my experience in being married to Jennifer, I think we have actually been able to both support each other. Feminism is not the reason we got married, but I certainly think that it helps promote support of each other. . . . I don't think I could have handled marriage any other way.

Couples reported the importance of five processes that collectively described a vigilance to the attending to or monitoring of their experiences of equality. All couples described engaging in three vigilant processes: critique of gender injustices, public acts of equality, and support of wives' activities. Of the 10 couples in this study, four couples considered themselves to share the work of the home equally and described satisfactory engagement in an additional two processes, reflective assessment and emotional involvement. The other six couples perceived imbalances in doing the work of the home and reported difficulties with these last two processes.

## Processes of Vigilance Common to All Couples

*Critique of gender injustices.* Feminism was a lens through which partners together critiqued sexism, gender stereotypes, and "cultural baggage" or gender expectations of their partners. Couples reported an ongoing dialogue based on their critique of messages they heard throughout the day, such as commercials that pigeonholed men as incompetent in the home and women as willing to give up their careers for marriage, male friends who expressed an inability to wash clothes, or men who denigrated their wives at parties. Calvin explained some of the topics he and Jennifer discussed in daily conversations.

CALVIN: Men are putting this image out of women, virtually anorexic and must have certain characteristics, marvelous skin and tremendous shape,

and it's absolutely unfair and very sexist. It is very bothersome to see that. The other thing that we comment on, we see so much of in the papers these days, in the news, is the abuse that goes on in the home situation, mostly of women.

The following example of sexism is typical of incidents related by all couples.

DAN: They actually asked me, when I made my appointment with the doctor, if I minded that she was female.

BARB: But I never get asked if I mind if the doctor is male.

DAN: I'm in there for ulcer treatment. "What is she going to do to me? Do I have to come in and do something strange?" I thought it was a very strange question to ask me.

BARB: That's when you become aware of it. That's when it becomes very evident to you. That's double standards.

All couples reported spending relationship time addressing the sexism or sexual harassment experienced by the women in educational, social, or work settings.

DAN: I was mad because I felt that Barb wasn't valued for what she was. She worked just as hard as anyone else, and she wasn't appreciated. It made me more supportive of her.

MILTON: There's a real awareness for me that women feel they don't have the authority in a classroom because they are women, which just blows me away. It helps me to understand sometimes Deborah's insecurities about teaching.

Women described feminism as offering a language to help them clarify their experiences of injustice, and thus make sense of their world and define themselves. Naming their experiences of discrimination, sexual harassment, and salary disparities enabled them to make choices to protect themselves, for instance, to demand higher wages or seek a better work environment.

DEBORAH: Feminism gives me a larger context for understanding my private sphere as dependent on a larger society.

Men's participation in identifying gender injustices and introducing them into topics of conversation was common throughout the couples. Women especially noted this activity on the part of their husbands.

DEBORAH: Milton is more likely to run across something [gender injustice] and tell me than the other way around. Probably I am several degrees more radical on a variety of topics including feminism living with Milton.

Men stated that feminism allowed them to better understand the experiences of others, and they expressed their attempts to empathize with women and validate their wives' experiences of gender injustice.

PATRICK: If I were a woman, I would have a much different outlook on life, absolutely. I think I would be a lot more cynical. I think I would be a lot more wary.

DAN: Where Barb works, it's got all sorts of discrimination problems. That affects us in the sense that on a daily basis Barb has to come home and unload her frustration because her work environment is extremely frustrating.

*Public acts of equality.* All couples were vigilant in their public demonstration of their concern for the wife's status in the marriage. Different last names and financial decisions were the most common expressions of the importance of the wives' equal status, although other public acts were common, such as John's defense of Mary's right to have lunch with male friends or Larry using flex-time in order to leave work in the middle of the afternoon to care for his son while his wife worked. The financial ability of these women to care for themselves and their minor children demon-

strated equality not only to others, but also to themselves.

Eight couples had different last names, a conscious effort to symbolize that their marriage was not based on traditional assumptions of male preeminence.

JENNIFER: My husband certainly didn't get anybody with his name. When I got divorced I dropped my ex-husband's name, and I dropped my father's name and I went back to my first and second names. My second name was my mother's father's name. The younger of the two girls now has that same last name. My older daughter kept her father's name. So we have three names in the family.

This act symbolizes the public dimensions of a relationship decision.

PAUL: We can witness to what we believe by living it. We don't make a big deal about it but it does make a statement to folks.

All couples were aware of the symbolic and concrete implications of common financial decisions. They put the wife's name first on the tax return or on a car registration. Some consciously decided to put half of the credit in the wife's name, while others had separate accounts even if they had a joint account for household bills. All couples described careful attention to ensuring that paperwork reflected their goals of equality. One public act that men were quite aware of doing was delaying decisions in order to consult with their partners, despite a tendency to make decisions on their own, especially when others expected them to assume this male privilege.

LARRY: Well, the world we're in still expects to see the male making all the decisions about what the family is going to do. So people ranging from a car salesman to everything else expect me to make any decision that is confronting what we should do. They talk to me, and I don't like that. I don't want them to talk to me, I want them to talk to both of us.

*Husbands' support of wives' activities.* Support of women's employment and feminist activities were important in these marriages. All the women said their husbands had directly supported their career or vocation. For example, Carl assisted Elizabeth in completing her book. Deborah's career was considered primary, and her employment prospects had determined the location of their residence. John arranged his work schedule to accommodate Mary's artistic vocation, which required many hours away from the family. During busy seasons, Calvin, the recognized cook of the family, brought dinner to his wife's business for them to share and then stayed to help her with the work load. In addition, he serviced the business computers, which required many hours of his free time.

Men described their support of their wives' feminist activities as "behind the scenes." For example, Shawn provided child care while Sarah went to marches. Carl supported Elizabeth's multiyear effort to change discriminatory pay practices at her workplace by opening up their home as a meeting place for research and strategy sessions. Other husbands such as Tony and Dan verbally supported their wives' participation in feminist organizations in front of family, friends, and coworkers.

## Two Additional Processes of Vigilance

While the three processes of vigilance described above were reported by all of the couples, only four couples reported the use of all five processes. Two additional processes of vigilance, reflective assessment and emotional involvement, were used by four couples who also reported equal sharing of parenting, household, and domestic management tasks. The other six couples, who reported little or one-sided monitoring of equality in their relationship and/or difficulty in emotional involvement, also had an imbalance in the division

of tasks. These six couples employed explanations of difference due either to gender or to personality (Hare-Mustin, 1991; Hochschild, 1989) to account for an unfair division of parenting and household tasks.

*Reflective assessment.* Reflective assessment indicates an ongoing monitoring of one's contribution to the relationship and family life. Among the four couples who described the equal sharing of parenting, household, and domestic responsibilities, both partners described a vigilance in assessing their marital contributions. When both partners participated in an ongoing reflective assessment, this process provided a way to identify and correct imbalances.

PATRICK: I think it is really possible to have equality or a nonoppressive marriage but it is not something that sort of happens and you say "Zap, now we got it" and you go on. You have to constantly communicate and sometimes it swings a little bit more toward the other. It is this fluid thing, it is just not static. You just don't say, "Well, we are feminists now so therefore our marriage is equal, and I won't physically hurt or verbally abuse you and so therefore we have equality in our marriage." I think without constant communication the notion of equality probably can't exist. You have to ensure that equality maintains itself. I am convinced that having a sense of equality about the marriage, that the notion that both of you have equal say about what's going on in decisions, makes for a better marriage and a better life.

Rose described her reaction to having a partner who attended to the relationship and who was vigilant in monitoring his contributions.

ROSE: I think about Patrick as another responsible partner, an equal person in carrying out this relationship. As I look back on the other marriage, I saw myself as an adult taking care of that relationship. For the first several years, I was continually surprised at what it was like to live with another adult who was also responsible for the work of the home. Because we both do a lot of the same things, we have an appreciation of each other. He's getting lots of good stuff out of this relationship; I think he puts a lot into our relationship.

Through assessments of their financial contributions to the relationship, Jennifer and Calvin created an understanding that "growing a business" is equivalent to bringing a stable salary into the family.

JENNIFER: Several times over the last several years I don't feel like I'm bringing in enough and there are times when I'm anticipating that he would be thinking, "Well, maybe she ought to quit that and go get a decent paying job." And I've said that. That's not his reaction to it at all. He reminds me that I'm growing a business, that it's not the same as getting a salary from someone else because everything in here I own. He's not more important or valuable because he makes more money than I do.

The importance of reflective assessment of the practice of equality was highlighted by the reports of the other six couples in which one partner did more reflective assessment than the other. These couples also reported more disparity in carrying out responsibilities of the home. Couples used justifications based on gender and personality differences to explain the imbalances. Men justified the arrangement by stating, "she has a higher standard," "she's more fussy," or "she's the more organized person." The two couples in which the husbands (Dan and Milton) did more of the domestic tasks explained this arrangement by citing the husbands' shorter work hours as a logical reason for this difference and by referring to one wife's recent illness and prolonged recuperation (Milton).

When reflective assessment was one-sided, wives were the ones who monitored their own and their partners' contributions to the relationship. While imbalances were identified, they were not corrected, leading to feelings of resentment and frustration.

RACHEL: I was disappointed, I felt ripped off. He didn't do 50% of the housework. He maintains that a lot of this stuff is totally unimportant to him, that he doesn't care if the bills are paid. It seems to me that it's a cop-out for him to just say, "Well, I don't care about these things so you do them all if you want them done." I think he certainly benefits a lot. I don't think our degree of commitment to those menial tasks is consistent with the degree to which they are important.

Sarah described two examples of how she is attempting to balance the work load, given she has the responsibility for all of the "planning" activities around the home.

SARAH: I am not afraid of a conflict. I tell him, "You do the expenses from now on, I am not going to do it." I run the household, the planning and the managing. It is more intensified when you have children. . . . A lot of it was me [telling him he needed to take on more responsibility]. "You are going to cook two nights a week, and not only that, you are going to know what we are going to have for dinner, and you are going to do the grocery shopping for it." You see what it gets down to? So, he calls at 4:30 and says, "What do you want for dinner?" putting it back to me. [I say] "I don't know. You decide. Good-bye. Figure it out for yourself."

Regarding discrepancies in parenting responsibilities, four couples with biological children who did not share parenting provided the following justifications: Work demands interfered with the husband's time at home, the special bond between mother and infant became apparent through the early months of an infant's life and so propelled the parents to interact with the infant to different degrees, and/or the mother knew more about emotionally caring for children and thus could provide children with better parenting. The two couples (Mary and John, Ruth and Paul) who used these explanations the most described the most unequal parenting arrangements. Two other couples (Rachel and Tony, Sarah and Shawn) relied on these explanations to a lesser extent. They described conflict when the wives advocated for more participation from their husbands in parenting and in assuming domestic responsibilities.

When these four women compared their husbands as fathers with other men, they voiced strong appreciation for the closeness and involvement their husbands had with the children. Yet when comparing themselves with their husbands as parents, these four women voiced disappointment (Mary and Ruth) and anger (Rachel and Sarah). They wanted their husbands to take on more of the responsibility, management, and awareness that is required for raising children (LaRossa, 1988). On balance, it is important to note that a typical week at Ruth and Paul's house would show him caring for their son on his day off while Ruth worked, visiting him at school, meeting the school bus at noon, and taking their son to day care on the days that both he and Ruth worked. Likewise, the other fathers demonstrated similar or higher degrees of involvement with their children.

*Emotional involvement.* Couples described the importance of communicating emotions verbally and not withdrawing from conflict. Every couple mentioned the importance of feeling close to the other partner, whether they experienced the presence or absence of this feeling. Those four couples who shared the work of the home equitably, however, described being able to meet each other's emotional needs. In their individual interviews both Miriam and Larry related feeling a special fit between them.

LARRY: I don't know if I could love someone the way that I love Miriam. I think marriage is the second best thing that ever happened to me, our son being the first right now. It's not hierarchy, this is the first and second. It's just two equal, good things.

MIRIAM: He's my soul mate, and I know I would never find anybody as perfect for me as he is. Other friends are for spice, for variety, for flavor, for a fuller emotional range. I get everything I need from him, but having other people is important, too. And I love him, no matter what. I knew he was the right guy for me.

Miriam explained how communication is related to the experience of equality.

MIRIAM: You always let the other one know what you're thinking and what you're doing. The way to keep the other person powerless is to deny them sufficient finances, sufficient knowledge. So if you're always open and you're always sharing, then you're not denying the other person what they need to establish their power, too.

The ability to use communication to build intimacy was not automatic for these couples. In the past, Calvin, Larry, and Carl had been confronted on the results of their communication and had worked at changing their interactional styles.

CALVIN: I had to learn that I intentionally send messages with my body language. When we have a quote "discussion" or argument or whatever, I tend to stand and pace and they [his wife and their daughters] tend to sit. That is a physical position where you're coming on as being superior. I didn't realize that, but I have tried to remind myself to be the first to sit down in such a situation.

Every couple talked about the importance of communication, including those six couples who described some difficulties. Emotionally shutting down was described as either a lack of communication skills or a power play.

DAN: One thing I can say for us, we talk.

BARB: We value the ability to talk to each other. We really don't seem to have a communication problem. If I'm pissed off at him, I'll tell him. If he's pissed off at me, he will usually tell me. Except he's worse at that, he keeps a lot of things inside. But, we definitely value that part of our relationship.

In Barb's reflections on their communication, she noted Dan's tendency to withhold intense feelings about a difficult issue involving his extended family. She attributed this keeping "things inside" to a lack of skills versus a power play; therefore, she did not feel emotionally vulnerable as some wives did, as noted below. However, Barb also voiced frustration over the greater amount of work she did in regard to this issue. Dan's holding back communication on this particular situation translated into Barb doing more work. This couple's experience highlights the varying degrees of emotional withdrawal in marriage, the variation in interpretation of such withdrawal, and the connection between withholding communication and the perception of workload.

Using communication to establish superiority, withholding talk to control a situation, or exploding in anger were contrary to the establishment of emotional closeness.

DEBORAH: If there are any problems, he shuts down or he wants to ignore them as long as possible. I want to get them resolved as quickly as possible. I am more comfortable talking out personal problems, and he is more, "Let's pull down the curtain, let's stop, let's do nothing." It is like I don't exist. It can be simply pulling up the newspaper, it can be just looking blank or giving me the feedback that he has heard, but what I have said isn't worth listening to.

As a result of this communication pattern, Deborah stated feeling emotionally unsafe at times, so she sought emotional understanding from friends.

Mary said that while her husband, John, was not empathetic and open with his feelings, she felt close to him. In contrast to Deborah and Milton, Mary did not experience John's lack of empathy as a control issue, but rather an inability to communicate in a particular way.

MARY: He also is not very up front about his feelings. Just because you are a feminist doesn't mean you are open with your feelings. You can still be very closed and very inward. He keeps everything inside. I wish I knew what his feelings were. So we'll go through this, "Well, how are you feeling?" and I try to drag things out of him at times when I know he should be depressed and he should be upset.

Yet, although Mary and John both felt very close to one another, like Deborah, Mary sought friendships to provide her with the empathy she wished she had in her marriage.

## DISCUSSION

This study confirms that the ideology of marital equality does not translate automatically into an outcome of marital equality. While this incongruency between ideology and practice is commonplace among couples in which the man holds to a traditional ideology, men who have egalitarian ideologies are more likely to share equally in the work of the second shift (Hochschild, 1989). This present study on feminist couples, who could be considered the most ideologically committed to marital equality, also reveals their difficulty in carrying out beliefs of equality, in that six of the 10 couples had difficulty in participating in two of the five processes of vigilance—reflective assessment and emotional involvement.

Yet this study does reveal the likelihood that a feminist ideology upgrades marriage for women. Wives and husbands who claim a feminist identity strive to enact their beliefs of equality through practices of vigilance, sometimes resulting in a mutual sharing of the second shift work. The second shift was shared by partners who, in addition to providing a safe and supportive location for women's feminist voices, were vigilant in the monitoring of their own contributions and had the interpersonal skills necessary to establish emotional closeness (Baber & Allen, 1992; Vannoy-Hiller & Philliber, 1989).

The men in this study spoke of their feminist beliefs and the benefits accompanying a marriage based on these beliefs and they sought, albeit in varying degrees, to put equality into practice. Upgrading marriage for women is possible; getting the "stalled revolution" into motion again is possible. However, both require the participation of men who are committed to a process of marital vigilance and to a guiding ideology of equality. While their numbers may be few, studies are beginning to note their presence. Recognition of them and their commitment to the creation of an "interdependent union of equals" (Schwartz, 1994, p. 2) is necessary in the ongoing study of heterosexual marriage.

## Processes That Upgrade Marriage

All 10 couples practiced the first three vigilant processes that functioned to support women and upgrade their marriages. The processes of critiquing gender injustices, publicly demonstrating marital equality, and supporting wives' career and vocational goals provided a context in which women's identities were validated. Marriages were not experienced as oppressive to women; rather they enabled women to pursue personal, relational, and professional goals.

First, husbands' feminist attitudes and behaviors served a necessary function in upgrading their wives' marriages. . . . At home, these women could express their mixed feelings of anger, hope, and fear about sexism and have their feelings' validated by their husbands. . . . Men's initiation and participation in a critique of gender injustices demonstrated their feminist commitment, reinforcing women's understanding of the marriage as a safe place for them to talk about their experiences and their feelings of anger. . . .

Second, couples' public acts of equality, such as different last names, stated to others their intentions of equality, thereby reinforcing their decision to do marriage differently. The women in this study were financially able and willing to leave their marriages, if necessary. Okin (1989) argued that women's ability to exit relationships, largely a factor of finances, is translated into more influence in relationships.

Third, support for women's careers, education, and vocational goals was commonplace as men adjusted their schedules and jobs to offer concrete demonstrations of their support. Such support provided these women with benefits they saw occurring in only a few other marriages.

## Processes That Promote the Practice of Equality

The ideology and practice of marital equality were congruent for those four couples who participated in two additional vigilant processes: reflective assessment of personal contributions to their marriage and meeting each other's emotional needs. Six couples who reported difficulty with these two processes also reported inequality in the work of the second shift. This study suggests that reflective assessment and emotional involvement are connected to the outcome of marital equality, supporting Vannoy's (1991) conclusion that, with less powerful social forces maintaining marriage, interpersonal skills and individual ability for emotional intimacy are required of couples.

First, reflective assessment requires the attainment of personal development to make commitments and to participate in mutual emotional support (Barber & Allen, 1992). When individuals in couples reflected on their own contributions and made necessary alterations—that is, when they went against gender prescriptions—they reported less conflict than couples who relied on the wife to monitor relational contributions, and they reported equality in sharing the second shift.

Second, emotional involvement corresponded to reports of equal sharing of the second shift and functioned to validate personal identity. Because of a shared feminist ideology with their husbands, these women's identities were supported, and they experienced marriage as an accepting and fortifying relationship. For some men, feminism revealed the barriers to emotional involvement and motivated them to develop closeness with their partners and children. However, when emotional vulnerability was one-sided, marital equality was inhibited.

## REFERENCES

Atkinson, M. P. & Boles, J. (1984). WASP (Wives as Senior Partners). *Journal of Marriage and the Family* 46, 861–870.

Baber, K. M. & Allen, K. R. (1992). *Women & families: Feminist reconstructions*. New York: Guilford Press.

Bernard, J. (1982). *The future of marriage*. New Haven, CT: Yale University Press. (Original work published 1972.)

Daly, K. (1992). Parenthood as problematic: Insider interviews with couples seeking to adopt. In J.F. Gilgun, K. Daly, & G. Handel (eds.), *Qualitative methods in family research* (pp. 103–125). Newbury Park, CA: Sage Publications.

Ferree, M. M. (1990). Beyond separate spheres: Feminism and family research. *Journal of Marriage and the Family* 52, 866–884.

Fishman, P. M. (1983). Interaction: The work women do. In B. Thorne, C. Kramarae, & N. Henley (eds.), *Language, gender and society* (pp. 89–101). Rowley, MA: Newbury House.

Gilbert, L. A. (1993). *Two careers/one family*. Newbury Park, CA: Sage.

Glenn, E. N. (1987). Gender and the family. In B. B. Hess & M. M. Ferree (eds.), *Analyzing gender* (pp. 348–380). Newbury Park, CA: Sage.

Haas, L. (1980). Role-sharing couples: A study of egalitarian marriages. *Family Relations* 29, 289–296.

Hare-Mustin, R. T. (1991). Sex, lies, and headaches: The problem is power. In T. J. Goodrich (ed.), *Women and power* (pp. 63–85). New York: W. W. Norton.

Hochschild, A. (1989). *The second shift*. New York: Viking.

Jump, T. L. & Haas, L. (1987). Fathers in transition: Dual-career fathers participating in child care. In M. S. Kimmel (ed.), *Changing men* (pp. 98–114). Newbury Park, CA: Sage.

LaRossa, R. (1988). Fatherhood and social change. *Family Relations* 37, 451–457.

Luepnitz, D. A. (1988). *The family interpreted*. New York: Basic Books.

Okin, S. M. (1989). *Justice, gender, and the family*. New York: Basic Books.

Perry-Jenkins, M., & Crouter, A. C. (1990). Men's provider role attitudes: Implications for household work and marital satisfaction. *Journal of Family Issues* 11, 136–156.

Rubin, L. B. (1983). *Intimate strangers: Men and women together*. New York: Harper & Row.

Schwartz, P. (1994). *Peer marriage*. New York: Free Press.

Stacey, J. (1990). *Brave new families*. New York: Basic.

Taylor, S. J. & Bogdan, R. (1984). *Introduction to qualitative research methods* (2nd ed.). New York: John Wiley & Sons.

Thompson, L. (1991). Family work: Women's sense of fairness. *Journal of Family Issues* 12, 181–196.

Thompson, L. & Walker, A. J. (1989). Gender in families: Women and men in marriage, work, and parenthood. *Journal of Marriage and the Family* 51, 845–871.

Vannoy, D. (1991). Social differentiation, contemporary marriage, and human development. *Journal of Family Issues* 12, 251–267.

Vannoy-Hiller, D. & Philliber, W. W. (1989). *Equal partners*. Newbury Park, CA: Sage.

## CRITICAL THINKING QUESTIONS

1. What do Blaisure and Allen mean by marital "vigilance"? Did all of the vigilance processes result in egalitarian marital practices?

2. How did the husbands' feminist attitudes and behaviors "upgrade" their wives' marriages? Was this upgrading mutual or one-sided?

3. Qualitative analyses, reflected in the Blaisure and Allen research, provide valuable insights from the respondent's point of view. Why, however, are the study's findings limited? Consider, for example, the sample size and selection process, possible interviewing biases, and the socioeconomic as well as racial and ethnic characteristics of the respondents.

# IV PARENTS AND CHILD

Conservatives and centrists are very similar in their views on single-parent families. Both groups believe that the increase in single-parent households has had only detrimental effects on children. Feminists and most liberals, in contrast, believe that the importance of the father's social contribution to the family has been exaggerated. Compared to conservatives and liberals, centrists have not taken a strong position on such topics as raising children and on gay and lesbian families. The debates on both of these latter issues are primarily between conservatives and liberals.

## Chapter 9: Single-Parent Families

Most conservatives and centrists view the increase in single-parent families as an indicator of a rise in individualism and a flight from parental obligations. There are several avenues to single-parenthood: getting divorced, being widowed, or not marrying. We hear very little about children who grow up with widowed mothers, probably because the percentage is small and many widows have incomes (from insurance policies, for example) that protect the family from poverty.

For some time conservatives have maintained that welfare encourages single-parent families (see Chapter 18). As Bryce J. Christensen argues in "Imperiled Infants," infant mortality rates are much higher among unmarried, black teen mothers than among married mothers. In contrast, Mexican-American infants, even in poor families, are protected by a "family ethic" that encourages marriage and two-parent families.

Centrists agree with conservatives that unmarried-mother families perpetuate crime, poverty, and drug use. They emphasize, moreover, that a "culture of fatherlessness" creates a wide range of problems, from crime to school failure. According to David Popenoe, in "The Carnage of Declining Marriage and Fatherhood," for instance, the absence of a biological father "has become the most prevalent form of child maltreatment in America today." Even in high-income, single-mother families, centrists maintain, children suffer because it takes two adult role models to inculcate such values as honesty, self-sacrifice, and responsibility.

Castigating unemployed, unmarried mothers and assuming that male-headed families are inherently superior are destructive and unwarranted, claim liberals.[1] Some feminists, furthermore, accuse conservatives and centrists of using "single mother" as a code word for "black, unmarried, welfare mother."[2] Most single mothers—whether unmarried, divorced, or lesbian—are child-oriented and raise happy, successful children. According to Judith Stacey, in "The Father Fixation," "harping on the superiority of married biological parents and the evils of fatherlessness injures children and parents in a wide array of contemporary families." Stacey and other feminists argue that it is not family structure but unemployment, our failed institutions, and declining real wages that destroy families and cut children adrift from their moorings.[3]

Does single motherhood harm children? In an examination of six nationally representative data sets, Sara S. McLanahan and Gary Sandefur found that family disruption is not the principal cause of high school failure, poverty, and delinquency. Because children in single-father homes do just as poorly as children living with a single mother, moreover, fatherlessness does not appear to be the crucial variable that endangers children's well-being. Family disruption does, however, lower children's well-being because it reduces the time parents spend with children and the control they have over them, undermines children's access to community resources due to greater residential mobility, and decreases the household's economic resources.[4]

Are welfare and a decline of family values to blame for the increase in single-mother households? According to McLanahan, three factors seem to be primarily responsible for the rise in single-mother families. First, the growing economic independence of women means that women who can support themselves can be more discerning about when and whom they marry. Second, the decline of men's earnings compared to women's earnings means that many low-skilled men are unable to play the breadwinner role. Third, a shift in societal (rather than family) norms and values during the 1960s reduced the stigma associated with divorce and nonmarital childbearing.[5]

## Chapter 10: Raising Children

As might be expected, all of the political and ideological groups express concern about raising happy, healthy, and responsible children. Some observers note that contemporary parenting is more difficult than in the past. Our society is more impersonal and more competitive, and "public schools, the courts, social service workers, gardeners, housekeepers, day-care providers, lawyers, doctors, televisions, frozen dinner, pizza delivery, manufactured clothing, and disposable diapers" continuously invade the family.[6] On the one hand, we are encouraged to provide more intensive parenting as the number of employed mothers increases. On the other hand, parents must compete for their children's attention in an "adult culture" that creates entertainment options (television, the Internet, music videos) over which parents have increasingly less control.[7]

Religious conservatives emphasize the importance of establishing strong Christian principles in childrearing.[8] And, generally, both secular conservatives and centrists agree that the most effective childrearing is within biological, two-parent homes (see Chapter 9). Although it does not represent an ideologically centrist position, the article by John P. Bartkowski and Christopher G. Ellison ("Conservative versus Mainstream Models of Childrearing in Popular Manuals") presents an overview of conservative and liberal views on several childrearing issues, such as parent-child relations and discipline strategies.

The most controversial aspect of discipline is spanking. A survey by the National Committee to Prevent Child Abuse found that 49 percent of Americans had spanked or hit their children in the preceding year.[9] Advocates of spanking (who are usually ideologically conservative), as reflected in Den A. Trumbull and S. DuBose Ravenel's "Spare the Rod?" article, feel that spanking is necessary and effective, prepares children for life's hardships, and deters misbehavior. Critics of spanking, who are usually liberal, argue that any physical punishment, including spanking, is harmful to a child's emotional development. According to Murray S. Straus, in "Ten Myths That Perpetuate Corporal Punishment," for example, spanking is rarely effective in changing undesirable behavior in the short term and can produce harmful side effects such as depression or violence in the long run.

## Chapter 11: Gay and Lesbian Families

As with the topic of raising children, the greatest disagreements about gay and lesbian families are between conservatives and liberals. Norval Glenn writes, in Chapter 1, that a fairly common position among centrists is that although marriage should be reserved for heterosexuals, legal recognition of homosexual pairings is warranted. Centrists are similar to liberals because they "rarely consider homosexuality to be a sin or believe that sexual orientation is a matter of choice." Conservatives and liberals hold opposing viewpoints about gay and lesbian issues on two fronts: whether gay parenting is harmful or beneficial to children's development and whether or not same-sex couples should be able to marry legally.

Conservative Christians argue that because marriage exists for the purpose of procreation, it follows that homosexual unions are "unnatural" and sinful. During the Southern Baptist convention in 1998 (described in the section introduction to Part II), for example, the statement on the family described marriage as the "uniting of one man and one woman" and as "the channel for sexual expression according to biblical standards, and the means for procreation of the human race." In recent years, many religious groups have encouraged homosexuals to "choose" heterosexuality and to renounce gay life.

Secular conservatives oppose gay unions and family life on different grounds. In "Gay Parenting and the Developmental Needs of Children," Lawrence F. Burtoft maintains, for example, that gay parents provide a bad example that children might imitate. Such modeling is especially harmful because it may result in risky sexual behavior that can result in AIDS and other disease risks.

Because centrists have not written about gay families (at least to my knowledge), I am using a selection from Barbara F. Okun, "Gay and Lesbian Parenting," that summarizes (from a nonideological perspective) some of the research on same-sex families. Okun cautions that much of the information about gay and lesbian parenting is recent and limited to small samples.[10] She shows, however, that the greatest parenting problems that lesbians and gay fathers encounter are due to homophobic attitudes rather than their own sexual orientation.

In 1993, the Supreme Court of Hawaii ruled that the denial of marriage licenses to same-sex couples violated the Hawaii constitution's equal rights protections. In response to this case, Congress passed the Defense of Marriage Act, which President Bill Clinton signed into law in 1996. This act permits states not to recognize same-sex marriages performed in other states or jurisdictions. Since 1993, a number of states have passed laws that prohibit same-sex marriages. As Thomas B. Stoddard discusses in "Why Gay People Should Seek the Right to Marry," the gay community itself is divided over the marriage issue. Some feel that lesbians and gay men should not "cave in" to heterosexual norms and laws. Others feel that legalizing same-sex marriage would provide gays "a litany of benefits and protections, rights and responsibilities" that they currently don't enjoy under either state or federal laws.[11]

## NOTES

1. See, for example, Susan L. Thomas, "From the Culture of Poverty to the Culture of Single Parenthood: The New Poverty Paradigm," *Women & Politics* 14, no. 2 (1994): 65–97.

2. See, for example, Charles Murray, *Losing Ground: American Social Policy, 1950–1980* (New York: Basic Books, 1984); and Lawrence M. Mead, *Beyond Entitlement: The Social Obligations of Citizenship* (New York: Free Press, 1986).

3. Ann Hartman, "Ideological Themes in Family Policy," *Families in Society: The Journal of Contemporary Human Services* 76 (March 1995): 182–192.

4. Sara S. McLanahan and Gary D. Sandefur, *Growing Up with a Single Parent: What Hurts, What Helps?* (Cambridge, MA: Harvard University Press, 1994).

5. Sara S. McLanahan, "The Consequences of Single Motherhood," *The American Prospect* 18 (Summer 1994): 48–58. In terms of changing societal norms, George A. Akerlof and Jane L. Yellen argue that, despite the availability of contraception and abortion, the demise of the shotgun marriage has increased out-of-wedlock births. See "New Mothers, Not Married," *The Brookings Review* 14 (Fall 1996): 18–21.

6. Sharon Hays, *The Cultural Contradictions of Motherhood* (New Haven, CT: Yale University Press, 1996), p. 11.

7. For a centrist perspective on the negative impact of an adult culture on children, see Peter Uhlenberg, "Changing Adulthood Changes Childhood," Working Paper No. 57 (New York: Institute for American Values, 1997).

8. See, for example, James C. Dobson, *Parenting Isn't for Cowards* (Dallas, TX: Word Publishers, 1987).

9. Reported in S. Banisky, "A Matter of Discipline," *Baltimore Sun*, July 10, 1994, pp. J1, J8.

10. Katherine R. Allen and David H. Demo examined 2,598 articles of three leading family research journals (*Journal of Marriage and the Family, Family Relations,* and *Journal of Family Issues*) published between 1980 and 1993. They found that only 12 articles (less than half of 1 percent) focused on the families of lesbians and gay men. See "The Families of Lesbians and Gay Men: A New Frontier in Family Research," *Journal of Marriage and the Family* 57 (February 1995): 111–127.

11. E. Wolfson, "Why We Should Fight for the Freedom to Marry: The Challenges and Opportunities That Will Follow a Win in Hawaii," *Journal of Gay, Lesbian, and Bisexual Identity* 1, no. 1 (1996): 79–89. For an opposing view, see V. A. Brownsworth, "Tying the Knot or the Hangman's Noose: The Case Against Marriage," *Journal of Gay, Lesbian, and Bisexual Identity* 1, no. 1 (1996): 91–98.

# 9 Single-Parent Families

## *Conservative:* Imperiled Infants

BRYCE J. CHRISTENSEN, "Imperiled Infants: A Legitimate Concern," *The Family in America* 5 (January 1991): 1–8. Reprinted with permission from *The Family in America*, a publication of the Howard Center, Rockford, IL.

*Does marriage protect infants and children? Bryce J. Christensen believes that the United States could reduce its high infant mortality rates if public health officials, government programs, and churches reinforced marriage. Children need two parents to survive and thrive. Instead of subsidizing illegitimacy, Christensen argues, our policies should promote a "moral coherence" that increases an infant's life chances after birth and beyond.*

Every fourteen minutes, an infant dies in the United States. Experienced as personal heartbreak by tens of thousands of parents, infant mortality poses a daunting challenge for medical and public health officials in the United States. For by international standards, America is not protecting the lives of its newborn infants very well. If a nation's infant mortality rate is, as one observer has put it, "one of the most revealing measures of how well a society is meeting the needs of its people," then many countries look decidedly better than the United States.[1]

According to a report completed in 1988 by the National Commission to Prevent Infant Mortality, "a baby born in 18 other industrialized countries, including Japan, Finland, and Singapore, has a better chance of surviving its first year than a child born in the United States." The report also found that "a baby born in Czechoslovakia or Bulgaria has a better chance of celebrating his or her first birthday than a black child in the United States." Labeling relatively high infant mortality in the United States a "disgrace," the editors of the British *Economist* wonder "whether America has the will to put an end to the anomaly of 40,000 infants dying each year in a proud and prosperous country." In response to such international criticism, President Bush told the United Nations in September 1990 that America is committed to reducing infant mortality.[2]

But continued progress in reducing infant mortality may depend heavily on an issue rarely addressed by the nation's leaders. Efforts to reduce infant mortality further may be retarded by the unwillingness of medical and public officials to speak out against childbearing outside of marriage. The most fundamental of social institutions, marriage powerfully protects children during infancy and after. Curiously, among officials involved in work against infant mortality, many tacitly accept illegitimacy in ways that put at risk the future of American children.

## STRANGE SILENCE

While the national trend in infant mortality continues downward, officials see little or no progress in some areas. Infant deaths remain particularly high among babies born to teen mothers and among blacks. In their analysis of infant mortality rates, the editors of the *American Journal of Public Health* voice concern that "the position of blacks relative to that of whites has remained unchanged or has deteriorated. This is the opposite of what might have been anticipated because the black rates were farthest away from some theoretically irreducible minimum." The latest available figures show infant mortality rates running over twice as high for blacks as for whites (17.9 vs. 8.6 deaths per 1,000 births). Indeed, Marian Wright Edelman reports that "by 1988 the black infant mortality rate in America's largest cities (population over 500,000) was actually on the increase." Epidemiologists also find "a strong association between young maternal age and high infant mortality," an ominous finding given the relatively high number of babies born to teenage mothers in the United States.[3]

Public officials loudly call for initiatives to reduce the number of vulnerable babies born to teenage mothers. They remain strangely silent about an upsurge in illegitimacy which likewise exposes babies to perilous risks. Public officials do not lack for documentation of the protective effects of marriage. Researchers have repeatedly demonstrated that infant mortality runs lower among infants born to married mothers than among infants born to unmarried mothers. In a study reported in August 1990, T. Bennett of the University of California, San Francisco, examined national birth and death files for 3.4 million infants born in 1983. Bennett concluded that "for both whites and blacks, unmarried motherhood was associated with an elevated overall infant mortality rate." Among whites, the mortality rate for babies born to unmarried women stood at 13. 1 deaths per 1,000 single births, compared to 7.8 deaths

per 1,000 single births to married mothers. Though less pronounced, the same pattern prevailed among blacks, among whom 19.6 babies died for every 1,000 babies born to unmarried mothers compared to 14.6 for every 1,000 babies born to married mothers. The linkage between the marital status of the mothers and infant mortality was especially strong for babies older than one month but less than one year old.[4] Oddly, when officials at the Centers for Disease Control (CDC) interpret Bennett's findings, they argue that "marital status of the mother confers neither risk nor protection to the infant; rather, the principal benefits of marriage to infant survival are economic and social support." But can or should the economic and social supports enjoyed by a married mother be analytically severed from wedlock itself? Clearly, marriage *does* protect infants, regardless of the skittishness of CDC officials in acknowledging that truth. Perhaps CDC officials do not take a strong stand against illegitimacy because they do not see it as their job to reverse social trends. And the trend in illegitimacy is clearly upward in the United States. In 1970, three years before the Supreme Court legalized abortion nationwide in *Roe v. Wade*, only 10.7 percent of all babies were born out of wedlock. In 1987, 24.5 percent of all births in the United States were to unmarried women. Although teenage mothers bore over half of all illegitimate infants in 1970, in 1987 teenage mothers bore less than one third of all illegitimate babies. The rising age of unwed mothers ought to raise concern among public health officials. For while researchers find no consistent link between infant mortality and maternal marital status among teenage mothers, they do find such a consistent link among mothers age 20 and over.[5] Public health officials may not relish the prospect of opposing a strong social trend, but available evidence makes it quite clear that protecting infants should mean affirming marriage.

Other recent studies further document the relationship between marriage and infant mortality. In a 1987 analysis of statistics for the state of California, sociologist James Cramer found that "large and significant differences in infant mortality" could be traced to differences in marital status, marital age, race, birth order, and maternal education. Likewise, in a national study published the same year, epidemiologists Joel Kleinman and Samuel Kessel discovered that compared to married women, unmarried women run "a substantially higher risk of having infants with very low or moderately low birth weights." (Low birth weights are a prime predictor of infant mortality.) In analyzing why very low birth weights became *more* common among black women between 1973 and 1983, Kleinman and Kessel note that this trend would not be expected by analysts who attend only to changes in educational achievement, which rose significantly for black women during the period in question. "The increase in education was not sufficient to offset the increase in births to unmarried women," the researchers explain. Kleinman and Kessel doubt that marriage exerts a "direct causal influence on the outcome of pregnancy," but that a life course that includes marriage is likely to be healthier for a number of reasons. For instance, unmarried mothers are more likely to smoke than married mothers.[6]

In a 1988 study of births in Texas, demographer Eve Powell-Griner reported "hazard rates for babies born out of wedlock to blue-collar mothers are 1.5 times as high as those among babies born in wedlock. For infants of white-collar mothers, death rates among the out of wedlock are 2.36 times as high as among the in wedlock." Powell-Griner theorized that marital status may affect infant mortality because of "tangible and intangible resources available [to a mother] during pregnancy to obtain good medical care, obtain proper nutrition, and regulate working hours and conditions. In addition, the ability of a married woman to provide an environment which fosters an infant's growth and development may be involved." Like Kleinman and Kessel, Powell-Griner also identified differences in "health behaviors" favoring married women (who gain more weight during pregnancy than unmarried women, but are less likely to smoke or drink).[7]

## THE MEXICAN-AMERICAN MIRACLE

To understand the importance of marriage as a cultural norm, it is helpful to consider the surprisingly low incidence of infant death among Mexican Americans. In her 1988 study of infant mortality in Texas, Powell-Griner reported that the risk of infant death is "lower for Hispanics than Anglos." Powell-Griner admitted that this finding was "paradoxical" considering the "high representation" of Hispanics in "at-risk categories." Similarly, in a 1986 study of infant mortality in California, researchers' "conventional risk factor assessment" did not work very well for "Spanish-surname women." The authors indeed admitted that the "favorable birth weight distribution among Latinos despite their adverse socioeconomic milieu is a contemporary public health enigma." The researchers found it particularly hard to account for the low infant mortality among Mexican Americans because "Latinos are considered to be one of the most medically underserved subpopulations in the United States" and because Mexican-American women bear more children later in life than women from other ethnic groups. "It might be expected, therefore, that Latinos would experience higher rates of infant mortality than do other ethnic groups," remark the researchers. In trying to account for the low rate for infant mortality among Mexican Americans, the California researchers raise the possibility that fewer Mexican-American infants die in part because of "a higher regard for parental roles" than found in other ethnic groups. "The lower incidence of nonmarital births among Latinos as compared with blacks is suggestive of a possible differential in parental attitudes," they write.[8]

Confirmation of the importance of marriage as an expression of parental attitudes comes from a 1987 study conducted in Chicago. The authors of this study found that despite comparable economic status, Mexican Americans suffer from far lower infant mortality rates than found among blacks. The researchers observed low birth weight in only 6 percent of Mexican-American babies, compared to 17 percent of black babies. In explaining this racial disparity, the Chicago investigators noted sharp differences in "cultural patterns and lifestyles," but no differences in income. "Mexican-American mothers tended to be older, married, less educated, and less likely to be recipients of welfare or food stamps during pregnancy than black mothers. Mexican-American fathers were more likely to be employed, but a higher percentage of black mothers were employed outside the home. There was, however, no significant difference in income during the pregnancy." The investigation also revealed that, compared to black mothers, "more Mexican-American mothers reported that the pregnancy was planned or that they were breast feeding." Unlike the thoroughly urbanized black population, "the Mexican-American population . . . is poor but not culturally urban—rather they are representative of individuals who were raised in a rural, somewhat preindustrial, social milieu." Wisely, the Chicago researchers recommended that Mexican Americans be "supported in their attempts to maintain those sociocultural attributes that are conducive to healthy infants."[9]

Unfortunately, in their efforts to reduce infant mortality, public officials evince a timidity about acknowledging the protective advantages of marriage and traditional family life. With rare exceptions, government programs for reducing infant mortality do nothing to reduce illegitimacy or to reinforce marriage. Adopting the usual approach, Dipali Apte won a national award in 1986 from the Department of Health and Human Services for outlining a program for reducing infant mortality in Chicago. Apte acknowledged that "being unmarried" increased the risk that a woman would bear a short-lived infant. Yet her program did nothing to foster marriage through its "three components: sex education, medical services, and community awareness and support." Apte did call for churches to help support Partnership-in-Health programs to help disseminate information about proposed health clinics and to encourage parents to become "involved in educating their child about sexual development." However, Apte does not suggest that church leaders or parents should encourage marriage or stigmatize illegitimacy. Nor does Apte express any intent that marriage be ratified by those who offer the family planning services and school-based health clinics that she believes will reduce infant mortality.[10]

Expanding the welfare state, not reinforcing the family, similarly appears to be the formula of the editors of *Public Health Reports*. In a 1987 editorial, they urge that vital records of the 50 states be linked into one national data base in part so that maternal participation in Medicaid, WIC, prenatal outreach can be monitored and assessed. The *PHR* editors say nothing about falling marriage rates or rising illegitimacy rates.[11]

Similarly, social worker Terri Combs-Orme calls upon her colleagues to "claim infant mortality as a social problem that is of direct and immediate concern to the profession" and to start "planning and lobbying for needed legislation and programs" to address the issue. Combs-Orme notes in passing that unmarried mothers are at "increased risk" of bearing a short-lived infant, but she says nothing about encouraging marriage in her discussion of how social workers should help pregnant women receive Medicaid and other welfare benefits.[12]

The same glaring omission distorts a plan developed by The Commonwealth Fund for reducing infant mortality. The Commonwealth Fund plan stresses family planning, prenatal care, nutritional supplements, and avoidance of smoking and other harmful practices, yet it says nothing whatever about fostering marriage or discouraging illegitimacy.[13]

Congressional measures to reduce infant mortality to date have followed the same lines. In 1989, Congress passed a measure "aimed at reducing the nation's infant mortality rate" by "expanding coverage to poor women and children under the joint state-federal Medicaid program." In 1989, Congress also acted on legislation "to enlarge and coordinate programs aimed at preventing disease and promoting health among minorities," particularly at reducing "the incidence of infant mortality among blacks."[14]

## SUBSIDIZING ILLEGITIMACY

When government spending on teen mothers (overwhelmingly unmarried) rose to $21.5 billion in 1988, the Center for Population Options called the increase "welcome," explaining that "expanded [welfare benefit] coverage may help more women to get adequate prenatal care, ensuring more healthy pregnancies and births." But Americans can expect disappointment from government programs that attempt to reduce infant mortality without encouraging marriage or discouraging illegitimacy. During the 1970's, health officials in North Carolina observed a much greater decline in infant mortality among Indians than among blacks, even though there were no "significant improvements in the Indian socioeconomic status" during this period. The North Carolina officials did note, however, that Indian mothers were less likely to be at risk through being of "early age," being unmarried, making a low number of prenatal medical visits, or making a late prenatal medical visit. The North Carolina officials also stressed "organizational differences in the Indian communities which produce these advantages." The North

Carolina authorities identify a lower likelihood of bearing a child out of wedlock as only one characteristic distinguishing Indian mothers from black mothers, but it may reasonably be supposed that marriage is essential to the social vitality of Indian communities. It is also worth noting that Mississippi officials report markedly better progress in reducing mortality among infants born to married nonwhite mothers in their state than among infants born to unmarried nonwhite mothers between 1975 and 1980.[15]

Of course, without good nutrition and medical care, marriage in itself will not protect infants from premature death. As already noted, maternal marriage appears to offer little protection against infant death among teen mothers, especially black teen mothers. However, the overall pattern is clear: among whites and nonwhites, babies born to unmarried mothers are more likely to die in infancy than babies born to married mothers. Besides, a child enjoys far better long-term prospects in life if born and reared in an intact family than if born and raised in a single-parent household. Compared to children reared in intact families, children in single-parent families are more likely to live in poverty, to fail in school, to commit delinquent acts, to use drugs, to bear or to father a child out of wedlock, and to become dependent upon welfare as adults.[16] Concern for a child's welfare should not be so narrowly focused on survival during infancy that long-term prospects are neglected. Children need two parents.

Government programs may actually be putting more babies at risk by fostering illegitimacy and by legitimizing the mother-state-child family. Confirming a popular perception, economist Robert Plotnick published a national study in 1990 demonstrating that welfare policy fostered illegitimacy in the 1980's.[17] When public officials seek to reduce infant mortality simply by expanding Medicaid and other welfare programs, they further encourage illegitimacy.

Encouraging teenage girls to become welfare mothers not only puts their own children at risk, it also imperils the next generation, since the teenage daughters of unmarried mothers are themselves more likely to bear a child out of wedlock than teenage daughters of intact marriages.[18] When public officials try to reduce infant mortality by relying upon the welfare state, they actually endorse a formula for putting babies at risk generation after generation. Even from an economic perspective, public officials have reason to wonder whether further expanding the welfare state will protect many infants. In a San Antonio study published in 1982, researchers could find no consistent relationship between infant mortality and the socioeconomic class of the mothers. The researchers theorized that because of "greater relative increases" in illegitimate births and births to teenage mothers among women of higher socioeconomic class, socioeconomic class was now less useful for predicting infant mortality than in the past.[19] But if socioeconomic class does not help predict infant mortality, how can expanded welfare programs help reduce it?

On the other hand, the results of the 1982 San Antonio study may not adequately represent the country as a whole because of the relatively high number of Mexican Americans in that area. One of the researchers responsible for the San Antonio study helped write a different study in 1985, based on statistics from Corpus Christi, showing that socioeconomic status can be used to predict infant mortality among whites, but that among Mexican Americans *no* link between socioeconomic status and infant mortality can be found.[20]

Public officials appear reluctant to consider what Mexican-American exceptionalism can teach about reducing infant mortality. Yet this relatively impoverished minority population, poorly served by medical practitioners, has managed to keep infant mortality remarkably low *without* the benefit of many of the programs officials now want to expand. As an ethnic group,

Mexican Americans display a distinctively strong commitment to family life. Compared to non-Hispanic whites, Mexican-American women are significantly more likely to marry young and more likely to bear three or more children. Mexican-American women are more likely to bear a child out of wedlock than non-Hispanic white women, but that reflects a much stronger aversion to abortion, as well as less prevalent use of contraceptives. Mexican-American women are actually significantly less likely than non-Hispanic whites to engage in sexual intercourse before marriage. Considering their relative impoverishment, the illegitimacy rate of 29 percent among Mexican Americans is lower than might be expected and is less than half of the rate of 62 percent among blacks. In fact, the Mexican-American youth most likely to engage in premarital sexual activity come from the wealthiest homes and have the most highly educated mothers.[21]

The strong commitment to family life which protects Mexican-American infants was not learned from public-health manuals. Rather, for most Mexican Americans, strong family life reflects religious faith, generally Catholic, and an essentially rural and premodern outlook. If they think about it at all, Mexican Americans probably recognize the remarkable health of their infants as a blessing from God, whose laws they follow by avoiding fornication and abortion and by devoting their lives to marriage and child rearing.

## TOWARD MORAL COHERENCE

Public health officials are resolute in their commitment to protecting the lives of infants. But in their reliance upon government welfare programs and medical technology, they offer no support to marriage, the institution upon which the future of children critically depends, during infancy and beyond. Public health officials use epidemiological evidence to justify their efforts to persuade women not to smoke, drink, or use drugs during pregnancy. Yet they generally ignore the evidence that marriage protects infants while illegitimacy imperils them. For instance, in 1989 Dr. Edwin Brandt, assistant secretary for Health, Department of Health and Human Services, outlined national government policy for reducing infant mortality. He stressed the need to help women plan pregnancies to "coincide with optimal maternal age," to receive "proper medical care," and to "avoid behavior known to be related to untoward pregnancy outcomes, such as smoking, alcohol consumption, drug abuse, and improper nutrition." Dr. Brandt said nothing about marriage or illegitimacy.[22]

This curious reticence about marriage may reflect a reluctance to speak out on a life choice rooted in moral preferences. But the commitment to preserving infant life itself expresses a moral preference—one not shared by the ancient people who worshipped Moloch, for instance (see 2 Ki.23:10). Acting with vision and intelligence in fulfilling this commitment to infant life requires a willingness to see the interconnectedness of choices. Public officials who fight to preserve infant lives while regarding the abortion of the unborn with indifference may not be seeking moral coherence. But policies premised in moral incoherence can only further weaken family life in ways that will put many infants and children at risk. Moral coherence in protecting infants may require raising disturbing but necessary questions about not only the deaths of infants, but the *disappearance* of infants caused by the current "birth dearth." Untimely death is not the only way, nor even the most common way, babies vanish from society. Moral coherence in protecting infants will require an acknowledgment that social attitudes determine an infant's life chances at least as much as medical technology.

Efforts to prevent infant death deserve both praise and support. But if severed from the moral principles that undergird family life, such efforts will ultimately expose future babies to deplorable risks during infancy and after. In their fight to protect infants, public officials need to reaffirm the primacy of family commitments. With good reason, Basil Mitchell, formerly Nolloth professor of the Christian religion at the University of Oxford, warns against the consequences if public officials refuse to speak out in defense of moral principles while devoting themselves solely to the pragmatic task of serving the needs of individuals. "The adoption of this pragmatic policy alone is bound to weaken the moral ties which bind society together, thus further eroding the system and placing an increasingly heavy burden upon the state apparatus. . . . [T]he greater the number of sexual relationships contracted in which no definite responsibilities are assumed, the greater the insecurity of any children born to them; while in turn official acceptance of such relationships, combined with an emphasis upon the needs of children as the sole consideration of importance, tends inevitably to diminish the standing of marriage. . . . So there are more casualties for the state to rescue and the more single-mindedly it concentrates upon this task, the more unmanageable the task becomes."[23]

No medical equipment or government program can provide unfailing protection against the death of infants. From first breath, humans live in the shadow of mortality. Too often, babies born to conscientious married parents die in infancy. But the lives of future infants will be powerfully safeguarded if their parents have learned to speak vows long before practicing exercises for breathing during delivery.

### NOTES

1. See U.S. Bureau of the Census, *Statistical Abstract of the United States: 1990*, 110th ed. (Washington, D.C.: U.S. Government Printing Office 1990), Table 80; James C. Cramer, "Social Factors and Infant Mortality: Identifying High Risk Groups and Proximate Causes," *Demography* 24 [1987]: 299.

2. See Julie Rovner, "Commission Urges New Steps to Combat Infant Mortality," *Congressional Quarterly Weekly Report* 46 (August 6, 1988), 2188; "Shameful figures," *The Economist*, September 3, 1988, pp. 25–28; Victoria Graham, "Bush urges worldwide effort against scourges of childhood," Associated Press, *The Rockford Register-Star*, October 1, 1990, p. 5A.

3. "What Infant Mortality Tells Us," *American Journal of Public Health* 80 (1990): 653; U.S. Bureau of the Census, *Statistical Abstract of the United States: 1990*, Table 110; Marian Wright Edelman, Memorandum to the National Commission on Children, October 5, 1990; Andrew Friede *et al.*, "Young Maternal Age and Infant Mortality: The Role of Low Birth Weight," *Public Health Reports* 102 (1987): 192.

4. T. Bennett, "Infant Mortality by Marital Status of Mother—United States, 1983," *Morbidity and Mortality Weekly Report* (August 3, 1990): 521–523.

5. Bennett, "Infant Mortality by Marital Status of Mother," 522–523; U.S. Bureau of the Census, *Statistical Abstract of the United States: 1990*, Table 90; Cramer, "Social Factors and Infant Mortality," 303–309.

6. Cramer, "Social Factors and Infant Mortality," 303–309; Joel C. Kleinman and Samuel S. Kessel, "Racial Differences in Low Birth Weight: Trends and Risk Factors," *New England Journal of Medicine* 317 (1987): 750–753.

7. Eve Powell-Griner, "Differences in Infant Mortality Among Texas Anglos, Hispanics, and Blacks," *Social Science Quarterly* 69 (1988): 461–465.

8. Powell-Griner, "Differences in Infant Mortality Among Texas Anglos, Hispanics, and Blacks," 460–464; Ronald L. Williams, Nancy J. Binkin, and Elizabeth J. Clingman, "Pregnancy Outcomes Among Spanish-surnamed Women in California," *American Journal of Public Health* 76 (1986): 387–390.

9. Patrick T. Dowling and Michael Fisher, "Maternal Factors and Low Birth Weight Infants: A Comparison of Blacks with Mexican Americans," *The Journal of Family Practice* 25 (1987): 153–158.

10. Dipali V. Apte, "A Plan to Prevent Adolescent Pregnancy and Reduce Infant Mortality," *Public Health Reports* 102 (1987): 80–85.

11. "Seeking Answers to the Slowing Progress in Lowering Infant Mortality," *Public Health Reports* 103 (1987): 121.

12. Terri Combs-Orme, "Infant Mortality: Priority for Social Work," *Social Work* 32 (1987): 507–511.

13. J. Brooks-Gunn, Marie C. McCormick, Margaret C. Heagarty, "Preventing Infant Mortality and Morbidity: Developmental Perspectives," *American Journal of Orthopsychiatry* 58 (1988): 288–295.

14. See *Congressional Quarterly Almanac: 101st Congress, 1st Session, 1989* (Washington, D.C.: Congressional Quarterly, Inc., 1990), 172–173, 177.

15. See Sherry Jacobsen, "Funding for Teen Moms Hits $21.5 B," Gannett News Service, *Rockford Register-Star*, September 24, 1990, p. 3A; Fernando Bertoli, Clyda S. Rent, George S. Rent, "Infant Mortality by Socioeconomic Status for Blacks, Indians, and Whites: A Longitudinal Analysis of North Carolina, 1968–1977," *Sociology and Social Research* 68 (1984): 364–373; Donna M. Strobino, "Declines in Nonwhite and White Neonatal Mortality in Mississippi, 1975–80," *Public Health Reports* 100 (1985): 420.

16. See Sara S. McLanahan, "Family Structure and Dependency: Early Transitions to Female Household Headship," *Demography* 25 (1988): 1–16; Sheila F. Krein and Andrea H. Beller, "Educational Attainment of Children from Single Parent Families: Differences by Exposure, Gender, and Race," *Demography* 25 (1988): 221–234; Ross L. Matsueda and Karen Heimer, "Race, Family Structure, and Delinquency: A Test of Differential Association and Social Control Theories," *American Sociological Review* 52 (1987): 826–840; Richard H. Needle, S. Susan Su, and William J. Doherty, "Divorce, Remarriage, and Adolescent Substance Abuse: A Prospective Longitudinal Study," *Journal of Marriage and the Family* 52 (1990): 157–159. William Marsiglio, "Adolescent Fathers in the United States: Their Initial Living Arrangements, Marital Experience and Educational Outcomes," *Family Planning Perspectives* 19 (November/December 1987): 240–251.

17. Robert D. Plotnick, "Welfare and Out-of-Wedlock Childbearing: Evidence From the 1980's," *Journal of Marriage and the Family* 52 (1990): 735–746.

18. See McLanahan, "Family Structure and Dependency," 1–16.

19. Kyriakos S. Markides and Connie McFarland, "A Note on Recent Trends in the Infant

Mortality-Socioeconomic Status Relationship," *Social Forces* 61 (1982): 271–274.

20. Jeffrey S. Levin and Kyriakos S. Markides, "Socioeconomic Status and Infant Mortality Among Hispanics in a Southwestern City," *Social Biology* 32 (1985): 61–63.

21. U.S. Bureau of the Census, *Statistical Abstract of the United States: 1990*, Tables 87, 95; Carol S. Aneshensel, "Onset of Fertility-Related Events During Adolescence: A Prospective Comparison of Mexican American and Non-Hispanic White Females," *American Journal of Public Health* 80 (1991): 959–963; Carol S. Aneshensel, Eve P. Fielder, and Rosina M. Becerra, "Fertility and Fertility-Related Behaviors Among Mexican-American and Non-Hispanic White Female Adolescents," *Journal of Health and Social Behavior* 30 (1989): 56–76.

22. Edward N. Brandt, "Infant Mortality—A Progress Report," *Public Health Reports* 99 (1984): 284–288.

23. Basil Mitchell, *Why Social Policy Cannot Be Morally Neutral: The Current Confusion About Pluralism*, The Social Affairs Unit, 1989.

**CRITICAL THINKING QUESTIONS**

1. If marriage protects babies, why are the infant mortality rates much higher for black married mothers than their white counterparts? For unmarried mothers age 20 and over compared to unmarried teenage mothers? For unmarried white-collar mothers compared to unmarried blue-collar mothers? That is, why are there variations by age, race, and socioeconomic status?

2. Christensen attributes the "Mexican-American miracle" of low infant deaths to marriage and traditional family life. Do the studies he cites support his conclusion? What other variables might explain the lower Mexican-American infant mortality rates?

3. What does Christensen mean by "moral coherence"? Do you agree that there is a relationship between moral coherence and infant mortality rates?

# 9    Single-Parent Families

## *Centrist:* The Carnage of Declining Marriage and Fatherhood

DAVID POPENOE, *Life Without Father: Compelling New Evidence That Father-hood and Marriage Are Indispensable for the Good of Children and Society* (New York: Free Press, 1996), pp. 2–10, 13–14. © 1996 by David Popenoe. Reprinted and abridged with the permission of The Free Press, an imprint of Simon & Schuster, Inc.

*Both conservatives and centrists are alarmed by the rise of single-parent families. Many conservatives focus on out-of-wedlock births as an indicator of family decline (see the article by Christensen). Centrists, moreover, continuously empha-size the negative effects of father absence—due to out-of-wedlock births, divorce, or the man's losing authority in a traditional household. In this selection, David Popenoe asserts that American fathers are more removed from family life than ever before and that the "massive erosion" of marriage and fatherhood contributes to many of our societal problems.*

With all the concentration on "role equality" in the home, the larger and more ominous trend of modern fatherhood has been mostly overlooked. We have been through many social revolutions in the past three decades—sex, women's liberation, divorce—but none more significant for society than the startling emergence of the absent father, a kind of pathological coun-terpart to the new father.

While the new father has been emerging gradually for most of this century, it is only in the past thirty years that we have wit-nessed the enormous increase in absent fathers. In times past, many children were left fatherless through his premature death. Today, the fathers are still alive and out there somewhere; the problem is that they seldom see much, if anything, of their chil-dren.

The main reason for contemporary father absence is the dramatic decline of marriage. Divorce rates have skyrocketed in the past thirty years, and even more recently we have seen a veritable explosion in the rate of unwed motherhood. What this means, in human terms, is that about half of today's children will spend at least a portion of their growing-up years living apart from their fathers.

As a society, we can respond to this new fatherlessness in several ways. We can, as more and more of us seem to be doing, simply declare fathers to be unnecessary, superfluous. This is the response of "single parents by choice." It is the response of those who say that if daddies and mommies are expected to do precisely the same things in the home, why do we need both? It is the response of those who declare that unwed motherhood is a woman's right, or that single-parent families are every bit as good as two-parent families, or that divorce is generally beneficial for children.

In my view, these responses represent a human tragedy—for children, for women, for men, and for our society as a whole. I am writing this book to tell you why. My main emphasis will be on children. I hope to convince you, especially those of you who rely on empirical evidence before you make up your mind, that the evidence is strong: Fathering is different from mothering; involved fathers are indispensable for the good of children and society; and our growing national fatherlessness is a disaster in the making.

## THE DECLINE OF FATHERHOOD

The decline of fatherhood is one of the most basic, unexpected, and extraordinary social trends of our time. The trend can be captured in a single telling statistic: in just three decades, from 1960 to 1990, the percentage of children living apart from their biological fathers more than doubled, from 17 percent to 36 percent. If this rate continues, by the turn of the century nearly 50 percent of American children will be going to sleep each night without being able to say good night to their dads.

No one predicted this trend, few researchers or government agencies have monitored it, and it is not widely discussed, even today. But its importance to society is second to none. Father absence is a major force lying behind many of the attention-grabbing issues that dominate the news: crime and delinquency; premature sexuality and out-of-wedlock teen births; deteriorating educational achievement; depression, substance abuse, and alienation, among teenagers; and the growing number of women and children in poverty. These issues all point to a profound deterioration in the well-being of children. Some experts have

suggested, in fact, that the current generation of children and youth is the first in our nation's history to be less well-off—psychologically, socially, economically, and morally—than their parents were at the same age. Or as Senator Daniel Patrick Moynihan has observed, "the United States . . . may be the first society in history in which children are distinctly worse off than adults."[1]

Along with the growing father absence, our cultural view of fatherhood is changing. Few people have doubts about the fundamental importance of mothers. But fathers? More and more the question is being raised, are fathers really necessary? Many would answer no, or maybe not. And to the degree that fathers are still thought necessary, fatherhood is said by many to be merely a social role, as if men had no inherent biological predisposition whatsoever to acknowledge and to invest in their own offspring. If merely a social role, then perhaps anyone is capable of playing it. The implication is one of arbitrary substitutability. Not just biological fathers, but any competent actor who has studied the part can easily step in: mothers, partners, stepfathers, uncles and aunts, grandparents. Perhaps the script can even be rewritten and the role changed—or dropped.

## FATHERS: ESSENTIAL BUT PROBLEMATIC

Across time and cultures, fathers have always been considered by societies to be essential—and not just for their sperm. Indeed, until today, no known society ever thought of fathers as potentially unnecessary. Biological fathers are everywhere identified, if possible, and play some role in their children's upbringing. Marriage and the nuclear family—mother, father, and children—are the most universal social institutions in existence. In no society has nonmarital childbirth been the cultural norm. To the contrary, a concern for the "legitimacy" of children is another cultural near universal: The mother of an illegitimate child virtually everywhere has been regarded as a social deviant, if not a social outcast, and her child has been stigmatized.

At the same time, being a father is universally problematic for men and for their societies in a way that being a mother is not. While mothers the world over bear and nurture their young with an intrinsic acknowledgment and, most commonly, acceptance of their role, taking on the role of father is often filled with conflict, tension, distance, and doubt. Across societies, fathers may or may not be closely engaged with their children, reside with the mother, or see their father role as highly important.

The source of this sex-role difference can be plainly stated. Men are not biologically as attuned to being committed fathers as women are to being committed mothers. Left culturally unregulated, men's sexual behavior can be promiscuous, their paternity casual, their commitment to families weak. Yet in virtually all societies, especially modern societies, both child and social well-being depend on high levels of paternal investment: the time, energy, and resources that fathers are willing to impart to their children.

That men are not perfectly attuned to fatherhood in biological terms is not to say that fathering behavior is foreign to the nature of men. Far from it. Evolutionary scientists tell us that the development of the fathering capacity and high paternal investments in offspring—features not common among our primate relatives—have been a source of enormous evolutionary advantage for human beings. Because human young are more dependent on adults for a longer period of their lives than any other species and human mothers require a great deal of help if their children are to survive, a key to human evolution was the capturing of male effort to the goal of childrearing. It is almost certainly the case that the human family is the oldest social institution, at heart a biological arrangement for raising children that has always involved fathers as well as mothers.

In recognition of the fatherhood problem—that fatherhood is essential but also somewhat problematic—human cultures have realized that sanctions are necessary if paternal investments are to be maximized. The main cultural carrier of sanctions is the institution of marriage, a major purpose of which is to hold men to the reproductive pair bond. Simply defined, marriage is a relationship within which a community socially approves and encourages sexual intercourse and the birth of children. It is society's way of signaling to would-be parents of children that their long-term relationship together is socially important. As evidenced by the vows of fidelity and permanence that almost universally are part of the wedding ceremony, an important purpose of marriage is to hold the man to the union. Margaret Mead once said, with the fatherhood problem strongly in mind, that there is no society in the world where men will stay married for very long unless culturally required to do so.

## FATHERHOOD AND MARRIAGE

Today, because the great social complexity of modern societies requires longer periods of socialization and dependency for children than ever before, the need for adult investments in children has reached new heights. In order to succeed economically in an increasingly technological society, children must be highly educated. In order to succeed socially and psychologically in an increasingly complex and heterogeneous culture, children must have strong and stable attachments to adults. Nonfamily institutions can help with education, but family and close-kin groups are essential for socioemotional success. Parents and other close relatives are still the persons most likely to have the motivational levels necessary to provide the time and attention that children need to feel loved and special.

Yet at the time when the childrearing task is ever more demanding and male assistance with the task is ever more important, cultural sanctions holding men to marriage and children have dramatically weakened. Marriage, once both sacred and economically essential for survival, is today based solely on the fragile tie of affection for one's mate. And whereas the institution of marriage once legally bound a couple with a high degree of permanence, marriages can now be broken unilaterally on a whim.

The United States has by far the highest divorce rate in the industrialized world. The chance that a first marriage occurring today will end in divorce stands at around 50 percent—by some estimates as high as 60 percent. The chance in the middle of the last century was around 5 percent. In the past three decades alone, the divorce rate has doubled or tripled, depending upon how one calculates it.

Marriages are not only breaking up in large numbers, but the institution itself is in decline. The marriage rate is dropping. In place of marriage we are witnessing the rapid rise of nonmarital cohabitation, which by its very nature implies a lower level of commitment. More problematic still is the increase in "single parenting by choice."

There has emerged in the last decade or two a tendency for women to go it alone. It would be nice, many of these women report, if the perfect man came into the picture. But he is not around, so I am going to have a child anyway. This phenomenon was made culturally memorable by the *Murphy Brown* television episode in which Murphy decided to have a nonmarital child and that fact was celebrated nationwide. Like Murphy, but typically without her level of economic resources, more and more women report with each passing year that they, too, might have a child if they are unable to find the right man.

The lifestyle of the single parent, rather than being eschewed, is becoming socially accepted as part of a new wave of tolerance befitting the contemporary celebration of diversity. Even marriage and family-relations professionals have come to extol "alternative lifestyles." Textbooks that used to be entitled *Marriage and the Family* (read: married-father-included) are now entitled *Intimate Relationships* or the all-inclusive *Families*. The growth of unmarried mothers on welfare has raised some national ire, but many on the Left believe that there is a new national "right" for such mothers to have as many children as they want and immediately receive support for those children from taxpayers.

With this kind of cultural acceptance, it is little wonder that the percentage of out-of-wedlock births in America has increased 600 percent in just three decades, from 5 percent of all births in 1960 to 30 percent in 1991.[2] If the percentage keeps climbing at its current rate, 40 percent of all births (and 80 percent of minority births) will take place out of wedlock by the turn of the century.[3]

## THE SHRINKING FATHER

Contemporary fatherhood faces an additional challenge. The father's role has shrunk drastically over the years. American fathers have been losing authority within the family and psychologically withdrawing from a direct role in childrearing almost since colonial times.

The Puritan father was a domestic patriarch; he was not only the family's chief provider and protector but also the moral authority and chief educator, at least of his older children. In the last century, however, the focus of the family turned to mothers. With the rise of a major new family form— what historians label "the modern nuclear family" but what most people today know as "the traditional family"—the father's main role became family breadwinner. Legally and socially fathers became the second parent, and their direct role in the home increasingly was marginalized. Finally, with the waning of the modern nuclear family in this century, even the breadwinner role has eroded.

Today men are being asked to return to domestic roles. Fathers are badly needed as comprehensive childrearers on an equal basis with mothers. Not only does this represent a radical shift from recent history, but increasingly men are asked to become major caretakers for infants and toddlers, a role they never before in history have had to embrace.

## THE FATHERHOOD DEBATE

Could it be that the era of fatherhood is at an end, that the fatherhood problem can be resolved by simply getting rid of fathers and perhaps substituting someone or something else in their stead? Is there something new and different about modern societies that makes single parenthood a reasonable option and makes these societies increasingly immune from the age-old proscription against illegitimacy? Have we become so free and individualized and prosperous that the traditional social structures surrounding family life no longer have the importance that they have had in all of human history to date?

Positive answers to these questions have been forcefully argued. The argument contains these key elements:

- Women no longer need men for provision or protection, the traditional male family roles. For provision, most women now have independent access to the labor market; and if they don't, they have access to government-supported welfare programs. For protection, women have the police, and in any event it is usually their male partner from whom they must be protected.
- Both single mothers and their children have been unfairly stigmatized over the generations. This has been grossly unfair to mothers as well as to the children who did absolutely nothing to bring about their plight. Societies today are able, thankfully, to correct this age-old injustice.
- Male-female family life is inherently inequitable, a patriarchal institution wherein men have always dominated

women. Men are selfish, irresponsible, psychologically untrustworthy, even intractable. If women are to achieve true equality, therefore, we must find some alternative to the nuclear family.
- Men frequently leave their wives and children in the lurch, especially in times of crisis, either through psychological withdrawal or outright desertion. It is safer for a woman never to begin counting on a man.
- It is not clear that fathers any longer provide something unique to their children. There is not much they do that mothers do not, or cannot, do just as well.

There is some truth, of course, to each of these points. Many women today are perfectly capable, in economic and other terms, of raising children by themselves. The traditional stigma against illegitimacy is something that few people want to bring back. There does seem to be some kind of inherent inequality between men and women, if nothing more than that men are bigger and stronger and more aggressive. The selfish, irresponsible male is not uncommon. And since some fathers and mothers do carry out the same childrearing activities, the question of why we need both is a reasonable one to ask.

But the aim of this [reading] is to try to convince you that this no-father argument is fundamentally wrong. If we continue down the path of fatherlessness, we are headed for social disaster.

## FATHERS AND MOTHERS

It is the rare child who does not wish to grow up with both a father and a mother. We should ask the question, why do children have this desire? Despite their sometimes wanting candy for breakfast, children do have, after all, a certain wisdom about life. Is it simply that they don't want to be any different from their friends? Is it merely something they have been taught to say? I think not.

Every child comes into the world totally dependent upon adults, especially the parents to whom they were born. To a large extent children's life chances come from who cares for them and how they are cared for. Of course, children are surprisingly flexible and malleable; some can thrive in the most intolerable of circumstances. But this fact says nothing about the life chances for the multitude. I suspect that children instinctively realize that the world is made up almost equally of two sexes, that each sex possesses biological and psychological traits that balance and complement the other, and that each sex brings something unique and important to children's lives.

Whatever the basis for children's primal desire for a father and a mother, the weight of social science evidence strongly supports the rationality of their wish. In my many years as a functioning social scientist, I know of few other bodies of evidence whose weight leans so much in one direction as does the evidence about family structure: On the whole, two parents—a father and a mother—are better for the child than one parent.[4]

There are, to be sure, many complicating factors to the simple proposition that two parents are best. Family structure is only a gross approximation of what actually goes on within a family. We all know of a two-parent family that is the family from hell. A child can certainly be well-raised to adulthood by one loving parent who is wholly devoted to that child's well-being. But such problems and exceptions in no way deny the aggregate finding or generalization. After all, to take another much-publicized area of research, plenty of three-pack-a-day smokers live to a ripe old age and die of natural causes.

What does the social science evidence about family structure and child well-being actually show? Researchers Sara McLanahan and Gary Sandefur recently examined six nationally representative data sets containing over twenty-five thousand children from a variety of racial and social-class backgrounds. Their conclusion:

> Children who grow up with only one of their biological parents (nearly always the mother) are disadvantaged across a broad array of outcomes . . . they are twice as likely to drop out of high school, 2.5 times as likely to become teen mothers, and 1.4 times as likely to be idle—out of school and out of work—as children who grow up with both parents.[5]

Sure, you may say, that is because one-parent families are poorer. But here is the researchers' conclusion about the economic factor:

> Loss of economic resources accounts for about 50 percent of the disadvantages associated with single parenthood. Too little parental supervision and involvement and greater residential mobility account for most of the rest.[6]

Many other researchers, whose work is reviewed in this book, have come up with similar conclusions. The evidence covers the full range of possible effects, from crime to school achievement. Social analysts William A. Galston and Elaine Ciulla Kamark report, for example, that

> The relationship [between family structure and crime] is so strong that controlling for family configuration erases the relationship between race and crime and between low income and crime. This conclusion shows up again and again in the literature.[7]

Based on such evidence, a strong case can be made that paternal deprivation, in the form of the physical, economic, and emotional unavailability of fathers to their children, has become the most prevalent form of child maltreatment in America today.[8]

Is the missing ingredient in the single-parent family simply a second adult who can provide "parental supervision and involvement"? It is in part, but only in part. Consider this conclusion of McLanahan and Sandefur: "Children of stepfamilies don't do better than children of mothers who never remarry."[9]

The main missing ingredient in a growing number of families today, I shall argue, is the biological father. He can be replaced adequately here and there, and obviously not all biological fathers are good fathers, but in general males biologically unrelated to their children cannot be expected to have the same motivation and dedication to raising those children as males raising their own biological offspring. The incidence of sexual abuse among stepfathers, for example, is far higher than among biological fathers.

It is not my intent to stigmatize step- and adoptive parents. Those alternative family forms where parents are doing their job well deserve our deepest respect; those experiencing difficulties should be provided both compassion and tangible assistance. My point is this: Being a father is much more than merely fulfilling a social role. Engaged biological fathers care profoundly and selflessly about their own children; such fatherly love is not something that can easily be transferred or reduced to the learning of a script. Why many biological fathers themselves are now becoming disengaged from their children is, of course, a puzzling phenomenon.

### THE UNATTACHED MALE

Apart from enhancing children's lives, there are other good reasons why it is important for men to be engaged in parenting. One socially crucial reason is contained in this caveat: Every society must be wary of the unattached male, for he is universally the cause of numerous social ills. The good society is heavily dependent on men being attached to a strong moral order centered on families, not only to help raise children but to discipline their own sexual behavior and to reduce their competitive aggression.

Family life is a considerable civilizing force for men. It is not uncommon to hear men say, for example, that they will give up certain deviant or socially irresponsible behavior only when they have children, for then they feel the need to set a good example. Long ago the great sociologist Emile Durkheim noted that married men

experience a "salutary discipline"; marriage forces men to master their passions, but it also encourages the regular work habits and self-sacrifice required to meet the family's material needs.[10]

A high proportion of male criminals are unattached. Unattached men are more likely to behave criminally and violently than attached men; they are also more likely to die prematurely through disease, accidents, or self-neglect. Men with various social and physical handicaps obviously find it more difficult to attract a spouse, and it is these same traits that may result in criminal behavior or shorter lives. Yet careful epidemiologic studies have shown that marriage has a protective effect for men independent of the "marriage-selection" factor.[11]

So even those who disagree that fathers are essential to sound childrearing and feel sanguine about unmarried women taking on the task by themselves still should worry about how the men left out will be spending their time. Do we really want a society filled with single men, unattached to children, leading self-aggrandizing and often predatory lives?

### FATHERHOOD, MARRIAGE, AND THE GOOD SOCIETY

Today in America the social order is fraying badly; we seem to be on a path of continuing social decline. The past three decades have seen steeply rising rates of crime, declining interpersonal and political trust, growing personal and corporate greed, deteriorating communities, and increasing confusion over moral issues.[12] I am referring not only to the situation of the inner city poor, with which most Americans have little contact, but to the overall quality of daily life. The average American seemingly has become more anxious, unsettled, and insecure.

Our societal decline can be phrased in terms of a failure of social values. People no longer conduct themselves, to the same extent as prior generations, according to the civic virtues of honesty, self-sacrifice, and personal responsibility. People have become strong on individual rights and weak on community obligations.[13] In our ever-growing pursuit of the self—self-expression, self-development, self-actualization, and self-fulfillment—the social has become increasingly problematic.

At the heart of the problem lies an erosion of personal relationships. People no longer trust others as they once did; they no longer feel the same sense of commitment and obligation to others. This is certainly not a new or original observation. The perceived erosion of "primary relationships" that is associated with modernity was one of the formative conceptions of the discipline of sociology in the last century.[14] But the early sociologists could not have known the great extent to which their conception would prove correct.

Fathers are one of the two most important role models in children's lives. Some children across America now go to bed each night worrying about whether their father will be there the next morning. Some wonder what ever happened to their father. Some think to themselves, who is my father? Is it a stretch to believe that the father-neglected or father-abandoned child is more likely to have a jaundiced view of such values as honesty, self-sacrifice, and personal responsibility, to say nothing of trust?

The decline of fatherhood and of marriage cuts at the heart of the kind of environment considered ideal for childrearing. Such an environment, according to a substantial body of knowledge, consists of an enduring two-parent family that engages regularly in activities together, has many of its own routines and traditions, and provides a great deal of quality contact time between adults and children. The children have frequent contact with relatives, active neighboring in a supportive setting, and contact with their parents' world of work. In addition, there is little concern on the part of children that their parents will break up. Finally, each of these ingredients comes together in the development of a rich family subculture that has lasting meaning and strongly promulgates such family values as responsibility, cooperation, and sharing.

In our society, as in all others so far as we know, the family is the seedbed of trusting and socially responsible personal relationships. The family is also, not coincidentally, the seedbed of those civic virtues that we are losing. Children do not hold such virtues as honesty and self-sacrifice at birth; these virtues must be purposefully taught and reinforced through close personal relationships and good example. Children learn many things, including values, through imitation or modeling. The more consistently caring and altruistic the parent is, the more likely it is the child will be so. If such virtues are not taught within the family, they normally are not taught at all.

What the decline of fatherhood and marriage in America really means, then, is that slowly, insidiously, and relentlessly our society has been moving in an ominous direction—toward the devaluation of children. There has been an alarming weakening of the fundamental assumption, long at the center of our culture, that children are to be loved and valued at the highest level of priority. Nothing could be more serious for our children or our future.

Our national response, therefore, should be the reestablishment of fatherhood and marriage as strong social and cultural realities. If we are to make progress toward a more just and humane society, a major national objective should be no less than this: To increase the proportion of children who are living with and cared for by their married, biological fathers and to decrease the proportion of children who are not.

### NOTES

1. *New York Times*, September 25, 1986, p. C7.

2. U.S. Department of Health and Human Services. *Vital Statistics of the United States, 1991*. Vol. 1, *Natality*. Washington, DC: GPO, 1993. Among blacks, the increase has been from 23% to 68%.

3. Congressional testimony of Lee Rainwater, Harvard University. Cited in William J. Bennett.

1994. *The Index of Leading Cultural Indicators.* New York: Simon & Schuster, p. 47.

4. It should be noted that social science evidence is never conclusive, on this or any other matter we will be taking up in this book. The world is too complex; the scientific method can only imperfectly be applied to the study of human beings; researchers have biases; and people may not always be telling investigators the truth. These are but a few of the many problems endemic to the social sciences. The best use of the social science evidence is to help confirm or disconfirm. Does the evidence generally support a proposition or not? If it does, fine; if it does not, one had better have a good explanation as to why that proposition may still be true.

5. Sara S. McLanahan. 1994. "The Consequences of Single Motherhood." *The American Prospect*, 18:48–58, esp. 49. Article is drawn from Sara McLanahan and Gary Sandefur. 1994. *Growing Up with a Single Parent.* Cambridge, MA: Harvard University Press.

6. McLanahan. *Consequences*, p. 52.

7. Elaine Ciulla Kamark and William A. Galston. 1990. *Putting Children First: A Progressive Family Policy for the 1990s.* Washington, DC: Progressive Policy Institute, pp. 14–15.

8. See Henry B. Biller. 1993. *Fathers and Families: Paternal Factors in Child Development.* Westport, CT: Auburn House.

9. McLanahan. *Consequences*, p. 51.

10. Emile Durkheim. 1951. *Suicide: A Study in Sociology.* New York: Free Press.

11. Arthur Kraus and Abraham Lilienfeld. 1959. "Some Epidemiologic Aspects of the High Mortality Rate in the Young Widowed Group. *Journal of Chronic Diseases* 10:207–217. Walter Gove. 1973. "Sex, Marital Status, and Mortality." *American Journal of Sociology* 79:45–67.

12. Two general books on this topic are: James Lincoln Collier. 1991. *The Rise of Selfishness in America.* New York: Oxford University Press; and Art Carey. 1991. *The United States of Incompetence.* Boston: Houghton Mifflin. See also: Louis Harris. 1987. *Inside America.* New York: Vintage Books; and William J. Bennett. 1994. *The Index of Leading Cultural Indicators.* New York: Simon & Schuster. In the light of such changes, some observers have called into question the very idea of social progress itself. See Christopher Lasch. 1991. *The True and Only Heaven.* New York: W. W. Norton.

13. Mary Ann Glendon. 1991. *Rights Talk: The Impoverishment of Political Discourse.* New York: Free Press.

14. Robert A. Nisbet. 1966. *The Sociological Tradition.* New York: Basic Books.

## CRITICAL THINKING QUESTIONS

1. Why, according to Popenoe, have both fatherhood and marriage declined?

2. Do you agree that "if we continue down the path of fatherlessness, we are headed for social disaster"? Are there other possible reasons—such as crime, delinquency, poverty, and deteriorating educational achievement—that help to explain the decline of fatherlessness?

3. Centrists say they embrace egalitarian gender roles (see, for example, Chapters 1 and 3). Popenoe maintains, however, that "family life is a considerable civilizing force for men," that marriage "disciplines" men's sexual behavior, and that "even the [male] breadwinner role has eroded." How different are these views from those expressed by conservatives in Chapters 3, 5, and 8?

# 9 Single-Parent Families

## *Liberal/Feminist:* The Father Fixation

JUDITH STACEY, "The Father Fixation: Let's Get Real About American Families," *Utne Reader* 77 (September/October 1996): 72–73. Reproduced with permission of the author.

*Most conservatives and centrists contend that father absence explains many societal problems. Many liberals, especially feminists, argue, instead, that macro-level problems—such as poverty and employment—generate single-parent households. For example, Judith Stacey maintains that the father's influence in the family has been exaggerated, that divorce is better for children than living in high-conflict two-parent families, and that "family diversity is here to stay."*

As the electoral season hits full throttle, more and more voices are intoning the mantra of "family values." The Institute for American Values and its offshoot, the Council on Families in America, and other groups crusade on behalf of the supposed superiority of married-couple nuclear families, branding all other kinds of families second-rate—or worse. They are using the apparently objective language of social science to preach a sermon that we used to hear mainly in the fire-and-brimstone tones of the religious right. This quieted-down approach is having a major effect on Democratic Party and media rhetoric on family issues.

These groups pretend to speak for an overwhelming consensus of social scientists when they blame family "breakdown"—by which they mean primarily the rise of divorce and unwed parenting—for just about every social problem in the nation. David Blankenhorn, president of the Institute for American Values, for example, calls fatherlessness "the most

harmful demographic trend of this generation." He writes that "it is the leading cause of declining child well-being in our society. It is also the engine driving our most urgent social problems, from crime to adolescent pregnancy to child sexual abuse to domestic violence against women." The somewhat more temperate David Popenoe [see the previous article] concedes that there are many sources of social decay but insists that "the evidence is now strong that the absence of fathers from the lives of children is one of the most important causes."

However well intentioned and appealing, most of the claims made by family values crusaders are blatantly false as well as destructive. As a sociologist, I can attest that there is absolutely no consensus among social scientists on family values, on the superiority of the heterosexual nuclear family, or on the supposed evil effects of fatherlessness. In fact, the best research and the most careful, best-regarded researchers, among them Andrew

Cherlin at Johns Hopkins University, confirm that the quality of our family relationships and resources is far more important than gender or structure. The claim that intact two-parent families are inherently superior rests exclusively on the misuse of statistics and on the most elementary social science sins—portraying correlations as though they were causes, ignoring mediating factors, and treating small, overlapping differences as gross and absolute.

Take, for example, the hysteria that the family values campaign has whipped up about the "doomsday" effects of divorce. Certainly, no sociologist—no reasonable adult I can think of—would argue that divorce is a meaningless or minor event for a family. No one among the many scholars of the family who share my views would deny that some divorces unfairly serve the interests of one or both parents at the expense of their children. Still, the evidence resoundingly supports the idea that a high-conflict marriage injures children more than a divorce does. Instead of protecting children, the current assault on no-fault divorce endangers them by inviting more parental conflict, desertion, and fraud.

Moreover, research shows again and again that poverty and unemployment can more reliably predict who will marry, divorce, or commit or suffer domestic or social violence than can the best-tuned measure of values yet devised. A study conducted by University of California-Berkeley psychologist Ralph Catalano found, for example, that workers laid off from their jobs were six times more likely than employed workers to commit violent acts and that losing one's job was a better predictor of violence than gender, marital status, mental illness, or anything else. Those who really want to shore up marriages should fight for secure jobs and a living wage.

You don't need to be a social scientist to know that living with married biological parents offers children no magic shield against trouble. Indeed, a recent Kaiser Permanente study of youth and violence found that 68 percent of "youth highly exposed to health and safety threats" were living in two-parent households. Poignantly, even in two-parent families, fathers were among the last people troubled teens said they would turn to for help: 44 percent said they would turn to their mothers for advice; 26 percent chose their friends; and only 10 percent picked their fathers.

Harping on the superiority of married biological parents and the evils of fatherlessness injures children and parents in a wide array of contemporary families, including the millions of children who live with gay or lesbian parents. Blankenhorn castigates lesbian couples who choose to have children for promoting "radical fatherlessness" and advocates restricting access to sperm banks and fertility services to married heterosexual couples. Popenoe claims that biological fathers make distinctive, irreplaceable contributions to their children's welfare.

Yet here the social science record is truly uniform. Nearly three decades of research finds gay and lesbian parents to be at least as successful as heterosexuals. Dozens of studies conclude that children reared by lesbian or gay parents have no greater gender or social difficulties than other children, except for the problems caused by homophobia and discrimination. Ironically, some of the worst risks these children suffer stem from our failure to legally recognize the actual two-parent families in which many live. For example, a child whose lesbian birth mother dies often loses a second parent too, as Kristen Pearlman did in 1985 when a Florida court placed her in the custody of her grandparents rather than her surviving co-mother, Janine Ratcliffe, who had helped parent her since birth. Anyone who cares about the welfare of children should campaign to extend full marriage and custody rights to their parents rather than belittle them for lacking a father or mother.

It is time to face the irreversible historical fact that family diversity is here to stay. Of course, two good parents of whatever gender generally are better than one. But no one lives in a "general" family. Our unique, often imperfect, real families assume many shapes, sizes, and characters. Each type of family has strengths, vulnerabilities, and challenges, and each needs support and deserves respect. We can't coerce or preach people into successful marital or parenting relationships, but we can help them to succeed in the ones they form. What we need to promote instead of divisive, self-righteous family values are inclusive, democratic, and compassionate *social* values.

**CRITICAL THINKING QUESTIONS**

1. Why does Stacey argue that the father's influence in the family is exaggerated?

2. Stacey maintains that the claims made by such centrists as Popenoe and other "family values crusaders" are "false as well as destructive." Since both Stacey and Popenoe are sociologists, why do they disagree about the importance of two-parent families?

3. Do you agree or disagree with Stacey's argument that "family diversity," including gay and lesbian households, is here to stay? Explain your position.

# 10 Raising Children

## *Conservative:* Spare the Rod?

DEN A. TRUMBULL AND S. DUBOSE RAVENEL, "Spare the Rod? New Research Challenges Spanking Critics," *Family Policy*, Family Research Council, January 22, 1999. Reproduced with permission of The Family Research Council.

*One of the most controversial issues between conservatives and liberals is whether sparing the rod will spoil the child. In this selection, Den A. Trumbull and S. DuBose Ravenel argue that opponents of spanking base their conclusions on eleven unfounded arguments. The authors maintain that caring discipline, including spanking, is effective in changing inappropriate behavior if the spanking is age-appropriate, used selectively, and is motivated by love for the purpose of teaching and correcting, not revenge or rage.*

Opposition to parents spanking their children has been growing significantly in elite circles over the past 15 years.[1] No doubt much of this opposition springs from a sincere concern for the well-being of children. Child abuse is a reality, and stories of child abuse are horrifying. But while loving and effective discipline is quite definitely *not* harsh and abusive, neither is it weak and ineffectual. Indeed, disciplinary spanking can fall well within the boundaries of loving discipline and need not be labeled abusive violence.[2]

Or so most Americans seem to think. According to a recent Voter/Consumer Research poll commissioned by the Family Research Council, 76 percent of the more than 1,000 Americans surveyed said that spanking was an effective form of discipline in their home when they were children.[3] These results are made all the more impressive by the fact that nearly half of those who answered otherwise grew up in homes in which they were never spanked. Taken together, more than four out of five Americans who were actually spanked by their parents as children say that it was an effective form of discipline.

In addition, Americans perceive lack of discipline to be the biggest problem in public education today, according to a recent Gallup poll.[4] Several studies show strong public support for corporal punishment by parents.[5]

Critics claim that spanking a child is abusive and contributes to adult dysfunction. These allegations arise from studies that fail to distinguish appropriate spanking from other forms of punishment. Abusive forms of physical punishment such as kicking, punching, and beating are commonly grouped with mild spanking. Furthermore, the studies usually include, and even emphasize, corporal punishment of adolescents, rather than focusing on preschool children, where spanking is more effective. This blurring of distinctions between spanking and physical abuse, and between children of different ages gives critics the illusion of having data condemning all disciplinary spanking.

There are several arguments commonly leveled against disciplinary spanking. Interestingly, most of these arguments can be used against other forms of discipline. Any form of discipline (time-out, restriction, etc.), when used inappropriately and in anger, can result in distorting a child's perception of justice and harming his emotional development. In light of this, let us examine some of the unfounded arguments promoted by spanking opponents.

### Argument #1: Many psychological studies show that spanking is an improper form of discipline.

*Counterpoint:* Researchers John Lyons, Rachel Anderson, and David Larson of the National Institute of Healthcare Research recently conducted a systematic review of the research literature on corporal punishment.[6] They found that 83 percent of the 132 identified articles published in clinical and psychosocial journals were merely opinion-driven editorials, reviews, or commentaries, devoid of new empirical findings. Moreover, most of the empirical studies were methodologically flawed by grouping the impact of abuse with spanking. The best studies demonstrated beneficial, not detrimental, effects of spanking in certain situations. Clearly, there is insufficient evidence to condemn parental spanking and adequate evidence to justify its proper use.

### Argument #2: Physical punishment establishes the moral righteousness of hitting other persons who do something that is regarded as wrong.

*Counterpoint:* The "spanking teaches hitting" belief has gained in popularity over the past decade, but is not supported by objective evidence. A distinction must be made between abusive hitting and nonabu-

sive spanking. A child's ability to discriminate hitting from disciplinary spanking depends largely upon the parents' attitude with spanking and the parents' procedure for spanking. There is no evidence in the medical literature that a mild spank to the buttocks of a disobedient child by a loving parent teaches the child aggressive behavior.

The critical issue is *how* spanking (or, in fact, any punishment) is used more so than *whether* it is used. Physical abuse by an angry, uncontrolled parent will leave lasting emotional wounds and cultivate bitterness and resentment within a child. The balanced, prudent use of disciplinary spanking, however, is an effective deterrent to aggressive behavior with some children.

Researchers at the Center for Family Research at Iowa State University studied 332 families to examine both the impact of corporal punishment and the quality of parental involvement on three adolescent outcomes—aggressiveness, delinquency, and psychological well-being. The researchers found a strong association between the quality of parenting and each of these three outcomes. Corporal punishment, however, was *not* adversely related to any of these outcomes. This study proves the point that quality of parenting is the chief determinant of favorable or unfavorable outcomes.[7] Remarkably, childhood aggressiveness has been more closely linked to maternal permissiveness and negative criticism than to even abusive physical discipline.[8]

It is unrealistic to expect that children would never hit others if their parents would only exclude spanking from their discipline options. Most children in their toddler years (long before they are ever spanked) naturally attempt to hit others when conflict or frustration arises. The continuation of this behavior is largely determined by how the parent or caregiver responds. If correctly disciplined, the hitting will become less frequent. If ignored or ineffectively disciplined, the hitting will likely persist and even escalate. Thus, instead of contributing to greater violence, spanking can be a useful component in an overall plan to effectively teach a child to stop aggressive hitting.

**Argument #3: Since parents often refrain from hitting until the anger or frustration reaches a certain point, the child learns that anger and frustration justify the use of physical force.**

*Counterpoint:* A study published in *Pediatrics* indicates that most parents who spank do not spank on impulse, but purposefully spank their children with a belief in its effectiveness.[9] Furthermore, the study revealed no significant correlation between the frequency of spanking and the anger reported by mothers. Actually, the mothers who reported being angry were not the same parents who spanked.

Reactive, impulsive hitting after losing control due to anger is unquestionably the wrong way for a parent to use corporal punishment. Eliminating all physical punishment in the home, however, would not remedy such explosive scenarios. It could even increase the problem. When effective spanking is removed from a parent's disciplinary repertoire, he or she is left with nagging, begging, belittling, and yelling, once the primary disciplinary measures— such as time-out and logical consequences—have failed. By contrast, if proper spanking is proactively used in conjunction with other disciplinary measures, better control of the particularly defiant child can be achieved, and moments of exasperation are less likely to occur.

**Argument #4: Physical punishment is harmful to a child.**

*Counterpoint:* Any disciplinary measure, physical, verbal or emotional, carried to an extreme can harm a child. Excessive scolding and berating of a child by a parent is emotionally harmful. Excessive use of isolation (time-out) for unreasonable periods of time can humiliate a child and ruin the measure's effectiveness. Obviously, excessive or indiscriminate physical punishment is harmful and abusive. However, an appropriately-administered spanking of a forewarned disobedient child is not harmful when administered in a loving controlled manner.

Without the prudent use of spanking for the particularly defiant child, a parent runs the risk of being inconsistent and rationalizing the child's behavior. This inconsistent manner of parenting is confusing and harmful to the child and is damaging to the parent-child relationship. There is no evidence that proper disciplinary spanking is harmful to the child.

**Argument #5: Physical punishment makes the child angry at the parent.**

*Counterpoint:* All forms of punishment initially elicit a frustrated, angry response from a child. Progression of this anger is dependent primarily upon the parent's attitude during and after the disciplinary event, and the manner of its application. Any form of punishment administered angrily for purposes of retribution, rather than calmly for purposes of correction, can create anger and resentment in a child. Actually, a spanking can break the escalating rage of a rebellious child and more quickly restore the relationship between parent and child.

**Argument #6: Spanking teaches a child that "might makes right," that power and strength are most important, and that the biggest can force their will upon the smallest.**

*Counterpoint:* Parental power is commonly exerted in routine child rearing, and spanking is only one example. Other situations where power and restraint are exercised by the average parent include:

- The young child who insists on running from his parent in a busy mall or parking lot.
- The toddler who refuses to sit in his car seat.
- The young patient who refuses to hold still as a vaccination is administered, or as a laceration is repaired.

Clark, Lynn C. *SOS! Help for Parents.* 1985; 181–185. Kentucky: Parents Press.

Baumrind, Dr. Diana. "The Development of rumental Competence Through Socializa-." *Minnesota Symposia on Child Psychology.* ; 7:3–46.

Austin, Glenn. *Love and Power: How to Raise petent, Confident Children.* 1988. California: rt Erdmann Publishing. Also, Dobson, Dr. es. *The Strong-Willed Child.* 1985. Illinois: dale House Publishers, and Coopersmith, ley. *The Antecedents of Self-Esteem.* 1967. w York: W. H. Freeman & Co. Reprinted 1. California: Consulting Psychologists ss, Inc.

Larzelere, Dr. Robert E. "Should the Use of poral Punishment by Parents Be Considered ld Abuse?" Mason, M., Gambrill, E. (eds.). ating Children's Lives. 1994; pp. 204–209. Cali-nia: Sage Publications.

Eron, Dr. Leonard D. "Theories of Aggres-n: From Drives to Cognitions." Huesmann, L. (ed.). *Aggressive Behavior, Current Perspectives.* 4; pp. 3–11. New York: Plenum Press.

Straus, Murray A. "Discipline and Deviance: ysical Punishment of Children and Violence d Other Crime in Adulthood." *Social Problems.* 1; 38:133–152.

National Committee to Prevent Child use. *Memorandum.* May 1995; 2(5).

White, Kristin. "Where Pediatricians Stand Spanking." *Pediatric Management.* September 3: 11–15.

25. Larzelere, Dr. Robert E., *op. cit.*

26. Socolar, Rebecca R. S., M.D. and Stein, Ruth E. K., M.D., *op. cit.*

27. Baumrind, Dr. Diana, *op. cit.*

28. Wolfe, David A. "Child-Abusive Parents: An Empirical Review and Analysis." *Psychological Bulletin.* 1985; 97(3): 462–482.

29. Wissow, Dr. Lawrence S. and Roter, Dr. Debra. Letter to the editor, in reply to corporal punishment letter. *Pediatrics.* 1995; 96(4): 794–795.

30. Larzelere, Dr. Robert E., *op. cit.*

31. Statistics Sweden. *K R Info.* May 1995; pp. 1–6. Stockholm, Sweden.

## CRITICAL THINKING QUESTIONS

1. Why do Trumbull and Ravenel argue that corrective measures such as time-outs and restriction of privileges can be more harmful to a child than a spanking?

2. How do Trumbull and Ravenel justify spanking in terms of act, intent, attitude, and effects?

3. Develop a set of guidelines for spanking based on this article. Compare your guidelines to the article on corporal punishment by Murray S. Straus. What are the biggest differences between the two perspectives?

Power and control over the child are necessary at times to ensure safety, health, and proper behavior. Classic child rearing studies have shown that some degree of power, assertion,[10] and firm control[11] is essential for optimal child rearing. When power is exerted in the context of love and for the child's benefit, the child will not perceive it as bullying or demeaning.

### Argument #7: Spanking is violence.

*Counterpoint:* Spanking, as recommended by most primary care physicians,[12] is not violence by definition ("exertion of physical force so as to injure or abuse").[13] Parents who properly spank do not injure or abuse their child.

The use of this term "violence" in the spanking debate only serves to deepen the confusion. Why do anti-spanking authors repeatedly fail to distinguish between abusive violence and mild spanking? The distinction is so fundamental and obvious that its omission suggests that these authors use such terminology for its propaganda value, not to clarify issues.

### Argument #8: Spanking is an ineffective solution to misbehavior.

*Counterpoint:* Though the specific use of appropriate spanking has rarely been studied, there is evidence of its short-term and long-term effectiveness. When combined with reasoning, the use of negative consequences (including spanking) does effectively decrease the frequency of misbehavior recurrences with preschool children.[14] In clinical field trials where parental spanking has been studied, it has consistently been found to reduce the subsequent frequency of noncompliance with time-out.[15] Spanking, as an effective enforcer of time-out, is a component of several well-researched parent training programs[16] and popular parenting texts.[17]

Dr. Diana Baumrind of the Institute for Human Development at the University of California-Berkeley conducted a decade-long study of families with children 3 to 9 years old.[18] Baumrind found that parents employing a balanced disciplinary style of firm control (including spanking) and positive encouragement experienced the most favorable outcome in their children. Parents taking extreme approaches to discipline (authoritarian-types using excessive punishment with less encouragement or permissive-types using little punishment and no spanking) were less successful. Baumrind concluded that evidence from this study "did not indicate that negative reinforcement or corporal punishment per se were harmful or ineffective procedures, but rather the total patterns of parental control determined the effects on the child of these procedures."

This approach of balanced parenting, employing the occasional use of spanking, is advocated by several child rearing experts.[19] In the hands of loving parents, a spanking to the buttocks of a defiant toddler in appropriate settings is a powerful motivator to correct behavior and an effective deterrent to disobedience.

### Argument #9: Adults who were spanked as children are at risk for using violence as a means of resolving conflicts as adults.

*Counterpoint:* This theory comes from work done by Murray Straus of the Family Research Lab at the University of New Hampshire. Straus's conclusions are based upon theoretical models and survey results of adults recalling spankings as teenagers. His work is not clinical research, and many experts believe that his conclusions go far beyond his data. As with most of Straus's survey research, teenage spanking is the focus, not the selective use of spanking of young children by reasonable parents. The evidence for his conclusion disappears when parental spanking is measured between the ages of 2 and 8 years, and when childhood aggression is measured at a later age.

In a 1994 review article on corporal punishment, Dr. Robert E. Larzelere, a director of research at Boys Town, Nebraska, presents evidence supporting a parent's selective use of spanking of children, particularly those 2 to 6 years old.[20] After thoroughly reviewing the literature, Larzelere concludes that any association between spanking and antisocial aggressiveness in children is insignificant and artifactual.

After a decade of longitudinal study of children beginning in third grade, Dr. Leonard Eron found no association between punishment (including spanking) and later aggression. Eron, a clinical psychologist at the University of Michigan's Institute for Social Research, concluded, "Upon follow-up 10 years after the original data collection, we found that punishment of aggressive acts at the earlier age was no longer related to current aggression, and instead, other variables like parental nurturance and children's identification with their parents were more important in predicting later aggression."[21] Again, it is the total pattern of parenting that determines the outcome of a parent's efforts.

### Argument #10: Spanking leads a parent to use harmful forms of corporal punishment which lead to physical child abuse.

*Counterpoint:* The abuse potential when loving parents use appropriate disciplinary spanking is very low. Since parents have a natural affection for their children, they are more prone to underutilize spanking than to overutilize it. Both empirical data and professional opinion oppose the concept of a causal relationship between spanking and child abuse.

Surveys indicate that 70 to 90 percent of parents of preschoolers use spanking,[22] yet the incidence of physical child abuse in America is only about 5 percent. Statistically, the two practices are far apart. Furthermore, over the past decade reports of child abuse have steadily risen while approval for parental spanking has steadily declined.[23]

More than 70 percent of primary care pediatricians reject the idea that spanking

sets the stage for parents to engage in forms of physical abuse.[24]

Teaching parents appropriate spanking may actually reduce child abuse, according to Larzelere, in his 1994 review article on corporal punishment.[25] Parents who are ill-equipped to control their child's behavior, or who take a more permissive approach (refusing to use spanking), may be more prone to anger[26] and explosive attacks on their child.[27]

Parental child abuse is an interactive process involving parental competence, parental and child temperaments, and situational demands.[28] Abusive parents are more angry, depressed, and impulsive, and emphasize punishment as the predominant means of discipline. Abused children are more aggressive and less compliant than children from nonabusive families. There is less interaction between family members in abusive families, and abusive mothers display more negative than positive behavior. The etiology of abusive parenting is multifactorial with emphasis on the personalities involved, and cannot be simply explained by a parent's use of spanking.

In a letter to the editor in a 1995 issue of *Pediatrics*, Drs. Lawrence S. Wissow and Debra Roter of Johns Hopkins University's pediatrics department acknowledge that a definitive link between spanking and child abuse has yet to be established.[29]

Finally, the Swedish experiment to reduce child abuse by banning spanking seems to be failing. In 1980, one year after this ban was adopted, the rate of child beatings was twice that of the United States.[30] According to a 1995 report from the government organization, Statistics Sweden, police reports of child abuse by family members rose four-fold from 1984 to 1994, while reports of teen violence increased nearly six-fold.[31]

Most experts agree that spanking and child abuse are not on the same continuum, but are very different entities. With parenting, it is the "user" and *how* a measure is used much more than the measure used that determines the outcome of the disci-

plinary effort. Clearly, spanking can be safely used in the discipline of young children with an excellent outcome. The proper use of spanking may actually reduce a parent's risk of abusing the child.

### Argument #11: Spanking is never necessary.

*Counterpoint:* All children need a combination of encouragement and correction as they are disciplined to become socially responsible individuals. In order for correction to deter disobedient behavior, the consequence imposed upon the child must outweigh the pleasure of the disobedient act. For very compliant children, milder forms of correction will suffice, and spanking may never be necessary. For more defiant children who refuse to comply with or be persuaded by milder consequences such as time-out, spanking is useful, effective, and appropriate.

### CONCLUSION

The subject of disciplinary spanking should be evaluated from a factual and philosophical perspective. It must be distinguished from abusive, harmful forms of corporal punishment. Appropriate disciplinary spanking can play an important role in optimal child development, and has been found in prospective studies to be a part of the parenting style associated with the best outcomes. There is no evidence that mild spanking is harmful. Indeed, spanking is supported by history, research, and a majority of primary care physicians.

### NOTES

1. Fathman, Dr. Robert E. "Corporal Punishment Fact Sheet." July 1994.

2. Lyons, Dr. John S., Anderson, Rachel L., and Larson, Dr. David B., memo.

3. Voter/Consumer Research Poll, National Values. Commissioned by the Family Research Council, 1994.

4. "School Poll." *The Washington Times.* 28, 1995, p. A-2.

5. Flynn, Clifton P. "Regional Differe Attitudes Toward Corporal Punisl *Journal of Marriage and the Family* 56 (Ma 314–324.

6. Lyons, Dr. John S., Anderson, Rache Larson, Dr. David B. "The Use and E Physical Punishment in the Home: A Sy Review." Presentation to the Section Ethics of the American Academy of Ped annual meeting, November 2, 1993.

7. Simons, Ronald L., Johnson, Chris Conger, Rand D. "Harsh Corporal Pur versus Quality of Parental Involveme Explanation of Adolescent Maladju *Journal of Marriage and Family.* 1994; 56:

8. Olweus, Dan. "Familial and Tempe Determinants of Aggressive Behavior i cent Boys: A Causal Analysis." *Dev Psychology.* 1980; 16:644–660.

9. Socolar, Rebecca R. S., M.D. and S E. K., M.D. "Spanking Infants and Maternal Belief and Practice." *Pediat* 95:105–111.

10. Hoffman, Martin. "Parental Disc Child's Moral Development." *Journal Social Psychology.* 1967; 5:45–57.

11. Baumrind, Diana, Ph.D. "Rearin tent Children." Damon, W. (ed.). *Chi ment Today and Tomorrow.* 1989; pp. 34 Francisco, Calif.: Jossey-Bass.

12. McCormick, Kenelm F., M.D. "A Primary Care Physicians Toward Cor ishment." *Journal of the American Medi tion.* 1992; 267:3161–3165.

13. *Webster's Ninth New Collegiate Dict* p. 1316. Massachusetts: Merriam-Web:

14. Larzelere, Dr. Robert E. and Mer A. "The Effectiveness of Parental Di Toddler Misbehavior at Different Lev Distress." *Family Relations.* 1994; 43 (

15. Roberts, Mark W. and Power: "Adjusting Chair Time-out Enforcei dures for Oppositional Children.' *Therapy.* 1990; 21:257–271, and Bean and Roberts, Mark W. "The Effect Release Contingencies on Change Noncompliance." *Journal of Abnorm chology.* 1981; 9:95–105.

16. Forehand, R. L. and McMahon, *the Noncompliant Child.* 1981; pp. York: Guilford Press.

# 10 Raising Children

*Centrist:* Conservative versus Mainstream Models
of Childrearing in Popular Manuals

JOHN P. BARTKOWSKI AND CHRISTOPHER G. ELLISON, "Divergent Models of Childrearing in Popular Manuals: Conservative Protestants vs. the Mainstream Experts," *Sociology of Religion* 56 (Spring 1995): 21–34, the official journal of the Association for the Sociology of Religion, Inc. © 1995 Association for the Sociology of Religion. Reprinted by permission.

*Most of the recent family debates have focused on the conflicting perspectives over family gender roles (see Chapters 1–5). There are also some sharp divisions between political and ideological groups about "good" childrearing practices. John P. Bartkowski and Christopher G. Ellison's research shows that conservative Protestants and mainstream (i.e., liberal) "experts" disagree on four key childrearing issues—long-term parenting goals, parent-child relations, the definition of parental roles, and discipline strategies.*

## INTRODUCTION

Contemporary conflicts over the American family have attracted widespread popular commentary and academic research (Thorne and Yalom, 1982; Berger and Berger, 1983; Dornbusch and Strober, 1988; Stacey, 1990; Faludi, 1991; Hunter, 1991). To date, however, these and other social scientists have constructed the "battle over the family" almost exclusively in terms of debates regarding gender roles. Indeed, many have dismissed other dimensions of this conflict, including conflicts over parenting issues, asserting that they are insignificant. . . .

While we readily grant the importance of ongoing debates over gender roles, we also believe that disagreements over parent-child relations are much more fun-

damental and significant than previous discussions have recognized. A sharply polemical literature on parenting surfaced within conservative Protestant circles in the 1970s, extolling the virtues of "traditional" parenting techniques and challenging the views of mainstream experts (see Boggs, 1983; Lienesch, 1991; Ellison and Bartkowski, 1995). Since that time, sales of popular literature on "Christian" (generally conservative Protestant)[1] parenting have mushroomed, and the core themes of this parenting ideology have been widely circulated via broadcast media and organizations devoted to family issues, such as Focus on the Family. Conservative Protestant writers and commentators have clearly emerged as the leading spokespersons for "traditional" hierarchical childrearing practices (e.g., Gordon, 1989; Osborne, 1989).

Our study explores this conservative Protestant parenting ideology in greater detail. . . . Our analysis suggests that conservative Protestant parenting specialists part company with their mainstream counterparts in four key areas: (1) long-term parenting goals; (2) the structure of parent-child relations; (3) the definition of parental roles; and (4) strategies of child discipline and punishment. . . .

## CONSERVATIVE PROTESTANT THEOLOGY AND CHILDREARING

The childrearing beliefs of many conservative Protestants begin with their commitment to a "literal" interpretation of the Bible. . . . Literalists generally consider the Bible to be the absolute Word of God purposively conveyed to humankind, and many believe that the Bible provides failsafe, empirically verifiable, and sufficient truths to guide the conduct of all human affairs, including childrearing (e.g., Fugate, 1980). Proceeding from such assumptions, networks of conservative Protestant theologians, pastors, and influential laity generate the specific scriptural understandings that prevail among rank-and-file adherents, with recourse to a handful of carefully selected commentaries. . . .

The widespread preoccupation with establishing and defending the legitimacy of biblical authority is one facet of a broader conservative Protestant worldview that Kenneth Wald and his colleagues (1989) have termed "authority-mindedness." Many commentators maintain that the general concerns of authority and obedience permeate virtually every aspect of conservative Protestant life (see Peshkin, 1986; Ammerman, 1987; Hunter, 1987; Rose, 1988).

In addition to this affinity between biblical literalism and "authority-mindedness," it is also important to recognize the links between contemporary constructions of literalism and basic conceptions of human nature. . . . Contemporary conservative Protestants accord particular significance to the doctrine of original sin, reflected in the Fall of Adam and Eve from the Garden of Eden (Genesis 2–5). According to this view, all individuals are born sinful—that is, predisposed toward selfish, egocentric conduct and inclined toward rebellion against authority in all forms (Dobson, 1978; LaHaye, 1977; Fugate, 1980).

In sum, we argue that contemporary understandings of biblical "literalism," and their affinity with both "authority-mindedness" and beliefs that human nature is fundamentally sinful, legitimate conservative Protestant childrearing practices that diverge sharply from those recommended by contemporary mainstream experts. The remainder of this study explores this parenting debate, analyzing a number of popular manuals written by conservative Protestants and mainstream experts.

## SELECTION OF POPULAR CHILDREARING MANUALS

Three concerns guided our selection of childrearing manuals for examination. First, for mainstream and conservative Protestant specialists alike, we have focused primarily on the writings of the most prominent, bestselling childrearing experts, as determined via sales figures and interviews with publishers' representatives. Second, although our analysis is concerned with childrearing advice presented in popular manuals, the influence of many conservative Protestant and mainstream parenting specialists is not restricted to this medium. Many of these authors appear on radio and television programs, contribute to various parenting periodicals, and communicate with their constituency via local seminars or direct mailings.[2]

Third, because we are aware that trends in parenting advice can change over time, we have selected childrearing manuals which reflect a cross-section of both classic

Power and control over the child are necessary at times to ensure safety, health, and proper behavior. Classic child rearing studies have shown that some degree of power, assertion,[10] and firm control[11] is essential for optimal child rearing. When power is exerted in the context of love and for the child's benefit, the child will not perceive it as bullying or demeaning.

### Argument #7: Spanking is violence.

*Counterpoint:* Spanking, as recommended by most primary care physicians,[12] is not violence by definition ("exertion of physical force so as to injure or abuse").[13] Parents who properly spank do not injure or abuse their child.

The use of this term "violence" in the spanking debate only serves to deepen the confusion. Why do anti-spanking authors repeatedly fail to distinguish between abusive violence and mild spanking? The distinction is so fundamental and obvious that its omission suggests that these authors use such terminology for its propaganda value, not to clarify issues.

### Argument #8: Spanking is an ineffective solution to misbehavior.

*Counterpoint:* Though the specific use of appropriate spanking has rarely been studied, there is evidence of its short-term and long-term effectiveness. When combined with reasoning, the use of negative consequences (including spanking) does effectively decrease the frequency of misbehavior recurrences with preschool children.[14] In clinical field trials where parental spanking has been studied, it has consistently been found to reduce the subsequent frequency of noncompliance with time-out.[15] Spanking, as an effective enforcer of time-out, is a component of several well-researched parent training programs[16] and popular parenting texts.[17]

Dr. Diana Baumrind of the Institute for Human Development at the University of California-Berkeley conducted a decade-long study of families with children 3 to 9 years old.[18] Baumrind found that parents employing a balanced disciplinary style of firm control (including spanking) and positive encouragement experienced the most favorable outcome in their children. Parents taking extreme approaches to discipline (authoritarian-types using excessive punishment with less encouragement or permissive-types using little punishment and no spanking) were less successful. Baumrind concluded that evidence from this study "did not indicate that negative reinforcement or corporal punishment per se were harmful or ineffective procedures, but rather the total patterns of parental control determined the effects on the child of these procedures."

This approach of balanced parenting, employing the occasional use of spanking, is advocated by several child rearing experts.[19] In the hands of loving parents, a spanking to the buttocks of a defiant toddler in appropriate settings is a powerful motivator to correct behavior and an effective deterrent to disobedience.

### Argument #9: Adults who were spanked as children are at risk for using violence as a means of resolving conflicts as adults.

*Counterpoint:* This theory comes from work done by Murray Straus of the Family Research Lab at the University of New Hampshire. Straus's conclusions are based upon theoretical models and survey results of adults recalling spankings as teenagers. His work is not clinical research, and many experts believe that his conclusions go far beyond his data. As with most of Straus's survey research, teenage spanking is the focus, not the selective use of spanking of young children by reasonable parents. The evidence for his conclusion disappears when parental spanking is measured between the ages of 2 and 8 years, and when childhood aggression is measured at a later age.

In a 1994 review article on corporal punishment, Dr. Robert E. Larzelere, a director of research at Boys Town, Nebraska, presents evidence supporting a parent's selective use of spanking of children, particularly those 2 to 6 years old.[20] After thoroughly reviewing the literature, Larzelere concludes that any association between spanking and antisocial aggressiveness in children is insignificant and artifactual.

After a decade of longitudinal study of children beginning in third grade, Dr. Leonard Eron found no association between punishment (including spanking) and later aggression. Eron, a clinical psychologist at the University of Michigan's Institute for Social Research, concluded, "Upon follow-up 10 years after the original data collection, we found that punishment of aggressive acts at the earlier age was no longer related to current aggression, and instead, other variables like parental nurturance and children's identification with their parents were more important in predicting later aggression."[21] Again, it is the total pattern of parenting that determines the outcome of a parent's efforts.

### Argument #10: Spanking leads a parent to use harmful forms of corporal punishment which lead to physical child abuse.

*Counterpoint:* The abuse potential when loving parents use appropriate disciplinary spanking is very low. Since parents have a natural affection for their children, they are more prone to underutilize spanking than to overutilize it. Both empirical data and professional opinion oppose the concept of a causal relationship between spanking and child abuse.

Surveys indicate that 70 to 90 percent of parents of preschoolers use spanking,[22] yet the incidence of physical child abuse in America is only about 5 percent. Statistically, the two practices are far apart. Furthermore, over the past decade reports of child abuse have steadily risen while approval for parental spanking has steadily declined.[23]

More than 70 percent of primary care pediatricians reject the idea that spanking

sets the stage for parents to engage in forms of physical abuse.[24]

Teaching parents appropriate spanking may actually reduce child abuse, according to Larzelere, in his 1994 review article on corporal punishment.[25] Parents who are ill-equipped to control their child's behavior, or who take a more permissive approach (refusing to use spanking), may be more prone to anger[26] and explosive attacks on their child.[27]

Parental child abuse is an interactive process involving parental competence, parental and child temperaments, and situational demands.[28] Abusive parents are more angry, depressed, and impulsive, and emphasize punishment as the predominant means of discipline. Abused children are more aggressive and less compliant than children from nonabusive families. There is less interaction between family members in abusive families, and abusive mothers display more negative than positive behavior. The etiology of abusive parenting is multifactorial with emphasis on the personalities involved, and cannot be simply explained by a parent's use of spanking.

In a letter to the editor in a 1995 issue of *Pediatrics*, Drs. Lawrence S. Wissow and Debra Roter of Johns Hopkins University's pediatrics department acknowledge that a definitive link between spanking and child abuse has yet to be established.[29]

Finally, the Swedish experiment to reduce child abuse by banning spanking seems to be failing. In 1980, one year after this ban was adopted, the rate of child beatings was twice that of the United States.[30] According to a 1995 report from the government organization, Statistics Sweden, police reports of child abuse by family members rose four-fold from 1984 to 1994, while reports of teen violence increased nearly six-fold.[31]

Most experts agree that spanking and child abuse are not on the same continuum, but are very different entities. With parenting, it is the "user" and *how* a measure is used much more than the measure used that determines the outcome of the disciplinary effort. Clearly, spanking can be safely used in the discipline of young children with an excellent outcome. The proper use of spanking may actually reduce a parent's risk of abusing the child.

## Argument #11: Spanking is never necessary.

*Counterpoint:* All children need a combination of encouragement and correction as they are disciplined to become socially responsible individuals. In order for correction to deter disobedient behavior, the consequence imposed upon the child must outweigh the pleasure of the disobedient act. For very compliant children, milder forms of correction will suffice, and spanking may never be necessary. For more defiant children who refuse to comply with or be persuaded by milder consequences such as time-out, spanking is useful, effective, and appropriate.

## CONCLUSION

The subject of disciplinary spanking should be evaluated from a factual and philosophical perspective. It must be distinguished from abusive, harmful forms of corporal punishment. Appropriate disciplinary spanking can play an important role in optimal child development, and has been found in prospective studies to be a part of the parenting style associated with the best outcomes. There is no evidence that mild spanking is harmful. Indeed, spanking is supported by history, research, and a majority of primary care physicians.

## NOTES

1. Fathman, Dr. Robert E. "Corporal Punishment Fact Sheet." July 1994.

2. Lyons, Dr. John S., Anderson, Rachel L., and Larson, Dr. David B., memo.

3. Voter/Consumer Research Poll, National Values. Commissioned by the Family Research Council, 1994.

4. "School Poll." *The Washington Times.* August 28, 1995, p. A-2.

5. Flynn, Clifton P. "Regional Differences in Attitudes Toward Corporal Punishment." *Journal of Marriage and the Family* 56 (May 1994): 314–324.

6. Lyons, Dr. John S., Anderson, Rachel L., and Larson, Dr. David B. "The Use and Effects of Physical Punishment in the Home: A Systematic Review." Presentation to the Section on Bio-Ethics of the American Academy of Pediatrics at annual meeting, November 2, 1993.

7. Simons, Ronald L., Johnson, Christine, and Conger, Rand D. "Harsh Corporal Punishment versus Quality of Parental Involvement as an Explanation of Adolescent Maladjustment." *Journal of Marriage and Family.* 1994; 56:591–607.

8. Olweus, Dan. "Familial and Temperamental Determinants of Aggressive Behavior in Adolescent Boys: A Causal Analysis." *Developmental Psychology.* 1980; 16:644–660.

9. Socolar, Rebecca R. S., M.D. and Stein, Ruth E. K., M.D. "Spanking Infants and Toddlers: Maternal Belief and Practice." *Pediatrics.* 1995; 95:105–111.

10. Hoffman, Martin. "Parental Discipline and Child's Moral Development. " *Journal of Personal Social Psychology.* 1967; 5:45–57.

11. Baumrind, Diana, Ph.D. "Rearing Competent Children." Damon, W. (ed.). *Child Development Today and Tomorrow.* 1989; pp. 349–378. San Francisco, Calif.: Jossey-Bass.

12. McCormick, Kenelm F., M.D. "Attitudes of Primary Care Physicians Toward Corporal Punishment." *Journal of the American Medical Association.* 1992; 267:3161–3165.

13. *Webster's Ninth New Collegiate Dictionary.* 1987; p. 1316. Massachusetts: Merriam-Webster, Inc.

14. Larzelere, Dr. Robert E. and Merenda, Dr. J. A. "The Effectiveness of Parental Discipline for Toddler Misbehavior at Different Levels of Child Distress." *Family Relations.* 1994; 43 (4).

15. Roberts, Mark W. and Powers, Scott W. "Adjusting Chair Time-out Enforcement Procedures for Oppositional Children." *Behavioral Therapy.* 1990; 21:257–271, and Bean, Arthur W. and Roberts, Mark W. "The Effect of Time-out Release Contingencies on Changes in Child Noncompliance." *Journal of Abnormal Child Psychology.* 1981; 9:95–105.

16. Forehand, R. L. and McMahon, R. J. *Helping the Noncompliant Child.* 1981; pp. 79–80. New York: Guilford Press.

17. Clark, Lynn C. *SOS! Help for Parents.* 1985; pp. 181–185. Kentucky: Parents Press.

18. Baumrind, Dr. Diana. "The Development of Instrumental Competence Through Socialization." *Minnesota Symposia on Child Psychology.* 1973; 7:3–46.

19. Austin, Glenn. *Love and Power: How to Raise Competent, Confident Children.* 1988. California: Robert Erdmann Publishing. Also, Dobson, Dr. James. *The Strong-Willed Child.* 1985. Illinois: Tyndale House Publishers, and Coopersmith, Stanley. *The Antecedents of Self-Esteem.* 1967. New York: W. H. Freeman & Co. Reprinted 1981. California: Consulting Psychologists Press, Inc.

20. Larzelere, Dr. Robert E. "Should the Use of Corporal Punishment by Parents Be Considered Child Abuse?" Mason, M., Gambrill, E. (eds.). *Debating Children's Lives.* 1994; pp. 204–209. California: Sage Publications.

21. Eron, Dr. Leonard D. "Theories of Aggression: From Drives to Cognitions." Huesmann, L. R. (ed.). *Aggressive Behavior, Current Perspectives.* 1994; pp. 3–11. New York: Plenum Press.

22. Straus, Murray A. "Discipline and Deviance: Physical Punishment of Children and Violence and Other Crime in Adulthood." *Social Problems.* 1991; 38:133–152.

23. National Committee to Prevent Child Abuse. *Memorandum.* May 1995; 2(5).

24. White, Kristin. "Where Pediatricians Stand on Spanking." *Pediatric Management.* September 1993: 11–15.

25. Larzelere, Dr. Robert E., *op. cit.*

26. Socolar, Rebecca R. S., M.D. and Stein, Ruth E. K., M.D., *op. cit.*

27. Baumrind, Dr. Diana, *op. cit.*

28. Wolfe, David A. "Child-Abusive Parents: An Empirical Review and Analysis." *Psychological Bulletin.* 1985; 97(3): 462–482.

29. Wissow, Dr. Lawrence S. and Roter, Dr. Debra. Letter to the editor, in reply to corporal punishment letter. *Pediatrics.* 1995; 96(4): 794–795.

30. Larzelere, Dr. Robert E., *op. cit.*

31. Statistics Sweden. *K R Info.* May 1995; pp. 1–6. Stockholm, Sweden.

**CRITICAL THINKING QUESTIONS**

1. Why do Trumbull and Ravenel argue that corrective measures such as time-outs and restriction of privileges can be more harmful to a child than a spanking?

2. How do Trumbull and Ravenel justify spanking in terms of act, intent, attitude, and effects?

3. Develop a set of guidelines for spanking based on this article. Compare your guidelines to the article on corporal punishment by Murray S. Straus. What are the biggest differences between the two perspectives?

# 10 Raising Children

*Centrist:* Conservative versus Mainstream Models
of Childrearing in Popular Manuals

JOHN P. BARTKOWSKI AND CHRISTOPHER G. ELLISON, "Divergent Models of
Childrearing in Popular Manuals: Conservative Protestants vs. the Mainstream Experts," *Sociology of Religion* 56 (Spring 1995): 21–34, the official
journal of the Association for the Sociology of Religion, Inc. © 1995 Association for the Sociology of Religion. Reprinted by permission.

*Most of the recent family debates have focused on the conflicting perspectives over
family gender roles (see Chapters 1–5). There are also some sharp divisions
between political and ideological groups about "good" childrearing practices. John
P. Bartkowski and Christopher G. Ellison's research shows that conservative
Protestants and mainstream (i.e., liberal) "experts" disagree on four key childrearing issues—long-term parenting goals, parent-child relations, the definition of
parental roles, and discipline strategies.*

## INTRODUCTION

Contemporary conflicts over the American
family have attracted widespread popular
commentary and academic research
(Thorne and Yalom, 1982; Berger and
Berger, 1983; Dornbusch and Strober, 1988;
Stacey, 1990; Faludi, 1991; Hunter, 1991). To
date, however, these and other social scientists have constructed the "battle over the
family" almost exclusively in terms of
debates regarding gender roles. Indeed,
many have dismissed other dimensions of
this conflict, including conflicts over parenting issues, asserting that they are
insignificant. . . .

While we readily grant the importance
of ongoing debates over gender roles, we
also believe that disagreements over
parent-child relations are much more fun-

damental and significant than previous discussions have recognized. A sharply
polemical literature on parenting surfaced
within conservative Protestant circles in the
1970s, extolling the virtues of "traditional"
parenting techniques and challenging the
views of mainstream experts (see Boggs,
1983; Lienesch, 1991; Ellison and
Bartkowski, 1995). Since that time, sales of
popular literature on "Christian" (generally
conservative Protestant)[1] parenting have
mushroomed, and the core themes of this
parenting ideology have been widely circulated via broadcast media and organizations devoted to family issues, such as
Focus on the Family. Conservative Protestant writers and commentators have clearly
emerged as the leading spokespersons for
"traditional" hierarchical childrearing practices (e.g., Gordon, 1989; Osborne, 1989).

Our study explores this conservative Protestant parenting ideology in greater detail. . . . Our analysis suggests that conservative Protestant parenting specialists part company with their mainstream counterparts in four key areas: (1) long-term parenting goals; (2) the structure of parent-child relations; (3) the definition of parental roles; and (4) strategies of child discipline and punishment. . . .

## CONSERVATIVE PROTESTANT THEOLOGY AND CHILDREARING

The childrearing beliefs of many conservative Protestants begin with their commitment to a "literal" interpretation of the Bible. . . . Literalists generally consider the Bible to be the absolute Word of God purposively conveyed to humankind, and many believe that the Bible provides failsafe, empirically verifiable, and sufficient truths to guide the conduct of all human affairs, including childrearing (e.g., Fugate, 1980). Proceeding from such assumptions, networks of conservative Protestant theologians, pastors, and influential laity generate the specific scriptural understandings that prevail among rank-and-file adherents, with recourse to a handful of carefully selected commentaries. . . .

The widespread preoccupation with establishing and defending the legitimacy of biblical authority is one facet of a broader conservative Protestant worldview that Kenneth Wald and his colleagues (1989) have termed "authority-mindedness." Many commentators maintain that the general concerns of authority and obedience permeate virtually every aspect of conservative Protestant life (see Peshkin, 1986; Ammerman, 1987; Hunter, 1987; Rose, 1988).

In addition to this affinity between biblical literalism and "authority-mindedness," it is also important to recognize the links between contemporary constructions of literalism and basic conceptions of human nature. . . . Contemporary conservative Protestants accord particular significance to the doctrine of original sin, reflected in the Fall of Adam and Eve from the Garden of Eden (Genesis 2–5). According to this view, all individuals are born sinful—that is, predisposed toward selfish, egocentric conduct and inclined toward rebellion against authority in all forms (Dobson, 1978; LaHaye, 1977; Fugate, 1980).

In sum, we argue that contemporary understandings of biblical "literalism," and their affinity with both "authority-mindedness" and beliefs that human nature is fundamentally sinful, legitimate conservative Protestant childrearing practices that diverge sharply from those recommended by contemporary mainstream experts. The remainder of this study explores this parenting debate, analyzing a number of popular manuals written by conservative Protestants and mainstream experts.

## SELECTION OF POPULAR CHILDREARING MANUALS

Three concerns guided our selection of childrearing manuals for examination. First, for mainstream and conservative Protestant specialists alike, we have focused primarily on the writings of the most prominent, bestselling childrearing experts, as determined via sales figures and interviews with publishers' representatives. Second, although our analysis is concerned with childrearing advice presented in popular manuals, the influence of many conservative Protestant and mainstream parenting specialists is not restricted to this medium. Many of these authors appear on radio and television programs, contribute to various parenting periodicals, and communicate with their constituency via local seminars or direct mailings.[2]

Third, because we are aware that trends in parenting advice can change over time, we have selected childrearing manuals which reflect a cross-section of both classic treatments of parenting (e.g., Dobson, 1970; Christenson, 1970; Dodson, 1970; Gordon, 1970) and more recent best-selling publications (e.g., Dobson, 1987; Swindoll, 1991; Brazelton, 1992; Spock and Rothenberg, 1992). In our careful readings of these texts, we have detected few noteworthy changes in the parenting prescriptions advocated by each group over this twenty-year time period. . . . Our analysis mainly focuses on childrearing advice directed at the parents of toddlers and pre-adolescents. This distinction is especially salient with regard to prescriptions for the discipline and punishment of children.

## DIVERGENT MODELS OF PARENTING: MAPPING THE CONTOURS OF THE DEBATE

### Long-Term Goals

What constitutes successful parenting? Mainstream and conservative Protestant advice manuals emphasize strikingly different outcomes. Almost without exception, leading mainstream writers focus on "healthy" personality development and social competence. Most mainstream parenting manuals underscore the importance of helping children develop desirable personality profiles: self-esteem, self-confidence, self-discipline, creativity, and intellectual curiosity (Brazelton, 1992; Dodson, 1970; Leach, 1989; LeShan, 1985). . . . Although it is recognized that parents must elicit compliance from youngsters in various settings, they are strongly urged to refrain from employing any childrearing or disciplinary techniques which might undermine the development of these personality traits in their children (e.g., Balter, 1989; Spock, 1988).

In a related vein, many mainstream parenting specialists stress the importance of teaching empathy and verbal communication skills. . . . For instance, Balter (1989) suggests that teaching empathy to toddlers reduces parent-child conflicts, allows the child to become more considerate of the needs and desires of others, and promotes

self-control and self-discipline. LeShan (1985) recommends that parents should teach their children to interpret the moods and actions of others effectively, because this will foster greater tolerance of human frailty. Taken together, the interrelated social skills of empathy and communication help children to create a common understanding between two interacting individuals—the very definition of a "healthy" relationship.

Although most conservative Protestant specialists grant the value of "healthy" personalities and social competence, these traits are not seen as the most important outcomes of successful parenting. Instead, conservative Protestant writers emphasize that to succeed in adult roles, children must be trained to embrace the divinely-ordained principles of authority and hierarchy (Christenson, 1970; Fugate, 1980; LaHaye, 1977; Swindoll, 1991). This emphasis on authority is vital because of the view that children are born with sinful natures, prone to challenge authority in all forms. Conservative Protestants contend that a child who is not taught to submit to familial authority (1) will not develop a respect for superordinate figures outside the family (e.g., teachers, employers, guardians), and (2) will be unable to exercise rightful authority when assuming a superordinate role in human relationships (e.g., as a father, parent, or employer).

Moreover, the kind of authority training advocated by conservative Protestant writers is also believed to convey a crucial spiritual lesson to children. According to these writers, Christian parents are responsible for leading their children toward righteousness and salvation (e.g., Deuteronomy 6:6–7; Proverbs 22:6). Given their belief that human nature is fundamentally sinful, conservative Protestants maintain that training children to submit their selfish desires to the will of God, the creator and supreme authority of the universe, is central to this project of salvation (Fugate, 1980; LaHaye, 1977; Swindoll, 1991). In short, conservative Protestant parents are warned that abrogating their divinely-ordained parenting responsibilities—i.e., failing to command respect from their child—may substantially decrease the likelihood that the developing youngster will be inclined to "humble" him/herself before the divine authority of God (Dobson, 1978).

## Structure of Parent-Child Relations

Many mainstream specialists believe that *all* human institutions—including the family—should be guided by democratic and egalitarian principles (e.g., Gordon, 1970, 1989; Leach, 1989). Consequently, the dominant discourse in much of the mainstream literature centers on the "rights" and "interests" of family members. Most mainstream parenting manuals suggest that conflicts within the family should be resolved through negotiation, and that ideal solutions to these conflicts are solutions that maximize the joint satisfaction of the conflicting parties. By teaching children to (1) identify interests, (2) articulate demands and grievances, (3) understand the feelings of others, and (4) negotiate to achieve desired ends, democratic families are believed to help children develop skills that are essential for effective participation in modern society. . . .

Some mainstream writers have elaborated the concept of children's rights, arguing that children should be accorded many of the same rights currently enjoyed by adults. . . . Some have likened the disempowered status of children in modern America to that of slaves in earlier periods in history (Holt, 1974; Farson, 1974). These bolder voices argue that the use of power and authority is "unethical," and that parents who continue to use their power to control others must lack expertise in alternative forms of conflict resolution. In their view, children should be liberated from the oppression of their erstwhile caretakers.

In sharp contrast to the prevailing mainstream perspectives on the structure of parent-child relations, conservative Protestants view the family as an organic whole, rather than a compilation of potentially conflicting "rights" and "interests." Conservative Protestants assert the moral superiority of one "timeless," divinely-ordained blueprint for parent-child relations, a model based on (and legitimated by) the biblical principles of authority and hierarchy that are articulated within contemporary literalist communities (e.g., Daniel 4:35; Romans 13:1; see Christenson, 1970; Fugate, 1980).

Not surprisingly, conservative Protestant parenting writers have reacted with alarm and hostility to calls for democracy within the family. Families, in their view, are characterized by specific sets of superordinate and subordinate roles (Fugate, 1980). Conservative commentators cite an array of passages from Old and New Testament sources underscoring the respective obligations of children and parents (e.g., Ephesians 6:1–4). Conservative Protestant writers frequently stress the imperative of intergenerational hierarchy within the family. They repeatedly exhort children to honor and obey parental authority (Exodus 20:12; Colossians 3:20; 1 Timothy 3:4–5), and they call attention to Old Testament writings that threaten disobedient children with familial and societal ostracism, and even death (Exodus 21:15–17; Deuteronomy 21:18–21, 27:16; Proverbs 30:17). . . .

Popular notions of children's "rights" especially rankle these conservative religious writers. As Dobson (1978:170) puts it, "I find no place in the Bible where our little ones are installed as co-discussants at a conference table, deciding what they will and will not accept from the older generation." Yet some religious writers appropriate the language of "rights" and "interests" in the service of conservative parenting ideals, countering that religious Scripture accords children the right to receive love, protection, religious training, and responsible leadership from their parents (Christenson, 1970:115; Dobson, 1970:42, 161; Fugate, 1980:31). These writers commonly contend that children, regardless of what they may say, actually want and expect these benefits from their parents, and that these crucial children's rights are undermined by the egalitarian impulses of mainstream experts.

Further, conservative religious writers believe that popular democratic and egalitarian family models also have undesirable spiritual consequences. Virtually all of the Christian parenting specialists reviewed for this study claim that children develop their initial images of God based on the behavior of parents (Dobson, 1978; LaHaye, 1977; Swindoll, 1991). This belief makes the preservation of hierarchical parent-child relations crucial. Those adults who opt for egalitarian households are denounced by conservative Protestant parenting specialists for abrogating their divinely-ordained parental responsibilities, and for sabotaging their youngsters' respect for parental, institutional, and (ultimately) divine authority (Christenson, 1970; Dobson, 1978; Fugate, 1980).

## Parental Roles

Perhaps the most common image of the ideal parent in mainstream parenting literature is that of the proactive tactician or manager. . . . This ideal parent is knowledgeable about child development issues, and consequently holds "reasonable" expectations of the child, consonant with the child's developmental stage (e.g., Leach, 1989; LeShan, 1985). In addition, the ideal parent remains sensitive to the feelings of the child and permits him/her considerable latitude for the expression of these feelings. . . . The parent is advised to encourage desired behavior through love, praise, and various forms of positive reinforcement (hence the hackneyed phrase "catch 'em when they're doing good"). According to mainstream experts, competent parents plan lessons and games to communicate values and promote desired behavior, and they find ways to engage children in their own training whenever possible (e.g., by having children make choices or help to decide on disciplinary measures). Finally, the parent-as-tactician organizes household life in ways that max-

imize "win-win" situations among family members, instilling egalitarian values while carefully reconciling the needs and interests of various parties.[3]

Although parenting advice has generally been directed toward mothers, on the assumption that they have primary responsibility for child care, mainstream experts have increasingly promoted ungendered parenting roles. It seems that a growing number of mainstream parenting manuals acknowledge that childrearing should be understood as a partnership between equals. . . . Some volumes are wholly dedicated to the subject of "shared parenting," emphasizing the importance of an equal division of household tasks, administrative duties, and parenting responsibilities (e.g., Kimball, 1988). Many others greet the trends toward ungendered parenting with alacrity. Indeed, some mainstream specialists suggest that, when the father assumes a more active nurturing role in the family, children develop more flexible notions of gender roles (Pruett, 1987; Brazelton, 1992). Therefore, some reason that these youngsters are better equipped to participate fully and successfully in a society experiencing slow but steady progress toward gender equality in the workplace, political arena, and other institutions.

Like their mainstream counterparts, many conservative Protestant family experts urge parents to become knowledgeable about childrearing. However, instead of relying primarily upon the fads and fashions of academic theories or popular psychology (Dobson, 1978, 1987), Christian parents are encouraged to consult what is believed to be the most reliable parenting manual, the Bible. The lessons to be learned from Scripture apparently differ notably from the information conveyed by mainstream parenting experts.

While some conservative Protestant specialists occasionally acknowledge the value of parental cleverness, empathy, and communication, on the whole these themes receive far less attention from conservative religious writers than from their mainstream counterparts. Tactical parenting, negotiation, and avoidance of conflict are not prized parental skills in the conservative childrearing literature. Instead, conservative Protestants are repeatedly advised to demonstrate firm leadership. Because children are perceived to be naturally sinful and rebellious, according to these specialists, the Christian parent should "shape the will," training the child to submit to authority figures (Christenson, 1970; Fugate, 1980; LaHaye, 1977; Swindoll, 1991). Parents are told to expect conflict and respond decisively, often with physical force, to the youngster's inevitable expressions of willful defiance. . . . Dobson (1978) maintains that parents who shrink from this challenge will be hard-pressed to elicit obedience from their children later.

Finally, unlike mainstream experts, conservative Protestant writers generally do *not* approve of ungendered parental roles. In keeping with the normative significance of subordinate and superordinate relationships, these trends toward shared parenting concern conservative Protestant writers for at least three reasons. First, they argue that the de-gendering of parental roles undermines the authority of the Bible as the word of God, because some scriptural passages place the father as the divinely-ordained head and protector of the family (e.g., Colossians 3:18; 1 Corinthians 11:3; Genesis 2:18; 1 Timothy 3:4–5; see Christenson, 1970; Dobson, 1970, 1978; Fugate, 1980; LaHaye, 1977; Swindoll, 1991). Second, the absence of a clear, biblically-inspired gender hierarchy within the household is thought to undermine the child's ability to learn submission to authority from watching his/her parents interact. . . . Finally, some worry that ungendered parental roles will erode the allegiance of youngsters to more traditional gender roles, thus exacerbating what they see as a societal devaluation of masculinity (Christenson, 1970; Swindoll, 1991).

## Discipline and Punishment

Central to the ongoing debate over parent-child relations are the sharp disagreements over appropriate strategies of discipline and punishment. Mainstream specialists overwhelmingly oppose the use of physical discipline. . . .[4] In place of corporal punishment, mainstream specialists advocate setting firm guidelines accompanied by various pragmatic disciplinary techniques, including combinations of positive reinforcement, logical consequences and/or natural consequences, time-out, and empathetic communication and reasoning. Specialists who endorse these myriad strategies argue that they promote the internalization of moral judgment and self-discipline (e.g., Brazelton, 1992; Leach, 1989). By contrast, "excessively harsh" forms of punishment, including corporal punishment, are believed to inhibit parent-child communication and produce counterproductive degrees of guilt and aggression in youngsters (e.g., Balter, 1989).

In contrast to their mainstream counterparts, conservative Protestant parenting specialists strongly endorse the use of corporal punishment, albeit under specific conditions. . . . In general, they recommend that physical punishment should be administered regularly: (1) on occasions of willful defiance to parental authority, (2) promptly after the defiant act, (3) with the use of a "rod," specifically designated for the purpose of physical chastisement, and (4) only to pre-adolescents (see Greven, 1990; Ellison and Bartkowski, 1995).

Most conservative Protestant specialists support the use of corporal punishment for a variety of reasons. First, they believe that chastisement is commanded by scripture (e.g., Proverbs 13:24, 22:14, 23:13–14, 29:15; 2 Samuel 7:14). Indeed, they interpret some passages as indicating that chastisement is a sign of parental love and caring (see especially Hebrews 12:5–11). Thus, in addition to serving as a behavioral corrective, corporal punishment is believed to promote youthful security by communicating both a deep concern for the child's welfare and an unswerving commitment to biblical principles (e.g., Fugate, 1980; LaHaye, 1977; Swindoll, 1991).

Further, because children initially understand God in terms of parental images, conservative Protestants suggest that children will infer God's view of them based on the treatment they receive from their parents. These writers are quick to point out that parents should teach their children by example that God is loving, merciful, and forgiving. At the same time, however, because God's punishment of sin is understood as both inevitable and consistent, they also believe that parental discipline should embody these characteristics as well. Given such convictions, conservative Protestants argue that the experience of loving physical discipline (1) helps the child to develop an appropriate, accurate image of God, and (2) underscores the importance of obedience to His authority. Thus, corporal punishment is believed to demonstrate to the young child that deviation from biblical principles will provoke consistent and inevitable reproof from authorities in this life and from God in the next ("the wages of sin is death"). By contrast, obedient children who are able to avoid chastisement are said to learn that a strict adherence to biblical principles will insure God's blessing (Fugate, 1980; LaHaye, 1977).

### SUMMARY AND CONCLUSION

This study has argued that debates over childrearing beliefs and practices deserve more attention from scholars interested in the contemporary "battle over the family." In particular, we noted that conservative Protestants have emerged as the standard-bearers for "traditional" hierachical and authority-centered parenting models. We identified two core theological tenets that legitimate these distinctive conservative Protestant parenting orientations: (1) the doctrine of biblical literalism, and the concomitant preoccupation with worldly and spiritual authority relations; and (2) the belief that human nature, including the nature of children, is inherently sinful, and therefore ultimately subject to divine judgment.

A careful reading of parenting advice manuals produced by conservative Protestant and mainstream experts indicates that views within these two camps tend to diverge in four key areas. With respect to *long-term parenting goals*, we found that mainstream specialists focus on meeting the psychosocial needs of the child, while conservative Protestant family experts focus on the child's spiritual needs, particularly submission to human and divine authority. In addition, conservative Protestants and their mainstream counterparts differ in their prescriptions for the *structure of parent-child relations*. In contrast to the mainstream specialists, who tend to support the implementation of democratic values in parenting, conservative Protestant writers propose relatively hierarchical and authoritarian parent-child relations. Moreover, these two camps also clash in their views of *parental roles*, with mainstream experts touting the benefits of tactical, proactive, ungendered parenting, and conservative Protestants advocating Bible-based child training, decisive parental leadership, and male headship of the family unit. Finally, while mainstream specialists recommend a range of pragmatic strategies of *child discipline*, conservative Protestants strongly encourage the judicious use of physical punishment in response to "willful disobedience" on the part of youngsters.

A growing literature uses survey data to document religious differences in various family-related attitudes and practices (McCutcheon, 1988; Beck, Cole, and Hammond, 1991; Peek, Lowe, and Williams, 1991; Ellison and Sherkat, 1993a, 1993b). However, it is important to supplement these empirical patterns with research into the differing presuppositions of various religious and cultural communities, because it is these presuppositions that make social organization and human action meaningful (McNamara, 1985b; Thomas and Wilcox, 1987; Thomas and Roghaar, 1990). Careful exploration of these presuppositions may be especially appropriate and valuable in the case of conservative Protestants, given the prevalence of negative stereotypes in popular media and in many strands of social scientific research (Warner, 1979).

## REFERENCES

Ammerman, N. T. 1987. *Bible believers.* New Brunswick, NJ: Rutgers University Press.

Balter, L. (with A. Shreve). 1989. *Who's in control: Dr. Balter's guide to discipline without combat.* New York: Poseidon Press.

Beck, S. H., B. S. Cole, and J. A. Hammond. 1991. Religious heritage and premarital sex: Evidence from a national sample of young adults. *Journal for the Scientific Study of Religion* 30:173–80.

Berger, B., and P. L. Berger. 1983. *The war over the family.* Garden City, NY: Anchor Press/Doubleday.

Boggs, C. J. 1983. An analysis of selected Christian child-rearing manuals. *Family Relations* 32:73–80.

Boone, K. C. 1989. *The Bible tells them so: The discourse of Protestant fundamentalism.* Albany: SUNY Press.

Brazelton, T. B. 1992. *Touchpoints: Your child's emotional and behavioral development.* New York: Addison-Wesley.

Christenson, L. 1970. *The Christian family.* Minneapolis: Bethany House.

Dobson, J. 1970. *Dare to discipline.* Wheaton, IL: Living Books/Tyndale House.

———. 1978. *The strong-willed child: Birth through adolescence.* Wheaton, IL: Living Books/Tyndale House.

———. 1987. *Parenting isn't for cowards.* Dallas: Word.

Dobson, J., and G. Bauer. 1990. *Children at risk.* Dallas: Word.

Dodson, F. 1970. *How to parent.* New York: Penguin.

Dornbusch, S., and M. Strober (eds.). 1988. *Feminism, children, and the new families.* New York: Guilford Press.

Ellison, C. G., and J. P. Bartkowski. 1995. Religion and the legitimation of violence: The case of conservative Protestantism and corporal punishment. In *The web of violence: From interpersonal to global,* edited by L. R. Kurtz and J. Turpin. Urbana: University of Illinois Press.

Ellison, C. G., and D. E. Sherkat. 1993a. Conservative Protestantism and support for corporal punishment. *American Sociological Review* 58:131–44.

———.1993b. Obedience and autonomy: Religion and parental values reconsidered. *Journal for the Scientific Study of Religion* 32:313–79.

Faludi, S. 1991. *Backlash: The undeclared war against American women.* New York: Basic Books.

Farson, R. 1974. *Birthrights.* New York: Macmillan.

Fugate, J. R. 1980. *What the Bible says about child training.* Tempe, AZ: Alpha Omega.

Gordon, T. 1970. *P.E.T.: Parent effectiveness training.* New York: Peter H. Wyden, Inc.

———. 1989. *Discipline that works: Promoting self-discipline in children.* New York: Penguin.

Greven, P. 1990. *Spare the child: The religious roots of punishment and the psychological impact of abuse.* New York: Alfred A. Knopf.

Holt, J. 1974. *Escape from childhood.* New York: E. P. Dutton.

Hunter, J. D. 1987. *Evangelicalism: The coming generation.* Chicago: University of Chicago Press.

———. 1991. *Culture wars: The struggle to define America.* New York: Basic Books.

Kadushin, A., and J. A. Martin. 1981. *Child abuse: An interactional event.* New York: Columbia University Press.

Kimball, G. 1988. *50/50 parenting: Sharing family rewards and responsibilities.* Lexington, MA: Lexington Books.

LaHaye, B. 1977. *How to develop your child's temperament.* Eugene, OR: Harvest House.

Leach, P. 1989. *Your baby and your child: From birth to age five.* New York: Alfred A. Knopf.

LeShan, E. 1985. *When your child drives you crazy.* New York: St. Martin's Press.

Lienesch, M. 1991. Train up a child: Conceptions of child-rearing in Christian conservative social thought. *Comparative Social Research* 13:203–24.

McCutcheon, A. L. 1988. Denominations and religious intermarriage: Trends among white Americans in the twentieth century. *Review of Religious Research* 30:213–27.

McNamara, P. H. 1985a. Conservative Christian families and their moral world: Some reflections for sociologists. *Sociological Analysis* 46:93–99.

———. 1985b. The New Christian Right's view of the family and its social science critics: A study in differing presuppositions. *Journal of Marriage and the Family* 47:449–58.

Osborne, P. 1989. *Parenting for the nineties.* Intercourse, PA: Good Books.

Peek, C. W., G. D. Lowe, and L. S. Williams. 1991. Gender and God's word: Another look at fundamentalism and sexism. *Social Forces* 69:1205–21.

Peshkin, A. 1986. *God's choice: The total world of a fundamentalist Christian school.* Chicago: University of Chicago Press.

Power, T. G., and M. L. Chapieski. 1986. Childrearing and impulse control in toddlers: A naturalistic observation. *Developmental Psychology* 22:271–75.

Pruett, K. D. 1987. *The nurturing father.* New York: Warner Books.

Roof, W. C., and W. McKinney. 1987. *American mainline religion.* New Brunswick. NJ: Rutgers University Press.

Rose, S. D. 1988. *Keeping them out of the hands of Satan: Evangelical schooling in America.* New York: Routledge, Chapman, and Hall.

Simons, R. L., L. B. Whitbeck, R. D. Conger, and Chyi-In Wu. 1991. Inter-generational transmission of harsh parenting. *Developmental Psychology* 27:159–71.

Spock, B. 1988. *Dr. Spock on parenting: Sensible advice from America's most trusted child care expert.* New York: Simon & Schuster.

Spock, B., and M. B. Rothenberg. 1992. *Dr. Spock's baby and child care.* New York: Simon & Schuster.

Stacey, J. 1990. *Brave new families.* New York: Basic Books.

Strathman, T. 1984. From the quotidian to the Utopian: Child rearing literature in America, 1926–1946. *Berkeley Journal of Sociology* 29:1–34.

Straus, M. A. 1991. Discipline and deviance: Physical punishment of children and violence and other crime in adulthood. *Social Problems* 38:133–54.

Swindoll, C. 1991. *The strong family.* Portland, OR: Multnomah.

Taylor, L., and A. Maurer. 1985. *Think twice: The medical effects of corporal punishment.* Berkeley: Generation Books.

Thomas, D., and J. E. Wilcox. 1987. The rise of family theory: A historical and critical analysis. In *Handbook of marriage and the family,* edited by M. B. Sussman and S. K. Steinmetz, 81–102. New York: Plenum Press.

Thorne, B., and M. Yalom (eds.). 1982. *Rethinking the family: Some feminist questions.* New York: Longman.

Tomczak, L. 1982. *God, the rod, and your child's bod: The art of loving correction for Christian parents.* Old Tappan, NJ: Fleming H. Revell Co.

Wald, K. D., D. E. Owen, and S. S. Hill. 1989. Habits of the mind? The problem of authority in the New Christian Right. In *Religion and behavior in the United States,* edited by T. G. Jelen, 93–108. New York: Praeger.

Warner, R. S. 1979. Theoretical barriers to the understanding of evangelical Christianity. *Sociological Analysis* 40:1–9.

## NOTES

1. By "conservative Protestants," we refer broadly to evangelical, fundamentalist, and charismatic Protestants. Thus, our use of the "conservative Protestant" label dovetails with the work of Roof and McKinney (1987) and others. To be sure, other religious conservatives, including charismatic Catholics (e.g., Tomczak, 1982), have occasionally articulated similar views concerning childrearing issues. However, we focus on conservative Protestant manuals because conservative evangelicals have emerged during the past two decades as the most vociferous proponents of these "traditional" childrearing approaches.

2. The following information can be furnished by the authors upon request: (1) a complete list of the manuals consulted during the course of this research; (2) all available sales figures for both mainstream and conservative evangelical manuals; (3) information on the visibility of these specialists in media other than book publications (e.g., the electronic media, parenting periodicals).

3. For an analysis of the shift in popular and academic parenting ideologies away from

"authoritarian" models and toward "permissivist" models, see Strathman (1984).

4. In largely rejecting physical punishment, mainstream popular writers are again mirroring the conventional wisdom among academics. A growing body of research suggests that mild-to-moderate corporal punishment may cause physical injury to children (Taylor and Maurer, 1985), may escalate into full-fledged child abuse (Kadushin and Martin, 1981), may cause psychological damage (e.g., loss of self-esteem and self-confidence) among children, may be ineffective and even counterproductive in fostering behavioral compliance (e.g., Power and Chapieski, 1986), may promote aggression among children, and may increase the risk that they will perpetrate family violence (i.e., child abuse, spousal abuse, elder abuse) as adults (Simons et al., 1991; Straus, 1991).

## CRITICAL THINKING QUESTIONS

1. How do the authors define "conservative Protestants" and "mainstream experts"? Why does this research focus, largely, on 1970s and 1980s parenting manuals?

2. Why do Bartkowski and Ellison believe that the popular media and "many strands of social scientific research" convey negative stereotypes of conservative Protestants' childrearing practices?

3. Compare this article with that of Trumbull and Ravenel. Would Trumbull and Ravenel agree with Bartkowski and Ellison's description of conservatives' parent-child relations, the definition of parental roles, and child discipline strategies?

# 10 Raising Children

## *Liberal/Feminist:* Ten Myths That Perpetuate Corporal Punishment

Murray A. Straus, *Beating the Devil Out of Them: Corporal Punishment in American Families* (San Francisco: Jossey-Bass, 1994), excerpts from pp. 149–162. Reproduced by permission of the author.

*In the first article in this chapter, Trumbull and Ravenel contend that liberals proliferate numerous myths about the harmful effects of spanking. Liberals maintain that conservatives propagate numerous myths about the benefits of spanking. Murray A. Straus argues, for example, that every time we strike a child, we are passing on the message that violence is acceptable. Instead of changing a child's or youth's behavior, Straus claims, corporal punishment is damaging in both the short and long term.*

Hitting children is legal in every state of the United States and 84 percent of a survey of Americans agree that it is sometimes necessary to give a child a good hard spanking. Almost all parents of toddlers act on these beliefs. Study after study shows that almost 100 percent of parents with toddlers hit their children. There are many reasons for the strong support of spanking. Most of them are myths.

### Myth 1: Spanking Works Better

There has been a huge amount of research on the effectiveness of corporal punishment of animals, but remarkably little on the effectiveness of spanking children. That may be because almost no one, including psychologists, feels a need to study it because it is assumed that spanking is effective. In fact, what little research there is on the effectiveness of corporal punishment of children agrees with the research on animals. Studies of both animals and children show that punishment is *not* more effective than other methods of teaching and controlling behavior. Some studies show it is less effective.

Ellen Cohn and I asked 270 students at two New England colleges to tell us about the year they experienced the most corporal punishment. Their average age that year was eight, and they recalled having been hit an average of six times that year. We also asked them about the percent of the time they thought that the corporal punishment was effective. It averaged a little more than half of the times (53 percent). Of course, 53 percent also means that corporal punishment was *not* perceived as effective about half the time it was used.

LaVoie (1974) compared the use of a loud noise (in place of corporal punishment) with withdrawal of affection and verbal explanation in a study of first- and second-grade children. He wanted to find out which was more effective in getting the children to stop touching certain prohibited toys. Although the loud noise was more effective initially, there was no difference over a longer period of time. Just explaining was as effective as the other methods.

A problem with LaVoie's study is that it used a loud noise rather than actual corporal punishment. That problem does not apply to an experiment by Day and Roberts (1983). They studied three-year-old children who had been given "time out" (sitting in a corner). Half of the mothers were assigned to use spanking as the mode of correction if their child did not comply and left the corner. The other half put their non-complying child behind a low plywood barrier and physically enforced the child staying there. Keeping the child behind the barrier was just as effective as the spanking in correcting the misbehavior that led to the time out.

A study by Larzelere (in press) also found that a combination of *non*-corporal punishment and reasoning was as effective as corporal punishment and reasoning in correcting disobedience.

Crozier and Katz (1979), Patterson (1982), and Webster-Stratton et al. (1988, 1990) all studied children with serious conduct problems. Part of the treatment used in all three experiments was to get parents to stop spanking. In all three, the behavior of the children improved after spanking ended. Of course, many other things in addition to no spanking were part of the intervention. But, as you will see, parents who on their own accord do not spank also do many other things to manage their children's behavior. It is these other things, such as setting clear standards for what is expected, providing lots of love and affection, explaining things to the child, and recognizing and rewarding good behavior, that account for why children of non-spanking parents tend to be easy to manage and well-behaved. What about parents who do these things and also

spank? Their children also tend to be well-behaved, but it is illogical to attribute that to spanking since the same or better results are achieved without spanking, and also without adverse side effects.

Parents who favor spanking can ask, If spanking doesn't work any better, isn't that the same as saying that it works just as well? So what's wrong with a quick slap on the bottom? There are at least three things that are wrong:

- Spanking becomes less and less effective over time and when children get bigger, it becomes difficult or impossible.
- For some children, the lessons learned through spanking include the idea that they only need to be good if Mommy or Daddy is watching or will know about it.
- As the preceding chapters show, there are a number of very harmful side effects, such as a greater chance that the child will grow up to be depressed or violent. Parents don't perceive these side effects because they usually show up only in the long run.

## Myth 2: Spanking Is Needed as a Last Resort

Even parents and social scientists who are opposed to spanking tend to think that it may be needed when all else fails. There is no scientific evidence supporting this belief, however. It is a myth that grows out of our cultural and psychological commitment to corporal punishment. You can prove this to yourself by a simple exercise with two other people. Each of the three should, in turn, think of the most extreme situation where spanking is necessary. The other two should try to think of alternatives. Experience has shown that it is very difficult to come up with a situation for which the alternatives are not as good as spanking. In fact, they are usually better.

Take the example of a child running out into the street. Almost everyone thinks that spanking is appropriate then because of the extreme danger. Although spanking in that situation may help *parents* relieve their own tension and anxiety, it is not necessary or appropriate for teaching the child. It is not necessary because spanking does not work better than other methods, and it is not appropriate because of the harmful side effects of spanking. The only physical force needed is to pick up the child and get him or her out of danger, and, while hugging the child, explain the danger.

Ironically, if spanking is to be done at all, the "last resort" may be the worst. The problem is that parents are usually very angry by that time and act impulsively. Because of their anger, if the child rebels and calls the parent a name or kicks the parent, the episode can escalate into physical abuse. Indeed, most episodes of physical abuse started as physical punishment and got out of hand (see Kadushin and Martin, 1981). Of course, the reverse is not true, that is, most instances of spanking do not escalate into abuse. Still, the danger of abuse is there, and so is the risk of psychological harm.

The second problem with spanking as a last resort is that, in addition to teaching that hitting is the way to correct wrongs, hitting a child impulsively teaches another incorrect lesson—that being extremely angry justifies hitting.

## Myth 3: Spanking Is Harmless

When someone says, I was spanked and I'm OK, he or she is arguing that spanking does no harm. This is contrary to almost all the available research. One reason the harmful effects are ignored is because many of us (including those of us who are social scientists) are reluctant to admit that their own parents did something wrong and even more reluctant to admit that we have been doing something wrong with our own children. But the most important reason may be that it is difficult to see the harm. Most of the harmful effects do not become visible right away, often not for years. In addition, only a relatively small percentage of

spanked children experience obviously harmful effects.

Another argument in defense of spanking is that it is not harmful if the parents are loving and explain why they are spanking. The research does show that the harmful effects of spanking are reduced if it is done by loving parents who explain their actions. However, a study by Larzelere (1986) shows that although the harmful effects are reduced, they are not eliminated. The harmful side effects include an increased risk of delinquency as a child and crime as an adult, wife beating, depression, masochistic sex, and lowered earnings.

In addition to having harmful psychological effects on children, hitting children also makes life more difficult for parents. Hitting a child to stop misbehavior may be the easy way in the short run, but in the slightly longer run, it makes the job of being a parent more difficult. This is because spanking reduces the ability of parents to influence their children, especially in adolescence when they are too big to control by physical force. Children are more likely to do what the parents want if there is a strong bond of affection with the parent. In short, being able to influence a child depends in considerable part on the bond between parent and child (Hirschi, 1969). An experiment by Redd, Morris, and Martin (1975) shows that children tend to avoid caretaking adults who use punishment. In the natural setting, of course, there are many things that tie children to their parents. I suggest that each spanking chips away at the bond between parent and child.

Contrary to the "spoiled child" myth, children of non-spanking parents are likely to be easier to manage and better behaved than the children of parents who spank. This is partly because they tend to control their own behavior on the basis of what their own conscience tells them is right and wrong rather than to avoid being hit. This is ironic because almost everyone thinks that spanking "when necessary" makes for better behavior.

## Myth 4: One or Two Times Won't Cause Any Damage

The evidence in this book indicates that the greatest risk of harmful effects occurs when spanking is very frequent. However, that does not necessarily mean that spanking just once or twice is harmless. Unfortunately, the connection between spanking once or twice and psychological damage has not been addressed by most of the available research. This is because the studies seem to be based on this myth. They generally cluster children into "low" and "high" groups in terms of the frequency they were hit. This prevents the "once or twice is harmless" myth from being tested scientifically because the low group may include parents who spank once a year or as often as once a month. . . . [Studies] show that even one or two instances of corporal punishment are associated with a slightly higher probability of later physically abusing your own child, slightly more depressive symptoms, and a greater probability of violence and other crime later in life. The increase in these harmful side effects when parents use only moderate corporal punishment (hit only occasionally) may be small, but why run even that small risk when the evidence shows that corporal punishment is no more effective than other forms of discipline in the short run, and less effective in the long run.

## Myth 5: Parents Can't Stop Without Training

Although everyone can use additional skills in child management, there is no evidence that it takes some extraordinary training to be able to stop spanking. The most basic step in eliminating corporal punishment is for parent educators, psychologists, and pediatricians to make a simple and unambiguous statement that hitting a child is wrong and that a child *never*, ever, under any circumstances except literal physical self-defense, should be hit.

That idea has been rejected almost without exception every time I suggest it to parent educators or social scientists. They believe it would turn off parents and it could even be harmful because parents don't know what else to do. I think that belief is an unconscious defense of corporal punishment. I say that because I have never heard a parent educator say that before we can tell parents to never *verbally* attack a child, parents need training in alternatives. Some do need training, but everyone agrees that parents who use *psychological* pain as a method of discipline, such as insulting or demeaning the child, should stop immediately. But when it comes to causing *physical* pain by spanking, all but a small minority of parent educators say that before parents are told to stop spanking, they need to learn alternative modes of discipline. I believe they should come right out, as they do for verbal attacks, and say without qualification that a child should *never* be hit. . . .

Given the fact that parents already know and use many methods of teaching and controlling, the solution is amazingly simple. In most cases, parents only need the patience to keep on doing what they were doing to correct misbehavior. Just leave out the spanking! Rather than arguing that parents need to learn certain skills *before* they can stop using corporal punishment, I believe that parents are more likely to use and cultivate those skills if they decide or are required to stop spanking.

This can be illustrated by looking at one situation that almost everyone thinks calls for spanking: when a toddler runs out into the street. A typical parent will scream in terror, rush out and grab the child, and run to safety, telling the child, No! No! and explaining the danger—all of this accompanied by one or more slaps to the legs or behind.

The same sequence is as effective or more effective *without the spanking*. The spanking is not needed because even tiny children can sense the terror in the parent and understand, No! No! Newborn infants can tell the difference between when a mother is relaxed and when she is tense (Stern, 1977). Nevertheless, the fact that a child understands that something is wrong does not guarantee never again running into the street; just as spanking does not guarantee the child will not run into the street again.

If the child runs out again, non-spanking parents should use one of the same strategies as spanking parents—repetition. Just as spanking parents will spank as many times as necessary until the child learns, parents who don't spank should continue to monitor the child, hold the child's hand, and take whatever other means are needed to protect the child until the lesson is learned. Unfortunately, when non-spanking methods do not work, some parents quickly turn to spanking because they lose patience and believe it is more effective: But spanking parents seldom question its effectiveness, they just keep on spanking. . . .

## Myth 6: If You Don't Spank, Your Children Will Be Spoiled or Run Wild

It is true that some non-spanked children run wild. But when that happens it is not because the parent didn't spank. It is because some parents think the alternative to spanking is to ignore a child's misbehavior or to replace spanking with verbal attacks such as, Only a dummy like you can't learn to keep your toys where I won't trip over them. The best alternative is to take firm action to correct the misbehavior without hitting. Firmly condemning what the child has done and explaining why it is wrong are usually enough. When they are not, there are a host of other things to do, such as requiring a time out or depriving the child of a privilege, neither of which involves hitting the child.

The importance of how parents go about teaching children is clear from a classic study of American parenting—*Patterns of Child Rearing* by Sears, Maccoby, and Levin (1957). This study found two actions by parents that are linked to a high level of aggression by the child: permissiveness of the child's aggression, namely ignoring it when the child hits them or another child, and spanking to correct misbehavior. The

most aggressive children are children of parents who permitted aggression by the child and who also hit them for a variety of misbehavior. The least aggressive children are children of parents who clearly condemned acts of aggression and who, by not spanking, acted in a way that demonstrated the principle that hitting is wrong.

There are other reasons why, on the average, the children of parents who do not spank are better behaved than children of parents who spank:

- Non-spanking parents pay more attention to their children's behavior, both good and bad, than parents who spank. Consequently, they are more likely to reward good behavior and less likely to ignore misbehavior.
- Their children have fewer opportunities to get into trouble because they are more likely to child-proof the home. For older children, they have clear rules about where they can go and who they can be with.
- Non-spanking parents tend to do more explaining and reasoning. This teaches the child how to use these essential tools to monitor his or her own behavior, whereas children who are spanked get less training in thinking things through.
- Non-spanking parents treat the child in ways that tend to bond the child to them and avoid acts that weaken the bond. They tend to use more rewards for good behavior, greater warmth and affection, and fewer verbal assaults on the child (see Myth 9). By not spanking, they avoid anger and resentment over spanking. When there is a strong bond, children identify with the parent and want to avoid doing things the parent says are wrong. The child develops a conscience and lets that direct his or her behavior. . . .

## Myth 7: Parents Spank Rarely or Only for Serious Problems

Contrary to this myth, parents who spank tend to use this method of discipline for almost any misbehavior. Many do not even give the child a warning. They spank before trying other things. Some advocates of spanking even recommend this. At any supermarket or other public place, you can see examples of a child doing something wrong, such as taking a can of food off the shelf. The parent then slaps the child's hand and puts back the can, sometimes without saying a word to the child. John Rosemond, the author of *Parent Power* (1981), says, "For me, spanking is a first resort. I seldom spank, but when I decide . . . I do it, and that's the end of it."

The high frequency of spanking also shows up among the parents described in this book. The typical parent of a toddler told us of about 15 instances in which he or she had hit the child during the previous 12 months. That is surely a minimum estimate because spanking a child is generally such a routine and unremarkable event that most instances are forgotten. Other studies, such as Newson and Newson (1963), report much more chronic hitting of children. My tabulations for mothers of three- to five-year-old children in the National Longitudinal Study of Youth found that almost two-thirds hit their children during the week of the interview, and they did it more then three times in just that one week. As high as that figure may seem, I think that daily spanking is not at all uncommon. It has not been documented because the parents who do it usually don't realize how often they are hitting their children.

## Myth 8: By the Time a Child Is a Teenager, Parents Have Stopped

Parents of children in their early teens are also heavy users of corporal punishment, although at that age it is more likely to be a slap on the face than on the behind. . . . [M]ore than half of the parents of 13– to 14–year-old children in our two national surveys hit their children in the previous 12 months. The percentage drops each year as children get older, but even at age 17, one out of five parents is still hitting. To make matters worse, these are minimum estimates.

Of the parents of teenagers who told us about using corporal punishment, 84 percent did it more than once in the previous 12 months. For boys, the average was seven times and for girls, five times. These are minimum figures because we interviewed the mother in half the families and the father in the other half. The number of times would be greater if we had information on what the parent who was not interviewed did.

## Myth 9: If Parents Don't Spank, They Will Verbally Abuse Their Child

The scientific evidence is exactly the opposite. Among the nationally representative samples of parents in this book, those who did the least spanking also engaged in the least verbal aggression.

It must be pointed out that non-spanking parents are an exceptional minority. They are defying the cultural prescription that says a good parent should spank if necessary. The depth of their involvement with their children probably results from the same underlying characteristics that led them to reject spanking. There is a danger that if more ordinary parents are told to never spank, they might replace spanking by ignoring misbehavior or by verbal attacks. Consequently, a campaign to end spanking must also stress the importance of avoiding verbal attacks as well as physical attacks, and also the importance of paying attention to misbehavior.

## Myth 10: It Is Unrealistic to Expect Parents to Never Spank

It is no more unrealistic to expect parents to never hit a child than to expect that husbands should never hit their wives, or that no one should go through a stop sign, or that a supervisor should never hit an employee. Despite the legal prohibition, some husbands hit their wives, just as some drivers go through stop signs, and a supervisor occasionally may hit an employee.

If we were to prohibit spanking, as is the law in Sweden, there still would be parents who would continue to spank. But that is not a reason to avoid passing such a law here. Some people kill even though murder has been a crime since the dawn of history. Some husbands continue to hit their wives even though it has been more than a century since the courts stopped recognizing the common law right of a husband to "physically chastise an errant wife" (Calvert, 1974).

A law prohibiting spanking is unrealistic only because spanking is such an accepted part of American culture. That also was true of smoking. Yet in less than a generation we have made tremendous progress toward eliminating smoking. We can make similar progress toward eliminating spanking by showing parents that spanking is dangerous, that their children will be easier to bring up if they do not spank, and by clearly saying that a child should *never*, under any circumstances, be spanked.

## REFERENCES

Calvert, Robert. 1974. "Criminal and Civil Liability in Husband-Wife Assaults." Chapter 9 in *Violence in the Family*, edited by S. K. Steinmetz and M. A. Straus. New York: Harper & Row.

Crozier, Jill, and Roger C. Katz. 1979. "Social Learning Treatment of Child Abuse." *Journal of Behavioral Therapy and Psychiatry* 10: 213–20.

Day, Dan E., and Mark W. Roberts. 1983. "An Analysis of the Physical Punishment Component of a Parent Training Program." *Journal of Abnormal Child Psychology* 11: 141–52.

Hirschi, Travis. 1969. *The Causes of Delinquency*. Berkeley: University of California Press.

Kadushin, Alfred, and Judith A. Martin. 1981. *Child Abuse: An Interactional Event*. New York: Columbia University Press.

Larzelere, Robert E. 1986. "Moderate Spanking: Model or Deterrent of Children's Aggression in the Family?" *Journal of Family Violence* 1: 27–36.

LaVoie, Joseph C. 1974. "Type of Punishment as a Determination of Resistance to Deviation." *Developmental Psychology* 10: 181–89.

Newson, John, and Elizabeth Newson. 1963. *Patterns of Infant Care in an Urban Community*. Baltimore: Penguin Books.

Patterson, Gerald R. 1982. "A Social Learning Approach to Family Intervention: III." *Coercive Family Process*. Eugene, OR: Castalia.

Redd, William H., Edward K. Morris, and Jerry A. Martin. 1975. "Effects of Positive and Negative Adult-Child Interactions on Children's Social Preference." *Journal of Experimental Child Psychology* 19: 153–64.

Rosemond, John K. 1981. *Parent Power, A Common Sense Approach to Raising Your Children in the '80s*. Charlotte, NC: East Woods Press.

Sears, Robert R., Eleanor C. Maccoby, and Harry Levin. 1957. *Patterns of Child Rearing*. Evanston, IL: Row, Peterson.

Stern, Daniel. 1977. *The First Relationships: Mother and Infant*. Cambridge, MA: Harvard University Press.

Webster-Stratton, Carolyn, Mary Kolpacoff, and Terri Hollinsworth. 1988. "Self-Administered Videotape Therapy for Families with Conduct-Problem Children: Comparison with Two Cost-Effective Treatments and a Control Group." *Journal of Consulting and Clinical Psychology* 56: 558–66.

Webster-Stratton, Carolyn. 1990. "Enhancing the Effectiveness of Self-Administered Videotape Parent Training for Families with Conduct-Problem Children." *Journal of Abnormal Child Psychology* 18: 479–92.

## CRITICAL THINKING QUESTIONS

1. Since much of the research shows that spanking does *not* change behavior, why do almost 100 percent of parents hit their toddlers and one out of five parents hit their teenage children?

2. How does Straus's view of a child's human nature differ from that of Trumbull and Ravenel?

3. Straus would like to prohibit spanking legally (as in Sweden). Who—according to the Trumbull/Ravenel and Straus articles—would probably oppose such laws?

# 11 Gay and Lesbian Families

## *Conservative:* Gay Parenting and the Developmental Needs of Children

*Many conservatives oppose gay and lesbian households on religious grounds. Others reject gay families because—like cohabiting couples and unmarried mothers—they don't mirror traditional family structures. Lawrence F. Burtoft argues, moreover, that gay parents harm their children by depriving them of a biological parent, by influencing their sexual behavior and identity, and by exposing them to medical risks associated with homosexual behavior.*

There is relatively little research indicating the long term effects of being raised in an exclusively homosexual home. What research is confirming, however, is that the domestic environment most conducive to the well-being of children has both a mother and a father.[1] While cases may be found in which children of gay or lesbian parents demonstrate general psychological and social adjustment, the overall behavioral and psychological profile of homosexuals gives ample reason for extreme caution in this regard. Granting legal status and social approval to homosexual adoption constitutes a social experiment with potentially tragic results. Given the negative aspects and consequences of homosexuality, we would do well to heed the words of Joseph Nicolosi:

> One of the beautiful things about a democracy is that social scientists can ruin a generation, and then come back 20 years later with our objective measures to validate what common sense should have told us.[2]

Common sense, unfettered by politically correct ideology, would predict that many children, under homosexual parentage, could echo the words of Jaki Edwards, who spent her critical adolescent years, along with her younger brother, in a home with her lesbian mother and her various lovers. She reflects on the effects of this experience:

> I realize that homosexuals feel they can give a child love and support that even many straight families can't provide. But I've been there. I know the finger-pointing and the shame one carries. For years, you struggle with the thought that you might be a homosexual. People say "like mother, like daughter." Most of us become promiscuous to prove we're straight.

Edwards then raises a most important question:

> How will a man raised by two men know how to relate to a woman? A woman brought up like this doesn't know how to emotionally connect with men. I had to struggle for years to believe a man could really love me.[3]

## CHILDREN NEED THE UNIQUE NURTURING INFLUENCES OF BOTH A MOTHER AND A FATHER

The last great experiment on marriage, no-fault divorce, has proven to be a disastrous mistake, spawning more problems than it has solved, particularly the victimization of women and children. Inadvertently, however, it has given us the opportunity to study the effects upon children of growing up without both a mother and a father. The results show that children need the influence of parents of both sexes, and that there are significant medical risks when this influence is lacking.

### Supporting Data

Dr. Deborah A. Dawson of the National Center for Health Statistics studied data from the 1988 National Health Interview Survey of Child Health. She discovered that children living with either never-married mothers, formerly married mothers, and in mother/stepfather families evidenced "elevated scores for behavioral problems and health vulnerability." More specifically, Dr. Dawson discovered that:

Health vulnerability scores from 20% to 35% higher than those for children living with both biological parents.
Children living with formerly married mothers had a 50% greater risk of having asthma in the preceding 12 months.
An increased risk of frequent headaches among both children living with formerly married mothers and those living with mother and stepfather.
The observed proportion reported to have received professional help for emotional or behavioral problems in the preceding year varied from 2.7% for children living with both biological parents to 8.8% for children living with formerly married mothers. For children living with never-married mothers or with mothers and stepfathers, the respective proportions were 4.4% and 6.6%.[4]

Thus, there is strong empirical support for any legislation that would have the effect of encouraging traditional marriage between a man and a woman.

## FATHERS ARE AS IMPORTANT AS MOTHERS

There is less popular resistance to the idea of lesbian couples as parents. However, there is exceedingly strong evidence that demonstrates that children—both girls and boys—need the influence of a father.

### Supporting Data

In his testimony before the House Select Committee on Children, Youth, and Families (February 12, 1986), Dr. George Rekers, who is currently professor of neuropsychiatry and behavioral science at the University of South Carolina School of Medicine and who specializes in psychosexual disorders, summarized the research as follows:

Research has documented that children without fathers more often have lowered academic performance, more cognitive and intellectual deficits, increased adjustment problems, and higher risks for psychosexual development problems. . . .
In girls, research studies by [E. Mavis] Heatherington and her colleagues have compared girls with two parents [a mother and a father] with girls who grew up without a father because of divorce or death of a father. Compared with girls with intact nuclear families, girls who lost their father by death were more inhibited in their relationships with males in general, but girls who lost their father by divorce were overly responsive to males, were more likely to be sexually involved with males in adolescence, married younger, were pregnant more often before marriage, and became divorced or separated from their eventual husbands more frequently.[5]

There is a large body of evidence that indicates that men and women are inherently different in more than just biology, and that these differences are crucial for the well-being of children. Studies of the effects of "androgynous parenting"—where the mother and father share domestic and child-rearing responsibilities equally—have led to interesting findings. Dr. David Popenoe, professor of sociology and associate dean of the Faculty of Arts and Sciences at Rutgers University, writes,

> Although it is neither possible nor desirable to return to the traditional nuclear family exemplified by *Ozzie and Harriet*, we must take care not to jettison traditional mother-father roles entirely. Unlike the workplace, family organization is based on very real, biological differences between men and women. Parental androgyny is not what children need. . . .
>
> There appear to be sound biological and sociological reasons why some gender differentiation of roles within childrearing families is necessary for the good of society. Gender differentiation is important for marital stability. While the fully equal participation of both parents in childrearing is essential, fathers are not the same as mothers, nor should they be.[6]

The bottom-line point: children need the influence of both a mother and a father, and our marriage laws ought to reflect this empirical fact. It is not in the interest of individuals, society, or the state, to sanction familial arrangements that disadvantage our most vulnerable citizens, children. States ought not be forced to recognize legalized same-sex marriage, and certainly our federal agencies should not.

### TENDENCY OF HOMOSEXUAL PARENTS TO ENCOURAGE HOMOSEXUAL BEHAVIOR IN THEIR CHILDREN

Not only are same-sex parenting environments detrimental from a basic medical health perspective, there are empirical indications that such arrangements inordinately influence children raised within them to experiment with homosexual behavior and to identify as gay or lesbian as adults.

### Supporting Data

In the January 1996 issue of *Developmental Psychology*, London researchers Susan Golombok and Fiona Tasker compared children raised by mothers who were in lesbian relationships with those raised by single mothers in heterosexual relationships.[7] In both cases the fathers were absent. Whereas none of the children who grew up in a heterosexual setting engaged in homosexual behavior, 24 percent (6) of the lesbian-raised children had done so, and 8 percent (2) later identified as bisexual, lesbian, or gay as adults. These figures significantly exceed the normal percentage of homosexuality within the general population.

Based on their findings, Golombok and Tasker acknowledge that "by creating a climate of acceptance or rejection of homosexuality within the family, parents may have some impact on their children's sexual experimentation as heterosexual, lesbian, or gay."

This conclusion agrees with the opinion of Dr. Diana Baumrind of the Institute of Human Development at the University of California, Berkeley. In an article in the 1995 issue of *Developmental Psychology*, Dr. Baumrind questioned the conclusion of other researchers who claimed that the children of homosexuals are not more likely than children of heterosexuals to adopt a homosexual orientation. Baumrind writes,

> I question their conclusion on theoretical and empirical grounds. Theoretically, one might expect children to identify with lifestyle features of their gay and lesbian parents. One might also expect gay and lesbian parents to be supportive rather than condemnatory of their child's nonnormative sexual orientation.[8]

Baumrind goes on to show that the research does in fact reveal that children raised by homosexuals demonstrate a higher likelihood of adopting homosexuality.

Statistically, this means that a child raised in a home in which homosexuality is treated positively is more likely to be exposed to all of the soundly documented negative factors associated with homosexuality: higher rates of promiscuity, exposure to sexually transmitted and other diseases, premature death, relational and psychological instability, and social ostracism. The last point discusses this matter in more detail.

## THE INHERENT MEDICAL RISKS
## OF HOMOSEXUAL BEHAVIOR[9]

There is a direct relationship between the sanctioning of same-sex marriage and the sanctioning of homosexual behavior in general. To say that same-sex marriage is socially acceptable is to say that homosexual behavior is socially acceptable. Medically speaking, this is a tragic assumption, for the evidence shows homosexuality to involve exceptionally high risk behaviors.

### Supporting Data

*The Anatomical Risks of Homosexual Behavior*  In contrast to normal, monogamous heterosexual intercourse, homosexual behavior in all its forms is risky at best. Consider anal intercourse. Without any reference to disease, the insertion of the penis into another's rectum is inherently injurious from a purely anatomical perspective. The rectum consists of a highly absorbent, single-layered wall of columnar epithelial cells. It is far more fragile than the multilayered vaginal wall made up of squamous cells and, thus, a more flexible and protected organ. The rectum is subject to rupture and tearing under the physical force of penal thrusting or the less common practice of "fisting," which involves the insertion of the hand or arm into the rectum. Ongoing anal intercourse often leads to the breakdown of normal rectal functions due to trauma to the anal sphincter muscle.[10] This is an activity that is risky, whether practiced in homosexual or heterosexual context. Thus, basic anatomical facts demonstrate that the lower intestinal tract was not intended to be used as a sex organ. But if body design isn't a sufficient argument against anal intercourse, the tragic reality of AIDS ought to be conclusive.

*AIDS and Anal Sex*  Its physical structure also makes the rectum highly susceptible to the infiltration of disease. With a thin cellular wall, infectious organisms more easily penetrate into the blood stream.

In addition, the tearing and rupturing which can take place during anal intercourse exposes the individual to infection by manifold serious and fatal diseases. Of these, AIDS is the most well-known and the most dangerous. As of the end of June 30, 1993, 315,390 cases of AIDS have been reported.[11] Of these, 191,642 were homosexual and bisexual men.[12] That equals 61% of all AIDS cases. The remaining 39% is a combination of heterosexuals, intravenous drug users, hemophiliacs, recipients of blood transfusions, children of HIV infected mothers, and others. Given that exclusively homosexual males make up only approximately 2% of the population, this means that they are 30 times more likely to contract HIV. Anal intercourse, receptive or insertive, second only to oral copulation as the most practiced homosexual behavior, has been identified as especially conducive to HIV infection.[13]

Studies have also indicated that the body's natural immune system is broken down by repeated exposure to sperm during anal intercourse. The reason rests again in the difference between anal and vaginal membranes: sperm can penetrate the former but not the latter.[14] Facts such as these led Dr. C. Everett Koop, the former Surgeon General of the United States, to declare that anal intercourse, even with a condom, "is simply too dangerous a practice."[15]

It is not only homosexuals who are at risk through anal intercourse. This is an essentially dangerous behavior for all who participate in it, be they homosexual or heterosexual. Studies have shown that more than 10% of American women and their male partners engage in anal sex with some regularity.[16] While males are more likely to pass on HIV infection than females, women are at far greater risk of contracting AIDS through anal intercourse than vaginal.[17]

*Other Disease Risks*  However, HIV/AIDS is only one of the many infections to which homosexuals are significantly prone. Since either oral-anal or penile-anal sex involves contact with human feces, such behavior carries with it a high risk of contracting such diseases as hepatitis A, hepatitis B, Kaposi's sarcoma, anal carcinoma, and other rectal infections involving gonorrhea, herpes simplex, syphilis, and human papillomavirus.[18] Because of the extremely high rate of incidence among homosexuals, a group of rare intestinal diseases have been grouped together under the title "gay bowel syndrome."[19] According to Dr. Glen E. Hastings of the University of Kansas School of Medicine, this group of conditions occurs "among persons who practice unprotected anal intercourse, anilingus, or fellatio following anal intercourse."[20] Many homosexuals, alarmed by the documented relationship between penile-anal intercourse and HIV infection, have chosen the less risky course of oral-anal intercourse ("rimming"). Yet since the transmission of HIV and HBV (the hepatitis B virus) is primarily through the exchange of blood or body fluids, rimming, along with other acts such as fisting and urinal sex, are also extremely high risk behaviors.[21]

The more extreme forms of homosexual behavior, including such sado-masochistic acts as scarring (cutting of the flesh), whipping, and breath-control (strangulation), are obviously inherently injurious and potentially fatal.[22]

While it is true that all of the diseases discussed above can be found among heterosexuals, statistics support the conclusion that homosexuals, *precisely because of their sexual behavior*, are significantly more susceptible to infection, sickness, and death.[23] In the case of almost any other medical condition—coronary artery disease, for instance—behavioral characteristics that place the individual at significantly higher statistical risk are recognized without quarrel as "causative," hence the legitimate object of public-health campaigns to eliminate or modify; certainly not to support as "neutral." Homosexual behavior is as direct a "cause" of the above-discussed conditions in precisely the same sense that overeating, lack of exercise, and smoking are "causes" of coronary-heart disease. Indeed, from a purely medical perspective, homosexual behavior is repeatedly

identified as the single most important risk factor for a large number of diseases, only one of which is AIDS. In 1988 *The Atlantic* reported that since the mid-1970's, gay and bisexual men account for nearly half of the reported cases of syphilis [24] This corresponds to similar statistics regarding gonorrhea of the throat and various intestinal diseases. Studies have indicated that among heterosexual men infected with gonorrhea, 3% to 7% suffer infection of the pharynx (pharyngeal gonorrhea); for homosexual men, the figures more than triple (10% to 25%).[25] This disease is spread primarily through fellatio, which is also why heterosexual women who practice oral sex are also at risk.[26] Of men enrolled in a antimicrobial study by the Disease Control Service of the Denver Department of Health and Hospitals, chosen because they either were attending a sexually transmitted disease clinic, showed positive for anogenital gonorrhea, or had been exposed to gonorrhea, 78% (89) were homosexual.[27] According to Dr. Franklyn N. Judson of the University of Colorado Health Sciences Center, anorectal gonorrhea is the "primary reservoir of infection" for homosexual men, who are also far more likely than heterosexuals to be co-infected with both gonorrhea and syphilis.[28]

As one review article[29] demonstrated, the medical risks faced by active homosexual males fall into four main categories:

- Classical sexually transmitted diseases (gonorrhea, syphilis, herpes simplex, etc.)
- Enteric diseases (hepatitis A & B, Shigella species, cytomegalovirus, etc.)
- Trauma (fecal incontinence, hemorrhoids, anal fissure, penile edema, etc.)
- HIV/AIDS

### SUMMARY

For the sake of America's children, there are significant developmental and medical reasons for social policies biased in favor of the natural, biological parent-child relationship. No other familial environment demonstrates the capacity to promote the welfare of children. In contrast, homosexual relationships involve behaviors and psychosexual dynamics which can be shown to be detrimental to children by 1) depriving them of the unique influence of both a mother and a father, 2) by influencing toward homosexual behavior and identity which in turn 3) exposes them to the medical risks associated with such behavior.

## NOTES

1. Whitehead, Barbara Dafoe, "Dan Quayle Was Right," *The Atlantic Monthly*, April 1993.

2. Quoted by Don Feder, "Gay Adoptions Flout Simple Common Sense," *Colorado Springs Gazette-Telegraph*. September 28, 1993, 5B.

3. *Ibid.*

4. Dawson, Deborah A., "Family Structure and Children's Health and Well-Being: Data from the National Health Interview Survey on Child Health," *Journal of Marriage and the Family*, August 1991, 53, 573, 578–579.

5. *The Diversity and Strength of American Families*, Hearing Before the Select Committee on Children, Youth, and Families, House of Representatives, Ninety-ninth Congress, Second Session, Washington, D.C., 1986, 59–60.

6. Popenoe, David, "Parental Androgyny," *Social Science and Modern Science* 30, no. 6, September/October 1993, 6, 11.

7. Golombok, Susan, and Tasker, Fiona, "Do Parents Influence the Sexual Orientation of Their Children? Findings from a Longitudinal Study of Lesbian Families," *Developmental Psychology*, 1996, 32, no. 1, 3–11.

8. Baumrind, Diana, "Commentary on Sexual Orientation: Research and Social Policy Implications," *Developmental Psychology*, 1995, 31, no. 1, 134.

9. This section excerpted and adapted from Larry Burtoft, *Setting the Record Straight: What Research Really Says About the Social Consequences of Homosexuality*, Focus on the Family, 1995, 32–34.

10. Mildvan, D., et al., "Opportunistic Infections and Immune Deficiency in Homosexual Men," *Annals of Internal Medicine*, 1982, 96, 700–704; Ostrow, D., et al., eds., *Sexually Transmitted Dis-*

*eases in Homosexual Men* (New York: Plenum Medical Book Co., 1982), 989–90; Miles, A. J. et al., "Effect of anoreceptive intercourse on anorectal function," *Journal of the Royal Society of Medicine* 86:3 (March 1993), 144–7.

11. *HIV/AIDS Surveillance Report*, July 1993, 5, no. 2, U.S. Department of Health and Human Services, 12.

12. *Ibid.*, 6.

13. Coates, Randall A., et al., "Risk Factors for HIV Infection in Male Sexual Contacts of Men with AIDS or an AIDS-Related Condition," *American Journal of Epidemiology*, 1988, 128, no. 4; Winkelstein, Warren, Jr., et al., "Sexual Practices and Risk of Infection by the Human Immunodeficiency Virus," *Journal of the American Medical Association*, January 16, 1987, 257, no. 3, 321, 325; Melbye, Mads, and Robert J. Biggar, "Interactions Between Persons at Risk for AIDS and the General Population in Denmark," *American Journal of Epidemiology*, March 15, 1992, 135, no. 6, 601.

14. Ratner, Herbert, "Semen and AIDS," *Child and Family Quarterly*, Part I, 20, 275–82, and Part II, 21, 90–96; Mavglit, Giora M., et al., "Chronic Immune Stimulation by Sperm Alloantigens," *Journal of the American Medical Association*, January 13, 1984, 251, no. 2, 237–41. See also Richards, J., "Rectal Insemination Modifies Immune Responses in Rabbits," *Science*, 1984, 224, 390–92.

15. Hooper, Cecila, "Surgeon General Advises Doctors to Teach Patients About Condoms," *United Press International*, October 13, 1987.

16. Voeller, Bruce, "AIDS and Heterosexual Anal Intercourse," *Archives of Sexual Behavior*, 1991, 20, no. 3, 233–76; Voeller, Bruce, "Heterosexual Anal Intercourse: An AIDS Risk Factor," in Voeller, B., Reinisch, J. M., and Gottlieb, M., eds., *AIDS and Sex—An Integrated Biomedical and Behavioral Approach* (New York and Oxford: Oxford University Press, 1990), 276–310.

17. Voeller, *op. cit.*

18. Beral, et al., *op. cit.*; Corey, L., and Holmes, K. K., "Sexual Transmission of Hepatitis A in Homosexual Men," *New England Journal of Medicine*, February 21, 1980, 302, no. 8, 435–8; Daling, J. R., et al., "Sexual Practices, Sexually Transmitted Diseases, and the Incidence of Anal Cancer," *New England Journal of Medicine*, October 15, 1987, 317, no. 16, 973–7; H. Jaffee, et al., "National Case Control Study of Kaposi's Sarcoma," *Annals of Internal Medicine*, 1983, 99, 145–51; Quinn, Thomas C., et al., "The Polymi-

crobial Origin of Intestinal Infections in Homosexual Men," *New England Journal of Medicine*, September 8, 1983, 309, no. 10, 576–82.

19. Hastings, G. E., and Weber, R. W., "Inflammatory Bowel Disease: Part I. Clinical Features and Diagnosis," *American Family Physician*, 1993, 47:598–608; Laughon, Barbara E., Druckman, Dolph A., et al., "Prevalence of Enteric Pathogens in Homosexual Men with and without Acquired Immunodeficiency Syndrome," *Gastroenterology*, 1988, 94:984–93; Quinn, T. C., "Gay Bowel Syndrome. The Broadened Spectrum of Non-Genital Infection," *Postgraduate Medicine*, 1984 76:197–8, 201–10.

20. Hastings, Glen E., M.D., and Weber, Richard, M.D., "Letter to the Editor," *American Family Physician*, February 15, 1994, 49, no. 3, 581.

21. Gill, S. K., C. Loveday, and R. J. C. Gilson, "Transmission of HIV-1 Infection by Oroanal Intercourse," *Genitourinary Medicine*, 1992, 68, 254–7; McKusick, L., W. Horstman, and T. J. Coates, "AIDS and Sexual Behavior Reported by Gay Men in San Francisco," *American Journal of Public Health*, May 1985, 75, no. 5, 493–6; Shook, Lyle L., et al., "Rectal Fist Insertion," *American Journal of Forensic Medicine and Pathology*, December 1985, 6, 319–424.

22. Michalodimitrakis, M., et al., "Accidental Sexual Strangulation," *American Journal of Forensic Medicine and Strangulation*, 1986, 7, no. 1, 74–75.

23. Judson, F. N., et al., "Comparative Prevalence Rates of Sexually Transmitted Diseases in Heterosexual and Homosexual Men," *American Journal of Epidemiology*, 1980, 112, 836–43.

24. Leishman, Katie, "AIDS and Syphilis," *The Atlantic*, January 1988, 261, no. 1, 20.

25. Hutt, David M., and Judson, Franklyn, N., "Epidemiology and Treatment of Oropharyngeal Gonorrhea," *Annals of Internal Medicine*, 1986, 104:655–658.

26. Soper, David E., and Merrill-Nach, Suzanne, "Successful Therapy of Penicillinase-Producing *Neisseria Gonorrhea* Pharyngeal Infection During Pregnancy," *Obstetrics and Gynecology*, August 1986, 68, no. 2, 290–91; Cavenee, Michael R., et al., "Treatment of Gonorrhea in Pregnancy, " *Obstetrics and Gynecology*, January 1993, 81, no. 1, 33–38.

27. Judson, Franklyn N., Ehret, Josephine M., and Handsfield, H. Hunter, "Comparative Study of Ceftriaxone and Spectinomycin for Treatment of Pharyngeal and Anorectal Gonorrhea," *Journal of the American Medical Association*, March 8, 1985, 253, no. 10, 1417–1419.

28. *Ibid.*

29. Owen, Jr., W. F., "Medical Problems of the Homosexual Adolescent," *Journal of Adolescent Health Care* 6, no. 4 (July 1985), 278–85, cited in Jeffrey Satinover, *Homosexuality and the Politics of Truth* (Grand Rapids: Baker, 1996), 68.

## CRITICAL THINKING QUESTIONS

1. If children need the influence of a father and a mother, why does Burtoft reject "androgynous parenting"?

2. According to some of the research, children with same-sex parents are more likely to experiment with homosexuality than children with heterosexual parents. Does this mean that same-sex parenting *causes* children's sexual orientation?

3. Lesbians, unlike gay men, rarely engage in high-risk sexual behavior. Would Burtoft agree, then, that lesbians could be good parents? Or "better" parents than gay men?

# 11 Gay and Lesbian Families

## *Centrist:* Gay and Lesbian Parenting

BARBARA F. OKUN, *Understanding Diverse Families: What Practitioners Need to Know* (New York: Guilford Press, 1996), pp. 131–35. Reprinted with permission of Guilford Publications, Inc.

*Because most gays were raised in traditional heterosexual, nuclear families, they encounter more parenting problems than their heterosexual counterparts. As Barbara F. Okun shows, for example, they must deal with homophobic attitudes, a lack of social support, possible denial of child custody, and ostracism by family members. Okun also cautions that the impact of gay and lesbian parenting on children's development is sketchy, is limited to specific geographic locations, and focuses on problems rather than strengths.*

### GAY AND LESBIAN PARENTING

Gay and lesbian parents and families typically encounter all or nearly all of the issues of heterosexual parents and families in addition to those that are the unique by-products of their specific sexual orientation and living and parenting arrangements. Because almost all gays and lesbians were raised in traditional heterosexual, nuclear families (Harris & Turner, 1985–1986), as parents they are at a disadvantage because of the absence of relevant gay and lesbian parent role models. Each, therefore, must navigate new territory without benefit of the familiar signposts that aid heterosexual families. Homophobic attitudes classify gays and lesbians as inferior, even dangerous, parents. Falk (1994) and Barrett and Robinson (1994) document the gap between empirical research and societal assumptions in gay and lesbian custody cases. In 1994, there was a controversial case in Virginia in which custody of a child was given to the maternal grandmother solely on the judge's belief that a lesbian mother could not be a competent parent. In the same year, a Massachusetts court allowed a lesbian to adopt her lover's biological daughter.

Irrational fears about homosexual parents include concern that a child will be sexually molested by a same-gender parent (even though the data reveal that most sexual abuse is heterosexual), that gender and sexual identity formation will somehow be deviant among children of homosexuals, and that children of gays and lesbians will be subjected to continuous harassment by their peers and, therefore, will experience a general social ostracism. Popular mythology also holds that lesbians lack a maternal instinct and, therefore, are not suited to parent. Gays are considered the least fit parents of all. Fear also exists, to some extent, that children of gays will be at higher risk for contracting HIV (Harris & Turner, 1985–1986).

It is clear that gay and lesbian families lack standard social supports, rights, and financial benefits, and that these lacks can exert a deleterious effect upon family cohesion and longevity. Gay and lesbian parents who had their children in a previous heterosexual union commonly live in a state of dread that they will lose custody or visitation rights should the courts discover their sexual orientation. The secrecy this realistic dread exerts upon the social adjustment of family members can debilitate individual and family development. Also, extended family members often disown gay and lesbian relatives, leaving the homosexual family without a crucial source of support (Baptiste, 1987). Against such a menacing and deeply rooted backdrop of fear, ignorance, and hatred, it would appear that social stigmatization, ostracism, and stereotyping present formidable external roadblocks to gay and lesbian parents and families.

Gay and lesbian parents coming out of heterosexual marriages may need to work through their coming-out process prior to realizing a harmonious gay or lesbian parent identity. That is assuming that they are allowed visitation or coparenting opportunities, because they are rarely allowed custody if their sexual orientation becomes known. They may have difficulty in forming a new couple relationship, as do any blended or reconstituted families. But for someone coming out of a heterosexual marriage, the inexperience in and novelty of having a same-gender couple relationship, the guilt and self-doubts around divorce, along with internalized and societal homophobia create more intense vulnerability for a homosexual blended family than for a heterosexual blended family.

Most of the literature about the psychological issues of homosexual parenting focuses on lesbian parenting. As pointed out by Schwartz-Gottman (1989), fathers tend to be relegated to the shadows compared to mothers, and gays are often stereotyped as antifamily. The research on lesbian parents asserts that lesbian women are not more likely than heterosexual women to be mentally ill; in fact, the results of various studies indicate that lesbian women are more self-confident, independent, composed, and self-sufficient than heterosexual women (Baumrind, 1995; Falk, 1989; Patterson, 1994; Turner et al., 1990). This would have a positive impact on their parenting. Other comparative studies (Patterson, 1992) suggest that there are no substantial differences between the maternal attitudes and caregiving behaviors of lesbian and heterosexual mothers. And, as reported by P. J. Falk (1989), considering all of the obstacles that lesbians face, a woman who is willing to overcome these difficulties in order to parent is likely to be a highly motivated and very committed parent. The same can be said for gay fathers. Because of their own struggles with marginalization, both gay and lesbian parents are likely to be particularly sensitive to diversity. They tend to foster the development of tolerance in their children (American Psychological Association, 1995).

The complexity of gay and lesbian family concerns increases dramatically with the homosexual couple's choice to have children. And, as with heterosexual couples, the decision to have children can place strains upon the couple relationship. Gay and lesbian couples have added issues, such as the method of becoming parents, and which parent will have the biological input, in addition to legal and financial constraints.

## IMPACT OF GAY AND LESBIAN PARENTING ON CHILDREN'S DEVELOPMENT

In the past few years, considerable attention and research efforts have focused on the psychosocial development of children of homosexual parents. Concerns about the emotional development, sexual orientation, and day-to-day psychological well-being of these children come from all sides, both from those who have the power to decide custody and parenting rights and may be influenced by overt or masked homophobia, heterosexism, and ignorance; and from those who are determined to find results supporting the parenting rights of gays and lesbians. Most of the studies are based on children born within heterosexual marriages. The samples are further limited because many gays and lesbians remain in heterosexual marriages, hiding their homosexuality from their families, and are obviously not available for study.

The phenomenon of gay and lesbian couples choosing to have and raise children solely within the gay or lesbian family structure is too recent to provide sufficient samples to study. In the first statistical study of gays who chose to parent, Sbordone (1993) studied 78 gay fathers who chose to parent as gay couples or as single gay men via adoption or by contracting with a surrogate mother, and compared these men to a group of 83 gays choosing not to parent. Compared to gays who chose not to parent, those choosing to parent displayed higher levels of self-esteem and lower levels of internalized homophobia, although both groups had similar perceptions about intimacy and autonomy in their families of origin during childhood. This is one of the few studies about gays who became parents as gay men. Scallen (1993) also studied gay fathers, finding them less traditional in parental attitudes, with a higher psychological investment in their roles as fathers than as economic providers.

The existing studies of lesbians who became parents as lesbians (Green, Mandel, Hotvedt, Gray, & Smith, 1986; Harris & Turner, 1985–1986; Kirkpatrick, 1987; McCandlish, 1987; Patterson, 1992; Steckel, 1987) found the children to be as healthy as those in heterosexual families. The children of lesbians reported more stress due to homophobia as well as having a greater sense of well-being and feeling more sensitive, lovable, and emotionally responsive than did the children of heterosexual mothers. Patterson (1992) also found that lesbian mothers are more diligent in creating opportunities for their children to have relationships with adult males than are heterosexual single mothers. Golombok, Spencer, and Rutter (1983) found that lesbian mothers arranged for their children to have more contact with their fathers than did heterosexual single or divorced mothers. R. L. Barret and Robinson (1994, pp. 168–169) found children of gay fathers to be (1) like all kids, some with problems, some well adjusted, some doing well in just about all activities; (2) living in unique family situations requiring the development of coping strategies; (3) needing help sorting out their feelings about homosexuality and their anxieties (shared by most youth) about their own sexual orientation; (4) possibly isolated and angry and perhaps having poor relationships with their gay fathers; (5) in little danger of sexual abuse and unlikely to "catch" homosexuality; (6) mostly adjusting well to their family situation and using the family as a means to develop greater tolerance of diversity; (7) advocates of human and gay rights; and (8) having the potential for greater honesty and openness in their relationships with their fathers.

The majority of the research is limited to assessing sexual identity formation, including gender identity, sex role identity, sex-typed behavior, and sexual orientation. The methods by which "normality" versus "abnormality" are assessed vary from one study to another, but are consensually agreed to be resistant to any form of objective measurement, such as the available, valid, and reliable standard personality assessment batteries. Thus, the research must be considered within its political context. The research on both gay and lesbian parents, such as it is, is in virtually unanimous agreement that there are no significant differences thus far assessed between the children of homosexual and heterosexual parents on any dimension of personality functioning or personal development, issues of separation and individuation, self-concept, and locus of control

(American Psychological Association, 1995; Barret & Robinson, 1994; Falk, 1994; Gibbs, 1989; Golombok et al., 1983; Harris & Turner, 1985–1986; Hoeffer, 1981; Kirkpatrick, Smith, & Roy, 1981; Martin, 1993; Patterson, 1992, 1994; Riddle, 1978). The parental attitudes, behaviors, and child-rearing practices of gays and lesbians have been found to be essentially the same as those of their heterosexual counterparts. The focus of the research has been more on children's welfare than on parents' relationships.

The literature does acknowledge the impact on children of the pervasive pressure for secrecy, noting consideration of geographic location. Living in San Francisco as the child of gay or lesbian parents would be a different experience than living in Wichita, Kansas. The degree of acceptance of diversity is influenced by geographical exposure, values, and norms. Thus, it appears that fear of exposure and increased social isolation may burden at least some children of homosexual parents. Research on the impact of homophobia on children and adolescents is sketchy at best.

It is difficult to assess how many of these children are raised solely within a single-sex culture and how many parents consciously attempt to expose their children to opposite-gender role models, as suggested in the previously mentioned studies. Considerable social learning results, however, from extrafamilial models, such as television, school, peer groups, books, movies, clubs, and other community resources. The degree of the parents' heterophobia and comfort with diversity, their identity and coming-out experiences, and their current life experiences all influence their children's perceptions and interpretations of their experiences.

It is noteworthy that the general literature focuses on problems and limitations and minimizes or ignores strengths and assets. Laird (1993) suggests consideration of resiliency, which can develop from the experience of being marginalized and marching to the tune of a different drummer. Phenomenological studies and informal dialogues indicate that psychological benefits might include increased acceptance of one's sexuality, increased tolerance and empathy, increased willingness to come forward and talk about problems, and increased androgyny.

Another major research problem is that of comparison. Are the groups against which gays and lesbians are compared based solely on sexual orientation, on single parenting, on matched financial and occupational levels?

## REFERENCES

American Psychological Association. (1995). *Lesbian and gay parenting: A resource for psychologists* (A joint report of the Committee on Women in Psychology, the Committee on Lesbian and Gay Concerns, and the Committee on Children, Youth, and Family). Washington, D.C.: Author.

Baptiste, D. A. (1987). Psychotherapy with gay/lesbian couples and their children in "stepfamilies": A challenge for marriage and family therapists. *Journal of Homosexuality* 14(1/2), 223–228.

Barret, R. L., & Robinson, B. E. (1994). Gay dads. In A. E. Gottfried & A. W. Gottfried (eds.), *Redefining families: Implications for children's development* (pp. 157–171). New York: Plenum Press.

Baumrind, D. (1995). Commentary on sexual orientation: Research and social policy implications. *Developmental Psychology* 31(1), 130–136.

Falk, P. J. (1989). Lesbian mothers: Psychosocial assumptions in family law. *American Psychologist* 44, 941–947.

Falk, P. J. (1994). The gap between psychological assumptions and empirical research in lesbian-mother child custody cases. In A. E. Gottfried & A. W. Gottfried (eds.), *Redefining families: Implications for children's development* (pp. 132–152). New York: Plenum Press.

Golombok, S., Spencer, A., & Rutter, M. (1983). Children in lesbian and single-parent households: Psychosexual and psychiatric appraisal. *Journal of Child Psychology and Psychiatry* 24, 551–572.

Green, R., Mandel, J. B., Hotvedt, M . E., Gray, J., & Smith, L. (1986). Lesbian mothers and their children: A comparison with solo parent hetero-sexual mothers and their children. *Archives of Sexual Behavior* 15, 167–184.

Harris, M. B., & Turner, P. H. (1985–1986). Gay and lesbian parents. *Journal of Homosexuality* 12, 101–113.

Hoeffer, B. (1981). Children's acquisition of sex-role behavior in lesbian-mother families. *American Journal of Orthopsychiatry* 5, 536–544.

Kirkpatrick, M. (1987). Clinical implications of lesbian mother studies. *Journal of Homosexuality* 13, 201–211.

Kirkpatrick, M., Smith, C., & Roy, R. (1981). Lesbian mothers and their children: A comparative survey. *American Journal of Orthopsychiatry* 51, 545–551.

Laird, J. (January 23, 1993). *Gay and lesbian families: Strengths, resilience, and cultural diversity.* Paper presented at Harvard Medical School conference on Clinical Issues for Gay and Lesbian Families, Cambridge, MA.

Martin, A. (1993). *Lesbian and gay parenting handbook: Creating and raising our families.* New York: HarperCollins.

McCandlish, B. (1987). Against all odds: Lesbian mother family dynamics. In F. Bozett (ed.), *Gay and lesbian parents* (pp. 23–28). New York: Praeger.

Patterson, C. (1992). Children of lesbian and gay parents. *Child Development* 63, 1025–1042.

Patterson, C. (1994). Children of the lesbian baby boom: Behavioral adjustment, self-concepts and sex-role identity. In C. Patterson (ed.), *Contemporary perspectives of gay and lesbian psychology: Theory, research, and applications.* Beverly Hills, CA: Sage.

Riddle, D.I. (1978). Relating to children: Gays as role models. *Journal of Social Issues* 34(3), 38–53.

Sbordone, A. (July 24, 1993). *Gay men choosing fatherhood: Extending the parameters of inclusion.* Paper presented at the 15th National Lesbian and Gay Health Conference and 11th Annual AIDS/HIV Forum, Houston, TX.

Schwartz-Gottman, J. (1989). Children of gay and lesbian parents. *Marriage and Family Review* 14(3/4), 35–57.

Steckel, A. (1987). Psychosocial development of children of lesbian mothers. In F. Bozett (ed.), *Gay and lesbian parents* (pp. 75–85). New York: Praeger.

Turner, P., Scadden, M., & Harris, M. (1990). Parenting in gay and lesbian families. *Journal of Gay and Lesbian Psychotherapy* 1(3), 55–65.

## CRITICAL THINKING QUESTIONS

1. How do Okun's conclusions about the impact of gay and lesbian parenting on children's development differ from those of Burtoft? How are they similar?

2. How do gay and lesbian parents compare to their heterosexual counterparts in terms of raising healthy, well-adjusted children?

3. Burtoft focused on the problems of gay families. What, according to Okun, are some of the strengths of gay and lesbian parents?

# 11 Gay and Lesbian Families

## *Liberal/Feminist:* Why Gay People Should Seek the Right to Marry

Thomas B. Stoddard, "Why Gay People Should Seek the Right to Marry," *Out/look: National Lesbian and Gay Quarterly*, no. 6 (Fall 1989): 9–13.

*Same-sex marriage is as controversial within gay communities as among heterosexuals. Some lesbians and gay men oppose same-sex marriage because its legalization signals a retreat from recognizing a diversity of family structures. Others, like Thomas B. Stoddard, argue that gay people should have the right to marry for practical, political, and philosophical reasons.*

Even though, these days, few lesbians and gay men enter into marriages recognized by law, absolutely every gay person has an opinion on marriage as an "institution." (The word "institution" brings to mind, perhaps appropriately, museums.) After all, we all know quite a bit about the subject. Most of us grew up in marital households. Virtually all of us, regardless of race, creed, gender, and culture, have received lectures on the propriety, if not the sanctity, of marriage—which usually suggests that those who choose not to marry are both unhappy and unhealthy. We all have been witnesses, willing or not, to a lifelong parade of other people's marriages, from Uncle Harry and Aunt Bernice to the Prince and Princess of Wales. And at one point or another, some nosy relative has inevitably inquired of every gay person when he or she will finally "tie the knot" (an intriguing and probably apt cliché).

I must confess at the outset that I am no fan of the "institution" of marriage as currently constructed and practiced. I may simply be unlucky, but I have seen preciously few marriages over the course of my forty years that invite admiration and emulation. All too often, marriage appears to petrify rather than satisfy and enrich, even for couples in their twenties and thirties who have had a chance to learn the lessons of feminism. Almost inevitably, the partners seem to fall into a "husband" role and a "wife" role, with such latter-day modifications as the wife who works in addition to raising the children and managing the household.

Let me be blunt: in its traditional form, marriage has been oppressive, especially (although not entirely) to women. Indeed, until the middle of the last century, marriage was, at its legal and social essence, an extension of the husband and his paternal family. Under the English common law, wives were among the husband's "chattel"—personal property—and could not, among other things, hold property in their own names. The common law crime of adultery demonstrates the unequal treatment accorded to husbands and wives: while a woman who slept with a man who wasn't her husband committed adultery, a man who slept with a woman not his wife committed fornication. A man was legally incapable of committing adultery, except as an accomplice to an errant wife. The underlying offense of adultery was not the sexual betrayal of one partner by the other, but the wife's engaging in conduct capable of tainting the husband's bloodlines. (I swear on my *Black's Law Dictionary* that I have not made this up!)

Nevertheless, despite the oppressive nature of marriage historically, and in spite of the general absence of edifying examples of modern heterosexual marriage, I believe very strongly that every lesbian and gay man should have the right to marry the same-sex partner of his or her choice, and that the gay rights movement should aggressively seek full legal recognition for same-sex marriages. To those who might not agree, I respectfully offer three explanations, one practical, one political, and one philosophical.

## THE PRACTICAL EXPLANATION

The legal status of marriage rewards the two individuals who travel to the altar (or its secular equivalent) with substantial economic and practical advantages. Married couples may reduce their tax liability by filing a joint return. They are entitled to special government benefits, such as those given surviving spouses and dependents through the Social Security program. They can inherit from one another even when there is no will. They are immune from subpoenas requiring testimony against the other spouse. And marriage to an American citizen gives a foreigner a right to residency in the United States.

Other advantages have arisen not by law but by custom. Most employers offer health insurance to their employees, and many will include an employee's spouse in the benefits package, usually at the employer's expense. Virtually no employer will include a partner who is not married to an employee, whether of the same sex or not. Indeed, very few insurance companies even offer the possibility of a group health plan covering "domestic partners" who are not married to one another. Two years ago, I tried to find such a policy for Lambda and discovered that not one insurance company authorized to do business in New York—the second-largest state in the country with more than 17 million residents—would accommodate us. (Lambda has tried to make do by paying for individual insurance policies for the same-sex partners of its employees who otherwise would go uninsured but these individual policies are usually narrower in scope than group policies, often require applicants to furnish individual medical information not required under most group plans, and are typically much more expensive per person.)

In short, the law generally presumes in favor of every marital relationship, and acts to preserve and foster it, and to enhance the rights of the individuals who enter into it. It is usually possible, with enough money and the right advice, to replicate some of the benefits conferred by the legal status of marriage through the use of documents like wills and power of attorney forms, but that protection will inevitably, under current circumstances, be incomplete.

The law (as I suspect will come as no surprise to the readers of this journal) still looks upon lesbians and gay men with suspicion, and this suspicion casts a shadow over the documents they execute in recognition of a same-sex relationship. If a lesbian leaves property to her lover, her will may be invalidated on the grounds that it was executed under the "undue influence" of the would-be beneficiary. A property agreement may be denied validity because the underlying relationship is "meretricious"—akin to prostitution. (Astonishingly, until the mid-seventies, the law throughout the United States deemed "meretricious" virtually *any* formal economic arrangement between two people not married to one another, on the theory that an exchange of property between them was probably payment for sexual services; the Supreme Court of California helped unravel this quaint legal fantasy in its 1976 ruling in the first famous "palimony" case, *Marvin v. Marvin*). The law has progressed considerably beyond the uniformly oppressive state of affairs before 1969, but it is still far from enthusiastic about gay people and their relationships—to put it mildly.

Moreover, there are some barriers one simply cannot transcend outside of a formal marriage. When the Internal Revenue Code or the Immigration and Naturalization Act say "married," they mean "married" by definition of state statute. When the employer's group health plan says "spouse," it means "spouse" in the eyes of the law, not the eyes of the loving couple.

But there is another drawback. Couples seeking to protect their relationship through wills and other documents need knowledge, determination, and—most importantly—money. No money, no lawyer. And no lawyer, no protection. Those who lack the sophistication or the wherewithal to retain a lawyer are simply stuck in most circumstances. Extending the right to marry to gay couples would assure that those at the bottom of the economic ladder have a chance to secure their relationship rights, too.

### THE POLITICAL EXPLANATION

The claim that gay couples ought to be able to marry is not a new one. In the seventies, same-sex couples in three states—Minnesota, Kentucky, and Washington—brought constitutional challenges to the marriage statutes, and in all three instances they failed. In each of the three, the court offered two basic justifications for limiting marriage to male-female couples: history and procreation. Witness this passage from the Supreme Court of Minnesota's 1971

opinion in *Baker v. Nelson*: "The institution of marriage as a union of man and woman, uniquely involving the procreation and rearing of children within a family, is as old as the book of Genesis. . . . This historic institution manifestly is more deeply founded than the asserted contemporary concept of marriage and societal interests for which petitioners contend."

Today no American jurisdiction recognizes the right of two women or two men to marry one another, although several nations in Northern Europe do. Even more telling, until earlier this year, there was little discussion within the gay rights movement about whether such a right should exist. As far as I can tell, no gay organization of any size, local or national, has yet declared the right to marry as one of its goals.

With all due respect to my colleagues and friends who take a different view, I believe it is time to renew the effort to overturn the existing marriage laws, and to do so in earnest, with a commitment of money and energy, through both the courts and the state legislatures. I am not naive about the likelihood of imminent victory. There is none. Nonetheless—and here I will not mince words—I would like to see the issue rise to the top of the agenda of every gay organization, including my own (although that judgment is hardly mine alone).

Why give it such prominence? Why devote resources to such a distant goal? Because marriage is, I believe, the political issue that most fully tests the dedication of people who are *not* gay to full equality for gay people, and also the issue most likely to lead ultimately to a world free from discrimination against lesbians and gay men.

Marriage is much more than a relationship sanctioned by law. It is the centerpiece of our entire social structure, the core of the traditional notion of "family." Even in its present tarnished state, the marital relationship inspires sentiments suggesting that it is something almost suprahuman. The Supreme Court, in striking down an anticontraception statute in 1965, called marriage "noble" and "intimate to the degree of being sacred." The Roman Catholic Church and the Moral Majority would go—and have gone—considerably further.

Lesbians and gay men are now denied entry to this "noble" and "sacred" institution. The implicit message is this: two men or two women are incapable of achieving such an exalted domestic state. Gay relationships are somehow less significant, less valuable. Such relationships may, from time to time and from couple to couple, give the appearance of a marriage, but they can never be of the same quality or importance.

I resent—indeed, I loathe—that conception of same-sex relationships. And I am convinced that ultimately the only way to overturn it is to remove the barrier to marriage that now limits the freedom of every gay man and lesbian.

That is not to deny the value of "domestic partnership" ordinances, statutes that prohibit discrimination based on "marital status," and other legal advances that can enhance the rights (as well as the dignity) of gay couples. Without question, such advances move us further along the path to equality. But their value can only be partial. (The recently enacted San Francisco "domestic partnership" ordinance, for example, will have practical value only for gay people who happen to be employed by the City of San Francisco and want to include their non-marital spouses in part of the city's fringe benefit package; the vast majority of gay San Franciscans—those employed by someone other than the city— have only a symbolic victory to savor.) Measures of this kind can never assure full equality. Gay relationships will continue to be accorded a subsidiary status until the day that gay couples have *exactly* the same rights as their heterosexual counterparts. To my mind, that means either that the right to marry be extended to us, or that marriage be abolished in its present form for all couples, presumably to be replaced by some new legal entity—an unlikely alternative.

## THE PHILOSOPHICAL EXPLANATION

I confessed at the outset that I personally found marriage in its present avatar rather, well, unattractive. Nonetheless, even from a philosophical perspective, I believe the right to marry should become a stated goal of the gay rights movement.

First, and most basically, the issue is not the desirability of marriage, but rather the desirability of the *right* to marry. That I think two lesbians or two gay men should be entitled to a marriage license does not mean that I think all gay people should find appropriate partners and exercise the right, should it eventually exist. I actually rather doubt that I, myself, would want to marry, even though I share a household with another man who is exceedingly dear to me. There are others who feel differently, for economic, symbolic, or romantic reasons. They should, to my mind, unquestionably have the opportunity to marry if they wish and otherwise meet the requirements of the state (like being old enough).

Furthermore, marriage may be unattractive and even oppressive as it is currently structured and practiced, but enlarging the concept to embrace same-sex couples would necessarily transform it into something new. If two women can marry, or two men, marriage—even for heterosexuals— need not be a union of a "husband" and a "wife." Extending the right to marry to gay people—that is, abolishing the traditional gender requirements of marriage—can be one of the means, perhaps the principal one, through which the institution divests itself of the sexist trappings of the past.

Some of my colleagues disagree with me. I welcome their thoughts and the debates and discussions our different perspectives will trigger. The movement for equality for lesbians and gay men can only be enriched through this collective exploration of the question of marriage. But I do believe many thousands of gay people want the right to marry. And I think, too, they will earn that right for themselves sooner than most of us imagine.

## CRITICAL THINKING QUESTIONS

1. Since he views marriage as oppressive and usually unsuccessful, why does Stoddard argue that gay couples should have the right to marry?

2. How would legalizing same-sex marriages also improve heterosexual marriages?

3. In the two previous articles in this chapter, both Burtoft and Okun described some of the stigma that children in lesbian and gay male households encounter. Would legalizing same-sex marriage decrease such stigmatization and increase the children's sense of "fitting in"? Or would societal ostracism persist?

# V WORK, RACE, ETHNICITY, AND SOCIAL CLASS VARIATIONS

Conservatives and centrists appear to be more similar than different in their views on the relationship between work and family life. While centrists are more accepting of employed mothers than are conservatives and support family-friendly workplace policies, both groups see childrearing primarily as a mother's responsibility. In contrast, liberals, especially feminists, emphasize that women's employment is necessary to sustain a family financially. Thus, instead of blaming employed women for not spending more time with their children, many liberals propose implementing policies that help parents, especially poor women, to care for their families.

Conservatives generally accept racial and economic inequality because, they claim, people have choices in shaping their family lives. In contrast, liberals feel that U.S. economic structures disadvantage the poor and families of color. It is difficult to characterize centrists' positions on racial issues because "the communitarians have shied away from racial and ethnic diversity when discussing family relations."[1] It is difficult, similarly, to unearth centrists' views on social class (with the few exceptions that I will discuss shortly).

## Chapter 12: Work and Family Life

Most conservatives assert that full-time parental care of children is crucial. In "Children's Needs and Parents' Careers," the Family Research Council cites some of the psychological attachment studies which suggest that infants and mothers need time to bond and to form intimate ties. Many conservatives believe that such relationships won't develop if infants and young children are at day-care centers. Instead, conservatives urge, parents should have more discretion over how many hours they work and more freedom to pursue home-based employment. One way to ensure that parents, especially mothers, will stay home with their children is to raise the retirement age and to not penalize old-age employees. If women knew that they could work well past the current retirement age, this article suggests, perhaps they would feel less pressure to work while their children are young.

In "Parenting, Bureaucratic Style," Dana Mack points out that many employed mothers would like to be at home with their kids, that latchkey children get into trouble without adult supervision, and that both mothers and fathers feel stressed over juggling family and work responsibilities. Corporations push working parents to their limits, Mack writes, by requiring long work hours and frequent job transfers. Such workplace pressures create intense competition between work and family time. Instead of providing day-care services that trap parents into even longer hours in the workplace, employers should provide greater flextime and flex-place options.

In contrast to the Family Research Council and the Mack articles, Rosalind C. Barnett and Caryl Rivers argue that the 300 middle-class and working-class couples they interviewed are very pleased with their two-income lives ("Ozzie and Harriet Are Dead"). The authors cite such advantages as being able to live in low-violence neighborhoods, having the flexibility to change career patterns when necessary, enjoying good physical and mental health, and avoiding the possibility of slipping into poverty. In addition, according to Barnett and Rivers, gender-role differences are shrinking, and men and women are working together on both the work and home fronts.

These three articles are fairly representative of conservative, centrist, and liberal positions on work and family life. The concern over whether or not parents, especially mothers, should devote more time to childrearing is typically targeted at middle-class families. Working-class families are practically invisible, and wealthy families—at least according to the literature—don't exist. The exclusion of working-class parents from most discussions by all political factions is especially telling because it is primarily middle-class, professional families who have day care, somewhat flexible schedules, and home employment options. Middle-class families are not the norm, however. As one observer notes, "The ethic of hard work being rewarded with a decent standard of living for one's family is a fantasy for growing numbers of American workers and their families."[2]

One centrist proposes that women should encourage men to marry them because it will give men an incentive to work and "something to work for."[3] However, the real hourly wages of most workers have fallen, and the group experiencing the greatest wage decline has been non-college-educated workers, especially new entrants into the labor force. Because three-fourths of the work force has not earned a four-year college degree, the continuing deterioration of the wages of high school graduates means that the vast majority of men and many women are working at far lower wages that their counterparts did a generation earlier. Since 1987, moreover, wages have been falling among college graduates and white-collar workers, especially among men.[4]

It is not clear, then, that poor and working-class families would be able to take advantage of the flextime and flex-place policies that conservatives, centrists, and liberals advocate. Nor is there any evidence that these two-income families enjoy the more egalitarian gender roles as well as good mental and physical health that characterize at least some middle-class couples.


## Chapter 13: Racial and Ethnic Diversity


Much of the debate on racial and ethnic family diversity focuses on single motherhood: *Not* talking about single motherhood is scarcely an option. More than half of the children born in 1994 will spend some or all of their childhood with only one parent, typically their mother. If current patterns hold, they will likely experience higher rates of poverty, school failure, and other problems as they grow up. The long-range consequences could have enormous implications.[5]

One of the most serious consequences of the changing family, according to many conservatives, is that the proportion of black children born out of wedlock has mushroomed while the black two-parent family has declined. In "Black Family Structure and Poverty," Stephan Thernstrom and Abigail Thernstrom show that since the 1950s marriage and childbearing have become almost completely disassociated for much of the African-American population. As a result, child poverty is high and is related to other problems such as school failure and juvenile crime.

Although centrists reiterate that there's an association between family structure and poverty (see Chapter 9), they rarely frame such discussions in terms of racial and ethnic characteristics. In "Multiculturalism or One People?" for example, Amitai Etzioni urges Americans to stop emphasizing multiculturalism because, and despite some differences, "we are joined by the shared responsibilities of providing a good society for our children and ourselves."

Since we live in a racist society, however, it would be unrealistic for parents of color to pretend that their children won't have to deal with prejudice and discrimination. According to Lynet Uttal, in "Racial Safety and Cultural Maintenance in Childcare," for example, minority parents are concerned that child-care providers accept racist behavior (such as name-calling) or are insensitive to social class differences. Thus, being employed can increase a family's vulnerability because very young children may be exposed to racially and culturally unsafe environments outside the home. Parenting for two-income racial and ethnic families is a difficult task. The socialization of their children "involves the bicultural effort of attempting to promote self-esteem within one's own culture and to develop competencies to deal with the harsh realities of the wider society."[6]

## Chapter 14: The Impact of Social Class

Most of the debates about social class are directed at or about the poor (rather than the chasm between rich and poor families, for example), and especially at impoverished black urban families. Conservatives often view family issues through relatively privileged, middle-class lenses and conclude that behavioral or moral failure explains poverty. According to Carl F. Horowitz, in "Searching for the White Underclass," the black "underclass" behaves in ways that are self-destructive. In contrast to white-majority communities, he maintains, the black underclass has high unwed motherhood rates, low marriage rates, and "poor" values that lock them into poverty.

Centrists seem to detour social class issues. As a result, I selected "neutral" material that, while possibly controversial, represents neither conservative nor feminist perspectives. In "What Money Can't Buy," Susan E. Mayer concludes that parents' character—their skills, diligence, honesty—and good health probably matter more to children's positive prospects than money. "Income is not the only determinant of material hardship," she writes, because existing safety nets already cover most basic necessities, such as food and medical care, for poor families.[7]

Both liberals and conservatives might use Mayer's findings to reinforce their positions on the relationship between socioeconomic status and children's outcomes. Liberals might say, "Aha, I told you so. If we cut off assistance for the basic necessities, the results on children can be devastating." Conservatives might say, "Aha, I told you so. Children fail because they have irresponsible parents. Underclass, and not income, is the issue."

According to some liberals, the term *underclass* has become a code word for hiding antiblack or anti-Latino feelings.[8] Herbert Gans notes that instead of expressing racial antagonisms openly, references to the underclass can avoid targeting minority groups and hide "the existence of very poor whites who suffer from many of the same problems as poor blacks."[9] *All* racial groups experience poverty and hard times. As the selection by Kathryn Edin and Laura Lein ("Making Ends Meet") shows, however, many white, black, and Mexican-American mothers struggle in low-wage jobs to make ends meet even though they might be better off on welfare. According to Edin and Lein's research, most welfare mothers are not an underclass of lazy women who spend most of their time waiting for the next welfare check. Many work very hard to become self-sufficient and to enable their children to achieve the American Dream.

Although not entirely surprised, I was struck by the narrowness and paucity of the family-related debates' material on race, ethnicity, and social class issues. Most conservatives seem to think that there are two types of families in America—unmarried welfare mothers and "others." Centrists, as I noted earlier, sidestep race and ethnicity topics almost entirely. When some centrists incorporate social class characteristics in family-related discussion, the focus is narrow. There is either criticism of white, married, middle-class, employed mothers whose children are in day care or, less directly, of "underclass" (though centrists rarely use the word) unmarried fathers who don't provide financial support for their children (see Chapter 9).

In the early 1990s, Norma Williams and Andrée Sjoberg observed that "the dominant paradigm in gender studies has reflected a white privileged, largely middle-class perspective."[10] Since then, the paradigm has stretched considerably, because women of color have emphasized the importance of incorporating multicultural perspectives in feminist discourse. Nonetheless, it is still difficult to locate material on family issues that addresses social class *as well as* race and ethnicity, especially for minority families that are not black.

## NOTES

1. Gideon Sjoberg, Norma Williams, Elizabeth Gill, and Kelly F. Himmel, "Family Life and Racial and Ethnic Diversity: An Assessment of Communitarianism, Liberalism, and Conservatism," *Journal of Family Issues* 16 (May 1995): 255.

2. Marlene Johnson, "A Universal Agenda for Women and Their Families," *Vital Speeches of the Day* 58, August 15, 1992, p. 660.

3. Patricia Morgan, *Farewell to the Family? Public Policy and Family Breakdown in Britain and the USA* (London: IEA Health and Welfare Unit, 1995).

4. Lawrence Mishel and Jared Bernstein, *The State of Working America, 1994–95*, Economic Policy Institute Series (Armonk, NY: M. E. Sharpe, 1994). See also William Julius Wilson, *When Work Disappears: The World of the New Urban Poor* (New York: Knopf, 1997), esp. pp. 25–50.

5. Sara S. McLanahan, "The Consequences of Single Motherhood," *The American Prospect* 18 (Summer 1994): 48.

6. Teresa W. Julian, Patrick C. McKenry, and Mary W. McKelvey, "Cultural Variations in Parenting: Perceptions of Caucasian, African-American, Hispanic, and Asian-American Parents," *Family Relations* 43 (January 1994): 36.

7. Family income, however, has an impact on shaping children's ability and achievement, enhancing preschoolers' cognitive development, and improving children's subsequent chances of finishing high school. See Greg J. Duncan and Jeanne Brooks-Gunn, "Income Effects Across the Life Span: Integration and Independence," in Greg J. Duncan and Jeanne Brooks-Gunn, eds., *Consequences of Growing Up Poor* (New York: Russell Sage Foundation, 1997), pp. 596–610.

8. For a probing discussion of the debate on the urban underclass, "race vs. class," and the alleged pathology of black poverty, see Bill E. Lawson, ed., *The Underclass Question* (Philadelphia: Temple University Press, 1992).

9. Herbert J. Gans, *The War Against the Poor: The Underclass and Antipoverty Policy* (New York: Basic Books, 1995), p. 59.

10. Norma Williams and Andrée F. Sjoberg, "Ethnicity and Gender: The View from Above versus the View from Below," in Ted R. Vaughan, Gideon Sjoberg, and Larry T. Reynolds, eds., *A Critique of Contemporary American Sociology* (New York: General Hall, 1993), pp. 174–175.

# 12 Work and Family Life

## *Conservative:* Children's Needs and Parents' Careers

FAMILY RESEARCH COUNCIL, *Free to Be Family: Helping Mothers and Fathers Meet the Needs of the Next Generation of American Children* (Washington, DC: Family Research Council, 1992), pp. 49–51. Reproduced with the permission of the Family Research Council.

*Most conservatives feel strongly that mothers should not be employed or pursue a career until the children are "well-launched." Otherwise, children might grow up with profound feelings of insecurity and low self-esteem. Instead of promoting day care, legislation should encourage mothers of infants and young children to stay at home by providing tax credits for nuclear families, a more fluid job market, fewer restrictions on home-based employment, and a reordering of work priorities over the life cycle.*

Children go through different phases as they mature, each one with its own unique challenges. Therefore, families go through phases, too, as they confront each new hurdle and reward of their child's journey to adulthood. Families with children the same ages often feel like kindred spirits because the job of raising a child into an adult—though involving individualized needs—presents many universal difficulties and offers many common rewards.

Although there are certainly many different ways of categorizing the life of a child into phases, we have chosen to look at the challenges children face as they go through infancy, childhood, and adolescence.

### CHILDREN'S NEEDS AND PARENTS' CAREERS

Most parents know intuitively what reams of child development research have demonstrated—that young children need significant interaction with both parents and that maternal nurturance is particularly important during the early months and years of a child's life. (Paternal involvement becomes increasingly significant as children grow older.)

According to the late British psychoanalyst John Bowlby, "The young child's hunger for his mother's love and presence is as great as his hunger for food." Bowlby, who devoted much of his life's work to attachment theory, found that children form an intimate bond or attachment with their mother during the first three years of life, and that the strength and security of this bond greatly influence how children view themselves and how well they interact with others.

According to Bowlby, children with parents who are warm, nurturing, and accessible come to view themselves as worthy and lovable, while children with parents who are rejecting, unresponsive, or neglectful typically struggle with profound feelings of insecurity and low self-esteem. Not only do insecurely attached children question whether others can be counted on to meet their deepest needs, but Bowlby says they question positive input offered by nonparents since it contradicts their own self-perceptions.[1]

Another prominent psychologist, Mary Ainsworth, has used a laboratory experiment known as the Strange Situation (in which a child is initially separated and later reunited with his mother) to assess mother-child attachment. Ainsworth's research has determined that the second half of a baby's first year of life is an especially critical phase in the attachment process because this is when "clear-cut" attachment first blooms. During this phase, babies typically begin to approach, cling, and protest separations, as well as search for objects hidden from view and recall that an object continues to exist even though they cannot see, hear, feel, smell, or taste it. According to Ainsworth, this important phase in the attachment process continues well into the second and third years of life.[2]

In addition, Ainsworth has identified three different patterns of attachment: (1) securely attached infants, who are less troubled by separation from Mom than other children and more likely to respond positively to her return; (2) anxious-resistant babies, who are often emotionally torn by Mom's inconsistency and unpredictability; and (3) anxious-avoidant babies, who defensively avoid Mom because they have been deprived repeatedly of maternal affection.

According to a review of recent research on attachment by child psychologist Brenda Hunter, rising rates of maternal employment have resulted in a marked increase in anxious-avoidant babies since 1980. "When mothers resume employment for 20 or more hours per week, during the crucial first year of life, about 50 percent of the babies will be insecurely attached to mother and/or father," Hunter observes.

"The majority of these will be classified as anxious-avoidant."[3]

Moreover, a 1987 study by psychiatrist Peter Barglow found a mother's return to full-time employment during the child's first year increases the likelihood of anxious-avoidant attachment—even when the child is provided high quality nanny care in the home. Barglow concludes that babies placed in early non-maternal care may view the repeated, daily separations from Mom as rejection.[4]

Similarly, a much-publicized 1985 study by researchers Jay Belsky and Michael Rovine found that boys placed in infant day care for 20 or more hours per week developed insecure attachments to both parents.[5] Likewise, a 1985 University of North Carolina study found that children in kindergarten and first grade who had entered high quality day care at 12 weeks of age were more likely to "hit, kick, and push other children" than those who had been cared for at home by their mothers. The UNC study found that children who had been placed in substitute care during the first 12 months of life were more physically and verbally abusive, less cooperative, and less tolerant of frustration.[6]

Given the wealth of research data raising concerns about substitute care in the early stages of a child's development, facilitating parent-child interaction should be the overriding goal of public policies designed to improve the well-being of America's preschool children. Unfortunately, surprisingly little attention has been given to meeting this goal.

## PARENTAL PREFERENCE

Legislation introduced by Congressman Charlie Stenholm (D–TX) and Senator Orrin Hatch (R–UT) places greater priority on promoting extended parent-child interaction than on providing ironclad job security. The Family Protection Act of 1991 (H.R. 1270/S. 418) offers parents who quit their jobs to care for young children "parental preference" in re-hiring by their previous employer. Such a policy, which is patterned loosely after a "veteran's preference" law that dates back to the late 1930s, would give workers an opportunity to return to paid work for their previous employer provided there is a job available for which they are qualified.

The Stenholm-Hatch Bill recognizes that infants need more than just 12 weeks of undistracted time with their parents. It recognizes that many mothers would be willing to sacrifice some job security in order to be home with their children for more than 12 weeks—especially if their future employability were not jeopardized seriously. As columnist Judy Mann points out, "One of the reasons mothers stay in the work force is they are afraid they won't be able to rebuild their careers if they stay home with young children.[7]

Thus, the Family Protection Act strikes a balance between providing guaranteed job security (at a cost to time with children) and providing no job security (at a potential cost to future employability). It offers employees a guaranteed promise—a promise that their prior service with an employer will be recognized when they seek reemployment after taking extended time off to care for young children. For employed women interested in devoting more than just 12 weeks of full-time care to their young children, parental preference offers considerable "promise"—especially when linked to other legislative efforts (like increasing the Young Child Tax Credit) which make it more affordable for tax-paying families to devote more of their time to child-rearing responsibilities.

Such a linkage is important because employment policies designed to facilitate parental time with children are only as good as the family's ability to meet basic economic needs. Nevertheless, some critics sneer at the role of tax benefits in promoting family time, arguing that an $1,800 per child tax credit or an $8,200 per child tax exemption would not provide enough economic assistance to enable families to permanently forego a second income. While it is true that pro-child tax relief may not enable every family to live on a single income, families at the economic margin would most certainly be affected. In addition, families unable to live on one income indefinitely would still benefit considerably from pro-child tax relief. For such families, dramatically increasing the Young Child Tax Credit and greatly expanding the dependent exemption might enable one or both parents to reduce their hours of paid employment to devote more time to children. Or it might "buy" them an extra month or six months or two years of job interruption after the birth or adoption of a child.

Some policy makers and day care advocates argue that most families who care for their own children do so because they lack access to "high-quality" center-based day care. But a 1989 University of Michigan study shows that most employed mothers opt for care by fathers or other family members out of preference rather than necessity.[8] And Rep. George Miller (D–CA) acknowledged in *Mother Jones* magazine that socialized day care has no grass roots constituency:

> I spent eight years in getting the child-care bill passed in Congress, and at its zenith, there was never a child-care movement in the country. There was a coalition of child advocacy groups, and a few large international unions that put up hundreds of thousands of dollars, and we created in the mind of the leadership of Congress that there was a child-care movement—but there was nobody riding me. And not one of my colleagues believed their election turned on it for a moment.[9]

### THE FAMILY-FRIENDLY WORKPLACE: TIME OFF FOR GOOD PARENTING

Miller's confession—along with all of the research data on parental preferences—should give pause to government and business leaders being urged to increase day care services to children. Instead, policymakers should seek what Karl Zinsmeister calls a "more fluid, less rigid job market" that gives family-oriented workers significant discretion over when, where, and how many hours they work for pay.[10] Specifically, policymakers should encourage flexible hours, part-time work, job sharing, and most especially home-based employment opportunities. Not only is homework one of the more promising work-family solutions, but it also has the potential to put a dent in rush-hour traffic congestion, daytime home burglaries, automotive air pollution, and gasoline consumption.

The first step toward making home-based employment a more viable option would be to loosen restrictions on the deductibility of home office expenses. Under current law, taxpayers cannot write off home office expenses unless home office space is used exclusively for income-producing activities. In other words, overhead expenses for a room that doubles as an office and a guest bedroom cannot be claimed. This exclusive-use rule is particularly burdensome to families with children because they frequently have greater demands on household space than unmarried adults living alone. Thus, Congress should consider dropping the exclusive-use test for parents.

In addition, government policies should encourage a reordering of priorities over the life cycle. In recent years, families in America have increasingly: (1) had both spouses employed full-time while children are young; and (2) had one or both spouses retire before age 65. Taken together, these two trends have created a peculiar "middle-aged bulge" in the allocation of work and family responsibilities over the life cycle.

Author Arlene Rossen Cardozo and lawyer Edith U. Fierst believe the solution to this curious arrangement is "sequencing"—seeking to "do it all" over the course of one's life, instead of all at once. Cardozo and Fierst point to former United Nations Ambassador Jeanne Kirkpatrick as an example of a "sequencer" who took time off from employment when children were young and then returned to her career after her kids were "well-launched."[11]

Apart from facilitating full-time parental care of young children for extended periods of time, Congress should remove disincentives to old-age employment, or "twilighting." Specifically, Congress should eliminate the Social Security earnings test and allow "twilighters" to receive full benefits rather than have their benefits reduced in proportion to their income. At the same time, Congress should seek to reverse the growing trend toward early retirement by accelerating scheduled increases in the Social Security retirement age. Indeed, given the improving health and life expectancy of Americans, Congress should consider raising the retirement age beyond currently scheduled thresholds.

## NOTES

1. John Bowlby, *Attachment* (New York: Basic Books, 1969), p. xii.

2. Mary D. S. Ainsworth, "Patterns of Infant-Mother Attachments: Antecedents and Effects on Development," *Bulletin of New York Academy of Medicine* 61: 771–791.

3. Brenda Hunter, "Will Parental Leave Work?" Paper presented at Conference of Eagle Forum Education and Legal Defense Fund, Washington, D.C., February 12, 1991.

4. Peter Barglow et al., "Effects of Maternal Absence Due to Employment on the Quality of Infant Attachment in a Low-Risk Sample," *Child Development* 58 (1987): 945–54.

5. Jay Belsky and Michael Rovine, "Nonmaternal Care in the First Year of Life and the Security of the Infant-Parent Attachment," *Child Development* 56 (1985): 157–67.

6. Ron Haskins, "Public School Aggression among Children with Varying Day Care Experience," *Child Development* 56 (1985): 689–703.

7. Judy Mann, "Making Time for the Families," *The Washington Post*, January 9, 1991.

8. Karen Oppenheim Mason and Karen Kuhlthau, "Determinants of Child Care Ideals Among Mothers of Preschool-Aged Children," *Journal of Marriage and the Family* 51 (August 1989).

9. Douglas Foster and David Beers, "Clout," *Mother Jones* (May/June 1991): 36.

10. Karl Zinsmeister, "Brave New World: How Day-Care Harms Children," *Policy Review* (Washington, D.C.: The Heritage Foundation, Spring 1988).

11. See Edith U. Fierst, "Time Out for Motherhood," *The Washington Post*, May 14, 1989, p. C5; and also Linda Chion-Kenney, "Another Way to Have It All," *The Washington Post*, May 31, 1988; Cardozo is the author of *Sequencing*, published by Atheneum.

## CRITICAL THINKING QUESTIONS

1. If children form a bond with their full-time mothers during the first three years of life, how can we explain the close attachment between children and employed fathers? Between adoptive parents and children adopted after age three? Or the stay-at-home moms who abuse or murder their children?

2. This article points out that some studies have found an association between infant day care and behavioral problems of kindergartners and first graders. Are there other factors, besides day care, that might explain the behavioral problems?

3. What are the advantages and disadvantages of "sequencing"? Do you think that eliminating early retirement would encourage sequencing?

# 12 Work and Family Life

## *Centrist:* Parenting, Bureaucratic Style

DANA MACK, *The Assault on Parenthood: How Our Culture Undermines the Family*, pp. 194–203. Reprinted with permission of Simon & Schuster. Copyright © 1997 by Dana Mack.

*Dana Mack and other centrists are more likely than are conservatives to recognize that economic pressures require mothers to work for pay. Centrists also feel that current family policies (such as the Family and Medical Leave Act of 1993) are inadequate in meeting the needs of working families. The important question, according to Mack, is why mothers participate in the labor force in the first place, especially when we lead time-pressed lives and children are starved for attention.\**

Once upon a time, when our economy was primarily agrarian, the home was the center of work and family life. Mothers and fathers played fairly equal, if clearly differentiated, roles in child-rearing (women seeing to the custodial tasks of child-rearing and the nurturing of their children, men to children's education and training). Children helped out with economic production. With the increasing industrialization of the nineteenth century, men increasingly left home in order to earn their bread, and their participation in homemaking and child-rearing diminished. As goods and services—clothing, household products, even schooling—traditionally produced at home became available for purchase, women's responsibilities diminished as well.

Technology continued to streamline domestic tasks in the twentieth century; at the same time, some of the emotional responsibilities of family life became the province of professionals. In *The Second Shift*, sociologist Arlie Hochschild notes that "tasks women used to do at home have also gradually come to be done elsewhere for pay. Day care for children, retirement homes for the elderly, homes for delinquent children, mental hospitals and even psychotherapy are, in a way, commercial substitutes for jobs a mother once did at home."[1]

As domestic work diminished, home life no longer offered the challenges it once did, and the professionalization of many once

---

\* Dana Mack's research is based on about 250 parents in private interviews and focus groups in Baltimore, New York, New Jersey, Texas, northern California, and Connecticut. She notes that "My colleagues at the Institute for American Values, David Blankenhorn and Barbara Defoe Whitehead, have enabled me to glean the fruits of their focus group interviews in Ohio, New Jersey, and Mississippi. The mothers and fathers we have spoken to have in most cases been married and middle-income (typically, their annual household income lies between $25,000 and $60,000); they have at least one child between the ages of five and eigthheen living at home; and they tend to proportionally reflect the ethnic and racial demographic profile of the area in which they live" (p. 310).

domestic functions gradually led many women to feel that child-rearing was no longer the proper province of parents. As early as the 1950s sociologists noticed that many prosperous middle-class mothers were depending upon schools, clubs, and summer camps to raise their children for them.[2] In their exhaustive study of life in a Canadian suburb in the 1950s, *Crestwood Heights*, John Seeley, R. Alexander Sim, and Elizabeth W. Loosley offer some touching and disturbing examples of the extent to which a smug professional class of child-rearing experts, determined to "propagate current ideologies in education and child-rearing," were able to render "highly literate" women profoundly insecure—even superfluous—in their role as mothers:

> The school . . . is more certain of its methods than the parents are of theirs. . . . At Home and School meetings it was not uncommon for parents to ask teachers what the proper hour for bed should be, or how to prevent a child's telephone conversations during homework. The parents of one kindergarten child were contemplating a move . . . which was not undertaken until the teacher had given it as her opinion that the change would not be detrimental to the child. . . . Parents are educated by the school for their cultural obligation toward the child, which approaches, increasingly, the role of trusteeship for the school. . . . A favorite in-group joke of Crestwood Heights teachers states that "the ideal child is an orphan."[3]

By the early 1970s many middle-class women not only were convinced of the superfluity of stay-at-home mothering; they felt compelled by market pressures to work for pay—partly in order to purchase the very goods and services they once provided for themselves. Many eagerly rushed into the labor force with dreams of the good life. A great many of them were disappointed to discover, when they became mothers, that family life and household tasks, however shrunken, still demanded far more time and commitment than a working life allowed them. In 1988, a working mother with a full-time job worked an average of 57.3 hours a week on the job and at home, while a housewife worked an average of only 32.2 hours a week. That left the housewife with twenty-five hours more per week in which to interact with her children.[4]

Time-pressed lives and attention-starved children have led many American women to reassess the wisdom behind the working mother model. The fifteen-thousand-member national support organization Mothers at Home reported in a 1989 public policy pamphlet entitled "Mothers Speak Out on Child Care" that "the exceptionally candid letters we receive from mothers across the nation confirm . . . that most mothers today either do not need or do not want substitute child care. Firsthand experience with day care has shown mothers that it doesn't do the job; that no matter how 'quality' it becomes, it will never do the job."[5]

Aware of the conflicts women had about child care, some feminists of the 1980s attempted to make the movement more responsive to many women's aspirations for lives closer to home and children. In her 1981 book, *The Second Stage*, Friedan herself appealed for according family life a more prominent place in feminist doctrine.[6] But in general the "mommy issue"—especially as it relates to work-family conflicts—is a problem that the feminist movement has cavalierly brushed aside. Felice Schwartz, a longtime feminist and founder of Catalyst, a nonprofit group that promotes women in the workplace, came under strong criticism from the National Organization of Women and under widespread attack from feminists when she published work in the late 1980s and early 1990s advocating the creation of a career track for women that would allow them to take leaves of absence to raise young children. In her 1996 book *"Feminism Is Not the Story of My Life,"* Elizabeth Fox-Genovese captured the alienation today's working mothers feel from feminism, mainly as a result of such traditional feminist hostility and insensitivity to family issues.[7]

For the most part, feminism has remained deaf to the large numbers of women I've talked to who remember with fondness and some nostalgia that when they got home from school, "Mom was home." Many of these women feel guilty their own children do not enjoy what they took for granted in their own childhoods—the consistent presence of a parent in the household. A Baltimore mother remembers, "You know, when I grew up, the mother always stayed home and did everything for the kids. . . . She was there to show some kind of example." A Texas mother relates, "My parents divorced when I was eighteen and my brother was four—and he's, like, raised in a different family, because my mother was working and there was no parent at home with him. And he is spoiled. . . . My mother felt so guilty that she let him have his way with everything."

As Fox-Genovese puts it, "When we consider the lives of women and children, the feminist hostility to the 'mommy track' seems puzzling at best, irresponsible at worst." Traditional feminists, with their professional child care "scenarios," she implies, are snobs who lack "any sense of who will really take care of the children, unless, of course, you assume that children do not need much attention beyond that which can be provided by servants."[8] In fact, Fox-Genovese's characterization of feminists as spoiled is painfully accurate. Consider the tired, self-obsessed arguments for careerism and communal child-rearing that journalist Ellen Willis pursued in a 1994 *Glamour* article entitled, "Why I'm Not 'Pro-Family'": "I don't doubt the fragility of today's family life is hard on kids. . . . On the other hand, children are more narcissistic than most adults ever dream of being—if my daughter had her way, I'd never leave the house. They too have to learn that other people's needs and feelings must be taken into account."[9]

For women like Willis, who teaches journalism at New York University and no doubt gets tremendous emotional satisfaction and even significant material reward from her work, labor outside the home constitutes a woman's "right," a measure of her "happiness," and a symbol of her personal "freedom." A career satisfies her "needs" and "feelings." But if women like Willis are happier for their careers, are their daughters? And how representative is Willis? Most working others I've talked to do not think their jobs provide sufficient emotional compensation for the impediment they constitute to their work as parents. They feel their children's need for them is not "narcissistic" but an authentic demand they have a terrible time satisfying. A San Francisco working mother relates, "Personally, I'm feeling guilty with my kids. . . . How many hours do I spend . . . *productive* hours, with my kids?"

Heidi Brennan, director of social policy for Mothers at Home, says her impression in corresponding with hundreds of women about work-family issues is that American mothers as a whole have been "coerced against their will *into* the workplace." She adds, "There is a complete disconnect between the views of policy-makers and real people on the issue of working mothers." Policy-makers believe there is a dichotomy of opinion about at-home mothering between working and nonworking mothers, she says. But if there is a dichotomy, it is between elite working mothers (that is, professional women) versus the rest of the world. Many more women, Brennan claims, would stay home if there were more social support and less financial penalty for the decision to do so.[10]

Certainly the parents I have talked to are convinced that children suffer when both parents work, even when they are cared for in their own home by nannies or baby-sitters. Some parents I spoke with have consciously made financial sacrifices to stay home with their children. A Texas mother decided "after trying to work when my children were small that it really wasn't worthwhile. . . . They don't get your values; they get the baby-sitter's values." A San Francisco father said, "Financially we felt it when our kids were small . . . we really felt it . . . [and] we struggled through it. . . . But my wife was there when the kids came home, and it worked out nice—someone else didn't raise them." A Baltimore mother confessed that she "wanted to go back to work once my children were school age. But I realized that's when you really have to be home, to supervise them after school."

Working mothers echoed these sentiments, and many said they wished they could quit work. They found that their participation in the workforce has yielded more stress, more worries, and more domestic strife than they remember their nonworking mothers having faced. An African-American working mother of two teenage boys notes: "My mother was home with us. She could enforce the rules. I tell my son, don't go out till I get home, don't look at TV, make sure your chores are done. . . . He comes [home] from school at two-thirty, three. . . . By the time I get home it's five-thirty, it's almost too late. . . . He's done everything by then that I told him not to do!"

Hardly a wonder, then, that a 1994 Labor Department survey found that while 79 percent of working women liked their jobs, only 15 percent contended they would continue to work full-time if they could afford not to.[11] Far from achieving the happy independence feminism promised, working mothers labor under tremendous emotional pressures. Arlie Hochschild describes how women under the work gun often become "the target of children's aggression . . . the family 'heavy,' the 'time and motion' person of the family and work speed-up . . . hurry[ing] children through their daily rounds."[12]

When Hochschild went out in the late 1980s to talk to women and men in two-income families, she was dismayed to note that even successful career women suffered unbearable tensions between their roles as mothers and their roles as wage-earners— tensions that expressed themselves in chronic fatigue, illness, and depression. These tensions, she noted, might have been relieved were husbands more willing to pick up the slack, but men seemed reluctant to do their share, consigning women to a "second shift" of household and child-rearing burdens that made their lives a never-ending cycle of pressures.

When men remained uninvolved in homemaking and child-rearing, working women—strained beyond their limits— were also disengaging themselves from homebound demands. "In the race against time," Hochschild lamented, both parents often "inadvertently cut back on children's needs," "cutting corners" on both physical and emotional care. "Trying to rationalize her child's long hours in day care," Hochschild noted, "one working mother remarked about her nine-month-old daughter that she 'needed kids her age' and 'needs the independence.' It takes relatively little to cut back in house care, and the consequences of skimping on housework are trivial, but reducing one's notions of what a baby needs—imposing the needs of a fourteen-year-old onto a nine-month-old baby—takes a great deal of denial and has drastic consequences."[13]

Hochschild's prescription for picking up the parenting slack focuses on calling for more help from working husbands and better child care options. Despite the intractable conflict she unearthed between the work schedules of two-income parents and their ability to minister to children's needs, she remained convinced that for women, the laboring life was an opportunity, a magnificent revolution "stalled" by the remnants of household oppressions.[14]

But even in marriages where men are willing to take up a more significant share of the "second shift"—as in many marriages of people I interviewed for this book—it has become increasingly clear to both fathers and mothers that given the intense negative pressures on children from outside the home, at least one parent should devote the major portion of his or her energies to watching and raising the children.[15] Many two-income parents I've talked to worry that the lack of parental presence in the home during the daytime leaves children, in the words of a Texas father, "to their own devices with simply too many options." Such children, parents say, often develop problem behaviors out of sheer loneliness. A New Jersey mother puts the problem in a nutshell: "The feeling a child has when no one is at home. . . . There has to be something hollow inside."

In a 1989 study involving five thousand eighth-graders in Los Angeles and San Diego, "latchkey" children were twice as vulnerable to substance abuse as were children who were supervised by adults after school, a fact which many experts link to loneliness as well as lack of supervision.[16] To some extent after-school programs might be the answer, but given children's— even older children's—needs for down time and interaction with their parents, a more efficacious solution to the "home alone" syndrome might be the "home with mom (or dad)" answer. (A 1990 Search Institute survey revealed that about half of all sixth-graders and 60 percent of high school seniors are home alone for two hours a day or more.) As we will see later, the recent trend among parents to supervise their children in the workplace after school reflects their growing conviction that signing their kids up for after-school activities is not the ultimate answer to the problem of after-school supervision.

Given their awareness of the negative impact on their children, why do mothers work? Overwhelmingly, because of financial pressures. Many of the parents I've talked to find that even with two incomes, it is hard for them to make ends meet. The median income of the American family in inflation-adjusted dollars was no more in 1993 than in 1973; in fact, real wages for males fell from a median of $34,048 for full-time work to $30,407. In an age of rapid technological change, jobs are no longer as secure as they once were. At the same time, the cost of college and—where public schools have failed—private school strains even high-earning households. The average mortgage takes almost double the bite—up to 40 percent—out of family income it took twenty years ago.[17] And taxes have risen

from an average of about 2 percent of family earnings in 1950 to more than 30 percent today. Meanwhile, almost a third of men between the ages of twenty-four and thirty-four do not make enough money to maintain a family with two children above the poverty level.[18]

While working fathers do not experience as great a strain between the demands of work and family as working mothers do (most married men still see their primary role as financial provider, a role they view as "overlapping" with, rather than "conflicting" with, parenthood, according to David Blankenhorn, author of *Fatherless America*),[19] they also feel palpable tensions today between their obligations to work and to family. According to a *New York Times* survey of 1990, 72 percent of working fathers considered themselves "torn by conflict between their jobs and the desire to spend more time with their families." A poll conducted by the *Los Angeles Times* revealed that 57 percent of fathers felt that they did not spend enough time with their children.[20]

Hardly a wonder. The father of the 1990s is much more apt than the father of the 1950s to allow work pressures to infringe on domestic ritual, even though he is aware that he is putting his job before the kids. In fact the father of the 1950s, much maligned for his alleged detachment from the home and child-rearing, was the most domesticated in our century, according to Blankenhorn. William Whyte's 1956 work, *The Organization Man*, Blankenhorn contends, was actually a critique of the "turn toward familism among 1950s fathers," which to Whyte reflected "a decline of the Protestant ethic and . . . an overall weakening of the American male character."[21]

Most of us who are raising children today remember fathers who showed up at the dinner table at a preassigned hour without fail. How many of our children can boast the same? Says William R. Mattox Jr., director of research and policy for the Family Research Council and a specialist on work and family issues:

Contrary to the assertions of professional children's advocates in Washington, the number one problem facing American children today is not lack of subsidized day-care centers, nutrition programs, or after-school care for "latchkey" kids . . . [or] even economic poverty, although 20 percent of American children live below the official poverty line. The biggest problem facing American children is a deficit of another kind . . . a lack of time with and attention from their parents. Parents today spend 40 percent less time with their children than did parents in 1965. . . . In 1965, parents on average spent approximately 30 hours a week with their kids. By 1985, parent-child interaction had dropped to just 17 hours a week.[22]

A Texas father I spoke with compared his own childhood to that of his children:

Kids today are dropped off at seven, before school starts, they're in school all day, they stay in the after-school child care until five-thirty. Mom or dad comes and picks them up, then they go home, homework and shower, eat supper, go to bed. They don't have that unstructured time anymore . . . that interaction with the family where just everyone is sitting in the house doing their own thing—maybe talking, you know, the kids playing. . . . I don't know that that happens much. . . . I know I had a lot of that.

Part of the reason for what has become an intense competition between work and family time lies with the realities of the modern global marketplace. American corporations have been forced to push working parents to their limits, without regard to the attendant strains on family life and stability. In my Connecticut town, which has a large population of corporate employees in middle management, the average resident stays less than three years. The corporate penchant for frequent transfers creates a situation that even wives who do not work outside the home find extremely unsettling. An acquaintance of mine in a nearby town, the mother of a child about to enter elementary school, divorced her husband because she could not endure their frequent moves, and felt her daughter would suffer from the lack of a stable communal environment.

In the late 1980s and early 1990s, many large corporations bent on expansion were eager to attract qualified labor by offering employees family-friendly perks—among them day care, telecommuting, and flex-time options. Not surprisingly day care subsidies and on-site day care centers proved less popular in the long run than telecommuting and flex-time arrangements. In general, management found day care expensive, many parents seemed reluctant to take advantage of either subsidies or on-site day care centers except in emergencies, and employees who were not parents found support of day care inequitable.[23] Flex-time and flex-place arrangements, however, proved more attractive for the majority of businesses. They seemed to increase productivity, were bottom-line-friendly, and did not invite conflicts between parents and nonparents regarding equity in benefits. (Studies of home-based telecommuting show an increase of productivity from 20 to 40 percent, as well as enormous time and money savings in the long freeway commutes that separate affordable family housing with corporate office complexes.)[24]

But downsizing has stalled or slowed business's eagerness to pursue such family-friendly policies. Bill Mattox, of the Family Research Council, notes that in a time of shaky job security employees are far less assertive in pushing a pro-family agenda, for fear that their coveted jobs will go to hardworking singles who have no family responsibilities.

And there are indications that despite the bottom-line benefits of telecommuting and flex-time, some of the nation's largest corporations insist on pursuing family policy avenues that will assure them closer surveillance of employee activity, no matter the costs. The American Business Collaboration for Quality Dependent Care, launched in 1992, is an alliance of twenty-one corporate giants—including Aetna Life and Casualty, Allstate Insurance, American Express, AT&T, Bank of America, Deloitte and Touche, Hewlett Packard, IBM,

Johnson & Johnson, Mobil, Price Water-house, Exxon, Xerox, Citibank—who by 1996 had committed $127.4 million to "develop and strengthen school-age, child care and elder care projects in communities across the country." Funds from the project will be used to finance day care centers, to train day care workers, to standardize and accredit after-school child care programs, to extend child care hours in existing programs, and to set up voice messaging systems in schools so that parents do not have to take the time out from work to meet teachers face-to-face.[25]

It does not take much insight to see that the goal here is to trap parents in the workplace for as long as possible each day. Of course corporate managers are for day care rather than flex-time and telecommuting where it allows them to assign their employees overtime, "vary their work schedules, [assign] travel on business, and participate in additional schooling or training sessions after work hours."[26] A recent DuPont employee survey proudly noted that the company's dependent care policies (which provided backup care for ill children and reimbursements for child care while traveling on company business as well as child care referrals and some flexible work practices) enabled the average manufacturing employee to put in a forty-seven-hour week, with managers typically working fifty-five hours per week. While it was reported in the DuPont study that employees found it difficult to "'get everything done' for work and family," and that working mothers with working spouses spent "103 hours per week (out of a total of 168 hours a week) on a combination of work, commuting, child care, household and personal chores," the company congratulated itself on earning greater employee commitment by way of its "work/life" programs. "We've always said that people are our most important asset," effused John A. Krol, president and CEO-designate of DuPont. "This study demonstrates that when a company acts . . . by responding to employees' concerns, it is not

only good for our people but it's good for business."[27]

In December 1995, I read with dismay a story in the *Christian Science Monitor* that told of high workloads and low employee morale at many companies during the holiday season. Several corporations, the report said, had found it necessary to stage seminars to help employees cope with work-family stresses. The object of these seminars? To get workers to relinquish feelings of guilt for cutting corners on family time and holiday preparations. The thought of *relieving* work pressures at the holiday season in the interest of family time apparently did not occur to the personnel managers who set up these stress seminars; nor, obviously, did it occur to them that for employees, the hours spent in such quasi-therapeutic exercises might be spent more rewardingly with their families.[28]

Big business's determination to increase short-term productivity, even at the expense of family life, is apparent in the Family and Medical Leave Act, which suffered acutely from the advice of the big businesses whom it pretended to obligate in the name of family time. This bill, which enables men and women who work for companies with fifty or more employees to take a three-month leave without pay for childbirth or family illness, guarantees their position and medical benefits only if they return to work after their reprieve. As conservative author and syndicated columnist Maggie Gallagher remarked to me when the act was passed in the spring of 1993, it was "perfectly named, since it encouraged new mothers to leave their families." David Ruben, a liberally aligned contributing editor to *Parenting* magazine, was not much more impressed. He noted in an August 1993 article, "This law is no panacea for hard-pressed working families. . . . Because the leave is unpaid, it's a sure bet that many parents won't be able to afford the time off they're entitled to."[29] Both were right. A 1996 survey revealed that only two-fifths of those who took maternity leave under the act stayed home an entire three months with their new babies, and one in eight women who took maternity leave had to request public assistance for lack of financial resources.[30]

## NOTES

1. Arlie Hochschild with Anne Machung, *The Second Shift* (New York: Avon, 1990), p. 243.

2. John R. Seeley, R. Alexander Sim, and Elizabeth W. Loosley, *Crestwood Heights: A Study of the Culture of Suburban Life* (New York: Basic Books, 1956), p. 376.

3. Ibid., p. 284.

4. Statistics taken from David R. Francis, "Who Works Hardest? Psst, Working Wives," *Christian Science Monitor*, March 24, 1995, p. 8.

5. "Mothers Speak Out on Child Care" (Merrifield, VA: Mothers at Home, 1989), p. 11.

6. Betty Friedan, *The Second Stage* (New York: Summit, 1981).

7. For a concise summary of this conflict, see Elizabeth Fox-Genovese, *"Feminism Is Not the Story of My Life": How Today's Feminist Elite Has Lost Touch with the Real Concerns of Women* (New York: Nan A. Talese/Doubleday, 1996), pp. 213–15. Schwartz outlined her views in *Breaking with Tradition: Women, Work and the New Facts of Life* (New York: Warner, 1992).

8. Fox-Genovese, *"Feminism Is Not the Story of My Life,"* p. 224.

9. Ellen Willis, "Why I'm Not 'Pro-Family,'" *Glamour*, October 1994, p. 15.

10. Author telephone interview with Heidi Brennan, April 1995.

11. Michele Ingrassia and Pat Wingert, "The New Providers," *Newsweek*, May 22, 1995, p. 38.

12. Hochschild with Machung, *The Second Shift*, p. 262.

13. Ibid., pp. 197–98.

14. Ibid., p. 262.

15. In conjunction with Louis Harris Associates, Julie Brines of the University of Washington did a 1995 survey of housework in two-income families. She found that the biggest housework burden was on women who were housewives or whose earnings represented a minimal contribution to the household. In households where women's earnings were equal to men's, men contributed around ten hours to their wives'

fifteen. But in marriages where wives contributed significantly more than husbands to income, women had proportionately more of the household burden once again. See Ingrassia and Wingert, "The New Providers," p. 37.

16. Sylvia Ann Hewlett, "Tough Choices, Great Rewards," *Parade*, July 16, 1994, p. 5.

17. William R. Mattox Jr., "The Parent Trap: So Many Bills, So Little Time," *Policy Review*, Winter 1991, p. 9.

18. Lester C. Thurow, "Companies Merge; Families Break Up," *New York Times*, September 3, 1995.

19. David Blankenhorn, *Fatherless America* (New York: Basic Books, 1995), p. 110.

20. Mattox, "The Parent Trap," p. 10.

21. Blankenhorn, *Fatherless America*, pp. 105–106.

22. Mattox, "The Parent Trap," p. 6.

23. William R. Mattox Jr., "The Family Friendly Corporation: Strengthening the Ties That Bind," *Family Policy* (a publication of the Family Research Council), November 1992.

24. Several research projects undertaken in the late 1980s and early 1990s showed that home-based work arrangements were not only family-friendly, because they offered parents more time with children and the luxury of organizing their work schedules around family lives, but also that they revealed significant bottom-line benefits. For a summary of these flex-place pilot programs and demonstration projects, see "Productivity Benefits of Home-Based Work," *In Focus* (a publication of the Family Research Council, 1992). See also Caroline Hull, "The Flexible Workplace," *Insight* (publication ISIS94C2WF of the Family Research Council, 1994).

25. The preceding information was taken from an information package sent to me by Work/Family Directions, the Boston-based consulting firm that is coordinator of the American Business Collaboration for Quality Dependent Care.

26. Sandra L. Burud, Pamela R. Aschbacher, and Jacquelyn McCroskey, *Employer Supported Child Care* (Dover, MA: Auburn House, 1984), quoted in Mattox, "The Family Friendly Corporation," p. 6.

27. *DuPont Corporate News*, October 30, 1995, pp. 1, 4.

28. Marilyn Gardner, "Handling the Holiday Season's Time Crunch," *Christian Science Monitor*, December 4, 1995, p. 13.

29. David Ruben, "Clinton Scorecard: How's He Doing?" *Parenting*, August 1993, p. 66.

30. Marilyn Gardner, "U.S. Workers, Companies Give Family-Leave Law Good Grade: Study Finds Concerns of Cost, Burden Largely Unfounded," *Christian Science Monitor*, May 6, 1996, p. 15.

## CRITICAL THINKING QUESTIONS

1. Why, according to Mack, do mothers work outside the home?

2. On the one hand, Mack asserts that "at least one parent should devote the major portion of his or her energies in watching the children." On the other hand, she focuses on employed mothers rather than employed fathers to resolve family/work conflicts. Does this mean that, when both parents work, mothers but not fathers are ultimately responsible for raising healthy and well-adjusted children?

3. Mack's research is based on middle-income families. Might the conclusions be different about work/family conflicts if she had interviewed mothers and fathers in lower socioeconomic levels?

# 12 Work and Family Life

## *Liberal/Feminist:* Ozzie and Harriet Are Dead

ROSALIND C. BARNETT AND CARYL RIVERS, *She Works, He Works: How Two-Income Families Are Happy, Healthy, and Thriving* (Cambridge, MA: Harvard University Press, 1996), pp. 1–7. © 1996 by Rosalind C. Barnett and Caryl Rivers. Reprinted by permission of the publisher.

*In contrast to conservatives and centrists, many liberals—including feminists—maintain that dual-earner families are necessary to maintain a family's economic well-being. Rosalind C. Barnett and Caryl Rivers, for example, argue that two-income families and their children are happier, healthier, and better rounded than the traditional families where the father is the breadwinner and the mother is a full-time homemaker.\**

The new American family is alive and well.

Both partners are employed full time, and according to the latest research, the family they create is one in which all members are thriving: often happier, healthier, and more well-rounded than the family of the 1950s.

That's the message of this new, myth-shattering study of such couples, funded by a 1 million-dollar grant from the National Institutes of Mental Health. Our study shows that the full-time-employed, dual-earner couple is a success. It is an excellent fit with today's economic realities. The men and women are doing well, emotionally and physically, and the children are thriving. This is not to say that families don't face many problems; but on the whole, the news about the two-career couple today is very good indeed:

* Barnett and Rivers's research is based on interviews with a random sample of 300 middle-class and working-class married couples in two communities in the greater Boston area.

- The women are not experiencing the high depression and anxiety rates characteristic of women in the 1950s—and while they have busy lives and often feel stressed, they are in very good health overall.
- The men with whom they are partnered are not the distant, work-obsessed fathers of the 1950s, who often felt wistful about their lack of connection to their children; if they are fathers, they are closely involved with all aspects of their children's care.
- Both men and women report that their relationships with their children are close and warm, and they are generally satisfied with the jobs they are doing as parents.
- They know their children are facing the many pressures of a fast-moving, mobile society—drugs, violence, AIDS, and a competitive, uncertain job market in which the need to acquire skills means economic survival and creates pressures

to get into good schools and do well there. They worry about their children, but not obsessively.

- Because they have two full incomes that help buffer them against the terrible wrenches of a changing economy, they do not feel the gut-wrenching vulnerability of standing at the edge of a precipice, ready at any second to topple off the cliff if a company downsizes or relocates. The terrible anxiety of economic uncertainty that can cause so many tensions in families is eased by two incomes, and the health of two-earner couples is bolstered as a result.

- Two-income couples are most often pictured in the media as hard-charging yuppies, but in our sample, both partners seem very much invested in family life. While they often enjoy their jobs and get a health boost from being involved with productive work, they understand that the implicit contract Americans used to expect from their employers—lifetime security in exchange for loyal and productive service—is gone, perhaps forever. Both men and women are committed to working, and what happens on the job is critical to their health. Nonetheless, most see their families as the center of their emotional lives.

But all this good news is too often obscured by a veritable tide of gloom and doom about the modern family, and by a nostalgic longing for a past that no longer exists: the heyday of Ozzie and Harriet, the breadwinner father and the homemaker mom.

This book, we hope, will help to dull the nostalgic glow and bring a sense of reality and optimism to our view of the present. The two-earner couple that has become the norm today is a success story, and the adults and the children within it are thriving. We could do a lot more, as a society, to ensure their health and happiness if we stopped viewing the two-income family as a failed or aberrant life style. For that to happen, we have to see past the fog of the 1950s and dim the wattage on the images from that era that engage us yet.

They dance through our heads—smiling, dashing off snappy one-liners, and solving problems in the blink of an eye—and it is hard to ignore them. Ozzie and Harriet Nelson, Ward and June Cleaver, and Carol and Mike Brady—with their seemingly limitless brood—are with us still. Even though it has been a long time since their first incarnations in the television sitcoms of the 1950s and 1960s, their images assault us in endless reruns on cable. At almost every hour of every day around the world, someone is watching Beaver struggle over problems with his math homework, or seeing David and Ricky Nelson bickering or Marcia Brady brooding about a date for the prom.

This omnipresence might only be a minor problem—like the advertising jingle that gets stuck in your head—until you realize how much politics, how many ponderous papers from how many think tanks, how much social policy, and how many personal decisions are based on a world that never existed in the first place.

For even as Ozzie and Harriet and their peers reigned supreme over the realm of television, the world they were supposed to reflect was slipping away—and that world was never as vast as we assumed. We tend to think that all mothers in those days were baking cookies in their shiny new kitchens, happily domestic. But studies show that by 1960, 19 percent of mothers with children under six were in the workforce, along with 31 percent of those with children between six and seventeen.[1] At the very time that the sitcom families were burrowing into our subconscious, their real-life counterparts were already starting to fossilize.

Today the so-called "traditional" family, with the breadwinner father and the stay-at-home mother, accounts for less than 3 percent of American families. The number of two-income couples has skyrocketed in the last decade from 20.5 million to about 31 million. By the mid-

1990s, about 60 percent of all married couples were two-earner couples. In 1990, 40 percent of families had full-time-employed husbands and wives, up from 32 percent in 1980, and that percentage is expected to climb.[2] Figure 1 shows the dramatic way in which the face of the American workforce has changed.

The couples in our study were typical Americans, not some exotic breed. They were largely white and middle or working class; this book is not a picture of the urban poor or the underclass.

And while some critics may bemoan the fact that so many women are employed, the women in our study are helping to make life for their families, facing the uncertainty of the new global marketplace, free of white-knuckle worry. Because these families in our study have two full incomes, they are sheltered from some of the worst problems in American society today. They don't have to live in neighborhoods wracked by lethal violence; they can afford, for the most part, to live in areas that have schools where guns and metal detectors are

not part of the curriculum. They are not plunged into chaos or poverty if one partner loses a job; they do not have to depend on dwindling government services for food or shelter. In a time when the social safety net is rapidly shrinking, they are less likely to have to depend on it than other Americans. They have the flexibility to change career patterns, if need be. One partner can support the other if one has to go back to school or get new skills training or take a drop in income to enter a new field. They are less likely than single people or one-income families to drop out of the middle class and slip into near-poverty as the economy lurches from one extreme to another.

The dual-earner family offers economic stability, protection against financial disaster, and often offers both adults and children a close-knit, cooperative family style in which all members take an active part in keeping the household running. Men and women sometimes feel there isn't enough time in the day, that what drops off the map is personal and leisure time, and that they would trade job advancement for more time to manage their busy lives. But most would not trade their lifestyle for the Ozzie and Harriet one that gave women fewer opportunities—and today would give both partners much more economic vulnerability.

Is the two-earner lifestyle without problems? Of course not. No family style plays out on one vast flood plain of joy and light. But this book will puncture some of what has become the conventional wisdom about American families. We believe that we have to look at families today through a prism of data and reality, not through the lens of an exaggerated sunny past or the political prism of those who believe the only family values worth promoting are those of a brief, atypical era now past. Trying to examine today's issues through those outmoded lenses will bring us no solutions to current problems and no understanding of what is really happening inside the American family. In this book, we examine families as

**FIGURE 1. The Increasing Responsibility of Women Workers for Family Financial Needs**

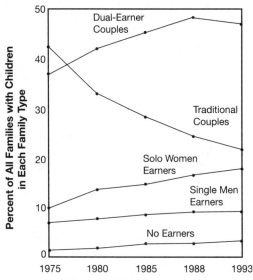

Source: U.S. Bureau of Labor Statistics, 1993.

they actually are today. These are some of the findings of our study and other cutting-edge research, which we will examine in the chapters to come:

- Working women are in excellent health—far better than homemakers—and are not getting sick from stress or dying from heart disease.
- American couples are cooperating in both work and parenting in a style we call the collaborative couple—and feel good about themselves and their lives.
- Working mothers are not destroying their children—in fact, there is little difference on any of the indices of child development between children of working moms and those of at-home mothers.
- Fatherhood has become more central to the lives of men in dual-earner couples, and critical to their emotional health. More men are willing to trade raises and promotions to spend time with their families.
- Work is just as important to women's health and well-being as it is to men's.
- The so-called mommy track can be bad for a woman's health.
- Marriage is just as central to men's identity and sense of well-being as it is to women's.
- Gender-role differences are shrinking as men's and women's lives become more alike.
- Men and women find exactly the same aspects of their jobs satisfying or distressing.

We found, in fact, that working couples are coping well with many of the changes that have made the two-earner couple the American norm today. The couples themselves have proved much more flexible than America's corporate culture. The corporate world, stuck in the mentality of the 1950s, too often still operates on the notion that the American worker is a male with a wife at home to tend to all the family issues. Workers today—be they men or women—are often in a generational sand-wich, facing problems with elderly parents and young children at the same time. The stress that such couples feel is often intensified by the rigidity of a corporate culture that for the most part refuses to adopt family-friendly policies that could do wonders for the bottom line as well as improve employees' quality of life. In this book, we'll argue forcefully that the outdated corporate culture has to change for the good of both the American family and American productivity.

If family issues continue to be seen as "women's-ghetto" problems, they will remain peripheral to the American workplace. Our research definitively shows that family issues are a major factor in men's health and productivity, and that failure to address them will have disastrous consequences not only for public health in this country but for our ability to effectively compete in world markets.

This book may be unsettling to some readers because the old ideas are so entrenched that we tend to believe them even while we are living the new realities of American life. Until fairly recently, men and women *did* lead very different lives. Men brought home the paycheck and delegated family responsibilities to their wives. Women saw to it that their husbands and children were happy and healthy. But life has changed with lightning speed. Today, *for the first time,* there is a generation of women whose lives parallel those of their husbands.

The authors of this book are examples of such women. We have each raised two children, now happy and healthy young adults. Juggling, to us, is more than a word; it's a life experience. We have been involved, all of our adult lives, with both the raising of children and with serious and sustained work in our careers. Like most women today, we have spent much of our lives in the workforce and have wrestled with balancing career and kids. Even though this lifestyle has become the norm today, we, as a nation, don't really know what it is like inside the new American family—because we haven't had time to look. Our book does just that. It documents new patterns in the lives of American men and women and the positive consequences for their health. Though the authors have written extensively in the past on the psychology of women, this book is addressed to men and women alike. We believe that the blame game ought to be retired to the dustbin of history. Women are not selfish careerists, destroying their children and their families and undermining society; nor are men brutish, uncaring, lazy slobs who are dead set against change and want women to wait on them hand and foot. The portrait that emerges from our study is one of men and women working together on both the work and home fronts to find personal challenge and satisfaction, to nurture each other, and, if they are parents, to raise children to be responsible citizens in a time of great change.

## NOTES

1. U.S. Census figures, 1960.
2. U.S. Census figures, 1990.

## CRITICAL THINKING QUESTIONS

1. What are some of the advantages and disadvantages of two-earner families for parents? For their children?
2. Barnett and Rivers's sample was based primarily on white families. Might their conclusions have been different if they had focused on families of color?
3. Barnett and Rivers state that "gender differences are shrinking as men's and women's lives become alike" and that "there is a generation of women whose lives parallel those of their husband." Are these conclusions consistent with the liberal/feminist articles on gender roles in Chapters 5 to 8?

# 13 Racial and Ethnic Diversity

## *Conservative:* Black Family Structure and Poverty

STEPHAN THERNSTROM AND ABIGAIL THERNSTROM, *America in Black and White: One Nation, Indivisible*, pp. 237–241. Reprinted with permission of Simon & Schuster, Inc., and Writers Representatives Inc. Copyright © 1997 by Stephan Thernstrom and Abigail Thernstrom.

*Conservatives assert that many family-related problems reflect a breakdown of the intact, two-parent household rather than, for example, economic inequality or racial discrimination. Stephan and Abigail Thernstrom argue, similarly, that it is family structure that divides the haves from the have-nots in the black community. More specifically, out-of-wedlock childbearing almost guarantees that many black children will grow up in poverty and experience problems commonly associated with being raised in a single-parent family.*

Growing up in a black female-headed household is not quite a guarantee that you will grow up poor, but it is pretty close to it. A recent review of the evidence in an article titled "Family Change Among Black Americans" concluded bleakly that "a majority of black children are now virtually assured of growing up in poverty, in large part because of their family status."[1]

### THE DECLINE OF THE BLACK TWO-PARENT FAMILY

Thus, it is family structure that largely divides the haves from the have-nots in the black community. The population in poverty is made up overwhelmingly of single mothers. And yet as recently as 1960, two-thirds of all black children lived in intact, two-parent families (Table 1). Two-thirds was well below the 91 percent rate

for white children in 1960, of course, but the racial difference was small in comparison with what it would soon become. The lower proportion of intact African-American families in 1960 was mainly due to higher rates of divorce or desertion, and to the fact that black women were more often widowed before their children were fully grown.

As early as 1965, Daniel Patrick Moynihan, then an assistant secretary in the Department of Labor, warned of the disintegration of the African-American family, and argued that "national action" of some kind was required to arrest the trend. Civil rights activists and other liberals attacked Moynihan savagely for suggesting that this trend was anything to worry about.[2] But Moynihan was prescient, as Eleanor Holmes Norton, an important civil rights voice, conceded twenty years later.[3] In the past three decades the proportion of intact

**TABLE 1.  Percent of Children Under 18 Living in Various Family Types, 1960–1995**

|  | 1960 | 1970 | 1980 | 1995 |
|---|---|---|---|---|
| Two parents |  |  |  |  |
| Black | 67 | 59 | 42 | 33 |
| White | 91 | 90 | 83 | 76 |
| Mother only |  |  |  |  |
| Black | 22 | 30 | 44 | 52 |
| White | 7 | 8 | 14 | 18 |
| Father only |  |  |  |  |
| Black | NA | 2 | 2 | 4 |
| White | NA | 1 | 2 | 3 |
| Neither parent |  |  |  |  |
| Black | NA | 10 | 12 | 11 |
| White | NA | 2 | 2 | 3 |

*Sources:* Figures for 1960 from U.S. Bureau of the Census, Current Population Reports, P-23–181, *Households, Families, and Children: A 30–Year Perspective* (Washington, D.C.: U.S. Government Printing Office, 1992), 37; the mother-only figures for 1960 are actually for children living with one parent. The vast majority of them would be living with their mothers, though, so this is a fair approximation of the true figure. Figures for 1970 and 1980 from U.S. Bureau of the Census, Current Population Reports, P-20–480, *The Black Population in the United States: March 1994 and 1993*, table G. Figures for 1995 from U.S. Bureau of the Census, *Statistical Abstract of the United States: 1996* (Washington, D.C.: U.S. Government Printing Office, 1996), 65.

married-couple families has declined precipitously, even though the fraction of black women aged fifteen to forty-four who were divorced, separated, or widowed also went down. That figure has risen a good deal for white women, from 7 to 13 percent, but not for blacks.[4] It is thus not divorce but the failure to marry that has led to such a momentous change in black family patterns. The marriage rate for African Americans has plummeted in the past third of a century.

In 1960 only a little over a quarter of black women aged fifteen to forty-four were unmarried and had never been married. Nearly three-quarters had been married, although a sizable proportion of their marriages had come to an end, as a result of divorce, separation, or the death of their spouse. Black women were only a

shade less likely to marry than white women; 72 percent of black females and 76 percent of white females had been married.

The contrast with the present day is stark. Today a clear majority of African-American women aged fifteen to forty-five have never been married, as compared with just a third of their white counterparts. Although American women are currently marrying about four years later than they did back at the height of the Baby Boom in the 1950s, by the time they reach their late twenties (ages twenty-five to twenty-nine), seven out of ten white women today have married. The figure for black females of the same age is only four out of ten.[5] Moreover, this huge racial gap in marriage rates continues to widen.

Many fewer black women are marrying, and yet they continue to have children—which was not the case in an earlier era. The proportion of black children born out of wedlock has mushroomed. In 1960 just over a fifth (22 percent) of the births to black women were out of wedlock. At the latest count—1994—the figure stood at a staggering 70 percent. If the trend continues at anything like the same pace, the proportion of black births that are out of wedlock will hit three out of four births by 1997.

For much of the African-American population, marriage and childbearing have become almost completely dissociated. Since 1987, astoundingly, fertility and marriage have been inversely rather than positively correlated for blacks. In 1987 the birth rate for married black women actually fell *below the birth rate for unmarried black women*, the first time that has ever happened for any ethnic group. It was not a one-time anomaly; the pattern has continued ever since.[6] The disconnect between marriage and childbearing could scarcely become any more complete than that. A great many African Americans appear to be living in what Daniel Patrick Moynihan calls a "post-marital society."

These changes—the huge decline in the proportion of intact, two-parent families, the corresponding surge in the number of single parents, and the explosion of out-of-wedlock births—have not been confined to the African-American population, of course. They are to some extent general trends that have influenced all elements of American society. The number of unmarried white women becoming mothers—"Murphy Browns"—has also increased notably, and white female-headed families have become increasingly common.

If similar changes have been taking place among whites, why point a finger at blacks? some have asked. The political scientist Andrew Hacker has noted that the proportion of female-headed households has been rising just as rapidly among whites in recent decades; the percentage of out-of-wedlock births has increased more rapidly among whites than blacks. The evidence on changing family patterns, then, reveals "not so much racial differences as concurrent adaptations to common cultural trends."[7]

The *percentage increase* in the proportion of births that take place out of wedlock has indeed been higher among whites than blacks in recent decades, and the proportion of single-parent families has multiplied at about the same rate for both races. And yet the rate of change is surely not the most important point. A quarter of white children, still a distinct minority, are born out of wedlock. In the case of blacks, it is the vast majority: seven out of ten black children. A black newborn with a married mother is as rare as a white child born to one who is unmarried. A social pattern with devastating economic consequences has become the norm in the black community, while it is still the deviant pattern among whites. To be born out of wedlock is a ticket to an impoverished childhood.[8]

"Single Mother and Proud," ran the title of a *Washington Post* op-ed article in the summer of 1996. "Working Two Jobs and Raising a Daughter; What's to Be Ashamed Of?" was the subtitle.[9] But shame is not the point. Poverty is—as we have already argued. The author (nearly through college) was juggling jobs and school and baby, but the majority of black single mothers are not

college-educated and have very limited earning capacity. Child poverty, female-headed families, and out-of-wedlock births are closely connected—especially among blacks. The poverty rate for African-American children living in single-parent families is nearly *five times* what it is for those living in married-couple families (62 percent versus only 13 percent). Poverty is in fact part of a cluster of closely related problems associated with single-parent families. Recent evidence indicates that children living with mothers but no fathers are two-and-a-half times more likely to repeat a grade in school, more than three times as likely to be suspended or expelled, and twice as likely to end up in juvenile correctional facilities.[10]

It once was common for skeptics to greet such numbers with the argument that they do not show that there is anything wrong with female-headed families per se; these differences all stem from the greater likelihood that such families will have a low income. If you controlled for income, the differences would vanish. There are two flaws in this argument. First, why should we control for income? When the connections between living in a female-headed household and living in poverty are as strong as they are, artificially holding income constant makes no sense. It is possible that a careful study would show that college athletes perform as well in the classroom as nonathletes *if* you control for the number of hours a week they devote to studying. But if most of them don't study nearly as much as other students, their GPA controlled for hours of study is not of great interest. What matters is how well they perform. Likewise, median income in 1995 was only $15,004 for female-headed black families, little more than a third of what it was in black married-couple families. That is not a fact that should be obscured by controlling for other related factors.[11]

Nevertheless, recent studies have done what the critics had asked for; they have held income and a variety of other socioeconomic variables constant. But they reveal that even when you do control for other variables, family structure has an independent effect that is measurable, and that, in important ways, the effect of growing up in a single-parent family is negative.[12]

## NOTES

1. David Ellwood and Jonathan Crane, "Family Change Among Black Americans: What Do We Know?" *Journal of Economic Perspectives* 4 (Fall 1990), 81.

2. The full text of "the Moynihan Report," which appeared officially as U.S. Department of Labor, *The Negro Family: The Case for National Action* (Washington, D.C.: U.S. Government Printing Office, 1965), is conveniently available in Lee Rainwater and William Yancey, *The Moynihan Report and the Politics of Controversy* (Cambridge: MIT Press, 1967). Rainwater and Yancey offer a useful analysis of the controversy and reprint key documents.

3. In "Restoring the Black Family," *New York Times Magazine*, June 2, 1985, 43. Norton deplored the fact that the attack on Moynihan resulted in "driving the issue from the public agenda and delaying for a generation the search for workable solutions." Savage criticism of the Moynihan Report is still appearing; for one example, see Carl Ginsberg, *Race and Media: The Enduring Life of the Moynihan Report* (New York: Institute for Media Analysis, 1989).

4. That the proportion of black women who were divorced, separated, or widowed did not rise but actually declined between 1960 and 1994 is somewhat misleading, though. The figures are for *all* women aged 15–44, not just those who were ever married, and only those who ever married, of course, are eligible to become divorced, separated, or widowed. The sharp decline in the proportion of African-American women who have been marrying at all has meant a steep fall in the number of those who *could* experience a broken marriage. If we look only at the rate of divorce, separation, or widowhood for *ever-married* black women, it has risen substantially—from 28 percent in 1960 to 41 percent in 1992; Ellwood and Crane, "Family Change, Among Black Americans," 67; U.S. Bureau of the Census, Current Population Reports, P-20-471, *The Black Population in the United States: March 1992* (Washington, D.C.:

U.S. Government Printing Office, 1993), table 4. The divorce rate is currently higher for black women than white women; U.S. Bureau of the Census, Current Population Reports, P-23-180, *Marriage, Divorce, and Remarriage in the 1990s* (Washington, D.C.: U.S. Government Printing Office, 1992), 5. Nevertheless, the declining marriage rate for African Americans is a more important source of family change than the increase in the rate of breakup of marriages that have already been formed.

5. U.S. Bureau of the Census, Current Population Reports, P-20-484, *Marital Status and Living Arrangements: March 1994* (Washington, D.C.: U.S. Government Printing Office, 1996), table 6.

6. Ellwood and Crane, "Family Change Among Black Americans," 68; U.S. Bureau of the Census, *Statistical Abstract of the U.S.: 1996* (Washington, D.C.: U.S. Government Printing Office, 1996), 75, 77.

7. Andrew Hacker, *Two Nations: Black and White, Separate, Hostile, Unequal* (New York: Scribner, 1992), 68, 80.

8. The journalist Michael Lind has recently dismissed concern about the spectacular rise in out-of-wedlock births by black mothers as "one of the great conservative hoaxes of our time"; Lind, *Up from Conservatism: Why the Right Is Wrong for America* (New York: Free Press, 1996), 167. According to Lind, the crucial fact about black unwed births is that the typical unwed mother today is not having more children than was the case a generation ago; the huge rise in the proportion of African-American births that occur outside of marriage is due mainly to the fact that the fertility of black married women has gone down very sharply. This point derives from Christopher Jencks's calculation that if married black women had continued to have babies between 1960 and 1987 at the same rate as they did in 1960, the proportion of black out-of-wedlock births would have risen much less— from 23 percent to 29 percent rather than from 23 percent to 62 percent; *Up from Conservatism*, 167–170. There would have been just as many babies born out of wedlock, but they would have been a much smaller proportion of all African-American births. Jencks's estimate seems a useful footnote that clarifies the demographic mechanisms responsible for the current pattern. That is all it was intended to be. Jencks did not use it to support the tendentious claim that it is therefore a "hoax" to speak of a crisis of illegitimacy in the black community. That is Lind's unique contribution to the dialogue, and it seems to us like

arguing that "if my grandmother had wheels she'd be a bus." The fertility of married black women did in fact decline very sharply in the post–Baby Boom period, while that of unmarried black women did not. The fact that seven in ten black children are born out of wedlock is what merits attention, not what the family circumstances of a hypothetical black baby might have been today if black married women had continued to bear children at the same rate that they did in the Baby Boom years. It does not really matter what particular combination of changes in marital and nonmarital fertility produced the current mess. What's important is the kind of family that a great many of the next generation of African-American children will grow up in. Lind does acknowledge (feebly) that "it may be that any number of out-of-wedlock births is a problem"; *Up from Conservatism*, 169. But if "any number" is a problem, then surely seven out of ten is a very big problem indeed. Denying that elementary point seems the real "hoax."

9. Stephanie Crockett, "Single Mother and Proud," *Washington Post*, July 14, 1996, C5.

10. David Whitman, "The War over 'Family Values,'" *U.S. News & World Report*, June 8, 1992, 35.

11. U.S. Bureau of the Census, Current Population Reports, P-60–193, *Money Income in the United States: 1995* (Washington, D.C.: U.S. Government Printing Office, 1996), table 3.

12. Much of the evidence is summarized in Sara McLanahan and Gary Sandefur, *Growing Up with a Single Parent: What Hurts, What Helps* (Cambridge: Harvard University Press, 1994).

## CRITICAL THINKING QUESTIONS

1. Why, according to the authors, is the African-American family disintegrating? What evidence do they provide to support this conclusion?

2. Why do the Thernstroms argue that controlling for income would not diminish the negative effects of being raised in female-headed households?

3. This article maintains that family structure leads to poverty. Is it also possible that poverty shapes family structure?

# 13 Racial and Ethnic Diversity

*Centrist:* Multiculturalism or One People?

AMITAI ETZIONI, "Some Diversity," *Society* 35 (July/August 1998): 59–61. Reproduced with permission of the author.

*To assume that skin tones reflect different visions and values is racist, according to Amitai Etzioni. Americans of different origins do not have the same views across or within racial and ethnic groups. Despite some differences, most Americans share many common values and attitudes on issues such as family life, morality, and welfare reform. Although intermarriage rates are increasing, the American creed should not be replaced, Etzioni maintains, by "something called 'multiculturalism'."*

Various demographers have been predicting for years that the end of the white majority in the United States is near, and that there will be a majority of minorities. CNN ran a special program on the forthcoming majority of the people of color in America. President Clinton has called attention to this shift in a recent address at the University of California, San Diego campus, for a renewed national dialogue about race relations. He argues that such a dialogue is especially needed as a preparation for the forthcoming end of the white majority, to occur somewhere in the middle of the next century. White House staffer Sylvia Mathews provides the projected figures as 53 percent whites and 47 percent mixtures of other ethnic groups by 2050. Pointing to such figures, Clinton asked rhetorically if we should not act now to avoid America being divided into "separate, unequal and isolated" camps.

## ONE PEOPLE

What is fundamentally wrong about this way of focusing the interracial dialogue is that it is implicitly and inadvertently racist: it assumes that people's pigmentation, or, more generally, racial attributes, determine their visions, values, and votes. Actually, very often the opposite is true. The fact is that America is blessed with an economic and political system, while far from flawless, that is embraced by most Americans of all races. It is a grievous error to suggest that because American faces or skin tones may appear more diverse some fifty years from now, that most Americans who hail from different social backgrounds will seek to follow a different agenda or hold a different creed than the white majority.

Two findings out of many that could be cited illustrate this point: A 1992 survey found that most black and Hispanic Americans (86 percent and 85 percent, respectively) seek "fair treatment for all, without prejudice or discrimination." The figure for all Americans is a close 79 percent. A poll of New York residents shows that the vast majority of respondents considered teaching "the common heritage and values that we share as Americans" to be "very important." Indeed, more minorities than whites endorse this position: 88 percent of

Hispanics and 89 percent of blacks, compared to 70 percent whites.

## NO SOLID CAMPS

The very notion that there are social groups called "Asian-Americans" or "Latinos" is largely a statistical artifact (reflecting the way social data are coded and reported), promoted by some ethnic leaders, a shorthand the media finds convenient, and something President Clinton may end up helping to perpetuate rather than challenge. Thus, most of the so called Asian-Americans do not see themselves, well, as Asian-Americans and many resent being labeled this way. Many Japanese-Americans do not feel a particular affinity to Filipino- or Pakistani-Americans, or to Korean-Americans. And the feeling is rather reciprocal. As Professor Paul Watanabe, from the University of Massachusetts, an expert on Asian Americans and himself an American of Japanese descent, puts it: "There's this concept that all Asians are alike, that they have the same history, the same language, the same background. Nothing could be more incorrect."

William Westerman of the International Institute of New Jersey complains about Americans who tend to ignore the cultural differences among Asian nations, which reflect thousands of years of tradition. He wonders how the citizens of the United States, Canada, and Mexico would feel if they were all treated as indistinguishable "North Americans."

The same holds for the so called Latinos, including three of my sons. Americans of Hispanic origin trace their origins to many different countries and cultures. Eduardo Diaz, a social-service administrator, puts it this way: ". . . there is no place called Hispanica. I think it's degrading to be called something that doesn't exist. Even Latino is a misnomer. We don't speak Latin." A Mexican American office worker remarked that when she is called Latina it makes her think "about some kind of island." Many

Americans from Central America think of themselves as "mestizo," a term that refers to a mixture of Amerindian and European ancestry. Among those surveyed in the National Latino Political Survey in 1989, the greatest number of respondents chose to be labeled by their country of origin, as opposed to "pan-ethnic" terms such as "Hispanic" or "Latino."

The significance of these and other such data is that far from dividing the country into two or three hardened minority camps, we are witnessing an extension of a traditional American picture: Americans of different origins identifying with groups of other Americans from the same country—at least for a while, but not with any large or more lasting group.

Far from there being a new coalition of non-white minorities soon to gain majority status (something President Clinton points to and Jesse Jackson dreams about as a rainbow, that contains all colors but white), the groups differ greatly from each other—and within each other.

Moreover, on numerous issues the differences among various minority groups are as big or bigger than those between these groups and "Anglo" Americans. For instance, fewer Cuban Americans agreed with the statement that U.S. citizens should be hired over non-citizens, than Anglo (42% Cubans compared to 51% of Anglos), other Hispanic groups agree more strongly than Anglos (55% of Puerto Ricans and 54% of Mexican Americans). Quotas for jobs and college admissions are favored only by a minority of any of these four groups studied, but Cubans differed from Mexicans and Puerto Ricans more (by 14%) than from Anglos (by 12%).

The fact that various minorities do not share a uniform view, which could lead them to march lock-step with other minorities to a new America (as some on the left fantasize), is also reflected in elections. Cuban-Americans tend to vote Republican, while other Americans of Hispanic origin are more likely to vote Democratic. Americans of Asian origin cannot be counted on to vote one way or another, either. First generation Vietnamese-Americans tend to be strong anti-Communists and favor the Republican Party, older Japanese and Chinese-Americans are more often Democrats, while Filipino-Americans are more or less equally divided between the parties. (Of the Filipino-Americans registered to vote, 40% list themselves as Democrats, 38% as Republicans, and 17% as independent.)

We often encounter the future first in California. In a 1991 election in Los Angeles for the California State Assembly, Korean-American, Filipino-American, and Japanese-American groups each ran their own candidate, thus splitting the so called "Asian-American" vote, not deterred by the fact that they thereby ensured the election of a white candidate. Candidates of all kinds of backgrounds may carry the day in the next century America, but the notion that all minorities, or even most members of any one minority, will line up behind them based on their pigmentation, is far from a reliable assumption for a national dialogue about our interracial future.

While African-Americans are the least mainstreaming group, there is a growing black middle class, many members of which have adopted rather similar lifestyles and aspirations to other middle class Americans. Even if one takes all African-Americans as a group, one could be swayed too far by the recent data on the great differences in the ways whites and blacks perceived the O.J. Simpson trial and other matters directly concerning racial issues. When it comes to basic tenets of the American creed, the overwhelming majority of blacks are surprisingly accepting of them. For instance, a national survey asked in 1994: "a basic American belief has been that if you work hard you can get ahead—reach your goals and get more"; 67% of blacks responded "yes, still true," only ten percent less than whites. Most blacks (77%) say they prefer equality of opportunity to equality of results (compared to 89% of whites). When it comes to "do you see yourself as traditional or old

fashioned on things such as sex, morality, family life, and religion, or not," the difference between blacks and whites was only 5%, and when asked whether values in America are seriously declining, the difference was down to one point. Roughly the same percentages of blacks and whites strongly advocate balancing the budget, cutting personal income taxes, reforming the welfare system, and reforming Medicare. Percentages are also nearly even in responses to questions on abortion and marijuana.

In a recent extensive national survey conducted at the University of Virginia, James Davison Hunter and Carl Bowman found that ". . . the majority of Americans do not engage in identity politics—a politics that insists that opinion is mainly a function of racial, ethnic, or gender identity or identities rooted in sexual preference." While there were some disagreements on specific issues and policies, this study found more similarities than discrepancies. Even when asked about such divisive issues as the direction of changes in race and ethnic relations, the similarities across lines were considerable: 35% of blacks, 37% of Hispanics, and 40% of whites feel these relations are holding steady; 36%, 53%, and 44% feel they have declined, respectively. (The rest feel that they have improved.) That is, on most issues four out of five—or more!—agreed with one another, while those who differed amounted to less than 20% of all Americans. No anti-anything majority here, or most likely, in our future.

### INTERMARRIAGE AND "OTHERS"

Last but not least, the White House figures are misleading. They are based on a simplistic projection of past trends, ignoring the rapidly rising category of racially mixed Americans, the result of the rising number of cross-racial marriages and a rejection of monoracial categories by some others, especially Hispanic-Americans. One out of 12 marriages in 1995 (8.4%) were interracial/ethnic marriages.

Intermarriage between Asian-Americans and whites are particularly common; marriages between Hispanic-Americans and whites are also rather frequent, while such marriages with African-Americans are the least common. Since 1970, the proportion of marriages among people of different racial or ethnic origin increased by 72%. And the number of children of interracial marriages has quadrupled since 1970 to reach the 2 million mark. Moreover, in the 1990 Census, 4%, or 9.8 million Americans, chose to classify themselves as others, i.e. not members of any particular racial group. Even if these trends do not accelerate and continue only at the present pace, the figures for 2050 may read something like the following: 51% white; 14% multiracial; 35% minorities. The rise of the "others"—far from dividing the country still further, along with the fact that more and more Americans will be of mixed heritage with relatives in two or more camps, as Tiger Woods has—will serve to blur the racial lines. That is, while there may well be more Americans of non-European origin, a growing number of the American white majority will have a Hispanic daughter- or son-in-law, an Asian stepfather or mother, and a whole rainbow of cousins.

## MULTICULTURALISM OR AMERICAN CREED?

All this does not mean that racial diversity is a figment of the president's imagination. But the changes in America's demography do not imply that the American creed is being or will be replaced by something called "multiculturalism." The American creed always had room for pluralism of subcultures, of people upholding some of the traditions and values of their countries of origin, from praying to playing in their own way. But the interracial dialogue would be better served if President Clinton would stress that pluralism was, is, and is likely to continue to be bound by a shared framework if America is to be spared the kind of ethnic tribalism that tears apart countries as

different as Yugoslavia and Rwanda, and raises its ugly head even in well established democracies such as Canada and the United Kingdom (where Scottish and Welsh separatism is on the rise).

The president could point to the social, cultural, and legal elements that constitute the framework that holds together the diverse mosaic: A commitment by all parties to the democratic way of life, to the Constitution and its Bill of Rights, and to mutual tolerance. It is further fortified by a strong conviction that one's station in life is determined by hard work and saving, by taking responsibility for one's self and one's family. And, most Americans still share a strong sense that while we are different in some ways, in more ways we are joined by the shared responsibilities of providing a good society for our children and ourselves, one free of racial and ethnic strife, and providing the world with a model of a country whose economy and polity are thriving.

## CRITICAL THINKING QUESTIONS

1. Thernstrom and Thernstrom asserted that family structure is associated with high rates of African-American poverty. Here, Etzioni argues that most of us share similar values about what we deem "very important." Is there a potential for racially based conflict if we hold similar values but experience unequal economic outcomes due to family structure?

2. Etzioni posits that the growth of intermarriages will dilute some of the current racial boundaries across groups. Is it possible, however, that the increasing numbers of biracial children will divide the country even further?

3. Many people in the United States celebrate the virtues of "diversity" and "multiculturalism." Do you think that an emphasis on "one people" rather than multiculturalism, as Etzioni advocates, would result in a greater acceptance or rejection of diverse family forms and practices?

# 13 Racial and Ethnic Diversity

## *Liberal/Feminist:* Racial Safety and Cultural Maintenance in Childcare

LYNET UTTAL, "Racial Safety and Cultural Maintenance: The Childcare Concerns of Employed Mothers of Color." The original expanded version of this essay appears in *Ethnic Studies Review* 19 (February 1996): 43–59. Reproduced by permission of the NAES.

*Some centrists (see the article by Etzioni) advocate focusing on our similarities rather than our differences. Are such suggestions realistic or desirable? According to Lynet Uttal, for example, parents of color must teach their children how to continuously navigate racist waters. And, however well intentioned, white child-care providers are often ignorant about providing "racial safety" or are insensitive to maintaining the children's cultural values and practices.\**

### INTRODUCTION

Childcare advocates are pressing for the professionalization of childcare work and the practice of a single model of developmentally appropriate care. Underlying this proposal is the assumption that childrearing can be stripped of cultural values and practices, and that the type of care a child receives can be offered independent of the social and cultural location of the child's family.

This model ignores how membership in historically subordinated racial ethnic groups creates a different experience for people of color than experienced by the White population. Childcare research has

\* Uttal's study is based on in-depth interviews with 15 employed mothers (7 Mexican American, 7 African American, 1 Guamanian American) of infants, toddlers, and pre-school-aged children in northern California during 1990–1992.

identified systematic differences in preferences by socioeconomic and racial ethnic groups. One difference frequently noted is that African American parents, specifically, and low income parents, generally, view childcare as an educational setting more so than do White parents. White parents, especially middle class ones, are more likely to view childcare as an opportunity for their children to have social interactions with other children.[1] African American parents express a greater preference for childcare that provides structured academic programs for preschool-aged children, whereas middle class White parents prefer loosely structured activities that expose their children to different concepts through play. This high valuation of education is rooted in beliefs that early education will prepare children for kindergarten and create a stronger foundation for social mobility through education.[2] African American parents are also more likely to advocate the use of authoritarian disciplining styles such as physical punishment and authoritarian commands by child care providers.[3] In contrast, White parents are less likely to support the use of corporal punishment in daycare, even though they may privately use these methods at home.

One study found that African American parents expected the daycare center's staff to be aware of and sensitive to racial issues and objected when the daycare center's programming violated this expectation.[4] In another study, Chinese American parents expressed concern about the conflicting messages children get when what is taught at home differs from what is taught at their daycares,[5] such as differing beliefs about how to address elders and eating practices (e.g. whether picking up a bowl and eating from it is acceptable). These concerns are important to take into account because early childhood education research has shown that presentations of positive ethnic images are important in the formulation of children's self-images and for the transmissions of cultural values. . . .[6]

Historical consciousness of their status as members of historically subordinated racial ethnic groups informs the types of concerns employed mothers of color have about leaving their children in other people's care. In this article, I explore two expressions of this historical consciousness in employed mothers' views of their childcare arrangements: racial safety and cultural maintenance. . . . This article not only identifies childcare problems related to overt forms of racism, but also discusses the problems that occur when well-intentioned White childcare providers lack the cultural competency to care for children of different racial ethnic groups.

## THE CONCERN FOR RACIAL SAFETY

According to Harriette Pipes McAdoo, "the 'extreme' difficulties which White society imposes on Black people by denying their identity, their values, and their economic opportunities are not unusual or extreme but 'mundane,' daily pressures for Blacks."[7] McAdoo compares living with racism to living in a harsh physical environment. . . .

Awareness of racism in U.S. society was a common topic when mothers of color talked about their childcare arrangements. Because of their own experiences with racism, they were concerned about how their children would be treated when the childcare providers were White. Often times, mothers discovered these problems only after they established childcare arrangements. For example, Gloria Thomas,[8] an African American waitress and mother of two children, observed behaviors that she defined as racist. Gloria said:

> I don't know if she was used to [Black people]. I think she was kind of narrow minded. I didn't feel comfortable, me being Black. [And] she looked like she put more energy into the White kids than the Black kids. I think she felt that I was on to her, because she said in a couple days, or actually I said, "this isn't going to work," and she pretty much knew also that it wasn't going to work.

Gloria expected White childcare providers to have knowledge of how to negotiate cross-racial interactions. She said:

> If you are dealing with my kids, I hope you do have some cultural skills. I don't like prejudiceness at all . . . You have to be not dumb. Some white people can be really stupid. They say the stupidest things.

When it was clear that childcare providers lacked these skills, mothers removed their children from the childcare setting. Frances Trudeau, an African American lawyer and the mother of two children, responded this way when the teachers and administrators at her five year old son's preschool-elementary school failed to acknowledge and address that the name calling and chasing of African American children was racism. When she and other parents spoke to the director, they were told that the school could not develop a policy to address these problems because families came from so many different walks of life and the school did not want to tell people how to behave. This response reduced cross-racial interactions to individual interactions and personal disagreements and failed to acknowledge the more systemic nature of racism. Mothers of color found this kind of response inadequate and frustrating because they are aware of the pervasiveness of the problem of racism. Because they know racism's regularity, commonness, and reoccurrence, they do not define unpleasant cross-racial interactions as occasional, individual disagreements, even in childcare settings.

The mothers of color also experienced racism when they used predominantly White childcare settings. Gloria Thomas described one such encounter:

This one woman was pretty annoying. She asked me this question and to this day I still want to ask her what did she mean by it. She said, "Oh, are you a single parent?" And I said, "Yes. " And she goes, "Oh, do you live around here?" And I said, "Yes, I live right around the corner. " You could tell her mind was [thinking], "She goes to this daycare? She's a single parent, Black, and she lives up here. How can she afford it?" It's really weird.

One of the strategies that the mothers developed to protect their children from racism was to find child care within their own racial ethnic communities. The use of kin and community networks protected the children and the mothers from having to deal with cross-racial interactions. When mothers of color were able to make childcare arrangements with childcare providers of their same racial ethnic group, the concerns about racial safety and cultural maintenance were eliminated. Yet, care within one's racial ethnic community did not guarantee a fit between the values and childrearing practices of mothers and childcare providers. Often times, mothers had several relatives and acquaintances from which to choose. When this was the case, the mothers carefully discriminated between their choices based on what they considered to be a good environment and good care. After ensuring their child's racial safety and exposure to traditional cultural practices and values, they invoked additional criteria to decide which childcare setting was the best. Sylvia Rodriguez, an office manager and the mother of two children, chose her cousin over her sister-in-law. She explained:

It depends on who the relatives are. Like for example, you know, financially [my husband's sister] could have used watch[ing for pay] my son and my daughter at her house. She's real good about feeding them and things like that. But she has a lot of marital problems that I wouldn't want my kids to be around, watching the arguments and fights. I know they use bad language, and that's another thing I don't like.

Like Sylvia, Lupe Gonzalez, an administrative assistant and the mother of an eleven month old, was discriminating in terms of which relative she chose to watch her young baby. She had two options: an elderly grandmother and an aunt who was the same age as herself. She was pleased that her aunt was available to care for the baby, although she would have left her baby in her grandmother's care if necessary, but her grandmother was elderly and was already watching several other grandchildren. Because of her grandmother's age, Lupe felt that she would not be as attentive or as physically able to pick up her baby. The advantage of care by the aunt was that her infant son would also be the only child for whom the aunt provided care.

Although Gloria Thomas had left a White childcare provider because she felt the White provider was unable to negotiate the cross-racial interactions, she found that simply finding an African American childcare provider did not necessarily create satisfactory childcare arrangements. Gloria had found a family daycare run by an African American woman, yet other factors prevented her from feeling comfortable with this arrangement. Gloria's views were informed by Black nationalism as well as the health foods movement. She expressed the political position that she would not hire a Latino immigrant because that resembled the racial exploitation of African Americans, and she also rejected high fat and high sugar cooking in favor of low fat and low sugar organic foods. She talked with the African American childcare provider about what kinds of foods were provided at the daycare, and she expressed her preference that her children be provided with fresh juices instead of sodas or drinks with sugar in them. In spite of this initial discussion, it was not unusual for Gloria to come to pick up her kids and find them drinking sugar drinks. Gloria defined what her childcare provider was doing as an African American cultural practice:

> Black people are raised different where they can eat the fried foods whatever. But I just wasn't trying to act like my kids were special. I was mainly just concerned about their nutrition, but it wasn't like I was acting they were more special. I was just doing it because I didn't want them to eat any sugar.

Unhealthy food was a piece of her cultural heritage that she did not want to continue to practice.

Similarly, Gloria and her provider had disagreements about what were appropriate disciplining practices. Gloria talked with her provider about these issues, but felt that her preferences were not validated by the childcare provider. She said:

> Well, I did, I said, "I don't believe in hitting." And she said, "What do you mean by hitting?" I said, "just swatting," and she said, "I do, you know, a slap on the hand." And I said, "pretty much even that I don't want." But I could feel like that she didn't want to hear that.

Since Gloria also wanted something different than what she perceived as traditional African American childrearing practices, she moved her children into a daycare center where she was the only African American parent, as well as of the lowest socioeconomic status and background, and one of only two single parents. She often found herself irritated with what she perceived as a White style of interaction, yet she felt the social, educational, and environmental advantages of the daycare center outweighed the need to have her child cared for by her previous African American childcare provider.

Young mothers often opposed some of the traditional childrearing practices used by the older and more traditional women in their communities. For example, Maria Hernandez, a Mexican American office manager and the mother of a four-year-old boy, expressed dissatisfaction with the care provided by her Mexican American mother-in-law. She said:

> I don't really like the idea of them being yelled at or spanked. I think if there is a behavior problem, they should be able to tell [the parents] and for us to deal with it. Luckily, I have been in the situation where my kid is pretty mellow, but I've seen her spanking her other grandchildren. I wouldn't like that.

Occasionally, Maria would consider moving her child to a daycare center. Yet, when Maria weighed out all factors (i.e. convenience, location, flexibility, cost, quality of care, being within the family for child care), she decided that this care by her mother-in-law was the best choice, in spite of the differences about disciplining practices.

One of the formal sources of childcare referrals was through the County's childcare referral service. This service provided referrals to licensed daycare centers, family daycares, and unlicensed individual caregivers. However, given the structure of the childcare market into informal and formal sectors, and the racial demographics of the region, the referral service was not often helpful for African American and Mexican American mothers. Even though the service was provided in both English and Spanish, several Mexican American mothers commented that the service was not a good source for Latino providers. One Mexican American mother pointed out that when she visited the referrals given to her by the County's referral service, she saw only

White childcare providers and very few non-White racial ethnic children in their care. Mexican American employed mothers reported that they had greater success locating Latino caregivers through informal sources, such as personal referrals and Spanish radio ads. Thus, Mexican American mothers often turned to their social and community-based networks to locate child care instead of using the childcare referral service. African American mothers in this study found it difficult to locate African American childcare providers in either the formal or informal sector of the childcare market.

Another consideration was that simply being of the same race did not guarantee racial safety. Gloria felt that her African American childcare provider was uncomfortable with the fact that her children's father was White. Being biracial located her children in a different category of race than being labeled as simply "Black." Similarly, other mothers found that their searches for child care were complicated by having mixed race children. Julie Lopez described how her background complicated what she look for in childcare:

I'm bilingual, but I'm not bicultural. My father was Black, my mother was White, my husband is Mexican. My child is half Mexican, Chicano. My grandparents are Jewish. We had all these different types of people all there and I picked parts of different cultures . . . My child is going to get a different concept of different people.

Since within-group care was problematic, another strategy that the mothers used to protect their children and themselves against racism was to choose childcare settings that were multiracial. Frances Trudeau said:

Whenever we look at places for the kids, we always look at what's the number of minority kids, specifically black kids but also minorities. We're also Jewish so what's the make-up in terms of Jews . . . [He's going] to be spending most of his day with these people, what do they believe in? What is it that he's

gonna get either subtle or not so subtle in terms of their teachings?

Several of the middle class, predominantly White daycares had made a formal commitment to diversify the ethnic composition of their staff and families they served, as well as to develop a multicultural curriculum. They offered full scholarships to children of color in order to diversify the race and ethnicities of the children in their care. Yet, even when the daycare center had a formal commitment to multiculturalism, childcare providers' behaviors and attitudes often demonstrated a lack of cultural competency that resulted in racially unsafe environments for children of color and their mothers.

Racist encounters ranged from outright hostile relations with childcare staff and other parents at the daycare to incompetent interactions with well-intentioned White childcare providers who lack experience with caring for children of color and negotiating cross-cultural interactions. Aurora Garcia, a Mexican American mother, explained how this happens:

They're all White, and they come from that perspective . . . And they have blind spots. I don't know how else to put it. They're coming from their perspectives and their reality, their experiences, and so to change that, you have to ask them to. You have to help them do it, too.

And indeed, one of the consequences of being a parent of a child of color in a majority White daycare was the increased need for parental involvement. Aurora negotiated her child's racial safety by becoming, informally, the daycare center's multicultural consultant. She intervened when the staff at her daughter's daycare center did not interrupt behavior that was racist and stereotypical, such as when a White child pretended to be an Indian and came to school stereotypically dressed in feathers and headbands, wielding a toy tomahawk, and whooping war cries. First, she brought to their awareness that certain behaviors and practices were racist and stereotypical. In the case of the White boy who came to school dressed as a stereotypical American Indian, she told them that she objected to the child's practice as well as the staff's encouragement of it by painting stereotypical Indian war paint on him. When the daycare center was responsive to her concerns and asked her to work with them on it, she talked to the children and staff, and recommended multicultural readings.

Aurora acknowledged the daycare staff's effort to improve themselves, but at the same time she was aware of the cross-cultural gaffes that were a regular part of taking her child to a predominantly White daycare center. She said:

> They are very actively trying to deal with some of these issues, and to me that felt good, culturally, you know. They made some boo-boos. [Like] at one point one of these teachers was talking to one of the [Latino] kids in Spanish, and she said, "She's bilingual, right?" [The child wasn't.] Then you have to decode what you are and [let them know that] not all Chicanos speak Spanish. So, on one level, it was like you could ignore it. But I had to talk to her and explain who I am, and this has been my experience, and people assume that if you're a particular ethnicity then you're going to do what they perceive are the stereotypical things of that ethnicity.

Because of their awareness of racism in U.S. society, mothers of color were acutely aware of whether their children would be racially safe in their childcare settings. When one is a member of a historically subordinated racial ethnic group, finding child care that provides children with racial safety is an important concern. Yet, the search is complicated by other racial/ethnic factors than simply what is the child's race or ethnic group.

## THE SEARCH FOR
## CULTURAL MAINTENANCE

Many of the mothers expressed interest in child care by racially and ethnically similar caregivers. For some, this was

motivated by the desire to protect their children and create a racially safe situation. For others, it was an explicit strategy to ensure that their children would learn about their cultural heritage and histories. Many of the mothers had been young adults at a time in history when racial ethnic groups began to take pride in claiming their cultural histories and formed nationalist movements. Prior to the 1960s, historically subordinated racial ethnic groups were expected to socialize their children to the dominant Anglo Saxon Protestant values that undergird U.S. society. As far back as the 1920s, child care services were used to "Americanize" immigrant children and their parents.[9] Mothers of color were aware of these historical biases and purposefully sought out culturally similar providers because they saw child care as a site that would influence their children's understandings of their cultural heritages.

Several Mexican American mothers sought Spanish-speaking Mexican/Mexican American caregivers for this reason. For example, when Elena Romero, a Mexican American nutritionist, first needed child care, she used this strategy and found a Spanish-speaking provider through a referral from her husband's office. She said:

> We found out about this [family] day care that was run by a preschool teacher that had decided to open up her own day care. And she was Chicana and . . . I really wanted him to know Spanish. Since birth I had [talked] to him [in Spanish] . . . Anyway, so I went to this day care and I really was impressed with the daycare center because . . . she was really organized . . . and I liked her right away, you know. Then she had like señoras, mexicanas . . . come in and cook for her and like they would make a big ol' pot of albondigas . . . a meatball soup, you know. So like they would make really good Mexican food.

Similarly, Aurora Garcia said:

> I was hoping that, given that my child would be in the household for a significant number of hours during the day, that there be some [ethnic] similarity, you know. Not that I'm

traditional, I don't consider myself traditional, but those values I wanted, kind of implanted, you know, issues of discipline, you know, being really caring and nurturing and her being familiar with Spanish.

In describing what she looked for in child care, Julie Lopez, an African American mother whose ex-husband and stepfather are Latino, said:

There's a cultural thing . . . one of the things for me, and our family, it has been really important to have [my child] in a bilingual place where she can sit down with other kids and speak Spanish and have a teacher that speaks Spanish. They sit down at lunch and they speak Spanish together. And the writing they do is both in English and Spanish and the pictures on the walls and stuff, because that cultural thing to me is really important . . . I'm always more comfortable if they're bicultural as well, versus just being bilingual.

Thus, their concerns were not simply about language skills and types of food that their children would be eating, but also addressed a broader understanding that shared cultural practices were expressions of shared cultural values.

Another issue that confronted this group of mothers of color was whether to foster cultural maintenance and racial safety at the cost of middle class opportunities. In particular, mothers who had been raised working class and were now middle class grappled with this problem. When Aurora Garcia switched her daughter from a family daycare home with a Mexican American caregiver to a predominantly White daycare center, she felt like she had to make compromises. She said:

I'm not getting the ideal. I can't find the ideal . . . there are very few children of color there. I think diversity to them is Jewish. That's being diverse culturally . . . I mean, the ideal to me would be that she be in a school where she would be learning Spanish, she would be learning those things . . . And that's a tradeoff for me right now . . . I think of all the skills she's learning right now, but there's a cultural context to them that would be nice to have.

Aurora acknowledged that because she used a predominantly White daycare center, she was raising her child in a White environment. However, she pointed out that her daughter was exposed to traditional cultural values because of who her parents are. She said, "I'm very much entrenched in who I am and what my cultural values are and my experience, and my partner is in his." Similarly, Elena Romero reconciled herself to the fact that her children would learn about their culture and history at home. She said:

[My husband and I] are both real proud of being Mexicanos, Chicanos, you know. And we're both constantly involved in the Movement kind of things. And we both have friends who are bilingual and that have kids, and, you know, our families. If we have a birthday, we have a piñata and all that stuff. So we decided, well, that they would get it from us.

Yet Aurora and Elena both realized that placing children in White daycares removed them from being fully immersed in their traditional ethnic community. Aurora said:

It's the same for a child. I mean, it really is how you play, who you play with, what you play. It's what you eat, it's how people treat you, what they say to you . . . [Her teachers] are going to present it from a white perspective because they don't have bilingual teachers. They don't have African American teachers. So for me, it's a trade off.

. . . Although on the surface it may appear that mothers of color who place their children in predominantly White daycare settings are rejecting their own cultural practices and turning their backs on their racial ethnic group, this was not the case. They were highly self-conscious that their children's child care was not fulfilling one of their major criteria for their childcare arrangements. By providing their children with the social opportunities and formal education that they had come to expect for any well-educated child of the middle class, they had to work harder at home to ensure their children learned about their cultures and histories. Furthermore, by placing themselves in predominantly White settings, they more frequently encountered racism and, more frequently and at a younger age, had to explain to their young children about race relations with White society and how to navigate them.

Both of these concerns—racial safety and cultural maintenance—reflect how membership in specific racial ethnic groups influence views of what constitutes appropriate caregiving. The concern of mothers of color for racial safety addresses their awareness that their children can be targets of racism by a society that has historically devalued their racial ethnic group. The concern for cultural maintenance reflects their preference to retain and/or retrieve traditional cultural practices and values. They recognize that childcare arrangements are an important site that serves as a source of what their children learn about their cultural practices and develop a historical consciousness.

## CONCLUSION

Mothers' concerns about racial safety and cultural maintenance call into question the current social construction of the professional model of developmentally appropriate child care as culturally neutral. The views of the mothers in this study do not reflect rigid adherence to traditional cultural practices, but rather a recognition of the significance of racism in U.S. society and their desire to have cultural learning be part of the childcare curriculum. First, they are concerned whether the caregivers are competent to negotiate cross-racial and cross-ethnic social relations, and whether their children will be treated with the same respect and positive assumptions made of white children. In short, they worried about

their children's racial safety. Second, they are concerned about whether the interpersonal interactions and formal and informal curriculum of the childcare setting supports and validates the cultural histories and practices of their racial ethnic group. This concern is beyond overt or subtle forms of racism, but also addresses the question of whether caregivers are culturally competent to positively educate children about their traditional cultures and practices. . . .

Hardly any realm of social life in the U.S. is not influenced in some way by racial ethnic stratification and racism. . . . Childcare choices is another example of how people of color experience the mundane extreme environment of racism.

Because childcare is a racially and class segregated system, a range of choices in types of child care for parents of color is limited. This is especially true for parents of color who want alternative practices and/or have been economically upwardly mobile, yet desire their children to be cared for by members of their own racial ethnic group. Mothers of color often must choose between childcare settings that provide cultural learning without the middle class opportunities and those that provide middle class educational opportunities without the cultural learning. Clearly, race and culture have great significance when mothers evaluate the quality of their childcare arrangements and choices.

## NOTES

1. Carole E. Joffe, *Friendly Intruders: Childcare Professionals and Family Life* (Berkeley: University of California Press, 1977).
2. Larner, Mary, and Anne Mitchell, "Meeting the Child Care Needs of Low-Income Families," *Child & Youth Care Forum* 21, 5 (1992):317–334; Rosier, Katherine Brown, and William A. Corsario, "Competent Parents, Complex Lives: Managing Parenthood in Poverty," *Journal of Contemporary Ethnography* 22, 2 (1993):171–204.

3. Carole E. Joffe.

4. Carole E. Joffe.

5. Stevanne Auerbach, "What Parents Want from Day Care," in *Child Care, A Comprehensive Guide: Philosophy, Programs and Practices for the Creation of Quality Services for Children,* Volume 1. *Rationale for Child Care Services, Programs vs. Politics,* ed. Stevanne Auerbach with James A. Rivaldo (New York: Human Sciences Press, 1975), 137–152.

6. Janice Hale, "The Transmission of Cultural Values to Young African American Children," *Young Children* (September 1991):7–14.

7. Harriet Pipes McAdoo, "Societal Stress: The Black Family," in *All American Women,* ed. Johnnetta B. Cole. (New York: Free Press, 1986), 189.

8. All names are pseudonyms.

9. Julia Wrigley, "Different Care for Different Kids: Social Class and Child Care Policy," *Educational Policy* 3, 4 (1989): 421–439; Wrigley has argued that different kinds of childcare are provided for kids of different socioeconomic status: enrichment opportunities that support middle class culture are provided to middle class children, whereas it is assumed that low income kids need care that interrupts their family's cultural practices.

## CRITICAL THINKING QUESTIONS

1. What does Uttal mean by "racial safety" and "cultural maintenance"? Why do both concepts reflect child-care concerns by historically subordinated racial and ethnic groups?

2. Uttal notes that "mothers of color must choose between childcare settings that provide cultural learning without the middle class opportunities and those that provide middle class educational opportunities without the cultural learning." Does this mean that parents of color must sacrifice their cultural values and practices to be upwardly mobile?

3. In your opinion, how might Uttal respond to Etzioni's argument that there are more similarities than differences across U.S. racial and ethnic groups? Are Uttal's findings limited, for example, because they're based on a very small sample of mothers? Or is Etzioni overlooking some important differences across racial/ethnic families?

# 14 The Impact of Social Class

## *Conservative:* Searching for the White Underclass

CARL F. HOROWITZ, "Searching for the White Underclass," *National Review* 47, September 11, 1995, pp. 52–56. Copyright © 1995 by National Review, Inc. Reprinted by permission.

*According to most conservatives, liberal social policies have exacerbated, rather than alleviated, inner-city ghetto values and behavior. As a result, Carl F. Horowitz argues, crime and poverty are largely problems of the black underclass. In contrast, white-majority communities are faring better because they have lower unwed motherhood rates and higher marriage and remarriage rates.*

"Every once in a while the sky really is falling," Charles Murray wrote in the October 29, 1993, *Wall Street Journal* in a guest editorial, "The Coming White Underclass." The sky was falling because whites, who make up more than four-fifths of the American population, were developing social pathologies at a fearful pace; whites might well wind up where blacks are today, and not too many years down the road either.

A decade earlier, Murray's book *Losing Ground: American Social Policy, 1950–1980* brought new thinking to the issue. The poor were made worse off by the very "anti-poverty" measures designed to improve their lot. Beginning around 1965, social pathology, from crime to drug abuse to illiteracy, took a sharp turn for the worse. It did so because we redrew the ground rules to bring out the worst in the poor—and potentially in all of us. Murray wrote:

The most compelling explanation for the market shift in the fortunes of the poor is that . . . we—meaning the not-poor and undisadvantaged—had changed the rules of the world. . . . The first effect of the new rules was to make it profitable for the poor to behave in the short term in ways that were destructive in the long term. Their second effect was to mask these long-term losses—to subsidize irretrievable mistakes. We tried to provide more for the poor and produced more poor instead. We tried to remove the barriers to escape from poverty, and inadvertently built a trap.

Now, late in 1993, Murray saw the jaws of that trap tightening further, despite disingenuous "work incentives" injected into the welfare system. The rising out-of-wedlock birth rate was the culprit. A family without a husband is simply not a viable economic unit. That is why anti-poverty assistance (roughly $350 billion in combined federal, state, and local government spending in fiscal 1994, according to the Heritage Foundation's Robert Rector) has continued to rise. The 1991 rate of births to black females out of wedlock was 68 percent, up from about 19 percent in 1955, 26 percent in 1965, 38 percent in 1970, and 55 percent in 1980. (Until 1969 "black" and "other" were included in the same category.) In many central-city neighborhoods, the figure is now around 80 percent.

This was appalling, but familiar enough. The shock was that while we were out partying, the rate among whites had reached 22 percent in 1991, more than triple the 1970 figure of 6 percent. The critical mass for a large white underclass is forming from this raw material, Murray argued. If in bygone eras "white trash" could be safely isolated from the rest of their community, to a growing extent this white underclass is coming to *define* its community. Welfare culture, and our tacit approval of it, are coming home with a vengeance. Ominously, he noted, the white illegitimacy rate is getting ever closer to where the black rate had stood in that pivotal year of 1965. In March of that year the U.S. Department of Labor released *The Negro Family: The Case of National Action*, whose author future New York Senator Daniel Patrick Moynihan, warned of a chaos that could engulf black America. Moynihan made few friends with that report, but the readers didn't have long to wait for the denouement, as rioting in Los Angeles and other cities made clear.

There is properly near-universal agreement that the 30 percent nationwide illegitimacy rate is too high. Yet consider some heresy: Suppose that whites are not doing as badly as we imagine, and that single white mothers in particular are doing better than single black mothers. In other words, let us suppose that the leading statistical indicator of an underclass, unwed motherhood, reveals less than we think.

There is a difference between *creating* and *raising* a child out of wedlock. An unmarried couple that creates a baby, and marries soon after, cannot be lumped in with couples who choose not to marry, or for that matter to remain a couple. The birth of Tiffany Trump, daughter of Donald and Marla Maples Trump, to take an extreme example, was "illegitimate," but it shortly preceded marriage. In Sweden, where for at least a decade out-of-wedlock birth rates have been at or above 50 percent, the

mother usually marries the father. The problem in this country is with the great many females who bear an illegitimate child and aren't marrying, period.

Research suggests a racial dimension here. White women, once having become mothers, appear more willing than black women to marry or find some alternative arrangement, according to a September 1992 Census Bureau study, *Studies in Household and Family Formation*. Using the Bureau's own *Survey of Income and Program Participation* and the University of Michigan's *Panel Study of Income Dynamics*, the study found in the mid Eighties that white single-mother households with children under 18 had a 16.5 percent rate of becoming another type of household within one year, and a 27.3 percent rate of becoming one within two years. The respective figures for black female-headed families with children under 18 were only 7.6 percent and 13.4 percent. Among families where the female head of household was between 15 and 29 years old, the white and black two-year rates were, respectively, 41.7 and 21.3 percent.

The difference becomes even more marked when we consider educational attainment. Among white mothers, no age specified, with 1 to 3 years of high school, the two-year rate was 29.9 percent, whereas for black mothers with the same level of education, the figure was only 11.0 percent.

Census data indicate that among divorcees, white women are more likely than black women to remarry. In 1990 61.4 percent of previously divorced white women aged 30 to 34, and 66.5 percent of such white women aged 35 to 39, had remarried. For divorced black women in these cohorts the rates were 42 and 54 percent.

Now, let us be fair to black women: The lower tendency toward marriage and remarriage among black females has a lot to do with a decline in potential mates of the same race. Census figures show that in 1970 the combined total of never-married and divorced white males stood at 11.5 million, whereas the female figure that year was only 10.5 million. By 1993 the figures had climbed to 24.4 million and 22 million. Thus, in both instances, there was a "man surplus" of about 10 percent.

For blacks, it is a different story. Whereas the figures for both single males and females were about 1.6 million in 1970, by 1993 the male and female totals were 4.7 million and 5.5 million, respectively. Excluding the widowed, eligible black females now outnumber eligible black males by about 17 percent.

The white–black differences become even more stark if we take into account the Hispanic factor. "Hispanic" is not a separate race on the standard Census form. For birth statistics, Hispanics are nearly always counted as "white." In 1991, for example, 97 percent of Hispanic mothers were reported as white, 2 percent as black, and 1 percent as other.

In 1992 there were 3,201,678 births to white mothers. But the figure for *non-Hispanic* white mothers was 2,527,207. That leaves a gap of around 675,000. And 39.1 percent of Hispanic births were out of wedlock. A quick calculation: The Hispanic out-of-wedlock rate was 16.5 percentage points above the overall white rate of 22.6 percent. Since Hispanic mothers account for roughly 20 percent of all white births the non-Hispanic-white illegitimacy rate in 1992 was about 18.5 percent.

In the youth culture today, whites imitate blacks more than vice versa. Take a trip to your local shopping mall or school grounds, and note the common fashion accoutrements of white youths—baggy shirts, baggy shorts, and baseball caps. The August 22, 1994 cover story of *New York* magazine took note of such style as indicative of a massive attitude adjustment: white youths are internalizing modern black youths' disdain for achievement. Studying hard, planning for the future, and staying out of trouble are examples of—God forbid—"acting white." Youths instead emulate a dumbed-down, French-fry celebrity circuit whose opinion leaders

include Jessica Hahn, Tonya Harding, Roger Clinton, and Roseanne Barr.

Even assuming that flashy trend is destiny, it is questionable that it has all that much relation to out-of-wedlock births. The two defining features of parenthood—vulgarity and provincialism—can take many forms, none necessarily inimical to forming nuclear families or taking steady work. Are whites really becoming an underclass, or just slumming around more conspicuously these days? Murray believes the former. He is fearful that the social policy and cultural forces let loose thirty years ago are now being institutionalized. The signs of white social regression can be seen first hand, he argued in the *Wall Street Journal*:

> Look for certain schools in white neighborhoods to get a reputation as being unteachable, with large numbers of disruptive students and indifferent parents. Talk to the police; listen for stories about white neighborhoods where the incidence of domestic disputes and casual violence has been shooting up. Look for white neighborhoods with high concentrations of drug activity and large numbers of men who have dropped out of the labor force. Some readers will recall reading the occasional news story about such places already.

*Look for those neighborhoods.* Ronald Mincy, then with the Urban Institute and now with the Ford Foundation, has done just that. He uncovered 880 tracts in the 1980 Census that fit a four-part definition of an "underclass" neighborhood (high proportions of un- or under-employed males over 16, single mothers, welfare dependency, and teenaged high-school dropouts). In these tracts, containing some 2.5 million people, Mincy found a racial breakdown of 59 percent black, 28 percent non-Hispanic white, and 10 percent Hispanic.

Susan Wiener, a research associate at the Urban Institute, found that the increase from 1980 to 1990 wasn't dramatic. The number of underclass Census tracts rose from 880 to 928, with the number of people in them increasing to only a little under 2.7 million. The 1990 racial breakdown was 59 percent black, 20 percent non-Hispanic white, and 20 percent Hispanic. The non-Hispanic-white proportion actually *declined* during the Eighties. Even more tellingly, the percentage of blacks, whites, and Hispanics in underclass areas, as a proportion of their entire respective nationwide population, fell during the Eighties. Where non-Hispanic whites in underclass tracts constituted 0.37 percent of U.S. whites in 1980, for example, they constituted only 0.29 percent in 1990. While all these numbers refer more to *concentration* than to size, they do suggest that the geographic spread of the underclass is approaching a limit.

If there is a long swing of history, it would seem to be a *lessening* of the coarser forms of behavior typical of "white trash." Have we forgotten the Irish "Westies" of Manhattan's Hell's Kitchen? Are we to believe that depictions of violent whites in bygone decades—*West Side Story, Blackboard Jungle,* the working-class/middle-class whiteboy confrontations of S. E. Hinton's 1960s Tulsa (*Rumblefish, The Outsiders*)—bore no relation to reality then? "With two generations of prosperity, white trash looks like gentry," Harper Lee once observed. A lot of ex-trash may be way beyond that point.

Look for . . . Davenport, Iowa, where six white teenagers were convicted of the murder of a local teenaged girl. An honor student, Michelle Jensen was a naive, thrill-seeking Girl Who Knew Too Much (about a planned convenience-store robbery—she refused to lend a getaway car). The killers were members of a local gang who had dubbed themselves the Vice Lords, after a notorious black Chicago gang. Much was made of the fact that five of the youths had grown up in female-headed homes (though they were not necessarily born out of wedlock). Only *Spin* magazine's Marc Cooper took the time to note that the real wheels in the gang were blacks, many from out of town.

According to a recent survey by George Knox, a professor at Chicago State University's criminal-justice department, law-enforcement officials in a majority of Illinois rural counties now complain of local gang activity. But are "heartland" and "white" synonymous? In Davenport, police estimate there are over two dozen gangs, comprising some 2,500 members. The estimated racial breakdown: 50 percent black, 40 percent white, 10 percent Latino and Asian. "These little white s---heads act black, they talk black, they think they're tough, but they are mutts without their gangs, just idiots. They get recruited by the older black gang members who run them like tops," noted Davenport police detective Lynn Kindred.

Where are all the female-headed households, the gunpowder for tomorrow's underclass? Unpublished data on some 23,000 U.S. communities gathered by the Census Bureau for the Associated Press in 1994 indicate they're mostly outside white-majority communities. Nationwide, black children are more than twice as likely as whites to be living with a single parent. Benton Harbor, Mich., a declining industrial community with a population of 12,800, held the dubious honor in 1990 of ranking highest in single-parent families as a proportion of all family households—83 percent—among the nation's roughly 3,000 largest communities. Benton Harbor High School is known locally as "Maternity High." Benton Harbor, according to the 1990 Census of Population, was 92.2 percent black.

The nine other communities making the top ten for single-parent families were Brownsville, Fla., Highland Park, Mich., Gladeview, Fla., Opa-locka, Fla., Camden, N.J., East St. Louis, Ill., East Cleveland, Ohio, Asbury Park, N.J., and Tuskegee, Ala. In not one did whites account for anything close to a majority of its female-headed families. Asbury Park and Camden had the *lowest* black populations, at 59.4 percent and 56.4 percent, and five had black populations in excess of 90 percent. The ten communities with the *lowest* proportions of single parents were: Western

Springs, Ill., Lighthouse Point, Fl., Morton Grove, Ill., Bel Air North, Md., Scarsdale, N.Y., Winnetka, Ill., Westchester, Ill., Colleyville, Tex., Lincolnwood, Ill., and Massapequa Park, N.Y. Scarsdale's 1990 black population of 2.2 percent was the highest of any of these communities, and eight of them had black populations of under 1 percent.

These enormous discrepancies in racial composition cannot help but cast severe doubt upon predictions that mainly white communities all across the U.S. will soon be in much the same straits as black ones today. The sky is not falling.

**CRITICAL THINKING QUESTIONS**

1. What, according to Horowitz, is an underclass? Do families from all racial and ethnic groups make up the underclass?

2. Why does Horowitz blame the antipoverty policies of the 1960s and 1970s for creating an underclass?

3. Why does Horowitz conclude that white communities across the United States are unlikely to become an underclass? Would the conclusions be different if a definition of underclass included such measures as unemployment or low wages?

# 14 The Impact of Social Class

## *Centrist:* What Money Can't Buy

Susan E. Mayer, *What Money Can't Buy: Family Income and Children's Life Chances* (Cambridge, MA: Harvard University Press, 1997), pp. 143–156. Copyright © 1997 by the President and Fellows of Harvard College. Reprinted by permission of the publisher.

*Many people believe that parental income is the single most important influence on children's life chances. In contrast, Susan E. Mayer argues that material hardship is not the only factor that determines how children fare. Once children's basic material needs are met, parental behavior and characteristics are more important in how children turn out than anything that additional money can buy.\**

### RAISING PARENTAL INCOME

My review of the evidence suggests three major conclusions. First, though the effect of parental income is nowhere near as large as many political liberals imagine, neither is it zero, as many political conservatives seem to believe. Second, though the effect of parental income on any one outcome appears to be fairly small, higher income has some effect on most outcomes, so its cumulative impact across all outcomes may be substantial. Third, one reason that parental income is not more important to children's outcomes is probably that government policies have done a lot to ensure that poor children get basic necessities most of the time. Each of these conclusions calls for some elaboration.

\* Mayer's study is based on cross-sectional and longitudinal surveys of U.S. households: the Current Population Survey (CPS), the Panel Study of Income Dynamics (PSID), and the National Longitudinal Survey of Youth (NLSY).

### Modest Effects

If the results in this book are correct, young children's test scores are likely to improve by one or two points when their parents' income doubles. Both teenage childbearing and high school dropout rates might decline, but the magnitude of the expected decline is uncertain (between one-tenth and one-quarter for teenage childbearing, and about half that much for dropping out). Doubling parental income probably raises a child's eventual years of education by about a fifth of a year. It might also improve male workers' wages and earnings, but it could increase men's chances of being idle. Doubling parents' income seems to reduce young single motherhood by between 8 and 20 percent. Increasing welfare benefits does not appear to improve children's outcomes.

To put these results in perspective, it is helpful to estimate what would happen to children's outcomes if we could double the household income of the poorest 20 percent of children through income transfers, tax credits, higher wages, guaranteed work, or some other strategy. The 1989 CPS suggests that this would require increasing the average income of the poorest quintile from about $10,000 to about $20,000 (in 1992 dollars). By historical standards, this would be a huge increase. The purchasing power of the poorest 20 percent of Americans has never been near $20,000. In absolute terms, such an increase would move almost all children above the poverty line and would move most of them above 125 percent of the poverty line, which was $14,228 for a family of four in 1992. For simplicity, I assume that we can accomplish this change by doubling income from all sources and that this leaves parents' choices about work, welfare, and fertility unchanged. This assumption is obviously not realistic, because all strategies for increasing income create incentives that alter people's choices. But this is still a useful mental experiment.

Among the poorest 20 percent of American teenage girls, about 40 percent have babies before they turn twenty years old. The largest estimate of the true effect of income suggests that doubling parents' income would reduce teenage childbearing by about 10 percentage points, from 40 to 30 percent. Given this change, the overall teenage childbearing rate in the United States would fall from 20 to 18 percent.

One reason the overall teenage childbearing rate would fall so little is that 60 percent of teenage births are to girls whose families are not low income. Raising the income of low-income families will not reduce teenage births to these families (and could actually increase them if redistributing income to low-income families required reducing the income of more affluent families). Doubling everyone's income should, of course, have a much greater effect on the teenage childbearing rate. But we do not know how to do that, and if what really matters is relative income, doubling everyone's income might not have any effect anyway.

Using these same assumptions, we can calculate that doubling low-income families' income would reduce the overall high school dropout rate from 17.3 to 16.1 percent, and increase the mean years of education from 12.80 years to 12.83 years. Male idleness would increase, and the percentage of young women who become single mothers would hardly change. From this we can conclude that any realistic income redistribution strategy is likely to have a relatively small impact on the overall incidence of social problems. For example, the EITC [Economic Income Tax Credit] increases family income by at most about 10 percent. Nonetheless, the overall benefit to children from extra income could still be greater than the benefits of any other policy that costs the same.

## Diverse Effects

In its 1964 annual report, the Council of Economic Advisors wrote, "[Poverty's] ugly by-products include ignorance, disease, delinquency, crime, irresponsibility, immorality, and indifference. None of these social evils and hazards will, of course, wholly disappear with the elimination of poverty. But their severity will be markedly reduced" (*Economic Report of the President*, 1964). As this list suggests, income-support policies are supposed to solve many social problems at once by changing one thing that seems common to them all. Income is the ultimate "multipurpose" policy instrument.

In contrast, what I call "targeted" solutions try to solve a narrowly defined problem, such as hunger, with one solution, such as Food Stamps. All noncash transfer programs are targeted policies. Another approach, which was characteristic of welfare policies at the local level until the 1960s and is still often used by state and local governments, is what I call "micro intervention." By this I mean one-on-one services for individuals or families. These services can include education, medical care, family therapy, homemaker services, school counseling programs, drug and alcohol treatment, and so on. Psychologists, who see problems in individual terms, tend to favor such programs. Most other social scientists dislike them because they are expensive, often paternalistic, and frequently create incentives for abuse.

Multipurpose solutions assume that one cause has many different effects. Changing that cause can thus solve many problems at once. Raising income is not the only candidate for this role. Just as many liberals believe that low income causes most of the problems that are correlated with poverty, many conservatives believe that single parenthood causes most of the problems correlated with it. Conservatives therefore expect that getting parents to marry and stay married will solve the problems that liberals propose to cure with higher wages or more generous public assistance. Racism and racial discrimination often play a similar role in discussions of minority children's problems.

Multipurpose policies will only work if three conditions are met: a single cause must really affect many outcomes; we must correctly identify this cause; and we must be able to change it. Yet even when multipurpose policies meet all these conditions, they often fail politically because they are impossible to evaluate.

### HOW MUCH IS ENOUGH?

I have argued that one reason income does not have a large effect on any one outcome is that programs such as Food Stamps, housing subsidies, and Medicaid have helped most American families meet their basic material needs. Once basic material needs are met, factors other than income become increasingly important to how children fare. But I have not tried to estimate how much money is enough to meet these needs.

It is not easy to decide how much is enough. The more resources families have, the less likely they are to face serious material hardships. But no one has found a breakpoint in the income distribution below which material hardship becomes much worse; nor are any of the material hardships for which I have data completely absent in the top half of the income distribution. This is because income is not the only determinant of material hardship. A family's income needs depend on its size, the health of its members, the efficiency with which it consumes goods and services, and the local cost of living. Tastes also vary from family to family.

Imagine again the two identical families headed by Mrs. Smith and Mrs. Jones. Mrs. Smith has all the attributes of an average middle-class American, but has fallen on hard times. When we give her $600 a month plus Food Stamps, she can find a way to shelter and feed her family. Mrs. Jones suffers from serious depression. She lacks the energy to search for cheap housing or travel to a cheap grocery store. Her depression may also have isolated her from friends and family who could help. The same resources do not buy as much for her children as for Mrs. Smith's children.

When the poor have the same values and skills as everyone else but cannot afford to buy food, housing, and other basic necessities, either income transfers or transfers of basic necessities can help their children substantially. But when the poor are considerably less competent than the middle class, income transfers may not help as much. Consequently, the important question for policy makers is not how much is enough, but rather what is the right kind of help. This depends on the social context of poverty.

If poverty occurred randomly, parental traits would by definition be unrelated to poverty. At least in the short run, the poor would be just like the middle class except that they would have less money. In the long run, however, poverty itself could alter parental traits.

But poverty is never completely random, even though it can sometimes be caused by more or less random events. When large numbers of fathers were killed in the Civil War, for example, poverty among their widows and children was not strongly associated with undesirable parental characteristics. Some Civil War widows escaped destitution because their husbands left them money, because they could work, or because they lived with relatives. Still, widowhood did plunge mothers from very different backgrounds into poverty. In the Great Depression, when unemployment was as high as 50 percent in some cities, poverty again struck all kinds of families. It was not completely random, but it was common enough for most people to think it could happen to them or to members of their family. Under such circumstances the poor were more like everyone else than they are today.

As countries get richer, they often implement policies that reduce poverty among families hit by random catastrophes such as the death of a spouse, protracted illness, or job loss. When countries do this, poverty declines. But those who remain poor also become less like everyone else. When barriers to work are lowered, as they have been for both women and racial minorities in this century, those who remain jobless are more exceptional than they were when these barriers were higher. When almost all employers discriminated against blacks, it was not surprising that blacks were more likely than whites to be poor. The fact that most blacks now escape long-term poverty leads to the suspicion that those blacks who remain poor today are different from those who do better.

A talented child born to bright, diligent, well-meaning parents who are too poor to feed the family might have trouble in school. When the government makes it possible for most parents to feed their children, other investments become more important in determining who succeeds and who does not. When poor children can get enough to eat but often cannot afford to go to school, variations in access to schooling rather than a nutritious diet will predict success. If the government then requires everyone to attend free public school up to age sixteen, variations in schooling after age sixteen will predict success. Thus if the state equalizes most important material and pedagogic investments in children, social and psychological differences between parents will explain a larger percentage of the variation in the success of their children. The marginal returns to additional market resources will also fall.

## What Kind of Help?

. . . Most families that become poor are headed by competent parents who can care for their children quite adequately during normal times. When they fall on hard times due to unemployment, a change in family composition, or illness, they need short-term cash assistance just as they would if their homes were destroyed by a flood or an earthquake. Most of them will never need any other kind of help, so writing a government check on behalf of their children is quicker, cheaper, and more effective than any other form of help. Short-term cash help does not appear to create serious incentives for adults to behave in ways that hurt their children.

Unlike the short-term poor, the long-term poor tend to be quite different from the nonpoor. When families fall on hard times and stay there for years, this means they cannot or will not find a way to support themselves. The children in such families often need outside help that goes beyond economic support. This does not mean that the persistently poor are all lazy, ignorant, uncaring, or neglectful—they are not. Some are chronically ill or have children who are chronically ill. Some are depressed or disturbed. Some have very low cognitive abilities. As one sympathetic teacher in an impoverished school put it, "We should not confuse families' inability to do with their desire to do. That always bothers me. It makes me uncomfortable talking about these problems. It makes me feel like we are saying that folks don't care. One of the most astounding things to me since I've been here is how few parents there are—in fact I could only think of one or two if I thought real hard—that don't seem to care. Folks care. They want for their kids."

Some of the chronically poor are drug addicts and alcoholics. An assistant principal in an economically mixed elementary school in the South told this story:

> Drugs are a really big problem here. I had a little girl, a tough little girl who always had her guard up. One day she just let it all down and began to cry. When I asked her why she was crying, she said she just wanted everything to be like it had been in the third grade. I asked what it had been like in the third grade. She said she had gotten a certificate for good attendance and some other award and her mom had hung them up on the refrigerator. She said her mom had been so happy. That was before the crack. "Since the crack my mommy doesn't care any more," she cried. This mom was not a bad mom. She cared, and she had been good, but she just got into trouble and there is no help for her—no place for her to turn, and now this little girl is miserable.

It is hard to imagine that giving this girl's mother more money will help much. It is also hard to imagine that providing additional programs for this little girl will help her much unless we also find a way to help her mother.

Some persistently poor parents are shiftless and neglectful. The homes in which they raise their children attain neither the moral nor the material standards that most Americans believe children require. Political pressure to improve the behavior of these parents is an inevitable and appropriate response. Nonetheless, it seems clear that one thing we should not do is refuse to provide any help at all. That solution would give the most troubled parents less money to buy basic necessities for their children. It would also remove the most disorganized and incompetent families from the supervision of agencies that could potentially help the family follow community norms about how parents should raise

their children. If the most vulnerable and inadequate families are deprived of any legal source of economic support, at least some will turn to illegitimate sources, such as prostitution, selling drugs, or other crimes, to make ends meet. Absent any state support, some women and children will be more likely to remain in abusive and destructive relationships with men. Others will turn to "social prostitution," serial relationships with men willing to help pay their bills.[1] Thus the fact that increases in parental income cannot be expected to improve any one outcome greatly does not mean that if we *reduce* cash or noncash transfers children will not suffer as a consequence. . . .

## CHANGING PARENTS' NONECONOMIC CHARACTERISTICS

I have argued that the stable parental characteristics that affect children's outcomes are often the same characteristics that employers value. Based on my data, I can only guess what these might be. Indeed, even the use of the term "stable" may be misleading. These parental characteristics are only stable in the context of a particular person's life. They may be partly innate, but even then their expression depends on parents' own childhood experiences and their adult attitudes, values, goals, and predispositions, which are in turn influenced by social structure and institutions. The fact that a trait is relatively stable certainly does not mean we cannot change it. Height is stable in adulthood, but changing children's diets can change their adult height. Occupations are also quite stable, but they can still be changed. . . .

If we want to improve children's outcomes we need to study the effect of these noneconomic characteristics as carefully as we study the effect of income. Parents' education, age when their children are born, and race account for up to half of the observed correlation between children's outcomes and parental income. Understanding each of these relationships would require careful study.

## Parents' Education

We know that each additional year of parental education is associated with better outcomes for children. But, as with income, views about why parental education predicts children's outcomes fall on a spectrum. Liberals tend to believe that individuals learn skills in school that make them better workers and better parents. The extreme version of this "skills" model holds that if mothers who currently have, say, ten years of schooling had spent two additional years in school, their children's outcomes would be like those of children whose mothers had a high school diploma.[2]

Many conservatives believe that character and competence are primarily inherited from parents. They therefore see parental educational attainment mainly as a proxy for genetic propensities or effective upbringing. Parents pass these advantages on to their children. Children with these advantages get higher test scores, find school more rewarding, and stay in school longer than those with fewer advantages.[3] From this perspective, getting high school dropouts to stay in school longer will not appreciably improve either their job prospects or their children's outcomes. Almost no one believes the extreme version of this argument, but many believe that the benefits of schooling are considerably smaller than simple comparisons between dropouts and graduates imply. Empirical estimates also suggest that parental education has some important effects on children's outcomes even when many parental characteristics are controlled.[4]

## Young Mothers

Children born to very young mothers have worse outcomes than children born to older mothers. Teenage mothers receive less education and earn less money than mothers who delay childbearing until they are at least twenty. Many people think that if we could get all teenage mothers to delay childbearing, their education and earnings would improve, which would help their children. Yet the best available evidence, based on comparisons between pregnant teenagers who have babies and those who have spontaneous miscarriages, suggests that delaying motherhood does not actually lead to much more maternal education or earnings (Hotz et al. 1995). Once again, the unobserved characteristics that cause teenagers to become pregnant also influence their education and wages. These same characteristics presumably influence children's outcomes, too.

## Race

Black children fare worse than white children on all outcomes. But when I control parents' income, black children are less likely than white children to drop out of high school. Black children also receive more post-secondary education than whites with the same family income. Parental income also appears to account for some of the other differences between black and white children's outcomes, but the difference in [cognitive assessment] scores, single motherhood, men's wages, and male idleness remains large.[5]

If low income is mainly a proxy for unmeasured parental characteristics that reduce parental income and hurt children, increasing the income of black parents through income transfers, child tax credits, child-support payments, or increased earnings would not by itself improve their children's life chances very much. The fact that income is lower among black parents implies that the unobserved parental characteristics that employers value and that affect such outcomes as children's test scores and teenage childbearing are more prevalent among white parents. These parental characteristics depend partly on parents' own childhood experiences. They also depend on the attitudes, values, and goals that parents acquire in the course of dealing with a predominantly white society. It should therefore come as no surprise that more black families than white families in the United States end up at a competitive disadvantage, both in the race for good jobs and in preparing their children for that race.

Values and attitudes are like habits: the longer one adheres to them, the harder they are to change. When the stakes are high enough, people can break many habits and acquire new ones. But because most government interventions are small compared with all the other things that influence parental behavior, policy makers who want to change adults' attitudes about work and family by changing the economic incentives built into government programs are usually disappointed. This is especially true if the attitudes they want to change are constantly reinforced by parents' relatives and friends.

## Single Parenthood

Americans have always thought that growing up with only one parent is bad for children. The rapid spread of single-parent families over the past generation does not seem to have altered this consensus much. Many people see eliminating single parenthood as a panacea for children's problems. . . .

Everyone agrees that when parents live apart their children are poorer. Once we hold income constant, moreover, the adverse effect of growing up in a single-parent family drops by roughly half (McLanahan and Sandefur 1994). This does not mean that we should control income when we estimate the effect of living arrangements. Low income is a direct consequence of single parenthood, so if we want to know the effect of single parenthood, we want to include the income effect. But the key role of income in accounting for the effect of single parenthood on children does imply that we could sharply reduce the adverse effect of single parenthood on children if we were to transfer large sums of money to custodial parents

(or if we could devise a way of making absent parents do this).

As we have seen, however, it is risky to take calculations of this sort at face value. If income predicts children's later success because it is a proxy for other unmeasured parental characteristics, transferring money to single mothers will not help children as much as standard statistical models imply. Both low income and single parenthood may in fact be correlated with poor outcomes for children because they are proxies for unmeasured parental characteristics. This suspicion is bolstered by the well-established finding that when single parenthood is a by-product of death rather than divorce or failure to marry, children do about as well as children living with two parents who have comparable incomes (McLanahan and Sandefur 1994).

## WHERE THE TROUBLE BEGINS

Trying to figure out what the government can do to help poor children is not a task to be taken lightly. The results in this book suggest that although children's opportunities are unequal, income inequality is not the primary reason. Despite the fact that liberals have worked hard to reduce the influence of family income on children, they are unlikely to believe the claim that they have largely succeeded, much less greet the claim with a sense of accomplishment. Liberals worked hard for the cash and noncash transfers that have helped reduce the most serious material deprivations. These programs appear to have narrowed the gap between rich and poor children's material living conditions. Liberals also lobbied for Head Start, compensatory education, and guaranteed student loans for college in order to narrow the gap in educational opportunities. These programs appear to have reduced the impact of parental income on children's life chances; eliminating them could increase the effect of parental income on children's outcomes.

But if advantage comes from having parents whose depression is treated rather than left untreated, from having parents who speak English rather than another language, from having parents who love to read or do math, or parents who love rather than tolerate their children, it will be much harder to equalize opportunity. As a teacher who had taught in both the affluent north shore and the poverty-ridden west side of Chicago put it, "Money can ease the path, but it doesn't hit deep down where the trouble begins."

## NOTES

1. See Edin and Lein (1997). The phrase "social prostitution" was used by a welfare recipient interviewed by Edin and Lein to describe her relationships with men, which were not for love, but not just for money either.

2. See Angrist and Krueger (1991); Ashenfelter and Krueger (1994); Ashenfelter and Rouse (1995); and Becker (1993) for discussions of this debate and support for the "skills" hypothesis.

3. See Herrnstein and Murray (1994); Plomin et al. (1988); and Scarr and Weinberg (1978) for support of the "hereditarian" view.

4. In controlling mothers' [intelligence test] scores, each additional year of maternal education increases test scores by between one half and one point.

5. The PSID sample I use does not include Hispanic respondents, but in the NLSY, children of Hispanic parents score lower than children of white parents on the three cognitive assessments. In fact, the scores of Hispanic children are similar to the scores for black children once parental characteristics and family size are controlled.

## REFERENCES

Angrist, Joshua, and Alan Krueger. 1991. "Does Compulsory Schooling Attendance Affect Schooling and Earnings?" *Quarterly Journal of Economics* 56(4):979–1014.

Ashenfelter, Orley, and Alan Krueger. 1994. "Estimating the Returns to Schooling Using a New Sample of Twins." *American Economic Review* 84:1157–1173.

Ashenfelter, Orley, and Cecilia Rouse. 1995. "Income, Schooling, and Ability." Unpublished manuscript.

Becker, Gary. 1993. *Human Capital. A Theoretical and Empirical Analysis with Special Reference to Education*. Chicago: The University of Chicago Press.

*Economic Report of the President*. 1964. Washington, D.C.: Government Printing Office.

Edin, Kathryn, and Laura Lein. 1997. *Making Ends Meet: How Single Mothers Survive Welfare and Low-Wage Jobs*. New York: Russell Sage Foundation.

Herrnstein, Richard, and Charles Murray. 1994. *The Bell Curve: Intelligence and Class Structure in American Life*. New York: Free Press.

Hotz, V. Joseph, Susan Williams McElroy, and Seth Sanders. 1995. "The Costs and Consequences of Teenage Childbearing for Mothers." In *Kids Having Kids: The Consequences and Costs of Teenage Childbearing in the United States*. Report to the Robin Hood Foundation.

McLanahan, Sara, and Gary Sandefur. 1994. *Growing Up with a Single Parent*. Cambridge, Mass.: Harvard University Press.

Plomin, Robert, John DeFries, and David Fulker. 1988. *Nature and Nurture during Infancy and Early Childhood*. New York: Cambridge University Press.

Scarr, Sandra, and Richard Weinberg. 1978. "The Influence of 'Family Background' on Intellectual Attainment." *American Sociological Review* 43:674–692.

## CRITICAL THINKING QUESTIONS

1. Why does Mayer contend that income inequality is not the primary explanation in children's positive or negative outcomes?

2. How might Mayer respond to Horowitz's argument that unwed motherhood is the major "cause" of poverty and crime?

3. Is Mayer suggesting that all forms of welfare assistance should be abolished?

# 14 The Impact of Social Class

## *Liberal/Feminist:* Making Ends Meet

KATHRYN EDIN AND LAURA LEIN, *Making Ends Meet: How Single Mothers Survive Welfare and Low-Wage Work* (New York: Russell Sage Foundation, 1997), pp. 127–136. © 1997 Russell Sage Foundation. Used with permission of the publisher.

*As you saw in Chapter 12, many conservatives and centrists believe that employed middle-class mothers should stay home and raise their children. In contrast, conservatives, especially, contend that poor mothers should get a job instead of staying at home and raising their children (see the article by Horowitz). As Kathryn Edin and Laura Lein show, some mothers go to extraordinary lengths to stay off welfare. Living on low wages is extremely difficult, however, and poses significant risks to both mothers and their children. In this selection, Edin and Lein describe some of the liabilities of single mothers who are struggling to become financially independent.\**

### THE LIABILITIES OF WORKING

Many of the wage-reliant women [those in low-wage jobs] said that they were no better off financially than they would have been on welfare, that there was little prospect of promotion in their jobs, that they worked in industries characterized by unstable employment, and that working full time placed substantial strains on their ability to be a good parent. These were the same concerns that welfare-reliant mothers [those receiving cash welfare] had about trading work for welfare.

\* This study is based on in-depth interviews with 379 white, black, and Mexican-American single mothers— 214 welfare recipients and 165 low-wage earners—in Boston, Chicago, San Antonio, and Charleston, South Carolina.

### No Better Off

One mother summed up the experiences of the majority of our wage-reliant mothers when she told us,

Five dollars an hour is nothing to live on. When I was on AFDC I was really scraping. Even with my job now, if I told people my income now, people would look at me and say, "How come you can't budget your money better?" Even though I pay [market] rent, they say I should still have enough money [to make ends meet every month]. I don't mind working, but I feel bad [when I have to go to my relatives for money]. They feel that I shouldn't need it because I'm working now. I [need] to make $10 an hour because I have to pay rent, clothes, food.... [Now that] I'm working for $5 an hour, people tell me that I am doing better for myself [than I was on welfare]. But I'm not.

I'm not getting anything more than when I was on aid.

Another mother expressed similar frustrations. When she ran out of money for food at the end of the month, she had to rely on an upstairs neighbor to feed her children. In addition, her landlady let her clean the apartment building and grounds in exchange for a reduction in rent. She also employed other money-saving strategies:

> We have a lot of beans and rice. I make a lot of bread. We don't have any luxuries. My sister cuts my son's and my hair for free. We can't afford real milk so we drink powdered. I mean, I am on a very strict budget. By the time I get that lousy check and pay rent, electricity, and gas, I have to make that last dollar stretch across the street. I usually do [laundry] by hand. I keep things washed out in the sink. For [my clothes] I go to the thrift store. For cigarettes, sometimes I roll my own.

National data suggest that the financial hardships our wage-reliant mothers reported were the rule rather than the exception. Longitudinal data on mothers who leave welfare for a job suggest that one in three will remain below the official poverty threshold after one year. In the second year, these mothers' chances of falling below the official threshold *increase* to about 46 percent. Moreover, most of the other mothers are only slightly above the official threshold and far below the amount mothers really need to achieve self-sufficiency (U.S. House of Representatives 1994, 724).[1]

## No Long-Term Payoff

Not only were wage-reliant women struggling to make ends meet in the present, they saw little prospect for improvement in the future. The types of positions these women held offered little opportunity for promotion and few rewards for job experience, and their employers seldom offered any training or education.

One Charleston woman who had just started working in a factory told us, "There have been people who have been there like two or three years, and they're not making very much. They're making like fifty or seventy-five cents [more per hour than I am]." Another wage-reliant mother told us that she had fourteen years of low-wage work experience and had never received assistance from a government welfare program. Even though she had worked virtually every day of her adult life, she had never made more than she was earning at her current job—$5 an hour. She told our interviewers,

> I always worked—the longest was maybe four months I'd stay at home. I kept us going. . . . I worked in a shoe factory. I took care of an old lady that had a stroke. I worked in a circuit place, where you hook up circuit [boards]. When I lived in Philadelphia I worked in a luncheonette. I was a short-order cook. I worked in a sewing factory to make leather jackets that the police wear in Philadelphia. I ended up getting laid off because I worked too fast. I worked in a factory that made curtains. Worked in another factory that made [neck braces]. I worked for a home supply store [as a stock clerk]. I worked in day care for two years [while my daughter was an infant, because I could take her with me for free].

> QUESTION: HAVE YOU EVER EARNED MORE THAN $5 AN HOUR?
> All lower, everything has been lower. This is the best-paying job I ever had.

One wage-reliant mother told us that no matter how many times she had switched jobs, she could never seem to escape the $5-an-hour ghetto. When we met her in 1991, she had been working steadily at a variety of low-wage jobs for more than a decade. Her first job was in a clerical position at a military contracting firm, where she made $4.75 an hour. When cuts in the federal defense budget forced the company to lay her off, she took another clerical position at a law office, where she was paid $5 an hour. When her boss at the law office told her she could not get promoted without training as a legal secretary or a paralegal, she took a clerical job with a large teaching hospital that offered its employees assistance with tuition. She never managed to enroll in school, however, because she could not find an affordable babysitter to take care of her children while she was away at evening classes.

Frustrated by the lack of opportunity for promotion at the hospital, she quit that job for yet another clerical job at the county courthouse that paid the same hourly wage but included benefits. When the county budget was tightened, she was laid off again. When we spoke with her one year later, she had signed up with a temporary agency and had managed to get work for nine of the last twelve months. She said she would have been satisfied with any of the jobs she had held during that time, but none of the employers could afford to take her on year-round.

One of our Chicago respondents had a work history illustrating the same constraints:

My first job I had, I worked at a hamburger place. . . . I didn't like it there much because there wasn't a chance for advancement, and they didn't want to give you raises. If they did, it was like five and ten cents, and it wasn't very often. At the restaurant place, I got paid every week. It was like $4 an hour and I made like $175 to $200 a week. So I stopped working there, and I got a job at the Cookie Factory. I really liked that because I made a little more money. But they really didn't give me benefits there. I made like $4.25 an hour. . . . Then my girlfriend, she was waitressing at this restaurant [and I went there to work]. I liked it a lot because I made like $50 [on a good day] in tips beside my regular paycheck. [But they didn't have any benefits either]. And the tips varied, you know. [In a good week], I made almost $400, [but in a bad week I made less than $200]. I couldn't take the uncertainty.

Then I was a receptionist for a guy for a year, but then he went out of business. I really liked that [job]. I got to talk to people. He had benefits and everything. When he went out of business it really hurt me. I made $5 when I first started. Then while I was there I got up to $7 an hour. So that was like $300 a week [plus the benefits].

So then I was on AFDC for a while after I stopped working there [because I couldn't find a job].

Right now, I'm a sandwich maker for [a college] food service. I make like $350 every two weeks plus $50 a week for [the babysitting I do on weekends]. I'll get a $1 raise in another six months. No promotion though. They really don't give promotions too much. They'll give you a raise before they'll give you a promotion, because the next promotion up is like the assistant director or the director, and you have to go back to school for that.

This mother's experience typifies the problems faced by low-wage single mothers in the late 1980s and early 1990s. They frequently moved from one position to another as one job evaporated and another appeared. These were primarily lateral moves, and wage-reliant single mothers rarely saw much improvement in their wages, benefits, or career prospects as a result. For these working mothers the labor market was not a ladder leading upward to better wages and opportunities but a carousel on which they went around and around in circles, with an occasional change of horses.

**Precarious Nature of Work**

Not only does low-wage work pay as badly as welfare without much opportunity for advancement, it is much less reliable. First, labor markets in many cities contain a large number of seasonal jobs. In order to remain employed full-time, year-round, our mothers who worked in seasonal occupations had to move among three or four jobs. Even jobs that were not seasonal were often unstable, either in hours or in tenure. Some industries such as fast food restaurants and retail sales rarely offered incumbents enough hours to make ends meet, and many workers could not predict how many hours they would be assigned in a given week. Other industries were subject to frequent layoffs, mergers, or other shake-ups. One wage-reliant mother had been laid off three times between April 1990 and October 1991. She collected unemployment between these jobs and expected to continue this cycle. Another mother in a similar situation commented,

> Before I had [my baby], I worked at a stock-broker firm. [After I got off welfare,] I work[ed] putting computers together. I worked there off and on for a while before they hired me full time. Then I got laid off. Now I am working part time doing telemarketing. I was recently upgraded to full-time temporarily [but they say that won't necessarily last].

Like this mother, many of our low-wage mothers were employed fewer hours than they wished. One mother tried to resolve this problem by combining informal babysitting with work at a fast food restaurant. Although she doubled up with friends to save rent, and her roommates watched her child for free while she was working, she still could not make ends meet. She told us she planned to go back on welfare and babysit "under the table" until she could find a better job.

Corporate buyouts, mergers, and takeovers can affect the earning power of low-wage workers as well. One of our Charleston respondents had worked at a large hotel chain for ten years, where she was initially hired as a receptionist. During her first year of employment, she proved herself by showing up early, staying late, and never missing a day of work. As a result, she was promoted to the payroll division and then to a supervisory position in the payroll department, where she earned $8 an hour.

Three years before our interviews began, a large corporation bought the hotel chain. The new parent company decided to move the payroll operation to their corporate headquarters and demoted her to general receptionist, stripped her of her benefits, and reduced her pay to $6 an hour. This demotion had a disastrous effect on her budget. She had just bought a small house through a special HUD program for single parents that allowed her to forgo closing costs and finance her down payment. To her, home-ownership represented everything she had accomplished during her last seven years of hard work. She believed that owning her home represented new status and respectability. Because her new wage of $6 an hour would not allow her to keep up with her mortgage payments, she was forced to take a second job waitressing in the evenings and on weekends.

### Placing Children at Risk

Along with the financial risks these mothers faced, they also worried that full-time work placed their children in jeopardy because they could not provide adequate supervision. The mothers we interviewed viewed a lack of supervision as especially detrimental in bad neighborhoods, since they feared that their older children would make friends who would lead them into drugs, crime, or early sexual activity. [National] data show that only a small portion of all working mothers admit to survey researchers that they leave their children home alone while they work. Among parents with children ages five to eleven, for example, only 5 percent admitted to leaving their children alone while they worked. This percentage steadily increases with age. By the time their children are fourteen, one in five mothers report leaving their child home alone. Overall, survey data show that 8 percent of the children of working mothers were "latchkey kids" in 1991 (U.S. Bureau of the Census 1994). No doubt, this ratio is much higher for working single mothers, particularly those who work at low-wage jobs.

Most mothers with whom we spoke seldom left their preschool children home alone. Some mothers, however, felt they had no choice but to leave children alone for at least a couple of hours during the work week. One mother commented,

> I trained my kids when they were young to take care of themselves. They really know how to take care of themselves. They have been doing that . . . my son, he [has] been

trained basically to take care of himself, basically since he was four.

One mother said of her six-year-old daughter, "When my daughter was younger, I paid for babysitters, but now she no longer needs a babysitter." Another mother told us that when she was at work her eight-year-old daughter took care of her younger siblings. She commented, "I don't know what I would do if I didn't have her. She is very mature for her age."

This dilemma was particularly acute in the more dangerous neighborhoods, where many poor Mexican and African American mothers lived. An African American mother with an eight-year-old son who lived in a high-rise housing project told us,

> I am ashamed to say it, but I have a latchkey child. When he comes home from school, he locks himself in the house and waits for me to come home. In the summertime, he can go outside, but only if he calls me to check in every hour. I had to get him a little watch with a timer so that he would remember to check in with me. If I don't get that call, I leave work to go find him.

Another mother felt it was simply too dangerous to leave her children home alone after school and in the evening. This mother lived in a notorious Chicago neighborhood, across the street from a row of abandoned two-flats; one of which was used as a crack house. During the afternoon and evening hours, the street filled with young men who were either high or wanting to get high. Fights and drive-by shootings were common. Because of her concerns about leaving her children alone in this environment, the mother worked the graveyard shift at a local twenty-four-hour drugstore. Before she left for work at 11 P.M., she made sure the children had completed their homework and gone to bed. The children, ages five and seven, had her work number posted on a telephone between their beds. Because there had been three fires on their block that winter, she and her children would stage a fire drill each night after supper. She had also arranged for an upstairs neighbor to allow the children to come upstairs in case of an emergency she had not foreseen. . . .

As single parents, the working mothers we interviewed felt acutely the tension between their roles as mothers and employees. One mother, whose job at a discount store required that she work from noon to 8 P.M., felt she was losing control of her eight- and eleven-year-old children. She commented,

> With the one job, I'm not here with my children, so how can I control. . . . I mean, you can say, "You're not allowed to do this and you're not allowed to do that." But when you're not here, they're at an age where they're going [to] do what they want to. I was a child and I know how it is. You can threaten them, but they're going [to] do what they want to do [unless I'm there to stop them].

Sickness was also a major problem. As any parent of a young child knows, children who go to day care or school are exposed to more infectious diseases than children who stay at home. Most day care centers and schools, moreover, will not admit a child with the sniffles, much less a child with a fever. Thus, mothers of sick children often find that their only responsible option is to remain home. Not surprisingly, employers lose patience with employees who repeatedly miss work to nurse their sick children. One mother said,

> When Jay started at day care, he came home every week sick. One week it's an ear infection, the next week it's a cold. The doctor gives him ten days of medicine and when the ten days are up, he is sick again. But that was when he first went. He's pretty healthy now. We'll have to see how the winter goes.

Some mothers even told us that they had quit better paying jobs for jobs with employers who were more sympathetic to their child-minding responsibilities. One mother explained why she had left a $6 an hour job for a job paying only $5.50: "I have had better paying jobs than I have now, but none of them understood that my kids come first. At least this job understands that if my kids are sick, I just won't be in that day."

The same mother who had to take two jobs in the wake of a corporate takeover found that although this strategy allowed her to keep her newly purchased home, it had a deleterious effect on her fourteen-year-old daughter. With her mother away so much, the daughter began to have promiscuous and unprotected sex. The mother was caught in a difficult dilemma. On the one hand, she was convinced that if she did not decrease her hours, her daughter would end up pregnant. On the other, if she were to quit either of her jobs—even temporarily—she would be unable to keep up with her mortgage payments. Her solution was to dedicate what little spare time she had to looking for a new job that paid better wages—a strategy that took her away from home even more. Six months later, she had sent out over a hundred resumes, had gone on several dozen interviews, and still could not find a job that paid more than the one she already had. Though her daughter was not yet pregnant, she was in trouble with the law for repeated school truancy and shoplifting. When we followed up on this situation two years later, the daughter had just delivered her first child and had dropped out of high school.

Wage-reliant mothers also worried about how their absence affected their children's performance in school. One mother who worked a second job at night was notified by her child's teacher that her ten-year-old was failing. Alarmed, this mother quit her second job and began spending her evenings helping the child with homework and the extra reading and math exercises his teacher had assigned. She did not think she could live without the extra income for long, but she was determined to wait until summer recess before going back to her night job.

## NOTES

1. Recently, Judith Smith and Jeanne Brooks-Gunn (1995) have found that the cognitive abilities of children of welfare recipients who go to work and remain in poverty decrease significantly. Smith, Judith R., and Jeanne Brooks-Gunn. 1995. "Transitions Between Welfare and Work: Effects on Young Children and Mothers." Paper presented at Workshop on Welfare and Child Development. Sponsored by Board on Children, Youth, and Families and the National Institute for Child Health and Human Development. Washington, D.C. (December 5, 1995).

## REFERENCES

U.S. Bureau of the Census. 1994. *Financial Characteristics of Housing Units: 1990*. Washington, D.C.: Government Printing Office.

U.S. House of Representatives, Committee on Ways and Means. 1994. Overview of Entitlement Programs (Green Book). Washington, D.C.: U.S. Government Printing Office.

## CRITICAL THINKING QUESTIONS

1. Horowitz argued that, instead of working, the underclass—especially unwed mothers—depends on welfare handouts. Does the Edin and Lein research support Horowitz's assertion?

2. Mayer observed that federal programs have helped most American families meet their basic material needs. Why, then, do the wage-reliant mothers that Edin and Lein describe struggle so hard to stay off welfare, especially when the financial rewards are so negligible?

3. What work-related liabilities discourage single mothers from seeking or keeping jobs? What kinds of new policies or programs might help mothers work long term?

# VI FAMILY CRISES AND TRANSITIONS

Families experience a variety of crises and changes throughout the life cycle. How political and ideological groups view these crises and changes can launch political campaigns and promote government measures that affect most, if not all, American families. In this section, we examine conservative, centrist, liberal, and feminist debates on four important topics: family violence, divorce, remarriage and the formation of stepfamilies, and family policy.

As might be expected, all of the ideological and political groups express concern about family violence. The greatest disagreement, as you will see shortly, is between conservatives and feminists. Some conservatives believe that wives are as violent as their husbands. Feminists, on the other hand, contend that national figures of wife abuse are greatly underestimated because most wives don't report the violence.

In terms of divorce, centrist perspectives seem very similar to those of conservatives. Both groups view divorce as a major social problem. In contrast, liberals and feminists argue that divorce is liberating. Many conservatives who in other cases argue for less government interference (as in welfare) are now urging states to enact covenant marriage laws. Liberals, who often look to government to solve economic problems (such as welfare), feel that states would be encroaching on personal decisions if covenant marriages became law.

In terms of remarriage and stepfamilies, centrists appear to be more conservative than conservatives. While conservatives tend to have mixed reactions to the benefits of remarriage, centrists often describe stepfamilies as "not quite" families. Many liberals, on the other hand, endorse both remarriage and stepfamilies because they provide a second chance for establishing close relationships between adults and loving households for children.

The chapter on family policies focuses primarily on the 1996 welfare reform, landmark legislation that has already sparked a great deal of controversy about its impact on families. Again, the debates are largely between conservatives and liberals. So far, centrists haven't taken a position.

## Chapter 15: Family Violence

Since the mid-1980s, the literature and research on domestic violence has burgeoned.[1] Much of the material has focused on wife battering and child abuse. Feminist scholars and activists have promoted legislation on family violence by showing that adult women and children are more often the victims of domestic violence than are adult men, and that the latter are often immune from prosecution because of men's dominance in families.[2]

Some conservatives have recently argued that the emphasis on women as victims is misplaced. According to Patricia Pearson, in "Violent Women and the Myth of Innocence," for example, wives are just as violent as husbands and inflict just as much physical harm as do men. "We should stop pretending," she writes, "that domestic violence is not, somehow, the responsibility of fully half of its perpetrators."

Russell P. Dobash and his colleagues disagree ("The Myth of Sexual Symmetry in Marital Violence"). "A currently fashionable claim," they write, "is that violence against husbands is about as prevalent as violence against wives." The authors argue that marital violence is not symmetrical. If, according to Dobash and his colleagues, researchers used better measures of domestic violence that aren't flawed and often misinterpreted, they would conclude that claims about mutual violence are highly exaggerated.

To my knowledge, centrists have not published any position papers on domestic violence. Richard J. Gelles provides a "neutral" perspective in "Myths About Family Violence" that "is designed to explore many of the conventional myths about family violence." Gelles addresses some of the misconceptions, regardless of one's ideological stance, that he believes hinder effective policies and treatment for family and intimate violence.


## Chapter 16: Divorce

Many if not most conservatives see divorce as a threat to the prevailing social order. Though conservatives agree that divorce is sometimes unavoidable (due to physical abuse, desertion, or adultery, for example), they believe that the recent increase in divorce has led to numerous negative social consequences. Compared to children in intact marriages, conservatives maintain, children of divorce are much more likely to fail in school, to suffer poorer physical and mental health, to suffer abuse or neglect, to commit crimes or to be victims of crime, to have children out of wedlock, to use alcohol or drugs, to be unemployed as young adults and to experience work-related problems as adults, to commit suicide, and to suffer from depression and other psychological illnesses.[3]

Many conservatives point to high divorce rates as evidence that the family is falling apart because people are no longer making lasting commitments. No-fault divorce, especially, has effectively "abolished marriage" because remaining together "for richer for poorer, in sickness and in health, until death do you part" has no basis in reality: "Under current [no-fault divorce] law the bride and groom are in fact promising to be husband and wife only until one of them doesn't want to any more. The lifetime commitment, which defined marriage, is gone."[4]

On the conservative side, Glenn T. Stanton, in "Finding Fault with No-Fault Divorce," maintains that current divorce laws are unilateral because the faithful spouses are legally defenseless. He encourages pro-family leaders to persuade state legislatures to roll back no-fault divorce laws in order to decrease the negative impact of divorce on children and adults.

Most centrists don't propose rescinding no-fault divorce provisions. They agree with conservatives, however, that divorce results in many negative consequences. According to Barbara Dafoe Whitehead ("Dismantling the Divorce Culture"), because "divorce is not a solo act but one that has enormous consequences for children," scholars, clergy, therapists, lawyers, and other professionals should make a serious and sustained effort to prevent divorce.[5]

To prevent divorce, many centrists support efforts to "reform the reform" by lobbying legislators to change no-fault divorce laws, to extend the waiting periods before a divorce is granted, and to strengthen marriages through mandatory premarital counseling.[6] According to both conservatives and centrists, such "marriage-saving" programs have been "phenomenally successful."[7] Louisiana and Arizona have passed "covenant marriage" laws that make it more difficult to get married or harder to get divorced.[8] Most recently, Florida has passed the Marriage Preparation and Preservation Act of 1998 to stem the tide of divorces.[9] Since 1998, legislators in at least 17 states have pushed for covenant marriage laws.[10]

In contrast to conservatives and centrists, most liberals prefer that the government stay out of their bedrooms, marriages, and divorces. Some liberals point out that getting divorced is not the same thing as rejecting marriage:

> . . . three-quarters of divorced people remarry, and higher rates of divorce only indicate that marriage has become so important that people are no longer willing to put up with the kinds of unsatisfying, conflicted, or "empty-shell" marriages earlier generations tolerated.[11]

Feminists, especially, argue that women who seek divorce are hardly the self-absorbed and self-centered creatures that many conservatives and centrists accuse them of being. According to Demie Kurz, for example, mothers at all socioeconomic levels typically put up with violence, their husbands' infidelity, and marital dissatisfaction for many years before they decide to get a divorce ("Why Women Seek Divorce").

Many liberals see divorce as a solution to rather than a cause of family problems. They point to research that shows, for instance, that marital discord rather than the divorce itself may preoccupy parents and cause them to be more irritable and explosive in dealing with their children, may exacerbate children's behavior problems, and may result in an inability to develop and sustain intimate relationships with spouses and children.[12] Instead of trying to reduce divorce, many liberals propose, conservatives and centrists should be more interested in "compassionate reforms to soften the impact of divorce on children—stricter enforcement of child support payments, for example."[13]

## Chapter 17: Remarriage and Stepfamilies

When faculty members reviewed the proposal for this reader, several felt that the book would be incomplete without a chapter on remarriage and stepfamilies. I had initially omitted this topic from my table of contents because I assumed that conservatives, centrists, and liberals would enthusiastically endorse both remarriage and stepfamilies. Even though redivorce rates are higher than divorce rates, remarriage reflects Americans' belief in marriage, and stepfamilies provide children with two adults who can share parenting and pool their resources. No controversy there, I thought.

Wrong. In terms of published and Internet materials, centrists appear to be more conservative about remarriage and stepfamilies than many conservatives. Thus, the "family feuds" on remarriage and the formation of stepfamilies seem to be between centrists and liberals.

To my knowledge, conservatives don't have a "representative" position on remarriage and stepfamilies. A few secular scholars imply that stepfamilies are defective because child abuse is higher in stepfamilies than in "biological-married-parents" families.[14] These views, however, are embedded within the larger issue of "family values." Consequently, there are only bits and pieces, here and there, about remarriage and stepfamilies. Some Christian conservatives, as the article by William A. Heth, "Why Remarriage Is Wrong," shows, may reject remarriage because it is deemed adulterous and contrary to biblical writings. Some conservative Christians, on the other hand—or at least those who publish material in conservative periodicals—cite the Bible as *not* forbidding remarriage.[15] In addition, a survey of *Christianity Today* readers (most of whom are church leaders) found that while 20 percent of the respondents believed that a divorced and remarried person should not be a deacon or elder, 73 percent accepted the remarriage of a Christian if the former spouse had committed adultery or remarried.[16] It appears, then, that both religious and secular conservatives have mixed reactions to remarriage.

Centrists, in contrast, seem to reject remarriage and stepfamilies. In a review of 20 recently published undergraduate marriage and family textbooks, for example, an eminent family sociologist on the Council of Families board implied that there are "acceptable" and "nonacceptable" family structures and relationships. The latter include "cohabiting couples, divorced non-couples, *stepfamilies*, and gay and lesbian couples" (emphasis added).[17] He also noted that many textbooks "fail to draw the obvious conclusion that the rapid increase in single parent families and *stepfamilies* has very likely increased the amount of child abuse in the United States" (emphasis added).[18]

Some centrists have suggested that violence in stepfamilies is biological rather than reflecting cultural factors such as economic stress, the family's low socioeconomic status, or the partners' emotional instability:

> The underlying trigger [for family violence], the evolutionists believe, lies within our inherently selfish genes, which are biologically driven to perpetuate themselves. Genetically speaking, stepparents have less of an investment in unrelated offspring and may even regard them as detrimental to their chances of passing along their own genes, through their own biological children. Citing examples among animals—from birds and bees to lions and baboons—that share our propensity to live in family groups, the evolutionists maintain that conflicts and incestuous relations are more common among stepparents and stepchildren and among children and their half-siblings and step-siblings because they are less closely related to one another than are parents and children in a traditional family.[19]

It's not clear how many centrists subscribe to the notion that stepfamily violence is genetic. Many, however, seem to agree that stepfamilies are devastating for children. One centrist, for example, describes stepfamilies as "lumpy families" because family membership is ambiguous and family obligations and family loyalties are fragmented, and says that children in stepfamilies are much more likely than children in intact, biological families to complete less education and to experience a variety of problems (such as poorer psychological health).[20]

Most importantly, according to centrists such as David Blankenhorn, in "The Stepfather as Nonfather," children in stepfamilies, especially where the mother has custody, are fatherless. Blankenhorn maintains that the outcomes for children in stepfamilies are "almost uniformly bleak" because remarriage hastens the process of disengagement between a biological father and his children and because stepfather-stepchild relationships are typically lukewarm, noncommunicative, and detached.

Most liberals acknowledge that the effects of parental remarriage on children are mixed: Some outcomes are positive and some are negative. They believe, however, that the children's overall well-being and development in stepfamilies, as in intact families, depend on the quality of parenting and the degree of conflict between spouses and ex-spouses. Liberals also emphasize that most children's negative responses to a remarriage are temporary.[21] In contrast to centrists, many liberals and feminists see remarriage and stepfamilies as providing another chance to develop a happy marriage and a healthy and happy family life.

Despite the ups and down, liberals claim, a stepfamily provides members with opportunities that may be missing in an unhappy, intact home: When children see happy adults, they have positive models of marriage.[22] A well-functioning stepfamily increases the self-esteem and well-being of divorced parents and provides children who have lost touch with noncustodial parents with a caring and supportive adult. As Sarah Turner shows ("My Wife-in-Law and Me"), for example, stepparenting relationships can improve the lives of children and ex-spouses. If, especially, we view stepparenting from a feminist perspective, Turner maintains, we can enhance the connections between divorced biological parents, biological mothers and their wife-in-laws, and the well-being of children.

## Chapter 18: Family Policies

The purpose of family policy, according to Shirley L. Zimmerman, is *"to stabilize and support family life by meeting needs that the market cannot or will not meet for large segments of the population."*[23] Although family well-being is the goal of family policy, she writes, "the current debate over family values is not about family well-being. It is about one-parent and two-parent families."[24] I would add that the debate seems to be about poor one-parent families, especially poor *single-mother* families.

The passage of the Personal Responsibility and Work Opportunity Reconciliation Act of 1996 (PRWORA) was targeted, almost entirely, at poor, mother-only families. The central feature of PRWORA is the replacement of Aid to Families with Dependent Children (AFDC) by block grants. The states set their own eligibility criteria and benefit levels. Three other important changes include the following: (1) federal money cannot be used to provide cash assistance to unmarried women under the age of 18 or to children born to mothers who are already receiving assistance; (2) adults are expected to work after receiving welfare for two years; and (3) a family cannot receive cash assistance for more than five years.

Many (if not most) conservatives feel that generous federal assistance policies have encouraged welfare and out-of-wedlock births (see Chapters 2, 7, 9, 13, and 14). Some conservatives believe that the recent welfare reform does not go far enough in reducing welfare. Charles Murray, in "What Government Must Do to Reduce Welfare," maintains that welfare mothers are not used to working, are not motivated to seek employment, and are not worried about the future because they feel they can slip through bureaucratic loopholes despite more restrictive welfare regulations.

In terms of a centrist position, Norval Glenn (see Chapter 1) writes that centrists "generally do not favor a major dismantling of the welfare state." Glenn may be right. I was unable, however, to locate materials that represent a centrist position. As a result, Laura A. Wilson and Robert P. Stoker wrote a "neutral" article on PRWORA for this chapter ("Is Federal Welfare Reform Helping or Hurting Poor Families?"). Wilson and Stoker describe PRWORA, the politics and general perceptions about welfare families that led to PRWORA's passage, and the act's implications for poor families.

In the last article in this chapter, "Abandoning Poor Families," Ruth Sidel maintains that poor, unmarried mothers and their children are scapegoats, being blamed for undermining the work ethic and weakening the traditional American family. Instead, Sidel maintains, many of our difficulties are due to "severe structural problems that afflict American society," such as increasing economic inequality, diminishing jobs that provide decent wages and benefits, and growing poverty among young, two-parent families.

How effective has PRWORA been in reducing the number of people on welfare? Many policy analysts feel that it's too early to tell. During his 1999 State of the Union address, however, President Clinton announced that the number of people on welfare had fallen to its lowest level in 30 years, implying that the new welfare reform was working. Some observers point out, however, that the number of welfare recipients started declining several years before PRWORA was passed. After PRWORA was implemented, recipients with some education or work skills moved off welfare, leaving behind those with deeper problems like substance abuse, domestic violence, and very little education.[25] Many people leaving welfare don't really find work. They simply move in with or depend on already poor relatives.[26]

Some aspects of PRWORA are already being challenged. In January 1999, for example, the U.S. Supreme Court heard its first case on the new law regarding a "two-tier" welfare system. Fifteen states limit new residents in their first year to the level of welfare aid they received in their former state, if the former state's level is lower than the new state. Under the two-tier system, for instance, if a family of four moves from Mississippi to California, its first-year assistance remains $144, compared with $673 for longer-term California residents. States implemented the two-tier system to discourage "interstate migration" to the states that pay the highest welfare benefits. The Supreme Court will rule on the constitutionality of the two-tier system during the summer of 1999. During the hearing, however, several of the justices questioned the states' authority to "treat their citizens differently," because Americans should be able to settle wherever they want.[27]

The United States is the only developed country in the world, except for South Africa, without universal family supports.[28] Barbara Bergmann accuses both Republicans and Democrats of implementing inadequate welfare reforms because "the United States has the worst record of any of the developed countries in allowing children to grow up in poverty."[29] Using France and Sweden as examples of countries that have low child poverty rates (5 percent for both countries compared to 20 percent in the United States), Bergmann says that our government should implement child-care policies and health insurance for all families: "Even the poorest job . . . would support a standard of living above that allowed by current welfare grants, as long as child care and health care are provided."[30]

Bergmann estimates that we would have to spend about $100 billion a year over and above what we are now spending to subsidize childcare and health insurance. Some groups, especially conservatives, might object to such programs because we can't afford them. Money, however, is probably not the issue. Corporate welfare is the most expensive form of federal assistance. Taxpayers pay $150 billion a year for corporate subsidies and tax benefits. This is more than the $145 billion paid out annually for core welfare programs such as Aid to Families with Dependent Children (AFDC), student aid, housing, food and nutrition, and all direct public assistance (excluding Social Security and medical care).[31] Simply trimming corporate welfare would increase the revenues for lifting many families out of poverty.

If money isn't the problem, what is? As you saw in previous chapters, especially Chapters 3 and 4, most conservatives, a large number of centrists, and probably many liberals believe that U.S. society is on the brink of a moral breakdown because welfare encourages irresponsibility and dependency. According to one conservative, for example,

> I think the main problem with the welfare state is its *permissiveness*, not its size. Today poverty often arises from the functioning problems of the poor themselves, especially difficulties in getting through school, working, and keeping their families together. But the social programs that support the needy rarely set standards for them. Recipients seldom have to work or otherwise function *in return* for support.[32]

Some black scholars agree that money isn't the only solution in reducing poverty.[33] For example, Donna Franklin argues that remaking welfare won't work unless it addresses the needs of four types of African-American women on welfare. Of the four groups, the most disadvantaged are young unmarried mothers who started their parenting careers as teenagers, live in families with a multigenerational pattern of welfare dependence, reside in either public housing or a neighborhood of concentrated poverty, and who are the most likely to have children who aren't doing well developmentally. Franklin feels that this group of women is the most vulnerable to persistent poverty and will have the hardest time making the transition from welfare to work. Besides being given basic education, they will have to be socialized to the "culture of work":

> Many of [these mothers] have been reared in families where no one has ever held a permanent job, and thus have never observed firsthand the amount of discipline and the household routines that are needed to juggle the dual responsibilities of motherhood and employment. They will also have greater difficulty understanding the expectations of their employers—that it is important not only to get to work, but to get to work on time. A "culture" has been created in these mothers over time, a set of attitudes, values, and behaviors. A lot of individualized psychosocial support will be needed either from paraprofessionals or professionals because these women have more depressive symptoms and generally do not score as high on tests that measure psychological well-being. From a service perspective, this means increasing benefits and using support services to help young mothers care for children and households, as well as for themselves, as they are introduced to a new way of life.[34]

Although Franklin doesn't identify her political and ideological affiliation, her recommendations for reducing poverty and helping the most disadvantaged (typically black) mothers on welfare incorporate the concerns of the various ideological groups. Some of her suggestions for moving poor mothers out of welfare include the following: (1) social interventions provided by community-based family service agencies that combat the effects of isolation and helplessness on low-income mothers that move these women "from despair to action"; (2) expanded preschool programs, especially in the poorest neighborhoods, that include weekly visits with mothers; (3) provision of quality day care for working mothers living in poor neighborhoods; (4) a network of support services that prevent teenagers from becoming pregnant; (5) efforts by the black middle class to "reach across the class divide to address the poverty and despair found in urban ghettos"; and (6) government endeavors to promote open housing, create jobs, and enforce policies that will minimize the drug trade in poor black communities and bring about equal opportunity in the pursuit of jobs that will lift many families out of urban blight and poverty.[35]

## NOTES

1. Some of the most recent periodicals on domestic violence include the following: *Journal of Child Sexual Abuse, Journal of Interpersonal Violence, Journal of Family Violence, Child Abuse and Neglect, Violence and Victims, Aggression and Violent Behavior, Elder Abuse,* and *Sexual Abuse.*

2. One of the earliest and most influential books on wife battering was J. R. Chapman and M. Gates, eds., *The Victimization of Women* (Thousand Oaks, CA: Sage, 1978). A chapter by Lenore Walker, "Treatment Alternatives for Battered Women," pp. 143–174, has become a classic in describing the "cycle of battering incidents" experienced by wives.

3. Bryce J. Christensen, "Taking Stock: Assessing Twenty Years of 'No Fault' Divorce," *The Family in America* 5 (September 1991): 1–10; William A. Galston, "Divorce American Style," *The Public Interest,* no. 124 (Summer 1996): 12–26.

4. Robert L. Plunkett, "Vow for Now," *National Review,* May 29, 1995, p. 50.

5. Some centrists feel that marital therapists are too quick to encourage divorce. Instead, some centrists contend, therapists should emphasize the moral nature of marital commitment and promote the value of personal satis-

faction and autonomy within the marital relationship. See William J. Doherty, "How Therapists Threaten Marriage," in Amitai Etzioni, ed., *The Essential Communitarian Reader* (Lanham, MD: Rowman & Littlefield, 1998), pp. 156–166.

6. Julie Brienza, "At the Fault Line: Divorce Laws Divide Reformers," *Trial* (September 1996): 12–14.

7. See, for example, Michael J. McManus, "The Marriage-Saving Movement," *American Enterprise* 7 (May/June 1996): 78–133.

8. Though the laws differ somewhat in Louisiana and Arizona, a "covenant marriage" creates a two-tiered system of marriage licenses. Couples can choose a standard marriage certificate, which allows a "no-fault" divorce with only 60 days of separation, with no recourse by a partner who wants to save the marriage. Or the couple can choose a covenant marriage certificate in which the expectation is that the marriage will be for life. Both partners are agreeing that neither can unilaterally walk away from the marriage for any reason. If their marriage has problems, and either is considering divorce, the couple agrees in advance to seek professional help to save the marriage. A divorce is possible, but a person who wants a divorce has to prove that the partner is at fault—due to adultery; conviction of a felony; physical, drug, alcohol, or emotional abuse; or abandonment or separation for two years.

9. This law includes four components to strengthen marriage and discourage divorce: (1) high school students are required to take a course in "marriage and relationship skill-based education"; (2) engaged couples who take a "premarital preparation course" of at least four hours can get a $32.50 reduction in the cost of their marriage license, which normally costs between $88 and $200 depending on the county; (3) each couple applying for a marriage license is given a handbook prepared by the Bar Association to inform couples of "the rights and responsibilities under Florida law of marital partners to each other and to their children, both during a marriage and upon dissolution"; and (4) couples with children who file for divorce must take a Parent Education and Family Stabilization Course that covers the legal and emotional impact of divorce on adults and children, financial responsibility, laws on child abuse or neglect, and conflict resolution skills. Michael J. McManus, "Florida Passes Nation's Most Sweeping Reform of Marriage Law," May 16,

1998 (accessed on *smartmarriages@his.com*, May 17, 1998).

10. *Baltimore Sun*, "States Ponder Ways to Fortify Matrimony," February 14, 1999, p. 4A.

11. Arlene Skolnick, *Embattled Paradise: The American Family in an Age of Uncertainty* (New York: Basic Books, 1991), p. 221.

12. See, for example, Paul R. Amato and Alan Booth, "A Prospective Study of Divorce and Parent-Child Relationships," *Journal of Marriage and the Family* 58 (May 1996): 356–365.

13. Margaret Talbot, "Love, American Style," *The New Republic*, April 14, 1997, p. 36.

14. See, for example, Patrick F. Fagan, "The Child Abuse Crisis: The Disintegration of Marriage, Family, and the American Community," *The Heritage Foundation Roe Backgrounder No. 1115*, May 15, 1997, http://www.heritage.org:80//library/categories/family/bg1115.html (accessed November 8, 1998). Fagan bases his conclusions on British National Incidence Studies research. He notes, also, that the national U.S. studies on child abuse, such as those conducted by the National Center on Child Abuse and Neglect and the U.S. Department of Health and Human Services, probably mask "grave risks for children" because the data don't differentiate child abuse by marriage and remarriage.

15. See, for example, Craig Keener, "Remarriage: Two Views: Free to Remarry," *Christianity Today*, December 14, 1992, p. 34.

16. Haddon Robinson, "Sex, Marriage, and Divorce," *Christianity Today*, December 14, 1992, pp. 29–32. Robinson's findings were based on "over two-thirds" of the 1,500 readers of *Christianity Today* who responded to the survey. According to Robinson, the survey garnered "one of the highest response rates in over two decades of subscriber research" and that three out of four of the respondents were male.

17. Norval D. Glenn, *Closed Hearts, Closed Minds: The Textbook Story of Marriage* (New York: Institute for American Values, 1997), p. 5.

18. Ibid., pp. 14–15.

19. Jane E. Brody, "Genetic Ties May Be Factor in Violence in Stepfamilies," *smartmarriages@his.com* (accessed December 22, 1998).

20. Maggie Gallagher, *The Abolition of Marriage: How We Destroy Lasting Love* (Washington, DC: Regnery, 1996). See esp. pp. 69–82.

21. See, for example, Terry Arendell, "Divorce and Remarriage," in Terry Arendell, ed.,

Contemporary Parenting: Challenges and Issues (Thousand Oaks, CA: Sage, 1997), pp. 179–195. Also, the chapter on remarriage and stepfamilies (pp. 453–477) in Nijole V. Benokraitis, *Marriages and Families: Changes, Choices and Constraints*, 3rd ed. (Upper Saddle River, NJ: Prentice Hall, 1999) summarizes both the positive and negative effects of remarriage and stepfamilies on children. One of the reasons for the negative impact of remarriage may reflect the fact that divorced mothers, who are economically insecure, rush into a marriage instead of choosing a partner who might be a good stepfather for their biological children. See Sara S. McLanahan, "Parent Absence or Poverty: Which Matters More?" in Greg J. Duncan and Jeanne Brooks-Gunn, eds., *Consequences of Growing Up Poor* (New York: Russell Sage Foundation, 1997), pp. 35–48.

22. V. Rutter, "Lessons from Stepfamilies," *Psychology Today* 27 (May 1994), pp. 30–34.

23. Shirley L. Zimmerman, *Understanding Family Policy: Theories & Applications*, 2nd ed. (Thousand Oaks, CA: Sage, 1995), p. 18, italics in original.

24. Ibid., p. 240. One conservative has observed, for example, that "*What welfare did was to disrupt the process of family formation*" (italics in original). See William Tucker, "All in the Family," *National Review*, March 5, 1995, p. 44.

25. "Welfare Level Shrinks to Lowest in 30 Years," *Baltimore Sun*, January 25, 1999, p. 3A.

26. Neal R. Peirce, "Reformed Welfare Makes Big Gains, Faces Bigger Challenges," *Baltimore Sun*, August 24, 1998, p.7A.

27. Lyle Denniston, "Justices Take Dim View of States with 'Two-Tier' Welfare Systems," *Baltimore Sun*, January 24, 1999, p. 3A.

28. Marlene Johnson, "A Universal Agenda for Women and Their Families," *Vital Speeches of the Day* 58, August 15, 1992, pp. 660–662.

29. Barbara Bergmann, "Real Welfare Reform: Help for Working Parents," *Challenge* (September–October 1996): 34.

30. Ibid., p. 36.

31. Corporate Welfare Information Center, *http://www.enviroweb.org/enviroissues/corporate/welfare/* (accessed February 13, 1999). Another item on this site notes: "After World War II, the nation's tax bill was roughly split between corporations and individuals. But after years of changes in the federal tax code and international economy, the corporate share of taxes has declined to a fourth the amount individuals pay, according to the US Office of Management and Budget." *Boston Globe* series on Corporate Welfare.

32. Lawrence M. Mead, *Beyond Entitlement: The Social Obligations of Citizenship* (New York: The Free Press, 1986), p. ix, italics in original.

33. Glenn Loury, a black economist, has blamed the lack of progress in many African-American communities on the "social disorganization of blacks" and a lack of discipline rather than racism: ". . . the most important challenges and opportunities confronting any person arise not from his racial condition but from our common human condition. . . . Whatever our race, class, or ethnicity, we must all devise and fulfill a life plan . . . the challenge confronting blacks today is not racial at all. It is primarily the human condition, not our racial conditions, which we must *all* learn to cope." Glenn C. Loury, "Individualism Before Multiculturalism," *The Public Interest* (Fall 1995): 105. When, most recently, Loury changed his mind and started blaming conservatives for racism, especially in not implementing affirmative action guidelines, he has been described by some conservatives as engaging in "vacuous theoretical preachments and a blurring of focus on the realities that in the past he so sharply saw and so bravely described." Norman Podhoretz, "The 'Loyalty Trap,'" *National Review*, January 25, 1999, p. 36.

34. Donna L. Franklin, *Ensuring Inequality: The Structural Transformation of the African-American Family* (New York: Oxford University Press, 1997), p. 227.

35. Ibid., pp. 216–239.

# 15 Family Violence

## *Conservative:* Violent Women and the Myth of Innocence

PATRICIA PEARSON, *When She Was Bad: Violent Women and the Myth of Innocence* (New York: Viking Penguin, 1997), pp. 114–123.

*One of the most abiding myths of our time, according to Patricia Pearson, is that the domestic violence literature focuses on male aggression and portrays women as docile and submissive. Instead, she argues, women are as violent as men are, wives are as likely as husbands are to initiate battering, and women are just as likely as men are to cause much physical harm. Pearson offers several explanations for why we condone female violence.*

Before his life fell to ruins, Peter Swann inhabited a world that felt good to him, purposeful and clear. As he entered his thirties he had solid work as a municipal engineer and was raising his seven-year-old daughter, Grace, in a house perched high on the grassy bluffs of Lake Ontario, east of the city of Toronto. From that untroubled vista he could pursue his love of the natural world, taking Grace up onto the roof on clear summer nights to show her the stars through his telescope, riding their mountain bikes through the sprawling ravines of Toronto's Metro Zoo. He filled the house with small wonders—an aquarium full of rare fish, a collection of rocks. Sometimes he'd dig out the treasure of his mother's phonograph, to teach Grace what snatches of old songs he knew.

As Grace approached puberty, with all its attendant moods, he began to look for a relationship, hoping to find a woman who might act as a mother figure to her. Her own mother had vanished, not long after the Catholic Children's Aid charged her with abuse and transferred custody to

Peter. He had been immensely relieved to have Grace back. Her upbringing was his mission. He had been given up for adoption as an infant. His daughter would stay with her own flesh and blood. "Mr. Swann," a counselor wrote some years later, "presents [himself] as a mature, warm, and caring father."

In 1989, a mutual friend introduced Peter to a thirty-year-old clothing store manager named Dana, whose marriage was on the rocks. Dana was a bright and charming woman, and if her temper seemed extreme, Peter reasonably attributed that to her frustrations with her husband, who was something of a boor. "They fought all the time," he remembers. "She used to beat him up on the couch. Hit him in the face. He thought it was a joke. The rest of us . . ." Peter makes a face of consternation. "But I felt, I'm not like him, so it won't be like that for us. I'm more easygoing, not the same personality."

Once Peter and Dana got involved, their relationship deepened quickly. Within months she'd moved into his home on the bluffs, continuing to work in retail, a job that she loved and was good at. They appeared to be a well-adjusted couple: two professionals raising a child. Three full and busy lives. There was only one, very private problem. Dana's temper, which Peter had attributed to her anger at her first husband, didn't go away. Far from calming her down, his more peaceable (and avoidant) temperament seemed to fuel her. "She'd start making an anthill into a mole-hill into a mountain," he says. Then he abruptly switches to the present tense, as if he's returned to that place in their kitchen, or his basement office, where something he said or did tripped an invisible wire. "She comes home from work, comes downstairs, and starts screaming at me, kicking holes in the walls. I don't know what to do. What's bugging her now? Somethin' at work, or what? I cleaned the kitchen, I paid the bills. . . It's goin' through my mind, and I'm just sitting there stymied, you know? I just don't know what to do. How do I calm her down? It just didn't work. Wham, bam. I'm getting hit."

Peter was stunned by her anger. He tried to appease her. "I became more passive." Whatever wound Dana up to the point of violence, he would simply refrain from; it wasn't worth it. "Our honeymoon was the only time we got along. It was like passing through an empty space, and then, Bang! Back into the hard stuff again." The list of nixed activities grew longer. He didn't go off on his bike rides with Grace; he didn't go out with his friends by himself; he didn't go out with his friends at all. Eventually, he didn't even wander out of sight in the supermarket, lest it start another fight he couldn't win.

"She couldn't compromise," he explains. "It was her way or no way. She controlled me, hit me, controlled me, hit me. Any excuse would do. She told me I was no good, that I drank too much, my family's no good, I'm useless. She'd throw metal address books at my head, ashtrays. Oh, bruises, right?" He lights another cigarette and rubs his forehead, his embarrassment rising. "I go to work, and guys say: What happened? 'Oh, I fell down,' whatever. Later I told them. They said, 'Get out of it.'" He flicks his cigarette ash, missing the ashtray, then wanders over to pick up his pet guinea pig. "I tried to get out, but I didn't . . . I just didn't know how. We've got a town house, my daughter's there, between us we're making fifty-two grand a year, I started giving her the pay-checks. I had to ask her for a pack of cigarettes. 'Please?' you know, like a dog. I didn't realize it, I was stupid, okay? I'm a wuss, okay? It's hard to say it. It's hard for a man to say that."

But Swann has to say that now, because Grace is gone. So is his job, his house, his telescope, everything he owned, even the phonograph, and Swann is sleeping in a boardinghouse with the guinea pig as his sole family. One night in that paltry place, he fumbles with the screw-top of an unrefrigerated bottle of wine, pours another splash into a coffee mug, and stammers out the simpleness of what he'd hoped: "A family is supposed to be a family. You know? We all get along." He waves his hand feebly, his voice weepy, his words slurred. "I want to be responsible for my daughter. Is something wrong with that, did I do something wrong?" What Peter Swann did was to meet and marry a female batterer, a woman who was angry, controlling, abusive, and manipulative, and who ultimately walked away with everything in his life, including his thirteen-year-old daughter.

Husband abusers aren't supposed to exist, but they do.

The idea that domestic violence refers exclusively to wife abuse or to violence against women is so deeply ingrained in Western consciousness that it is impossible to grapple with Peter Swann's story without first unraveling some potent conventional wisdom. Most of us believe that masculine power is the fountainhead of private, as well as public, violence. Spouse assault is what *men* do to *women*, women from all walks of life, getting punched in the face by the dark fist of patriarchy. Even if we concede that women batter their children, we cannot take it a step further and picture them battering men. We might learn that a man's nose was broken, that he lost his job, that he was emotionally devastated, but we still think to ourselves: He's a man. He could have hit back. He could have hit *harder*.

On the whole, men do indeed have a more powerful left hook. The problem is that the dynamic of domestic violence is not analogous to two differently weighted boxers in a ring. There are relational strategies and psychological issues at work in an intimate relationship that negate the fact of physical strength. At the heart of the matter lies human will. Which partner—by dint of temperament, personality, life history—has the will to harm the other? By now it should be clear that such a will is not the exclusive province of men. If it were, we wouldn't have the news coming out of North America's gay community that violence by women against women in personal relationships occurs with a frequency approaching violence in heterosexual relationships—with the smaller, more conventionally feminine partner often being the one who strikes.[1]

A great source of skepticism for people confronting the concept of husband assault is the absence of visible injury. Few abused men or lesbians emerge from their relationships resembling Hedda Nussbaum, the New Yorker whose common-law husband, Joel Steinberg, was prosecuted in 1988 for the beating death of their adopted daughter, Lisa. When Hedda Nussbaum testified, her appallingly broken face, with its cauliflower ear and boxer nose, was so vividly captured by television cameras that she quickly became the iconographic figure of the battered woman. Every time an activist proclaimed that one in four American women were assaulted by their partners, the image of Nussbaum sprang to mind.

In reality, victims like Hedda Nussbaum dwell at the extreme end of a continuum of violence in marital and dating relationships, in which about 4 percent of women are that severely injured.[2] The majority of couples embroiled in intimate power struggles engage in a spectrum of violent acts, which women are statistically as likely as men to initiate: the slaps across the face, the glass suddenly hurled, the bite, the fierce pinch, the waved gun, the kick to the stomach, the knee to the groin. Add the invisible wave of violence that washes over American households in an acid bath of words, the children used as pawns, the destruction of property, the enlistment of community as a means of control, and all this paints a much more complex picture of domestic violence than that summoned by one woman's face in a heartbreaking trial.

That we have not been able to get at this complexity, in terms of the range of behavior, its causes, and its victims, has everything to do with how the issue evolved in the popular mind to begin with. Spousal assault was once a silent crime. The violence was private, like child assault. What people did behind closed doors was the business neither of their neighbors nor of the state. The first radical alteration of this paradigm came about in the early 1970s, through the work of Second Wave feminists. Because they were concentrating on the problems of women—transforming what were once considered personal issues into political concerns—they exposed the female victims of domestic assault. The subject made headlines with the publication of *Battered Wives* by the journalist Del Martin in 1976, one year after Susan Brownmiller opened the door on rape with her landmark book *Against Our Will*.

The first order of business, for many feminists like Martin, was to remove the stigma attached to battered women. Prior to *Battered Wives*, the few investigations that had been made into battery had been conducted by court-appointed male psychiatrists who were asked to assess male assailants for trial. Since the assailants refused to concede any problem, the psychiatrists refocused their attention on the wives who'd been assaulted and, in the grand tradition of pathologizing female behavior, came up with a host of victim-blaming labels: "masochists," "castrators," "flirts." From the outset of claiming this issue for women, it was critical to clear battered women of blame. As this mission gained momentum, with more and more women testifying about their experiences to feminists and journalists, the need to shield victims from blame gained currency. To pose the question "Why did she stay?" quickly became unacceptable. It emerged that there were a number of reasons why women stayed—for the sake of their children, or because of financial dependency, or because, even if they left, their husbands would track them down. Most people accepted such reasons as credible, as evidenced most recently by the funds allotted in 1994 by the United States federal Violence Against Women Act. Male approval of spousal assault has dropped 50 percent in this period, from 20 percent of men thinking it's acceptable to strike your wife to 10.[3]

Soon after the first battered women found safe haven in the feminist movement, research began to reveal that violence in the home actually claimed victims of both sexes. The most significant data came from a survey published in 1980 by three highly respected family violence scholars in New Hampshire, Murray Straus, Richard Gelles, and Suzanne Steinmetz. Their random survey of 3,218 American homes uncovered that severe abuse was committed equally by men and women. Minor, but recurring, violence was also on a par, with 11.6 percent of women and 12 percent of men reporting that they hit, slapped, or kicked their partners.[4]

At this point, people working on the subject of family violence had a choice. They could expand the field to include male victims—establishing that abused men were not the same men who were abusing, and vice versa for women—or they could do what they did: devote an extraordinary amount of energy to shouting male victims down. For feminists,

the idea that men could be victimized was nonsensical. It didn't square with their fundamental analysis of wife assault—that it was an extension of male political, economic, and ideological dominance over women. If women were so clearly subjugated in the public domain, through rape, sexual harassment, job discrimination, and so on, how could there be a different reality behind closed doors? Activists anticipated, moreover, that the New Hampshire data might be used to devalue female victims, in the manner of male lawyers, judges, and politicians saying, "See? She does it too"; case dismissed.

As a result, critics rushed to accuse Straus and Gelles, who were the primary authors, of shoddy research. They argued that their measurement tools were "patriarchal" and that they hadn't explored the context of the violence: If women were equally abusive, it was only in self-defense.[5] None could assert this as fact; nor did they criticize the lack of context for assaults against women. On the contrary, the Straus/Gelles survey method (called the conflict tactics scale) was quickly adopted as a tool for research into violence against women. But Straus and Gelles, put on the defensive, reworked their survey questions and sampled several thousand households again. Their findings, published in 1985, were virtually identical, with the additional discovery that women initiated the aggression as often as men. About a quarter of the relationships had an exclusively violent male, another quarter had an exclusively violent female, and the rest were mutually aggressive.[6]

Once again, there was a flurry of protest and scrutiny. Scholars set out to prove that male self-esteem was less damaged by abuse, that men took their wives' violence less seriously, and that injury had to be measured in terms of harm rather than intentions. A woman with a broken jaw could not be compared to a man like Peter Swann, who only got an ashtray to the head. In truth, both sides were guilty of using a male-centered measure of harm, in that neither was looking at the damage women could cause through indirect aggression. Moreover, Straus and Gelles, as well as subsequent scholars, have found that men often do, in fact, sustain comparable levels of injury. A 1995 study of young American military couples, arguably the most patriarchal of all, found that 47 percent of the husbands and wives had bruised, battered, and wounded each other to exactly the same degree.[7] The argument about harm versus intention has been confounded in recent years, at any rate, by the addition of "mental" and "emotional" abuse to the lexicon of female victimization. A spate of new books on the self-help market argue that verbal abuse damages women as badly as physical blows.[8] Picking up on this theme, California has added new provisions to its prisoner clemency policy, allowing women to apply for release for killing their mates due to "emotional" abuse. Since nobody can sensibly argue that women aren't capable of extremely artful and wounding verbal attacks (studies find high degrees of female verbal hostility in violent marriages), the whole question of "harm" gets turned on its head.[9]

Nevertheless, battered women's supporters are so invested in a gender dichotomy that some have even stooped to attacking male victim researchers on a personal level. After Suzanne Steinmetz proposed the battered husband syndrome in an article published in 1978 in *Victimology*,[10] a speech she was asked by the ACLU to give was canceled because the organization received a bomb threat. Steinmetz also received so many threatening phone calls at home that she had to get an unlisted number. Thirteen years later, in 1991, the chairwoman of a Canadian panel on violence against women, Pat Marshall, when asked if she was familiar with the Straus/Gelles studies, replied that she was familiar with Murray Straus as a man and insinuated that he abused his wife. Marshall repeated these comments so frequently that Straus had to write to the Canadian minister responsible for the

status of women to request a public apology.[11] He received one. His wife, the pawn in this pretty maneuver, did not.

Accompanying the resistance to statistics on men has been a tendency to suppress data altogether. A 1978 survey conducted by the Kentucky Commission on Violence Against Women uncovered that 38 percent of the assaults in the state were committed by women, but that finding wasn't included when the survey was released.[12] (The information was discovered some years later by scholars.) In Detroit, a tally of emergency medical admissions due to domestic violence was widely reported by activists as evidence of injuries to women.[13] No one told the media that 38 percent of the admissions were men. In Canada, the federal government allotted $250,000 to a research project on comparative rates of violence in dating relationships.[14] The lead researcher, Carleton University sociologist Walter DeKeseredy, released his data on women, generating a wave of violence against women headlines and conveying the impression that Canadian college campuses were bastions of violent misogyny. DeKeseredy didn't mention in his report that he had collected evidence of dating violence against men. If his data, which he intends to publish in 1997, reflect most other studies on dating violence, the rates will be equal. Physical aggression by young women in premarital romance is among the best documented.[15]

"The battered husband syndrome is a backlash," DeKeseredy said in a 1994 telephone interview. "Men are using this information to keep women out of shelters." In fact, men are not using the information for anything, because academics with a particular political agenda are keeping it to themselves.

Under the circumstances, it is not surprising that those who stumble across evidence of battered men and battered lesbians do so quite by accident. A Winnipeg social scientist named Reena Sommer conducted a citywide survey on alcoholism for the University of Manitoba in 1989. Out of curiosity, she included six questions about domestic violence, interested specifically in violence against women. Some years later, she went back to her data and looked at the rates she'd collected on violence against men. To her astonishment, she found that 39.1 percent of the women in her survey had responded that they had committed acts of violence against their spouses at some point in their relationships, with 16.2 percent of those acts defined as severe. Sommer went back to her original list, found the telephone numbers, called up her respondents, and interviewed 737 of them. Ninety percent of the women who'd reported being abusive told her that they hadn't struck in self-defense. They had been furious or jealous, or they were high, or frustrated. Rational or irrational, impulsive or controlling, they had hit, kicked, thrown, and bitten. Fourteen percent of the men went to the hospital.[16]

In Columbus, Ohio, two young sociologists, Laura Potts and Mary Reiter, were working in a "misdemeanor intake program" in the city attorney's office, criminal division, trying to settle minor charges through mediation, without bringing individuals to trial. Although nothing they'd read as feminists prepared them to expect it, they kept encountering men who'd been assaulted by women. One was an ailing, seventy-five-year-old man whose much younger wife had smashed him over the head with a porcelain vase. Another was a man attempting to break up with his girlfriend who got slashed in the temple with a screwdriver. In a third case, a man leaving his home to avoid an argument with his wife was chased down the street and stabbed in the back. "What we were seeing in reality," Potts told a meeting of the American Society of Criminology in 1994, "was a far greater use of [violence by women] than what we saw in the literature."

In Seattle, a therapist named Michael Thomas encountered the same gap between his schooling and his on-the-job experience. "My initial work was with a child abuse agency," he says. "When you start listening to the children's stories, you start to realize that there's an awful lot more violence by women than any of us had been trained to expect." Moving into private practice, Thomas began meeting "men who'd been sexually abused, often by their mothers." Within that distressing realm he heard his first accounts of husband abuse, for it is often men who witnessed or experienced violence in childhood who permit themselves to be assaulted as adults. As one battered husband who'd been abused in his boyhood explained: "We have not had control, as men, so we're not familiar with it and we're quite willing to give it over."[17]

## NOTES

1. See Claire Renzetti, *Violent Betrayal: Partner Abuse in Lesbian Relationships* (Newbury Park, Calif: Sage Publications 1992); Nancy Hammond, "Lesbian Victims of Relationship Violence," *Women and Therapy* 8 (1989), 89–105; M. J. Bologna, C. K. Waterman, and L. J. Dawson, "Violence in Gay Male and Lesbian Relationships: Implications for Practitioners and Policy Makers," paper presented at the Third National Conference of Family Violence Researchers, Durham, N.H., 1987 (the authors found that 18 percent of gay men and 40 percent of lesbians admitted to being victims of aggression in their current relationship); Gwat-Yong Lie and S. Gentlewarrior, "Intimate Violence in Lesbian Relationships: Discussion of Survey Findings and Practise Implications," *Journal of Social Service Research* 15 (1991), 41–59 (in their 1990 survey of 1,099 lesbians, Lie and Gentlewarrior found that 52 percent had been victims of aggression by their partners); G. Y. Lie et al., "Lesbians in Currently Aggressive Relationships: How Frequently Do They Report Aggressive Past Relationships?" *Violence and Victims* 6:2 (1991).

2. Murray Straus, Richard J. Gelles, and S. K. Steinmetz, *Behind Closed Doors: Violence in the American Family* (Garden City, N.Y.: Anchor Books, 1980), p. 40.

3. Murray Straus and Glenda Kaufman Kantor, "Change in Cultural Norms Approving Marital Violence from 1968 to 1994," paper pre-

sented at the annual meeting of the American Sociological Association, Los Angeles, August 1994.

4. Straus, Gelles, and Steinmetz, *Behind Closed Doors*, pp. 40–41.

5. See, for example, M. Bograd and K. Yllo, eds., *Feminist Perspectives on Wife Abuse* (Newbury Park, Calif: Sage Publications, 1988).

6. Murray Straus and Richard J. Gelles, "Societal Change and Change in Family Violence from 1975–1985 as Revealed by Two National Surveys," *Journal of Marriage and the Family* 48 (1986), 465–479. "We found that among couples where violence occurred, both partners are violent in about half of the cases, violence by only the male partner occurs one-quarter of the time, and violence by only the female partner occurs one-quarter of the time. . . . These results cast doubt on the notion that assaults by women on their partners primarily are acts of self-defense or retaliation." In terms of damage done, the study found that levels of medical care, days off work, and time spent bedridden were not significantly different between the sexes (162–163). Women, however, reported much higher levels of depression. See also "Physical Assaults by Wives: A Major Social Problem," in Richard J. Gelles and Donileen R. Loeske, eds., *Current Controversies in Family Violence* (Newbury Park, Calif: Sage Publications, 1993).

7. J. Langhinrichsen-Rohling, P. Neidig, and G. Thorn, "Violent Marriages: Gender Differences in Levels of Current Violence and Past Abuse," *Journal of Family Violence* 10:2 (1995), 159–175.

8. See, for example, Patricia Evans, *Verbal Abuse: Survivors Speak Out on Relationship and Recovery* (Holbrook, Mass.: Bob Adams, Inc., 1993).

9. See, for example, D. Vivian and K. D. O'Leary, "Communication Patterns in Physically Aggressive Engaged Partners," paper presented at the Third National Family Aggression Research Conference, University of New Hampshire, July 1987.

10. S. K. Steinmetz, "The Battered Husband Syndrome," *Victimology* 2:3/4 (1977).

11. Pat Marshall's remarks described by David Lees, "The War Against Men," *Toronto Life*, December 1992. Lee quotes Marshall as saying: "I know Murray. . . . I was speaking at an international conference a few years ago in Jerusalem. . . . Met a woman there and . . . didn't know her name . . . I have never met a woman who looked so victimized. Never in my whole, whole life. By coincidence, it happened to be Murray Straus's wife. I have never met somebody who was trying so desperately to be invisible in the space that she occupied. I mean, it was just dramatic."

12. M. Schulman, "A Survey of Spousal Violence Against Women in Kentucky" (Washington, D.C.: Government Printing Office, 1979). The raw data were reviewed by C. A. Hornung, B. C. McCullough, and T. Sugimoto, "Status Relationships in Marriage: Risk Factors in Spouse Abuse," *Journal of Marriage and the Family* 43 (1981), 675–692. The authors found that 38 percent of the violent attacks in the Kentucky survey were by women against men who had not assaulted them.

13. Christina Hoff Sommers, *Who Stole Feminism? How Women Have Betrayed Women* (New York: Simon & Schuster 1994), p. 201.

14. Walter DeKeseredy and K. Kelly, "The Incidence and Prevalence of Woman Abuse in Canadian University and College Dating Relationships: Preliminary Results from a National Survey," unpublished report to the Family Violence Prevention Division, Health and Welfare Canada, 1993.

15. See, for example, D. B. Sugarman and G. T. Hotaling, "Dating Violence: Prevalence, Context and Risk Markers," in M. A. Pirog-Good and J. E. Stets, eds., *Violence in Dating Relationships: Emerging Social Issues* (New York: Praeger, 1989); Diane Follingstad et al., "Sex Differences in Motivations and Effects in Dating Relationships," *Family Relations* 40 (January 1991), 51–57: Two and a half times more women than men cited "control" as a motive for assaults. More males cited jealousy. Twenty percent of females said they had the right to use violence, whereas no males did. See also A. DeMaris, "Male vs. Female Initiation of Aggression: The Case of Courtship Violence," in E. Viano, ed., *Intimate Violence: Interdisciplinary Perspectives* (Bristol, Pa.: Hemisphere Publishing, 1992); P. Marshall and L. Rose, "Gender, Stress and Violence in Adult Relationships of a Sample of College Students," *Journal of Social and Personal Relations* 4 (1987); Sarah Ben-David, "The Two Facets of Female Violence: The Public and the Domestic Domains," *Journal of Family Violence* 8:4 (1993).

For female sexual coercion in dating relationships, see, for example: L. O'Sullivan and S.

Byers, "Eroding Stereotypes: College Women's Attempts to Influence Reluctant Male Sexual Partners," *The Journal of Sex Research* 30 (1993); Kate Fillion, *Lip Service: The Truth About Women's Darker Side in Love, Sex and Friendship* (Toronto: HarperCollins, 1996).

16. Reena Sommer, "Male and Female Perpetrated Partner Abuse: Testing a Diathesis-Stress Model," unpublished doctoral dissertation, University of Manitoba, 1994. See also R. Sommer, G. E. Barnes, and R. P. Murray, "Alcohol Consumption, Alcohol Dependence, Personality and Female Perpetrated Spousal Abuse," *Personality and Individual Differences* 13:12 (1993), 1315–1323.

17. Therapist Michael Thomas: Interview with the author.

## CRITICAL THINKING QUESTIONS

1. Why, according to Pearson, do we rarely hear about battered husbands?

2. If "academics with a particular political agenda" are keeping data about male abuse to themselves, what kinds of studies does Pearson cite to show that women are violent?

3. Several conservative writers maintain that women are innately virtuous and nurturant (see Chapters 5, 6, and 8). How do you think Pearson would respond to such descriptions of women?

# 15 Family Violence

## *Centrist:* Myths About Family Violence

RICHARD J. GELLES, *Intimate Violence in Families*, 3rd ed. (Thousand Oaks, CA: Sage, 1997), pp. 2–12.

*Although we know more about family violence today than 20 years ago, many of our beliefs ignore information based on scholarly research. Richard J. Gelles examines eight of the most popular and persistent myths about family violence. These myths, he says, help explain why many of us view violent behavior as normal or as describing "them" rather than "us."*

How is it possible that families have been violent for centuries, all over the globe, yet we have only recently discovered and attended to family violence as a serious family and social problem? How is it that after 30 years of intensive research and practice in this field, we can still read newspaper accounts that talk about instances where children who were identified by social service agencies as abused, and whose cases have been followed by social workers for months, are killed, virtually under the nose of the person who was supposed to protect them? One answer to these two questions is that there are a number of myths and controversies about family violence that tend to hinder both public recognition and effective professional practice. . . .

### 1. Family and intimate violence is a significant social and public health problem but not an inevitable aspect of family relations.

Until the 1960s, most people considered family violence a rare phenomenon. What few official statistics there were tended to

bear out this assumption. Few states required professionals or public agencies to report known or suspected instances of child abuse. When David Gil (1970) surveyed the entire country in 1967 to determine how many valid cases of physical child abuse there were, he found about 6,000. The individual state definitions of abuse and the procedures used to investigate reports of child abuse influenced the total number reported. California had more than 3,500 reports; Rhode Island had none. Until recently, there were few localities or states that required reporting of domestic violence or adult abuse. Today, at least seven states have laws that specifically address the issue of reporting when domestic violence or adult abuse is suspected (Hyman, 1995). Prior to 1970, few hospitals bothered to categorize women patients they treated as either abused or nonabused. Police departments did keep records of how many domestic disturbance calls they received and investigated, but many times the records were inaccurate or incomplete. Sometimes a husband assaulting his wife would be recorded as a domestic disturbance, and other times it would be recorded as an assault.

The strong belief that families are places people turn *to* for help, and the perception that city streets hold the greatest risk for women and children, helped to continue the myth of the rareness of family violence even into the 1990s. As different types of family violence are discovered and examined, most people find it difficult to believe how many individuals and families are involved in violence in the home.

There has been no shortage of publicity about family violence in the 1990s. Public awareness about child abuse, sexual abuse, wife abuse, and elder abuse has been fueled by a combination of public awareness campaigns designed to educate the public about the dangers and costs of family violence and high-profile cases of family violence. Public discussion of and attention to family violence has included the sensational case of Lorena Bobbitt, who cut off her husband's penis after he allegedly raped her; the double murder of their parents by the Menendez brothers in California; self-disclosures of their own abuse victimization by celebrities such as Oprah Winfrey and former Miss America Carolyn Sapp; a nearly daily discussion of various forms and types of abuse on daytime television talk shows; and finally, the killing of Nicole Brown Simpson and Ronald Goldman and the trial and acquittal of O.J. Simpson.

The public awareness campaigns and the publicity attendant to the high-profile cases of family violence tend to be accompanied by claims of an "epidemic" of family violence, a rising tide of family violence, and the emergence of various "factoids" used to highlight the claim that family violence is growing, widespread, and harmful.

In the wake of the killings of Nicole Brown Simpson and Ronald Goldman and the allegation that the killer was Nicole Brown Simpson's former husband, O.J., there were a number of statistics that were repeated over and over about the extent of spouse abuse. Among the three most widely repeated "facts" were the following:

- More women are treated in emergency rooms for battering injuries than for muggings, rapes, and traffic accidents combined.
- Family violence has killed as many women in the past 5 years as the total number of Americans who were killed in the Vietnam War.
- The March of Dimes reports that battering during pregnancy is the leading cause of birth defects and infant mortality.

Not only were these widely repeated, they were attributed to "authoritative sources." For example, the first "fact" about emergency room visits was attributed to the Centers for Disease Control and former Surgeon Generals C. Everett Koop and Antonia Novello. The Centers for Disease Control has repeatedly backed away from being the source of this "fact," stating that it is actually based on a very small study of a single emergency room. Even the authors of that study were tentative about the proportion of women who seek emergency room treatment who are battered. The authors' actual conclusion was that battering *may* (emphasis added) be the single most common source of serious injury to women, accounting for more injury than auto accidents, muggings, and rape combined (Stark et al., 1981).

The second "fact" is attributed to Robert McAfee, the former president of the American Medical Association. The "fact" is not accurate, because approximately 1,500 women are killed each year by husbands or boyfriends, for a total of 7,500 in 5 years, whereas there were 50,000 American casualties in the Vietnam War.

Finally, the March of Dimes reports no study of theirs or any other reputable researcher that finds the results attributed to the March of Dimes in the above "fact."

These are but a few of what some call "advocacy" statistics in the area of family violence (see, e.g., Sommers, 1994). The statistics and quotes are not put forward with malevolent intent or to deliberately deceive people. They are cited and cited again in an attempt to focus public and policy attention on the problem of family violence. Unfortunately, inaccurate statistics can obscure the true nature of the problem. Moreover, some of those who oppose efforts to deal with family violence can undermine advocates' claims for resources and new public policies by demonstrating that the so-called facts are inaccurate.

Family and intimate violence is indeed a significant social and public health problem. It is not, however, an inevitable aspect of family relations. Although there are millions of victims of family violence each year and thousands of fatalities, severe instances of family violence that result in injury are still relatively low-base-rate behaviors that vary across groups and cultures.

## 2. Family violence is confined to mentally disturbed or sick people.

A woman drowns her twin 6-month-old daughters. Another mother throws her daughter off a bridge into icy water. A mother and father plunge their 4-year-old into a bathtub filled with boiling water. A father has sexual intercourse with his 6-month-old daughter. A woman waits for her husband to take a shower, then fires a bullet into his skull at close range with a .357 magnum. These descriptions, and accompanying color slides of the harm done to the victims, are usually enough to convince most people that only someone who is mentally disturbed or truly psychotic would inflict such grievous harm onto a defenseless child, woman, or man. One way of upholding the image of the nurturant and safe family is to combine the notion that family violence is rare with the myth that only "sick" people abuse family members. Combining the two assumptions allows us to believe that when and if violence does take place, it is the problem of "people other than us."

The manner by which people determine that abusers are sick undermines the claim of mental illness. "People who abuse women and children are sick," we are told. How do you know they are sick? "Because they abuse women and children." This explanation does nothing more than substitute the word *sick* for *abuse*. The key question is, without knowing what someone did to his or her spouse or child, could you accurately diagnose him or her as mentally ill? In most cases, this is impossible. The sociologist Murray Straus (1980) claims that fewer than 10% of all instances of family violence are caused by mental illness or psychiatric disorders.

## 3. Family violence is confined to the lower class.

One of the consequences of the massive publicity generated by the murder of Nicole Brown Simpson and the trial of her ex-husband, O.J. Simpson, was a focus on violence in affluent families. Although there is increased awareness about the extent of family violence and the fact that violence is not always caused by mental illness or psychopathology, many people still believe that violence in general, and family violence in particular, is confined to lower-class families and the families of racial and ethnic minorities. There was a small sensation produced in the week following the murder of Nicole Brown Simpson when *Newsweek* magazine ran an unretouched police mug shot of O.J. Simpson while *Time* magazine ran an artist's rendition of the same photograph. The *Time* picture portrayed O.J. Simpson with much darker skin, almost as if the purpose of the drawing was to portray O.J. Simpson closer to the public stereotype of the lower-class, minority abuser.

Next to the myth of mental illness, the next most pervasive myth about family violence is that it is confined to the lower class. Like all myths, there is a grain of truth behind this belief. Researchers do find more *reported* violence and abuse among the lower class. For example, in the Second National Family Violence Survey, the rate of abusive violence toward women in households with total incomes below $10,000 per year was about 70 per 1,000, whereas the rate in households with total incomes more than $40,000 per year was a little less than 20 per 1,000 (Gelles, 1992, 1995). Official reports of child abuse indicate an overwhelming overrepresentation of lower-class families being reported as abusers. However, by virtue of being in the lower class, families run a greater risk of being correctly *and falsely* labeled abusers if their children are seen with injuries (Newberger, Reed, Daniel, Hyde, & Kotelchuck, 1977). Believing that abuse of wives and children is confined to the lower class is yet another way people try to see acts of others as deviant and their own behavior as normal.

### 4. Family violence occurs in all groups—social factors are not relevant.

When the first medical practitioners began to notice and attend to cases of child abuse, one of the first things they were struck by was that the children came from every type of social, racial, economic, and age group. Those who work with battered women also point out that women of all cultures, races, occupations, and income levels are battered.

Indeed, offenders and victims of family violence come from every level of society. It is also true that most forms of family and intimate violence do not occur with equal frequency across social groups. Social factors are relevant in explaining family violence.

For a factor to be a cause of family violence does not mean that it has to be perfectly associated with abuse. For poverty to be a causal factor it is not necessary that only poor people abuse wives, children, or parents and that no well-to-do people are abusive. There are very few (perhaps no) perfect associations in social science. Thus, for social factors to be causal, they need only satisfy the four criteria of causality: (a) association (statistical, not deterministic); (b) time order (the cause must precede the consequences); (c) the relationship is not spurious (no third factor, preceding cause and effect in time, is related

to both cause and effect); and (d) rationale (the proposed relationship has to make logical sense).

Another problem with the observation that social factors are not related is that they are. Even though abuse can be found among the wealthy and the poor, it is more likely to be found among the poor. Even though most poor people do not abuse their children, wives, or parents, there is indeed a greater risk of abuse among those in the lowest income groups.

In addition, it is important to point out the dynamic nature of social factors. Changes in social circumstances, such as becoming unemployed or encountering economic problems, can raise the risk of abuse and violence in a family or an intimate relationship.

### 5. Children who are abused will grow up to be abusers.

This is a myth with some truth value to it. Most studies of wife and child abuse find that abusive adults were more likely to have been treated harshly and abused as children than adults who are not abusive. The problem with the statement that "children who are abused will grow up to be abusers" is that this is a deterministic statement and the relationship is probabilistic. People who experience abuse are more likely, but not preprogrammed, to become violent adults. Sadly, many people have begun to believe that all abused children grow up to be violent. This belief has two negative consequences. First, it scares people who have experienced violence as children into thinking that they are preprogrammed to be violent and that perhaps they should avoid marriage and having children. Second, those who are responsible for detecting and treating child abuse may see an unusual injury in a child and, on learning that a parent had been battered as a child, assume that the parent has caused the injury. False positive diagnoses (labeling someone an abuser when he or she is not) are a possible consequence of believing that violence determines violence.

Again, just as with social factors, it is important to remember that perfect associations rarely exist in social science. Abuse and violence grow out of a complex set of interrelated factors, and latching onto one commonsense factor misrepresents the causal explanation and can cause injustice.

### 6. Battered wives "like" being hit and/or are responsible for the violence; otherwise, they would leave.

In the wake of the killing of Nicole Brown Simpson and Ronald Goldman, a 911 tape was released by the Los Angeles Police Department. The tape revealed that Nicole Brown Simpson had been beaten by her ex-husband, O.J. During the trial, photographs of the results of one of those beatings were shown to the jury. Although many people reacted to the 911 tape and the photos with sympathy and empathy, others' reactions questioned why she would continue a relationship with a man who had battered her and whom she feared. Many battered women find that when they publicly reveal their victimization, rather than receive sympathy, they are blamed for not leaving their batterers.

One common question asked about battered women is, "Why don't they (the battered wives) just pack up and leave?" Battered women fail to attract the same attention and sympathy directed toward battered children because somehow, many people think that the women (a) provoked the violence and (b) must like it if they didn't leave after the first beating. Those who espouse this view (and it is a belief of both men and women) tend to be those with considerable education, good jobs, and extensive social networks. They cannot imagine that someone could be socially, legally, and materially entrapped in a marriage. They cannot imagine that a woman could literally have no place to go. Wives seem to bear the brunt of considerable "victim blaming." Quite a few people believe that battered wives are somehow culpable, and their culpability is enforced

by their decision not to leave. Nothing could be further from the truth.

### 7. Alcohol and drug abuse are the real causes of violence in the home.

The "demon rum" explanation for abuse in the home is nearly as popular as the mental illness explanation and perhaps more popular than the two social class myths. Again, certain facts help support the myth. Most studies find a considerable association between drinking and violence (Fagan, 1990; Gelles, 1974; Gillen, 1946; Guttmacher, 1960; Snell, Rosenwald, & Robey, 1964; Wolfgang, 1958). In cases of spousal violence, both offender and victim have frequently been drinking before the violence. Perhaps as many as half the instances of violence and abuse involve some alcohol or drugs—a very strong association. But do the drugs or the alcohol themselves cause people to be violent? Are drugs and alcohol disinhibitors that unleash violent behavior? And would solving the drug or drinking problem eliminate the violence? Common sense frequently says "yes" to these questions. Research argues "no."' There is little evidence that alcohol and drugs are disinhibitors. The best evidence against the disinhibitor theory comes from cross-cultural studies of drinking behavior. These studies find that how people react to drinking varies from culture to culture (MacAndrew & Edgerton, 1969). In some cultures, people drink and become violent; in others, people drink and are passive. What explains the difference? The difference is due to what people in those societies believe about alcohol. If they believe it is a disinhibitor, people become disinhibited. If they believe that it is a depressant, people become depressed. Because our society believes that alcohol and drugs release violent tendencies, people are given a "time out" from the normal rules of social behavior when they drink or when people believe they are drunk. Combine the time out with the desire to "hush up" instances of family violence, and you have the perfect excuse: "I didn't know what I was doing, I was drunk." Or from the victim's perspective, "My husband is a Dr. Jekyll and Mr. Hyde—when he drinks he is violent, when he is sober there is no problem." In the end, violent spouses and parents learn that if they want to not be held responsible for their violence, they should either drink before they hit, or at least say they were drunk.

Additional evidence comes from research on the link between alcohol and intimate violence. Murray Straus and his colleagues examined data from two national surveys of family violence. The first survey found that there was a strong relationship between alcohol abuse and family violence. However, extreme levels of alcohol abuse were not related to high levels of violence. Physical violence in families actually declined when drunkenness occurred "almost always" (Coleman & Straus, 1983). Glenda Kaufman Kantor and Murray Straus (1987) examined data from a second survey of family violence and again found that excessive drinking is associated with higher levels of wife abuse. However, in the majority of families, alcohol is not an immediate antecedent of violence.

More recently, drug abuse, especially "crack abuse," has been linked to extreme and severe cases of domestic violence. The issue of the possible link between drug abuse and violence is explosive, and fact is often mixed with myth. One problem is that there are multiple drugs that have been implicated in acts of violence, and each drug has a different physiological effect. In addition, there are varying social expectations for how specific drugs affect human behavior. Research on different forms of drugs and their possible effect on violent behavior has found some consistent evidence. Marijuana produces a euphoric effect and may reduce rather than increase the probability of violent behavior. Research on LSD also finds that the physiological effects of the drug are antithetical with violence. One drug does stand out as a possible cause of violent behavior: amphetamines. Amphetamines raise excitability and muscle tension. This may lead to impulsive behavior. The behavior that follows from amphetamine use is related to both the dosage and preuse personality of the user; high-dosage users who already have aggressive personalities are likely to become more aggressive when using this drug (Johnson, 1972). Studies of nonhuman primates, stump-tailed macaques, have found that the monkeys do become more aggressive when they receive a protocol of d-amphetamine (Smith & Byrd, 1987). Based on his program of research with monkeys and amphetamine, Neil Smith estimates that as much as 5% of instances of physical child abuse are related to amphetamine use and abuse (Smith & Byrd, 1987).

Except for the evidence that appears to link amphetamine use to violence, the picture of the alcohol- and drug-crazed partner or parent who impulsively and violently abuses a family member is a distortion. If alcohol and other drugs are linked to violence at all, it is through a complicated set of individual, situational, and social factors (Gelles, 1993).

### 8. Violence and love do not coexist in families.

Once people believe that families are violent, they tend to think that the violence occurs all the time. Moreover, the persistent belief is that if family members are violent, they must not love one another. Violence, although common in many families, is certainly not the most frequent behavior in the home. Although violence and abuse are typically chronic problems in families and not simply one-shot events, on average, abusive parents and partners are violent about once every other month. The remaining time the family functions nonviolently (although the threat of physical violence and abuse tends to hang heavy in the air). It is not only possible, but probable, that abused wives still have strong feelings for their husbands. Many battered children love their parents in spite of the beatings. In fact, most victims of family violence are taught that they deserve the beatings, and thus they have the problem, not the attacker. That violence and love can coexist in a household is perhaps the most insidious aspect of family violence, because we grow up learning that it is acceptable to hit the people we love.

## REFERENCES

Coleman, D., & Straus, M. (1983). Alcohol abuse and family violence. In E. Gottheil, K. Druley, T. Skoloda, & H. Waxman (Eds.), *Alcohol, drug abuse and aggression* (pp. 104–124). Springfield, IL: Charles C Thomas.

Dawson, J. M., & Langan, P. A. (1994). *Murder in families*. Washington, DC: Bureau of Justice Statistics.

Dutton, D. G., & Golant, S. K. (1995). *The batterer: A psychological profile*. New York: Basic Books.

Fagan, J. A. (1990). Intoxication and aggression. *Drugs and crime: Vol. 13. Crime and justice: An annual review* (pp. 241–320). Chicago: University of Chicago Press.

Gelles, R. J. (1974). *The violent home*. Beverly Hills, CA: Sage.

Gelles, R. J. (1992). Poverty and violence toward children. *American Behavioral Scientist*, 35, 258–264.

Gelles, R. J. (1993). Alcohol and other drugs are associated with violence—They are not its cause. In R. J. Gelles & D. Loseke (Eds.), *Current controversies on family violence* (pp. 182–196). Newbury Park, CA: Sage.

Gelles, R. J. (1995). *Family violence by income*. Unpublished data. Kingston, RI. (Mimeographed)

Gil, D. (1970). *Violence against children: Physical child abuse in the United States*. Cambridge, MA: Harvard University Press.

Gillen, J. (1946). *The Wisconsin prisoner: Studies in crimogenesis*. Madison: University of Wisconsin Press.

Guttmacher, M. (1960). *The mind of the murderer*. New York: Farrar, Straus, and Cudahy.

Hyman, A. (1995). *Reporting of domestic violence by health care providers: Overview of state statutes*. San Francisco: Family Violence Prevention Fund.

Johnson, R. (1972). *Aggression in man and animals*. Philadelphia: W. B. Saunders.

Kaufman Kantor, G., & Straus, M. A. (1987). The drunken bum theory of wife beating. *Social Problems*, 34, 213–230.

Kempe, C. H., Silverman, F. N., Steele, B. F., Droegemueller, W., & Silver, H. K. (1962). The battered child syndrome. *Journal of the American Medical Association*, 181, 107–112.

MacAndrew, C., & Edgerton, R. B. (1969). *Drunken comportment: A social explanation*. Chicago: Aldine.

National Research Council. (1993). *Understanding child abuse and neglect*. Washington, DC: National Academy Press.

Newberger, E., Reed, R., Daniel, J. H., Hyde, J., & Kotelchuck, M. (1977). Pediatric social illness: Toward an etiologic classification. *Pediatrics*, 60, 178–185.

Smith, E. O., & Byrd, L. (1987). External and internal influences on aggression in captive group-living monkeys. In R. Gelles & J. Lancaster (Eds.). *Child abuse and neglect: Biosocial dimensions* (pp. 175–199). Hawthorne, NY: Aldine de Gruyter.

Snell, J. E., Rosenwald, R. J., & Robey, A. (1964). The wifebeater's wife: A study of family interaction. *Archives of General Psychiatry*, 11, 107–113.

Sommers, C. H. (1994). *Who stole feminism? How women have betrayed women*. New York: Simon & Schuster.

Stark, E., Flitcraft, A., Zuckerman, D., Grey, A., Robison, J., & Frazier, W. (1981). *Wife abuse in the medical setting: An introduction for health personnel*. Monograph No. 7. Washington, DC: Office of Domestic Violence.

Straus, M. A. (1980). A sociological perspective on the causes of family violence. In M. R. Green (Ed.), *Violence and the family* (pp. 7–31). Boulder, CO: Westview.

Wolfgang, M. (1958). *Patterns in criminal homicide*. New York: Wiley.

## CRITICAL THINKING QUESTIONS

1. Why do myths about family violence exist? What purpose do they serve for the general public, practitioners who treat family violence, and people who don't believe that family violence exists?

2. Gelles notes that "certain facts" support myths about family and intimate violence. If there is a kernel of truth to myths, are they really myths? Or not?

3. What are "advocacy" statistics? In your judgment, does Pearson's article illustrate advocacy statistics or not? What about this selection by Gelles?

# 15 Family Violence

## *Liberal/Feminist:* The Myth of Sexual Symmetry in Marital Violence

RUSSELL P. DOBASH, R. EMERSON DOBASH, MARGO WILSON, AND MARTIN DALY, "The Myth of Sexual Symmetry in Marital Violence," *Social Problems* 39, no. 1 (February 1992): 71–91. Copyright © 1992 by The Society for the Study of Social Problems. Reprinted by permission of the University of California Press and Russell P. Dobash.

*In the first article in this chapter, Pearson contended that women are just as violent as men. Is violence against husbands as prevalent as violence against wives? No, according to Russell P. Dobash, R. Emerson Dobash, Margo Wilson, and Martin Daly. They argue that national data based on reliable and valid measurements of marital violence show that wives' and husbands' violent behavior differs greatly, both qualitatively and quantitatively.*

A number of researchers and commentators have suggested that assaults upon men by their wives constitute a social problem comparable in nature and magnitude to that of wife-beating (Farrell 1986, McNeely and Mann 1990, McNeely and Robinson-Simpson 1987, Shupe, Stacey, and Hazelwood 1987, Steinmetz 1977/78, Steinmetz and Lucca 1998, Straus and Gelles 1986, 1990a, Straus, Gelles, and Steinmetz 1980). Two main bodies of evidence have been offered in support of these authors' claims that husbands and wives are similarly victimized: (1) self-reports of violent acts perpetrated and suffered by survey respondents, especially those in two U.S. national probability samples (Straus and Gelles 1986); and (2) U.S. homicide data. Unlike the case of violence against wives, however, the victimization of husbands allegedly continues to be denied and trivi-alized. "Violence by wives has not been an object of public concern," note Straus and Gelles (1986:472). "There has been no publicity, and no funds have been invested in ameliorating this problem because it has not been defined as a problem."

We shall argue that claims of sexual symmetry in marital violence are exaggerated, and that wives' and husbands' uses of violence differ greatly, both quantitatively and qualitatively. We shall further argue that there is no reason to expect the sexes to be alike in this domain, and that efforts to avoid sexism by lumping male and female data and by the use of gender-neutral terms such as "spouse-beating" are misguided. If violence is gendered, as it assuredly is, explicit characterization of gender's relevance to violence is essential. The alleged similarity of women and men in their use of violence in intimate relationships stands in marked contrast to men's virtual monopoly on the use of violence in other social contexts. . . .

## THE CLAIM OF SEXUALLY SYMMETRICAL MARITAL VIOLENCE

Authoritative claims about the prevalence and sexual symmetry of spousal violence in America began with a 1975 U.S. national survey in which 2,143 married or cohabiting persons were interviewed in person about their actions in the preceding year. Straus (1977/78) announced that the survey results showed that the "marriage license is a hitting license," and moreover that the rates of perpetrating spousal violence, including severe violence, were higher for wives than for husbands. He concluded:

> Violence between husband and wife is far from a one way street. The old cartoons of the wife chasing the husband with a rolling pin or throwing pots and pans are closer to reality than most (and especially those with feminist sympathies) realize (Straus 1977/78:447–448).

In 1985, the survey was repeated by telephone with a new national probability sample including 3,520 husband-wife households, and with similar results. In each survey, the researchers interviewed either the wife or the husband (but not both) in each contacted household about how the couple settled their differences when they had a disagreement. The individual who was interviewed was presented with a list of eighteen "acts" ranging from "discussed an issue calmly" and "cried" to "threw something at him/her/you" and "beat him/ her/you up," with the addition of "'choked him/her/you" in 1985 (Straus 1990a:33). These acts constituted the Conflict Tactics Scales (CTS) and were intended to measure three constructs: "Reasoning," "Verbal Aggression," and "Physical Aggression" or "Violence," which was further subdivided into "Minor Violence" and "Severe Violence" according to a pre-

sumed potential for injury (Straus 1979, Straus and Gelles 1990a). Respondents were asked how frequently they had perpetrated each act in the course of "conflicts or disagreements" with their spouses (and with one randomly selected child) within the past year, and how frequently they had been on the receiving end. Each respondent's self-reports of victimization and perpetration contributed to estimates of rates of violence by both husbands and wives.

According to both surveys, rates of violence by husbands and wives were strikingly similar (Straus and Gelles 1986, 1990b, Straus et al. 1980). The authors estimated that in the year prior to the 1975 survey 11.6 percent of U.S. husbands were victims of physical violence perpetrated by their wives, while 12.1 percent of wives were victims of their husbands' violence. In 1985, these percentages had scarcely changed, but husbands seemed more vulnerable: 12.1 percent of husbands and 11 .3 percent of wives were victims. In both surveys, husbands were more likely to be victims of acts of "severe violence": in 1975, 4.6 percent of husbands were such victims versus 3.8 percent of wives, and in 1985, 4.4 percent of husbands versus 3.0 percent of wives were victims. In reporting their results, the surveys' authors stressed the surprising assaultiveness of wives:

> The repeated finding that the rate of assault by women is similar to the rate by their male partners is an important and distressing aspect of violence in American families. It contrasts markedly to the behavior of women outside the family. It shows that within the family or in dating and cohabiting relationships, women are about as violent as men (Straus and Gelles 1990b:104).

Others have endorsed and publicized these conclusions. For example, a recent review of marital violence concludes, with heavy reliance on Straus and Gelles's survey results, that "(a) women are more prone than men to engage in severely violent acts; (b) each year more men than women are victimized by their intimates"

(McNeely and Mann 1990:130). One of Straus and Gelles's collaborators in the 1975 survey, Steinmetz (1977/78), used the same survey evidence to proclaim the existence of "battered husbands" and a "battered husband syndrome." She has remained one of the leading defenders of the claim that violence between men and women in the family is symmetrical (Steinmetz 1981, 1986, Steinmetz and Lucca 1998, Straus et al. 1980). Steinmetz and her collaborators maintain that the problem is not wife-beating perpetrated by violent men, but "violent couples" and "violent people" (see also Shupe et al. 1987). Men may be stronger on average, argues Steinmetz, but weaponry equalizes matters, as is allegedly shown by the nearly equivalent numbers of U.S. husbands and wives who are killed by their partners. The reason why battered husbands are inconspicuous and seemingly rare is supposedly that shame prevents them from seeking help.

Some authors maintain not only that wives initiate violence at rates comparable to husbands, but that they rival them in the damage they inflict as well. McNeely and Robinson-Simpson (1987), for example, argue that research shows that the "truth about domestic violence" is that "women are as violent, if not more violent than men," in their inclinations, in their actions, and in the damage they inflict. The most dramatic evidence invoked in this context is again the fact that wives kill: spousal homicides—for which detection should be minimally or not at all biased because homicides are nearly always discovered and recorded—produce much more nearly equivalent numbers of male and female victims in the United States than do sublethal assault data, which are subject to sampling biases when obtained from police, shelters, and hospitals (McNeely and Robinson-Simpson 1987, Steinmetz 1977/78, Steinmetz and Lucca 1988, Straus et al. 1980). According to McNeely and Mann (1990:130), "the average man's size and strength are neutralized by guns and

knives, boiling water, bricks, fireplace pokers, and baseball bats.". . .

The existence of an invisible legion of assaulted husbands is an inference which strikes many family violence researchers as reasonable. Two lines of evidence—homicide data and the CTS survey results—suggest to those supporting the sexual-symmetry-of-violence thesis that large numbers of men are trapped in violent relationships. These men are allegedly being denied medical, social welfare, and criminal justice services because of an unwillingness to accept the evidence from homicide statistics and the CTS surveys (Gelles 1982, Steinmetz 1986).

## VIOLENCE AGAINST WIVES

Any argument that marital violence is sexually symmetrical must either dismiss or ignore a large body of contradictory evidence indicating that wives greatly outnumber husbands as victims. While CTS researchers were discovering and publicizing the mutual violence of wives and husbands, other researchers—using evidence from courts, police, and women's shelters—were finding that wives were much more likely than husbands to be victims (e.g., Byles 1978, Chester and Streather 1972, Dobash and Dobash 1977/78, 1979, Levinger 1966, Lystad 1975, Martin 1976, O'Brien 1971, Stark et al. 1979, Vanfossen 1979). After an extensive review of the research, Lystad (1975) expressed the consensus: "The occurrence of adult violence in the home usually involves males as aggressors towards females." This conclusion was subsequently supported by numerous further studies of divorce records, emergency room patients treated for non-accidental injuries, police assault records, and spouses seeking assistance and refuge (e.g., Fergusson et al. 1986, Goldberg and Tomlanovich 1984, McLeer and Anwar 1989, Okun 1986, Warshaw 1989). Analyses of police and court records in North America and Europe have persistently indicated that women constitute ninety to ninety-five percent of the victims of those assaults in the home reported to the criminal justice system (Dobash and Dobash 1977/1978, McLeod 1984, Quarm and Schwartz 1985, Vanfossen 1979).

Defenders of the sexual-symmetry-of-violence thesis do not deny these results, but they question their representativeness: these studies could be biased because samples of victims were self-selected. However, criminal victimization surveys using national probability samples similarly indicate that wives are much more often victimized than husbands. Such surveys in the United States, Canada, and Great Britain have been replicated in various years, with essentially the same results. Beginning in 1972 and using a panel survey method involving up to seven consecutive interviews at six-month intervals, the U.S. National Crime Survey has generated nearly a million interviews. Gaquin's (1977/78) analysis of U.S. National Crime Survey data for 1973–1975 led her to conclude that men "have almost no risk of being assaulted by their wives" (634–635); only 3 percent of the violence reported from these surveys involved attacks on men by their female partners. Another analysis of the National Crime Survey data from 1973 to 1980 found that 6 percent of spousal assault incidents were directed at men (McLeod 1984). Schwartz (1987) re-analyzed the same victimization surveys with the addition of the 1981 and 1982 data, and found 102 men who claimed to have been victims of assaults by their wives (4 percent of domestic assault incidents) in contrast to 1,641 women who said they were assaulted by husbands. The 1981 Canadian Urban Victimization Survey (Solicitor General of Canada 1985) and the 1987 General Social Survey (Sacco and Johnson 1990, Statistics Canada 1990) produced analogous findings, from which Johnson (1989) concluded that "women account for 80–90 percent of victims in assaults or sexual assaults between spouses or former spouses. In fact, the number of domestic assaults involving males was too low in both surveys to provide reliable estimates" (1–2). The 1982 and 1984 British Crime Surveys found that women accounted for all the victims of marital assaults (Worrall and Pease 1986). Self-reports of criminal victimization based on national probability surveys, while not without methodological weaknesses, are not subject to the same reporting biases as divorce, police, and hospital records.

The national crime surveys also indicate that women are much more likely than men to suffer injury as a result of assaults in the home (Schwartz 1987, Solicitor General of Canada 1985, Worrall and Pease 1986). After analyzing the results of the U.S. National Crime Surveys, Schwartz (1987:67) concludes, "there are still more than 13 times as many women seeking medical care from a private physician for injuries received in a spousal assault." This result again replicates the typical findings of studies of police or hospital records. For example, women constituted 94 percent of the injury victims in an analysis of the spousal assault cases among 262 domestic disturbance calls to police in Santa Barbara County, California (Berk et al. 1983); moreover, the women's injuries were more serious than the men's. Berk et al. (1983:207) conclude that "'when injuries are used as the outcome of interest, a marriage license is a hitting license but for men only.'" Brush (1990) reports that a U.S. national probability sample survey of over 13,000 respondents in 1987–1988 replicated the evident symmetry of marital violence when CTS-like questions about acts were posed, but also revealed that women were much more often injured than men (and that men downplayed women's injuries).

The CTS survey data indicating equivalent violence by wives and husbands thus stand in contradiction to injury data, to police incident reports, to help-seeking statistics, and even to other, larger, national probability sample surveys of self-reported victimization. The CTS researchers insist that their results alone are accurate because husbands' victimizations are unlikely to be detected or reported by any other method. It is therefore important to consider in detail the CTS and the data it generates.

## DO CTS DATA REFLECT THE REALITY OF MARITAL VIOLENCE?

The CTS instrument has been much used and much criticized. Critics have complained that its exclusive focus on "acts" ignores the actors' interpretations, motivations, and intentions; that physical violence is arbitrarily delimited, excluding, for example, sexual assault and rape; that retrospective reports of the past year's events are unlikely to be accurate; that researchers' attributions of "violence" (with resultant claims about its statistical prevalence) are based on respondents' admitting to acts described in such an impoverished manner as to conflate severe assaults with trivial gestures; that the . . . distinction between "minor" and "'severe violence" (whereby, for example, "tried to hit with something" is definitionally "severe" and "slapped" is definitionally "minor") constitutes a poor operationalization of severity; that the responses of aggressors and victims have been given identical evidentiary status in deriving incidence estimates, while their inconsistencies have been ignored; that the CTS omits the contexts of violence, the events precipitating it, and the sequences of events by which it progresses; and that it fails to connect outcomes, especially injury, with the acts producing them. . . .

### Problem with the Interpretation of CTS Responses

. . . In asking about such abstractions as "violence," the CTS is confined to questions about "acts": Respondents are asked whether they have "pushed" their partners, have "slapped" them, and so forth, rather than whether they have "assaulted" them or behaved "violently." This focus on "acts" is intended to reduce problems of self-serving and biased definitional criteria on the part of the respondents. However, any gain in objectivity has been undermined by the way that CTS survey data have then been analyzed and interpreted. Any respondent who acknowledges a single instance of having "pushed," "grabbed," "shoved," "slapped," *or* "hit or tried to hit" another person is deemed a perpetrator of "violence" by the researchers, regardless of the act's context, consequences, or meaning to the parties involved. Similarly, a single instance of having "kicked," "bit," "hit or tried to hit with an object," "beat up," "choked," "threatened with a knife or gun," or "used a knife or fired a gun" makes one a perpetrator of "severe violence."

Consider a "slap." The word encompasses anything from a slap on the hand chastising a dinner companion for reaching for a bite of one's dessert to a tooth-loosening assault intended to punish, humiliate, and terrorize. These are not trivial distinctions; indeed, they constitute the essence of definitional issues concerning violence. Almost all definitions of violence and violent acts refer to intentions. Malevolent intent is crucial, for example, to legal definitions of "assault" (to which supporters of the CTS have often mistakenly claimed that their "acts" correspond; e.g., Straus 1990b:58). However, no one has systematically investigated how respondents vary in their subjective definitions of the "acts" listed on the CTS. If, for example, some respondents interpret phrases such as "tried to hit with an object" literally, then a good deal of relatively harmless behavior surely taints the estimates of "severe violence." Although this problem has not been investigated systematically, one author has shown that it is potentially serious. In a study of 103 couples, Margolin (1987) found that wives surpassed husbands in their use of "severe violence" according to the CTS, but unlike others who have obtained this result, Margolin troubled to check its meaningfulness with more intensive interviews. She concluded:

While CTS items appear behaviorally specific, their meanings still are open to interpretation. In one couple who endorsed the item "kicking," for example, we discovered that the kicking took place in bed in a more kidding, than serious, fashion. Although this behavior meets the criterion for severe abuse on the CTS, neither spouse viewed it as aggressive, let alone violent. In another couple, the wife scored on severe physical aggression while the husband scored on low-level aggression only. The inquiry revealed that, after years of passively accepting the husband's repeated abuse, this wife finally decided, on one occasion, to retaliate by hitting him over the head with a wine decanter (1987:82).

## HOMICIDES

The second line of evidence that has been invoked in support of the claim that marital violence is more or less sexually symmetrical is the number of lethal outcomes:

> Data on homicide between spouses suggest that an almost equal number of wives kill their husbands as husbands kill their wives (Wolfgang 1958). Thus it appears that men and women might have equal potential for violent marital interaction; initiate similar acts of violence; and when differences of physical strength are equalized by weapons, commit similar amounts of spousal homicide (Steinmetz and Lucca 1988:241).

McNeely and Robinson-Simpson (1987:485) elevated the latter hypothesis about the relevance of weapons to the status of a fact: "Steinmetz observed that when weapons neutralize differences in physical strength, about as many men as women are victims of homicide."

Steinmetz and Lucca's citation of Wolfgang refers to his finding that 53 Philadelphia men killed their wives between 1948 and 1952, while 47 women killed their husbands. This is a slender basis for such generalization, but fuller information does indeed bear Steinmetz out as regards the near equivalence of body counts in the

United States: Maxfield (1989) reported that there were 10,529 wives and 7,888 husbands killed by their mates in the entire country between 1976 and 1985, a 1.3:1 ratio of female to male victims.

Husbands are indeed almost as often slain as are wives in the United States, then. However, there remain several problems with Steinmetz and Lucca's (as well as McNeely and Robinson-Simpson's) interpretation of this fact. Studies of actual cases (Campbell 1992, Goetting 1989) lend no support to the facile claim that homicidal husbands and wives "initiate similar acts of violence." Men often kill wives after lengthy periods of prolonged physical violence accompanied by other forms of abuse and coercion; the roles in such cases are seldom if ever reversed. Men perpetrate familicidal massacres, killing spouse and children together; women do not. Men commonly hunt down and kill wives who have left them; women hardly ever behave similarly. Men kill wives as part of planned murder-suicides; analogous acts by women are almost unheard of. Men kill in response to revelations of wifely infidelity; women almost never respond similarly, though their mates are more often adulterous. The evidence is overwhelming that a large proportion of the spouse-killings perpetrated by wives, but almost none of those perpetrated by husbands, are acts of self-defense. Unlike men, women kill male partners after years of suffering physical violence, after they have exhausted all available sources of assistance, when they feel trapped, and because they fear for their own lives (e.g., Browne 1987, Campbell 1992, Polk and Ranson 1991).

## HOW TO GAIN A VALID ACCOUNT OF MARITAL VIOLENCE?

How ought researchers to conceive of "violence"? People differ in their views about whether a particular act was a violent one and about who was responsible. Assessments of intention and justifiability are no less relevant to the labelling of an event as "violent" than are more directly observable considerations like the force exerted or the damage inflicted.

Enormous differences in meaning and consequence exist between a woman pummelling her laughing husband in an attempt to convey strong feelings and a man pummelling his weeping wife in an attempt to punish her for coming home late. It is not enough to acknowledge such contrasts (as CTS researchers have sometimes done), if such acknowledgments neither inform further research nor alter such conclusions as "within the family or in dating and cohabiting relationships, women are about as violent as men" (Straus and Gelles 1990b:104). What is needed are forms of analysis that will lead to a comprehensive description of the violence itself as well as an explanation of it. In order to do this, it is, at the very least, necessary to analyze the violent event in a holistic manner, with attention to the entire sequences of distinct acts as well as associated motives, intentions, and consequences, all of which must in turn be situated within the wider context of the relationship.

## REFERENCES

Berk, Richard A., Sarah F. Berk, Donileen R. Loseke, and D. Rauma. 1983. "Mutual combat and other family violence myths." In *The Dark Side of Families*, ed. David Finkelhor, Richard J. Gelles, Gerald T. Hotaling, and Murray A. Straus, 197–212. Beverly Hills, Calif.: Sage.

Browne, Angela. 1987. *When Battered Women Kill*. New York: Free Press.

Brush, Lisa D. 1990. "Violent acts and injurious outcomes in married couples: Methodological issues in the National Survey of Families and Households." *Gender and Society* 4:56–67.

Byles, Jack A. 1978. "Family violence: Some facts and gaps. A statistical overview." In *Domestic Violence: Issues and Dynamics*, ed.

Vincent D'Oyley, 53–83. Toronto: The Ontario Institute for Studies in Education.

Campbell, Jacqueline C. 1992. "If I can't have you, no one can: Issues of power and control in homicide of female partners." In *Femicide: The Politics of Woman Killing*, ed. Jill Radford and Diana E. H. Russell. New York: Twayne.

Chester, Robert, and Jane Streather. 1972. "Cruelty in English divorce: Some empirical findings." *Journal of Marriage and the Family* 34:706–710.

Dobash, R. Emerson, and Russell P. Dobash. 1977/78. "Wives: The 'appropriate' victims of marital violence." *Victimology* 2:426–442.

Dobash, R. Emerson, and Russell P. Dobash. 1979. *Violence Against Wives: A Case Against the Patriarchy*. New York: Free Press.

Farrell, Warren. 1986. *Why Men Are the Way They Are: The Male-Female Dynamic*. New York: McGraw-Hill.

Fergusson, David M., L. John Horwood, Kathryn L. Kershaw, and Frederick T. Shannon. 1986. "Factors associated with reports of wife assault in New Zealand." *Journal of Marriage and the Family* 48:407–412.

Gaquin, Deirdre A. 1977/78. "Spouse abuse: Data from the National Crime Survey." *Victimology* 2:632–643.

Gelles, Richard J. 1982. "Domestic criminal violence." In *Criminal Violence*, ed. Marvin E. Wolfgang and Neil A. Weiner, 201–235. Beverly Hills, Calif.: Sage.

Goetting, Ann. 1989. "Patterns of marital homicide: A comparison of husbands and wives." *Journal of Comparative Family Studies* 20:341–354.

Goldberg, Wendy G., and Michael C. Tomlanovich. 1984. "Domestic violence victims in the Emergency Department: New findings." *Journal of the American Medical Association* 251:3259–3264.

Johnson, Holly. 1989. "Wife assault in Canada." Paper presented at the Annual Meeting of the American Society of Criminology, November, Reno, Nevada.

Levinger, George. 1966. "Sources of marital dissatisfaction among applicants for divorce." *American Journal of Orthopsychiatry* 36:803–806.

Lystad, Mary H. 1975. "Violence at home: A review of literature." *American Journal of Orthopsychiatry* 45:328–345.

Margolin, Gayla. 1987. "The multiple forms of aggressiveness between marital partners:

How do we identify them?" *Journal of Marital and Family Therapy* 13:77–84.

Martin, Del. 1976. *Battered Wives*. San Francisco, Calif.: Glide Publications.

McLeer, Susan R., and R. Anwar. 1989. "A study of battered women presenting in an emergency department." *American Journal of Public Health* 79:65–66.

McLeod, Maureen. 1984. "Women against men: An examination of domestic violence based on an analysis of official data and national victimization data." *Justice Quarterly* 1:171–193.

McNeely, R. L., and CoraMae Richey Mann. 1990. "Domestic violence is a human issue." *Journal of Interpersonal Violence* 5:129–132.

McNeely, R. L., and Gloria Robinson-Simpson. 1987. "The truth about domestic violence: A falsely framed issue." *Social Work* 32:485–490.

O'Brien, John E. 1971. "Violence in divorce-prone families." *Journal of Marriage and the Family* 33:692–698.

Okun, Lewis. 1986. *Woman Abuse: Facts Replacing Myths*. Albany, N.Y.: SUNY Press.

Polk, Kenneth, and David Ranson. 1991. "The role of gender in intimate violence." *Australia and New Zealand Journal of Criminology* 24:15–24.

Quarm, Daisy, and Martin D. Schwartz. 1985. "Domestic violence in criminal court." In *Criminal Justice Politics and Women: The Aftermath of Legally Mandated Change*, ed. C. Schweber and C. Feinman, 29–46. New York: Haworth.

Sacco, Vincent F., and Holly Johnson. 1990. *Patterns of Criminal Victimization in Canada*. Ottawa: Statistics Canada.

Schwartz, Martin D. 1987. "Gender and injury in spousal assault." *Sociological Focus* 20:61–75.

Shupe, Anson, William A. Stacey, and Lonnie R. Hazelwood. 1987. *Violent Men, Violent Couples: The Dynamics of Domestic Violence*. Lexington, Mass.: Lexington Books.

Solicitor General of Canada. 1985. *Female Victims of Crime. Canadian Urban Victimization Survey Bulletin No. 4*. Ottawa: Programs Branch/Research and Statistics Group.

Stark, Evan, Anne Flitcraft, and W. Frazier. 1979. "Medicine and patriarchal violence: The social construction of a 'private' event." *Internal Journal of Health Services* 9:461–493.

Statistics Canada. 1990. "Conjugal violence against women." *Juristat* 10 (7):1–7.

Steinmetz, Suzanne K. 1977/78. "The battered husband syndrome." *Victimology* 2:499–509.

Steinmetz, Suzanne K. 1981. "A cross-cultural comparison of marital abuse." *Journal of Sociology and Social Welfare* 8:404–414.

Steinmetz, Suzanne K. 1986. "Family violence. Past, present, and future." In *Handbook of Marriage and the Family*, ed. Marvin B. Sussman and Suzanne K. Steinmetz, 725–765. New York: Plenum.

Steinmetz, Suzanne K., and Joseph S. Lucca. 1988. "Husband battering." In *Handbook of Family Violence*, ed. Vincent B. Van Hasselt, R. L. Morrison, A. S. Bellack, and M. Hersen, 233–246. New York: Plenum Press.

Straus, Murray A. 1977/78. "Wife-beating: How common, and why?" *Victimology* 2:443–458.

Straus, Murray A. 1979. "Measuring intra-family conflict and violence: The Conflict Tactics (CT) Scales." *Journal of Marriage and the Family* 51:75–88.

Straus, Murray A. 1990a. "Measuring intra-family conflict and violence: The Conflict Tactics (CT) Scales." In *Physical Violence in American Families*, ed. Murray A. Straus and Richard J. Gelles, 29–47. New Brunswick, N.J.: Transaction Publishers.

Straus, Murray A. 1990b. "The Conflict Tactics Scales and its critics: An evaluation and new data on validity and reliability." In *Physical Violence in American Families*, ed. Murray A. Straus and Richard J. Gelles, 49–73. New Brunswick, N.J.: Transaction Publishers.

Straus, Murray A., and Richard J. Gelles, eds. 1990a. *Physical Violence in American Families*. New Brunswick, N.J.: Transaction Publishers.

Straus, Murray A., and Richard J. Gelles. 1986. "Societal change and change in family violence from 1975 to 1985 as revealed by two national surveys." *Journal of Marriage and the Family* 48:465–480.

Straus, Murray A., and Richard J. Gelles. 1990. "How violent are American families? Estimates from the National Family Violence Resurvey and other studies." In *Physical Violence in American Families*, ed. Murray A. Straus and Richard J. Gelles, 95–112. New Brunswick, N.J.: Transaction Publishers.

Straus, Murray A., Richard J. Gelles, and Suzanne K. Steinmetz. 1980. *Behind Closed Doors: Violence in the American Family.* New York: Doubleday/Anchor.

Vanfossen, B. E. 1979. "Intersexual violence in Monroe County, New York." *Victimology* 4:299–305.

Warshaw, Carole. 1989. "Limitations of the medical model in the care of battered women." *Gender and Society* 3:506–517.

Worrall, A., and Ken Pease. 1986. "Personal crime against women: Evidence from the 1982 British Crime Survey." *The Howard Journal* 25:118–124.

**CRITICAL THINKING QUESTIONS**

1. What is the Conflict Tactics Scale (CTS)? How, according to the authors, does the CTS distort information about acts of physical violence?

2. How does the context of marital violence that results in homicide differ for women and men?

3. Why do Pearson (see the first article in this chapter) and Dobash and his colleagues reach such different conclusions about sexual symmetry in marital violence?

# 16 Divorce

## Conservative: Finding Fault with No-Fault Divorce

GLENN T. STANTON, "Finding Fault with No-Fault," *Focus on the Family Citizen*, January 15, 1996, pp. 14–15. Reprinted with permission.

*The United States has one of the highest divorce rates in the world, just behind Russia. Some family policy groups feel that states should tighten divorce laws. Glenn T. Stanton argues, for example, that rolling back no-fault divorce laws would provide women with greater economic security and protect children from financial and emotional hardship.*

Todd and Leslie were high-school sweethearts who married just after graduation. Leslie supported Todd through six years of college as he earned a bachelor's degree, then an MBA. When Todd saved enough money to start an oil-change business in a nearby town, Leslie—who was busy raising five children by this time—kept the books for her husband's new enterprise.

The business prospered, growing into a chain of eight stores with 50 employees. There were the usual labor problems—some substandard and dishonest employees were fired—but overall the work crews were productive, courteous, and cohesive. Not so with Todd and Leslie; their marriage disintegrated. Out of the blue, Todd asked Leslie for a divorce. He would not explain why, and Leslie refused to give her consent.

Todd couldn't be happier with the divorce laws in his state. He didn't need a reason—or Leslie's consent for that matter—in seeking a divorce. Leslie, however, was mortified, as she faced the formidable and unpleasant tasks of both finding a decent-paying job and affordable child-care arrangements for their kids.

She found it bitterly ironic that Todd could dissolve their marriage more easily than he could break an eight-month employment agreement with an ineffectual shop manager last year.

*Todd had to provide all kinds of paperwork showing cause for firing the manager,* Leslie thought, *but he wasn't required to show any cause to divorce me. I had less legal protection than Todd's manager had. Where's the justice in that?*

### VICTIMS EVERYWHERE

There are thousands—if not millions—of individuals like Leslie in America today. Their spouses have divorced them without cause, simply because the law no longer requires it.

The culprit? No-fault divorce.

Before 1969, when California became the first state to embrace no-fault, "society erected a formidable barrier, fault-based divorce law, to prevent (or at least hinder) the dissolution of a marriage," wrote three law professors in the *Journal of Marriage and the Family*.[1]

Under a fault-based system, courts would grant a divorce only if one spouse was found guilty of certain acts, such as adultery or cruelty, and the other spouse was found innocent. Divorce was denied if both parties were at fault or if the innocent party did not want the divorce—further indication that the state had an interest in preserving marriage.[2]

Determining guilt and innocence by providing proof—for example, that a spouse had been adulterous—became an ugly business, however. Lawmakers and the public were repelled by the spectacle of private irresponsibility made public. By 1985, all 50 states had adopted no-fault divorce; what they thought would be a much less acrimonious policy.

What lawmakers didn't recognize, however, was that the new laws put one spouse—the one who wanted to keep the marriage intact—at a distinct disadvantage.

"Women held a potent club [before no-fault]. If a man wanted his freedom, he would have to pay for it," wrote marriage-law expert Thomas Mulroy in the *American Bar Association Journal*. A fault-based system allowed women "to extract economic security through bargaining. A divorce decree was often an expensive commodity."[3]

Under no-fault, if one partner wants out, the spouse has no coercive power to hold the marriage together. That is why author and family commentator Maggie Gallagher calls no-fault divorce "the murder of marriage" because it elevated "wanderlust [to] a state-protected emotion, while loyalty was on its own."[4]

Beyond creating an extraordinary injustice, no-fault divorce has predictably led to more divorces. The *Journal of Marriage and the Family* recently reported that "the switch from fault divorce law to no-fault divorce law led to a measurable increase in the divorce rate" in America.[5] In fact, the divorce rate in the U.S. has risen 380 percent since 1970.[6] This increase has guaranteed the United States' dubious distinction of being the unchallenged divorce-rate leader in the industrialized world.[7]

## COLLATERAL DAMAGE

Every development that raises the divorce rate brings with it misery, because divorce itself is associated with a range of social pathologies, as countless studies demonstrate. The Council on Families in America, a diverse group of scholars from various academic disciplines, recently released a report detailing the failure of the "divorce revolution." They explain:

*The evidence of the failure is overwhelming. [This] revolution has created terrible hardships for children. It has generated poverty within families. It has burdened us with insupportable social costs. It has failed to deliver on its promise of greater adult happiness and better relationships between men and women.*[8]

An overwhelming body of social-science data support their conclusion:

- Divorced men and women experience far greater health problems than their married or never-married counterparts.[9]
- A greater number of divorced men and women are admitted for psychiatric care than married or single people, and their treatments are less successful.[10]
- Children of divorce do poorer in school, exhibit greater behavioral problems at home and in school, and engage in sexual activity and criminal behavior earlier in life than children whose parents remain married.[11]
- Compared with those from intact families, adults who experienced divorce as children have poorer psychological adjustment, lower socioeconomic attainment, and greater marital instability.[12]

Judith Wallerstein, founder and executive director of the Center for the Family in Transition, is one of few researchers who understands not just the statistical impact but also the emotional impact of divorce. She writes:

*Divorce has ripple effects that touch not just the family involved, but our entire society. As [one] writer observed when his own marriage broke up, "Each divorce is the death of a small civilization." Today, all relationships between men and women are profoundly influenced by the high incidence of divorce. Children from intact families are jittery about divorce. Teachers from all over the country tell me that their students come to school wide-eyed with fear, saying that their parents quarreled the night before and asking in terror, "Does that mean they are going to divorce?" Radical changes in family life affect all families, homes, parents, children, courtships, and marriages—silently altering the social fabric of the entire society.[13]*

## COUNTER-REVOLUTION

Armed with such research, pro-family leaders believe they can persuade state legislatures to roll back no-fault divorce laws. One of their initial targets is Michigan.

State Rep. Jessie Dalman, R–Holland, is the chief sponsor of a package of bills that would restore divorce law in Michigan to a fault-based system in cases where there is not mutual consent for the divorce. The Michigan Family Forum (MFF), a pro-family group, affiliated with Focus on the Family, enthusiastically supports this bill and is working diligently to enlist support among legislators.

"Our immediate goal in this effort is to restore some justice to an arena of law that is terribly unjust, and to begin a discussion of the negative impact divorce has on children and adults," said Dan Jarvis, research and public policy coordinator for MFF.

Another state pro-family group, the Rocky Mountain Family Council in Colorado, is planning a three-year initiative against no-fault. The first step would encourage a serious public discussion regarding the problem of current divorce law. Second, the council will seek to reduce divorce by helping churches more effectively counsel couples entering marriage. In the third step, the council will encourage introduction of divorce-reform legislation in the Colorado state legislature.

"No-fault divorce has spawned an entire generation of broken families and broken hearts; but there may yet be time to reach the next generation," said Tom McMillen, executive director of the Rocky Mountain Family Council and a lawyer. "If we can get people's eyes off of themselves and onto children, we believe we can achieve consensus about the destructiveness of divorce."

## NOTES

1. Paul A. Nakonezny, Robert D. Shull, and Joseph Lee Rodgers, "The Effect of No-Fault Divorce Law on the Divorce Rate Across the 50 States and Its Relation to Income, Education and Religiosity," *Journal of Marriage and the Family* 57 (May 1995): 477–488.

2. Lenore J. Weitzman, *The Divorce Revolution* (New York: The Free Press, 1985), p. 7.

3. Thomas M. Mulroy, "No-Fault Divorce: Are Women Losing the Battle?" *ABA Journal*, November 1989, p. 77.

4. Maggie Gallagher, *Enemies of Eros: How the Sexual Revolution Is Killing Family, Marriage and Sex and What We Can Do About It* (Chicago: Bonus Books, 1989), p. 192.

5. Paul A. Nakonezny, Robert Shull, and Joseph Rodgers, "The Effect of No-Fault Divorce Law on the Divorce Rate Across the 50 States and Its Relation to Income, Education, and Religiosity," *Journal of Marriage and the Family*, 1995, 57:477–488.

6. *Statistical Abstract of the United States: 1993*, U. S. Bureau of the Census (113th edition), Washington, DC, 1994, p. 53.

7. Ailsa Burns and Cath Scott, *Mother-Headed Families and Why They Have Increased* (Hillsdale, NJ: Lawrence Erlbaum Associates, 1994), pp. 2, 5.

8. "Marriage in America: A Report to the Nation," a report issued by the Council on Fam-

ilies in America; Institute for American Values, 1995, p. 3.

9. Robert H. Coombs, "Marital Status and Personal Well-Being: A Literature Review," *Family Relations*, 1991, 40:97–102.

10. Coombs, 1991.

11. Paul Amato and B. Keith, "Parental Divorce and Well-Being of Children: A Meta-Analysis," *Psychological Bulletin*, 1991, 110:26–46.

12. Paul Amato and B. Keith, "Parental Divorce and Adult Well-Being: A Meta-Analysis," *Journal of Marriage and the Family*, 1991, 53:43–48.

13. Judith S. Wallerstein and Sandra Blakeslee, *Second Chances: Men, Women and Children a Decade After Divorce* (New York: Ticknor & Fields, 1990), p. xxi.

## CRITICAL THINKING QUESTIONS

1. Why, according to Stanton, should we tighten no-fault divorce laws? Should we eliminate them altogether?

2. No-fault opponents argue that the partner who wants to keep the marriage intact should have the legal right to do so. What, however, about the legal rights of the wife or husband who wants to end the marriage?

3. Stanton maintains that divorce-reform legislation would decrease the negative impact of divorce on children and adults. However, what kinds of problems might such legislation create?

# 16 Divorce

## *Centrist:* Dismantling the Divorce Culture

*Most centrists support existing no-fault divorce laws. They contend, nonetheless, that many of the reasons for divorce are self-centered, irresponsible, and often frivolous. Barbara Dafoe Whitehead maintains, for example, that we have created a "divorce culture." Our high levels of divorce lead to less gender equality, decrease freedom for parents and children, weaken the social basis for altruism, and damage the nation's social fabric by eroding the idea of lasting commitments. Whitehead offers several suggestions for dismantling the divorce culture.*

At such high and sustained levels, divorce is not simply a legal mechanism for dissolving marriages but a social and cultural force that opportunistically reproduces itself everywhere. A high-divorce society is a society marked by growing division and separation in its social arrangements, a society of single mothers and vanished fathers, of divided households and split parenting, of fractured parent-child bonds and fragmented families, of broken links between marriage and parenthood.

The shift from a family world governed by the institution of marriage to one ruled by divorce has brought a steady weakening of primary human relationships and bonds. Men's and women's relationships are becoming more fleeting and unreliable. Children are losing their ties to their fathers. Even a mother's love is not forever, as the growing number of throwaway kids suggests.

Divorce is not the only force that has contributed to weaker family ties and more fragile families, but it has been the most important in shaping a new cultural disposition about the meaning of family breakup. Divorce has been damaging not only because it has contributed to the widespread trend toward family fragmentation and the paternal abandonment of children but also because it has won influential adherents in the society who defend family breakup as necessary for individual psychological growth and freedom.

When the divorce revolution began, no one could have predicted where it would lead, how it would change the shape and content of family relationships, or whether it would deliver on its promises of improving marriage and family life, especially for women. Thirty years later we have acquired a substantial body of social learning experience and empirical evidence on the impact of divorce on men and women, on children, and on the larger society. And this body of evidence tells us that the cultural case for divorce has been based on misleading claims, false promises, and bankrupt ideas.

## LESS EQUALITY, MORE INEQUALITY

One of the claims made for divorce was that with greater freedom to dissolve marriage, women would gain greater equality and independence in their family lives. Yet the evidence suggests that widespread divorce has generated new forms of inequality for women and children. It has contributed to greater economic insecurity and poverty among women and children, and it has been a principal generator of unequal opportunities and outcomes for children. Indeed, it is hard to think of any recent economic force that has been as brutally efficient as divorce in transforming middle-class haves into have-nots. In a high-divorce society—even if the wage gap continues to narrow, jobs continue to be plentiful, and child-support enforcement continues to be more efficiently and aggressively pursued—women are still likely to lose ground in their efforts to achieve economic equality.

Nor can it be said that widespread divorce has moved us closer to the social goal of greater gender equality. In a society marked by high and sustained levels of divorce, women not only bear double responsibilities for breadwinning and child-rearing but bear them alone. Thus, the achievement of a fair and equitable distribution of these tasks between men and women becomes ever more elusive. Moreover, in a high-divorce society the goal of involved, hands-on, nurturant fatherhood becomes more difficult to attain. Even for the most committed and determined divorced fathers, nonresidential fatherhood is a struggle. For those less heroic and resolute, solo fatherhood becomes close to impossible. Sadly, when extraordinary heroism is required, more men fail at fatherhood.

## LESS FREEDOM, MORE COERCION

Perhaps the most alluring and most powerfully sponsored claim for divorce has been its promise of greater personal freedom. One popular book promises women "the joy of handling your own money, learning to cope as a single mother, and the freedom to manage your time as you see fit."[1] Another proclaims that "there is joy in emancipating oneself." Yet in ways not fully anticipated, divorced women's freedoms and opportunities are often quite limited. Single mothers in particular may find it difficult to achieve a satisfying blend of work and family life, and to "be all that they can be." Society's principal cheerleaders for expressive divorce have been its most economically advantaged and well-educated women, but only their message, and not their privilege, has been transmitted to their working-class "sisters."

Divorce frees many men from the daily tasks of home and family life, and many men free themselves from the responsibilities of providing for their children. However, divorced fathers are not truly liberated. Their opportunities to share in the daily lives of their children and to enjoy the free and easy exchanges that come with daily life are lost. As they lose their franchise as fathers, many men also lose a central reason for working hard and participating in the life of the community. Divorced men also lose access to women's emotional and social intelligence in building and sustaining relationships. Men's social as well as family ties attenuate after divorce. They are less embedded in a network of relationships with kin and community, and less connected or committed to others. Although it is too soon to tell, fathers who abandon their children may be abandoned by their adult children when they become old, needy, and dependent, leaving elderly men to the care and custody of strangers.

In a culture of divorce, children are the most "unfree." Divorce abrogates children's right to be reasonably free from adult cares and woes, to enjoy the association of both parents on a daily basis, to remain innocent of social services and therapy, and to spend family time in ways that are not dictated by the courts.

More broadly, the divorce culture limits the family's freedom to conduct its own relationships without intrusion or coercion. The American family is founded on the principle of glorious voluntarism. The freedom to choose our love relationships without interference from outside parties or interests remains one of our most enduring "family values."[2] However, the freedom to choose is not unfettered freedom. Through marriage the individual becomes committed to a set of duties and obligations, not only to the spouse but to children, relatives, and the larger society. These obligations are voluntarily made and kept. There is no constabulary to patrol family households and to enforce the proper conduct of daily family life. There is no legal oversight of children's homework or bedtimes, no government authority dictating how much time parents should spend reading to their children or how much money they should invest in sneakers or music lessons.

However, in a culture captive to an expressive ethos of divorce, the family becomes less able or willing to govern itself. Parental commitments outside of marriage become increasingly involuntary and subject to regulation. The obligation of fathers to provide for their children, an obligation freely accepted and (generally) faithfully honored by married fathers, becomes the focus of state supervision and enforcement. Parent-child relationships, once conducted without legal oversight, are governed by court-established visitation and custody arrangements. Paternity itself—the voluntary recording of a father's name on a birth certificate, an occasion once celebrated with cigars and champagne—becomes a matter of court-ordered and state-reimbursed blood tests. Adoption, the voluntary system of reassigning children to families, loses ground to a system of reshuffling children from biological parents to foster or residential care and back again. In brief, divorce and single parenthood invite, indeed often require, more active supervision and regulation of family relationships by the state.

Even though the state can require certain forms of parental support, mainly for the economic upkeep of children, it can do so at only minimal levels. The state cannot force divorced fathers to take higher-paying jobs or work extra shifts for their children's sake. It cannot require divorced parents to set aside their anger and hostility and to assist each other in rearing their children. Consequently, compared with a system in which parents share a common household and voluntarily invest in their children, a family system characterized by a legally arranged and supervised parenthood is almost by definition one in which the levels of parental investment in children are likely to be low and somewhat fitful, even if the regulatory controls are steadily improved and tightened. Thus, Americans are moving away from a high-investment child-rearing strategy at exactly the time when the requirements of a postindustrial economy require even higher-level and longer-term parental and societal investments in children.

## LESS ALTRUISM, MORE INDIVIDUALISM

Another claim made for divorce is that disrupted families with diminished capacity to provide for their children will be able to recruit support from kindly strangers. There is a liberal version of this claim, and a conservative version. Liberals look to the kindly taxpayers and the public sector as a source of support while conservatives find their kindly strangers in the voluntary sector. Liberals suspect that the conservative faith in an invigorated voluntary sector is an excuse for cutting taxes while conservatives suggest that the liberal faith in a generous public sector is a rationale for big government. Nonetheless, both sides seek to tap sources of altruism outside the family itself.

What neither side acknowledges is that the extreme individualism sanctioned by expressive divorce weakens the social basis for altruism. When family relationships are governed by marketplace notions of individual self-interest, both the spirit of kindness and the supply lines of kindly strangers begin to shrink. How many Big Brothers and good-hearted Cub Scout leaders can be found to replace all the missing fathers? How many single men and women will voluntarily enlist in the ranks of "paraparents" to help stressed-out single mothers? How many more foster parents will step forward? How many grandparents are waiting in the wings? Will a deadbeat dad who has abandoned three children of his own suddenly step forward to help the children of another deadbeat?

In brief, Americans cannot sustain a vigorous voluntary sector or a generous public sector if the voluntary basis of family obligation erodes and if a radically individualistic ethic pervades thinking about family relationships. To be sure, many Americans are morally motivated to help needy children, while others are philosophically committed to public spending on children that is at least as generous as public spending on the elderly. So there will always be a community responsive to the needs of children. But in a culture of family breakup, it becomes increasingly difficult to make the arguments and win the support for public sacrifice for children. If parents are entitled to put their own psychological needs and interests first, why should others feel obliged to volunteer their resources and help? If fathers can reduce their financial contributions to their own flesh and blood, why should others be compelled to make up the difference? If families are not making hard sacrifices for their children's sake, why should corporations?

If the divorce culture continues, both parental and social altruism will decline. The kindness of strangers will be replaced by the coldness of the trustee. Indeed, as some conservatives acknowledge, the end of the welfare state may bring about the rise of the custodial state. A depleted voluntary sector may have to depend on an expanding "involuntary sector," made up of such institutions as prisons, orphanages, and residential homes. In the twenty-first century "commitment" may revert to its most literal and pejorative meaning: involuntary confinement to an institution.

Consequently, for all the efforts to liberate individuals from the psychological bondage of family ties, to achieve greater affective and expressive satisfactions in family life, to create warmer and closer partnerships, Americans find themselves in the grips of a cooling trend in relationships, a harsher climate of regulation and control, and a chillier and more inhospitable environment for children.

### A SOCIETY OF THE UNCOMMITTED

How many divorces over how many years can a nation sustain without serious damage to its social fabric? There is no precise way to answer that question, but it does not require sophisticated statistical projections to make the argument that Americans have already experienced too much divorce over the past twenty-five years and that the current trends cannot be sustained for another twenty-five years without profound loss and damage to children, families, and the society. If we do not act with deliberate speed to reduce divorces involving children, we will surely become a nation with a diminished capacity to sponsor the next generation into successful lives as citizens, workers, and family members. More alarmingly, we will lose the capacity to foster strong and lasting bonds between fathers and children, between older and younger generations, and between children and the larger society. A sense of permanence and trust will continue to erode, and with it, the commitment to invest in others. Self-investment will be the safer and saner bet.

For the past three decades American children have attended the school of divorce and learned its lessons. The main lesson is that families break up, relationships end, and love is not forever. One psychiatrist, studying the attitudes of young adults toward "committed relationships," noted that they displayed a "comparison shopper's mentality" which introduces the kind of calculation and guardedness that works against commitment and even against the ability to fall in love. As one young adult from a divorced family explained: "My own opinion is that if a man and a woman get along for five or ten years, that is as much as can be expected. People change and they stop sharing. It is much more sensible to plan on a series of relationships—perhaps three or four."[3] This view is widespread among younger Americans; it suggests that divorce not only erodes the social bases of commitment but also extinguishes the very idea of lasting commitment.

## DISMANTLING THE DIVORCE CULTURE

Divorce is necessary in a society that believes in the ideal of affectionate marriage, and particularly in a society that seeks to protect women from brutality and violence in marriage. But it is not necessary to do away with divorce altogether in order to dismantle the divorce culture. Rather, the goal should be to change the way we think about the meaning and purpose of divorce, especially divorces involving children. Just as the environmental movement required a new consciousness about how an individual's private decision to buy a car affected the natural world, so too a movement to dismantle the divorce culture must create a stronger awareness of how an individual's personal decision to divorce affects the family and social world.

For parents, divorce is not a solo act but one that has enormous consequences for children. A mounting body of evidence from diverse and multiple sources shows that divorce has been a primary generator of new forms of inequality, disadvantage,

and loss for American children. It has spawned a generation of angry and bereaved children who have a harder time learning, staying in school, and achieving at high levels. High and sustained levels of divorce have also raided children's piggy banks, depriving them of the full resources that they might have had growing up in an intact family. In middle- and upper-middle-class families the process of getting a divorce has also diverted family resources away from children toward the professional service sector, where an entire industry has sprung up to harvest the fruits of family discord.

Finally, divorce is never merely an individual lifestyle choice without larger consequences for the society. Divorce has contributed to welfare dependency and given rise to an entire public bureaucracy devoted to managing and regulating the parental tasks and obligations of raising children. It has imposed a new set of burdens and responsibilities on the schools, contributed to the tide of fatherless juveniles filling the courts and jails, and increased the risks of unwed teen parenthood.

Once we acknowledge that divorce is a family and social event involving other stakeholders and imposing costs on others, then we can begin to think and talk about high levels of divorces involving children as a social problem that must be addressed rather than as an expression of individual freedom that cannot be infringed. This will engender activism rather than passivity in the face of what some now say are irresistible and unstoppable trends. It was just such activism in the face of what seemed to be unstoppable trends toward environmental despoliation that inspired the effort for cleaner water and air.

A second and complementary step toward dismantling the culture of divorce is to repeal the language and ethic of expressive divorce and treat divorce as a morally as well as socially consequential event. The ethic of expressive divorce recognizes the rights and needs of the liberated self, but has nothing to say about the responsibilities of the obligated self. It has no language for talking about the special obligations of parents to children or about the social trust invested in marriages with children. Even after thirty years of sustained high levels of divorce, we are still reluctant to speak about the moral obligations involved in divorces with children for fear of "blaming" and thus psychologically burdening adults. Yet the truth is that divorce involves a radical redistribution of hardship, from adults to children, and therefore cannot be viewed as a morally neutral act.

Changing the way we think and talk about divorce will have several likely consequences. First, if children are treated as key stakeholders in their parents' marriage and as those most at risk in the dissolution of the marriage, then parents, clergy, therapists, judges, and policymakers will be more likely to attend to the claims and interests of children. Second, if divorce is regarded as a central source of disadvantage and father-loss for children, there may be a stronger effort at educating the public about the risks of divorce to children. Third, if marriages with children are considered a kind of special trust, there will be greater societal effort aimed at preventing the dissolution of such marriages. Not all marriages can or should be saved "for the sake of the children," but clearly, of the six out of ten divorces that involve children, some are salvageable. Yet the effort to strengthen and preserve marriage has been all but abandoned in recent years, either as a commitment by parents unhappy in their marriages or as a goal for family professionals. For example, among the hundreds of workshops offered at the annual conventions of the leading professional organization of family therapists, the American Association for Marriage and Family Therapy, marriage rarely appears as a topic; it showed up twice in 1992 and not at all in 1993. In 1994 the association gave a major press award to a magazine article arguing that fathers are not necessary in the home.

In 1995 the word "marital" appeared only twice on the program, and "marriage" not at all. Noting the curious disappearance of "marriage" from the marriage counselors' vocabulary, *U.S. News & World Report* columnist John Leo writes: "The therapeutic custodians of marriage don't believe in it any more and seem determined not to bolster, promote or even talk about it much."[4]

Members of the divorce establishment could demonstrate their commitment to children by taking leadership in divorce prevention. Therapists, lawyers, and other professionals who profit from divorces involving children might, through their professional associations, support projects specifically designed to reduce divorce among families with children. Others could make important contributions as well. Scholars might put marriage back on their research agenda and thereby add to our knowledge of what makes marriages succeed or fail.[5] Clergy might renew their commitment and redouble their efforts to provide pastoral care to married couples with children, especially at times when marriages are likely to be stressed. Within religious communities, older married couples might serve as mentors to younger couples.

A serious and sustained effort at divorce prevention would send an important message about marriage as a valuable but vanishing social resource which must be prized and protected. Such a message might encourage couples, husbands especially, to be more vigilant about the maintenance and care of their marriages. Indeed, if Americans treated their marriages as tenderly as their family cars, there might be more commitment to repairing rather than junking marriages. There might also be greater recognition of the need for special maintenance and care of marriages that are fragile, including second marriages and marriages with handicapped children. Finally, there might be greater honor attached to marriage as a human pursuit requiring struggle, intention, and work.

## NOTES

1. Catherine Napolitane with Victoria Pelligrino, *Living and Loving After Divorce* (New York: Signet, 1977), 236.

2. This freedom was particularly cherished by those who had been denied it. One of the ways black Americans marked their emancipation was to rush out to have their marriages registered and legalized. For example, in Vicksburg, Mississippi, between 1864 and 1866, 4,638 couples who had been married during slavery had their marriages registered. Of the 843 couples who registered their marriages in Washington, D.C., in the years 1866–67, 3 had been married for more than fifty years. Andrew Billingsley, *Climbing Jacob's Ladder: The Enduring Legacy of African-American Families* (New York: Simon & Schuster, 1992), 102.

3. Alan S. Stone, "Calculation and Emotion in Marriage," in *Contemporary Marriage: Comparative Perspectives on a Changing Institution*, ed. Kingsley Davis (New York: Russell Sage Foundation, 1985), 404.

4. John Leo, "Where Marriage Is a Scary Word," *U.S. News & World Report* (February 5, 1996), 22.

5. Two recent, empirically based studies offer useful insights and approaches. See John Mordechai Gottmann, *Why Marriages Succeed or Fail: What You Can Learn from the Breakthrough Research to Make Your Marriage Last* (New York: Simon & Schuster, 1994); Judith S. Wallerstein and Sandra Blakeslee, *The Good Marriage: How and Why Love Lasts* (Boston: Houghton Mifflin Co., 1995).

## CRITICAL THINKING QUESTIONS

1. Whitehead contends that divorce has generated greater inequality because divorced women bear double responsibilities for breadwinning and childrearing, and they bear them alone. Is remarriage the best solution for gender inequality after a divorce?

2. Both Stanton and Whitehead emphasize the negative consequences of divorce on children. Do other factors also determine children's happiness and well-being as well? Are both authors implying that divorce is acceptable in child-free marriages?

3. How does divorce erode "the social bases of commitment"? Is Whitehead suggesting that a loveless commitment should take precedence over an individual's unhappy marriage? If this is the case, should we encourage arranged marriages, as do many other societies?

# 16 Divorce

## *Liberal/Feminist:* Why Women Seek Divorce

DEMIE KURZ, *For Richer, for Poorer: Mothers Confront Divorce* (New York: Routledge, 1995), pp. 46–62. Copyright © 1995. Reproduced by permission of Routledge, Inc.

*As the two previous selections in this chapter illustrate, conservatives and centrists view divorce as one of the major causes of family breakdown. In contrast, many liberals, especially feminists, see divorce as a solution to family breakdown. Demie Kurz's research shows, for example, that there are four major reasons why women in unhappy marriages seek divorces: personal dissatisfaction, violence, "hard-living," and their husbands' infidelity.*

There were significant differences between reports of women in different classes. The higher their class position, the more likely the women were to cite personal dissatisfaction as a reason for their divorce, while the lower their class position, the more they reported leaving because of violence. "Hard-living" divorces were more prevalent among working-class and poverty-level women and were significantly more likely to occur among white women. There were no other statistically significant differences between women in terms of their race.[1]

* Kurz's study is based on interviews, during 1987 and 1988, with a random sample of 129 mothers who obtained divorces through the Philadelphia Family Court. Most of the respondents were white or black, some Hispanic. The mothers included middle-class, professional, working-class, and poverty-level women.

### PERSONAL DISSATISFACTION

I begin my discussion of the ending of these marriages with the category of what I have called "personal dissatisfaction," since this category is closest to the kinds of dissatisfaction that contemporary observers have said motivate Americans to divorce. The 19 percent of women who left their marriages for reasons of personal dissatisfaction stated that: they didn't love their husbands anymore; the communication in their marriages was not good; they fought too often with their husbands; their husbands had been too controlling; or they were tired of carrying the emotional load of the marriage. At the same time that they cited a variety of factors as critical to the ending of their marriages, however, women also identified certain patterns to the separation, particularly the importance of gender roles.

A few women spoke in gender-neutral terms about why they left their marriages. A 33-year-old white secretary, married twelve years, mentioned lack of communication in her marriage. A 31-year-old woman from a similar background said that she and her husband argued all the time:

> One of the problems with my ex-husband was that we didn't communicate well. I guess we were just different. He didn't talk much and he was very moody. I had to plan when I would say things to him. He did use drugs—but we all did, our generation. . . . But that wasn't the cause of our communication problem.

A 41-year-old working-class Hispanic woman, married seventeen years, said that she did not like or respect her husband. She claimed he had squandered their money on bad business ventures, and she didn't trust him anymore:

> I went to marriage counseling around the time of the separation. . . . It wasn't helpful. I knew the marriage was done. He had sold the house he bought with his mother right out from under her. . . . I thought, if he does that to her, what is he going to do to me?

Most of these women, however, gave what I call "gendered" accounts of how their marriages ended. By gendered I mean that women described leaving their marriages because of behaviors associated with the conventional male role. Typically, there is a division of family labor by gender, with women assuming emotional and caretaking functions and men expected to be the primary bread winners. In addition, despite norms favoring equality in marriage, men often still control decision-making in the family. Gender, of course, permeates all social interactions. As Joan Scott notes, gender is "a constitutive element of social relationships based on perceived differences between the sexes, and a . . . primary way of signifying relationships of power."[2]

First, women mentioned their ex-husbands' controlling behavior. One 34-year-old white middle-class woman, an administrator who had been married for eleven years, felt that because of her ex-husband's controlling behavior, she could not participate in decision-making during the marriage:

> I left him . . . he wasn't physically abusive, but he was emotionally abusive. . . . I didn't like how he made all the decisions. He always argued very logically with what I said. So it always seemed like what I said didn't make sense and what he said was right. I just didn't have respect for him anymore. I thought long and hard about leaving, for over a year. I tried to get him into counseling. He went but he didn't really participate. And when we got home it was just the same thing.

Some working-class women also spoke of their ex-husbands as being too controlling:

> I married him when I was young and dumb. I had a scholarship at [local university] I could have taken but I married him instead. He also wanted to control everything about my life. He wanted to control my friends, my time. [36-year-old black nurse, married for fifteen years with two children]

Second, women stated that they did not get enough emotional support from their husbands. A 33-year-old white psychiatrist, who had been married nine years, spoke about the issue of emotional support in very gendered terms:

> I had to do all the emotional work in the relationship and I wasn't getting anything back. I really tried to make it work for a couple of years. I kept thinking that it would change, that if I did the right thing he would become more emotionally active and responsive in the relationship. We went to therapy but things didn't seem to change. Finally I told him I wanted him to leave. He was very angry.
>
> I knew I couldn't stay with someone who was so completely unsupportive. He was only looking out for what was good for him. I don't think all men are the same, but I believe it was very male behavior. I guess he was angry that he wasn't getting enough emotional attention. First, because we had recently had a baby. And then because I went back to school.

A 34-year-old black poverty-level woman, a part-time classroom aide, spoke in a similar vein:

> I want a supportive relationship. One where I can give support and get support. My husband thought a man was supposed to be

a good provider and that was it. I want more than that. I want a real relationship.

Third, a small number of women voiced discontent with their husbands' failure to be adequate enough providers. These women are discontented because their husbands are not working, or are not working hard enough. Those who are themselves working for pay are particularly unhappy. One white middle-class woman, a registered nurse, stated she left her husband because he remained unemployed throughout the marriage. She claimed that he accumulated debts and smoked a lot of marijuana, and that he didn't spend time with the children or help her take care of them. One woman, a 36-year-old white middle-class mother of two, who was married for twelve years, felt that her husband did not try hard enough to be successful in his work:

> He is bitter. He feels he got kicked out. It was me that wanted the divorce. I didn't love him anymore. I didn't respect him anymore. He didn't have any ambition. I had to really push him to improve his business.

As Myra Marx Ferree notes, in accordance with prevailing gender norms, some women subscribe to the idea that men should be the primary providers and are uncomfortable when they believe their husbands do not live up to the primary breadwinner role.[3]

Those women who state that the decision to end their marriages was mutual also spoke of their husbands' controlling behavior. Anne, [an] educational consultant, at first spoke of how her divorce was the result of a "mutual split":

> We just couldn't get along. My ex-husband is a nut. He has a terrible temper. He . . . constantly fights and argues. He even told me "I'll miss fighting with you."

However, she then continued with a story about her ex-husband's controlling behavior:

> My ex-husband didn't have an emotional vocabulary. Everything was fine or he was very very angry. He used his anger to control. It scared me. I would really try to prevent it.

If I could tell it was coming, I would do things to prevent it.

> I was very frightened by the end. My friends were frightened too. He would throw and destroy things. My daughter was really upset too. She thought, if he can throw these things, what can happen to me?

A 38-year-old black senior computer program analyst stated that the decision to end her marriage was mutual; married for nine years, she had experienced a lot of violence before and during the marriage. She thought the separation would be peaceful, but found otherwise:

> When we first separated it was by mutual agreement, and I thought it would be amicable. But he would come over a lot and harass me in all kinds of ways. Like when he used to come to the house he would go to my bedroom and rummage through my drawers and throw all the clothes on my bed. He would say, "I want to find out about your love life." He's driven around my mother's house. They're afraid of him. They've never dealt with a person like him. . . . He almost caused me to lose my job. He really harassed people [at my workplace], including the guard.

In these cases, the report of a "mutual" decision to break up may conceal troubled circumstances that are far from mutual, and that reflect imbalanced power relations.

We need to know more about when women see their husbands as too controlling, since women raised this issue in all of the categories. Some women, like this 38-year-old black technician who did not give a reason why her marriage ended, described explicit controlling behavior:

> When I was married, I stayed in. I was home with my son and he was always out. He said, "You should be home with the baby."

A 35-year-old white clerical worker who left her husband of sixteen years because of his use of drugs stated:

> My ex-husband always got his way, even during our marriage. He'd ask me what I wanted to do about something. Then he'd do it his way. Then if I said anything he'd get

angry. He'd say, "Well, I asked you what you wanted." I'd be totally stuck. I just couldn't win.

Other women, like this 49-year-old middle-class white woman who left her husband of ten years because he was seeing another woman, described a more indirect kind of control.

In my marriage I was afraid of saying what I really thought. He could always just leave. Even at 36, knowing everything I knew, I still walked on eggshells about that. . . . I am much better now than I was while we were married at telling him what I think. He's moody and also he can always win in an argument. When we were married I used to bite my lip and not say anything.

[P]olling data show women want more equality in marriage, while men think there is enough. One group of researchers believes that the divorced population includes a higher percentage of men who have more traditional gender-role attitudes and women who have nontraditional views. They argue that particularly those women who are in the paid labor force are now in a position to leave a relationship in which they view their husbands' demands as unfair.[4]

### VIOLENCE

In this sample, 70 percent of women of all classes and races experienced violence at the hands of their husbands at least once. Fifty percent of women experienced violence at least two to three times. Women were asked to check off on a list the acts of violence which they and their husbands committed during their marriage, and the frequency of their use of violence. The list included: throwing things at a spouse, pushing, slapping, kicking, hitting, beating up, threatening with a knife or gun, and using a knife or gun. Of the 70 percent of women who reported violence, 16 percent reported that the violence occurred only once; 13 percent reported that it occurred two to three times during the marriage; 37 percent reported that the violence took place more than three times, or that there was one serious incident of violence; and 4 percent that there was violence during the separation only. An incident of violence was considered "serious" if a woman said she had been "beaten up" or she had sustained a physical injury.[5]

The accounts of these women resonate with fear and pain. One can easily imagine how the children who witnessed this violence were very fearful and deeply saddened. At the same time, a quiet courage runs through the accounts of these women as they assessed the costs and benefits of staying in their marriages.

While many women in the sample experienced violence, those who stated that they separated because of the violence had experienced much more serious physical violence than women who gave other reasons for separating. Many of these women stated that they left their husbands after a particularly serious fight. Some women, such as this 41-year-old white working-class mother of two, felt that their lives could have been in danger:

It took a year for the separation to come through. I filed. We separated for the last time after he beat me up. It was Mother's Day. He beat me up in front of the kids and his parents. I was really scared then. I thought, "if he'll do this in front of them, what could he do next?" I had to get a protection order at the time and that cost $300.

We had been going to a counselor. . . . The therapist called me one night and said to come right over. He said, "Your husband doesn't know right from wrong. He only thinks he is right. You'd better get away. He could kill you." I now believe that. At the time I thought he would still change.

This 31-year-old mother of one, a black woman living at poverty level, left an eleven-year marriage after a particularly serious incident of physical abuse. She addressed the question most frequently put to battered women, the question of why she didn't leave sooner, despite experiencing a lot of very serious violence throughout her marriage:

We separated after a big fight where he was physically abusive. First I went to the Emergency Room. Then I went to the Police Roundhouse. The police came to the house and made him leave. . . . I got a restraining order. It lasted for a whole year.

There was violence constantly for the 10 years. It would usually happen on the weekends. We would fight over small things like, if he would go out on Friday, I would say I want to go out on Saturday. But slowly over the years something was clicking inside. I said to myself, "Are you going to let someone else run your life?"

*Interviewer*: So what made you realize that you wanted to get out of this relationship?

I have thought about that a lot. Somebody told me people scheme on others but you scheme on yourself. First, I don't want to hurt or disappoint other people. So instead I get hurt. Also, there would be repercussions. Where would I go with three children? I didn't want to go back to my mother's. I get along with my mother but if I went home it would be like I had been a failure.

Some women left when the violence affected their children. One woman left when her husband sexually assaulted her son by a former marriage. She filed a criminal charge against her ex-husband, who is now serving time in prison for this crime. This poverty-level black woman left because of the effect of the violence on her children and on herself:

All the violence was hard on my son. He saw me injured when he was two years old. He saw blood, he saw a lot. It's affected my son. He's mixed up.

I left because I was afraid of what this was doing to my son. I left because of what it was doing to me. I realized I could have shot my ex-husband. But I couldn't do that for my son's sake.

I finally realized the marriage wasn't working. I really wanted a marriage. I wanted that marriage to work. But I finally realized it just wasn't working. [28-year-old black woman living at the poverty-level, mother of one, married six years]

[S]ome women also watched their husbands destroy property and found this

frightening. This 33-year-old white middle-class mother of two, who owned and ran a business with her husband, described his violence:

I was the one who left. My ex-husband had a terrible temper. He used violence a lot. He didn't hurt me physically very much but he destroyed property a lot. He flew off the handle a lot. He was also an alcoholic. He had an explosive angry temper.

## HARD-LIVING

Seventeen percent of women gave "hard-living" as the reason for the ending of their marriage. "Hard-living" is the term Joseph Howell used some time ago to describe certain behaviors, such as heavy drinking and frequent absences from the family, which men, particularly working-class and poverty-level men, exhibit when they feel frustrated by unstable work conditions and high unemployment. Since Howell first described hard-living, alcohol abuse has continued to plague men with weak employment histories. Hard-living is usually associated with male behavior. Lillian Rubin argues that some men continue to use alcohol as a way of coping with unemployment and Katherine Newman stresses that alcohol abuse is associated with the downward mobility and job insecurity of male workers at all socio-economic levels.[6] It is important, however, to highlight the role of gender in hard-living; more often than not, it is women who are the victims of these behaviors. . . .

Most of the women who left because of their ex-husbands' use of drugs or alcohol found their husbands' behavior very troubling and particularly disruptive of family life. The majority of women who reported leaving their marriages for reasons of hard-living are working-class and poverty-level women, although a few middle-class women reported that their ex-husbands abused alcohol, and one that her ex-husband used drugs. Said one woman living at the poverty level:

He's still an alcoholic and he's still into drugs. That was the problem in our marriage. At first he'd be gone one night a month. I would stay up all night worrying and he would come in at 6:30 in the morning and take a shower and leave. I didn't realize what it was at first. Then it became more and more frequent and he was gone a whole lot. . . . It started getting to the kids. [34-year-old white bookkeeper, mother of two, married twelve years]

In some of these cases the husbands also used violence:

He kicked me out of the house, violently. It was our house. By then there was a lot of violence. Things hadn't been that way to start. Initially there was none. But around the time my son was born I noted he was acting funny. I didn't know what it was. I thought maybe he was jealous of the baby because I was paying the baby more attention. But then I came to realize it was drugs. [33-year-old white secretary, mother of one, married seven years]

The women were particularly concerned about the effect of drugs on their children:

I was married a long time. Things were fine for six years. We got along pretty well. Then he decided he wanted other women. He wanted a wife and a girlfriend. But I won't be number two. I told him good-bye and good luck. I also found out during the last eighteen months of our marriage that he was selling drugs. Then I knew I wanted out. That's no way to raise a child. [38-year-old black middle-class office manager, mother of one, married fifteen years]

Women also reported that their ex-husbands were rarely home. These women say their husbands never took any responsibility for the marriage. Some men "hung out" on the street with other men. Said [one] white working-class wom[a]n:

I kicked him out finally. The problem was he was never here. He was always with his friends. He worked, but then he would go out. Or all his friends would be here. Sometimes I would wake up in the morning and his friends would be here. He was like a big kid. He just didn't want to be married. At first we had married friends. But then he made

friends with a single guy and after that all his friends were single. [26-year-old white data processing clerk, married four years]

This poverty-level woman thought her husband was "fooling around" with other women. He was also sometimes violent towards her:

Most of the time my husband wasn't even at home. He would go out with groups of people and screw around. Sometimes he was violent when he came home. I think he was guilty. If I asked where he'd been, he'd get mad. If I didn't ask, he'd say I didn't care.

He was gone weekends at a time. I was at my mother's most of the marriage. One time I went back for six months but it didn't work. It was tense. I got an addiction. I used to drink and take Valium just to forget he was there. I wish he had just left. [26-year-old white mother of two, married six years]

Eleven percent of the women in the sample said their husbands were never around. Their comments may reflect gender differences in commitment to the family. Various studies of poverty-level and working-class marriages indicate that husbands and wives have separate leisure-time activities, and that some men in these families prefer to spend their leisure time fraternizing with male friends, not staying at home.[7]

## OTHER WOMEN

Nineteen percent of the women reported that their ex-husbands were involved with other women. These women described two different kinds of experiences. One group of women stated they were left by their ex-husbands for other women. These women suffered a lot of emotional pain. A 51-year-old white middle-class woman with two college-age children who had been married for twenty-seven years said:

After he said he was leaving for another woman I was in very, very bad shape. I went into a depression. It continued into the separation. We were in counseling together and I was in alone at the same time. I personally suffered a lot and it can't be measured or weighed. It's taken a toll.

A 31-year-old black teacher with a two-year-old child explained how it was when her husband said he was leaving:

It was a horrible experience. I was on an unpaid maternity leave. I was a new mother. I had been hoping things would work out in the marriage. We had been having problems, but I thought we could work them out. But he was running around with another woman. And he had been, even while I was pregnant. I felt a lot of hurt and a lot of frustration. . . . The separation was the worst period of my life.

Women of all classes expressed the same feelings of rejection and emotional pain when they were left by husbands for other women:

I took my husband's finding another woman as rejection. I felt I failed. The other thing was money. I got really down. I was a candidate for [a local mental institution]. [33-year-old working-class black woman, part-time retail clothing, married seven years, one child]

There was a period of about nine months . . . I knew he was leaving . . . for the first six months I was okay but then I wasn't okay. By not okay, I mean not functioning. I was not a functioning parent, not a functioning daughter, nothing. It's an upheaval and then a tremendous adjustment. [41-year-old white working-class woman, legal secretary, married twelve years, three children]

I'd like to stay married to him . . . I still love him. He's the man I married. He will never change. He lives with that lady and he goes to bars. He's a macho man. He still doesn't want me to talk to any man and he finds out if I go out with any man. The year he left I tried to kill myself. I was really depressed cause I never thought this would happen. [40-year-old poverty-level Hispanic woman, married nineteen years, three children]

All of these women experienced great emotional pain, and spoke of being "devastated" and very depressed:

Emotionally it ripped me apart. I depended on him, and when he left me I felt rejected and lonely. The kids played a major part in my life. I lived for them. I didn't want them to get hurt by the divorce. I wish I had gone to counseling earlier to face the reality sooner. [33-year-old white working-class woman, part-time accountant, married twelve years, three children]

A few women mentioned that their ex-husbands wanted to come back when their affairs didn't work out, but these women had lost trust in their husbands and were not willing to try and reconstruct the marriage.

Within the category of women who reported that their marriages ended because their husbands became involved with other women, some women reported that they left their husbands because their husbands were seeing or "fooling around" with other women. Particularly poverty-level and African-American women reported having left for this reason, in contrast to the majority of white women, whose husbands left them. These women whose husbands were "fooling around" were upset not only because of their husbands' involvement with other women, but also because these men were rarely at home and did not take any responsibility for the household. Thus "fooling around" is related to the hard-living category of never being around. The quotation below reflects these women's concerns about their husbands' lack of responsibility:

My marriage began to change when I had my son. I stopped working then. Then I saw how things were. Without my income we couldn't pay for anything. I began to look at where the money my ex-husband was making was going. It was going into gambling.

The bills were not getting paid. Finally the electricity was cut off. When the electricity was cut off, he moved in with his mother. That's when I knew something was really wrong. Also, he threatened me a lot. And once he cracked up my car and just left it there. These things seemed to change at my son's birth. Even at the birth, my ex-husband wasn't supportive. I was in there going through labor and he was out in the hall talking to everyone, grandstanding.

Then I finally asked my ex-husband about his fooling around with other women. He was fooling around a lot. He finally admitted it and that's when I said I was going to get a divorce. This was important because I am a Jehovah's Witness, and in our religion that's the only grounds for divorce. Otherwise we believe that you should really work things out yourself. But because he admitted that I was able to get a divorce. Otherwise I would still be in the marriage. [34-year-old black child-care worker, married eight years, one child]

These women's accounts sound like Elijah Anderson's descriptions of relationships among poor, urban black youth. Anderson claims that if these young black men marry, they still do not plan to give up the freedom their peers have taught them to desire. Their goal is to conquer women, not to settle down and be breadwinners. Anderson argues that these young men want a reliable partner who will be like their mother and not question the time they spend with other "ladies" or with male friends. The women, who had hoped for a male breadwinner and a "typical" marriage, then leave when they see that their marriage will not conform to this ideal. According to Anderson, the origin of these conflicts lies in the fact that many young black men, due to high rates of discrimination and unemployment, have little hope of earning enough to support a family.[8]

On the whole, however, we don't know under what circumstances men and women choose to have affairs. Recent data show that 25 percent of men and 15 percent of women in marriages have affairs. Presumably they have affairs when they experience personal dissatisfaction with their partners and their marriages. In this sample, however, when women left for reasons of personal dissatisfaction, they did not leave for a man. Thus, according to these women, when they left they were becoming single parents, while their ex-husbands left to begin relationships with other women.[9]

## NOTES

1. Class remained a highly significant predictor for personal dissatisfaction and violence-related divorces after controlling for race. For hard-

living divorces, class was not significant, but black women were 90 percent less likely to cite hard living as the principal reason for divorce (after controlling for class).

2. Jean Scott, "Gender: A Useful Category of Historical Analysis," *American Historical Review* 91 (1986): 1067.

3. Myra Marx Ferree, "Beyond Separate Spheres" *Journal of Marriage and the Family* 52 (November 1990): 874.

4. Barbara Finlay, Charles E. Starnes, and Fausto B. Alvarez, "Recent Changes in Sex-Role Ideology among Divorced Men and Women: Some Possible Causes and Implications," *Sex Roles* 12 (1985): 637–53.

5. To measure acts of physical violence, a modified version of the Conflict Tactics Scales was used. See Murray Straus, "Measuring Intrafamily Conflict and Violence: The Conflict Tactics (CT) Scales," *Journal of Marriage and the Family* 41 (1979): 75–88.

6. Joseph Howell, *Hard Living on Clay Street*; Lillian Rubin, *Families on the Fault Line* (New York: Harper, 1994); Katherine Newman, *Falling from Grace* (New York: The Free Press, 1988); Rubin, *Worlds of Pain* (New York: Basic Books, 1976). While it is not clear how many people abuse alcohol or drugs, many use both. According to a survey conducted in 1988, 21.1 million Americans reported having used marijuana in the past year, and 65.7 had used it at least once. National Institute on Drug Abuse, "National Household Survey on Drug Abuse: Population Estimates 1988," DHHS Publication No. (ADM) 89–1636 (Washington, DC: U.S. Department of Health and Human Services, 1989).

7. See David Halle, *America's Working Man: Work, Home, and Politics Among Blue-Collar Property Owners* (Chicago: University of Chicago Press, 1984).

8. Elijah Anderson, *Streetwise: Race, Class and Change in an Urban Community* (Chicago: University of Chicago Press, 1990).

9. Data on marital fidelity come from a 1992 survey conducted by the National Opinion Research Center, University of Chicago, cited in *The New York Times*, October 7, 1994, Al.

## CRITICAL THINKING QUESTIONS

1. What does Kurz mean by women's giving "gendered" accounts of why their mar-

riages ended? Can men's reasons for ending marriages also be gendered? Or not?

2. In the previous article, Whitehead contends that divorce rates are high because of the rise of individualism and the abandonment of commitment to the family. Do Kurz's research findings support or challenge Whitehead's assertions?

3. Personal dissatisfaction, Kurz found, is one of the major reasons for women's getting a divorce. Is this, as Stanton and Whitehead also maintain, a frivolous reason for ending a marriage? A good reason for getting a divorce?

# 17 Remarriage and Stepfamilies

## *Conservative:* Why Remarriage Is Wrong

WILLIAM A. HETH, "Remarriage: Two Views: Why Remarriage Is Wrong," *Christianity Today*, December 14, 1992, p. 34. Reproduced by permission of the author.

*Secular and religious conservatives vary widely in their views about remarriage. Both those who support remarriage and those who oppose it often cite the Bible to defend their position. In this selection, William A. Heth uses biblical writers' words to show why remarriage can be construed as adultery.*

The most important reason for believing in lifelong marriage is rooted in Jesus' understanding of how God brought the first couple together (Gen 1:27; 2:24). Jesus said, "Consequently they are no more two, but one flesh. What therefore God has joined together, let no man separate" (Matt. 19:6; Mark 10:8–9, NASB). He therefore emphasizes the Genesis 2:24 teaching that marriage partners become closely related, that the marriage union is comparable to the kinship bond that exists between parents and children. Husband and wife, joined by God (Matt. 19:6), become a single kindred, a new family unit.

Sin may disrupt the marital *love* relationship; but sin does not nullify the marital *kinship*. Even though marital separation or legal divorce may be advisable under some circumstances (persistent adultery, abuse, incest), Jesus calls remarriage after any divorce adultery.

Mark (10:2–12) and Luke (16:18) seem to be unaware of the permission for remarriage after divorce for sexual sins that evangelicals often find in Matthew (5:32; 19:9). Some argue that Jesus spoke

in hyperbole and that Matthew makes explicit Mark and Luke's assumption that Jewish and Roman culture permitted divorce and remarriage for adultery.

But this assumes that Matthew has not made it clear Jesus is teaching a different kind of "divorce." Yet Matthew notes that Jesus rejects the Pharisees' proof text for their views (Deut. 24:1). Instead, Jesus appeals to Genesis 2:24 with its kinship understanding of marriage. Further, textual studies now confirm that the original text of both Matthew 19:9 and 5:32 contain Jesus' additional unqualified statement that finalizes his teaching on the subject: "And whoever marries a divorced woman commits adultery."

Paul's "let them remain unmarried or else be reconciled" (I Cor. 7: 10–11) says the same thing, and recent studies show that the likelihood that Paul's teaching on sexuality, marriage, and singleness in I Corinthians 6 and 7 stems from the same tradition shown in Matthew. Where Paul specifically mentions the possibility of remarriage, in both instances he notes quite explicitly that one of the spouses has died (I Cor. 7:39; Rom. 7:2–3).

Finally, in I Corinthians 7:27–48, Paul is not telling divorced individuals to feel free to remarry He is telling engaged or formerly engaged couples who have come under the ascetic teaching at Corinth to feel free to marry should they so desire (see vv. 33–38).

**CRITICAL THINKING QUESTIONS**

1. Why, according to Heth's interpretation of the Bible, is remarriage wrong?
2. Are there any conditions under which remarriage is acceptable?
3. If marital separation or divorce is advisable because of persistent adultery, why is remarriage considered adulterous?

# 17 Remarriage and Stepfamilies

## *Centrist:* The Stepfather as Nonfather

DAVID BLANKENHORN, *Fatherless America: Confronting Our Most Urgent Social Problems* (New York: HarperPerennial, 1995), pp. 188–195. Copyright © 1995 by the Institute for American Values. Reprinted by permission of Basic Books, a member of Perseus Books, L.L.C.

*Most centrists prefer "intact" families to stepfamilies because, they claim, the latter have negative consequences for children. According to David Blankenhorn, for example, stepfathers are "nonfathers who help raise other men's children." While it may offer adults a second chance for happiness, remarriage has few, if any, positive effects on children.*

Among married couples raising children, the growing prevalence of stepfathers is probably the most important transformation of U.S. family life in this generation. During the 1980s, the number of stepfathers continued to increase at an astonishing rate. By 1990, about 5.1 million stepfathers were living with dependent children in the United States, up from 3.7 million in 1980. In 1980, about 15 percent of all married-couple households with children contained a stepfather. By 1990, the figure had reached 21 percent—a 40 percent increase in ten years.[1]

Most current advice literature for remarried parents leans toward gender-neutral terminology, typically describing issues as they relate to "stepparents" and "stepfamilies." Yet as a daily presence in the lives of children, stepfathers are far more numerous and important than stepmothers. Up to 90 percent of all divorcing mothers maintain physical custody of their children.[2] In 1990, mother-stepfather couples with children outnumbered father-stepmother couples by

a factor of more than 17 to 1. Among all stepchildren, the vast majority live with their biological mother and a stepfather. In this sense, "stepparenting" in the United States has become an overwhelmingly male activity.[3]

Many analysts are quite optimistic about the rapidly growing number of stepfathers in the United States. In *Making Peace in Your Stepfamily*, Harold H. Bloomfield describes remarried parents as "the new wave of what family is all about in America." His conclusion is unequivocal: "There is no reason why stepparents cannot parent just as effectively as biological parents."[4]

Testifying before a congressional committee, the historian Tamara K. Hareven describes "blended families" as "a new source of adaptability and stability" in U.S. family life:

> As a result of the remarriage of one or both of their parents, children of divorce may have access to three or four sets of grandparents rather than just two. They also may have

access to many more aunts and uncles and cousins, and new relatives. Thus, there is encouraging evidence that divorce, in many cases, is followed by a recovery and reconstruction, as well as expansion of family ties.[5]

In *Making It As a Stepparent*, Claire Berman offers similar praise:

> Countless boys and girls are finding their lives broadened and enriched by the presence of four caring parents and by an untold number of new relatives and friends. They are enjoying the opportunity to experience a variety of life styles and to select from each that which seems to suit them best.[6]

Among scholars, Ross A. Thompson agrees with several other researchers who can find "no reliable evidence that children in stepfamilies differ significantly from children in other family structures in intellectual and cognitive development, personality and social behavior, adjustment, and family relationships." Consequently, Thompson suggests that "remarriage has no significant positive or negative effects on children."[7] Kyle D. Pruett goes further. In some ways, stepfathers may be better than fathers. For Pruett finds that

> stepfathers may be more attentive to the needs of their children and . . . less arbitrary in their parenting style than are fathers of many intact families, partly because their consciousness has been raised about the overriding significance of *two* parents in the lives of their children.[8]

This abstract language is revealing. Many of these authors insist on blurring or even erasing the distinction between relatives and nonrelatives. Consequently, to Berman, children in stepfamilies have "four caring parents." Pruett describes how stepfathers attend to the needs of "their" children. This same language is ubiquitous in books about stepfamilies written for children. In *The Wedding*, for example, a storybook, Mrs. Grant tells her son Robby that she has decided to marry Jack:

> "What's going to happen to my dad?" Robby asked.

> "Nothing. You'll see him just the way you do now," Mrs. Grant said.

> "Is he still going to be my father?" Robby wondered.

> "Sure he will. He'll always be your father," she answered. "In a way, you'll have two fathers."

> "Two fathers?" Robby repeated to himself, trying to understand.[9]

However they might "try to understand," very few real-life children actually believe that they have "two fathers." Or that stepparents "parent" just as well as biological parents. Or that living in a stepfamily constitutes a "new source of stability." Or that living in a stepfamily "has no significant positive or negative effects on children."

All these ideas reflect less the actual circumstances of children than the wishful thinking of adults. From a child's perspective, the truth about stepfamilies is more nearly the opposite of these feel-good descriptions. Stepfamilies comprise the most unstable and volatile family form in our society. They are inherently fraught with bad outcomes for children. More specifically, the great majority of stepfathers are not—cannot ever be—replacement fathers or even extra fathers. In almost all of the most important ways, they are not fathers at all.

Despite Ross A. Thompson's claim to the contrary, the social science data regarding outcomes for children in stepfamilies are remarkably consistent and almost uniformly bleak. In 1992, James H. Bray and colleagues presented findings from a seven-year study of approximately two hundred married-couple families, half of which contained a stepfather. The researchers found that the stepfamilies "reported and were observed to have more negative family relationships and more problematic family processes than nuclear families." Over the seven-year period, for example, "remarried husbands became more negative and less positive toward their wives than first-marriage husbands."

Children in these stepfather families had "more behavioral problems, less prosocial behavior, and more life stress." Moreover, stepfather-stepchild relationships "continued to be less positive and more negative and became more negative over time than did father-child relationships."[10]

Numerous studies demonstrate that children who live with stepfathers experience outcomes that are no better, and frequently worse, than children in mother-only homes. For example, does the arrival of an "additional adult" in a household reduce children's susceptibility to antisocial peer pressure and thus lower the risk of deviant behavior? The answer, it seems, is no. In his survey of 865 adolescents, Laurence Steinberg concludes that

> youngsters living in stepfamilies are equally at risk for involvement in deviant behavior as are their peers living in single-parent households. Although an additional adult is present in the adolescent's stepfamily, this may be a case in which two parents are not enough.[11]

Similarly, Nicholas Zill has documented some of the long-term consequences of parental divorce for children. Does remarriage, or the arrival of a stepfather, offer any protection against these harmful consequences? The answer, again, appears to be no:

> We found that remarriage, which usually brings a reliable second income to the family, did not appear to have an overall protective effect. It may be that any advantages in economic or parental resources are offset by the rivalry and increased conflict that stepparents and stepsiblings often bring with them.[12]

Frank F. Furstenberg, Jr., summarizes the current U.S. evidence: "Most studies show that children in stepfamilies do not do better than children in single-parent families; indeed, many indicate that on average children in remarriages do worse."[13]

These remarkable findings are reinforced by research from Great Britain and Australia. In Britain, results from a major longitudinal study of 17,000 children born in 1958 reveal that those in stepfamilies not only experienced far worse outcomes than did children who grew up with their two biological parents but also, on almost every measurement, experienced worse outcomes than did children from single-parent homes. For example, compared to girls from single-parent homes, girls from stepfamilies were more likely to drop out of school, to leave home early (frequently due to friction in the home), and to bear a child before reaching age twenty. Compared to boys from single-parent homes, boys from stepfamilies were more likely to drop out of school, to leave home early, to enter into a cohabiting relationship outside of marriage, and to become a father at an early age.[14] As the London *Daily Telegraph* described this study: "What emerges is the sad picture of young people becoming estranged from stepfamilies at an early age, and starting independent lives with little in the way of educational attainment and opportunities for work."[15]

In Australia, the Children in Families study, sponsored by the Australian Institute of Family Studies, conducted in-depth interviews with 402 children living in Victoria. Half of the children interviewed were age eight or nine years old; half were fifteen to sixteen. Children at both age levels "reported significantly less support from stepfathers than from biological fathers in intact families." Stepfathers were also "less likely than custodial mothers to play the role of disciplinarian." Indeed, some stepfathers, at least initially, "may even exercise no discipline at all in a policy of deliberate non-engagement."[16]

Comparing children from intact, single-parent, and stepfamily homes, the study concludes that "it appears to be children from stepfamilies that have a disadvantage. These children, compared with children in other family types, have lower levels of reading ability, self-control, and self-esteem. . . . These findings suggest that gaining a new parent can be more debilitating than losing an old one."[17]

What causes this special deprivation experienced by the children of stepfamilies? Certainly many features of stepfamily life, from its instability to its inevitable breeding of divided loyalties, contribute to this phenomenon.[18] But the primary underlying cause is fatherlessness. Indeed, unlike children in mother-only homes, children in stepfamilies commonly experience a twofold loss of fatherhood. In short, in the area of fatherhood many of these children are twice cursed.

First, the remarriage of either parent typically means the further erosion, and at times the cessation, of the child's relationship with his or her biological father. When a custodial mother remarries, for example, visits from the biological father typically become less frequent. Child-support payments become less likely.[19] Similarly, when the father remarries, he typically concentrates his attention and resources on his new home, not his old one. In retrospect, for the biological father, his divorce only began the process of disengaging from mother and child. As Furstenberg puts it: "Remarriage by either former partner usually hastens this process of disengagement."[20]

Second, and probably more important, the stepfather, precisely because he is not a father, can become for the stepchild a reminder of fatherlessness, an embodiment of fatherlessness. This guy is doing what my father should be doing. He is sleeping in the bed my father should be sleeping in. In this sense, his presence constitutes a rebuke of my father, a denial of my father. Moreover, if I let him "father" me, or if I agree with my mother that he is a great guy, I am admitting my father's guilt. If I let him win my affection, I may further lose my father's affection.

The result of this dynamic is not fatherhood or even a rough approximation of fatherhood. Fathers strive above all to protect their children, supporting and reassuring them, especially regarding the primacy of parental love. But what commonly results from the stepfather-stepchild dynamic is more nearly the opposite of paternal protection. Even in cases of good people with the best of intentions, what often emerges instead is a relationship that introduces children to new sources of divisiveness and anxiety regarding the most important questions in their lives.

Faced with such a stressful and largely insoluble problem, many stepfathers understandably respond by simply disengaging. Accordingly, many studies describe the stepfather-stepchild relationship, as against the father-child relationship, as less warm, less communicative, and significantly more detached. One study documents "a pattern in which the stepfather functioned as a more distant and detached observer."[21] Another concludes: "Both stepmothers and stepfathers take a considerably less active role in parenting than do custodial parents. Even after two years, disengagement by the stepparent is the most common parenting style."[22]

The advice literature for stepfathers clearly acknowledges, and frequently recommends, this strategy of disengagement. Indeed, this literature is quite revealing. For in many cases, alongside the boosterism and reassuring happy-talk—why your second family can be better than your first—these authors provide practical advice to stepfathers that is soberingly realistic and anything but reassuring.

Recall Harold H. Bloomfield's ringing assertion: "There is no reason why stepparents cannot parent just as effectively as biological parents." Yet in an article for *Parenting* magazine, Bloomfield divides his advice to stepparents into two categories. The first is "Grappling with Guilt." Divorced fathers, Bloomfield says, are "especially prone to guilt's debilitating effects because their children usually live with their former spouse, while they themselves may have become stepfathers to their second wife's children." He advises these stepfathers to "stop chastising themselves for the pain they've caused their children."

Under the topic of "Rolling with the Punches," Bloomfield writes: "Few stepparents are prepared to face just how much it hurts to be repeatedly spurned by their stepchildren." It is only natural to feel overwhelmed and trapped when you're raising children who aren't yours and who resent your presence. But the best tack for dealing with such frustration is to accept it, without letting it take over your family life.[23]

In an article called "Happily Remarried" in *Working Mother* magazine, Sandi Kahn Shelton argues that the "secret to a successful stepfamily is helping a new husband learn to be a good father." Toward this end, Shelton proposes a set of "tips" for mothers to pass along to their new husbands. First: "Help him realize that acceptance by the children is going to take a lot of time":

> Older kids may take years to become adjusted to a new parent in the household, and some may never really get beyond thinking of the stepfather as "my mother's husband." But don't be shocked if even very young children are resistant at first.

Second: "The mother should be the main disciplinarian for a while." Until "expectations are smoothed out" and "trust is formed," most psychologists agree that "it's probably best if the mother is the one who sorts out the temper tantrums and makes sure the rules of the household are followed."

Third: "Don't try to force a relationship to develop between your husband and your children." The main rule here is to "resist the urge to promote harmony." She quotes a psychologist: "Stepfathers and children have to respect each other, be civil to each other, and try to get along. But they don't have to love each other."

Shelton mentions four additional tips. Protect the stepfather's possessions. ("You can't ask the stepfather to make all the adjustments.") Make new traditions together. (But in doing so, remember to "drop anything that isn't working.") Try to patch up problems with your ex-husband. And make time for your marriage. (Although second marriages can be "complicated," they "really do provide a second chance at happiness.")[24]

Almost all the advice literature for stepfathers and stepchildren brings up the question of names. Here, as throughout this literature, the most frequently used word is *complicated*. For the child, there are two basic complications. First, what is my name?[25] Do I keep my father's last name or, as my mother has (probably) done, take on my stepfather's name? In fact, most stepchildren retain their father's name. Yet, as Bloomfield observes, stepchildren who keep their father's name "often feel embarrassed, particularly at school or church where the difference becomes conspicuous. The child suddenly finds himself or herself having to explain why he or she has a different name than his or her own mother!"[26]

Second, what do I call my stepfather? . . . [M]ost stepchildren do not call their stepfather "Dad" or "Daddy," or refer to their stepfather as their father. Recognizing this fact, the advice literature generally recommends that children either choose a nickname for their stepfather or simply address him by his first name.[27]

In general, the advice literature urges a practical, flexible approach to the problem of names. Talk things over. Consult the children. Do what feels best. In *What Am I Doing in a Stepfamily?* an advice book for young children, children are told: "Remember it isn't what you call someone that's important. It's how you feel about the person that matters."[28]

This approach is understandable, but it is based on a false idea. As an epistemological matter, and especially as a matter of child development, "what you call someone" cannot be separated from, much less pitted against, "how you feel about the person." The two go together. Or at least they ought to go together.

However well intended, adult casualness about the word *father* serves only to blur the main issue. For children, the core question is simple: Who is my father? The name matters because the father matters. Consequently, which man I call my father matters. Most children do not call stepfathers "Daddy" or "my father" precisely because they do not believe that these men are their fathers.

These children are right. Whatever their other virtues, these men are not their fathers. They are not even replacement fathers or second fathers. Remarriage may offer adults a second chance for happiness. But remarriage does not offer children a second chance for fatherhood.

## NOTES

1. For numbers of stepfathers, see Arthur J. Norton and Louisa F. Miller, "Marriage, Divorce, and Remarriage in the 1990s," U.S. Bureau of the Census, Current Population Reports, series P-23, no. 180 (Washington, D.C.: U.S. Government Printing Office, October 1992), 10. For married-couple households with children, see Steve W. Rawlings, "Household and Family Characteristics: March 1992," U.S. Bureau of the Census, Current Population Reports, series P-20, no. 467 (Washington, D.C.: U.S. Government Printing Office, April 1993), vii.

2. Lenore J. Weitzman, *The Divorce Revolution* (New York: Free Press, 1985), 256–57; and Ross A. Thompson, "The Role of the Father After Divorce," *The Future of Children* 4, no. 1 (Los Altos, Calif.: Center for the Future of Children, Spring 1994), 215.

3. Norton and Miller, "Marriage, Divorce, and Remarriage," 10.

4. Harold H. Bloomfield, *Making Peace in Your Stepfamily* (New York: Hyperion, 1993), 5, 63.

5. Tamara K. Hareven, testimony before the Select Committee on Children, Youth, and Families, U.S. House of Representatives, February 25, 1986 (Washington, D.C.: U.S. Government Printing Office, 1986), 31, 27.

6. Claire Berman, *Making It as a Stepparent: New Roles/New Rules* (New York: Harper & Row, 1986), 10.

7. Ross A. Thompson, "Fathers and the Child's 'Best Interests': Judicial Decision Making in Custody Disputes," in Michael E. Lamb, ed., *The Father's Role: Applied Perspectives* (New York: Wiley, 1986), 86.

8. Kyle D. Pruett, "The Paternal Presence," *Families in Society* 74, no. 1 (January 1993): 49.

9. Lawrence Balter, *The Wedding* (New York: Barron's, 1989). In Claire Berman's advice book for children, *What Am I Doing in a Stepfamily?* (New York: Carol Publishing, 1992), children

learn "how two families can be better than one." Near the end of the book, Berman writes: "Now you are finding out that children can love more than one set of parents."

10. James H. Bray et al., "Longitudinal Changes in Stepfamilies: Impact on Children's Adjustment" (Washington, D.C.: American Psychological Association, August 15, 1992), 7–8.

11. Laurence Steinberg, "Single Parents, Stepparents, and the Susceptibility of Adolescents to Antisocial Peer Pressure," *Child Development* 58 (1987): 275.

12. Nicholas Zill, Donna Ruane Morrison, and Mary Jo Coiro, "Long-Term Effects of Parental Divorce on Parent-Child Relationships, Adjustment, and Achievement in Young Adulthood," *Journal of Family Psychology* 7, no. 1 (1993): 101.

13. Frank F. Furstenberg, Jr., "History and Current Status of Divorce in the United States," *The Future of Children* 4, no. 1 (Los Altos, Calif.: Center for the Future of Children, Spring 1994), 37.

14. Kathleen E. Keirnan, "The Impact of Family Disruption in Childhood on Transitions Made in Young Adult Life," *Population Studies* 46, no. 2 (July 1992): 213–34.

15. Maggie Drummond, "Step This Way for the Growing Cause of Family Breakdown," *London Daily Telegraph*, December 2, 1991, 18.

16. Paul Amato, *Children in Australian Families: The Growth of Competence* (Englewood Cliffs, N.J.: Prentice Hall, 1987), 115, 118.

17. Ibid., 147–48.

18. For example, second marriages are significantly more likely to end in divorce than are first marriages. Among younger couples today, a redivorce may be as much as 25 percent more likely than a first divorce. One national survey finds that more than one-third of all children living in stepfamilies have already experienced a second parental divorce by the time they reach their early teens. As a result, about 15 percent of all the children in the nation today are likely to experience at least two parental divorces by the time they reach late adolescence.

19. Frank F. Furstenberg, Jr., and Andrew J. Cherlin, *Divided Families: What Happens to Children When Parents Part* (Cambridge, Mass.: Harvard University Press, 1991), 59.

20. Furstenberg, "Divorce and the American Family," 388.

21. John W. Santrock, Karen A. Sitterle, and Richard A. Warshak, "Parent-Child Relation-

ships in Stepfather Families," in Phyllis Bronstein and Carolyn Pape Cowan, eds., *Fatherhood Today: Men's Changing Role in the Family* (New York: Wiley, 1988), 159.

22. E. Mavis Hetherington, Margaret Stanley-Hagan, and Edward R. Anderson, "Marital Transitions: A Child's Perspective," *American Psychologist* 44, no. 2 (February 1989): 308. See also Lawrence A. Kurdek and Mark A. Fine, "The Relationship Between Family Structure and Young Adolescents' Appraisals of Family Climate and Parenting Behavior," *Journal of Family Issues* 14, no. 2 (June 1993): 279–90; Elizabeth Thomson, Sara S. McLanahan, and Roberta Braun Curtin, "Family Structure, Gender, and Parental Socialization," *Journal of Marriage and the Family* 54 (May 1992): 368–78; and Stephen Claxton-Oldfield, "Perceptions of Stepfathers," *Journal of Family Issues* 13, no. 3 (September 1992): 378–89.

23. Harold H. Bloomfield, "Stepparents: Getting to the Heart of Problems," *Parenting* (April 1993): 161–62.

24. Sandi Kahn Shelton, "Happily Remarried," *Working Mother* (April 1993): 62–64.

25. Even the word *stepchild* is so fraught with negative meaning that it is frequently used to suggest a state of deprivation. For example, one current dictionary defines *stepchild* as either "a child of one's wife or husband by a former marriage" or "one that fails to receive proper care or attention." See *Merriam Webster's Collegiate Dictionary* (Springfield, Mass.: Merriam-Webster, 1993).

26. Bloomfield, *Making Peace in Your Stepfamily*, 75.

27. See Emily and John Visher, *How to Win as a Stepfamily* (New York: Dembner Books, 1982), 67–69; and Berman, *Making It as a Stepparent*, 37–41.

28. Berman, *What Am I Doing in a Stepfamily?*

## CRITICAL THINKING QUESTIONS

1. Blankenhorn describes stepfamilies as "inherently fraught with bad outcomes for children." Does his material also suggest, however, that some of the bad outcomes may be due to few societal guidelines about rules, roles, and relationships rather than inherent stepfamily characteristics?

2. Blankenhorn argues that fatherlessness "causes" stepfamily problems. Why, then, don't biological fathers participate in their children's lives?

3. Is it possible that stepfamily relationships are more varied than Blankenhorn claims? Especially, for example, if we consider variations in terms of social class, race, ethnicity, age of children, custody decisions, and the relationship between the divorced parents?

# 17 Remarriage and Stepfamilies

## *Liberal/Feminist:* My Wife-in-Law and Me: Reflections on a Joint-Custody Stepparenting Relationship

SARAH TURNER, "My Wife-in-Law and Me: Reflections on a Joint-Custody Stepparenting Relationship," in *Women and Stepfamilies: Voices of Anger and Love*, ed. Nan Bauer Maglin and Nancy Schniedewind (Philadelphia: Temple University Press, 1989), pp. 310–320. © 1989 by Nan Bauer Maglin and Nancy Schniedewind. Reprinted by permission of Temple University Press. All rights reserved.

*Stepfamily relationships pose daunting problems, but are they doomed to failure, as the article by Blankenhorn suggests? Sarah Turner maintains that a feminist consciousness can create good working relationships between stepfamilies. She suggests several ways that adults can cooperate in co-parenting to achieve common goals and to foster the well-being of all concerned.*

Every two weeks my fifteen-year-old son loads his collection of three hundred comic books into two long cardboard boxes constructed for this purpose. These two boxes, together with his own and his eighteen-year-old sister's duffel bags and stereo boxes, get brought down to the car, and I take this cargo over to their father's house, about a half mile away. Two weeks later, they and their belongings come back to me. My husband and I separated seven years ago, after almost a year of intense and painful discussion. In retrospect, those discussions seemed to have paved the way for a fundamental renegotiation of our relationship, from husband and wife to co-parents. Even then we realized dimly that because of our children, our relationship would always be around in some form. Thus we were able to construct an amicable divorce based on a basic agreement over

two major points: money and custody. He, because he was able, would support the children's major expenses. And, perhaps equally as important, we would split their time with us half and half; neither of us was willing to have any less than half time with our kids, and each of us respected that wish in the other. Two years later, he remarried, and he and Ann subsequently became the parents of Sam, a two-year-old from El Salvador, who is now four.

I want to begin this chapter by acknowledging the importance of a basic fact: the major and often crippling difficult issues raised by disagreements over money and custody have not happened to us. There are three reasons for this, I think. For one thing, we were able to leave behind us, at least operationally, the mutual emotional entanglements that often persist after the relationship is officially "over." We were able to put aside issues of blame, guilt, recrimination, and the like at least partly, I think, because we had talked the whole relationship through already (even though, as I now know, the story of my marriage, like history, rewrites itself with each new development in my own life). Second, Jeff has always had the view that he is and should be an equally involved and responsible parent—until recently, a relatively unusual stance for males in our society. The importance of this equality cannot be overestimated, because it has given us a grounding of common involvement and trust. Third, he, through his family, has the financial resources to provide generously for our children, without anyone having to sacrifice. While I think it would be ideal if we were equal in this respect as well, the fact that his sense of responsibility has exactly matched his abilities to provide has made the potential conflicts in the financial area almost nonexistent.

These three factors—emotional distance, equality in co-parenting, and financial security—are important not only in themselves, but also because without them tremendous confusion can occur in people's interpretation of events. Emotional entanglements can play out in financial tugs-of-war, and inequalities of parental time are often exacerbated by financial dependencies (as in the case of the wife who has both less money and more childcare responsibilities). In our case, in sum, we were able relatively easily to come to a basic agreement about the form that our joint-custody lives would take. And in that sense we were able to set up two households with a basically compatible value system. My ex-husband and my "wife-in-law" have constructed a home that I am more than happy to have my children live in. I trust them implicitly and have absolute confidence in their judgment and concern. I expect that they would say the same for me. I am describing, in some ways, the best possible scenario.

However, the issues and feelings that have surfaced for me over the years, even in this situation, seem to be revealing and useful to describe. The very fact that ours is at bottom a healthy arrangement means that I am able to step back occasionally and reflect on some of its fundamental dynamics, dynamics that perhaps all co-parenting situations share to some degree. I am mainly going to write about my relationship with Ann, my "wife-in-law." Much of what goes on is negotiated by the two of us. It is Ann and I, rather than Jeff and I, who have tended to arrange schedules, doctors' appointments, and so on, although over the years those roles have declined as the children have begun to make their own plans. It is we who have the overlapping roles of mother—two people on one base, as it were—and we who sometimes get in each other's way. In terms of these issues, then, we can ask several questions. How do two women, united and at the same time divided by the same set of relationships, make sense of this situation? How can they construct their own relationship? How can they both make meaning out of their situation, so that they can derive a sense of efficacy and control, and be able to explain to themselves, and sometimes to each other, what is going on (as well as, of course, to Jeff)?

Thinking about specific issues that have come up for me, I find that several themes keep emerging, which I want to list, illustrate, and analyze from a feminist perspective. I will then conclude by suggesting ways that feminists can think about and deal with such co-parenting situations in general, so that the feelings, goals, and well-being of all concerned are fostered best. These themes, which are obviously related and occur in no particular order, are:

- The issue of a third person sharing the intimate daily life of your children.
- The construction of a required intimate relationship with someone you don't know at all, a woman who is "just like" your friends in many ways but who situationally cannot be your friend.
- The mutual invasion of familial boundaries of time and space, so that decisions that have been intrafamilial become contingent on two families.

- The necessary interplay between rules (such as two weeks here and two weeks there) and relationships (how the exceptions get constructed and allowed), and the complex interactions that take place in the journey back and forth between rights and responsibilities, to use Carol Gilligan's (1982) formulation.

## DEALING WITH YOUR CHILDREN

The first and most obvious issue is the fact that someone else is sharing the intimate role of parent to your children. As the "birth mother" I know that my perspective is different in important respects from that of the father, or the stepmother, or a stepfather. I feel this issue most strongly when Ann, who is extremely concerned about the welfare of my children, suggests music lessons, or less TV time, or more attention to course selection in high school, or more carefully constructed teenage summer plans. My immediate reaction (less so as I have come to understand this more) is anger at the intrusion and a profound guilt that I, the real mother, did not think of it. I think, "How dare she suggest he needs to do more homework or watch less TV? Is she impugning my role as a good mother? Well, actually, I am lazy about these things. They are lucky to have her. Why do they need me anyway. But, after all, how dare she . . . " and so on.

This particular scenario is exacerbated by the fact that indeed Ann is a careful and thorough planner who thinks of things that neither Jeff nor I would have thought of, and in this respect is a more organized parent than either Jeff or I. But Jeff as the *father* has never been expected to arrange music lessons. So my attitude becomes, from a feminist perspective, a complicated issue. Why, given that Jeff and I are both slightly cavalier parents in these respects, should I be the one to feel guilty and not him? Why do many (not all) conversations about the children's activities occur only between her and me? Once, several years ago, when I said I wanted to talk to Jeff

about some activity, Ann became hurt and Jeff became angry. "She felt you didn't trust her," he said. I said (and felt), "But you are the other parent."

On the other hand, there have been episodes in which having a co-mother around has been very supportive and useful. She and I agree about matters of teenage curfews; we combine sometimes in thinking about how to deal with boyfriends, and she can be a powerful ally.

In sum, there is a deep issue about sharing parenting, one I didn't really fully understand until I got to know the children of a man I have been seeing. I have had eager instincts to give them things or make other efforts to construct a relationship, and have recognized in myself an urge that must be partly about compensating for a feeling of intrusion, of not being their mother. With my own children I have not had to construct a relationship; I have been able to take for granted, in the deepest and best sense of that phrase, our connection to each other. I can be only myself; I have no choice. And them, too. What a task it must be to construct an analogue to that kind of intimacy! No wonder then that Ann was hurt that day. In my attempts to involve Jeff, I was denying her important struggle and accomplishments in relating to my children on her and their common turf. The feminist question here, I feel, is at some level a very deep one, connected as it is to the simultaneous gift and trap that motherhood is for women. I believe we have to learn how to share these kinds of connections with other adults, without giving up or ignoring the particular personal experiences entailed in being a mother.

## INTIMACY AS A REQUIRED COURSE

Ann and I have had to learn how to deal with each other's personalities and particularities on a level that is usually reserved for intimate friends and lovers. We are thrown, for example, into making plans together, as in getting the children ready for a trip. She likes them to be organized and packed a day in advance, and I don't care that much about preplanning. Once, we had a misunderstanding about arrangements I had made for a particular weekend, plans involving the vacation house (another joint-custody project). I had intended to use the house, and when my plans fell through I failed to let her know. She would have gone up there had she known it was free, but I didn't know about her anger and disappointment until I called her up on a completely different matter. She had been upset for several days. As I recall, we had an interesting conversation at that point about our different personality styles: my spontaneity and her careful planning. "When I'm upset," I said, "I want to deal with it right away, get it over with. I can't believe you were mad and I didn't know." She said she had been trying to deal with her anger on her own, that she, in turn, could not believe that I had failed to let her know that I wasn't going to use the house.

The point here is twofold; one, the most obvious, is the sudden intimacy of people thrown together by a situation central to both of their lives. The other is that, like many women, I construct relationships with other women quite easily. Particularly in my life as a women's studies teacher and professional, I am accustomed to making the personal political and the private public; I am comfortable and familiar with mutual self-disclosure. Yet, also like many women, I am more comfortable with connection than with conflict, more comfortable with commonalities than with differences. Here, in a closeup situation involving two people with a lot in common, we cannot easily be forthcoming with each other. The things that unite us also divide us. We are never going to be close friends because the situation imposes on us inherently different perspectives on the same events, people, and the situation itself. Whether, without our common situation, we would become friends, is not at issue here. (We have close mutual friends, and some say we would and others say we

wouldn't.) What is at issue is the construction of relationships across inherent differences and conflicts. How can we get there from here when, as sometimes happens, I don't get the vacation house precisely because they do? Perhaps the feminist approach is to acknowledge and compare the different perspectives, and allow the resolution to occur over time, and one episode at a time. We cannot usefully either fail to acknowledge the conflict or expect it to be resolved once and for all.

## BOUNDARIES OF TIME AND SPACE

When my children are at their father's house, I seldom call them up, except (as happens quite regularly) when I want them to come over for dinner in the middle of the two weeks. When they do come for dinner, they leave at about 8:30 "to go home and do homework," and I feel a pang similar to that which I feel when I drop them off every four weeks. These experiences feel like a draining off of an important part of me; but each time, once I am alone and have gotten used to it, I construct a life as a single person with work, friends, and a social life quite easily. The loss of my children for two weeks out of every four is like some kind of minor but consistent hole, or hiatus. I am aware of their absence, like a missing tooth, but, like a missing tooth, it's not exactly painful. As I said, this degree of comfort has a great deal to do with my basic trust in their other home situation.

On the other hand, when my children are with me and Ann calls for babysitting or some other plans, I sometimes experience this as an intrusion. I cannot say that I don't want them to babysit for Sam; that's their decision. I certainly don't interfere with their other babysitting plans; after all, it's a chance for them to earn money. But in these instances I sometimes feel as though the other family's life is spilling over into and onto mine.

Similarly, the vacation house: I have visiting rights to the house, built by both of us and now owned by Jeff. Jeff and Ann are very generous; basically I can go there whenever they don't want to. And we divide time at the house during summers and Christmas vacations more or less equally. But Ann was, reasonably enough, eager to redecorate the house on her terms, to her eye, and when I first saw the new curtains in the living room (bought to match a rug that I later took back but that Ann had assumed would stay there), I was really shaken up. "No big deal," I told myself, but my space, my ordering of it, and my definition of it, had been violated. (Here again, this felt to me more like an issue between me and Ann, not me and Jeff, who tends to be more neutral about his esthetic environment.)

Each visit to the house now involves for me a minuscule and very subtle reshuffling of china, cloth napkins, different quilts on different beds. These boundary issues, again, entail alterations and shifts in daily life patterns on an almost unconscious level. They have made me at times feel powerless to make assumptions about regularities and continuities in areas that ought, I feel, to be under my control—like when I serve dinner, or go on vacation. I share my space and my time with another family unit.

Am I implying here that people need control over their family lives that they can't have elsewhere? In a way, I am. In our society the home and the private sphere are touted as *the* place where people do have some control over the decisions that affect their lives, since work under capitalism cannot provide this for many people. In this view the family, as haven and indivisible unit, gives solace, individual agency, and personal recognition; it's where you can be yourself. As we know now, "the family" from insiders' perspectives is often a very different experience, and classically the woman has often provided these emotional boons to others at great cost to herself. It thus may be better, in fact, to see even the most successful families not as easy retreats *from* the world but as arenas in the world for people to support each other's needs for efficacy and connection. When I am saying,

then, that I resent outside incursions into my family, into my own sense of personal space and agency, I do not simply mean that I no longer want to be a sacrificial mother figure, a person who denies her own needs. Certainly I have a lot more power as an individual in my own house than I did when I was married; any single person does. But these incursions, when they take place, lack the crucial tradeoffs of intimacy and decisions made in common for a common goal that a successful family situation provides. To compromise on vacation time in order to be together with a spouse or children, or to preserve a relationship in some way, is different from compromising on vacation time from a distance, because people not included in your own plans demand it.

However, I have learned to say what I want in these situations less defensively and angrily as I have seen that there is a large middle ground to be negotiated between complete control and complete loss of it. In the absence of deep personal connection and a shared common purpose, boundary issues can be negotiated on principles of fairness and compromise (sometimes). And even *with* intimate personal connections, fairness and a sense of boundaries should be respected in families and among intimates more than I suspect they often are. Perhaps intimacy functions both healthily as a cushion, to ease over conflict, but also unhealthily, as a suppressor of conflicts that should occur and be resolved. The question becomes, then, how to foster both fairness and close connections in family life, particularly as the traditional family gives way to many alternative family patterns like ours.

## RULES AND RELATIONSHIPS

This brings me to the last issue that has come up in my thinking about joint custody, namely the connection, or relation, between rules and relationships. For example, we have some rules, which are extremely useful, about the children's time and what we call "the schedule" of two weeks at each home. As the children have gotten older, they themselves have determined the intervals to be spent at each house; in the beginning, we split the weeks into fractions, because they and we felt that more than three or four days was too long not to see the other parent. Later, at their instigation, we changed first to a whole week at one place and then to two weeks. ("I do *not* want to drag my stuff back and forth that often, Mum.")

There are also times when a parent has a conference or a trip, and the rules need to be bent. I have experienced at such times a semi-desperation when I realize that I am supposed to have the children at a time when I have to be away—or worse, don't absolutely have to but want to. At these times I feel that I am asking Jeff to bend the rules. He checks with Ann (or vice versa) and then gets back to me. Usually, it's fine. When it's not, I have learned that I can negotiate and that a compromise can usually be worked out. (Recently, in fact, we have been in a transition period, where the children have become old enough to stay home on their own. Jeff says, "They don't have to come to my house; they can be by themselves." I say, "But I think they are still too young," and if I really wanted to go away he would have me over a barrel!) However, the issue here was and is one of power and responsibility to each other, as well as one of rules. In this kind of situation, viewed completely rationally, if two people disagree and the rules are on one person's side, that person ought to win. Furthermore, I have often felt like an unequal player in the struggles over these matters. "There are two of them," I say to myself. "They are a whole family. There is only one of poor little me." Thus my misplaced sense of asking him permission to bend the rules.

But what has happened when they wanted me to bend the rules? Actually, of course, I have been happy to do so. Underneath the rules, and preserving them,

perhaps even making them possible in the first place, is a mutual sense of responsibility and, I have to admit, an equality of power. The rules are a way of organizing the relationship, but without the mutual trust they would not be enough in themselves. As many people in these situations know much better than I, rules don't work if people don't want the relationship they regulate to work. In fact, many such rules regulate relationships that are actually held together not by the rules alone but by inequalities of power. Thus many women have stayed in marriages because they lack the power, economically and emotionally, to leave, and until recently the rules, or laws, enforced the husbands' powers to keep them there. Now, when rules and powers sometimes go in different directions (as in laws about child support), we can see which is more important. Fathers escape support payments because their powers—both economic and political— override the rules.

Relationships of equality may thus need rules to regulate them (whereas in relationships of power rules play a different role). However, if the three of us didn't want to preserve our system, we could spend our time looking for the loopholes and counting up the compromised days and weekends in such a way that someone would always feel mistreated. What feminist scholars (like Carol Gilligan, 1982) have shown us about the importance of a responsibility and caring approach to decisions is important here. It is at least as much the desire and need to preserve our relationships as it is the desire to be fair that allows us our trust in each other's willingness to compromise. My situation is also fundamentally one of equality with my ex-husband; even though he supports the children, I support myself, and we are equally interested in their emotional welfare. Therefore I can negotiate the relationship with him and Ann as an autonomous person. When women lack such equality, relationships of domination tend to cloud and distort our need for connection and our concern with responsibility. We have to please other people, and must try to use rules in place of power when our reliance on the relationship fails. (This can happen with men, too, but I think less often.)

## CONCLUSION

I have had trouble with many aspects of my situation of bringing up my children in joint custody with their father and stepmother. I have not liked being told about appropriate extracurricular activities for them, although I have liked help and support about rule setting. I have not liked being personally involved with someone whose concerns, feeling, and interests I cannot share. I have not liked sharing my children's time, the decoration of my vacation living room, my own vacation schedule, although I have often been grateful for my times of solitude, built as they are on the basic assumption that my children were always all right. I have not liked needing "permission" before making some of my own plans.

I think, however, that all these negative experiences are relatively trivial. While I still feel them intensely when they occur, I have learned to step outside them later on, and analyze them as possible aspects of more general issues affecting women and men in families today. The new research on women, particularly that of Carol Gilligan (1982) and Jean Baker Miller (1976), has shown that women's lives (in fact, everyone's lives) rest in a network of relationships and responsibilities to individual people as well as participation in the more formal, impersonal, and rule-bound structures of institutions and jobs. When one family becomes two families, the questions of rules, boundaries, arrangements, and the differing goals and purposes of individuals become more formal and explicit, more institutional in a way, even as the relationships between and among the players become more complex. A feminist perspec-

tive on such a situation means an acknowledgment of both aspects of the constellation: the need for commonly agreed-on rules and the understanding that emotional connections both support and defy those rules. Thus the mother-child bond is unique and deep, but that doesn't mean that other adult-child relationships that have important and comparable meaning cannot be constructed. If we mothers rest too much on the uniqueness of this bond, we lose both our children as independent individuals and ourselves as fully rounded people, and we deny them other models of good parenting.

Similarly, women are often separated by the same structures (mother/stepmother, mother/teacher, teacher/student, employer/employee, etc., etc.) that bring them together, and we need to acknowledge where those roles need explications and guidelines to help those potentially conflictual relationships be resolved. Finally, boundaries and rules, while necessary in all relationships, probably mean little unless all involved want the relationship to continue. If we prefer relationships based on equalities of power, we are going to have to figure out how to balance such mixtures of rights and responsibilities, impersonal rules and personal connections, in some meaningful way.

In this regard, the question of joint custody with another parent and stepparent bears scrutiny from a feminist perspective, as one construction of the "divorce relationship." Divorces, when there are children, are ongoing relationships that survive, even beyond the children's growing up. We need to think of divorce, therefore, not only as a severing of connection but as a reconnection of different terms. Joint custody and stepparenting carry with them the connotation of joint responsibility and equality. My situation is unusual in that I can presume good will on both sides. When conflicts occur, as they inevitably do, I have the luxury of reflection on the issues that come up. When the situation involves financial hardship on one or both sides, old and unresolved marital hurts, basic inequalities of power, or fundamentally different value systems, the underlying dynamics of trying to construct a situation of fully equal responsibility across two families may become obscured or seem irrelevant. In such situations, the more basic issues may color every small transaction, giving them an inappropriate intensity that makes them harder to negotiate. Furthermore, most relationships in our society are built on power and domination, rather than equality, and so most divorces and many joint custody arrangements are therefore unequal ones.

But I think it is nevertheless possible to discern some approaches that reflect feminist values, even if we can't always live up to them. The first is the recognition of the need for equality. Father and mother and stepmother (and stepfather) should be co-parents, and as far as possible co-responsible for at least the emotional if not the financial aspects of their children's lives. The details of this equality, and the form that it actually takes, may vary, but the principle should be agreed on by all parties. The second factor is the need for rules and guidelines, ones that reflect and capture this equality and at the same time protect people's rights and expectations of fairness. An example from my own case would be the rule of equal time in each household, in which the children have had the right to determine what the length of that time would be.

The third factor, and the one that perhaps best reflects the recent concerns of feminist literature, is the recognition of the importance of relationships in people's lives, that each person and therefore each relationship is unique, and that the connections among people are crucial aspects of our experiences of ourselves. I want to be able to incorporate Ann's and Jeff's, and the children's perspectives on the issues, to see the situation on their terms and be mindful of the relations between and among us, even as I work to articulate my own views. The challenge, then, seems to be how to construct relationships of equality that honor differences, that connect us across our differences, and yet do not eradicate those differences in the name of alleged universal truths. Joint custody and stepparenting arrangements, ones that connect people across the divisions between two families, are one place to look for these values.

## REFERENCES

Gilligan, Carol. *In a Different Voice*. Cambridge, Mass.: Harvard University Press, 1982.

Miller, Jean Baker. *Towards a New Psychology of Women*. Boston: Beacon Press, 1976.

## CRITICAL THINKING QUESTIONS

1. How, according to Turner, can a feminist perspective help to transform potentially negative stepfamily relationships?

2. What does Turner mean when she describes biological and stepparenting roles as "gendered"? Does she imply that developing good co-parenting relationships is, in the last analysis, still a "woman's job"?

3. Does Turner's description of stepparenting support or challenge Blankenhorn's contention that divorced fathers become disengaged from their children?

# 18 Family Policies

## *Conservative:* What Government Must Do to Reduce Welfare

CHARLES MURRAY, "What Government Must Do: Make Welfare Unappealing or Reform Will Fail," *The American Enterprise* 9 (January/February 1998): 72–73. Reproduced with permission from The American Enterprise Institute for Public Interest.

*One of the most controversial issues of the 1990s was the passage of the Personal Responsibility and Work Opportunity Reconciliation Act of 1996. A major goal of the act was to get welfare recipients into jobs (see the next article). Charles Murray argues, however, that the act doesn't go far enough in reducing welfare.*

Years ago I worked for a research company that evaluated social programs for the federal government. One time I was heading a team assessing a program for troubled inner-city teenagers. As the evaluation approached its end, no quantitative measure showed the program had accomplished anything. I gave the draft of the report to the program's staff.

They were unhappy and angry. Maybe what they'd accomplished didn't show up in the numbers, they said, but dammit, they dealt in human lives, not numbers, and they knew they'd had an impact. I can't change the numbers, I replied, but we'll go through your files, pull out the ones that represent your biggest successes, and I'll write them up as case histories of what the program can accomplish at its best.

So we went through the files together. And we couldn't find any successes. The staff had been thinking about Sally, let's call her, who in the first year of the program had come back to school, pulled her grades up, and stayed away from drugs. But when we looked up what had happened to Sally since she'd left the program, it turned out she had dropped out of school and was back on drugs. It wasn't that our numbers had failed to capture important outcomes, but that the staff hadn't checked up on their success stories for a while, and they had regressed to where they started. In the end, I had to make what I could from a few examples of fragmentary progress.

This history is a cautionary tale for thinking about what we can expect from welfare devolution. It is hard even for the most well-meaning and dedicated people to change people's lives, and we must ask even of this scattered good news how many of the success stories will still be successes a year from now. It is time to return to a few hard realities that have been slipping from sight as we become accustomed to news about plunging welfare rolls.

The first reality is that welfare rolls have not gone down because of actual changes in law or the operation of welfare bureaucracies. As recent studies reveal, the rolls have been dropping at about the same rate before and after the provisions of any given welfare reform have gone into effect. What changed, if not the laws.

Don't rely on the growing economy for explanations. Look at the welfare rolls in the economic expansions of the 1960s and 1980s: In the Reagan years, welfare rolls remained steady; during the Johnson boom years, when unemployment stood at less than 4 percent, the welfare rolls soared. The growing economy of the 1990s has increased the ability of welfare recipients to get jobs if they want them, but the trigger for the change in wanting jobs must be sought somewhere besides growth in the GNP [Gross National Product].

In seeking that trigger, we know this much for sure: For a few years, the politicians, including the President, talked very tough indeed. Two years and out. No more entitlement to welfare. Get a job or you're going to find yourself on the streets. Legislation began to pass in individual states, then in Washington. The media gave headline coverage to the direst predictions—the coming of Calcutta on the Hudson, a million children thrown into poverty, etc. The word spread to the street. The least attentive welfare recipient could not avoid being bombarded with messages that her world was about to come crashing down.

My interpretation of the trends in welfare rolls is that the rhetoric worked. The welfare population includes a fairly large number of women who could work if they wanted to badly enough, and all the hoopla moved some proportion of those women to act. This is not a trivial accomplishment. But neither is it necessarily going to continue. Once we look beyond that top layer of competent and readily motivated women, we find another hard reality. The interventions of outsiders— whether they be government social workers or church volunteers or socially

conscious employers—require a receptive client. Receptive means first that she is not already deeply habituated to the life she lives. Receptive also means the client knows she is in dire trouble unless she gets her life in order. Absent either of those conditions, social interventions end up with evaluations concluding that the intervention had no statistical effect.

I write these pessimistic cautions as someone who believes that only the private realm of employers, philanthropy, churches, and neighbors can succeed in reducing the size of the underclass. [I doubt] a resurrection of the model I admire most: the extensive and energetic social philanthropy developed in late-nineteenth-century England by Victorians, a private system that enjoyed enormous success in propagating middle-class virtues down to the lowest ranks of the British working class. Neither of the conditions for a receptive clientele applies broadly today.

Consider the first condition for receptivity, that the client not be deeply habituated to the life she lives. Of those left on the rolls, many are so alienated from regular schedules, work habits, and responsible behavior that no one knows how to make them into good workers. If helping agencies of any kind are to be effective, they must perform triage. In language the Victorians would have used, they must not shrink from distinguishing between the deserving and undeserving poor.

This doesn't mean the undeserving must be abandoned. The Victorians accepted that they could feed and clothe them. But the Victorians focused their most energetic efforts on the deserving. America's helping agencies, public and private, have yet to accept that (1) from an ethical standpoint we should first help those who are trying to help themselves, and (2) from a practical standpoint they are just about the only ones we can help. A church shouldn't be putting its limited resources into helping young women who have to be pushed and cajoled to look for a job. It should be helping young women who have lined up a job but can't find a ride to work. A company shouldn't reserve job slots for employees who must be treated with kid gloves lest they get in a fight with their supervisors; it should be on the lookout for those whose job records may be bad but are saying, "Just give me a chance, and you can fire me the first time I'm five minutes late." Help those who are receptive to help, *let it be openly seen that those who are receptive to help receive preferential treatment*, and you will have begun the process whereby more and more people become receptive.

The second condition of receptivity, urgent motivation to change, is also weak. Even if it is true that today's private helpers need a dose of good old-fashioned judgmentalism, most of the blame for the difficulties they face falls on the government. The Victorians had the crucial advantage of working alongside a government that believed in the rule of "less eligibility," meaning that public assistance had to provide a standard of living less desirable (less eligible) than that enjoyed by the lowest-paid worker. The Victorians worked in an environment in which to have a baby without help from the baby's father or one's own parents was to be forced to rely on the kindness of strangers. Thus did the Victorians find a clientele motivated by the prospect of hovering disaster, and thus did they achieve great things.

In contrast, today's employers and church committees are finding that whatever momentary scare they had working for them is rapidly dissipating. The Clinton White House, with the collaboration of a Republican Congress, is busily gutting the tough aspects of the original welfare reform bill. Social workers, many of whom were hostile toward the welfare reform bill in the first place, are looking for excuses to relax the pressure to get jobs. Ways are being found, as they are always found with complex welfare systems, to slip through loopholes. These changes are known to the clientele—the street-level awareness of changes in atmosphere at the welfare office is as keen as Wall Street's sensitivity to changes in atmosphere at the Federal Reserve.

Women are already seeing through the propaganda. The welfare system still provides a better living than a low-wage job, it is still a more reliable source of money than the boyfriend, and if you know the ins and outs you can stay on it indefinitely. For the last few years, those who were trying to help move welfare women to work were dealing with women who were genuinely worried about what the future held. That is decreasingly true. Before the private helpers can do good, the government has to get the ground rules right. The government moved in that direction in 1996 but then lost its nerve.

My gloomy prediction? Faced with a difficult job at best, and trying to deal with an increasingly unreceptive clientele, churches and employers and local groups will have fewer and fewer successes to show for their efforts. The welfare rolls will start to move up again, and the pundits will say it proves that the private sector can't do the job after all. This can be avoided. But it will require a moral resolve about why welfare dependency is bad, why illegitimacy is bad, and why they must be reduced, that the President never had and that Congress has lost.

**CRITICAL THINKING QUESTIONS**

1. Why is Murray pessimistic that the recent reforms will reduce the number of welfare recipients?

2. Who, specifically, are the "unreceptive clientele"? The underclass?

3. If, as Murray argues, mothers with out-of-wedlock babies should not "rely on the kindness of strangers" (i.e., welfare), should conservatives support abortion to decrease the welfare rolls? Sex education in middle schools? Widespread distribution of condoms among high school students?

# 18 Family Policies

## Centrist: Is Federal Welfare Reform Helping or Hurting Poor Families?

Original paper written for this book by Laura A. Wilson and Robert P. Stoker. Reprinted by permission.

*The Personal Responsibility and Work Opportunity Reconciliation Act of 1996 (PRWORA) created new work requirements for welfare recipients. Laura A. Wilson and Robert P. Stoker describe the perceptions about welfare that led to the act, how PRWORA differs from previous welfare legislation, and the act's implications for millions of poor families.*

As a candidate for president of the United States, Bill Clinton promised to "end welfare as we know it." When he ran for reelection, no one could say President Clinton had failed to honor his campaign pledge. The 1996 federal welfare reform, the Personal Responsibility and Work Opportunity Reconciliation Act, was seen as a dramatic and controversial change in welfare policy.[1] The act created new work requirements for welfare recipients and redefined the historic relationship between the federal government and the states, affecting the lives of millions of needy American families.

### THE AMERICAN WELFARE SYSTEM

The welfare system the president hoped to transform is actually a loose collection of programs that provide benefits to people on the basis of income eligibility. Those who receive "welfare" may qualify for various types of benefits from different programs, so people may disagree about the boundaries of the welfare system. However, welfare benefits traditionally consist of three components: cash assistance (money the recipient may use for any purpose); medical assistance (reimbursement to health-care providers who treat welfare clients); and food assistance (coupons that may be exchanged for approved food products). Other programs that are often considered part of the welfare system include child-care grants to subsidize day care, housing subsidies, and energy assistance to help pay heating bills.

Until 1996, the primary cash assistance welfare program was Aid to Families with Dependent Children (AFDC). To be eligible for AFDC, it was necessary to be poor and to have a dependent child to support. Some states had an AFDC-UP (UP refers to Unemployed Parent) program that provided cash assistance to two-parent families with dependent children. However, most AFDC families were composed of unmarried women and their children. There was no limit on the length of time families could receive AFDC.

From the mid-1960s until the 1996 welfare reform, the typical welfare benefit package consisted of AFDC for cash assistance, Medicaid to defray the costs of health care, and Food Stamps to help purchase nutritious foods. AFDC was the gateway to the other benefits: By qualifying for AFDC, welfare recipients also qualified for Medicaid and Food Stamps. Some welfare recipients received child-care grants, housing assistance, and energy assistance, but participation in these programs was limited by funding constraints.

This chapter describes welfare policy in the United States, with an emphasis on how the Personal Responsibility and Work Opportunity Reconciliation Act (PRWORA) of 1996 has changed the welfare system and affected the lives of American families. In many cases, PRWORA was a reaction to the way that AFDC had evolved and the perceptions of policymakers about welfare recipients.

## SOCIAL POLICY IN THE UNITED STATES: ISSUES AND CONTROVERSIES

Recent changes in the welfare system reflect concern about the behavior of welfare recipients and the costs of welfare programs. However, to understand why and how the welfare system became a target for reform, it helps to distinguish two types of social welfare policies—welfare programs and social insurance programs. PRWORA brought many changes to welfare programs, but left social insurance programs unchanged.

The modern era in U.S. social policy is marked by the adoption of the Social Security Act of 1935. The Social Security Act created a number of "social insurance" programs and consolidated existing state "welfare" programs into a national welfare system. Social insurance and welfare programs are distinguished on the basis of eligibility. To be eligible for social insurance benefits, one must establish a work history, be the dependent of someone who has

worked, or be disabled. To be eligible for welfare benefits, one must have financial need, little income, and few assets.

Social insurance programs created by the Social Security Act include old age pensions, unemployment compensation, and disability insurance for groups generally considered worthy of government assistance because they were either disabled or had worked at one time in their lives. Over time, the social insurance system was expanded to include more of the population (such as widows and surviving children), new services were added (such as medical care), and benefit payments grew more generous. Expansion of the social insurance system had a profound effect on the welfare system. As opportunities to receive social insurance benefits expanded, eligible persons migrated from the welfare system to the social insurance system. The social insurance system became very popular, particularly Social Security payments to retirees. National political leaders refer to these payments as the "third rail of American politics."[2]

In contrast to its contemporary image, welfare cash assistance began as a popular program that provided benefits to needy children and their families, the elderly, and the blind. Until the 1950s, the typical welfare recipient was an elderly person who was in financial need despite a life history of work.[3] However, during the 1960s, the caseload and political climate of welfare changed. As the more "worthy" groups migrated to the social insurance system, the welfare caseload came to be composed primarily of never-married women with children.[4] A social stigma came to be attached to welfare, and recipients were frequently seen as unworthy of government support.

President Lyndon Johnson's Great Society programs, the welfare rights movement, and a series of federal court decisions helped to end a historic pattern of racial discrimination in making welfare eligibility decisions.[5] Consequently, families composed of racial minorities gained access to welfare benefits. This mixed the social stigma of welfare receipt with racial politics, making welfare programs a popular target for reform. Political leaders began proposing means to "rehabilitate" welfare recipients by proposing job requirements.[6]

The original purpose of welfare cash assistance was to allow mothers to remain at home so that their children could grow into "good and productive members of society."[7] By the 1960s, however, the role of women in society began to change, with more middle-class women entering the job market. Policy officials then faced a dilemma: If middle-class women are working, why should welfare mothers be idle? A variety of voluntary education and training programs and work incentives were tried. However, the limited success of these programs created frustration and the perception that welfare dependency—long-term receipt of cash assistance and other welfare benefits—was becoming more widespread. To this was added a new concern, intergenerational dependency—the tendency for children who grew up in the welfare system to end up in the welfare system as adult recipients.

By the 1980s, there was widespread frustration with the welfare system but no consensus about how to solve the problem. President Ronald Reagan invited states to apply for waivers of federal law and regulation to develop experimental welfare reforms. This practice was continued and encouraged by Presidents George Bush and Clinton. Throughout the late 1980s and early 1990s, many states implemented welfare reform experiments and took the lead in establishing welfare policy.

A consistent theme in the state welfare experiments was that welfare recipients had to demonstrate personal responsibility. The goal of these experiments was to create a reciprocal relationship between welfare clients and the state. As a point of contact between welfare clients and the state, the welfare system represented an opportunity to mold the behavior of welfare recipients.[8] The state would provide benefits, but only on the condition that welfare clients behaved responsibly. It was left to state officials to define what personal responsibility meant. States created and enforced a variety of different requirements for receipt of welfare. AFDC had been given without conditions, but states now linked cash assistance to welfare clients' looking for work or getting their children to school. Many states simply wanted AFDC recipients to find a job, any job.

Research evaluating state experiments convinced many policy analysts and political officials that mandatory work requirements could help end welfare dependency.[9] An influential report by the Manpower Development Research Corporation (MDRC) outlined the accomplishments of mandatory work requirements:

1. AFDC recipients saw mandatory work requirements as satisfactory and fair.
2. Participants in programs with mandatory work requirements were more likely to be employed than those who were not participants.
3. Over time, the benefits of these programs exceeded their costs.[10]

In essence, state "personal responsibility" reforms and mandatory work requirements became an attempt to transform the "unworthy" welfare recipients into "worthy" clients by fostering changes in behavior, especially self-sufficiency through work.

Federal officials embraced the emphasis on personal responsibility that was common in state experiments, but also had an additional concern, money. Although federal officials wanted to transform the behavior of welfare clients, concerns about money and the budget deficit also shaped the 1996 welfare reform. Prior to that reform, the programs that composed the welfare benefit package were entitlement programs. Such programs enjoy a special legal and budgetary status. States could not refuse to make payments to any individual who satisfied the eligibility requirements, and eligible individuals could sue to enforce these rights. In short, welfare was a legally enforceable, individual right to income maintenance, medical care, and food. The practical effects of entitlement status were that budgetary concerns could not prevent people from receiving welfare benefits and that the federal courts played a significant role in welfare administration. Status as an entitlement program also meant that Congress could not directly control welfare expenditures. If more people became eligible, the funds spent on welfare increased automatically.

Although many states had implemented mandatory work requirements and other behavioral reforms, concern about welfare dependency and the cost of federal welfare programs increased as welfare participation grew to historic levels in the early 1990s. This aggravated attempts to control the federal budget deficit.[11] In this context, the 1996 federal welfare reform was developed.

## PRWORA

The Personal Responsibility and Work Opportunity Reconciliation Act brought significant changes to the welfare system. The act repealed AFDC and created a new cash assistance program, Temporary Assistance for Needy Families (TANF). PRWORA provides federal welfare funds to the states with few conditions, thereby giving the states a great deal of discretion about requirements of welfare recipients.

### Cash Assistance, Personal Responsibility, and Work

PRWORA emphasized personal responsibility and work. While previous welfare reforms offered opportunities and incentives to work, work requirements with firm deadlines were first made national policy under PRWORA. TANF applicants who refuse to cooperate with work requirements may be sanctioned (their cash assistance payment may be suspended or reduced). Levels and conditions of sanction vary from one state to another.

The entitlement status of welfare cash assistance was removed when AFDC was repealed. The name of the new cash assistance program makes this point clear, *Temporary* Assistance for Needy Families. In 1997, TANF benefit payments ranged from $923 per month in Alaska to $120 per month in Mississippi.[12] The average TANF benefit in 1997 was $362.[13] Unlike AFDC, TANF benefits are not given unconditionally. Reflecting the emphasis on personal responsibility, recipients must satisfy several conditions, including work requirements and cooperation with child support enforcement.

Lawmakers have long been troubled by the image of people staying on welfare all of their adult lives, as well as intergenerational recipients, where a mother, a daughter, and a granddaughter are receiving welfare benefits.[14] PRWORA addressed this issue by limiting eligibility for cash assistance to only two years before clients must participate in some type of "countable work activity" such as employment or job training.[15] States may establish a more demanding requirement if they wish, and many have done so. In some states, TANF applicants must begin a job search as soon as they apply for benefits. Emphasis is placed on finding and accepting the first job available, because any job is a good job.

PRWORA limited lifetime eligibility for TANF cash assistance to five years. With few exceptions, people who are on the welfare rolls for five total years are ineligible for cash assistance.[16] Welfare clients are discouraged from lingering in the welfare system indefinitely because they cannot receive benefits for more than five years.

States enjoy some flexibility to define what a countable work activity is, and it is not always the same thing as being employed. In most states countable work activities include working in the private sector, with or without a wage subsidy; working in the public sector; doing community service; searching for a job; participating in literacy classes or other approved training classes; doing volunteer work; or even providing child care for someone else who is involved in a work activity.

Personal responsibility doesn't apply only to mothers on welfare. Troubled by the profile of the welfare population as never-married women, lawmakers began focusing on the obligations of absentee parents. Lawmakers believed that welfare dependency was caused in large part by the inability of never-married mothers to collect child support.[17] TANF recipients must cooperate with child support enforcement. This means that an applicant must name the father of her child and provide information to help the state find him and enforce child support payments. Under AFDC, mothers were paid a $50 bonus when child support enforcement was successful. Under PRWORA, cooperation with child support collection is mandatory, but most states have eliminated or reduced the bonus.[18] A penalty of at least 25 percent of the TANF grant is to be levied against anyone who refuses to cooperate in establishing paternity of a child or refuses to help the state locate the absent parent. PRWORA also instituted a number of reforms to the child support enforcement system to make it easier to track absent parents who leave the state where the child support order is in effect.

## Decoupling Cash and Other Welfare Benefits

In the past, AFDC served as the gateway to a package of benefits that could consist of Medicaid, Food Stamps, and other in-kind programs. Under PRWORA, the link between cash assistance and other in-kind benefit programs has been broken. In-kind benefit programs can still be awarded as a package that includes cash assistance under TANF, but the needy can now obtain these benefits without qualifying for TANF cash assistance.

Although new restrictions and requirements have been created for cash assis-

tance, many in-kind benefit programs have been liberalized. PRWORA eased eligibility for Medicaid benefits, allowing many to continue to receive benefits even after finding work. A new expedited Food Stamp program was created, but eligibility for Food Stamps was made more strict for some recipients, including work requirements for able-bodied beneficiaries.

Loss of medical benefits is often viewed as a significant barrier to exiting the welfare system.[19] Under AFDC, increased income from work or child support payments made many families ineligible for Medicaid. However, many of the jobs available to welfare clients do not offer medical benefits, so working is tantamount to surviving without health insurance. The situation is similar when child support is involved. Although child support payments can substitute for cash assistance, these payments do not provide medical benefits. PRWORA extends Medicaid coverage for 12 months for families who would otherwise be ineligible because of increased earnings due to work or child support payments. By extending Medicaid coverage, PRWORA encourages welfare recipients to exit the welfare system without losing medical assistance. It is too early to tell whether the 12-month extension will be sufficient to prevent former welfare clients from falling back into the welfare system.

Similar to medical assistance, the cost of providing child care when mothers return to work is also seen as a significant barrier to exiting the welfare system.[20] PRWORA combined previous child-care programs into a Child Care and Development Block Grant. Previous federal programs limited child-care subsidies to those receiving full or partial cash assistance benefits or those who had left welfare within the last 12 months. Child-care provisions under the 1996 welfare reform provide child-care subsidies for TANF recipients who are engaged in a work activity or education, child-care support for those who have recently left welfare or for "persons who are working but have very low income and would be at risk of becoming dependent on welfare in the absence of child care."[21]

## State Flexibility in Welfare Reform

PRWORA offers states a number of options and choices. In large part, this flexibility is desirable because states can customize their policy to meet the conditions that exist in their states. For example, Nevada has been very successful in placing former welfare recipients in jobs with the gaming industry, resulting in dramatic reductions in the state's welfare caseload. However, other states with different labor market conditions must develop different strategies. In addition, there is also the danger that states will try to erect significant barriers and conditions for welfare recipients to move persons off welfare quickly just to save money. States that save welfare funds can redirect some of those funds to other, more politically popular projects.

States can impose shorter time frames for welfare receipt than required by the federal government, and some have chosen this option. Reflecting tensions over the appropriate role of women in the family and the workplace, PRWORA permits states to exempt parents with children under one year of age from work requirements, and many have elected to do so.[22] States can specify the degree to which a recipient can be sanctioned for noncompliance with work requirements, although PRWORA sets the base amount of the penalty that can be imposed by any state. Sanction guidelines and amounts vary from state to state.

To address the problem of the "wandering poor," persons who move from one state to another in search of better benefits, PRWORA permits states to decide if they wish to provide newly arrived persons the same level of benefits that are available to established state residents. States have always been worried that if their welfare benefits appear too generous, the poor from other states may move to take advantage of the increased benefits. Some states have

decided to limit welfare benefits to newcomers to the level available in their home state for a fixed time. Other states allow newcomers to qualify for the same benefits available to established state residents.

States can also institute other behavioral requirements. One controversial option is a "family cap," denying or limiting increases in benefits to mothers who have additional children while on welfare. Again, the perception is that some welfare recipients had additional children just to increase the size of their cash benefits. Although the size of welfare families has been declining, AFDC benefit payments were increased when an additional child was born. Twenty-two states have enacted the "family cap."[23] New Jersey was the first state to enact a family cap (in 1991). New Jersey has continued its family cap program under TANF, denying additional benefits to mothers who have more children while on welfare. The state conducted an evaluation to determine whether or not the policy resulted in lower fertility among welfare recipients. There was a decrease in birth rates resulting from an increased use in family planning services and an increase in the number of abortions. New Jersey Governor Christine Todd Whitman praised the results: "The message of personal responsibility is working."[24]

In part, the flexibility in state welfare policy is encouraged by the way TANF is financed. TANF is a capped block grant to the states. This means that the amount of funding provided by the federal government is fixed and will not change over time. However, PRWORA is a block grant. This type of funding mechanism gives states a great deal of flexibility in the policies that they enact. As long as state policy complies with the minimal federal requirements dictated by PRWORA, states have a great deal of discretion in the requirements that they can impose on welfare recipients and how they spend welfare monies.

Although payments to the states are fixed, the shift from AFDC to TANF has been a financial boon for many states. Most states have experienced declines in their cash assistance caseloads.[25] For many states, the TANF block grant provides payments in excess of what was necessary to pay cash benefits. States enjoy some flexibility to decide what to do with the extra money. They may use it to provide additional services to TANF beneficiaries, or they may divert as much as 20 percent to other purposes (such as building schools or paving roads).

Although states have much flexibility under TANF, they are subject to conditions and requirements. By 1997, states were required to show a work participation rate of 25 percent. This requirement increases by 5 percent per year to 50 percent by 2002. States are given credit in this calculation if their overall caseloads drop. Suppose that a state had 10,000 welfare clients in 1996. The state places 500 of these clients in work activity slots while 2,000 people exit the welfare system during 1997. The state would be credited with filling 2,500 work activity slots, satisfying the federal requirement of 25 percent. As long as caseloads decline, targets for work participation are relatively easy to satisfy. However, if caseloads increase, especially if the increase results from an economic downturn, the work participation requirements will become much more difficult to achieve.

## IMPLICATIONS OF PRWORA

PRWORA is presented in the popular media as a triumph of conservative values and the Republican-controlled Congress. Senior staff of the Department of Health and Human Services resigned their positions in protest of President Clinton's decision to sign the bill into law. The controversy surrounding PRWORA obscures the fact that the effects of PRWORA on U.S. families are more complex and ambiguous than these easy characterizations and protests would suggest.

Some analysts were concerned that PRWORA would initiate a "race to the bottom," states competing to create the least generous welfare system. This concern reflects research that state governments confront a bind when they create relatively generous welfare policies.[26] Generous welfare policies may create migration to the state of those who need welfare benefits. To finance the generous benefits for the growing welfare-dependent population, the state must raise taxes. Tax increases discourage investment and job growth, undermining the state's revenue base. The state is caught in a vicious cycle that cannot be sustained. It is prudent, some claim, for states to guard against generous welfare policies.

This concern seems exaggerated. Although by some measures state policies have become more strict, particularly in the demand that welfare clients seek work, in other ways states have initiated more generous policies than were in place before the 1996 reform. Eligibility for cash assistance has been liberalized in many states. Thirty-nine states have changed their provisions regarding asset limits and 48 now exempt a vehicle in determining eligibility. Under TANF, welfare recipients can now accumulate savings, own a car, or obtain life insurance policies, all of which were restricted under AFDC.[27]

Child-care funding has been increased under PRWORA. Women who need child care are more likely to receive a grant to pay some of the costs of day care, based on income eligibility. This has had three effects on poor families. First, the additional funds have allowed more women who need day care to obtain it. Second, a barrier to work has been reduced. And finally, members of the extended family (aunts and grandmothers) may now be paid for child care.

Of course, not all the changes PRWORA has brought to the welfare system have been beneficial to welfare recipients. PRWORA allows and encourages states to erect barriers between the needy and cash assistance. Many states require that applicants begin job search activities and cooperate with child support enforcement weeks before they can actually receive cash payments. This creates a "hassle factor" for recipients. Some clients may exit the welfare system simply because of the time and effort required to overcome these hurdles. Others may elect simply to accept the in-kind benefits because many of the hassles are attached to cash assistance.[28] For example, with child support, if a woman is receiving money "under the table" from the father of her children, she may elect not to cooperate with child support efforts for fear of antagonizing the father and losing even the small amount of money that she is receiving.

In some ways PRWORA has reverted to administrative practices of the past. It was once common for welfare caseworkers to be actively involved in the lives of their clients, practices that were largely abandoned in the 1960s. Caseworkers had power over welfare clients because of the discretion they enjoyed and the subjective nature of their decisions. Discretion may help or hinder welfare clients.

PRWORA reinstated much of the discretion of the past. A current example is found in welfare diversion grants. Twenty-two states now offer such grants. These grants are given in circumstances deemed worthy by local welfare officials to divert people from entering the cash assistance program. In some localities in Maryland, for example, selected welfare clients received diversion grants to purchase surplus automobiles. But there was not enough money or surplus autos to provide a car for everyone who wanted one. Choices had to be made. Some clients received a benefit based on the discretion of the caseworkers and supervisors. This difference reflects a significant shift in the legal status of welfare discussed previously. If welfare were an entitlement, it would not be possible to provide a benefit only to selected clients; everyone who met the stipulated criteria would have an equal right to the benefit. This procedural equality was sacrificed when local caseworkers were given discretion.

Another effect of PRWORA was to break apart the traditional welfare benefit package of cash assistance, medical assistance, and food assistance. Under AFDC, a mother and child received cash, medical care, and food without conditions. PRWORA introduced several requirements. Rather than allowing the mother to stay home, PRWORA now demands that she go to work. A new profile of the welfare recipient's benefits has emerged as welfare mothers struggle to survive with a temporary low-wage job, medical assistance, Food Stamps, and a child-care grant.

Finally, it is important to realize that while PRWORA represented a significant shift in national policy, in many states it was of little consequence. As noted earlier, states had developed numerous experimental programs well before the adoption of PRWORA. The 1996 federal reform simply allowed states to make permanent, with a little fine-tuning, the waiver programs they had operated under AFDC. PRWORA formally endorsed the personal responsibility orientation that had already been taken by many states and symbolically signaled a shift in national policy as to how poor families would be treated in the United States.

## NOTES

1. Edleman, Peter. 1997. "The Worst Thing Bill Clinton Has Done." *Atlantic Monthly*; Solow, Robert. 1998. "Guess Who Pays for Workfare?" *The New York Review of Books*, www.nybooks.com.

2. The reference to the "third rail" is an inside joke in our nation's capital. The subway system in Washington, D.C., has three rails, two carry the trains and the third provides electrical power. Touch the third rail and you die. Politicians believe the same is true of Social Security.

3. Berkowitz, Edward. 1991. *America's Welfare State*. Baltimore: Johns Hopkins University Press.

4. For the impacts of the shift to never-married mothers, see Gabe, T. 1993. "Testimony Before the U.S. House of Representatives, Committee on Ways and Means" in *Trends in Spending and Caseloads for AFDC and Related Programs*, Washington, DC: U.S. Government Printing Office;

and Besharov, D. 1989. "Targeting Long-Term Welfare Recipients" in P. Cottingham and D. Ellwood, eds., *Welfare Policy for the 1990s*. Cambridge, MA: Harvard University Press.

5. Piven, F., and R. Cloward. 1993. *Regulating the Poor*. New York: Vintage Books.

6. Berkowitz, Edward.

7. Bremner, R. 1971. *Children and Youth in America*. Cambridge, MA: Harvard University Press.

8. Mead, Lawrence. 1986. *Beyond Entitlement: The Social Obligations of Citizenship*. Princeton, NJ: Princeton University Press.

9. Mead, Lawrence. 1997. "Welfare Employment." in L. Mead, ed., *Paternalistic Welfare Reform*. Washington, DC: Brookings Institution.

10. Gueron, Judith. 1987. *Reforming Welfare with Work*. New York: Ford Foundation Project on Social Welfare and the American Future.

11. Caseloads peaked in 1994 with 5,053,000 families and 14,276,000 recipients of AFDC.

12. Gallagher, L. Jerome, Megan Gallagher, Kevin Perse, Susan Schreiber, and Keith Watson. 1997. *One Year After Federal Welfare Reform: A Description of State Temporary Assistance for Needy Family Decisions as of October 1997*. Washington, DC: The Urban Institute.

13. U.S. Department of Health and Human Services. 1998. *First Annual Report of the Temporary Assistance to Needy Families Program*. Washington, DC: Government Printing Office.

14. See Handler, J., and Y. Hasenfeld, 1991. *The Moral Construction of Poverty* (Newbury Park, CA: Sage) on the importance of symbolism in forming welfare policy.

15. U.S. House of Representatives. 1996. *Summary of the Provisions of the Personal Responsibility and Work Opportunity Reconciliation Act of 1996*. Washington, DC: Government Printing Office.

16. States may exempt as much as 20 percent of their caseload from the requirements of PRWORA.

17. Roberts, Paula. 1994. *Ending Poverty as We Know It: The Case for Child Support Enforcement and Assurance*. Washington, DC: Center for Law and Social Policy.

18. Gallagher, L. Jerome, et al.

19. Edin, Kathryn. 1991. "Surviving the Welfare System: How AFDC Recipients Make Ends Meet in Chicago." *Social Problems*, 38: 462–473.

20. Ibid.

21. U.S. House of Representatives, 1996, p. 43.

22. Children's Defense Fund. 1997. *Selected Features of State TANF Plans. www.cdf.org*.

23. Gallagher, L. Jerome, et al.

24. Haveman, Judith. November 3, 1998. "Fewer Births for N.J. Welfare Mothers." *Washington Post*, p. A7.

25. A comparison of national figures indicates that from January 1993 to March 1998, welfare cash assistance caseloads declined 35 percent for families (from 4,963,000 to 3,224,000) and 37 percent among recipients (from 14,115,000 to 8,910,000), Department of Health and Human Services, 1998. The only state that did not register a decrease during this period was Hawaii. The declines are somewhat less dramatic if one takes 1996 as the base year, but the pattern is consistent.

26. For a discussion of concerns in the race to the bottom, see Volden, Craig, 1997, "Entrusting the States with Welfare Reform." In John Ferejohn and Barry Weingast, eds., *The New Federalism: Can the States Be Trusted?* Palo Alto, CA: Hoover Institute.

27. Gallagher, L. Jerome, et al.

28. There is some indication that while TANF caseloads are decreasing, Medicaid and Food Stamp caseloads are remaining constant, if not slightly increasing, with the implementation of PRWORA.

## CRITICAL THINKING QUESTIONS

1. How have perceptions about welfare assistance and its recipients changed since the 1950s?

2. What are some of the major differences between PRWORA and earlier welfare polices such as AFDC?

3. What are the advantages and disadvantages of PRWORA for welfare recipients? Why do Wilson and Stoker conclude that the legislation has had little impact on poor families in many states?

# 18 Family Policies

## *Liberal/Feminist:* Abandoning Poor Families

RUTH SIDEL, *Keeping Women and Children Last: America's War on the Poor* (New York: Penguin, 1998), pp. xvii–xviii, 222–227. Copyright © 1996 by Ruth Sidel. Used by permission of Viking Penguin, a division of Penguin Putnam, Inc.

*Most liberals, especially feminists, feel that welfare legislation, including PRWORA (see the previous article), is abandoning poor families. According to Ruth Sidel, politicians have exaggerated and stigmatized single-parent families— especially poor, black, female-headed households—to deflect attention from the severe economic and societal problems that many Americans face.*

Today we are in the midst of a widespread effort to denigrate and stigmatize poor single mothers, particularly welfare recipients. This effort is part of a more generalized drumbeat of criticism about one-parent families. The message is clear: the single-parent family breeds trouble, and poor single mothers breed catastrophe. "Illegitimacy," the term once again in vogue for out-of-wedlock birth, is being labeled a threat to American culture and to the very survival of our nation.

In this sequel to *Women and Children Last*, I suggest that the widespread campaign against poor single mothers is in reality a form of scapegoating, the singling out for blame and opprobrium of a group that is particularly vulnerable because of race, class, and gender. The designation of poor single mothers as the cause of America's ills deflects attention from the severe economic and societal problems we face and our unwillingness to deal with those problems: the growing gap between rich and poor; widespread employment insecurity;

increasing political apathy and alienation; extraordinary levels of violence, particularly among our young people; and our rapidly deteriorating infrastructure. This strategy in effect shifts blame from the affluent and powerful to the poor and powerless.

One of the functions of designating certain people as enemies is the bringing together of the rest of society. For the first time in over half a century the United States does not have significant external enemies. The relentless rhetoric against poor single mothers has provided an enemy against whom politicians and conservative ideologues can rally and against whom they can mobilize public opinion and the voting electorate.

The causes of the sharply increasing rate of mother-only families, of the rising number of teenagers becoming pregnant, and of the growing number of families living in poverty and near poverty are, in reality, neither the moral weakness of poor people nor the benefits provided by the social welfare system. Rather, the causes are profound changes in technology, in employment, in international trade, and in family structure that are occurring in the United States and in many other countries of the world, and the inadequacy of our economic, social, and family policies. These issues must be dealt with not through scapegoating and punishment but rather through fundamental structural change. . . .

A relentless campaign to stereotype, stigmatize, and demonize poor women, particularly poor, single mothers [has been] conducted to pave the way for the passage of harsh, restrictive new legislation. "Welfare mothers" [have been] repeatedly portrayed as lazy, dependent, and unwilling to work: they [have] also often [been] portrayed as promiscuous and even as unfit mothers. . . .

Since the passage of the Personal Responsibility and Work Opportunity Reconciliation Act of 1996, many politicians, Republicans and Democrats alike, as well as business leaders, have made gestures toward diminishing the stigma of receiving welfare benefits. An advertising campaign sponsored by the non-profit Welfare to Work Partnership, for example, has attempted to persuade employers to hire recipients by transforming the image of poor women. One print advertisement attempts to "present the stereotype and smash it at the same time." The stereotype, "Welfare mothers are irresponsible, is rewritten to read, "Welfare mothers make responsible employees." The idea hammered home in the mid 1990s, "Welfare is a program that creates dependence" is rewritten to read: "Welfare to work is a program that creates independence."[1] Can the attitudes of the American public in general and business leaders and employers in particular be shifted so fundamentally and in a relatively short period of time? And if not, what will the negative attitudes toward the poor mean for their chances of obtaining jobs once their benefits cease?

Such a dramatic shift is, I believe, highly unlikely. The hostile campaign against the poor fed into far too many entrenched prejudices and stereotypes about issues that are highly volatile in American society, particularly those involving race, class, and gender, to be erased by some clever, well-placed advertising campaigns or exhortations by political leaders. Individual recipients may well be given a chance, especially those who do not trigger all of the harshest stereotypes. Some have already been given such a chance by a variety of companies, many of which were able to provide extensive training and support services. Early reports indicate that retention rates have been relatively high, but these former recipients may be the easiest to place and to train.[2] Others have and will continue to obtain employment in those industries and regions of the country that need low-income workers, but millions of recipients and former recipients will be forced to search for jobs while simultaneously struggling to counteract deep-seated suspicions, fear, biases, and often outright hostility toward the poor—attitudes that were mercilessly and systematically encouraged just a short time ago by our national and local leaders.

It is especially disturbing that while poor women with children as young as three months are being forced to leave their infants to take jobs outside of the home or to participate in training or make-work programs, middle-class and upper-middle-class women who leave their children— even school-aged children—to participate in the labor market are increasingly looked upon with suspicion or in some instances with outright hostility. Leaving one's children with a nanny or an *au pair* or bringing them to day care is all-too-often seen as an abrogation of maternal responsibilities, a betrayal of "family values," while poor women who remain outside the labor market are vilified, their fundamental moral worth questioned, even their ability to raise their children debated in state legislatures and in the U.S. Congress.

In her recent book, *A Mother's Place: Taking the Debate About Working Mothers*

*Beyond Guilt and Blame*, Susan Chira, a *New York Times* reporter and editor, describes the "new conventional wisdom" for middle-class and upper-middle-class women: "When mothers forsake their rightful place at home, children are the victims." She continues, "The good mother who sacrifices, the selfish mother who works, the evils of day care, the obsessions with men's and women's different natures, the public laments by mothers torn from the arms of their children by jobs, the breast-beating over the state of children—these are the themes of the chorus bewailing a lost paradise, the days when mothers stayed at home."[3]

Headlines blare the evils of mothers working, articles recount the stories of female executives forsaking their high-level jobs for full-time motherhood, and radio talk shows bitterly criticize the mother of a baby allegedly killed by his *au pair* for working part-time as an ophthalmologist. As Chira states, this mother, and by implication all working mothers, was found guilty—guilty "of careerism, of callousness, of hiring someone to do a job only a mother should do."[4] Why should poor women be driven out of their homes to work in menial jobs that pay poverty wages while middle- and upper-middle-class working women are driven by the relentless questioning about the quality of their mothering to guilt, self-blame, and in some instances back to the home? Moreover, while affluent women are often berated for working and poor women for not working outside the home, working-class and middle-class mothers who do not have the options to remain at home or even to work part-time are encouraged by the politics of division to resent both those who are poorer and those who are richer than they.

Recent studies indicate, furthermore, that politicians and policy makers may be overestimating how much mothers of young children in the general population work for pay. Recent data indicate that only 30 percent of married mothers with children under the age of six worked full-time, year-round in 1997. If married mothers with young children have relatively low rates of full-time participation in the labor force, why are impoverished women being forced to enter the labor force and leave their children for full-time, year-round work? Why is the government intruding to this extent into the lives of poor women when adequate, alternate care-giving frequently does not exist?

What is to be done now that welfare policy is in the hands of the states and the thrust all over the country is to dramatically lower the number of recipients, to force remaining recipients into the workforce, or at very least to work for their benefits?[5] There are several directions advocates for the poor can take during this difficult time. First, we must continue to insist that the central problem faced by the poor is not welfare; it is poverty. If families are forced off of the welfare rolls and remain in poverty, what will they have gained? What will American society have gained? If parents are forced to work for meager wages and their income remains below the poverty line, they and their children will still face all of the deleterious effects of being impoverished in a very rich society. We must therefore redefine the problem—the United States must find ways of helping families out of poverty, not simply off the welfare rolls.

Second, advocates for the poor must fight at the state level to obtain as many essential benefits as possible for those in need. From food stamps to child care, from educational opportunities and job training to health care for the uninsured, we must pressure state legislatures for decent living conditions for the poor and near-poor. The struggle today is largely at the state level where legislators and local officials are often both accessible to organized lobbying and vulnerable to public opinion.

Third, unless the United States mobilizes to provide far greater access to first-rate child care and universal access to health care as well as extensive job training and possibly the creation of public sector jobs, we will not be able to truly reform our welfare system. So-called welfare reform must not force mothers to neglect the well-being of their children in order to fulfill the work mandate of the state. Moreover, parents cannot be expected to leave the welfare rolls and take jobs that will mean forfeiting their families' access to health care. We as a society must not insist that families make such cruel choices.

Fourth, we must both raise the minimum wage and expand the Earned Income Tax Credit so that all families with members who work will earn an income above the poverty line. The Earned Income Tax Credit, established in 1975 and expanded several times since, benefits low- and moderate-income working people, primarily those with children. In 1996, the EITC lifted 4.6 million people, including 2.4 million children, out of poverty.[6] If participation in the workforce is the key standard by which we choose to judge the moral worth of adults in American society, then we must at very least reward workers with a livable income. With the ever-widening gap between rich and poor, this is not only the most sensible policy but the moral one as well.

Finally, advocates for impoverished children and adults must consider the tactics of social protest. Massive letter writing, e-mail, fax, and telephone campaigns, lobbying state capitols en masse, demonstrations, and marches are not merely nostalgic reminders of the civil rights and anti-war movements of the 1960s but are effective and valuable ways of encouraging the poor to demand their rights, of mobilizing their supporters, of giving heart to individuals who are all too often discouraged at the pace of social reform, and of attempting to dramatically shift public opinion.

Developing an effective and humane safety net as well as guaranteeing basic living conditions for all people in the United States will require the efforts of generations of activists. But one day the United States can truly become a society in which all children grow and flourish, in which parents work and nurture, in which citizens and non-citizens, affluent and less affluent, whites and people of color, old and young, find meaningful roles and make significant contributions to the social, economic, and political life of the community.

## NOTES

1. Jason DeParle, "As Nation's Economy Hums, Welfare's Image Is Polished," *New York Times*, September 1997.

2. Robert Pear, "Welfare Workers Rate High in Job Retention at Companies," *New York Times*, May 27, 1998.

3. Susan Chira, *A Mother's Place: Taking the Debate About Working Mothers Beyond Guilt and Blame* (New York: HarperCollins, 1998), 4.

4. Ibid., 3.

5. Suzanne M. Bianchi and Philip Cohen, "Marriage, Children, and Women's Employment: Do We Know What We Think We Know?" Paper prepared for an Invited Session on "Gender Inequality at Work" at the annual meeting of the Eastern Sociological Association, Philadelphia, PA, March 20, 1998.

6. Kathryn Porter, Wendell E. Primus, Lynette Rawlings, and Esther Rosenbaum, *Strengths of the Safety Net: How the EITC, Social Security and Other Government Programs Affect Poverty* (Washington, D.C.: Center on Budget and Policy Priorities, March 1998), 20–21.

## CRITICAL THINKING QUESTIONS

1. Why does Sidel describe female-headed families as scapegoats?

2. According to Sidel, why are both poor women with children and middle-class employed mothers in a no-win situation when national and local leaders debate "family values"?

3. The three articles in this chapter show that family legislation, especially welfare issues, is directed at mothers. Does targeting women suggest that fathers and men aren't very important in childrearing?